"青年汉学家研修计划"
论文精选集 2018

A Selected Collection of Research Papers of Visiting Program
for Young Sinologists 2018

文化和旅游部国际交流与合作局
中外文化交流中心 编

中国社会科学出版社

图书在版编目（CIP）数据

"青年汉学家研修计划"论文精选集.2018 / 文化和旅游部国际交流与合作局、中外文化交流中心编.–– 北京：中国社会科学出版社，2020.5
ISBN 978-7-5203-7194-0

Ⅰ.①青… Ⅱ.①文… Ⅲ.①汉学—文集 Ⅳ.① K207.8-53

中国版本图书馆 CIP 数据核字 (2020) 第 171847 号

出 版 人　赵剑英
责任编辑　张冰洁
责任校对　孙砚文
责任印制　王　超

出　　　版　中国社会科学出版社
社　　　址　北京鼓楼西大街甲 158 号
邮　　　编　100720
网　　　址　http://www.csspw.cn
发 行 部　010 - 84083685
门 市 部　010 - 84029450
经　　　销　新华书店及其他书店

印刷装订　北京君升印刷有限公司
版　　　次　2020 年 5 月第 1 版
印　　　次　2020 年 5 月第 1 次印刷

开　　　本　710×1000　1/16
印　　　张　50
字　　　数　864 千字
定　　　价　299.00 元

2018 青年汉学家研修计划重庆班学员合影
Group photo of the participants in the Visiting Program for Young Sinologists(Chongqing) 2018

2018 青年汉学家研修计划重庆班专家集中授课现场
Young sinologists(Chongqing) listen to the lecture

2018 青年汉学家研修计划广州班学员赴深圳博物馆参观考察，了解中国改革开放辉煌成就
Young sinologists(Guangzhou) on visit to Shenzhen Museum to get to know the brilliant achievements of China's reform and opening up

2018 青年汉学家研修计划广州班学员合影
Group photo of the participants in the Visiting Program for Young Sinologists (Guangzhou) 2018

2018 青年汉学家研修计划北京班学员合影
Group photo of the participants in the Visiting Program for Young Sinologists (Beijing) 2018

2018 青年汉学家研修计划北京班学员参加 CCTSS 中外文化互译与传播论坛
Young Sinologists(Beijing) attend the CCTSS Forum on Sino-Foreign Cultural Translation and Dissemination

2018 青年汉学家研修计划（上海 7 月班）学员合影
Group photo of the participants in the Visiting Program for Young Sinologists(Shanghai·July) 2018

2018 青年汉学家研修计划（上海 7 月班）学员赴一大会址考察
Young sinologists (Shanghai·July) on visit to the Site of the 1st National Congress of the Communist Party of China

2018 青年汉学家研修计划西安班学员合影

Group photo of the participants in the Visiting Program for Young Sinologists(Xi'an) 2018

2018 青年汉学家研修计划西安班专家集中授课现场

Young sinologists (Xi'an) listen to the lecture

2018 青年汉学家研修计划杭州班开班仪式前学员进行自我介绍

Young sinologists (Hangzhou) make self-introduction before the opening ceremony

2018 青年汉学家研修计划杭州班学员参观考察 G20 会馆

Young sinologists (Hangzhou) visit the meeting Hall of G20

2018 青年汉学家研修计划（上海 9 月班）赴敦煌参观考察的学员一行参加第三届丝绸之路国际文化博览会

Young sinologists (Shanghai·September)on visit to DunHuang attend the 3rd Silk Road International Cultural Expo

2018 青年汉学家研修计划（上海 9 月班）专家集中授课现场

Young sinologists (Shanghai·September) listen to the lecture

主办：中华人民共和国文化和旅游部　中国社会科学院
承办：中外文化交流中心

Hosts：Ministry of Culture and Tourism of the People's Republic of China
　　　Chinese Academy of Social Sciences
Organizer: Network of International Culturalink Entities

目　录

CONTENTS

中国在巴西和德国的文化外交

安琳娜【德国】
巴西利亚大学研究员

一、中国文化外交

在中国，公共外交（Public Diplomacy）既是一种策略性工具，又是一种功能性工具（Hartig，2016），而文化外交（Cultural Diplomacy）则是从追求软实力和形象塑造的角度来理解的。此外，也有学者指出，中国人对西方人的公共外交的理解包含两个含义：（1）对外宣传，被认为是中国成功走向海外受众的全球传播，与国家宣传体系有关；（2）民间外交，人与人之间的"外交关系"。

很多研究集中于中国文化外交，强调这些词源的差异与外交思想和国家历史的不同传统有关。总的来说，中国的文化外交是由一个长期的和总体的价值体系驱动的，理想和战略取向相结合。在评估中国文化外交的结构时，有必要在中国的发展和外交政策的更广泛的历史背景下进行分析。在过去，中国的文化外交是相当温和的，近年来展示了该国如何加强其软实力的主动权和更宏大的叙事倾向。

文化外交的组织与主体

中国的文化外交是通过一系列活动、文化交流、地方政府倡议和社会倡议来表达的。总体而言，文化外交的本质是两个核心要素。首先，文化外交与更大的叙事、原则性的逻辑和中央政府决策者的政策导向有关。国家的长期规划在经济发展和意识形态基础上的结合，创造了灵活的平台和强大的适应能力。其次，文化外交不够协调性，反映了国家行政体制和政治体制的不同层次和制度文化的复杂性。这强调的是利用集体的力量和努力作为杠杆，来促进所期望的结果为关键。因此，文化外交可以在不同的层面上发生，如高层或工作层面，并针对不同的受众群体，如学者、政治决策者或公共政策制定者、商业部门或公众。此外，在中国政治体系中也可观察到公共事务与公共外交的交融渊源。

以下概述了中国文化外交的主体：

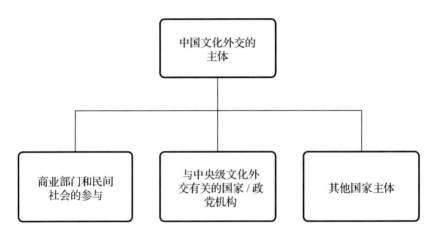

根据分析，中国文化外交是由一个多中心的基础设施组成，在广泛的网络中运作，而国家行为主体反映了政党国家和经济利益，非国家行为体可以在有文化、学术或文化利益的地方遇到。以下部分进一步详细阐述了国家的文化外交行为体结构。

二、与中国文化外交有关的国家 / 政党结构

文化外交的重点是政府和政党组织，包括中宣部、全国人大、全国政协、外交部、国务院新闻部办公室等。既定数量的行为体不是遵循公共外交或文化外交的具体国家战略，而是受制于具体的纲领。中国共产党在思想定位上有发言权，根据："中共中央政治局委员、国务委员等"之间的沟通协调。与公共外交有关的非政府组织……他们的立场和行动常常为最高领导人和具体方案提供至关重要的参考。

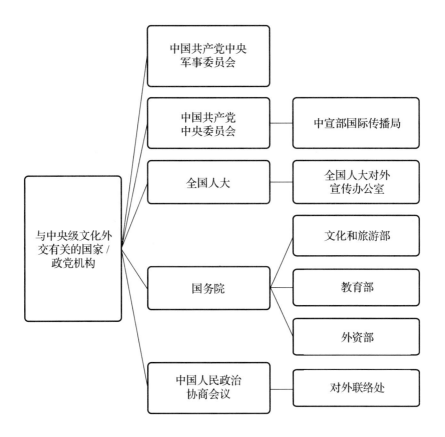

其他国家行为体有省市级机关、民间社会团体、对外友协、知识精英、学术机构、侨办机构。在这方面，提及中国政府推动的智库战略也是有效的。2013年中国共产党第十八次代表大会鼓励创建有中国特色的智库。2015年，中共中央和国务院共同努力，中国特色的智库进一步巩固。为了是到2020年底，中国将建成国际上有影响力的高端智库。这意味着科研、政策和政治之间有着密切的联系。例如，"一带一路"（BRI）智库联盟即由国务院发展研究中心、复旦大学和中国社会科学院（CASS）在2015年发起。同样，丝绸之路智库协会于2016年启动，目的是"加深人们对发展主动权的理解，避免国家之间的误解"。

虽然中国对私营部门的理解可能与西方不同，但中国企业在积极连接外交政策客体和商业利益团体的过程中，也涉及公共和文化外交当中。例如，中国国有企业和企业社会责任计划的存在，正在文化上实施中国文化导向的项目。

通过传播语言和文化意识，了解中国，也对中国的形象产生持久的影响，并影响不同语境下的舆论建设。通过各种交流活动，促进双方的理解。

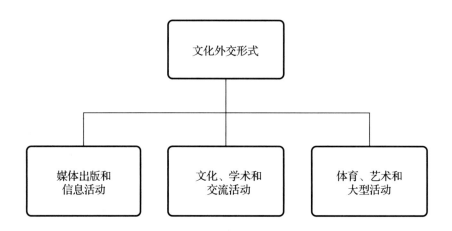

文化、学术和交流活动: 海外中国文化外交的主要形式之一是孔子学院, 它由中国教育委员会国际办公室（汉办）管理, 隶属于中国教育部, 并由各部委的其他代表组成政府机构和其他研究机构或机构的临时合作。截至 2017 年, 孔子学院在 142 个国家和地区设立了 516 所孔子学院和 1076 所孔子课堂, 根据孔子学院总部发布的消息。孔子学院创立于 1974 年, 并于 2004 年在韩国开设了第一所孔子学院。哈蒂格（Hartig）在对德国孔子学院的研究中强调, 由于文化外交是行使"软实力"的手段, 因此, 孔子学院可以被视为中国文化外交的工具, 试图在全球范围内施加中国"软实力"。此外, 海外中国文化中心在欧洲设有七个中心（巴黎、马耳他、柏林、莫斯科、马德里、哥本哈根和布鲁塞尔）; 非洲（毛里求斯、贝宁、开罗、尼日利亚和坦桑尼亚）、亚洲（首尔、东京、乌兰巴托、曼谷、老挝、斯里兰卡、巴基斯坦、尼泊尔和新加坡）; 墨西哥, 悉尼, 新西兰和斐济。研究和举办不同的项目和活动, 主要关注传统文化。根据同一研究者, 中国文化研究所与孔子学院的区别在于利用官方和非正式的国内资源, 与国有组织和私营企业合作, 包括表演团体和艺术从业者, 并与海外侨胞有联系。

媒体、出版和信息活动: 国家大力开展媒体信息活动, 通过国务院新闻办公室、各驻外使、领馆、新华社、中国全球电视网、中国国际广播电台、中国日报、环球时报、社会媒体等传播信息。许多中国媒体频道都有多语言电视频道和网站, 他们的声音在全球各地与全球办公室进行传播。双边和多边媒体合作、培训和专业交流协议是扩大中国在全球通信中占据更大份额的基础。因此, 建立与外国公众的关系也可以在更直接的层面上进行。例如, 由《今日中国》付费的插播"ChinaWatch"在《纽约时报》和《华尔街日报》等全球主要报纸上都有报道。

从这个意义上说，"借船出海"也说明了影响海外市场的努力。

同时，中国出版业加大力度"造船出海"，以进一步创新方式，不断开拓世界之路。在这方面，许多国家都有比较成熟的经验值得借鉴。在欧洲和美国的一些发达国家，"走出去"的出版不仅限于实物图书、专用基金和专业人才"走出去"的出口，而且利用"软实力"来影响"硬实力"已经成为一种模式。此外，世界各地的展览和非贸易出版物也可以通过文化传播到世界各地。只有不断构建新的平台，开辟新的渠道，才能拓展中国优秀图书的国际覆盖，使中国出版真正成为全世界了解中国的窗口。"此外，到世界各地办会展、以非贸易方式赠予出版物，同样能把中国文化传递给世界。只有不断建设新的平台、开通新的渠道，才能扩大中国优秀图书的国际覆盖面，让中国出版真正成为世界了解中国的窗口。"[1]

强调对中国文学和出版业进行框架化的要求表明：积极寻求对媒体内容产生影响的举措日益增多，并影响到政治讨论和议程设置的基调，以及参照建立话语体系支持政府在海外的成功定位。

体育、艺术和大型活动：这里列举一些在一定程度上涉及中国形象塑造和提升文化外交对话活动机会的中国文化外交事件：北京奥运会、上海世博会、亚太经合组织北京峰会、2016 年 G20 杭州峰会，2017 年"一带一路"倡议在北京举行的首脑会议和 2017 年金砖国家厦门峰会[2]。

三、在德国的中国文化外交

1. 德国与中国的双边关系

双边合作表现为德国政府对德中关系的认同和中国地位的提高。最重要的机制之一是双边磋商，自 2011 以来，德国总理安吉拉·默克尔欢迎中国总理温家宝在柏林举行的第一次德国——中国政府间协商会议。2014 年，德中关系从"全球责任战略伙伴关系"升级为"全面战略伙伴关系"。

大量的合作机制主要集中在科技、经济和教育合作方面，如官方双边磋商中的官方声明，或如德国联邦研究部（BMF）的中国战略等关键文件。德国外交部因此加强了对中国的个人努力，旨在实现"更具结构性的亚洲政策和增加中国相关知识和技能"。

1　新华社，2016.

2　然而，应该强调的是，这些活动主要是指中国国内的文化外交，而不是国际事件。因此，体育和大型赛事将不包括在分析中。

中国和德国之间的文化合作可以追溯到 20 世纪 70 年代末。1978 年，德国联邦科学技术研究所的代表团访问了北京，这就开始了关于政府间科技合作协议的讨论。1978 年 10 月，两国政府签署了《德意志联邦共和国政府与中华人民共和国政府关于科技合作的协议》，这是两国间首要合作协议之一。《经济合作协定》和《文化合作协定》在随后的两年内生效。从那以来，文化领域的合作得到了显著的加强。2017 年 5 月 24 日，德中高层人民对话促进和支持社会文化交流第一次会议在北京举行。出席会议的有 500 余人，会议由德国外交部长西格玛尔·加布里尔（Sigmar Gabriel）和中国副总理刘延东共同主持。此次对话旨在改善德国和中国在教育、文化、语言、媒体、体育和青年等领域的公民社会交流环境。

2. 中国在德国的文化外交活动

以下概述了中国文化外交举措，或更好地介绍了在德国进行文化外交有关的倡议和行动。虽然这个概述可能不完整，但它提供了对中国参与进程的理解。我们选择了几个不同的领域：文化、学术和交流活动，媒体、出版和信息活动。随后，对中国在德国的文化外交倡议的一部分总结了德国当前关于中国舆论的数据。

3. 文化、学术和交流活动

直到今天，全国有近 20 所孔子学院，其中大部分是通过合作协议在大学建立的，每年的预算约为 200,000 到 350,000 欧元（Thies, 2015）。除了语言之外，研究所本身在其非语言课程方面也有所不同，包括以企业为中心的文化能力课程、中职职业生涯日、特别关注哥廷根中学教师培训、专注于柏林的展览、书法与烹饪课程，太极拳班，中国的绿色经济，中国法律制度介绍等。以下是德国联邦各州孔子学院的名单：

表 1：孔子学院在德国的分布

所在州	孔子学院
柏林	柏林自由大学孔子学院
不来梅	不来梅孔子学院
北莱茵威斯特伐利亚	杜伊斯堡 - 埃森大学鲁尔都市孔子学院
北莱茵威斯特伐利亚	杜塞尔多夫大学孔子学院
图林根	埃尔福特应用科技大学孔子学院
黑塞	法兰克福大学孔子学院
下萨克森	哥廷根大学孔子学院
汉堡	汉堡大学孔子学院

所在州	孔子学院
下萨克森	汉诺威孔子学院
巴登堡	海德堡大学孔子学院
巴登堡	弗莱堡大学孔子学院
萨克森	莱比锡大学孔子学院
巴伐利亚	慕尼黑孔子学院
北莱茵威斯特伐利亚	帕德博恩大学孔子学院
梅克伦堡前波莫瑞州	施特拉尔松德应用技术大学孔子学院
巴伐利亚	奥迪英戈尔施塔特孔子学院
巴伐利亚	纽伦堡—埃尔兰根孔子学院
莱茵兰腭	特里尔大学孔子学院
图林根州	图林根州外国语学校孔子课堂
北莱茵威斯特伐利亚	波恩大学孔子学院

在哈蒂格对德国孔子学院的研究中指出，学院在教材方面保持一定程度的自主性，将它们与官方的汉办材料和他们自己的材料相结合。就德国而言，可以进一步评估促进中国和形象建设的多维结构。墨卡托中国研究院 2018 年的报告评估了德国与中国合作的需要，并强调战略定位良好的国家做法和熟练的专业人员对深入中国知识的重要性。作者评估了处于 Y 水平上的中国大学已经从 20 世纪 90 年代中期以来逐步增长，包括汉学和跨学科课程更加侧重于中国，额外的优惠和证书，德语中文学习项目和双学位。截至 2017 年 11 月，德中大学共有 1347 项正式合作计划。

报告还指出，虽然有超过 100 个支持中国持续时间延长的支持项目，但中国机构作为实施者的目标是增加文化和教育交流的支持项目，例如中国奖学金理事会颁发给中国教育部的补助，该奖项是以中国政府为研究对象颁发的，旨在瞄准不同的目标群体，包括学生、研究生、志愿者、科学家和年轻专业人员。因此，越来越多的中国机构直接位于德国，如孔子学院或中国民营企业，如德国科技集团德国的华为分部，该公司为德国目标集团推出了自己的支持项目。

这一观察与中国文化外交的其他研究相关联，这说明私营部门公司在代表锻造文化和教育关系方面的作用越来越大。在中学阶段，大约 5000 名学生目前在德国学校学习汉语，过去几年的数字有所下降。这与德国附近的法国形成了鲜明的对比，在那里，大约 38000 名学生正在中学学习汉语。然而，总的说来，中国的研究工作已经取得了一定的成果，并指出了该领域的明确专业化。也就是说，与中国接触的高等教育水平的基础设施可能与其他主要欧洲国家如法国和英国不同，甚至比其他欧洲国家落后，但仍有很强的基础。

4. 促进艺术和传统文化交流

德国首都柏林是中国文化中心的东道主，在 2008 成立，作为中国歌德学院的一员。与中国和德国的多维关系进一步被文化交流所证实，如 2017 年 9 月在北京开幕的"德国 8"展览，继 2015 莱茵北部威斯特伐利亚举行的"中国 8"展览之后。进一步的例子表明，在德国推广中国文化的行为体的多样性，例如，青海省政府新闻办公室在青海省文化、艺术和景观方面举办的 2018 届德国杜塞尔多夫城市展览（Xinhua News Agency, 2018）。更大范围的事件，例如 2007 年至 2010 年的事件系列。"德意志和中国在一起运动"，2012 年的中国文化年，德国与中国语言年以及德华青年学生交流年。

在媒体合作和影响力方面，由中国最大的英文报纸 China Daily 制作的英文报纸副刊"China Watch"在德国的两份报纸《汉德布拉特》和《德意志新闻报》（Deutsche Welle, 2018）中刊登。

在理想的情况下，公共和文化外交对国家的看法和态度起着积极的作用。德国对中国公众舆论的代表性研究反映了一个整体的正面形象，但对双边政治和经济关系仍有意见分歧。2016 年，对中国经济实力的偏见比前两年少（2014：49% 和 2016:44 %）。2016 年 59% 的德国人认为中国的经济对德国有相当大的（42%）或非常大的（17%）的影响。在经济决策者群体中，这一比例是 69%，而决策者中甚至有 90% 的受访者（Huawei, 2016）。虽然总体上增加了兴趣并提高了偏好形成，但"一带一路"倡议的兴起进一步引起了人们对中国关于德国的角色的改变，对双边的影响，以及在更广泛的欧盟背景下对德国产生的影响。

四、中国文化外交对德中关系的影响

公共外交在中国与德国的关系中具有重要作用。在德国 G20 峰会之前，德国总理安吉拉·默克尔和中国国家主席习近平出席了柏林动物园的大熊猫到访仪式，并收到来自中国的贷款。这吸引了媒体的关注。在德国文化外交活动的议程设置方面，强调中国文化传统、历史根源和非政治成分。分析表明孔子学院的分布和中国演员在教育交流计划中的参与程度有所提高。但有时文化外交可能会产生与其预期相反的效果。另一方面媒体也会关注谁伸出援助之手。而行为体主要是中央政府或中央政府附属机构（如国家媒体、孔子学院或中国文化中心），省级文化外交活动是通过展览等方式进行的。

五、巴西的中国文化外交

1. 巴西与中国的双边关系

1974 年，巴西和中国建立了外交关系。1993 年，两国建立战略伙伴关系，2006 年，巴中高级协调合作委员会（以下简称 COSBAN）作为两国间经常政治对话和合作的机构发起。COSBAN 将是联合行动计划和其能力领域的十年合作计划的主要决策机构。各小组委员会每年举行会议，以推动联合行动计划的执行，或提出可能的合作领域。两国坚持在文化艺术、广播影视、新闻出版、体育文化等领域开展合作，加强文化交流，加强合作。在全面的公共外交努力方面，中巴领导人的高层互访强调"南南合作"关系与"互利"的互补性。

2. 中国在巴西的文化外交活动

中国文化外交举措，更好地反映了与巴西文化外交有关的倡议和行动。我们选择了几个不同的领域，如：文化、学术和交流活动，以及媒体、出版和信息活动。

3. 文化、学术和交流活动

由于文化外交举措尚未在全国推广，尽管中国语言和文化的提升，中国驻巴西大使李金章评价了双方的积极认可："近年来，我看到了两国人民在相互了解和理解中成长的兴趣和热情。如文化月、电影周、摄影展、展览和美术表演等活动，以及 2016 年里约奥运会和其他体育赛事，都有助于增进相互了解和促进友好相处。这将加强双边文化交流的基础，创造新的机制和形成更长远的视野。"[1]

2018 年，巴西国民大会决定将 8 月 15 日设为"中国移民日"，这种承认可能进一步有助于塑造中国形象。

2008 年，巴西第一所孔子学院在国立圣保罗大学（圣保罗州立大学）开设。据中国驻巴西大使李金章介绍，目前巴西有 10 个孔子学院和 4 个孔子课堂，有 20,000 多名在校生，使巴西成为拉丁美洲拥有孔子学院数量最多的国家。从地理分布上看，巴西的孔子学院分布在全国 5 个地区，重点是东南地区。

1　从葡萄牙原文翻译。

表 2：巴西孔子学院分布表

地区	大学
中西部	巴西利亚大学孔子学院（UNB）
北方	帕拉州立大学孔子学院（UEPA）
东北地区	伯南布哥大学孔子学院（UPE），塞阿拉联邦大学孔子学院（UFC），
南方	南大河州联邦大学孔子学院（UFRGS）
东南部	FAAP 商务孔子学院（FAAP），里约热内卢天主教大学孔子学院（PUC-RIO）；米纳斯.吉拉斯联邦大学孔子学院；圣保罗州立大学孔子学院，坎皮纳斯大学孔子学院（Unapunov）

总的来说，孔子学院的目标是为学生提供教育、文化和语言实践。正如在德国的案例中，在巴西的受访者证实，所使用的语言可以将汉办教材和葡萄牙语教材结合起来，因为"有必要使教材适应学生的本地需求"。此外，研究所的一位前工作人员说："中国的文化元素和国家形象有着很鲜明的元素，但学生可以批判性地讨论和参与这一内容。"[1] 最后，虽然私人语言服务的数量正在增加，但扩大汉语教学的倡议有很大的潜力，特别是当涉及初级或中级水平教学，比如在里约热内卢州的尼特罗伊公立中学。

4. 促进艺术和传统文化发展

展示中国艺术一直是巴西孔子学院的特色。例如，在 2014 年，中国首次在圣保罗巴中美术馆举行了国际著名艺术家作品展。2017 年，中国以库里蒂巴国际双年展为主题，展示了中国文化和旅游部选定的作品。此外，还支持中国文化活动和节庆活动，如在圣保罗举办的中国新年庆祝活动或元宵节，由中国驻圣保罗领事馆支持。

5. 媒体、出版和文化活动

就中国媒体在巴西的存在而言，CGTN（中国环球电视网），前身是中央电视台（CCTV），也是中国全球电视网络集团的一部分，于 2010 在圣保罗开设了一个办事处，负责协调其在拉丁美洲美国的业务，主要使用西班牙语和葡萄牙语。2016 年，中国官方通讯社新华社推出了一个葡萄牙语的门户网站。这次发射正值里约热内卢奥运会开幕式。除了新华社，人民日报、中国中央广播电台和中国国际广播电台的数字版也有葡萄牙语的服务。2018 年，中国最大的外语出版机构中

1　访谈录（24.06.2018）。

国国际出版集团（CIPG）在巴西举办了一次写作竞赛，主题是撰写其与中国有关的经历。谈到文化背景下同巴西的具体合作，中国与葡语城市（澳门）的经贸合作论坛（也称为澳门论坛）是另一个可以开展合作的场所。

6. 巴西媒体印象中的中国

在巴西公众舆论中，没有对中国形象的长期系统性的研究，也没有评估中国文化外交对巴西有积极影响的研究。然而，由于中国公司在巴西的实际的存在，使巴西对中国重要性的理解有所增加。在衡量对中国有利观点的程度上，皮尤中心进行的全球态度调查，评估了巴西对中国的看法，其中 44% 是有利的，44% 是不利的（Pew Center, 2014）。就不同年龄阶段的人群对中国的观点而言，年轻人对中国的态度比年龄稍大的人更为积极，在 18—29 岁年龄组（53%）、30—49 岁年龄组（43%）和 50 岁及以上（36% 岁）（Pew Center, 2014）。同样，阿蒙尼和维拉斯奎兹（2016）表明在拉丁美洲（包括巴西）的公众舆论中呈现出积极的趋势。虽然这些数字仅是简要说明，并且仍需对中国形象的塑造和对公众舆论的影响进行更深入的研究，但中国所受到的不断上升的关注与它在国外的经济表现息息相关。未来可能会进一步影响中国移民和华人社区数量的增加，这有助于实现国家形象的多样化和个性化。

六、中国文化外交对中巴关系的影响

公共外交在中国与巴西的关系中具有重要作用。在整个公共外交手段的保护下，中国文化外交在中国与巴西的关系中产生了中等程度的影响，即它塑造了一个更大的公众的观念，为进一步增加中国经济机会的达成打开了大门。就教育交流领域的文化外交而言，语言学习活动，以及与国家相关的专业知识有助于塑造中国在巴西建立专门知识的方式。这具体地表明了政治和经济领袖、学术界、媒体以及在中国新年如春节等事件上更广泛的公众舆论的作用。在积极形象塑造和民族品牌塑造方面，孔子学院在制定中国形象策划和传播信息方面发挥了重要作用。就巴西而言，文化外交的方法是一种"做中学"的做法。另一个例子是中国环球电视网（CGTN），中国中央电视台（CCTV）在葡萄牙语中提供了积极的中国形象。

中国在巴西开创的"中国移民日"，是为了进一步建立一个更宽阔的平台来唤起人们的关注，同时也进一步动员了巴西日益壮大的华人社区。这也应该在更广泛的背景下看到，动员在其他地理环境中海外华人的努力也应如此。

七、结论

中国抓住机遇通过文化外交增加其存在的能力，证明了其文化外交的有效性和使用"软实力"的能力。本文以巴西和德国为例，探讨了中国近年来文化外交的发展。在分析的基础上，归纳了 5 点结论。

（1）在国内，中国的文化外交在官方政治话语中采取了更为直接的政治形式，强调了国内因素在公共外交研究中的重要性。

（2）巴西和中国的文化外交举措在规模和框架上有所不同。在巴西，其被嵌入到"南南合作"叙事中。

（3）两国文化外交活动的议程设置有相似之处。形象和身份是围绕着传统、价值观和文化艺术的历史根源而建立的，强调"非政治"的文化外交方式，如强调在外交政策的文化，并和政治方面保持一定的距离。

（4）行为体主要属于中央政府，而省级政府则是促进区域的发展。

（5）在双边合作的保护伞和中国的总体政策指导下，文化外交行为体在为中国利益创造有利条件时，有时会进行一些重叠的活动。建立关系的措施与日益增长的经济利益并行不悖。

就德国而言，在文化外交开展中，中国分散的行为体结构被复制。不同的行为体，尤其是孔子学院和中国文化中心，率先在语言和文化活动领域传播与中国有关的节目。最重要的是，孔子学院因其在中、高等教育领域的广泛活动而发挥着重要的作用。与此同时，汉语和文化已经被锚定在德国高等教育体系的更广泛的结构中，并进入中等教育。在其他文化外交场所，艺术一直是中国在德国定位和向更广泛的受众介绍国家的主要方式。我们可以注意到省级行为体的存在。德国政府略有不安，"一带一路"倡议为德国和欧盟层面的文化外交拓展提供了更多机会。

谈到中国与巴西的关系，中国的文化外交还没有得到明显的发展。与德国在公共外交领域的不同之处在于，中国在巴西的公共外交以"南南合作"叙事为中心，强调了这种新兴关系的机会和共同利益。同样，对德国来说，孔子学院是跨区域推广的主要参与者。与中德关系相比，尽管两国在职业、中学和高等教育方面的合作潜力巨大，但两国之间几乎没有学术合作。此外，在巴西的中国媒体

（Xinhua、CGTN 等）的存在以及在媒体领域的合作协议的实施，进一步反映了促进中国有利观点的努力。

　　总体而言，未来的研究将有必要在不同的国家背景下考察中国文化外交的更为具体的安排。同样重要的是，我们需要进一步了解文化外交的有效性。正如指出的那样，因为文化外交是公共外交的一个组成部分，"为了拓宽外交政策的客观主体而支持输出国家文化的代表性样本"。文化外交实践如何被感知和转化为输出的理论，是满足国内外日益增长的期望的决定性因素。

China's Cultural Diplomacy in Brazil and Germany

Alena Profit Pachioni / Germany

University of Brasilia, Researcher

Introduction

Building relationships and the perceptions of businesses, political leaders, and everyday citizens of the countries China is engaging with will be key to consolidate China's role globally. Behind all the achievements of China's international economic development, the role of cultural diplomacy and soft power initiatives are fundamental pillars to increasing a greater sense of understanding in the international community. With a diversified actor structure in China, the ways and forms cultural diplomacy works in the different national settings is tied to more complex realities. This paper explores the institutional set-ups and mechanisms guiding cultural diplomacy in China and China's cultural diplomacy in two different geographical regions: Brazil as an emerging and Germany as an industrialized country.[1]

---

1   This paper does not draw an entire picture of all cultural diplomacy activities in Brazil and Germany. It shows limitations due to the difficulty to get an into-depth picture of the scope of China's cultural diplomacy initiatives in the respective national contexts, we also did not consider the German or Brazilian cultural diplomacy activities towards China. It also does not evaluate the economic cooperation between the countries, or the wider multilateral forum in which cultural diplomacy also may take place. It would require a larger study to explicitly link the home and host context links between Chinese cultural diplomacy in Brazil and Germany.

To begin with, there are few comparative studies available on comparative cultural diplomacy impacts in the setting of Chinese foreign policy and wider public diplomacy efforts. Hartig (2014) shows that Confucius Institutes in African countries differ when compared to the settings of Confucius Institutes on other continents. For example, the role of foreign aid has been specifically linked to Confucius Institutes and China's foreign policy agenda (Hartig, 2014). This just underscores how important it is to engage in cross-regional explorative research by asking how China's cultural diplomacy contributes to China's desired international image-building and how this differs across different countries. To address these issues, this approach will situate cultural diplomacy in Chinese political and academic thinking; assess Chinese cultural diplomacy efforts in Brazil and Germany and review data on the image of China in Brazilian and German public opinion.[1]Given that cultural diplomacy is multidimensional, underpinned by different socio-political issues, the paper by no means is exhaustive. Rather, it aims to contribute to a growing field of comparative studies on China's cultural diplomacy abroad.

Cultural Diplomacy

Public diplomacy, according to Cull (2009, p.18) involves "collecting and collating data about publics and their opinions overseas" (Cull 2009a, p. 18); efforts to make "cultural resources and achievements known overseas" (Cull, 2009a, p.19); "international communication activity to actively promote a particular policy and ideas… " (Cull, 2009, ap.18);"technologies of radio, television and Internet to engage with foreign publics" (Cull 2009, p.21). Cultural diplomacy is a component of public diplomacy and may entail a national approach "to support the export of representative samples of that national culture in order to further the objectives of foreign policy" (Gienow-Hecht & Donfried, 2010, p.15).More traditionally, cultural diplomacy, refers to the ability to persuade through value, ideas and culture (Nye, 2004), intangible power resources based on culture, ideology and institutions (Nye,

---

1   Drawing on a comparative, qualitative approach, the paper assesses the country-contexts supported by both Chinese, English, German and Portuguese data sources, bibliographic review and two interviews in Brazil and two interviews in Germany with practitioners or experts on the issue.

1990). From this perspective, cultural diplomacy is part of foreign affairs and international relations,a key ingredient to success in world politics (Nye 2004).

It is thus vital to assess the environment in which cultural diplomacy is set to be effective, meaning that the historical local and national conditions of a particular country must be considered in order to make cultural diplomacy impact effective (Schneider, 2003). What makes cultural diplomacy further effective is that should maintain a separation from the political issues of diplomacy, and as Cull (2009b, p. 24) illustrates: "be credibly connected to the source of culture rather than policy and helped by distance from the makers of foreign policy".This makes cultural diplomacy, in its different forms, particularly effective for diplomatic outreach and a basis to construct long-term relations.

In terms of structure, the first section discusses a conceptual outlook on cultural diplomacy and reviews the foundations of the country's strategic and ideational thinking, as well as the scattered actor structure. Second, Chinese cultural diplomacy initiatives are reviewed in Germany through media, language promotion and art initiatives. In the same section, available data on German public opinion regarding China is assessed. Third, Chinese cultural diplomacy initiatives are reviewed in Brazil through media, language promotion and art initiatives. In the same section, available data on Brazilian public opinion regarding China is assessed. Lastly, the conclusion brings the two different contexts into perspective.

Chinese Cultural Diplomacy

In China, public diplomacy (公共外交) is both a strategic and functional tool (Hartig, 2016), in contrast to which cultural diplomacy cultural diplomacy (文化外交) is to be understood in terms of striving towards soft power and image-building efforts. In addition, Zhao (2015) notes that Chinese refer to two notions of the Western understanding of public diplomacy:

(1)External propaganda (对外宣传): understood as global diffusion of Chinese success towards over seas audience and thus related to the system of state publicity; (2)

People-to-people diplomacy(民间外交).

Different studies have focused on China's cultural diplomacy (e.g. Zhang, 2017) and emphasized that these etymological differences are related to the different traditions of diplomatic thought and history of the country, being shaped by blending the country's vision of development, opening up and modernization with the revival of more traditional Confucionist and Daoist values and references (Zhang, 2015). That said, scholars highlight the role of ideational leadership as orienting factor on international politics, such as in the case of China. In assessing the structures of China's cultural diplomacy, it is necessary to locate the analysis in the wider historical context of China's development and foreign policy. While in the past, cultural diplomacy was pursed rather moderately, the recent years demonstrate how the country has stepped up its soft power initiatives and the greater inclination to grand narratives.

A brief history of Chinese cultural diplomacy

Chinese cultural development can briefly be divided into three phases: (1) The period from 1949-1978, during which the engagement with other countries is reduced, maintaining a focus on the Cultural Revolution, with culture as a tool to influence ideology; (2) The period from 1978-2000, during which the opening strategy led to increasing international interest; and the period from 2000 until now, which features the emphasis of the promotion Chinese culture and ideas abroad as a means of positioning and rebranding the image of the country. While in the past, cultural diplomacy was pursed rather moderately, the recent years demonstrate how the country has stepped up its soft power initiatives and inclination towards grand narratives. The rising narrative of China as not only a leader of economic development, but also as county with a rich cultural heritage has been further bolstered at political level. 'Building cultural soft power' was mentioned in the 12th Five-Year-Plan (2011-2015) and Chinese President Xi Jinping incorporated the concept of cultural soft power into the vision of the Chinese Dream(Liu, 2017). The leadership of President Xi furthermarked overall a stronger influencing of the rhetoric's of international affairs and the Western-oriented liberal order, Huàyǔ quán (话语权) is concerned with the establishment of a discourse containing Chinese values and concepts. This has been outlined by Prof. Zhang Zhizhou(张志洲):

To promote China's international discourse power and break the basic pattern of international discourse power of "Western strong and we weak" requires strategic planning and reasonable and effective policy measures (State Council, 2017).[1]

Moreover, in 2016, the 29th meeting of the Leading Group for the Central Deepening of All-round Reforms was convened, and the "Guiding Opinions on Further Strengthening and Improving Chinese Cultural Outreach" was reviewed and adopted. This brief oversight shows that the cultural diplomacy has been tied to an ambitious agenda of getting its share at the global level.

Organization and actors of cultural diplomacy

China's cultural diplomacy is expressed through an array of activities, cultural exchanges, local government initiatives, and civil society initiatives. Overall, the nature of cultural diplomacy features two central elements. First, cultural diplomacy is tied to the greater narratives, principles-based logic and policy guidance of central government actors. The combination of a long-term national agenda in terms of economic development as well as ideational/ideological underpinnings with diverse players creates a flexible platform and strong adaptive capabilities. Second, cultural diplomacy is less coordinated and reflects the complexity of the country's national administrative and political system with the different layers and institutional cultures. This emphasizes the role of leveraging the collective weight and efforts to promote the desired outcomes as key. Thus, cultural diplomacy may happen at different levels, such as high-level or working-level and target different set of audiences, such as scholars, decision-makers in politics or public policy, business sector or the general public. In addition, Wang (2008) observes the origin of the

---

1 要提升中国国际话语权，打破"西强我弱"的国际话语权基本格局，需要有战略性筹划和合理有效的政策措施。

blending of public affairs and public diplomacy in the Chinese political system.

The following offers an overview of actors of Chinese cultural diplomacy.

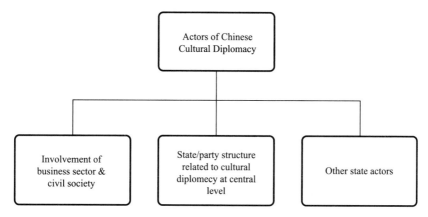

According to Cappelletti (2017), Chinese cultural diplomacy operates in a multi-centric infrastructure across broad networks, and while the state actors reflect the Party-state and economic interests, non-state actors can be encountered where there is a cultural, scholarly or cultural interest for China.

Key agents of cultural diplomacy are the government and party structures, including the International Communication Bureau of the Department of Publicity of the CPC Central Committee, the International Communication Office of the NPC (National People's Congress) and the CPPCC (Chinese People's Political Consultative Conference), the Bureau of External Cultural Relations of the Ministry of Culture and of Education, and the news department of the Ministry of Foreign Affairs, among others. With the number of actors, rather than following rather than following a national strategy of public or cultural diplomacy specifically, organizations follow rather specific under the umbrella of the general outline (Zhao, 2015). The CPC has the say in the ideological positioning, and according to Zhao (2015, p.181): "communication and coordination between the Member of the Politburo of the CPC Central Committee, the State Councillor, and ministers responsible for foreign affairs, as well as various official, semi-official, and non-governmental organizations related to public diplomacy…their positions and actions often provide crucial linkages between the top leader and specific programmes."

Other state actors provincial and municipal organs, civil society groups, "people's diplomacy" associations, intellectual elites, academic institutions, overseas Chinese institutions. In this regard, it is also valid to mention the Think Tank Strategy driven by the Chinese government (State Council, 2015). The 18th CPC Party Congress in 2013 encouraged the creation of think tanks with Chinese characteristics and in 2015 both State Council and CCP Central Committee joined efforts in forging the further consolidation of think tanks with Chinese characteristics (China News, 2017), towards the establishment of internationally influential think tanks by the year of 2020. This implies close ties between research, policy and politics. For example, the Belt and Road (BRI) think-tank alliance was launched in 2015 State Council's Development Research Center, Fudan University and the Chinese Academy of Social Sciences (CASS). Equally, the Silk Road Think Tank Association was launched in 2016 with the objective to "deepen people's understanding for the development initiative, and avoid misunderstandings between countries"(China Daily, 2016).

● Involvement of business sector and civil society

Whereas the understanding of private sector in China may differ from Western contexts, Chinese companies have been involved in public and cultural diplomacy to the extent that they actively link foreign policy objectives and business interests. For example,the presence of Chinese SOEs and their corporate social responsibility programs are culturally implementing Chinese culture-oriented programs.

● Programmes and forms of cultural diplomacy

Diffusing language and cultural awareness and learning about China, but also to create a lasting effect on their image in China and influence opinion-building across different contexts.

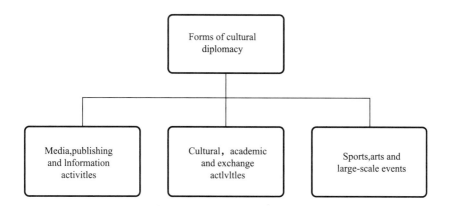

Cultural, academic and exchange activities: One of the main instruments of Chinese cultural diplomacy abroad refers to the role of Confucius Institutes, administered by the Office of Chinese Language Council International (Hanban), affiliated with the Chinese Ministry of Education and composed of various other representatives from ministries and government agencies and occasional cooperation with other research institute's or agencies. In 2017, there were a total of 516 Confucius Institutes and 1,076 Confucius Classrooms have been established in 142 countries and regions, according to the Confucius Institute Headquarters (China Daily, 2017), founded in 1974 and opened its first Confucius Institute in South Korea in 2004 (China Daily, 2017). As Hartig emphasis in his study on German Confucius Institutes that since cultural diplomacy is the means through which soft power is exercised, consequently, Confucius Institutes ca be grasped as instrument to China's cultural diplomacy seeking to wield and bolster Chinese soft power globally (Hartig, 2010, p.11). Moreover, the Cultural Centre holds location in Europe with seven centres (Paris, Malta, Berlin, Moscow, Madrid Copenhagen and Brussels); Africa (Mauritius, Benin, Cairo, Nigeria and Tanzania), Asia (Seoul, Tokyo, Ulaanbaatar, Bangkok, Laos, Sri Lanka, Pakistan, Nepal and Singapore) and in Mexico, Sidney, New Zealand and Fiji (Zhang, 2016). The institutes pursue different programmes and activities with a main focus on traditional culture. According to the same author what distinguishes the China Cultural Institute from the Confucius Institutes is the use of both official and informal domestic resources, collaborating with state-owned organizations and private enterprises, including performing groups and martial arts practitioners and contacts with the overseas Chinese diaspora (Zhang, 2016).

Media, publishing and information activities: The country has strongly invested in media and information activities. Dissemination through State Council Information Office, embassies, Xinhua, China Global Television Network, China Radio International, China Daily, Global Times, Social Media. Many Chinese media channels have multi-language TV channels and websites, taking their voice in the landscape of global communication with offices across the globe. Bilateral and multilateral media cooperation, trainings, and professional exchange agreements are the base for the expansion of China search to take a bigger stake in global communication. Thus, establishing relationships with foreign public can also take place at a more direct level. For example, an insert paid by China Daily, "China Watch" was featured in major global newspapers, such as the New York Times and the Wall Street Journal, amongst others.

In this sense, the slogan "Borrow a Ship to Reach the Sea" summarizes the efforts to impact on overseas markets. This can be for example seen in a recent case ofthepublishingindustry:

> However, in order to truly achieve the world, the Chinese publishing industry must increase its efforts to "build ships to the sea", further innovate ways, and constantly open up the road to the world. In this regard, many countries have relatively mature experience for reference. In some developed countries in Europe and America, the publication of "going out" is not limited to the export of books in kind, special funds and specialized talents "going out", and using soft power to influence hard power has become a model. In addition, the publication of exhibitions and non-traded publications around the world can also pass on the culture to the world. Only by continuously building new platforms and opening new channels can we expand the international coverage of China's excellent books and make Chinese publishing truly a window for the world to understand China. (Xinhua News Agency, 2016).

This emphatic demand for framing China in literature and the publishing industry shows:There is a growing tendency for initiatives seeking to exercise influence on media content, as well influence the tone of political discussions and agenda-setting, referring back to the establishment of a discourse-system supporting the successful positioning of the government abroad.

Sports and large-scale events: There are also events which to a certain degree dialogue with Chinese cultural diplomacy, the possibility for image-building and the opportunity for bringing in cultural diplomacy events: Beijing Olympic Games, Shanghai Expo, APEC Beijing Summit, 2016 G20 Hangzhou Summit in 2016, 2017 Belt and Road Summit in Beijing and 2017 BRICS Summit in Xiamen.[1]

To conclude, this section outlined the forms Chinese cultural diplomacy is practiced abroad, as well as the foundational ideas and positions behind it. In the following part, an explorative approach follows Wyszomirski et al.(2003, p. 3) in specifically looking out for the following activities and mechanisms, the exchange for educational and cultural purposes; exhibitions and performances abroad; sponsoring seminars and conferences both in-country and abroad that include international participants; promotion of language studies and cultural related programmes and institutions, including staff and personnel; support for country studies programmes; cooperation on cultural issues as well as trade activities for cultural goods and services.

Chinese Cultural Diplomacy in Germany

Bilateral cooperation is expressed by the increased status and recognition the German government attributed to Sino-German relations. One of the most important mechanisms are the bilateral consultations, in place since 2011 when German Chancellor Angela Merkel welcomed Chinese Premier Wen Jiabao to the first German-Chinese intergovernmental consultations in Berlin (Auswärtiges

---

1   It should be stressed, however, that these activities mainly refer to China's cultural diplomacy domestically, in the event of international events in the country, rather than abroad. For this reason, sport and large-scale events will not be included in the analysis to be followed.

Amt, 2016). In 2014, the Sino-German relations were upgraded from a "strategic partnership in global responsibility" to a "comprehensive strategic partnership".

The multitude of cooperation mechanisms focus mainly on technology, economic and educational cooperation, as expressed in the official statement of bilateral intergovernmental consultations or e.g. in key documents such as the China Strategy of the German Federal Research Ministry (BMF). The German Foreign Office has thus stepped up efforts and personal on China, aiming to aim for a more structured Asian policy and an increase in China related knowledge and skills (Auswärtiges Amt, 2017).

Cultural cooperation between China and Germany dates back to the late seventies. In 1978, a delegation from the German Federal Ministry of Research and Technology visited Beijing. This started discussions on an intergovernmental agreement on cooperation in science and technology (Wan Gang, 2016). In October 1978, both governments signed the "Agreement between the Government of the Federal Republic of Germany and the Government of the People's Republic of China on Scientific and Technological Cooperation", one of the first cooperation agreements between both countries. The agreement on economic cooperation and the agreement on cultural cooperation came into force within the two following years. Since then, cooperation in the field of culture has been stepped up significantly. The first meeting of the Sino-German High-Level People-to-People Dialogue to promote and support social and cultural exchange was held in Beijing on 24 May 2017. Attended by more than 500 people, the meeting was cochaired by Germany's then Foreign Minister Sigmar Gabriel and China's Vice-Premier Liu Yandong. The dialogue aims to improve the environment for civil society exchange between Germany and China in the areas of education, culture, language, media, sports and youth.

Cultural, Academic and Exchange Activities

● **Promotion of Chinese language**

Until today, there are nearly twenty Confucius Institutes in the country, most of them established at universities through cooperation agreements, with a budget of around 200,000 to 350,000 Euros annually (Thies, 2015). Apart from the language focus, the institutes themselves show differences in their further non-language programme, including cultural competency courses with a corporate focus, SinoJobs Career Days, a special focus on secondary teacher training in Göttingen, a focus on exhibitions in Berlin, courses in calligraphy and cooking , Tai Chi classes, Green Economy in China and introductions to the Chinese legal system. What follows below is a list of Confucius Institutes across the Federal States:

Table1 : Distribution of Confucius Institutes in Germany

Federal states	Confucius Institutes
Berlin	Konfuzius-Institut Berlin
Bremen	Konfuzius-Institut Bremen
North Rhine-Westphalia	Konfuzius-Institut Metropole Ruhr
North Rhine-Westphalia	Konfuzius-Institut Düsseldorf
Thuringia	Konfuzius-Institut an der Fachhochschule
Hesse	Konfuzius-Institut Frankfurt
Lower Saxony	Akademisches Konfuzius-Institut Göttingen
Hamburg	Konfuzius-Institut Hamburg
Lower Saxony	Konfuzius-Institut Hannover
Baden-Württemberg	Konfuzius-Institut Heidelberg
Baden-Württemberg	Konfuzius-Institut Freiburg
Saxony	Konfuzius-Institut Leipzig
Bavaria	Konfuzius-Institut München
North Rhine-Westphalia	Konfuzius-Institut Paderborn
Mecklenburg-Vorpommern	Konfuzius-Institut der Fachhochschule Stralsund
Bavaria	Audi-Konfuzius Institut Ingolstadt
Bavaria	Konfuzius-Institut Nürnberg-Erlangen
Rhineland-Palatinate	Konfuzius-Institut Trier
Thuringia	Konfuzius-Klassenzimmer an der Salzmannschule Schnepfenthal
North Rhine-Westphalia	Konfuzius-Institut Bonn

In his study on Confucius Institutes in Germany, Hartig (2010, p.11) notes that the institutes maintain a degree of autonomy when it comes to teaching materials, combining the official Hanban materials with their own materials.In the case of Germany, a multi-dimensional structure on which the promotion of China and image-building can be, built and can be further assessed. A 2018 report by the Mercator Institute for China Studies assessed the needs of Germany engaging with China and emphasized the importance of strategically well-positioned country approach and skilled professionals with an into-depth China knowledge. The authors assess that the focus on China at university y level has universities has grown since the mid-1990s, including sinology and interdisciplinary courses focusing on China, additional offers and certificates, German-Chinese study programs and double degrees. As of November 2017, there were 1347 formal cooperation schemes between Chinese and German universities (Stepan, Frenzel, Ives & Hoffmann, 2016,p.53).

The report also notes that while there are over 100 support programs that support China stays of varying duration, the increase of Chinese institutions as implementers for support programs targeting cultural and educational exchange, as for example the China Scholarship Council (CSC) awarding of grants to the Chinese Ministry of Education, which is awarded on behalf of the Chinese government for study and research stays targeting aiming at different target groups, including, students, graduate students, volunteers, scientists and young professionals. Thus, an increasing number of Chinese institutions are located directly in Germany, such as the Confucius Institutes or Chinese private companies, such as the German section of the technology giant Huawei, which has launched its own support programs for the German target group (Stepan et al, 2016, p. 83).

This observation correlates with other studies on Chinese cultural diplomacy which notes the increasing role of private sector companies in representing and forging cultural and educational ties. At secondary level, about 5000 students are currently learning Chinese at German schools, with a decline in numbers throughout the last years. This is in a stark contrast to France in the immediate vicinity of Germany, where around 38,000 students are learning Chinese at secondary level (Stepan et al, 2016, p.41). Overall, however, there have been efforts in stepping up Chinese studies and a clear professionalization of the field is noted (Stepan et al, 2016, p.10). That said, the tertiary education level infrastructure to engage with China in terms may differ or even lack behind other major European countries, such as France and the UK, but nevertheless rests on a strong foundation.

● **Promotion of art and traditional culture**

Germany's capital Berlin is host to a China Cultural Center, opened in 2008, as a counterpart of the Goethe-Institute in China. The multi-dimensional relations with China to Germany are further substantiated by cultural exchange continue, such as the "Deutschland 8" exhibition that opened in Beijing in September 2017. It follows the "China 8" exhibition that was staged in North Rhine-Westphalia in 2015. Further examples show the diversity of actors involved in promoting Chinese culture in Germany, as for example a 2018 exhibition in the German city of Düsseldorf held by the information office of the Qinghai provincial government on the culture, art and landscape of Qinghai Province showed (Xinhua News Agency, 2018). Bigger scale events, such as the 2007-2010 event series "Deutschland und China – Gemeinsam in Bewegung" [Germany and China – Together in Motion], the 2012 "Chinesisches Kulturjahr" [Chinese Culture Year] in 2012, and the "Deutsch-Chinesisches Sprachenjahr"[German-China Language Year] and the 2016 "Deutsch-Chinesische Jahr für Schüler-und Jugendaustausch"[German-China Year for Student and Youth Exchange].

Media, publishing and information activities

In terms of Media cooperation and influence, the English-language newspaper supplement "China Watch", produced by China's largest English-language newspaper, state-owned China Daily has been featured in two German newspapers, the Handelsblatt, and the Süddeutsche Zeitung (Deutsche Welle, 2018). Further cooperation has been underway in the entertainment industry, as for example in the recent cooperation agreement between Studio Babelsberg and Wuxi Studio.

● China in the German public opinion

In an ideal scenario, public and cultural diplomacy exercise a positive effect on country perceptions and attitudes towards the country. A representative study on public opinion in Germany towards China reflected an overall positive image with diverging results for opinion on bilateral political and economic relations. In 2016, opinions on Chinese economic power is viewed with less preoccupation than two years before (2014: 49% and 2016:44%). In 2016, 59% of Germans believe that China's economy 31 has a rather large (42%) or very large (17%) influence on Germany. Within the group of economic decision-makers, this share is 69%, and among policy-makers even 90% of respondents (Huawei, 2016). And while there is an overall increased interest and rise in preference formation, the rise of the Belt and Road Initiative further drew attention to the changing role of China for Germany, exercising impacts bilaterally as well as in the wider EU context with consequences for Germany (Harnisch, 2018). In the end, there needs to be more specific empirical evidence until which extend German public is responsive to Chinese cultural diplomacy and open to influence over the long-run. Building up credibility and building up trust, the views of the public opinion and support for particular issues can be triggered.

● The impact of Chinese cultural diplomacy on Sino-German Relations

Public diplomacy has an important function in the relations China maintains with Germany. Ahead of the G20 in Germany, the arrival ceremony of the pandas at Berlin Zoo, in the form as loans from China, was attended by German Chancellor Angela Merkel and Chinese President Xi Jinping. This received high-level media attention and reinforced a narrative of an empowered China with global and strategic self-presentation. In terms of agenda-setting of Chinese cultural diplomacy activities in Germany are emphatic about Chinese culture and traditions, their historical roots and the non-political component to these elements. The analysis shows the distribution of Confucius Institutes and the increased engagement of Chinese actors in educational exchange schemes. One of the impacts of these recent developments are voices in German media and civil society concerning a potential surge in Chinese influence-taking in Germany (Stepanet al, 2008), being sceptical of the motivations underlying Chinese cultural diplomacy. Possibly creating reputational issues for China, cultural diplomacy could achieve the opposite of its desired effect. Lastly, another aspect concerns who reaches out. Whereas actors are mainly central government or central government affiliated (e.g. state-media, Confucius Institutes or the China Culture Centre), provincial level cultural diplomacy activities occur through exhibitions, etc.

Chinese Cultural Diplomacy In Brazil

• Bilateral relations between Brazil and China

In 1974, Brazil and China RPC initiated their diplomatic ties. In 1993, both countries established a strategic partnership and in 2006 the Sino-Brazilian High-Level Coordination and Cooperation Commission (hereinafter COSBAN) was initiated as the body for regular political dialogue and cooperation between the two countries. COSBAN will be the main decision-making body of the Plan of Joint Action and the Ten-Year Cooperation Plan in its areas of competence. The respective Subcommittees meet each year to advance the implementation of the Joint Plan of Action or propose possible areas of cooperation.Concerning bilateral cultural cooperation, both countries agreed to uphold their cooperation in the fields of culture and the arts, radio, film and television, press and publishing, sports and cultural heritage, and foster more frequent cultural exchanges and more intensive collaboration in these areas (Funag, 2016, p.475). In terms of overall public diplomacy efforts, high-level visits between Chinese and Brazilian leaders stress the complementarity of the"South–South"relationship with"mutual benefits".

• Analysis of China's cultural diplomacy activities in Brazil

The following provides an overview of China's cultural diplomacy initiatives, or better, the cultural-diplomacy-related initiatives and actions in Germany. While this overview may not be complete, it provides an understanding of the progress of Chinese engagement. We choose to look at three different fields: (a) cultural, academic and exchange activities and (b) media, publishing and information activities. Subsequently, the part on China's cultural diplomacy initiatives in Brazil concludes with a review on current data on Brazilian public opinion on China.

● Cultural, academic and exchange activities

As cultural diplomacy initiatives are yet to spread nationally although the promotion of Chinese language and culture, Li Jinzhang, Chinese ambassador to Brazil evaluates the positive endorsement at bilateral level:

In recent years, I have seen the interest and enthusiasm of the two peoples grow in knowing and understanding each other. Activities such as Cultural Month, Film Week, photo exhibitions, shows and fine art shows, as well as the Rio 2016 Olympic Games and other sporting events, have contributed to mutual understanding and rapprochement. This will strengthen the basis for bilateral cultural exchanges, creating new mechanisms and a longer horizon.

In 2018, Brazilian National Congress established August 15th as the Chinese Immigration Day in Brazil, such recognition may further contribute to forge the image of China.

● Promotion of Chinese language

In 2008, the first Confucius Institute was opened at the State University of Sao Paulo (UNESP). According to the Chinese ambassador to Brazil, Li Jinzhang, today, there are 10 Institutes and 4 Confucius Classrooms with more than 20.000 enrolled students, making Brazil the country with the largest number of these institutions in operation in Latin America (Li, 2017). Geographically, the Confucius Institutes in Brazil are distributed across the five regions of the country, with a strong emphasis of the South-East region.

Table2: **Distribution of Confucius Institutes in Brazil**

Region	University
Center-West	University of Brasília (UNB);
North	State University of Pará (UEPA)
Northeast	University of Pernambuco (UPE), Federal University of Ceará (UFC),
South	Federal University of Rio Grande do Sul (UFRGS
Southeast	Armando Alvares Penteado Foundation (FAAP), Pontifícia Universidade Católica do Rio de Janeiro (PUC-RIO); Federal University of Minas Gerais UFMG; State University of São Paulo (UNESP), State University of Campinas (UNICAMP)

Overall, the Confucius Institutes aim to provide an educational, cultural and linguistic experience to the student. Just as in the German case, interviewees in Brazil confirm that the language sources used may combine Hanban teaching materials with Portuguese language ones, as there "is a need to adapt the materials to the local needs of the student". Moreover, as a former staffer of the institute describes: "There are strong elements of cultural elements and national images of mainland China, but the students can discuss and engage with this content critically." [1]Lastly, while the number of private language services is increasing, there is a great potential for expanding Chinese language and culture initiatives, specifically when it comes to primary or secondary levels, such as a public middle school in Niteroi, Rio de Janeiro State.

● Promotion of art and traditional culture

Chinese art and artists have been featured by Brazilian institutions. For example, in 2014, China Arte Brasil was held for the first time held in São Paulo with an exhibition of works of internationally renowned Chinese artists. In 2017, China was the thematic focus of the International Biennial of Curitiba, presenting works chosen by the Ministry of Culture and Tourism of China. Moreover, there is also support for Chinese cultural events and festivals, such as the Chinese New Year Celebration or the Lantern Festival in São Paulo, supported by the Chinese Consulate in São Paulo.

1　Interview conducted in 2018-06-24.

Media, publishing and information activities:

In terms of Chinese media presence in Brazil, CGTN (China Global Television Network), formerly known as China Central Television (CCTV) and part of the China Global Television Network group, opened an office in São Paulo in 2010, with the mission of coordinating its operations in Latin America, in Spanish and Portuguese. In 2016, the official Chinese news agency Xinhua launched a portal in Portuguese. The launch coincided with the start of the Olympic Games in Rio de Janeiro. In addition to Xinhua, also the digital version of the People's Daily, the central body of the Chinese Communist Party, and China's International Radio (CRI), have a service in Portuguese. In 2018, the China International Publishing Group (CIPG), the largest foreign-language publishing organisation in China, launched a writing competition for Brazilian participants to write on their China-related experience. When it comes to the specific cooperation between Brazil in the context of culture, the Forum for Economic and Trade Co-operation between China and Portuguese-speaking Countries (Macao), also known as Forum Macao, is another venue through which cooperation can take place.

China in the Brazilian public opinion

As previously mentioned, the impact of preference-shaping by cultural diplomacy has been discussed by several authors. There is no systematic long-term study on the reception of the China image in Brazilian public opinion and no study available to assess whether Chinese cultural diplomacy in Brazil had positive impact. However, the understanding of the importance of China has increased due to the substantive presence of Chinese companies in the country. In terms of measuring the degree of favourable views on China, the Global Attitudes survey undertaken by the Pew Center assessed the views on China in Brazil with 44% of ratings being favourable and an equal percentage of 44% being unfavourable (Pew Center, 2014). In terms of differences in age gaps on views on China, young people tend to have more positive attitudes toward China than older respondents within the age group of 18-29 years (53%), the age group of 30-49 years (43%) and the age group of 50 and older

(36%) (Pew Center, 2014). Similarly, Armony & Velasquz (2016) suggest a positive trend in public opinion in Latin America, including Brazil. While these numbers are merely snapshots and greater research into how the China-image is being built and impacts on public opinion is needed, the rising attention China has received is utterly linked to its economic performance abroad. What may further impact in the future is the increased number of Chinese migrants and community in the country who contribute to diversify and personalize an image of the country.

The Impact of Chinese Cultural Diplomacy on Sino-Brazilian Relations

Public diplomacy has an important function in the relations China maintains with Brazil. Under the umbrella of the overall public diplomacy approach, Chinese cultural diplomacy has a medium impact on China-Brazil relations in the sense that it shapes the perception of a larger public and opens the door to further increase the reach of China's economic opportunities. In terms of cultural diplomacy in the field of education and exchange, language learning initiatives but also country-related expertise help shape the way China expertise is built up in Brazil. This shows specifically the role of targeting political and economic leaders, academia, as well as media and the wider public opinion at events, such as the Chinese New Year and Spring Festival. In terms of active image building and nation-branding, the Confucius Institute has a solid role in setting an agenda of China's projected image and disseminate messages. In the case of Brazil, the cultural diplomacy approach is a learning-by-doing approach in which the different actors of the Chinese system complement and contribute towards the greater objective. Another example is China Global Television Network (CGTN), of state broadcaster China Central Television(CCTV), offering apositive China image in Portuguese language.

The inauguration of a Day of Chinese Migration in Brazil is a further step towards generating a wider platform to call attention, but also to further mobilize the growing Chinese community in Brazil. This has to be also seen in the wider context of the efforts to mobilize the ethnic Chinese overseas as it has been the case in other geographic contexts, being a useful way to furthering the national agenda.

Conclusion

China's ability to seize opportunity and increase its presence through cultural diplomacy attests to its effectiveness and increased capability to wield its soft power. This paper explored both Brazil and Germany as contexts where China has increased its cultural diplomacy presence during the past years. Drawing on the analysis, the paper summarizes the five mainpoints.

Domestically, China's cultural diplomacy has taken a more direct political form in the official political discourse, underscoring the importance of domestic factors in public diplomacy studies.

Cultural diplomacy initiatives in Brazil and China differ in terms of scale and framing. In the case of Brazil, they are embedded in a South-South narrative.

Similarities can be found in the agenda-setting of Chinese cultural diplomacy activities in both countries. Image and identity are built around the historical roots of traditions, values and cultural arts, stressing an "apolitical" approach to cultural outreach, as illustrated by Cull (2009), when emphasizing the need to maintain a distance between the cultural and political aspects of foreign policy.

Fourth, actors mostly belong to the central government structure; however, provincial governments engage in the promotion of their regions.

Under the umbrella of bilateral cooperation and China's overall policy guidance, cultural diplomacy actors pursue sometimes overlapping activities in setting up enabling conditions for Chinese interests. Cumulatively, relationship-building measures work side by side with the growing economic interests.

Summarizing the respective country contexts demonstrate the importance of analysing cultural diplomacy from a cross-country perspective. In the case of Germany, the scattered actor structure in China is replicated in the cultural diplomacy outreach. Different actors, most notably the Confucius Institutes and the China Culture Centre spearhead initiatives disseminating China-related programmes in the field of language and cultural activities. Most importantly, the Confucius Institutes hold an important role due to its widespread activities at the secondary and tertiary education level. At the same time, Chinese language and culture has already been anchored into the broader structure of the German higher education system and into secondary education. In terms of other venues of cultural diplomacy, arts have been a major way of positioning China in Germany and introducing the country to a wider audience. We can note the presence of provincial actors. Received with a certain discomfort by the German government, the Belt and Road Initiative brings further opportunities for cultural diplomacy outreach, involving Germany and national and EU-level.

When comes to China–Brazil ties, Chinese cultural diplomacy is yet to expand significantly. Different than in its public diplomacy outreach in Germany, China's public diplomacy in Brazil operates on a South-South narrative to stress the common interests and venues for opportunities of this burgeoning relationship. Similarly, to Germany, the Confucius Institute is the main actor with a cross-regional outreach. In contrast to Sino-German ties, there is little academic collaboration between both countries despite potential in terms of cooperation in vocational, secondary and higher education. A growing Chinese community is targeted through the introduction of the national Chinese Immigration Day, while an unconsolidated "China Studies" field and severe cuts to educational funding in Brazil leave room for Chinese diplomacy actors to mould knowledge production and the framing of China-related issues in academia. Moreover, the presence of Party-state media (Xinhua, CGTN, etc.) in Brazil, as well as the implementation of cooperation agreements in the field of media further reflect the efforts of promoting favourable views on China.

Overall, future research will be necessary to look into the more specific arrangements of China's cultural diplomacy in different national contexts. Equally important is the need to further understand the effectiveness of cultural diplomacy. As pointed out, since cultural diplomacy is a component of public diplomacy "to support the export of representative samples of that national culture in order to further the objectives of foreign policy" (Gienow-Hecht & Donfried, 2010, p.15), the role of knowledge about how the practice of cultural diplomacy is perceived and translated into outcomes is a determining factor to meet the rising expectations, both domestically and abroad.

References

Armony, Ariel; Velásquez, Nicolás. (2016). A Honeymoon with China? PublicPerceptions in Latin America and Brazil. Revista Tempo do Mundo, 2 (2):17-34.

Auswärtiges Amt. (2016, June 12). Enhancing cooperation: fourth German-Chinese intergovernmental consultations held in Beijing. Retrieved June 12, 2018, from: https://www.auswaertiges-amt.de/ en/aussenpolitik /laenderinformationen/china-node/160613-regkonsultationen/281194(2017, May 08).

Einrichtung einer Abteilung Asien und Pazifik. Retrieved June 12, 2018,from:https://fragdenstaat.de/files/foi/67292/OE-Abt.AP.pdf.

China Daily. (2017, October 07). Over 500 Confucius Institutes founded in 142 countries. Published. Retrieved July 13, from:http://www.chinadaily.com.cn/ china/2017-10/07/content_32950016.htm.

Cappelletti, Alessandra. (2017). The "Construction" of Chinese culture in a globalized world and its importance for Beijing's smart power: Notes and concepts on a narrative shift, Working Papers on East Asian Studies, No. 115/2017. Retrieved from https://www.econstor.eu/bitstream/10419/162559/1/890790310.pdf.

China Daily. (2016, February 23). Think tank to support Belt and Road Initiative. Retrieved July 13, from: http://www.chinadaily.com.cn/china/2016-02/23/ content_23611258.htm.

Cull, Nicholas. (2009a). Public Diplomacy: Lessons from the Past. LA: USC Centre for Public Diplomacy. (2009b). How We Got Here. In: Toward a New Public Diplomacy: Redirecting U.S. Foreign Policy. Philip Seib,ed.Pp.23-47.PalgraveMacmillan:NewYork.

Deutsche Welle. (2018, February 13). Chinas Medien offensive in Europa. Retrieved July 07 2018, from:https://www.dw.com/ de/chinas-medienoffensive-in-europa/ a-42497198.

Federal Ministry of Education and Research (BMBF). (2015). The China Strategy 2015-2020.https://www.bmbf.de/pub/China_Strategy_Longversion.pdf.

Fundação Alexandre de Gusmão. (2016). Brasil e China: 40 anos de relações diplomáticas: análisese documentos. Brasília: FUNAG, 2016.

Gienow-Hecht, Jessica and Donfried, Mark (2010). The Model of Cultural Diplomacy-Power, Distance, and the Promise of Civil Society, in Searching for a Cultural Diplomacy.

New York: Berghahn.

Gill, Bill; Huang, Yanzhong (2006). Sources and limits of Chinese 'soft power'. Survival,48(2),17-36.doi:10.1080/00396330600765377.

Hartig, Falk. (2010). Confusion about Confucius Institutes: Soft Power Push or Conspiracy? A Case Study of Confucius Institutes in Germany. Paper presented at the Biennial Conference of the Asian Studies Association of Australia, July 2010, Adelaide. Retrieved from citeseerx.ist.psu.edu/viewdoc/download?doi=10.1.1.458.49&rep=rep1&t ype=pdf (2012).

Soft Power in China: Public diplomacy through communication. Chinese Journal of Communication, 477-480.(2014, March 17). The Globalization of Chinese Soft Power. Retrieved from https://www.youtube.com/watch?v=iIbAUUR07xg (2016).

How China Understands Public Diplomacy: The Importance of National Image for National Interests. International Studies Review,18(4), pp.655–680.

Harnisch, Sebastian (2018). Deutschlands Politik gegenüber der Belt-and-Road-Initiative der Volksrepublik China 2013-2018, Yearbook, Chinese Academy of Social Sciences, 2017, Beijing. Retrieved https://www.uni-heidelberg.de/md/politik/harnisch/ person/ publikationen/harnisch_deutschlands_reaktion_auf_die_seidenstrasseninitiativen_ zeitschrift_asien.pdf.

Huawei. (2014). Deutschland und China – Wahrnehmung und Realität. Die Huawei-Studie 2014, Retrieved from http://www.huaweistudie.de/downloads/HuaweiStudie-2014-DE.pdf(2016). Deutschland und China – Wahrnehmung und Realität. DieHuawei-Studie2016,Retrievedfrom http://www.huawei-studie.de/downloads/Huawei-Studie-2016-DE.pdf.

Kong, Da. (2015) Imaging China: China's cultural diplomacy through loan exhibitions to British museums. PhD Dissertation.University of Leicester, United Kingdom.

Li Jinzhang .(20 July 2017). Speech at the Curitiba Biennial 2017 edition. Retrieved June 23, 2018 from: bienaldecuritiba.com.br/2017/china/.

Liu, Xin. (2017). Look Beyond and Beneath the Soft Power:An Alternative Analytical Framework for China's Cultural Diplomacy. Cambridge Journal of China Studies,12(4) https://doi.org/10.17863/CAM.21537.

Nye, Joseph.(1990).Softpower. ForeignPolicyNr. 80,pp.153-171. (2004). Soft Power: The Means to Success in World Politics. New York: Public Affairs.

Pew Research Center. (2014). Global Opposition to U.S. Surveillance and Drones, but Limited Harm to America's Image. Washington: Pew Research Center. Retrieved fromhttp://www.pewglobal.org/files/2014/07/2014-07-14-Balance-of-Power.pdf.

Stepan, Matthias; Frenzel,Andrea; Ives, Jaqueline; Hoffmann, Marie. (2018). China Kennen, China Können. Ausgangspunkte für den Ausbau von China-Kompetenz in Deutschland.

Mercator Institute for China Studies (MERICS).Retrieved from https:// www.merics. org/sites/default/files/201805/MERICS_China_Monitor_45_ China_kennen_China_ koennen.pdf.

Thies, Erich. (2015). Goethe ja, Konfuzius nein? Bemerkungen zu den Konfuzius Instituten in Deutschland. Konrad Adenauer Foundation. Nr. 535, November/Dezember 2015, 60. Jahrgang. Retrieved from: http://www.kas.de/wf/doc/kas_43584-544-1-30. pdf?151207112750.

Wan Gang. (2014). Die deutsch-chinesische Zusammenarbeit in Wissenschaft und Technologie als erfolgreiches Beispiel für den internationalen wissenschaftlichtechnologis chenAustausch.In:ErichThies/Nicola Leibinger.

Kammüller (Ed.), Politik für Wissenschaft und Forschung in Deutschland. Herausgegeben im Auftrag der Konrad-Adenauer-Stiftung. Munich 2014. pp. 13-27. Retrievedfrom:http:// www.kas.de/upload/dokumente /2014/06/Politik_WuF_82.pdf.

Wang, Yiwei. (2008). Public Diplomacy and the Rise of Chinese Soft Power. The Annals of the American Academy of Political and Social Science 616(1): pp. 257-73.

Wyszomirski, Margaret J., Burgess, Christopher, Peila, Catherine (2003). International cultural relations: A multi-country comparison. Columbus: The Ohio State University.

Xinhua News Agency. (2016, June 14). Zhōngguó chūbǎn yào "jiè chuán chūhǎi" gèng yào "zàochuán chūhǎi". 中国出版要 " 借船出海 " 更要 " 造船出海 ", Retrieved June 23, 2018, from http://www.xinhuanet.com/overseas/2016-06/14/c_129061070.htm.

Xinhua News Agency. (February 02, 2018). Art exhibition in Germany displays traditional culture, art in northwest China. Retrieved July 12, 2018, from: http://www. xinhuanet.com/ english/2018-02/02/c_136943248.htm.

Zhao,Kejin(2015).The Motivation Behind China's Public Diplomacy.The Chinese Journal of International Politics, Volume 8, Issue 2, 1 June 2015, pp. 167-196, https:// doi. org/10.1093/cjip/pov005.

Zhang, Feng. (2015). Confucian Foreign Policy Traditions in Chinese History, The Chinese Journal of International Politics, Volume 8, Issue 2, 1 June 2015, Pages 197– 218,https:// doi.org/10.1093/cjip/pov004.

Zhang, Xiaoling. (December 02, 2016). The Effectiveness of the Chinese Cultural Centres and Confucius Institutes. Retrieved June 21, from: theasiadialogue. com/2016/12/02/the-effectiveness-of-the-chinese-cultural -centres-and-confucius-institutes/.

Zhang,Guozuo. (2017). Research Outline for China's Cultural Soft Power. Singapore:Springer.

旅游目的地国家的中国游客形象研究——以泰国为例

冯志伟【泰国】

素叻他尼皇家大学国际旅游学院讲师，中山大学旅游学院博士研究生

一、问题的提出

随着中国农业、工业的现代化建设，以及改革开放政策带来的经济发展，中国硬实力得到极大提升。中国多年来不断参与国际及地区事务，国际地位和软实力也逐渐提升。2013 年中国提出"一带一路"倡议，不断加强与丝绸之路沿线国家的合作，成为国际跨区域合作的重要影响者。而伴随着中国在国际舞台扮演着越来越重要的角色，中国国家形象的重要性也逐渐显现。中国国家形象是中国软实力和影响力的基础，根据《中国国家形象全球调查报告 2015》[1] 显示，2015 年中国整体形象稳步提升，经济国际影响力位居世界第二。

2015 年中国国际广播电台环球资讯广播联合中国旅游研究院共同发布《中国游客海外形象全球调查报告》[2]，对中国游客海外行为进行研究，侧重于外国人对中国游客海外旅行不文明行为的认知。

长期以来，由于区域地理及语言文化因素的制约，国际社会了解中国信息的渠道仍然是以媒体报道为主，通过直接与中国人交往了解中国的仍占少数。《中国国家形象全球调查报告 2015》显示，海外受访者中，选择通过当地传统媒体和

---

1 《中国国家形象全球调查报告 2015》。
2 　中国国际广播电台环球资讯广播、中国旅游研究院：《中国游客海外形象全球调查报告》。

当地新媒体了解中国的，分别占到 62% 和 51%，而选择直接与中国人交往了解中国的仅为 14%。

而在泰国，由于中国游客数量大幅增加，与中国游客接触、交往已经成为泰国人了解中国的主要途径。这也意味着，中国游客行为传递出的信息，将直接影响泰国民众对于中国形象的认知。

本文中的中国游客形象，是指出境游以泰国作为旅游目的地的中国籍游客的总体形象。中国游客形象，是中国国民形象在海外的体现，同时也是中国国家形象的重要影响因素。

近年来，随着泰国中国游客数量的增加，中国游客在泰国社会中的形象反而下降。不良的中国游客形象，导致泰国社会对中国游客和中国旅游市场呈现抵触情绪。最终不仅制约了中泰两国旅游行业的发展，而且对中国国家形象和公共外交造成负面影响。

中国游客形象的形成，不仅局限于游客的行为，而且受到旅游行业和市场等综合的影响。本文通过调查问卷数据和泰国网站上泰国人对中国游客的评论，对泰国的中国游客形象的塑造进行解析，并针对其问题提出相应的建议。

二、文献综述

中国对于游客形象与国家形象有一定的研究，廖四顺在《游客不文明行为研究》中就认为，游客不文明行为不仅是个人形象，而且对他人、公共空间和环境造成破坏。张业遂在《旅游别把"脸"丢了》[1] 的文章中认为，海外中国游客不文明行为的负面影响（危害）突出表现在四个方面：一是引发其他国家民众对中国人反感，影响我的国家形象和"软实力"；二是对我在有关国家企业、侨民、留学生的生存和发展空间造成潜在负面影响；三是部分出境游客的不文明行为和过度维权违反当地法律，给其自身带来不必要的麻烦和损失；四是涉及境外游客旅游纠纷等群体性事件经微博等渠道在国内片面传播和炒作影响国家形象，给驻外使领馆工作带来压力。

有钱、"大手笔、爱炫富"、疯狂购物——这是中国游客在海外给人留下的印象。中国客在海外的形象，与他们钱袋子鼓起来的速度不成正比。经由游客一言一行，别人认知着那个伟大的国度。

---

1 张业遂：《旅游别把"脸"丢了》，《人民日报》，2013-08-01。

杨磊 (2014)《游客形象对中国公共外交的影响分析》[1] 中也提出，中国游客存在形象危机，中国个人不雅行为降低中国人整体形象与公共外交可信度。

泰国针对中国游客的研究包括，อัจฉรา สมบัตินันทนา 在 2012 年《来泰国的中国游客行为》[2] 中对影响中国游客目的地选择、中国游客旅游消费喜好等方面进行研究。泰国学者 นางกรวรรณ สังขร 在 2013 年《新一代中国游客——以清迈的中国游客为例》[3] 中对中国游客在清迈的旅游行为进行研究。

นางศรีสุดา วนพิญโญศักดิ์ 在《中国游客增长对泰国社会的影响》[4] 中，对中国游客对泰国社会的影响，泰国社会对中国游客问题的应对措施进行研究。研究承认泰国本身缺乏接纳大量中国游客的经验。少数中国游客的不文明行为，通过媒体放大效应，导致泰国社会对中国游客形象的偏见。

但至目前为止，泰国仍没有专门针对中国游客形象方面的研究，同时也缺乏游客形象与国家形象关系方面的研究。

综合来看，目前泰国和中国对赴泰国旅游的中国游客的研究主要集中在游客游动机、行为决策、消费行为、旅游满意度等方面，有针对中国游客形象的相关文章，但尚无针对赴泰国旅游的中国游客形象的专门研究。泰国是东盟最热的旅游目的地，中国游客也对泰国旅游市场乃至泰国社会有着重要的影响，因此本文的研究对丰富这一领域的研究有积极的作用。

三、方法数据

（一）选取研究样本

泰叻网[5]是泰国发行数量最大、最权威的泰叻报[6]（Thairath）经营的网站，网站以刊登泰叻报的新闻为主。泰叻报在人口 6700 万的泰国，发行量达到将近 100 万份，并覆盖泰国全境，是泰国最有影响力的媒体平台。泰叻报在新闻报道上秉承中立的态度，能够对事件进行全面、客观的分析，同时拥有持续报道的能力，保证对社会新闻事件的及时跟进、跟踪。泰叻网具有客观、量大、资料集中的特点。泰叻网站报道因此作为本文样品的抽取点。

1　杨磊：《游客形象对中国公共外交的影响分析》，《中国发展》，2014 年 8 月第 4 期。

2　พฤติกรรมการท่องเที่ยวของนักท่องเที่ยวชาวจีนที่เดินเข้ามาท่องเที่ยวในประเทศไทย，อัจฉรา สมบัตินันทนา，2012.

3　พฤติกรรมนักท่องเที่ยวจีนยุคใหม่: กรณีศึกษานักท่องเที่ยวจีนในจังหวัดเชียงใหม่，นางกรวรรณ สังขร，2013.

4　การเติบโตอย่างก้าวกระโดดของนักท่องเที่ยวจีนกับผลกระทบต่อสังคมไทย，นางศรีสุดา วนพิญโญศักดิ์,2015.

5　http://www.thairath.co.th/.

6　หนังสือพิมพ์ไทยรัฐ.

本研究选取泰叻网有关中国游客的文章，经过关键词检索中国游客[1]、中国旅游团[2]、"中国旅游"共 191 篇关于中国游客的新闻报道，以及 11 篇评论专栏。

（二）样品的预处理规则

通过关键词检索从泰叻网获得的资料中，包含信息过多，为获得与中国游客形象问题研究相关的资料，因此对样品进行预处理筛选。

样本根据以下范围进行筛选：1. 时间。时间筛选范围从 2010 至 2016 年 10 月 20 日，泰叻网最早样本时间为 2010 年，样本时间一直持续到 2016 年 10 月。

2. 目标群体。样品的目标群体是前往泰国旅行的中国游客群体。预处理后，新闻报道样品为 147 篇，评论样品为 11 篇。

（三）筛选后的样品

分析类目是内容分歧的基本单位，根据本次研究的目的，分析类目将包含 3 个方面：中国游客行为、中国游客形象以及泰中旅游市场。

中国游客行为，是中国游客在泰国的所有行为表现，同时也是直接影响泰国人形成中国游客形象的主要因素。泰叻网新闻报道中出现的中国游客行为，也是泰国人实际感知到的中国游客行为，具有一定的普遍性和代表性。

中国游客行为，在游客数量不断上升后，成为是塑造新中国游客形象的最主要因素。

中国游客形象，泰叻网新闻中对于中国游客形象的直接表现，反映泰国人对于中国游客的感知和认识。

泰中旅游市场动态，旅游时泰国的国家支柱型产业，而中国已经成为泰国第一大旅游客源国，因此中国游客对于泰中旅游市场占据重要的地位。同时，泰中旅游市场的波动，也对中国游客在泰国的形象造成影响。

筛选后的样品中，新闻报道共 146 篇，其中涉及中国游客行为的样品共计 58 篇，涉及中国游客形象的样品共计 17 篇，涉及泰中旅游市场的样品共计 79 篇。评论报道共 10 篇，其中涉及中国游客行为的样品共计 1 篇，涉及中国游客形象的样品 2 篇，涉及泰中旅游市场的样品 7 篇。

---

1 นักท่องเที่ยวจีน.

2 ทัวร์จีน.

四、研究分析

（一）泰国对中国游客的关注程度分析

泰国长期以来对于中国关注程度较低，但 2014 年以来，随着中国游客在泰国旅游产业中占据越来越重要的地位，以及中国游客与泰国社会的矛盾冲突加剧，中国游客在泰国的关注程度逐年上升。泰国社会对中国游客行为，特别是游客不文明行为新闻的关注程度增加。而中国游客新闻数量的增加，也不断促使泰国社会形成新的中国游客形象。新的中国游客形象，也成为中国形象塑造的重要影响因素。

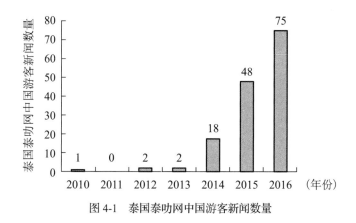

图 4-1   泰国泰叻网中国游客新闻数量

（二）泰国对中国游客的总体态度分析

根据泰叻报的新闻样本共 146 篇，其中对中国游客行为、中国游客形象、泰中旅游市场给予肯定评价的共 62 篇，中性评价的 59 篇、否定评价的 21 篇。

根据泰叻报的评论样本共 10 篇，其中对中国游客行为、中国游客形象、泰中旅游市场给予肯定评价的共 5 篇，中性评价的 2 篇、否定评价的 3 篇。

泰国主流新闻媒体对于中国游客的态度总体持肯定态度，这与泰国社交网络和中国新闻报道的态度并不相同。泰国社交媒体针对中国游客持否定态度，总体持否定态度。泰国社交媒体不仅有以个人名义传播中国游客负面新闻的行为，而且有部分已经形成组织化，包括脸书（Facebook）上存在的"我们爱中国游客（เรารักนักท่องเที่ยวจีน）"、"清迈反中国人"（Anti Chinese in Chiang Mai ต่อต้านนักท่องเที่ยวจีนในเชียงใหม่）等团体。同时，泰国主流媒体对中国游客的态度，与中国自媒体、中国主流媒体的报道呈现相反趋势，中国媒体的报道中普遍认为泰国人对中国游客持否定态度。

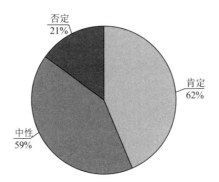

图 4-2   泰叻网新闻对中国游客的态度

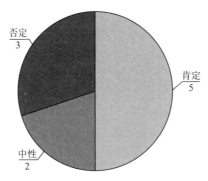

图 4-3   泰叻网评论对中国游客的态度

泰国主流媒体的评论主要仍以肯定为主，评论集中在中国游客对于旅游市场的影响方面。评论中对泰国人反对、攻击中国游客的行为进行批评，同时对泰中旅游市场不规范和中国资本进入泰国旅游市场给予否定评价。

（三）泰国对中国游客正面形象的报道

泰国主流媒体对中国游客形象也进行积极正面的报道。泰国主流媒体认为，中国游客能够积极促进泰国经济增长，中国政府也通过出台法律积极约束游客不文明行为。同时，能够客观地对泰国商家欺诈中国游客的纠纷事件进行报道，认为造成纠纷的并非中国游客，而是泰国非法商家。

中国游客不文明行为减少，中国政府积极解决问题。中国首部《旅游法》于2013年颁布后，泰国也进行报道并持肯定和支持的态度。泰国认为中国政府在亚航中国游客与空姐纠纷事件等问题中，积极打击游客不文明行为，并对存在不文明行为的中国游客进行约束。泰国认为中国游客不文明行为新闻的增加，也是因为中国游客数量增加。随着泰国对中国游客群体的关注程度上升，基础设施建设增强和双方文化交流增加，中国游客更加理解泰国，不文明行为在持续减少。

中国游客成为泰国非法商家的受害者。泰国认为中国游客同时也受到泰国不法商家的欺骗，成为受害者。泰国非法商家通过哄抬物价向中国游客销售产品，或在租赁车辆、摩托艇等过程中收取中国游客过高的费用。中国游客也有被泰国旅行社、导游弃团，景区针对中国游客涨价的事件，导致中国游客的利益受损。泰国认为，中国游客在维权方面是弱势群体，应该受到政府保护。

（四）泰国的对中国游客负面的形象报道

泰叻网新闻报道共 146 篇，其中涉及中国游客行为的新闻共计 58 篇，占总数的 39.7%。评论共 10 篇，其中涉及中国游客行为的新闻共 1 篇，占总数的 10%。泰国对中国游客负面的形象报道包括两类，一方面是中国游客因为文化、制度差异造成的不当行为，一方面是中国游客违反社会基本礼仪的不文明行为。

泰国社会对中国游客因为文化、制度差异造成的不当行为表示理解，但无法接受中国游客违反社会基本礼仪的不文明行为。

1. 泰国社会对中国游客因为文化、制度差异造成的不当行为表示理解。

中国游客在清迈乘坐双条车跳车、导致自己死亡。中国游客在芭提雅报案表示遭到百万岛商家强买强卖鳄鱼钱包，但最终泰国警方调查后认为，中国游客存在诈保的嫌疑。中国游客在攀牙府将受到保护的鱼类装到塑料袋中拍照、在 kaino 岛喂鱼等事件，都是对泰国社会规则的破坏。

泰国是一个耻感文化社会，泰国人对遵守社会规则非常看重，一般情况都会自觉遵守规则。泰国的车站、地铁站、电梯等需要排队的情况下，泰国人都会互相礼让和排队等候。因此，中国游客不遵守规则的行为，在泰国人看来不能理解。

中国游客在清迈大学穿大学校服拍照，他们并不了解大学校服的意义。泰国大学校服是学生身份的象征，同时也代表学校的荣誉，因此如果不是大学生不能够随便穿着。中国游客在清迈机场晾晒内衣的事件，也是不了解泰国习俗的表现，泰国文化中内衣是极其私密和不雅的物品，甚至晾晒内衣都放在外人看不到的空间，不会放在阳台等地方晾晒。因此，中国游客在机场座椅上晾晒内衣，被认为是对他人的冒犯。

泰国的文化中不仅包含传统道德，而且也受到佛教规定影响。中国游客在寺庙拍照中衣着暴露、摆拍姿势过于暧昧，都是对泰国佛教规定的触犯。中国游客在白庙旅游时，并没有意识到白庙是一座寺庙，因此缺少尊重。

泰国文化中认为，吸烟是影响他人的行为，不支持吸烟，烟草在销售的时候不能公开陈列，电视电影中出现吸烟的镜头时都会用马赛克遮盖。公共场合建筑内不允许吸烟，吸烟者一般会避开人群或到专门的吸烟区吸烟，而且不会公开展示自己的香烟。但一部分中国游客仍然在人群聚集的地方抽烟，虽然没有违反法律，但却会被认为是不尊重大家的行为。

泰国对于中国游客的不当行为，在表示理解的同时，也积极寻求解决的方式。泰国清迈大学在中国游客大量进入校园，并出现不文明行为后，一度封闭学校，不允许中国游客进入。但清迈大学随后进行调整迎接中国游客，学校每天开放 500 名参观名额，并开通电动车游览线路、配学生导游讲解，中国游客影响学校正常教学秩序的情况被解决。中国游客也愿意购买 60 铢的电动车游览票，为学校带来收入和旅游专业学生带来实习机会。

2015 年 8 月 15 日，清迈大学还专门为第 111,111 名游客举行庆祝活动，免费发放礼品和乘车券。中国游客也对清迈大学安排的线路感到满意。

2. 泰国对于中国游客违反社会基本礼仪的不文明行为则难以接受。

中国游客违反社会基本礼仪的不文明行为，集中在使用公共设施方面。清迈府中国游客不文明行为尤其突出，包括中国游客在清迈护城河小便（后证实并非中国游客），中国游客使用厕所后不冲水，未得到允许参加酒店举行的活动，在清迈大学宿营等事件。中国游客在黑庙游览时，为了拍跳起的照片，将 30 年历史的木质的黑色栏杆踢断，同时使用厕所后并没有保持卫生。

中国游客在游览清莱府白庙时，也有类似的行为。中国游客同样使用厕所不冲洗干净，导致白庙一度关闭厕所，并禁止中国游客进入白庙。中国游客在 pp 岛使用厕所洗手池洗鞋子和洗脚，导致负责厕所管理的自然保护区，专门派人将洗手池进行全面清理。

中国游客在龙虎园喂小老虎的时候，用力踢铁笼让小老虎遭受惊吓以取乐。此外，中国游客也存在需要保持安静的环境大声说话、不遵守交通规则、与服务人员爆发冲突等不文明行为。

同时，泰国对中国人利用泰国北部、东北部申请身份的便利，冒用泰国人身份经商进行批判和打击。泰国部分旅行社业者存在冒用泰国人身份的情况，特别是普吉、芭提雅的旅行社。同时大量旅行社共同组成零团费利益链，导致低品质的旅游团大量进入泰国，消耗泰国公共资源，却未给泰国旅游带来相对应的收益。

泰国认为冒用泰国人身份和零团费经营模式，破坏了泰国的经济秩序，对泰国旅游行业造成严重的不良影响。

（五）泰国的对中国游客现象的反思

1. 理解中国游客行为，认为文化冲突占主要因素。

泰国观点认为，中国游客的不文明行为仅存在于少数人中，不了解泰国文化是造成中国游客不文明行为的主要原因。中国游客在清迈机场晾晒内衣事件中，泰国社交网络对于中国游客的行为口诛笔伐，但清迈机场负责人在新闻中明确指出，中国游客的行为并没有违反法律，仅仅是不了解泰国的习俗和文化。中国游客穿着校服在泰国清迈大学照相事件中，清迈大学方面在与中国游客沟通后，也认为中国游客并非专门违反规定，仅仅是因为不了解彼此文化。中国游客清迈护城河小便事件（后被证明为假新闻）中，也被认为是文化冲突，并表示应该加强宣传，消除文化隔阂。

同时认为，文化冲突的情况普遍存在，泰国人在日本等国家旅游的时候，也面临不了解当地文化，违反规则的情况。

2. 泰国旅游接待能力有限，认为不应该谴责中国游客。

泰国观点认为，泰国旅游接待能力有限，本身并没有做好接待大量中国游客的准备。中国游客在黑庙照相弄坏栏杆事件中，黑庙方面认为旅行社、黑庙接待能力有限。事后黑庙方面要求导游增加讲解兰纳文化方面的内容，同时增加 10 名保安负责引导游客和保护游客安全。

白庙的建造者察冷差[1]之前一直攻击中国游客，表示中国游客不文明使用厕所、在白庙内抽烟等不文明行为。但在 2016 年 3 月 27 日接受采访中反思，并表示"中国游客没错，是我们自己没准备好"。[2]察冷差表示经过考虑，认为之前不应该抱怨中国游客，因为白庙缺乏与中国游客的沟通，并没有中文指示牌、没有足够的人员、没有导游的支持。正是因为缺乏接待能力，导致不能够很好地照顾中国游客，无法为中国游客提供指导。

泰国中文导游缺失也是造成接待能力不足的原因，泰国能够说中文的导游共4856 人，难以应付每年数百万的游客。[3]同时，泰国的基础设施建设不足，运输、

1　อ.เฉลิมชัย.

2　"นักท่องเที่ยวจีนไม่ผิด มึงต่างหากทีไม่พร้อม" เฉลิมชัย โฆษิตพิพัฒน์…. http://www.posttoday.com/analysis/interview/423753.

3　ย้ำชัด!อาชีพไกด์สงวนให้คนไทยเท่านั้น, thairath.co.th, 2015.06.27, www.thairath.co.th/content/507801.

酒店、景点接纳中国游客的能力有限，特别是曼谷的素万那普机场和廊曼机场，旅客接纳人数已经数年超过设计上线。素万那普机场通关迟缓，高峰期旅客往往需要 3—4 个小时才能够通关。

3. 泰国基础设施超负荷运转

2006 年以来，除了泰国政治动乱的 2008~2009 和 2014 年，外国游客数量持续增长。与此同时泰国基础设施建设缓慢，素万那普国际机场的旅客吞吐量已经超过其最大设计值。2012 年泰国将廉价航空公司和大多数飞国内航线的航空公司迁往廊曼机场，以缓解素万纳普机场的压力。但游客数量持续增加，素万那普国际机场每年接待的旅客数量，仍然超过 4500 万人 / 年的最大设计值[2]。旅游行业占据了绝大多数素万那普机场的资源，泰国政府针对素万纳普机场的投资扩建迟缓，同时也未采取限制游客数量的措施，导致素万那普机场基础设施难以满足需求。

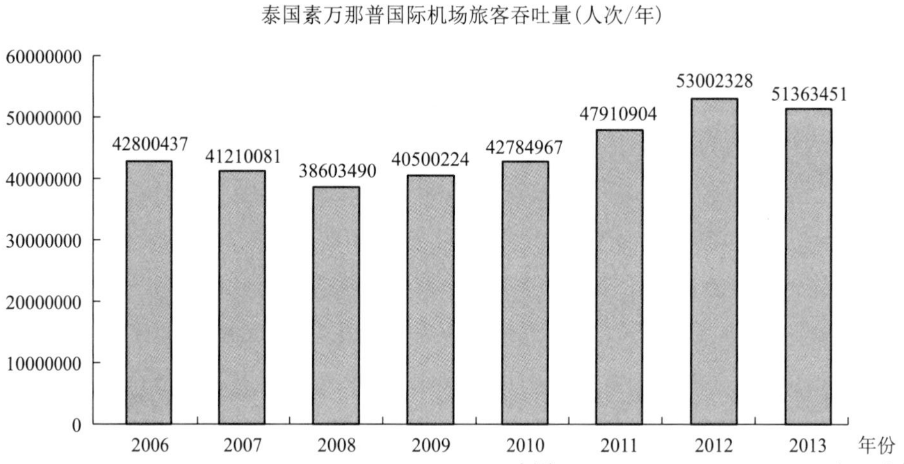

泰国素万那普国际机场旅客吞吐量（人次/年）

来源：Airports Council International（ACI）[1]

图 4-4　泰国素万那普国际机场旅客吞吐量

面对素万那普国际机场超负荷运转，泰国航空业界也向泰国政府提出停止启用新航班，以防止机场更加拥挤。泰国航空营运商委员会 (AOC) 指出，已用尽所有可行方法增加机场容量，如改善泊机位管理等，所以无法再应付额外旅客。[2]

1　Airports Council International（ACI），http://www.aci.aero/Data-Centre.

2　曼谷机场持续超负荷 航空业促其停开新航班，http://world.huanqiu.com/exclusive/2015-10/7797127.html.

泰国旅游业协会顾问席迪瓦差拉·其瓦拉那蓬[1]认为，泰国持证导游水平有待提高，一部分导游甚至无法用中文介绍景点。清迈的旅游经营者，也针对导游和工作人员进行中文和中国文化的培训。

甲米中国游客使用厕所洗手池洗脚事件中，新闻中也认为泰国在自然保护区沙滩附近的这个厕所，缺乏人性化的设施，应该增加洗脚池，以满足游客的需求。

泰国观点认为，不应该谴责中国游客，特别是在网上谩骂中国游客，需要互相了解，泰国并没有出现抵制中国游客的情况。同时希望民众不要拍摄中国游客，并将中国游客不雅观的照片视频发到网上，因为少数人的行为将造成彼此间的矛盾。

4. 肯定中国游客对泰国经济的贡献，希望保持良好关系。

泰国观光与体育部、泰国旅游局以及旅游协会始终肯定中国游客对泰国经济的贡献，2010 年随着中国游客数量大幅度增加，中国游客在泰国外国游客中所占的比重逐年上升。中国游客数量也开始成为影响泰国经济的重要因素。

泰国肯定中国游客的质量，认为中国游客处于外国游客群体的中上层，中国游客平均的旅游消费，高于外国游客的平均水平。2016 年统计的数据显示，中国游客人均消费是 5800 铢，而外国游客的平均消费为 5072 铢。泰国政府也认为，中国游客中 60% 是高质量游客，20% 是中档消费游客，仅有 20% 是零团费低消费游客。

2015 年开始，网络上因为清迈、清迈府中国游客的不文明行为，导致泰国社交网络上爆发多次针对中国游客不文明行为的语言攻击。实际上，一些不文明事件的当事人并非中国游客。在通过中国自媒体、传统媒体将泰国新闻事件曝光后，泰国人不喜欢中国游客的思想同时开始在中国传播。2016 年，来泰国旅游的中国游客下降，泰国担心中国游客减少，专门向中国政府说明情况，并邀请中国旅游促进会等机构，来到泰国进行实地考察。清迈旅游业者甚至打出中文横幅"我爱中国人"，以表示并没有对中国游客有任何成见。

泰国认为中国游客将为泰国带来巨大的经济收益，因此希望能够保持良好关系，营造欢迎中国游客的大环境以促进游客人数增长。

中国游客大幅增加，2015 年赴泰旅游的中国游客数量达到 7,934,781 人（次），

1　นายศิษฏิวัชร ชีวรัตนพร.

占泰国外国游客总数的 26.5%[1]。中国已经成为泰国第一大游客来源国，中国游客的数量也已经超过泰国人口[2]的十分之一。与此同时，中国游客数量仍在逐年递增。

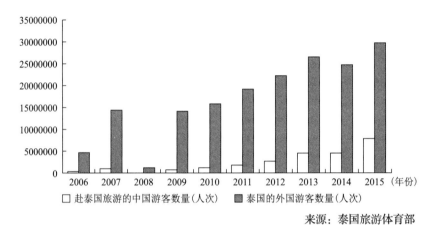

来源：泰国旅游体育部

图 4-5　泰国的中国游客数量

表 4-1：中国游客平均消费增加

中国游客平均日均消费增加（泰铢 / 天）				
年份	2012	2013	2014	2015
泰国中国游客日均消费	4,883.74	4,826.24	5,097.20	47386.42
泰国外国游客日均消费	4,687.81	4,392.81	4,616.49	48430.56[3]

来源：泰国旅游体育部

5. 中立观点。泰国对中国游客在泰国发生的事故、纠纷采取中立观点。

泰国对中国游客发生的纠纷采取中立观点，并没有偏袒本国民众一方。2014 年在清迈 5 岁中国小孩撕坏"古画"事件中，度假村一方向中国游客索赔 8 万铢，但最终警方介入，让度假村归还游客过度的赔款，最终仅赔款 2.5 万铢。

中国游客被导游抛弃在芭提雅事件中，泰国警方也迅速介入，抓捕弃团的导游，并要求旅行社进行赔偿。2015 年中国游客在清迈玩丛林飞跃致死事件中，泰

1　2015 年赴泰国旅游的中国游客占世界游客总量的 26.5545558560763%。
2　泰国国家管理厅统计数据，2015 年人口数量达到 65,729,098 人。：http://stat.bora.dopa.go.th/ stat/y_stat58.htm 2555. สืบค้น 16 กุมภาพันธ์ 2559.
3　สรุปสถานการณ์นักท่องเที่ยว มกราคม-ธันวาคม2555 2556 2557 2558 , กระทรวงการท่องเที่ยวและกีฬา กรมการท่องเที่ยว.

国警方也最终判定是工作人员操作不当，最终保险赔付死者家属 250 万铢。

2016 年攀牙府中国游客抓鱼拍照事件中，攀牙府县长马上证实，所谓中国游客抓鱼拍照的照片已经是 3 年前的老照片，攀牙府已经出台保护措施，未再发生类似事件。

泰国对零团费经营者，抬高商品价格、逼迫中国游客购买的行为也进行谴责，认为破坏泰国旅游形象。

五、结论

目前针对中国出境游游客和泰国中国游客的研究中，大多集中在游客带来的经济影响、游客旅游行为方面的研究，而针对中国游客对于旅游目的地国的影响、中国游客的形象研究仍较少。相信本论文能够为未来这一方向的研究提供参考。

中国目前已经成为泰国第一大入境游客源国，随着中国游客数量和影响力的增加，泰国对于中国游客的关注程度不断上升。研究发现，泰国主流媒体关于中国游客文章数量增加，关注程度上升。但同时发现，泰国对于中国游客的主要关注程度仍集中在经济方面，社会影响关注度较低。从泰国主流媒体的新闻报道来看，中国游客对泰国社会文化存在实质性的影响，但影响力和影响范围并没有想象中的大。

泰国社会对于中国游客不文明行为仍采取宽容的态度，这一方面是因为泰国本身善良和忍耐的民族性格，一方面是因为中国游客带来的经济利益。泰国主流媒体对中国游客不文明行为，并没有放大和扩大传播，而是更多地采取中立和正面的报道，甚至对将一部分中国游客不文明行为归结为本国基础设施建设和服务落后。

中国游客对泰国的文化、习俗不了解，导致文化冲突。中国游客在泰国一方面是因为不文明行为遭到指责，另一方面则是不了解泰国文化习俗的行为。泰国对这一现象表示理解，并增加更多渠道宣传泰国，让中国游客更加了解泰国。

泰国旅游市场针对中国游客做出改变。泰国针对中国游客制作中文指示牌，增加人员引导中国游客。特别是在泰国的机场，中文指示牌已经成为标配，同时泰国也在培训更多会说中文的泰国旅游从业人员。

泰国重视中国游客和中国旅游市场，希望能够向中国游客传递欢迎的态度。

希望泰国社交网络否定中国游客的信息不要对中国游客造成影响。泰国希望能够打造可持续发展的旅游产业，打击零费团，让中国游客拥有更好的旅游环境。

但泰国对于中国游客的态度，并不在其他国家普遍存在。相对而言，中国游客不文明行为对于一部分国家（包括中国）的社会文化影响更为突出。

A Study on the Image of Chinese Tourists in Destination Country—Taking Thailand as an Example

Wirun Phichaiwongphakdee / Thailand

Lecturer, International School of Tourism, Suratthani Rajabhat University / PhD Candidate, San Yat-sen University

1. Raising of Problems

With the modernization of agriculture and industry in China and economic development brought by the Opening-up Policy, China's hard power has been greatly improved. China has been always participating in international and regional affairs for many years and its international status and soft power have been also gradually improved. In 2013, China put forward the Belt and Road Initiative and then has strengthened cooperation with countries along the Silk Road continuously and become an international leader of cross-regional cooperation. China's role in the international stage is increasingly important and the importance of its image becomes apparent gradually. China's national image is a basis for China's soft power and influence. In accordance with the 2015 Global Survey on China's National Image[1],

---

1   2015 Global Survey on China' s National Image, Communication Strategy Laboratory, CIPG Sino-foreign Communication Research Center.

China's overall image in 2015 has been improved steadily and its international economic influence ranked second in the world.

In 2015, CRI News Radio published Global Survey of Chinese Tourists' Overseas Image[1] with China Tourism Academy and made a research on Chinese tourists' overseas behaviors and emphasized foreigners' understanding to Chinese tourists' uncivilized behaviors in overseas travel.

For a long time, international societies mainly know the information on China through media report due to the restriction of regional geography and language culture and rarely know China through direct communication with Chinese people. Shown in 2015 China National Image Global Survey, among overseas interviewees, the persons who chose to know China through local traditional media and local new media accounted for 62% and 51% respectively, while the persons who chose to know China through direct communication with Chinese people accounted for 14% only.

But in Thailand, due to rapid increase in the number of Chinese tourists, it has become a main channel for Thai people to know China through contact and communication with Chinese tourists. This means that, information sent by Chinese tourists' behaviors will influence Thai people's understanding to China's image directly.

Chinese tourists' image mentioned in this text, refers to overall image of Chinese tourists who go abroad to travel in Thailand. Chinese tourists' image is a reflection of China's national image at abroad, and also an important factor which influences China's national image.

In the recent several years, with the increase in the number of Chinese tourists in Thailand, Chinese tourists' image in Thai society has been declined. Bad image of Chinese tourists has caused Thai society to have an antipathy towards Chinese tourists and Chinese tourist market. Finally, it has not only restricted the development of tourist industry of both China and Thailand, but also brought

---

1 Global Survey of Chinese Tourists' Overseas Image, CRI News Radio, China Tourism Academy.

negative influence to China's national image and public diplomacy.

The shaping of Chinese tourists' image, is not only limited to tourists' behaviors, but is effected by tourist industry and market comprehensively. This text has analyzed the shaping of the image of Chinese tourists to Thailand and given corresponding suggestions concerning relevant problems through the data of questionnaire and Thai people's comments to Chinese tourists on Thai websites.

2. Literature Review

China has made some research on tourist image and national image. Mr. Liao Sishun held that tourists' uncivilized behaviors have not only shown personal image, but also brought damage to others, public space and the environment in Research on Tourists' Uncivilized Behaviors.

Mr. Zhang Yesui held in the article Don't Lose "Face" in The Travel[1] that, negative influence (damage) of Chinese tourists'uncivilized behaviors at abroad is mainly shown in four ways: firstly, it brings an antipathy of the people in other countries towards Chinese people and effects our country's national image and "soft power"; secondly, it brings potential negative influence to the life and development space of our enterprises, expatriates and overseas students settling in relevant countries; thirdly, some outbound tourists' uncivilized behaviors and excessive right protection are in breach of local laws and has brought unnecessary troubles and losses to themselves; fourthly, our outbound tourists' group events such as travel disputes are spread and speculated one-sided at abroad through such channels as Twitter and this has influenced the image of the Party and the government and brought pressure to over seas embassy.

Rich, generous, display of wealth and crazy shopping—this is the impression which Chinese tourists have given to people at abroad. The image of Chinese tourists at abroad is not proportional to their money. Other people know the great nation through tourists'words and deeds.

---

1   Wang Ke, Don't Lose "Face" in The Travel. *People's Daily*, Aug. 1, 2013.

Mr. Yang Lei also mentioned in Analysis to Influence of Tourist Image to China's Public Diplomacy[1] in 2014 that, image crisis is existed among Chinese tourists and Chinese people's indecent behaviors have reduced Chinese people's overall image and credibility of public diplomacy.

Thailand's research to Chinese tourists includes, อัจฉรา สมบัตินันทนา's research to factors effecting Chinese tourists' selection of destination and Chinese tourists' travel consumption hobbies in Behaviors of Chinese Tourists to Thailand[2] in 2012. Thai scholar นางกรวรรณ สังขกร made the research on Chinese tourists' travel behaviors in Chiang Mai in New Generation of Chinese Tourists——Taking Chinese Tourists to Chiang Mai As An Example[3] in2013.

นางศรีสุดา วนภิญโญศักดิ์ made the research on the influence of Chinese tourists to Thai society and countermeasures which Thai society has taken concerning Chinese tourists' problems in The Influence of Increase in The Number of Chinese Tourists To Thai Society[4]. It's acknowledged in the research that Thailand is lack of the experience in accepting plenty of Chinese Tourists. A few of Chinese tourists' uncivilized behaviors has resulted in Thai society's prejudice to the image of Chinese tourists through amplification effect by the media.

But there is no special research on the image of Chinese tourists up to now in Thailand. Meanwhile the research on the relation between tourist image and national image is still short.

On the whole, Thailand and China's research to Chinese tourists to Thailand mainly focuses on tourists' motives, behavior decision, consumption behavior, tourist satisfaction and so on currently. There is relevant articles on Chinese tourists' image, but there is no special research on the image of Chinese tourists who go to

---

1 Analysis to Influence of Tourist Image to China' s Public Diplomacy, China Development, Volume 14, Period 4, Aug. 2014.

2 พฤติกรรมการท่องเที่ยวของนักท่องเที่ยวชาวจีนที่เดินทางเข้ามาท่องเที่ยวในประเทศไทย, อัจฉรา สมบัตินันทนา, 2012.

3 พฤติกรรมนักท่องเที่ยวจีนยุคใหม่: กรณีศึกษานักท่องเที่ยวจีนในจังหวัดเชียงใหม่, นางกรวรรณ สังขกร, 2013.

4 การเติบโตอย่างก้าวกระโดดของนักท่องเพียวจีนกับผลกระทบต่อสังคมไทย,นางศรีสุดา วนภิญโญศักดิ์, 2015.

Thailand for travel yet. Thailand is the most popular tourist destination in ASEAN and Chinese tourists bring important influence to Thai tourist market, even Thai society. Therefore, this text play an active role in enriching the research in this field.

3. Method Data

3.1 Selection of Research Samples

Thai Rath[1] is the website operated by Thai Rath[2] (Thairath) which is most popular and authoritative in Thailand and mainly publishes the news of Thai Rath. Thai Rath enjoys issue volume of nearly 1 million pieces in Thailand with the population of 67 million and covers all the areas of Thailand, falling within the most influential media platform in Thailand. Thai Rath holds an neutral attitude to news report and could make overall and objective analysis to events. Meanwhile it has the ability in persistent report and ensures prompt tracking to social news events. Thai Rath has the characteristics of being objective, plentiful and concentrated. Therefore, the reports on the website of Thai Rath is used as extraction point of samples in this text.

The articles on Chinese tourists from the website of Thai Rath are chosen in this research. There are total 191 news reports on Chinese tourists and 11 comment columns by searching key words Chinese tourists[3], Chinese tourist group[4] and "Chinese tourism".

3.2 Pre-processing Rules for Samples

Among information obtained by searching key words on the website of Thai Rath, there is excessive information and samples are pre-processed and selected accordingly to obtain information relating to Chinese tourists' image problems.

Samples are selected according to the following scope: 1. Time. Time selection scope is from 2010 to Oct. 20, 2016, as the time of earliest samples on the website

---

1   http://www.thairath.co.th/ .

2   หนังสือพิมพ์ไทยรัฐ.

3   นักท่องเทียวจีน.

4   ทัวร์จีน.

of Thai Rath is started from 2010 and the time of other samples continues to Oct. 2016. 2. Targeted group. Samples'target group refers to the group of Chinese tourists who go to Thailand for travel.

After pre-processing, there are 147 news report samples and 11 comment samples.

3.3 Samples After Selection

Analysis category is basic unit for divergences in contents.According to the purpose of this research, analysis category here includes 3 aspects: Chinese tourists' behaviors, Chinese tourists'image and Thai and Chinese tourist market.

Chinese tourists' behaviors are all the behaviors and actions of Chinese tourists in Thailand and it refers to main factor which effects Thai people to shape Chinese tourists' image directly. Chinese tourists'behaviors mentioned in the news reports on the website of Thai Rath, are also Chinese tourists' behaviors which Thai people feel and know actually and are general and typical. Chinese tourists' behaviors have become the most important factor to shape Chinese tourists' new image after continuous increase in the number of tourists.

Chinese tourists' image, are direct expression of Chinese tourists' image in the news of Thai Rath and Thai people's perception and understanding to Chinese tourists are reflected.

The trend of Thai and Chinese tourist market. Tourism is national pillar industry in Thailand, while China has already become the biggest country of tourist source in Thailand. Therefore, Chinese tourists are important in Thai and Chinese tourist market. Meanwhile, the fluctuation in Thai and Chinese tourist market, also brings influence to Chinese tourists' image in Thailand.

Among samples after selection, there are total 146 news reports, including 58 samples involving Chinese tourists' behaviors, 17 samples involving Chinese tourists' image and 79 samples involving Thai and Chinese tourist market. There are total 10 comment reports, including one sample involving Chinese tourists' behaviors, 2 samples involving Chinese tourists' image and 7 samples involving Thai and Chinese tourist market.

4. Research and Analysis

4.1 Analysis to Thailand's Focus Level to Chinese Tourists

Thailand has paid few focus on China for a long period. But since 2014, focus level on Chinese tourists in Thailand has ascended year by year with more and more important role of Chinese tourists in Thai tourist industry and aggravation of conflicts between Chinese tourists and Thai society. Thai society has paid more focus on Chinese tourists' behaviors, especially the news of tourists' uncivilized behaviors. The increase in the number of news on Chinese tourists has urged Thai society to shape new image of Chinese tourists. New image of Chinese tourists, has also become an important influencing factor to shape China's image.

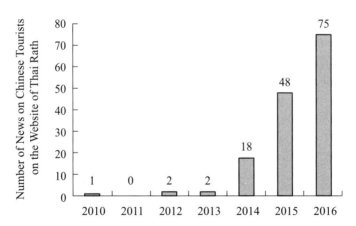

4.2 Analysis to Thailand's General Attitude to Chinese Tourists

There are total 146 news samples from Thai Rath, including 62 samples which make positive comments to Chinese tourists' behaviors, Chinese tourists' image and Thai and Chinese tourist market, 59 samples which make neutral comments and 21 samples which make negative comments.

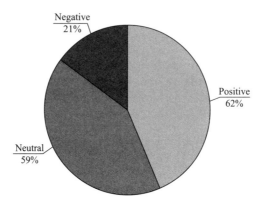

There are total 10 comment samples from Thai Rath, including 5 samples which make positive comments to Chinese tourists' behaviors, Chinese tourists' image and Thai and Chinese tourist market, 2 samples which make neutral comments and 3 samples which make negative comments.

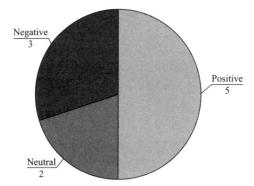

Thailand's leading news media holds a positive attitude to Chinese tourists for a whole, which is not same as the attitude of Thai social network and Chinese news report. Thai social network holds a negative attitude to Chinese tourists for a whole. Chinese tourists' negative news are not only spread on Thai social media in the name of individuals, but also some of them are spread by organizations, including groups such as "we love Chinese tourists（เรารักนักท่องเที่ยวจีน）" and "Chiang Mai opposes Chinese" (Anti Chinese in Chiang Mai ต่อต้านนักท่องเที่ยวจีนในเชียงใหม่) existed on Facebook. Meanwhile, Thailand's leading media's attitude to Chinese tourists is contrary to the reports on China's self-media and leading media. It's generally held in the report of Chinese media that Thai people holds a negative attitude to Chinese tourists.

Comments on Thailand's leading media are mainly positive and focus on the influence of Chinese tourists to tourist market. Thai people's behavior to oppose and reproach Chinese tourists is criticized in the comments, meanwhile negative comments to non-standardization of Thai and Chinese tourist market and Chinese capital's penetration into Thai tourist market are also given.

4.3 Thailand's Report on Chinese Tourists' Positive Image

Thailand's leading media makes the active and positive report to Chinese tourists' image. Thailand's leading media holds that, Chinese tourists could promote Thailand's economic growth actively and Chinese Government also constraints tourists' uncivilized behaviors actively through promulgation of laws. Meanwhile, it could report disputes on Thai merchants' cheating Chinese tourists objectively, and holds that the parties to result in such disputes is not Chinese tourists, but Thailand's illegal merchants.

Chinese tourists' uncivilized behaviors have been reduced and Chinese Government has solved the problems actively. After China's first tourism law was promulgated in 2013, Thailand has made corresponding report and holds a positive and support attitude. Thailand holds that Chinese Government has cracked down tourists' uncivilized behaviors actively in the problems such as the dispute between Chinese tourists and air hostess of Airasia Airlines and restrained Chinese tourists' uncivilized behaviors. Thailand holds that the increase in the news on Chinese tourists' uncivilized behaviors is also caused by the increase in the number of Chinese tourists. With Thailand's more focus on the group of Chinese tourists, infrastructure construction has been enhanced and mutual cultural exchange has also been increased and Chinese tourists have had a better understanding to Thailand and uncivilized behaviors are cut down continuously.

Chinese tourists have become the victims of Thailand's illegal merchants. Thailand holds that Chinese tourists have also cheated by Thailand's illegal merchants and become victims. Thailand's illegal merchants sell products to

Chinese tourists through bidding up price or charge Chinese tourists too high expenses in the process of leasing vehicles and motorboats. Some Chinese tourists are thrown away by Thai travel agencies and tour guides and scenic sites' marking up price to Chinese tourists has also caused Chinese tourists'benefits to be damaged. Thailand holds that Chinese tourists fall within vulnerable groups in right protection and should be protected by the government.

4.4 Thailand's Report on Chinese Tourists' Negative Image

There are total 146 news reports on the website of Thai Rath, including 58 news involving Chinese tourists' behaviors, accounting for 39.7% of the total. There are total 10 comments, including 1 news involving Chinese tourists' behaviors, accounting for 10% of the total. Thailand's reports on Chinese tourists' negative image include two kinds, one is Chinese tourists' improper behaviors caused by differences in culture and system, and the other one is Chinese tourists' uncivilized behaviors breaching social basic etiquette.

Thai society indicates its understanding to Chinese tourists' improper behaviors caused by differences in culture and system, but can't accept Chinese tourists' uncivilized behaviors breaching social basic etiquette.

4.4.1 Thai society understands that Chinese tourists'improper behaviors are caused by differencesincultureandsystem.

Chinese tourists jumped off the songthaew in Chiang Mai and caused death. Chinese tourists reported a case in Pattaya to show that they were forced by merchants to buy crocodile leather wallets in Ko Pha Ngan, but Thai police held that Chinese tourists were on suspicion of cheating insurance after investigation finally. Chinese tourists put the fishes under protection to plastic bags in Phang Nga Province to take photos and fed fishes in kainoIsl and, all of which has damaged Thai society's rules.

Thailand is a cultural society and Thai people pay much attention to following social rules and will follow the rules consciously under general circumstances. When it needs to wait in line in the station, metro station and elevator in Thailand, Thai people will be very polite and wait in line. Therefore, it's very difficult for Thai people to understand Chinese tourists' behaviors of not following rules.

Chinese tourists wore university uniform to take photos in Chiang Mai University and they didn't understand the meaning of university uniform. Thailand's university uniform is the symbol of studentship and also represents the university's honor, so those who are not university students can't wear the uniform. The event that Chinese tourists hung out underwear in Chiang Mai Airport is also a behavior of not knowing Thai custom.Underwear in Thai culture refers to very private and in elegant articles and should be hung in the space out of the sight of strangers and shouldn't be placed in the balcony. Therefore, Chinese tourists'hanging underwear in the airport's seat, has been regarded as offensive to others.

Thai culture has not only included traditional morality, but also influenced by rules of Buddhism. Chinese tourists wore skimpy clothes and made poses too ambiguously to take photos in the temple and these has breached rules of Thai Buddhism. When Chinese tourists visited the White Temple, they were not conscious that the White Temple is a temple and lacked of respect.

It's thought in Thai culture that smoking is a behavior to effect others and not accepted. Cigarettes can't be publicly displayed at the time of selling and the shots of smoking appeared in the TV and film could be pixilated. Smoking is not allowed in public buildings and smokers will keep away from the crowd or go to special smoking area for smoking generally and will not display their own cigarettes publicly. But some Chinese tourists smoked in the crowed place. Though this is not in breach of laws, it will be regarded as a behavior of not respecting others.

Thailand has also sought solutions actively at the same time of showing understanding to Chinese tourists'improper behaviors. Chiang Mai University was once closed and Chinese tourists were not allowed for entry after lots of Chinese tourists entered into the campus and made uncivilized behaviors. But Chiang Mai University made adjustment in the following and welcomed Chinese tourists and accepts 500 visitors every day. And the tour route with electric vehicles is open and student guides are equipped. The problem that Chinese tourists effect normal teaching order has been solved. Chinese tourists are also willing to buy the tour ticket at the price of 60Thai baht and this has brought income to the university and internship opportunities for students in the major of Tourism.

On Aug. 15, 2015, Chiang Mai University organized a celebration activity for the tourist who ranks 111,111 especially and distributed gifts and tour ticket freely. Chinese tourists were also satisfactory with the route arranged by Chiang Mai University.

4.4.2 It's difficult for Thailand to accept Chinese tourists' uncivilized behaviors breaching social basic etiquette.

Chinese tourists'uncivilized behaviors breaching social basic etiquette mainly focus on how to use public facilities. Chinese tourists' uncivilized behaviors in Chiang Mai Province were very serious, including Chinese tourists' peeing in Chiang Mai's moat (checked to be not Chinese tourists after investigation), Chinese tourists'no flushing after leaving the toilet, joining in the activities organized by the hotel without permission and camping in Chiang Mai University. When Chinese tourists visited the Black Temple, they kicked off black wooden handrail with the history of 30 years for taking the photos of jumping up and didn't keep the toilet clean after leaving.

There were also similar behaviors when Chinese tourists visited the White Temple in Chiang Rai. Chinese tourists also didn't flush the toilet and caused the White Temple to close the toilet once and forbid Chinese tourists from entry.

Chinese tourists washed their shoes and feet in the wash basin of the toilet in PP Island and caused the natural protection area managing the toilet to dispatch special personnel to clean the washbasin completely.

When Chinese tourists fed the little tiger in Sriracha Tiger Zoo, they kicked the iron cage violently and caused the little tiger to suffer scare for fun. Additionally, Chinese tourists also had uncivilized behaviors such as speaking loudly at the places of keeping quiet, not following traffic rules and conflict with service staff.

Meanwhile, Thailand has criticized and reproached Chinese people's behavior to engage in business by fraudulent use of Thai people's status through the convenience of applying for status in the north and northeast of Thailand. Some persons in part of Thai travel agencies used the status of Thai people fraudulently, especially those travel agencies in Phuket and Pattaya. Meanwhile, lots of travel agencies made up the benefit chain charging no fees together and caused lots of tourist group of low quality to enter in Thailand and consume Thailand's public resources but with no corresponding benefit brought to Thai tourist industry. Thailand holds that fraudulent use of Thai people's status and operation mode of charging no fees have destroyed Thailand's economic order and brought very bad influence to Thai tourist industry seriously.

4.5 Thailand's Rethinking to Chinese Tourists' Phenomena

4.5.1. It's thought that cultural conflict is the main factor in understanding of Chinese tourists' behaviors

Thailand holds that, only a few Chinese tourists have uncivilized behaviors and not knowing Thai culture is the main reason to cause Chinese tourists to have uncivilized behaviors. In the accident that Chinese tourists hung underwear in Chiang Mai Airport, Thailand's social network has criticized Chinese tourists' behavior seriously, but the responsible person in Chiang Mai Airport pointed out in the news that Chinese tourists' behavior is not in breach of laws, just not knowing

Thailand's custom and culture. In the accident that Chinese tourists wore the university uniform to take photos in Chiang Mai University, Chiang Mai University also held that Chinese tourists are not in breach of regulations purposely and just don't know mutual culture after communication with Chinese tourists. In the accident of Chinese tourists'peeing in Chiang Mai's moat (proved to be false news thereafter), it's regarded as cultural conflict and mutual culture shall be publicized to remove cultural gap.

Meanwhile, it's thought that cultural conflict is generally existed and Thai people also face with many circumstances of not knowing local culture and breaching the rules at the time of travel in other countries such as Japan.

4.5.2. Thailand's tourist reception ability is limited and it's thought that Chinese tourists shall not be condemned

Thailand holds that, Thailand's tourist reception ability is limited and it has made good preparation for accepting lots of Chinese tourists. In the accident that Chinese tourists kicked off black wooden handrail in Black Temple to take photos, the Black Temple held that the the travel agency and the temple's reception ability is limited. After that, the Black Temple asked the tour guides to increase explanation to Lanna culture and equipped 10 safeguards to be responsible to guide the tourists and protect them to be safe.

Chalermchai Kositpipat, the architect of the White Temple[1], always criticized Chinese tourists before and showed Chinese tourists'uncivilized behaviors such as using the toilet uncivilly and smoking in the White Temple. But he rethought in the interview on Mar. 27, 2016 and showed that "Chinese tourists are not wrong, we have not made good preparation"[2]. After consideration, Chalermchai Kositpipat showed that he should not complain Chinese tourists before, as the White Temple is lack of communication with Chinese tourists and there is no indication board in

---

1   อ.เฉลิมชัย.

2   "นักท่องเที่ยวจีนไม่ผิด มึงต่างหากที่ไม่พร้อม» เฉลิมชัย โฆษิตพิพัฒน์.... http://www.posttoday.com/analysis/interview/423753.

Chinese, no enough personnel and no the support by tour guides. Lack of reception ability has caused Chinese tourists to be not well cared and it's impossible to provide guide for Chinese tourists.

Lack of Chinese tour guides in Thailand has also resulted in lack of reception ability. There are 4856 tour guides in Thailand who can speak Chinese and it's difficult to accept millions of tourists each year.[1] Meanwhile, infrastructure construction in Thailand is not sufficient and reception ability for Chinese tourists is limited in the ways of transport, hotels and scenic sites, especially Suvarnabhumi Airport and Don Muang Airport in Bangkok. The number of accepted tourists has exceeded the upper limit as designed for several years. The customs clearance in Suvarnabhumi Airport is slow and tourists often need to wait for 3-4 hours to be cleared by the customs during peak hours.

4.5.3 Thailand's basic facilities are under overloaded operation

Since 2006, except political turmoil in Thailand in 2008-2009 and 2014, the number of foreign tourists has increased continuously. Meanwhile, Thailand is slow in infrastructure construction and the passenger throughput in Suvarnabhumi Airport has exceed the maximum designed value. In 2012, Thailand moved low-cost airline companies and most of airline companies flying domestic flights to Don Muang Airport to relieve the pressure of Suvarnabhumi Airport. But with continuous increase in the number of tourists, the number of passengers accepted by Suvarnabhumi Airport each year still exceeds the maximum design value[2] of 45 million persons/year. Tourist industry occupies most of resources in Suvarnabhumi Airport, and Thai government has not taken measures of restricting the number of tourists as to slow expansion of Suvarnabhumi Airport, which has caused Suvarnabhumi Airport's infrastructures to be difficult to meet the demands.

1　ย้ำชัด!อาชีพไกด์สงวนให้คนไทยเท่านั้น,thairath.co.th,2015.06.27,www.thairath.co.th/content/507801.

2　AOT, http://www.suvarnabhumiairport.com/cn/1092-about-airport16.

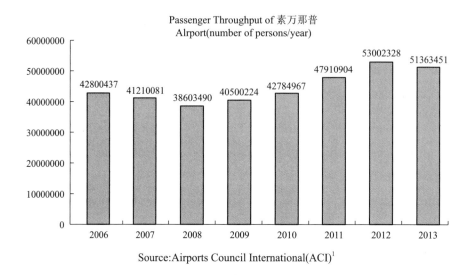

Passenger Throughput of 素万那普
Alrport(number of persons/year)

Source:Airports Council International(ACI)[1]

Faced with Suvarnabhumi Airport's overloaded operation, Thailand's airline industry also asked to stop starting new flights to the Thai government to prevent the airport from being more crowded. Aviation Operation Commission of Thailand (AOC) pointed out that it has used all the feasible methods to increase the capacity of the airport. In case of improving parking management, additional passengers couldn't be accepted.[2]

The adviser of Thailand's Tourist Association, Sidiwachala Chivaranapon[3] holds that, the level of Thai tour guides with certificates needs to be improved and part of Chinese tour guides can't introduce scenic sites in Chinese. Tourist operators in Chiang Mai has also organized the training on Chinese and Chinese culture for tour guides and workstaff.

In the accident that Chinese tourists washed shoes and feet in the wash basin of the toilet, it's reported in the news that humanized facilities is insufficient and footbath shall be added to meet the demand of tourists in this toilet near to the sand beach in natural protection area in Thailand.

1　Airports Council International(ACI),http://www.aci.aero/Data-Centre.

2　Airline Industry asked to stop starting new flights due to BangkokAirport's Continuous Overload, http://world. huanqiu.com/exclusive/2015-10/7797127.html.

3　นายศิษฏ์วัชร ชีวรัตนพร.

Thailand holds that Chinese tourists should not be condemned, especially vituperation to Chinese tourists online. Both parties need to know each other and Thailand has not resisted Chinese tourists. Meanwhile Thai people are hoped to not take photos of Chinese tourists and send Chinese tourists'inelegant photos and videos online as a few persons' behaviors have resulted in the contradiction between both parties.

4.5.4 Chinese tourists' contribution to Thai economy is affirmed and it's hoped to keep good relations

Ministry of Tourism and Sports, Tourism Authority of Thailand and Tourism Association always confirm Chinese tourists' contribution to Thai economy. With rapid increase in the number of Chinese tourists from 2010, the ratio of Chinese tourists among foreign tourists in Thailand has ascended year by year. The number of Chinese tourists has become an important factor to effect Thai economy.

Thailand confirms the quality of Chinese tourists and holds that Chinese tourists rank in the middle and supper level among foreign tourist groups and Chinese tourists'average tourist consumption level is higher than average level of foreign tourists. Shown from the statistics data in 2016, Chinese tourists'per capita consumption is 5800 baht, while foreign tourists'per capita consumption is 5072 baht. Thai government also holds that, 60% of Chinese tourists refer to high quality tourists, while 20% of them are middle-level consumption tourists and only 20% of the mare low consumption tourists charging no fees.

From 2015, Chinese tourists' uncivilized behaviors in Chiang Mai and Chiang Mai Province online, has resulted in language criticism to Chinese tourists'uncivilized behaviors on Thailand's social network for many times. In fact, parties concerned in some uncivilized events are not Chinese tourists.After Thailand's news event is exposed through China's self-media and traditional media, the idea that Thai people don't like Chinese tourists becomes to be spread in China. In 2016, the number of Chinese tourists to Thailand descended and

Thailand explained the situation to Chinese Government especially due to worrying the descending in Chinese tourists and invited such authorities as China Tourism Association to come to Thailand for survey on site. Tourist operators in Chiang Mai even carried the banner in Chinese "I love Chinese people" to show no prejudice to Chinese tourists.

Thailand holds that Chinese tourists will bring huge economic benefit to Thailand, so it hopes to keep good relation and create the broad environment to welcome Chinese tourists so as to promote the increase in the number of tourists.

Chinese tourists have increased greatly and the number of Chinese tourists to Thailand in 2015 came to 7,934,781 persons, accounting for 26.5%[1] of total foreign tourists in Thailand. China has become the biggest tourist source country for Thailand and the number of Chinese tourists has exceeded one tenth of Thai people[2]. Meanwhile, the number of Chinese tourists is increasing year by year.

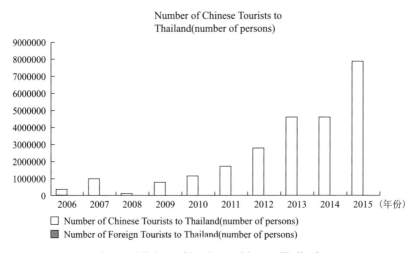

Number of Chinese Tourists to Thailand(number of persons)

□ Number of Chinese Tourists to Thailand(number of persons)
■ Number of Foreign Tourists to Thailand(number of persons)

Source: Ministry of Tourism and Sports, Thailand

---

1   The number of Chinese tourists toThailand in 2015 accounted for 26.5545558560763% of total global tourists.

2   Statistics Data of Department of NationalAdministration, the number of population in 2015 came to 65,729,098 persons. http://stat.bora.dopa.go.th/stat/y_stat58.htm2555. สืบค้น 16 กุมภาพันธ์ 2559.

Chinese Tourists' Per Capita Consumption Increases

Chinese Tourists' Per Capita Consumption per day increases (Thai baht/day)				
Year	2012	2013	2014	2015
Chinese tourists' per capita consumption per day in Thailand	4,883.74	4,826.24	5,097.20	47386.42
Foreign tourists' per capita consumption per day in Thailand	4,883.74	4,392.81	4,616.49	48430.56[1]

Source: Ministry of Tourism and Sports,Thailand

4.5.5 Neutral attitude. Thailand holds neutral attitude to Chinese tourists' accidents and disputes occurred in Thailand

Thailand holds neutral attitude to disputes on Chinese tourists and doesn't favor its own people. In the accident that a Chinese child of 5 years old tore up "ancient painting" in Chiang Mai in 2014, the resort claimed 80,000 baht against Chinese tourist, but the police interfered with such accident finally and asked the resort to return excessive compensation to the tourist and only claim only 25,000 baht.

In the accident that Chinese tourists were thrown away by the tour guide in Pattaya, Thai police interfered with such accident quickly and arrested the tour guide throwing away the tourist group and asked the travel agency to make compensation. In the accident that Chinese tourist died at the time of playing the game of flying in the jungle in Chiang Mai in 2015, Thai police also interfered with such accident and judged finally that it's caused by the work staff's improper operation and the bereaved was compensated for 2,500,000 baht.

In the accident that Chinese tourists caught fishes to take photos in Phang Nga Province in 2016, the magistrate in Phang Nga Province proved at once that, so-called photos on Chinese tourists' catching fishes are old photos 3 years ago and Phang Nga Province has taken protective measures to prevent similar accidents.

Thailand also condemned its operators'behaviors such as charging no fees,

---

1　สรุปสถานการณ์นักท่องเที่ยว มกราคม–ธันวาคม2555 2556 2557 2558 , กระทรวงการท่องเที่ยวและกีฬา กรมการท่องเที่ยว

bidding up the price of products and forcing Chinese tourists to buy products. It holds that these have destroyed Thailand's tourist image.

5. Conclusion

Among the researches on China's outbound tourists and Chinese tourists to Thailand at present, most of them focus on economic influence brought by tourists and behaviors of tourists, rare of them focuses on Chinese tourists and their influence to the place of tourist destination and Chinese tourists' image. I believe that this thesis will provide reference for the research in this field in the future.

China has become the largest source country of outbound tourists for Thailand currently. With the rapid increase in the number of Chinese tourists and the influence of Chinese tourists, Thailand has focused on Chinese tourists continuously. It's found out in the research that, the number of articles on Chinese tourists increases and the focus level ascends on Thailand's leading media. And Thailand's focus on Chinese tourists mainly concentrates on economy and the focus on social influence is less. Seen from news reports on Thailand's leading media, Chinese tourists has substantial influence to Thai social culture, but such influence level and influence scope are not so large as imaged.

Thai society takes a tolerant attitude to Chinese tourists' uncivilized behaviors still, which is derived from Thailand's kind and tolerant national character from one side and economic benefits brought by Chinese tourists from the other side. Thailand's leading media has not amplified and excessively spread Chinese tourists' uncivilized behaviors, but made neutral and positive report.

Chinese tourists don't know Thai culture and custom and result in cultural conflict. Chinese tourists are criticized due to uncivilized behaviors in Thailand from one side and they don't know Thai culture and custom from the other side. Thailand shows that it understands this phenomenon and advertises Thailand through more channels to enable Chinese tourists to know Thailand better.

Thai tourist market has made changes in Chinese tourists. Thailand has made indication board in Chinese for Chinese tourists and increased the staff to guide Chinese tourists. Especially in Thailand's airports, indication board in Chinese has become necessary. Thailand is training more Thai tourist professionals who can speak Chinese.

Thailand pays attention to Chinese tourists and Chinese tourist market and hopes to deliver a welcome attitude to Chinese tourists. It also hopes that the negative information on Chinese tourists on Thailand's social network will not effect Chinese tourists. Thailand hopes to create a tourist industry in the manner of sustainable development and criticize the behavior of charging no fees to enable Chinese tourists to enjoy better tourist environment.

But Thailand's attitude to Chinese tourists is not generally existed in other countries. Comparatively speaking, the influence of Chinese tourists'uncivilized behaviors to some countries' (including China) social culture is more obvious.

References

中国国际广播电台环球资讯广播、中国外文局中外传播研究中心传播战略研究室:《中国国家形象全球调查报告 2015》, 2016。

อัจฉราสมบัติน้นทนา, พฤติกรรมการท่องเที่ยวของนักท่องเที่ยวชาวจีนที่เดินเข้ามาท่องเที่ยวในประเทศไทย, กรุงเทพ,มหาวิทยาลัยศรีนครินทรวิโรฒ, 2012.

นางกรวรรณ สังขกร, พฤติกรรมนักท่องเที่ยวจีนยุคใหม่: กรณีศึกษานักท่องเที่ยวจีนในจังหวัดเชียงใหม่, จังหวัดเชียงใหม่,สถาบันวิจัยสังคม มหาวิทยาลัยเชียงใหม่, 2013.

นางศรีสุดาวนภิญโญศักดิ์,การเติบโตอย่างก้าวกระโดดของนักท่องเพียวจีนกับผลกระทบต่อสังคมไทย, กรุงเทพ,ประทรวงต่างประเทศ, 2015.

杨磊:《游客形象对中国公共外交的影响分析》,《中国发展》第 14 卷第 4 期 ,2014 年。

王珂:《旅游别把"脸"丢了》,《人民日报》, 2013 年 8 月 1 日。

การท่องเที่ยวแห่งชาติ, คู่มือการบริหารและจัดการท่องเที่ยวในพื้นที่รับผิดชอบองค์การบริหารส่วนตำบล(อบต.) และสภาตำบล(สต.). การท่องเที่ยวแห่งชาติ, กรุงเทพ, 2000.

แสงเดือน รตินธร,ปัจจัยผลักดันและปัจจัยดึงดูดที่ มีผลต่อนักท่องเทียวชาวจีนในการตัดสินใจเลือก มาท่องเที่ยวในประเทศไทย, กรุงเทพ,วารสารวิชาการสมาคมสถาบันอุดมศึกษาเอกชนแห่งประเทศไทย (สสอท.),2012.

ฉลองศรี พิมลสมพงษ์, การวางแผนและพัฒนาการตลาดการท่องเที่ยว. พิมพ์ครั้งที่ 6 กรุงเทพฯ: มหาวิทยาลัยเกษตรศาสตร์,
2007.

กรุณาบุญมาเรือน,ปัจจัยที่มีผลต่อการเดินทางเข้ามาท่องเที่ยวในประเทศไทยของนักท่องเที่ยวชาวต่างชาติ.สารนิพนธ์ ศ.ม.
กรุงเทพ,มหาวิทยาลัยเชียงใหม่, 2011.

กัลยกรศุภธราธาร, การวิเคราะห์พฤติกรรมการท่องเที่ยวของนักท่องเที่ยวชาวจีนในประเทศไทย. วิทยานิพนธ์,กรุงเทพ,
มหาวิทยาลัยหอการค้าไทย, 2005.

ทิฆาสมพร, อุปสงค์ของนักท่องเที่ยวชาวต่างประเทศที่เดินทางมาท่องเที่ยวประเทศไทยสารนิพนธ์, ศ. ม.กรุงเทพ,มหาวิทยาลัยรามคำแหง,
2003.

มา วงศ์ยัง,ปัจจัยที่มีผลต่อจำนวนนักท่องเที่ยวจีนที่มาประเทศไทย, 2012.

พนินทรเจริญธีระสกุลเดช1และเชียวกุ่ยหลง2, มัชฌิมำการเปลี่ยนแปลงของพฤติกรรมนักท่องเที่ยวจีนในประเทศไทย,
วารสารวิชาการมหาวิทยาลัยนอร์ทกรุงเทพ, กรุงเทพ, ปีที่ 3 ฉบับที่ 2 เดือนกรกฎาคม – ธันวาคม 2557.

文春艳:《我国游客不文明旅游行为研究综述》,《中国西部科技》,2015 年 3 月第 3 期。

谭岳坤:《泰中旅游贸易中的零团费问题研究》,对外经济贸易大学博士论文,2007 年。

庄国土、张禹东:《泰国蓝皮书泰国研究报告》,社会科学文献出版社 2016 年版。

史国栋等:《泰国政治体制与政治现状》,苏州大学出版社 2016 年版。

中德新闻报道中关于"一带一路"倡议关键词的跨范畴化研究

卡塔利娜【波兰】

波恩大学硕士研究生

一、研究背景

"一带一路"倡议是习近平主席于 2013 年提出的,由陆上"丝绸之路经济带"和海上"21 世纪海上丝绸之路"组成。来自亚洲、非洲、欧洲和大洋洲的 70 多个国家参加了这个庞大的基础设施和贸易项目。近年来,"一带一路"引起了世界范围的广泛关注,同时"一带一路"沿线国家的相关研究也在如火如荼地进行着。然而,相关研究主要集中于政治学、经济学、国际关系等领域,语言学领域的研究十分有限,并且很少有学者尝试对中外新闻报道中关于"一带一路"的话语进行对比分析。德国是中国在"一带一路"中的主要贸易伙伴之一,两国在合作中完成了渝新欧铁路等重大项目,然而,两国媒体在报道中对"一带一路"在用词选择和语言表达上完全不同。因此,本文旨在从认知语言学角度出发,基于动态范畴理论,对中德"一带一路"新闻报道中的差异性语言表达进行对比分析。

二、"一带一路"相关研究成果回顾

近年来,随着人们对"一带一路"的兴趣日益增加,关于它的相关研究蓬勃发展起来,中文类学术文章多从政治学视角出发,而英文类研究较为多样化,但仍以政治或经济类文章为主。

关于"一带一路"相关研究的一个主要话题是"中国文化外交",正如 Winter（2016）、Wei（2017）、Sterling（2018）以及欧洲亚洲研究所（2017）分析的那样，中国将"一带一路"作为一种软实力工具来提升自己在世界上的形象。另一个重要的话题是关于国外对"一带一路"观点的研究，尤其是从美国（Chance 2016）、俄罗斯（Smirnova 2017）和欧盟（Misiagiewicz 2016，Ma 2017）的角度来看，他们的研究主要涉及政治、经济和传媒领域。同样，中国关于"一带一路"的报道和描述也是很多研究者分析的对象，如（Sidaway/Woon 2017，波兰战争研究大学2017，Lubina 2017，Dadabeaev 2018），他们主要从地缘政治、国际关系等方面探讨了他们对"一带一路"的认识以及"一带一路"对各个国家的影响。虽然中国人和外国人对该倡议的看法是不同的，但应该指出的是，几乎每个研究的观点都代表了各个国家主要的看法。

到目前为止，已有一部分学者从语言学角度对中外媒体关于"一带一路"的报道做出了对比研究。Dutoit（2017）以批评性话语分析为基础，从论证、修辞手法、词汇风格和叙事方式等方面探析了中外媒体对中国"软实力"的不同认知，从社会政治角度探究这一差异的原因。Wangs（2017）通过对中美媒体关于"一带一路"新闻报道中关键词的词汇选择的对比研究，分析中美媒体在社会意识形态、价值观、立场上的差异，运用系统功能语法进行语言分析并解释语言和社会意识形态之间的关系。Zhang 和 Wu（2017）利用语料库辅助方法也进行了类似的对比研究，文章分析了中英媒体的标题和关键段落，并比较了词汇分类的主题。迄今为止，大多数类似的研究主要关于汉语媒体与英语媒体的比较，而其他语言学相关的文章描述了参与国的英语种类（Xu, 2017），丝绸之路沿线的多语言和语言政策（Sunuodula，2017）或与该倡议相关的翻译项目(Yang, Wang, 2016)等研究，但并没有汉语媒体和德语媒体关于"一带一路"的对比研究。

为了弥补这一研究之不足，本文基于动态范畴理论，对中德新闻报道中关于"一带一路"关键词的表达和词汇选择进行对比分析，该研究的主要意义有四：第一，拓宽动态范畴理论的应用范围并丰富其理论应用；第二，将对比分析应用于中德新闻报道中关于"一带一路"相关表达的研究；第三，探讨德国媒体对"一带一路"认知存在偏见的原因；第四，从语言学视角以中立的观点重新认识"一带一路",尝试改变德方对该倡议的正确理解,并希望本研究将有助于实现"一带一路"所提出的愿景,并促进今后中德之间的和平与合作。

三、理论框架

基于相关研究的空白,本文从认知语言学视角出发,运用动态范畴理论对中德"一带一路"相关报道中的关键词进行对比分析。

自人类诞生以来,人类就通过分类的方法来认识客观世界,这个过程被称为"范畴化",在此基础上,我们能够形成概念,赋予语言符号意义。古希腊哲学家亚里士多德提出了一种基于相似属性来对物体进行分组的方法,经典范畴理论由此诞生。在经典范畴理论看来,范畴之间边界明确,范畴成员之间地位平等。1953 年,奥地利哲学家维特根斯坦大胆地对经典范畴理论提出挑战,并提出了家族相似性,他认为,范畴的边界是模糊的,范畴成员之间地位不同。基于此,20 世纪 70 年代,美国学者 Rosch 和 Lakoff 提出了原型范畴理论,认为事物范畴的划分是根据其原型特征为基础并基于相似性而展开的,范畴不是一分为二的,范畴边界是不确定的,范畴内成员具有家族相似性。认知语言学家 Langacker 和 Taylor 等人进一步提出了图式范畴理论,并将"原型"解释为范畴核心的抽象或图式心理表征。近年来,范畴化理论研究出现了一个新趋势,Smith and Samuelson(1997),Croft and Cruse(2004),Zhang(2004),Goldberg(2016),Li(2006) 和 Fan(2010) 做了关于范畴的动态研究,他们意识到:一个词本身是没有固定意义的,它的意义是根据实际使用过程中心理变化的过程而形成的。然而,当前大多数的研究还不够全面,未能指出动态范畴变化的具体规律,而动态范畴研究大多集中在去范畴化上,忽略了其他过程,如聚范畴化、跨范畴化和再范畴化等动态变化现象。

为了对动态范畴理论做出进一步分析,王天翼(2017)基于哲学、语言学、社会学等领域的相关理论,系统构建了"动态范畴"的理论框架。首先,从后现代哲学的角度来看,动态范畴理论体现了反基础主义、非理性主义、多元主义和过程哲学的原则;其次,从语言学的角度来看,动态范畴理论可以用构式压制,隐转喻等元认知机制来解释;最后,从社会学和社会语言学的角度,探讨了社会性的动态范畴化,有效地解阐释了语言如何适应不同时代、社会和文化的改变而进行动态变化。王天翼(2017)指出,动态范畴化包含不同的过程,包括去范畴化、跨范畴化、再范畴话等。在范畴动态变化的过程中，范畴内某一成员的属性不断减少和被边缘化，它被迫从一个范畴中心成员向范畴边缘或范畴外转移，这一过程被称为去范畴化，反之，如果范畴成员范畴属性不断增加，从范畴外或范畴边缘向范畴内或范畴中心移变，则被称为聚范畴化；而如果该范畴成员在移变过程中位于两个范畴交集范围之内，这一过程被称为跨范畴化；而如果一个范畴的成员由于丢失了原初范畴的属性而转移到了另一个范畴之内，那么这一过程被称为再范畴化，我们将在下一章用实例来详细阐释。

本研究采用定性和定量相结合的研究方法，在选定的时间段内，从中德两种语言的相关新闻报道中收集了 87 个关于"一带一路"的相关表达，并建立封闭语料库。语料选取自中国的《人民日报》中文版，德国的《法兰克福汇报》、《德国之声》、《德国广播电台》、《明镜周报》等德语版 2015 年 3 月至 2018 年 5 月的相关新闻报道。本研究首先从上述报纸的标题和关键段落中选取关键词，然后根据词汇含义和词汇选择做出比较分析。研究发现，汉语相关新闻报道对"一带一路"持积极肯定的态度，使用的汉语词汇大多为褒义含义；而德国新闻报道对"一带一路"持消极否定的态度，使用的德语词汇大多为贬义含义，甚至用与军事或战争相关的词汇来解释"一带一路"。本研究尝试运用动态范畴理论详细阐释这一语言现象。

四、用动态范畴理论解释中德媒体中关于"一带一路"关键词的意义动态变化

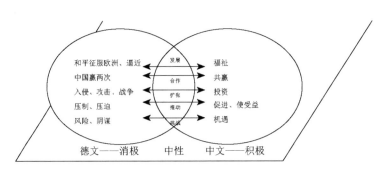

图 1　关键词的意义动态变化

如图 1 所示，从中德两国媒体对"一带一路"的报道可以发现，两国对于该倡议所持观点迥然不同。本研究分析的所有中文语料均取自中国官方报纸《人民日报》，报道显示，中国是一个爱好和平、睦邻友好的国家，而"一带一路"提倡和谐合作，互惠互利；相反，德语媒体却将中国描绘成西方国家的敌人和潜在威胁，德媒对中国和"一带一路"概念的整体认知只是一个模糊的框架，非常有限，这也增加了德国人民对于未知事物的恐惧感。这一差异主要体现在报道中关键词的不同表达。

我们认为可以运用动态范畴理论阐释这一语言现象的原因。本研究将通过以下 5 个例子对其进行详细阐释：本研究选取了五个高频关键词"发展"、"合作"、"扩张"、"推动"、"挑战"。

1."发展"

本研究选取的第一个高频关键词为"发展"（Friedliche Eroberung）。图 1 所示，"发展"作为中性词义，位于两个范畴的交集，左边一个范畴表示"发展"的贬义范畴，右边一个范畴表示"发展"的褒义范畴，两个范畴内部成员分别具有消极和积极的感情义属性。在"一带一路"相关中文报道中，"发展"一词完全具有积极肯定的特征。这表明"一带一路"不仅是中国的发展机遇，也是德国乃至世界的发展机遇，它为各国带来了和平与繁荣。另一方面，从上图也看出德国媒体对"发展"一词的理解复杂而消极。

"发展"的中性含义为事物由小到大、由简单到复杂、由低级到高级的变化过程。中德两国对于"一带一路"倡议的理解是从"发展"的中性义开始的。在中媒看来，"一带一路"倡议是中国有志于为"造福全世界"，"为人类谋福祉"的举措，中国的"一带一路"必将成为全球共同发展的机遇。因此，对中国媒体而言，"发展"一词的感情义属性就是积极正面的，因此它移变至右边的褒义范畴。然而，在德媒看来，中国的"一带一路"倡议是中国打着"推动全球共同发展"的幌子，而实际上却是一场想要"和平征服欧洲"的阴谋，对德国而言，"发展"一词的感情义属性是消极的，因此它移变至左边的贬义范畴。如：

中文示例：

（1）中国坚持和平发展、携手合作，在"一带一路"建设上不打地缘博弈小算盘、不搞封闭排他小圈子、不做凌驾于人的强买强卖，远远超越了西方地缘思维。

（2）随着"一带一路"的发展，沿途的贸易、金融、旅游等行业，也势必会逐渐跟上步伐。

德文示例：

In Peking feiert China mit der "neuen Seidenstra.e" das gr..te Entwicklungsprogramm seit dem Marshallplan.

众所周知，迄今为止"一带一路"是一个巨大的、成功的项目，它将塑造未来世界的政治和经济新格局，"发展"一词的属性也由"中性义"移变至"褒义"；与此同时，中国作为正在崛起的大国，引发了德国媒体对其动机的恐惧和误解，甚至将中国的"发展"视为一种"和平征服"、"向欧洲大陆入侵"等，"发展"一词的感情义属性也就从"中性义"范畴动态移变为"贬义"范畴。

2．"合作"

本研究选取的第二个高频关键词为"合作"。

图 1 所示："合作"一词的中性涵义为互相配合做某事或共同完成某项任务，指"一带一路"倡议是需要在中国与沿线国家通过相互配合来实现的。对中国媒体来说，"一带一路"倡议是中国希望通过"合作"来实现"双赢"的一项举措，由此，该词的范畴便从中性词转移到褒义词。而对德国媒体而言，"一带一路"是中国谋取私利的一种手段，是在牺牲欧洲人民利益的前提下为实现自身"赢两次"的阴谋，因此，该词的感情义属性从其本身的中性义范畴转移到贬义范畴。

中文示例：

（1）"一带一路"倡议提出以来，已从理念转化为行动、从愿景转变为现实——政策沟通不断深化、设施联通不断加强、贸易畅通不断提升、资金融通不断扩大、民心相通不断促进，"一带一路"建设将带来更多的合作共赢。

（2）中国坚持和平发展、携手合作，在"一带一路"建设上不打地缘博弈小算盘、不搞封闭排他小圈子、不做凌驾于人的强买强卖，远远超越了西方地缘思维。

德文示例：

（1）Es mehren sich allerdings die Zweifel, ob wirklich immer beide Seiten profitieren oder ob "Win-win" nicht bedeutet, dass China zweimal gewinnt.

（2）"Ich glaube an Win-Win-Situationen, doch da stellt sich schnell die Frage, wer gewinnt wieviel? Die Staaten Zentralasiens oder Russland gewinnen vielleicht 10,

15 Prozent, dann bekommt China 85 oder 90 Prozent - eine problematische Bilanz. Die Alternativen sind: Entweder nehme ich daran teil oder nicht, entweder gewinne ich

15 Prozent oder gar nichts.

正如中国媒体所述,"一带一路"充分显示中方与参与该项目各方的共同利益息息相关;然而,德国媒体并不认同这一观点,所以他们的报道将"双赢"理解为"中国赢两次"。于是,他们将"中国赢两次"这一感情义作为认知参照点,将"合作"义由"共同发展"的褒义范畴转移到与其相反的贬义范畴,由此"合作"便由积极的含义转移到了消极的含义。德媒通常补充到,"双赢局面"实际上是中国的双重胜利,而其他一些报道虽然支持互惠互利的观点,但同时也指出,随着中国在未来收益中获得最大份额,很可能不会平均分配,反讽和讽刺是西方尤其是德国媒体中使用频率很高的修辞手段。因此,"合作"一词的感情义在中国媒体的描述下由中性义范畴移变至褒义范畴。而在德国媒体的报道中却由中性义范畴移变至贬义范畴。

3."扩张"

图 1 所示,"扩张"一词的中性涵义为扩大(势力、疆土等)。"一带一路"倡议如此宏大的计划,必然会扩大中国的地缘政治经济空间,对国家间地区间的政治、外交等产生影响。在中媒看来,"一带一路"是开放合作的产物,而不是地缘政治的工具,更不能用过时的冷战思维去看待,"一带一路"实际上是中国对于沿线国家的投资,从而带动沿线国家共同富裕的项目。因此,"扩张"一词的感情义是积极的。但是,在德媒看来,"一带一路"倡议实际上是"中国帝国扩张"的手段,倡议的实施也就意味着中国的"入侵、攻击和战争","扩张"一词也被赋予了消极的感情义。

中文示例:

大摩预计,未来十年中国向一带一路沿途国家对外直接投资的年复合增长率将反弹至13%,总计达到1.2万亿美元。

德文示例:

Letztlich geht es darum, wie Europa sich darauf vorbereitet, den neuen Jahrhundertdeal zwischen offenem Handel einem regelbasierten System und Chinas expandieren den Ambitionenmit zu gestalten.

"扩张"是另一例证,它有和平发展和积极发展的感情义属性。《人民日报》的报道中将其释义为"投资"。相比之下,德国媒体所描述的"扩张"由于动态范畴变化的影响,它的积极感情义属性随着与"战争扩张"相关的消极属性的出现而减少。在德媒的报道中,人们对"一带一路"的扩张感到恐惧,在他们看来,"扩张"实际上就是"入侵"、"攻击"或"战争"。德媒报道者认为,"一带一路"实际上是中国不借助军事力量,采用的一种和平征服方式。事实上,他们忽略了一个事实,即中国是唯一没有殖民或领土野心的国家。他们使用"扩张"一词,是认为该词的感情义属性为中性义,由于认知的范畴动态变化,导致德国人民潜意识里对"一带一路"感到恐惧,自然而然地将"扩张"的感情义理解为"入侵、攻击或战争。"

4."推动"

用于描述"一带一路"完成情况的关键词之一是"推动"。如图 1 所示,"推动"一词的中性感情义为向前用力使物体前进。"一带一路"倡议旨在推动建立"共商、共建、共享"的人类命运共同体。在中媒看来,它将促进各国之间的合作交流,使更多国家获益,该词的属性便从中性义范畴转移到褒义范畴。而在德媒看来,"一带一路"倡议实际上是一种压制,是中国对于企图称霸的方式,"推动"也就被赋予了消极的含义,其属性也从中性转移到贬义。

中文示例:

(1)习近平强调,"一带一路"建设是推动构建人类命运共同体的重要实践平台。

(2)推动构建新型国际关系,推动构建人类命运共同体。

德文示例:

Chinesen wollten Projekte einfach durchdrücken, ohne Rücksicht auf Umweltaspekte oder gesellschaftliche Konsequenzen.

图 1 所示,范畴中"推动"一词的积极感情义属性如"加速增长"、"受益"等增加,这就是由中性词义向右边褒义范畴的范畴化移变。同一关键词在德国新闻报道中却经历了一个反向的范畴变化过程,虽然中国因按时完成某项大型项目而受到赞扬,但也有人指出,该项目能够在如此短的时间内完成是由于漠视环境和工人权利,因此,"推动"一词逐渐失去其积极感情义,而获得了"压迫"和"压制"的感情义。这就是"促进"一词的感情义在德媒语境中慢慢进入到对应的消极感情义范畴。

5."挑战"

本研究选取的最后一个例子是"挑战(challenge)"。"挑战"的中性涵义为激使敌方出战；谓首开衅端。中国作为"一带一路"的发起者，面对外部环境复杂的变化、国际金融危机深层次的影响、国际投资贸易格局和多边投资贸易规则酝酿的深刻调整，"一带一路"带来的不仅是前所未有的机遇，同时也面临着巨大的挑战。在中媒看来，"一带一路"倡议是相互依存下的合作共享，它所带来的前所未有的机遇大于挑战。因此，该词的感情义属性也从中性转移到褒义。而在德媒看来，"一带一路"倡议于中国而言是中国在以牺牲其他国家利益的前提下谋取自身利益的手段，因此风险大于机遇，是中国策划的一场"赢两次"的阴谋。该词的感情义属性也就转移到贬义的范畴。

中文示例：

面对复杂变化的世界，人类社会向何处去？亚洲前途在哪里？"一带一路"倡议将为世界带来了无可比拟的机遇，为陷入死胡同的多边主义带来独特而务实的新活力，为欧亚贸易和政治上的融合带来动力。

德文示例：

Ausgel.st durch einen gemeinsamen Brief von Berlin, Paris und Rom im Februar 2017 hat die Europ.ische Kommission einen Screening-Mechanismus vorgeschlagen, um bei Investitionen in sensiblen Sektoren Alarm zu schlagen. Dies verkennt jedoch den Umfang der eigentlichen Herausforderung.

由于"一带一路"项目规模庞大，中国媒体经常将其称为是一个挑战。然而，它更是未来经济增长和共同分享利润的机会，该词的感情义转向积极范畴。在德语中，"挑战"一词还被视为是一种"发展的机会"。尽管如此，在德媒看来，"挑战"一词并不仅仅是一个发展的机会，它体现的更多感情义属性显示出一种向其消极范畴移变的倾向。德媒称"一带一路"可能是欧盟经济发展的一个机会，与此同时，"危险"、"风险"或"阴谋"等属性也就体现出来了。

本章以"发展"、"合作"、"扩张"、"推动"、"挑战"为例，基于动态范畴理论，对比分析中德对"一带一路"相关新闻报道的关键词感情义和词汇选择的差异，并探讨了差异产生的原因。其意义在于：首先，动态范畴理论可以用来解释这一语言现象；其次，中德对于"一带一路"的范畴化认知差异主要是社会性和政治性因素所导致的，人们对其陌生和不了解使得范畴内部成员的褒义含义移变为贬义含义。

五、总结

本文从认知语言学的角度出发，通过对比中德"一带一路"相关报道的分析得出以下结论：

首先，本文通过对中德媒体报道中关键词感情义范畴动态变化的分析，为动态范畴的研究提供了全新的案例，同时拓展了动态范畴研究的应用范围；

其次，本文将对比分析应用于中德新闻报道"一带一路"相关表达的研究，通过对比分析发现中德媒体对于"一带一路"倡议态度迥异；

再次，借助认知语言学的前沿理论——跨范畴理论探究差异存在的原因，最终发现是由于两国认知范畴的差异导致看法上的差异；

最后，本文从认知语言学的视角中性感情义的立场出发，尝试帮助德国人民正确看待"一带一路"，以期促进中德合作，便于"一带一路"实现造福全人类的终极目标。

基于动态范畴理论下的跨范畴化，我们发现中国媒体倾向于强调"一带一路"倡议主动积极的属性，树立国家形象，为世界带来和平与繁荣。相比之下，德国媒体的观点与强调可能性的经济报纸以及主流报纸混杂在一起，后者将中国和"一带一路"倡议描述为一个潜在的威胁。认知是通过描述而形成的，而对"一带一路"的截然相反的态度主要是由于认知范畴在特定关键词上的差异而导致的。德国媒体因对未知的恐惧而产生的偏见可以通过扩大对"一带一路"倡议和中国的了解而得到修正。此外，从语言学的角度继续研究跨范畴化的过程和中德比较研究，有助于培养具有国际视野的媒体实践，加强相互了解和双边合作。

A Study on the Trans-categorization of Sino-German Vocabulary with Keywords from Chinese-German News Reports Regarding the "Belt and Road" Initiative as an Example

Katarzyna Rozalia Babinska / Poland

Postgraduate of University of Bonn

1. Research Background

The "Belt and Road" initiative (shorted in B&R) is a comprehensive political and economic development project launched by President Xi Jinping in 2013, consisting of the land-based "Silk Road Economic Belt" and the sea-based "21st Century Maritime Silk Road". More than 70 countries from Asia, Africa, Europe and Oceania are taking part in this massive infrastructure and trade project. In recent years it has sparked worldwide interests and researches began to flourish in countries along the B&R. However, the relevant researches are mainly conducted from a political, economic, social science and international relations point of view. The linguistic research is very limited, few scholars have so far attempted a comparative study of B&R keywords used in Chinese and foreign news reports. Germany is one of China's leading trade partners and major projects such as the Chongqing-Xinjiang-

Europe railway are realized in cooperation. However, the perception of the initiative differs greatly between those two countries which is reflected by the choice of words selected by the media. The aim of this study is to conduct a comparative analysis of the differences between Chinese and German B&R news reports from the perspective of cognitive linguistics, based on the dynamic categorization theory.

2. Research Achievements Regarding the B&R

In recent years, with the increasing interests in B&R, relevant researches on it have developed vigorously. Chinese academic articles are mostly from the perspective of political science, while English studies are more diverse, but it is still dominated by political or economic articles.

One of the main topics is the Chinese cultural diplomacy with the B&R serving as a soft power tool to promote China's image in the world as analyzed by Winter (2016), Wei (2017), Sterling (2018) or the European Institute for Asian Studies (2017). Another important topic is the study of foreign perspectives regarding the initiative, especially from the point of view of the United States (Chance 2016), Russia (Smirnova 2017) and the European Union (Misiągiewicz 2016, Ma 2017), which are mostly related to the field of politics, social science and media studies (Sidaway/Woon 2017, Polish War Studies University 2017, Lubina 2017, Dadabeaev 2018). While the Chinese and non-Chinese view regarding the project are in opposition to each other, it should be pointed out that in the respective countries there are almost no opinions different from the official rhetoric.

So far there have been a few attempts to compare Chinese and foreign media coverage of the B&R. Dutoit (2017) examines the discrepancy between the Chinese and Western European image based on the interdisciplinary theory of critical discourse analysis with a focus on sociopolitical discourse. The analysis is mainly focused on argumentation, rhetoric figures, lexical style and the way of storytelling. The object of Wangs' (2017) study is Chinese and American news reports about the initiative. Again the methodology applied is critical discourse analysis as well as systemic functional grammar. The keywords and the lexical choice from the reports are used to explore the implicit social ideologies. A similar study was presented by Zhang and Wu (2017), utilizing critical discourse analysis with corpus-assisted methods. It investigatedheadlines and key paragraphs in Chinese and British media and compared the classification theme of the lexis. The majority of similar studies has so far been limited to a comparison with English-language media, with no articles focusing on German-language news about the B&R. Other articles related to the field of language studies describe English varieties of participating countries (Xu 2017), multilingualism and language policy along the Silk Road (Sunuodula 2017) or translation projects connectedwiththeinitiative(Yang,Wang: 2016). But there is no comparative study of "B&R" in Chinese and German media.

In order to make up for the inadequacies of the research, based on the dynamic category theory, this paper compares and analyzes the choices of "B&R" keywords and vocabulary in Sino-German news reports. The main significance of the study is four: First, broaden the application scope of dynamic category theory and enrich its theoretical application; Second, the comparative analysis was applied to the research on the expression of "B&R" in the Sino-German news report; Third, explore the reasons for the German media's prejudice against "B&R" cognition; Fourth, from the linguistic perspective, we will re-understand "B&R" from a neutral point of view, try to change the German understanding of the initiative, and hope that this study will contribute to the realization of the vision proposed by "B&R" and promote peace and cooperation between China and Germany in the future.

3. Theoretical Framework

Due to the research gap, this paper based on cognitive linguistics, using dynamic category theory to conduct a comparative analysis of Sino-German related reports on B&R.

Since the beginning of mankind humans have been processing the reality by means of classifying and categorizing all things in the objective world, a process which could be called "categorization". On this basis, we were able to form concepts and give language symbols a meaning. Even in ancient times, Greek philosophers like Plato and Aristoteles introduced an approach of grouping objects based on their similar properties, which led to the classical categorization theory. These categories have clearly defined boundaries and are mutually exclusive. Categorization became a popular research topic again in the 19th and 20th century when the Austrian philosopher Wittgenstein questioned the traditional approach in 1953. Instead of common features shared by the category members, he suggested many ways of family resemblance. In the 1970s American scholars Rosch and Lakoff proposed the prototype theory, which suggested that categorization is constructed around specific prototypes. According to their cognitive approach natural categories are graded and have fuzzy boundaries. Likewise, the status of their members is inconsistent. Cognitive linguists like Langacker and Taylor further suggested a theory of schemata categorization on the basis of the archetype categorization theory and interpreted the "prototype" as an abstract or schematic mental representation of the category core. In recent years there has been a new trend in categorization theory, namely the dynamic construction of categories researched by Smith and Samuelson (1997), Croft and Cruse (2004), Zhang (2004), Goldberg (2016), Li (2006) and Fan (2010).Those studies point to a number of deficiencies in the aforementioned theories and adopt a different view from the past on the basic features of the category. Modern linguists realized that a word itself has no fixed meaning, and its meaning is formed according to the psychological process of change in actual use. However, most of the research is not comprehensive enough and faces shortcomings in the form of not pointing out the law of dynamic category changes. What is more, the majority of studies from the field of dynamic categorization is focused on the process of de-categorization ignoring other processes such as initial categorization, poly-categorization, trans-categorization and re-categorization.

To further analyze this subject Wang Tianyi (2017) systematically constructed the theoretical framework of "dynamic categorization", which involves related theories from the fields of philosophy, linguistics, and sociology. First, from the perspective of post-modern philosophy, the dynamic categorization embodies the principles of antifoundationalism, irrationalism, pluralism, and process philosophy; secondly, based on cognitive linguistics, dynamic categorization can be explained by metacognitive mechanisms as structural suppression, metaphor and metonymy. Finally, based on the perspective of sociology and cognitive sociolinguistics, it discusses the dynamic categorization of sociality, which can effectively explain how language adapts to the given development trends of respective times, societies and cultures.

As mentioned above, the dynamic categorization consists of different processes, which include de-categorization and trans-categorization. During the process of trans-categorization, the attributes of members in a certain category continue to decrease and they are constantly marginalized, forcing them to move from one category to another, which will be described in this study. "Trans-categorization" (Wang 2017) refers to the phenomenon when the meaning of a member changes from one category to another one. If the member of a category shifts to a different one due to losing the attributes of his original one, it possesses the attributes of both the original category and the new one. The attributes of the category become a member of the intersection of the two categories. This theory will be illustrated with examples in the following chapter.

Qualitative and quantitative research methods were used to collect 87 related expressions about B&R from relevant news reports published in the Chinese and German language in a specified time frame and to establish a closed corpus. A sample of news reports by the Chinese version of People's Daily and the German version of Frankfurter Allgemeine Zeitung, Deutsche Welle, Heise Online, Die Zeit, Deutschlandfunk, Produktion, Le Monde Diplomatique, Der Spiegel, Die Süddeutsche, Tagesschau and Manager Magazin dated between March 2015 and May 2018, was collected. The study first investigated keywords from the headlines and key paragraphs in the corpora of afore mentioned newspapers and then compared the categorization scheme of the vocabulary according to their connotation. It was found that the Chinese vocabulary used in the relevant reports was predominantly positive, while the German reports mainly included negative, and even used vocabulary connected with the military orwarfaretoexplainthe initiative.The trans-categorizationtheorywas applied to explain the semantic mechanism of attributes changing from commendatory to derogatory.

4. Explanation of Sino-German Meaning Changes Regarding the B&R with the Use of the Dynamic Categorization Theory

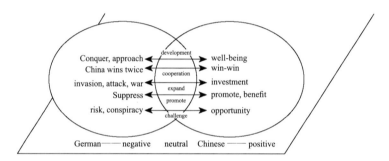

As is suggested in the figure, the media coverage in China and Germany regarding the B&R differs considerably. All Chinese-language corpora analyzed in this study were retrieved from *People's Daily* – the official newspaper of the CCP – and share a similar way of describing the initiative and China's foreign policy. China is portrayed as a peace-loving nation pursuing a friendship with other countries, while the B&R promotes a harmonious cooperation with mutual benefits for all participants. By contrast, different German-language media depict China as an antagonist to Western countries as well as a potential threat.The knowledge about China in general and the B&R, whose concept is that of a framework rather than a detailed plan, is limited. This adds to the Western fear of the unknown. The difference is mainly reflected in different expressions of the keywords in the report.

Dynamic categorization can be used to explain this linguistic phenomenon. This study will explain it in detail through the following five high frequency keywords: "development" (Friedliche Eroberung); "cooperation" (China ist die Gewinner);

"expansion" (eindringen); "promote" (unterdrüken); "challenge" (Herausforderung).

4.1 "Development" (Friedliche Eroberung)

The process of trans-categorization can serve as an explanation for the meaning changes of keywords in the respective newspapers. One of the examples appearing in the majority of articles is "development" (Friedliche Eroberung in German). As can be seen in the picture above this neutral word is located at the intersection of two categories and therefore combines attributes from both negative and positive development. In Chinese articles regarding the B&R it is gaining a growing number of positive attributes. The initiative is seen as a development chance not only for China but for the whole world, bringing peace and prosperity to all participating countries. On the other hand, the picture above illustrates that German media have a mixed and rather negative understanding of the word "development". It is acknowledged that the B&R is a giant and so far successful project which will shape future world politics and economy, gaining attributes from the "positive" category. At the same time China's emergence as a global player causes fear and misunderstanding about the motives, so far as to perceive the development as a "peaceful conquer" and "making an advance" towards the European continent. At the present moment, the word "development" is unlikely to leave its intersection position due to the existence of many different implications. However, we can observe a de-categorization trend in Chinese as well as German media which might lead to a trans-categorization and finally re-categorization process in the future.

The neutral meaning of "development" is the process of change from small to large, from simple to complex, from low to high. As far as the term "development" is concerned, China and Germany's understanding of "B&R" begins with the neutral meaning of "development". In the view of the Chinese media, "B&R" is "for the benefit of the whole world" and "for the well-being of mankind" and it will surely become an opportunity for the common development of the whole world. Therefore, for the Chinese media, the emotional meaning of the word "development" is positive, so it shifts to the right-handed category. However, in the view of German media, it seems that "B&R" is China in the guise of "promoting the common development", but in fact it is a conspiracy to "peacefully conquer Europe". For example:

Chinese examples:

（1）中国坚持和平发展、携手合作，在"一带一路"建设上不打地缘博弈小算盘、不搞封闭排他小圈子、不做凌驾于人的强买强卖，远远超越了西方地缘思维。

（2）随着"一带一路"的发展，沿途的贸易、金融、旅游等行业，也势必会逐渐跟上步伐。

German example:

In Peking feiert China mit der "neuen Seidenstraße" das größte Entwicklungs programm seit dem Marshallplan.

4.2 "Cooperation" (China ist die Gewinner)

Another example illustrating this principle is the neutral word "cooperation" (China ist die Gewinner). The neutral meaning of the word "cooperation" is to cooperate with each other to do something or to accomplish a certain task together, which means that "B&R" needs to be achieved through mutual cooperation between China and the countries along the line. For the Chinese media, "B&R" is an initiative that China hopes to achieve "win-win" through "cooperation", as a result, the scope of "cooperation" is transferred from neutral to commendatory. On the contrary, for the German media, "B&R" is a means for China to seek self-interest, and it is a conspiracy to achieve "win two times" on the premise of sacrificing the interests of the European. Therefore, the emotional meaning of "cooperation" shifts from its neutral meaning to derogatory. For example:

Chinese examples:

（1）"一带一路"倡议提出以来，已从理念转化为行动、从愿景转变为现实——政策沟通不断深化、设施联通不断加强、贸易畅通不断提升、资金融通不断扩大、民心相通不断促进，"一带一路"建设将带来更多的合作共赢。

（2）中国坚持和平发展、携手合作，在"一带一路"建设上不打地缘博弈小算盘、不搞封闭排他小圈子、不做凌驾于人的强买强卖，远远超越了西方地缘思维。

German examples:

(1)Es mehren sich allerdings die Zweifel, ob wirklich immer beide Seiten profitieren oder ob "Win-win" nicht bedeutet, dass China zweimal gewinnt.

(2) "Ich glaube an Win-Win-Situationen, doch da stellt sich schnell die Frage, wer gewinnt wieviel? Die Staaten Zentralasiens oder Russland gewinnen vielleicht 10, 15 Prozent, dann bekommt China 85 oder 90 Prozent - eine problematische Bilanz. Die Alternativen sind: Entweder nehme ich daran teil oder nicht, entweder gewinne ich 15 Prozent oder gar nichts.

As illustrated above in Chinese news reports about the B&R it usually belongs to the positively perceived category of "win-win-situation", highlighting the fact that a participation in this project is connected with mutual benefits for all parties. German media do not share this point of view, so it was a surprise to find a reference to "win win-situation" in their articles. However, they used it as a cognitive reference point to jump to a category opposite to the rather negatively perceived "cooperation" to express sarcastic humor. It was usually added afterward that the meaning of "win-win-situation" is that the initiative is a double victory for China. Other articles supported the view of mutual benefits, but at the same time suggested that they most likely will not be evenly distributed with China gaining the lion's share of future profits. Irony and sarcasm are very frequently used linguistic devices in Western and especially German media. Therefore, the emotional meaning of the word "cooperation" has been changed from the neutral meaning category to the commendatory category under the description of the Chinese media, but in the German media report it has changed from the neutral meaning category to the derogatory category.

4.3 "Expansion" (Eindringen)

The neutral meaning of the word "expansion" (Eindringen) is to expand (power, territory, etc.). As is known to us all that "B&R", which is such an ambitious plan will inevitably expand China's geopolitical and economic space and have an impact on politics and diplomacy among countries. In the view of Chinese media, "B&R" is a product of openness and cooperation, rather than a tool of geopolitics, and cannot be treated with outdated Cold War mentality. Actually, "B&R" is China's investment in the countries along the border, thus promoting the common prosperity of the countries along the line.Therefore, the emotional meaning of the word "expansion" is positive.However, in the view of the German media, "B&R" is actually a means of "expansion of the Chinese empire". The implementation of the initiative means China's "invasion, attack and war", and the word "expansion" has also been given a negative emotional meaning. For example:

Chinese example:

大摩预计，未来十年中国向一带一路沿途国家对外直接投资的年复合增长率将反弹至 13%，总计达到 1.2 万亿美元。

German example:

Letztlich geht es darum, wie Europa sich darauf vorbereitet, den neuen Jahrhundertdeal zwischen offenem Handel einem regelbasierten System und Chinas expandieren den Ambitionenmit zu gestalten.

The neutral word "expansion" located at the intersection of two categories is another illustration, it has both the attributes of a peaceful and an aggressive growth. In articles from People's Daily it has gained the meaning of "investment". In comparison, as depicted above in German news reports the positive attributes are decreasing with the simultaneous appearance of such connected with warfare in the negative category. The extension of the B&R is observed with fear and described as an "invasion", "attack" or "war". The authors of the German articles suggest that instead of using military strength China found a way of peaceful conquer, ignoring the fact that the Chinese empire was the only one without a history of colonial or territorial ambitions. They use the word "expansion" whose emotional attributes belongs to both categories to evoke mixed feelings and even subliminal fear towards the initiative.

4.4 "Promote" (unterdrüken)

One of the keywords used for describing the completion of different projects is "to promote"(推动, unterdrüken). The neutral emotional meaning of the word "promote"is to push the object forward. "B&R" aims at promoting the establish ment of a community of human destiny that "cooperates, builds, and shares". In the view of Chinese media, it will promote cooperation and exchanges among countries and benefit more countries. The emotional meaning of the word will be transferred from neutral to commendatory. However, In the view of German media, "B&R" is a kind of suppression. It is China's way of seeking hegemony. The word "Promote" is also given a negative meaning, and its emotional meaning is also transferred from neutral to derogatory. For example:

Chinese examples:

（1）习近平强调，"一带一路"建设是推动构建人类命运共同体的重要实践平台。

（2）推动构建新型国际关系，推动构建人类命运共同体。

German example:

Chinesen wollten Projekte einfach durchdrücken, ohne Rücksicht auf Umweltaspekte oder gesellschaftliche Konsequenzen.

As is shown above in the Chinese-language articles the negative attributes were reduced and at the same time positive attributes such as "accelerate the growth" and "benefit from" were obtained. The same keyword underwent a reversed process in German news reports. Although the B&R was praised for completing even large projects on time, it was also pointed out that their realization was possible due to the lack of care about the environment or workers' rights. Gradually losing the positive connotations and obtaining the sense of "oppression" and "suppression" would suggest a slow shift in the meaning of the word "promote" in the context of German media to the negative category.

4.5 "Challenge" (Herausforderung)

The last example shown in above picture is the word "challenge" (挑战, Herausforderung). The neutral meaning of "challenge" is to provoke the enemy to fight. As the initiator of "B&R", China faces unprecedented changes of the external environment, the deep-seated impact of the international financial crisis, the international investment and trade pattern, and the profound adjustments in the rules of multilateral investment and trade. "B&R" brings not only unprecedented opportunities, but also great challenges. In the view of the Chinese media, "B&R" is an interdependence of cooperation and sharing, and it brings unprecedented opportunities more than challenges, therefore, the emotional meaning of "challenge" is transferred from neutral to commendatory. In the view of German media, "B&R" is China's means to seek its own interests at the expense of other countries' interests. Therefore, risks are greater than opportunities, and China is planning a "win twice" conspiracy. The emotional meaning of "challenge" is transferred to the category of derogatory. For example:

Chinese example:

面对复杂变化的世界，人类社会向何处去？亚洲前途在哪里？"一带一路"倡议将为世界带来了无可比拟的机遇，为陷入死胡同的多边主义带来独特而务实的新活力，为欧亚贸易和政治上的融合带来动力。

German example:

Ausgelöst durch einen gemeinsamen Brief von Berlin, Paris und Rom im Februar 2017 hat die Europäische Kommission einen Screening-Mechanismus vorgeschlagen, um bei Investitionen in sensiblen Sektoren Alarm zu schlagen. Dies verkennt jedoch den Umfang der eigentlichen Herausforderung.

Chinese reports often refer to the B&R as a challenge due to the large scale of the planned projects. Yet it is rather perceived as an opportunity for future growth and common profit than a potential defeat, thereby moving to the right to the positive category. In German, the word "challenge" also has the connotation of a chance for improvement. Nonetheless, the emerging of many attributes in the negative category shows a tendency towards re-categorization as a word with pejorative meaning. German news reports suggest that the B&R might become an opportunity for the economy of the European Union. At the same time attributes like "danger", "risk" or "conspiracy" appear, which similar as in the case of "expansion" take advantage of the subliminal fear of the unknown and of being conquered.

Taking "development" (Friedliche Eroberung), "cooperation"(China ist die Gewinner), "expansion"(eindringen), "promote" (unterdrüken), "challenge" (Herausforderung) as examples, based on the dynamic categorization, this paper compares and analyzes the differences between Chinese and German on the keywords and vocabulary choice of "B&R" related news reports, and probes into the causes of the differences. The significance lies in: Firstly, the dynamic categorization can be used to explain this linguistic phenomenon; secondly, the cognitive differences between China and Germany towards "B&R" is mainly caused by social and political factors.

5. Summary

From the perspective of cognitive linguistics, the following conclusions can be drawn from the analysis of the relevant reports of "B&R" in China and Germany:

First of all, through the analysis of the dynamic changes of the emotional meaning category of keywords in the media reports of China and Germany, this paper provides a brand-new case for the study of the dynamic categorization, and expands the application scope of dynamic categorization;

Second, this paper applies comparative analysis to the research on the related expressions of "B&R" in the Sino-German news reports. Through comparative analysis, it is found that the Chinese and German media have different attitudes towards "B&R";

Third, with the help of trans-categorization, the author explores the reasons for the differences and finds that the differences in perceptions are caused by the differences in cognitive categories between the two countries;

Finally, from the perspective of cognitive linguistics, this paper attempts to help the German people to correctly treat "B&R" in order to promote Sino-German cooperation and facilitate it to achieve the ultimate goal of benefiting the whole of mankind.

In conclusion, it has been found that Chinese media tend to emphasize the positive attributes of the initiative and to build the image of China as a nation bringing peace and prosperity to the world. By contrast, the opinions in German media are mixed with economic newspapers highlighting the possibilities and mainstream newspapers describing China and the initiative as a potential threat. Perception is shaped by depiction and the diametrically opposite attitude towards the B&R is mainly due to differences in the cognitive categories regarding specific keywords. The prejudice of German media stemming from the fear of the unknown could be amended by widening the knowledge about the initiative and about China in general. Moreover, it would be advisable to continue research about the process of trans-categorization as well as Sino-German comparative studies from the field of linguistics to help develop a globally minded media practice as well as strengthen the mutual understanding and bilateral cooperation.

References

Andersen, Lars Erslev, Anoush Ehteshami, Mamtimyn Sunoudula and Yang Jiang (ed.). 'the Belt and Road' and China's Westward Pivot. Past, Present and Future. Conference Report –November 2017.DIIS -Danish Institute of International Studies.

Adele E. Goldberg. Partial productivity of linguistic constructions: Dynamic categorization and statistical preemption[J]. *Language and Cognition*. 2017(8):369-390.

Anne-Sophie Dutoit. *The Chinese Self, the Other and Western European Media: A Cross-Media Critical Discourse Analysis on Chinese Soft Power Narratives in the Context of the "One Belt, One Road" Initiative and the Asian Infrastructure Investment Bank* [D], 2017.

Chance, Alek. *American Perspectives on the Belt and Road Initiative: Sources of Concern, Possibilities for US-China Cooperation.* Institute for China-America Studies, 2016.

China-Programm der Stiftung Asienhaus (ed.). Wohin führen die Neuen Seidenstraßen? China's Belt and RoadInitiative. Stiftung Asienhaus, 2017.

Croft, W. & D. Alan Cruse (2004). *Cognitive Linguistics*[M]. Cambridge: Cambridge University Press.

Timur Dadabaev. "Silk Road"as Foreign Policy Discourse: The Construction of Chinese, Japanese and Korean Engagement Strategies in Central Asia[J]. *Journal of Eurasian Studies.* 2018:(9),30-41.

Rosch E, Mervis C B. Family Resemblances: Studies in the Internal Structure of Categories[J]. *Cognitive Psychology.* 1975(7):573-605.

Rosch E, Mervis C B, Gray W, et al. Basic Objects in Natural Categories[J]. *Cognitive Psychology.* 2016(8):382-439.

Linda B. Smith and Larissa K. Samuelson. Perceiving and remembering: category stability, variability and development[J]. 1997(1):161-195.

Ma, Junchi. The Challenge of Difference Perceptions on the Belt and Road Initiative[J]. *Croatian International Relations Review,* 2017, 23(78):149-168.

Michał Lubina. From Geopolitical Chance to Security Treat: Polish Public Political Discourse on the One Belt One Road Initiative[J]. *Polish Political Science Yearbook,* 2017(1):221-238.

Misiągiewicz, Justyna and Misiągiewicz, Marcin. China's „the Belt and Road" Initiative – the Perspective of the European Union[J]. *Annales Universitatis Mariae Curie-Skłodowska,* 2016(23):34-42.

Lakoff, G. *Women, Fire, and Dangerous Things: What Categories Reveal Aboutthe Mind*[M] .Chicagoand London: University of Chicago Press, 1987.

Li,Jun. Zhang, Yong and Richard E. Nisbett. Is It Culture or Is It Language? Examination of Language Effects in Cross-Cultural Research on Categorization[J]. *Journal of Personality and Social Psychology.* 2004(1):57-65.

Sidaway, James D. and Woon, Chih Yuan. Chines Narratives on "the Belt and Road" inGeopolitical and Imperial Contexts[J]. *The Professional Geographer,* 2017(0):1-13.

Larisa Smirnova. Perception of China's "One Belt, One Road" in Russia: "United Eurasia" Dream or "Iron Circle" of Containment? [N]. *21st Century,* 2017-03, No.1(20).

Sterling, Dahlia Patricia. A New Era in Cultural Diplomacy: Promoting the Image of China's "Belt and Road" Initiative in Asia, *Open Journal of Social Sciences*[J].2018(6):112-116.

Tim Winter. One Belt, One Road, One Heritage: Cultural Diplomacy and the Silk Road[N]. The Diplomat, 2016-04-02.

Wei, Li. Construction of Humanistic Silk Road with Sharing Cultures and Intercommunicating Souls Based on Chinese Civilization Wisdom[J]. *IOSR Journal of Research & Method in Education*, 2017(7):1-5.

Wu, Doreen and Zhang, Lejin. Media Representations of China:A Comparison of China Daily and Financial Times in Reporting on the Belt and Road Initiative[J]. *Critical Arts,2017*(6):29-44.

Wang, Dong.AMixed Methodology Study of Media Coverage of the "the Belt and Road Strategy"[J]. *Scholars Journal of Arts, Humanities and Social Sciences*, 2017(5): 349-356.

Xu, Xiaohui. Study on the English Varieties of "One Belt, One Road" Countries[J]. *Theory and Practice Language Studies*, 2017(7): 201-208.

李小飞、范振强：《具身哲学视域下的范畴动态构建观》,《山东社会科学》2010 年第 12 期。

李小飞、《范畴边界的动态建构研究》,《山东外语教学》, 2006 年第 5 期。

王晨佳：《"一带一路"概念下的文化传播与译介》,《人文杂志》, 2016 年第 1 期。

王天翼：《动态范畴化初探 —— 基于现代汉语 "还 " 字构式的研究》, 浙江大学 2017 年博士论文。

杨迎华：《"一带一路"建设下的中国语言战略》,《人民论坛》, 2016 年第 15 期。

城市发展与环境保护——以重庆市为例

萨琳娜【德国】

波恩大学硕士研究生

一、引言

在过去 30 年中，可持续发展变得越来越重要，成了全球各个角落很多领域的热门话题。尽管可持续性这一概念可能是德国矿区矿长兼税务会计汉斯·卡尔·冯·卡尔洛维茨首次提出，关于要谨慎可持续地对待林业。300 多年后，可持续性概念的意义更为明确。在"1987 年环境与发展会议"、"1992 年里约地球峰会"、"21 世纪行动计划"、2000 年的"千年发展目标"及 2015 年的"可持续发展目标"之后，可持续发展已成为全球计划。本文通过对重庆可持续发展的调查，希望从重庆在平衡发展和环境过程中面临着诸多困难，却能够消除污染，并成功应对伴随 21 世纪挑战而来的各项问题的经验，对未来城市发展与环境保护提出建议。

二、文献综述

本文中除来源于《重庆统计年鉴》的测量数据外，作者参考的德文、英文和中文文章对本文研究也有重要价值。卡尔·维尔纳·布兰德的 Der deutsche Diskurs zu nachhaltiger Entwicklung 一书对可持续发展这一主题给出了详细的见解。

布兰德指出，制定我们今天采用的行动计划时，考虑了不同的衡量手段。阿兰姆·子爱的"发展词典出现 25 年后的发展情况"文章，则对过去 20 年发展论述的成果进行了全面批判性概述，分析了西方可持续性实现方法，并确认了存在的其他概念，但也指出并非每种解决方案在其他各国都适用。秦经伟（音）和周玲（音）的"中国重庆新型城镇化的方式：整体设计和战略框架研究"中，全面报告了重庆在西南地区的重要性。中国科学家谢辉提供了重庆所面临环境挑战的相关深度信息，在 2012 年的《中国重庆市环境的可持续性》一文中，剖析了生态和经济指标。中国政府在《改善重庆空气质量的措施》一文中提出了消除污染的详尽行动计划。此外，还结合了实证调查、访谈及图片使用，以更好地了解重庆如何通过努力适应最新的发展。

三、研究方法

本文采用了几种不同的研究方法。除文献回顾外，统计数据收集为主要的信息来源。为了获取广泛的各种资料，作者选择了 15 种指标来衡量重庆市的发展和环境保护水平，包括：

1. 国内生产总值（GDP）（1996 年与 2016 年）

2. 常住人口与城镇化率（1996 年与 2016 年）

3. 施工项目数量（2016 年）

4. 施工项目投资（2016 年）

5. 生态保护和环境控制投资（2016 年）

6. 城市基础设施统计数据（2016 年）

7. 市区公园和绿地（2016 年）

8. 市区公共交通统计数据（2016 年）

9. 市容与环境卫生投资（2016 年）

10. 自然资源（2016 年）

11. 气候基础统计数据（1996 年与 2016 年）

12. 空气质量指数（2016 年）

13. 自然保护区（2015 年与 2016 年）

14. 环境保护投资（2016 年）

15. 工业污染处理（2015 年与 2016 年）

作者在文中使用的所有数据均来自《重庆统计数据年鉴》[1]。所有指标成为从1996年到2016年20年间的发展说明，或为过去三年的测量值，以确保研究资料为最新有效的资料。为了更好了解重庆的最新发展情况，参与式观察及焦点小组讨论也十分重要。

四、对可持续发展论述的概述

可持续发展被视作一个全球概念。《2030年可持续发展议程》和"17项可持续发展目标（SDG）"为各国指明了方向及具体行动内容。不过，这些都不是新的做法：早在1983年，联合国大会召集了"世界环境与发展委员会"，以制定"全球变化计划"。该委员会主席由挪威首相格罗·哈莱姆·布伦特兰担任，主要目的是为了解决两个方面的问题：

一是世界大部分地区的贫困和存在的"欠发达"情况，二是由于环境破坏和资源消费对社会发展构成了威胁。现在必须要创建一个全球发展行动战略，确保克服贫困及长期自然资源保护问题，并从这些目标出发，创造利益。自然资源问题是代表性工业化国家的前景问题。鉴于北方国家依靠资源走向繁荣的道路，南方国家担心资源保护会阻碍他们的发展。布伦特兰委员会通过提出符合所有利益的解决策略，可将发展与环境利益相联系。例如，它不提倡从根本上背离经济增长模式，但要求提高发展的质量——"在环境约束下寻求全球发展"。"布伦特兰报告"主要是批判很多环境组织从根本上背离了经济增长模式，同时也为了获得企业和政府的认可。发展目标与环境和资源保护相结合即催生了"可持续发展"。

这也建立了一种模式，引起了人们针对环境与发展政策的辩论。"发展"、"增长"和"进步"被"可持续"修饰后即成了不仅要满足当代人的需求，还要满足后代人的需求。"可续持"包括保护自然资源和环境。不过根据杜登词典（德文拼读与正字词典），"可持续"仅表示在较长时间内具有很大影响。《布伦特兰报告》指出，环境和资源保护本身本不是目标，而只是从"发展可持续性"总体目标间接推导得出的。在"可持续发展"概念中，自然和环境的承受能力并无内在价值，而只是社会发展的载体。根据《布伦特兰报告》，屏障和界限并非由环境确定，而是由使用环境的技术水平和社会组织决定。最后，在维持当前发展道路同时确保自然资源安全的目标下，可得出一项矛盾的任务陈述：同时进行发展的保留与转变。

1　http://www.cqtj.gov.cn/tjnj/2017/indexeh.htm.

五、重庆

1. 背景信息

重庆位于中国西南地区东部，距上海约 2500 公里，在长江和嘉陵江交汇处。重庆曾是抗日战争（1937~1945）期间的陪都，且在 1997 年成为了继北京、上海和天津之后的第四个直辖市。重庆辖区面积 82000 平方公里，总人口 3100 万人，下辖 25 个区和 13 个县，东西最大距离为 470 公里，南北最大距离为 450 公里。重庆历史悠久，文化底蕴深厚，是长江流域上游的经济中心[1]。

2. 近期发展

重庆在 20 世纪取得了快速发展。2016 年，该市的 GDP 增长了 10.7 个百分点，达到 17600 亿元，而该市在 1996 年 GDP 才 13 亿元。2018 年，经济增长目标为 8.5 个百分点，结束了过去 15 年的两位数增长。尽管重庆的 GDP 增长速度放慢，但仍然高于全国 GDP 6.9 个百分点的增幅。重庆市长唐良智对重庆的愿景如下：

"重庆在未来五年内的主要目标是从高速发展转变为高质量发展。重庆的发展仍不均衡，需要加快工业结构调整，通过创新驱动发展"[2]。

重庆的目标是促进实体经济与大数据、云计算和人工智能的融合，发展智慧产业。此外，重庆在进行中的"一带一路"项目中具有重要作用。重庆—新疆—欧洲国际铁路将中国与德国运输中心杜伊斯堡相连，因此，重庆对中国的国际贸易也有非常重要的作用。

除经济发展外，重庆还面临着大规模的城市化。1996 年，重庆城镇化率达到 29.5%，而在 2016 年，城镇化率接近 63%。对于这些数据，有趣的是过去 20 年中常住人口数量几乎没有增加。1996 年，常住人口约为 2870 万人，而 2016 生活在大重庆区域的人口为 3040 万人。所以，总人口并未增加太多，但人口分布却发生了很大变化。1996 年，约 800 万人生活在市区，大约 2000 万人生活在农村地区。但在 2016 年，情况几乎完全相反：生活在市区的人口为 1900 万人，生活在农村的为 1100 万人。这种从农村到城市的转移，改变并体现了该城市的发展情况，同时也给重庆带来了新的机遇和挑战。

为了应对快速城镇化，建设和基础设施项目在重庆随处可见。2016 年，约开

1　http://www.cqtj.gov.cn.
2　http://www.chinadaily.com.cn/a/201801/26/WS5a6ae287a3106e7dcc136edf.html.

展了 27000 个项目，而同年完成的项目就超过了 15000 个。2016 年，建设项目总投资超过了 13500 万元。而 2015 年的投资仅为 11600 万元。2016 年，基础设施融资金额约为 5600 万元；2015 年约为 4300 万元。基础设施不仅涉及道路和公共交通，还涉及电、热、气和水的生产和供应，以及公共设施管理、生态保护和环境控制，而对后者的投资为 608000 元，不足总投资的 1.1%。

重庆是有大规模建筑群、超过 1800 座桥梁及成千上万摩登大楼的大都市。城市坐落于山与山之间，绿地面积大。公共绿地人均面积为 16.2 平方公里，总绿地面积超过 72000 公顷。不但城市中心被群山和大的绿地带环绕，建筑群中也融入了树木植物，让这座城市更为环境友好，此外还有助于消除污染。下一章将更详细介绍重庆面临的环境挑战及解决方案。

3. 环境挑战

像重庆这样经历快速发展的城市自然会面临着各种挑战，空气污染是其中之一。由于人们大规模地从农村转移到城市，汽车数量大幅增加，每天有超过 500 万辆汽车行驶在重庆的大街小巷。但不管怎样，该城市在 2017 年成功地将空气中 PM2.5 含量降低了 16.3 个百分点。2015 年和 2016 年，重庆在环境保护方面的投资分别接近 4 亿元和 3.55 亿元。在应对气候变化方面，值得注意的是，1996 年和 2016 年期间的年均温度仅升高了 0.7 度。森林覆盖面积超过 370000 公顷，如上所述，城市管理部门沿道路两侧及房屋顶部植树。相比之下，自然保护区面积从 85000 公顷减少至 82000 公顷。此外，工业污染处理项目数量及投资金额也有所减少。2015 年，有 92 个项目立项，总投资 6000 万元，而 2016 年只有 84 个项目，总投资 3700 万元。

总体上讲，重庆已成功消除污染，并能够采取进一步措施保护环境，以实现可持续发展。不论如何，环境保护是一个持续的过程，不容轻视。下一章将分析重庆取得的成果，及其将要克服的挑战。

六、分析与展望

从前文叙述可以感到，重庆在发展方面取得了很大进步。GDP 增长、高增长新技术的使用及不断创新，都堪为中国乃至世界其他城市的典范。不过可持续发展道路仍然在持续，重庆还有很长的路要走。当地政府也承认，环境保护是城市安全、幸福和繁荣的一项主要特征。在短时间内降低空气污染不仅对环境具有重要意义，也是挽救人们的生命的保证。

1992年《里约环境与发展声明》有两条原则，即：

（1）人类是可持续发展问题的中心。人类可享有与自然协调一致的健康且有作为的生活。

（2）为了实现可持续发展，环境保护应作为发展过程不可分割的一部分，且不可孤立看待。

第一条原则明确表明，人们在享有健康生活的同时，需要努力实现其自身的可持续发展。这包括政府和公民团体。第二条说明了将环境保护融入发展的重要性。只有结合两个目标，方可实现可持续发展。尽管重庆在环境保护方面投入了大量人力财力，过去几年中的投资比例下降及自然保护区的减少还是令人担忧。尤其是在重庆人口密集，又在"一带一路"倡议中起着重要作用的情况下，其可持续发展尤为重要。因此，需要始终考虑两个因素，即发展和环境。如果该过程成功，重庆不但有希望成为世界上发展较快的城市，还能成为环境保护方面的典范。

City Development and Environmental Protection – A Case Study on Chongqing

Sharleena Goerlitz / Germany

Postgraduate of University of Bonn

1. Introduction

Over the last 30 years sustainable development has become more and more important and a so called hot topic in many fields all across the world. Although the concept of sustainability dates back to the german mining administrator and tax accountant Hans Carl von Carlowitz, who in his book *Sylvicultura Oeconomica* from 1713 demands a conscientious and sustainable handling with forestry.[1] More than 300 years later the concept of sustainability has become significantly more relevant. After the "Conference of Environment and Development 1987", the "Rio Earth Summit 1992", the "Agenda 21", the "Millenium Development Goals" in 2000 and finally the "Sustainable Development Goals" in 2015, sustainable development has become a global agenda. Therefore it is only reasonable to take a look at one of the world's largest cities, Chongqing, which is situated in the People's Republic of China. Chongqing faces a lot of difficulties when it comes to balance

---

1   Hans Carl vonCarlowitz (1713): Sylvicultura Oeconomica.

development and environment. However the city has also been able to combat pollution and successfully manages the issues that go along with the challenges of the 21 century.

The academic value of this paper actually arises from the social value of sustainable development itself. The definition of sustainable development from the Brundtland Report from 1987 states:

Sustainable development is development that meets the needs of the present without compromising the ability of future generations to meet their own needs.

In this sense, Chongqing can certainly be a good example to show what challenges are faced throughout rapid urbanization and how valuable the combination of developmental and environmental processes are.

2. Literature Review

Apart from measuring data from the *Chongqing Statistical Yearbook*, various German, English and Chinese articles have been a valuable addition to this research paper. The book *Der deutsche Diskurs zu nachhaltiger Entwicklung* from Karl-Werner Brand gives a detailed insight into the topic of sustainable development. Brand points out the different measures that have been taken into account to develop the action plan we are using today. The article "Post-development 25 years after The Development Dictionary" byAram Ziai presents a good and critical overview over the achievements regarding the development discourse in the last two decades. Ziai critices the western sustainability approach and recognizes that other concepts exist and that not every solution is applicable

in every country. The article "Paths for new urbanization in Chongqing, China: Study on overall design and strategic framework" by Qing Jingwei and Zhou Ling provides a comprehensive report on the importance of Chongqing for the southwestern region. The chinese scientist Hui Xie offers in-depths information about environmental challenges in Chongqing. His article "Environmental sustainability in Chongqing Municipality, China" from 2012 examines the ecologic and economic indicators. In addition to that, the article on "Measures to improve air quality in Chongqing" by the chinese government gives a very detailed action plan on how to combat pollution. Besides that, participatory observation, interviews and the usage of pictures played a huge role in better understanding how the city tries to adapt to there cent development.

3. Methodological Approach

For the purpose of writing this paper several different research methods have been used.Apart from literature review, statistical data collection has been the main source of information. In order to have a wide variety of materials the author chose 15 different indicators to measure the level of development and environmental protection in the city of Chongqing. The list includes the following:

① GDP(1996vs.2016)

② Resident Population and Urbanization Rate (1996vs.2016)

③ Number of Construction Projects (2016)

④ Investment in Construction Projects (2016)

⑤ Investment in Ecological Protection and Environment Control (2016)

⑥ Statistics on Urban Infrastructure(2016)

⑦ Parks and Green Land in Urban Area(2016)

⑧ Statistics on Public Transportation in Urban Area (2016)

⑨ Investment in City Appearance and Environmental Sanitation (2016)

⑩ Natural Resources(2016)

⑪ Basic Statistics on Climate (1996 vs. 2016)

⑫ Air Quality Index (2016)

⑬ Area of Nature Reserves (2015 vs. 2016)

⑭ Investment on Environmental Protection (2016)

⑮ IndustrialPollutionTreatment(2015vs.2016)

All data were collected from the *Chongqing Statistical Yearbook.*[1]

---

1   http://www.cqtj.gov.cn/tjnj/2017/indexeh.htm.

As shown in the list above, all indicators are either comparable between 1996 and 2016 to demonstrate the progression over the last 20 years, or measured during the last three years to ensure the research is still valid and up-to-date. In order to get a better understanding of the city's recent development, participatory observation as well as a focus group discussion have been a valuable asset.

4. Sustainable Development Discourse – Brief Overview

Sustainable development is seen to be a world wide concept. With the Agenda 2030 and the 17 Sustainable Development Goals (SDGs) countries now have a guideline on how to act and what to put into practice. However, this is not a new approach: As early as 1983, the United Nations General Assembly convened a "World Commission on Environment and Development", which was to formulate a "global program of change". It was to be an independent commission chaired by Norwegian Prime Minister Gro Harlem Brundtland. The commission focused mainly on two problem areas:

On the one hand poverty and existing "underdevelopment" in large parts of the world, on the other hand the endangering of social development due to environmental destruction and resource consumption. Now, a global action strategy for a development process had to be created, which should ensure both the overcoming of poverty and the long-term conservation of natural resources (Brand, p. 20). From these objectives, different interests can be derived. While the concern for natural resources was in the foreground for the representatives of the industrialized nations, the countries of the South feared that resource conservation would deny them the development that had helped the north to prosperity. The Brundtland Commission was able to correlate developmental and environmental interests in such a way that the proposed solution strategies met all interests. For example, it did not call for a fundamental departure from the economic growth model, but a change in the quality of growth —a "growth worldwide with regard to environmental constraints". Adhering to this growth model was a major criticism of the Brundtland report for many environmental organizations and, at the same time, an important point in order to gain acceptance in business and government circles. The combination of the growth target with simultaneous respect for the environment and resources led to the concept of " Sustainable Development" (Brand, p. 21).

This has created a model that has since then determined the environmental and developmental policy debate. The terms development, growth and progress were supplemented by the adjective "sustainable" and thus ensured not only the present, but also the future satisfaction of needs. The term "sustainable" includes the goal of preserving natural resources and the environment. According to the Duden (german spelling and orthography dictionary), however, the adjective "sustainable" only means that something has a strong impact on a longer period of time. According to Brand (p.23), environmental and resource protection is not an objective per se, but is derived only indirectly from the overall objective of the "durability of development". In the concept of "sustainable development" the endurance of nature and environment is not an intrinsic value, but only serves as a function of social development. In the view of the Brundtland report, barriers and boundaries are not set by the environment, but by the state of technology and social organization to use such environment. Ultimately, with the aim of securing natural resources while at the same time maintaining the current development path, a paradoxical mission statement was created: preservation and change of development at the same time (Ziai, p 2550).

5. Chongqing

After this very brief overview, the paper will now focus on the connection between development and environment in the city of Chongqing. Therefore background information will be provided as well as an in-depths analysis of the already mentioned "development indicators" in chapter three.

5.1 Background information

Chongqing is situated in the east of southwest China, about 2,500 kilometers from Shanghai, directly at the point where the Yangtze and the Jialing river merge.

Chongqing was serving as a capital during the Second Sino-Japanese War (1937-1945) and became the fourth municipality directly under the rule of the central government in 1997 after Beijing, Shanghai and Tianjin. Chongqing covers an area of 82,000 square kilometers with a total population of 31 million people. The municipality is divided into 25 districts and 13 counties. It reaches a maximum width of 470 kilometers from east to west, and a maximum lenght of 450 kilometers from north to south. Chongqing has a long and significant history and culture and the city serves as the economic centre of the upstream Yangtze basin.[1]

5.2 Recent development

(Disclaimer: All data in these chapters is derived from the Chongqing Statistical Yearbook and will therefore not be cited everytime.) Chongqing has developed rapidly during the 21st century. The GDP of the municipality grew by 10.7 percent in 2016, hitting 1.76 trillion yuan compared to 1.3billion in1996.The economic growth target for 2018 is at 8.5 percent, which puts an end to the double-digit growth over the past 15 years. But despite the slowdown, hongqing still exceeds the 6.9 percent national GDP growth. The mayor of Chongqing, Tang Liangzhi, has the following vision for his city:

The main goal for Chongqing in the next five years will be shifting from high growth to quality growth. […] Chongqing is still uneven in development and needs to accelerate the pace of industrial restructuring and make innovation a driving force for growth.[2]

Chongqing aims to promote the integration of the real economy with big data, cloud computing and artificial intelligence to develop smart industry. Furthermore, Chongqing plays a key role in the ongoing "Belt and Road" project. The Chongqing-Xinjiang-Europe International Railway connects inland China to Germany`s transportation hub Duisburg. Therefore Chongqing is of major importance when it

---

1   Government of Chongqing (2018):http://www.cqtj.gov.cn.
2   "Chongqing sets 2018 Growth Target at 8.5%" . http://www.chinadaily.com.cn/ a/201801/26/ WS5a6ae287a3106e7dcc136edf.html.

comes to China`s global trade (Qing/Zhou, p. 24).

Apart from the economic growth, Chongqing faces a massive urbanization rate. While in 1996 the urbanization rate amounted to 29,5 percent, in 2016 the urbanization rate approached 63 percent. Regarding these data it is interesting to see, that the resident population in the last 20 years has barely increased. In 1996 the resident population counted about 28,7 million people. In 2016 however, the population counted 30,4 million people living in the general Chongqing area. So the overall population hasn`t increased very much, but the distribution has changed drastically. In 1996 around eight million people lived in the city and around 20 million lived in rural areas. But in 2016 these numbers have nearly been reversed, with 19 million living in the city and 11 million living in the countryside (Qing/Zhou, p. 27). The shift from rural to urban changed and shaped the development of the city and at the same time brought new opportunities and challenges to Chongqing.

To cope with the rapid urbanization, construction and infrastructure projects can be seen throughout the city. In 2016 more than 27 thousand projects were carried out and over15 thousand were completed in the same year. In total the investment inconstruction projects in 2016 exceeded 135 million yuan. Compared to 2015, where 'only' 116 million yuan were invested. The financing of infrastructure projects amounted to roughly 43 million yuan in 2015 and 56 million yuan in 2016. Infrastructure does not only concern roads and public transportation, but also the production and supply of electricity, heat, gas and water, as well as the management of public facilities and ecology protection and environmental control (Xie, p. 3). For the later 608 thousand yuan were invested. Which is less than 1.1 percent from the overall investment.

Although Chongqing can be described as a megacity with massive buildings, over 1800 bridges and thousands of skyscrapers, the city, situated between mountains, has large green areas. The per capita area of public green land is 16,2 square kilometers. In general the green covered area is more than 72 thousand hectares. Not only is the city center surrounded by mountains and large green areas, but also the buildings incorporate trees and plants to make the city more environmentally friendly and additionally help to combat air pollution (Xie, p.5). The next chapter will look at the environmental challenges and solutions in Chongqing more thoroughly.

5.3 Environmental challenges

It is only naturally, that a city which has experienced development as rapid as Chongqing has to face various challenges. One of the most problematic challenge is air pollution.

Due to the massive migration from rural to urban the number of cars has increased drastically. More than 5 million cars are driving on the streets of hongqing everyday.

But somehow the city managed to cut back on the harmful PM2.5 (particulate matter) levels by 16.3 percent in 2017. The municipality invested nearly 400 million yuan in 2015 and 355 million yuan in 2016 in environmental protection. When it comes to climate change it is important to mention, that the yearly average temperature increased by 0,7 degrees between 1996 and 2016. In general the forest area covers more than 370 thousand hectares and as mentioned before, the city administration is planting trees and plants all along the roads and on top of buildings. In contrast to that the area of nature reserves decreased from 85 thousand hectares to 82 thousand hectares. Another decreasing figure can be found by looking at the projects and investments in industrial pollution treatment. In 2015, 92 projects were set up with an overall investment of 60 million yuan, whereas in 2016 only 84 projects with an investment of 37 million yuan had been established.

In general, Chongqing has successfully managed to combat pollution and was able to take a step forward in protecting the environment in order to contribute to sustainable development. Nevertheless, environmental protection is an ongoing process and should not be taken lighty. The next chapter aims to analyse the achievements Chongqing has made and the challenges the city has yet to overcome.

6. Analysis and outlook

As one can see from the last two chapters, Chongqing has made remarkable progress when it comes to development. The growth of the GDP, the use of new high-growth technologies and constant innovations are an example for other cities, not only in China, but worldwide.Although the route to sustainable development is still an ongoing process, Chongqing has come a long way. The municipality acknowledged, that environmental protection is a key feature for a safe, happy and prosperous community. Reducing air pollution in this short amount of time, was not only important for the environment, but literally saved the lives of people.

If we look at the "Rio Declaration on Environment and Development" from 1992 the first and fourth principles state the following:

(1) Human beings are in the centre of concerns for sustainable development. They are entitled to a healthy and productive life in harmony with nature.

(4) In order to achieve sustainable development, environmental protection shall constitute an integral part of the development process and cannot be considered in isolation from it.[1]

The first principle clearly shows that while people are entitled to a healthy life, they must strive for sustainable development themselves at the same time. This includes both the government and civil society. The fourth principledemonstrates the importance of the integration of environmental protection into development. Sustainable development is only possible if these two aims are combined. Despite the fact, that Chongqing invested a lot of capital and workforce into protecting the environment, the dropping investment percentages and the decreased nature reserves during the last few years are a course for concern. Especially as Chongqing is one of the most densely populated melting pots on earth and playing a crucial role in the ongoing 'One Belt One Road' initiative. Therefore it is important to always consider both factors: development and environment. If this process is going to be successful,

---

1   The United Nations Conference (1992):The Rio Declaration on Environment and Development.

Chongqing has not only the opportunity to be one of the fastest developed city of the world, but also to lead by example when it comes to environmental protection. Because it is not possible to holistically address a complex topic like this in a short article, I would suggest to further investigate on recent projects which are effecting the city as a whole, and to do further research on the impact of environmental degradation and the possibilities to stop and reverse it.

现代汉语语气词的认知语义功能分析 [1]

优丽雅【乌克兰】

基辅国立语言大学孔子学院副院长

一、引言

选择哪个语句来完成交际，说话人首先须对交际语境做出正确的分析，考虑自己与听话人在权位、熟悉度等方面的相对关系，然后决定选用哪些语言手段来传达语句内容以及自己的态度。而语气词就是汉语表情达意的重要手段之一。

人类意识作为复合多层结构，在其范围内表现为世界知觉、意向性、社会关系等。语气（mood; modality）体现说话人的情绪、口气和对语境的认知。我们平常说话都带有一定的语气，如果一个句子没有语气，也就不称其为句子了。语气的实现有不同的方式。在汉语里，同一个句子加上不同的语气词，可以表示各种微妙而丰富的语气。运用语气词表达语气是汉语语法的一大特点。因此，语气词在汉语语法中占有重要的地位，是语气范畴所要讨论的主要内容。

从交互主观性角度来看，语气词用于表达说话人对听话人的态度，表达一定的认知语义功能。总而言之，作为一个语法范畴，语气词的认知语义功能研究尚且不足，且少有人做过实际的语料调查分析。

1　本文所使用语料来自北京大学 BCC 语料库。
　　本文在撰写过程中得到刘玉梅教授的悉心指导，且得到井自纯、徐海宁师妹的帮助开展问卷调查，在此一并表示感谢。

二、现代汉语语气词的研究现状

语气词古来有之。古代汉语的"乎、也、矣、哉",现代汉语的"啊、吧、呢、吗、哈"等,构成了汉语语气词系统。在古汉语中,语气词常被作为虚词。不少学者对古代汉语语气词进行研究。如王力(2003)在研究语气词的发展中,介绍了古汉语中最主要的语气词的语义功能。按照他的说法,汉语中作为虚词的语气词借助语调使各种情绪表达更加明显。虽然语气词不是情态范畴中最核心的表达手段,但其明示情绪的作用不容忽视。

现代汉语语言研究者对此问题也很关注。他们主要以功能、认知语言学为视角研究此问题。如房玉清(1992)在研究现代汉语语气词的过程中,介绍了语气词的分类及其与语气类型的关系,其中,强调了以下 9 种语气类型:确定语气、夸张语气、停顿语气、疑问语气、反问语气、假设语气、测度语气、祈使语气和感叹语气。刘月华在考察现代汉语最常用的语气词时,更注重考察语气词的功能(如使句子变长、节奏减慢,使语气舒缓下来)。左思民(2009)主要关注现代汉语基本语气词在句中的语法作用,认为语气词所表示的并不是语气,而是口气。换言之,使受话者能在更大的程度上接受说话者所说的话语内容。徐晶凝从认知语义学角度指出,就语言特性而言,语句内容、情态、意义分别属于语言客观性(objectivity)、主观性(subjectivity)及交互主观性(intersubjectivity),因此,应注意的不仅是说话人对所说内容的态度,而且要关注交际双方的感情交互。

综上可见,语气词是一种非常抽象、复杂的现象,而且是表达语气的手段之一,它们在情态范畴中起着重要的作用。即是说,语气词作为情态范畴的一个成员,其表达的意义取决于说话人对相关交际情景的认知,传达不同意义,语气词使用则各异。语气词的情态范畴和交互主观性密切相关,因此,此研究对象不仅包括说话人的意图和对相关交际情景的态度,还需研究其对听话人的认识和态度。

三、现代汉语主要语气词的认知语义功能

1. 现代汉语情态范畴

学者们对情态范畴有不同的理解,这与对本问题的解释有很大关系。比如Halliday(1985)研究认知情态和非认知情态时,提到认知情态和非认知情态之间的模糊、融合和中位的情况。Lyons 区分了主观情态和客观情态,根据 Lyons

对情态的分析，凡是表示说话人主观态度且与可能性和必然性相关的命题成分，表达的都是情态意义，因此，情态意义可以用多种形式来表达。按照他的理论，情态动词、情态副词、情态形容词、语气词等都能作为情态范畴的表达手段（朱冠明，2005）。Perkins（1983）更全面地讨论了情态的表达方式，除 Lyons 提到的以外，还有准情态助动词、情态名词、有情态意义的动词、疑问句、反问句等。

上述学者都主张研究情态范畴应以语法化为主。比如 Palmer（1986）认为，尽管人类语言的情态表达手段非常丰富，但是，因为情态研究本身是一种语法研究，所以他将情态表达形式的语法化（grammaticalization）作为一个重要的标准，主要研究情态助动词、语气（mood）、小词（particle）和附着形式（clitics），而将形容词、副词、名词、动词等词汇形式及语调等韵律特征，排除在情态研究的范围之外。

尽管汉语表达情态意义的方式多种多样，但如果把情态作为一个语法范畴来考虑，则要求这个范畴的成员是个封闭的系统，由一组具有共同形式特征的语言成分构成。汉语界把情态作为一个语法范畴的研究并不多见，但对主要表达情态意义的助词的研究早已开始。后来，吕叔湘（1944）、赵元任（1979）对此话题也很关注。在现代汉语情态范畴的研究中，最重要的是通过汉语语言的特色，来分析情态表达系统和能够表达说话人 / 听话人对语句内容的态度。

2. 现代汉语语气词在情态范畴中的地位

上文我们已经说过，表达情态的手段丰富多样，而汉语中的语气词是语法化最高的表达形式。语气词作为句尾虚词而装饰全部命题。作为标记，语气词也极有可能和时体标记间存在着关联，其作用为情态标记和话语标记。徐晶凝（2008）提出，现代汉语语气词有三个重要的特点：1）在语法上，它不是语法结构必须的成分，不会影响语法结构；2）有或没有不会影响命题；3）在情态上，它是必需的成分，因此其目的在于表示句子与语境的关联性以及满足听话人的面子需要，更好地保证交际成功。由此可见，语气词虽然不会影响句子结构，也不能完全改变句子意思，但它会提示出命题的涵义并让说话人和听话人明白对话的微妙细节。简言之，语气词反映了说话人对命题的心理态度以及说话人对听话人交际身份的主观定位。语言最重要的一个功能就是交际，能够恰当地使用和理解语气词，可以推动交际更加流畅地进行。

3. 五种主要语气词的认知语义功能分析

现代汉语语气词系统比较庞大，鉴于篇幅，本文仅讨论现代汉语最常用的语气词。按照相关文献，汉语主要的语气词有"啊"（其变体"啦"、"哇"、"呀"、"哪"）、"吗"、"吧"、"呢"等。我们要讨论的语气词有"啦"、"吗"、"吧"、"呢"和最近变成流行的"哈"。我们将对上述语气词的认知语义功能分别进行分析。

语气词"吗"的认知语义功能

"吗"的历史由来学界并不清楚，但不可否认它是一个被公认的最典型的语气词，表示单纯的疑问语气，能单独传达询问信息，是一个"疑问标记"。例如：

（1）他来了【吗】？

例（1）是一个是非问句，"吗"是一个疑问标记词。该句表明，说话人对是非的判断比例是均等的，答案有可能是，也有可能不是。刘月华则提出，"吗"除构成是非问句（说话者一般有预想的答案）外，有时表示说话人的肯定（否定句），也可表示质问、责备、分辨的意味（反问句），例如：

（2）他不会游泳【吗】？

（3）看你，这还是领导【吗】？

例（2）形式上是一个是非问句，但是实际上表达了发话人对所言内容的一种自我肯定，即发话人认为"他会游泳"。同样，例（3）形式上也是一个是非问句，但却不需要作出是非判断，而表达发话人对所言内容的质问、责备的语气和态度。

总体而言，"吗"语气用法既可表明说话人对所言的一种是非判断，也可表明说话人想通过疑问形式表达其对所言内容的语气和态度。当"吗"置于句中停顿后，也可唤起听者的注意或考虑下面该怎么说（语调低而缓），例如：

（4）你说的这件事【吗】，我完全不同意。

例（4）形式上是一个陈述句，说话者"吗"后面用语音上的间歇，该句说明他想让听者更注意地听，而自己明白对方想表达的内容。

语气词"呢"的认知语义功能

"呢"出现在疑问句的句尾也作为疑问语气助词，例如：

（1）这是谁【呢】？

例（1）形式上是一个疑问句，说话者用"呢"希望得到关于"谁"的信息，"呢"就有了探索的意思。有时，用在疑问句句尾"呢"还表示请求的意思，虽然本句类意义不依赖语调而得到传递，但句子本身通常带疑问语调，其作用似乎在于使句子听起来更像一个请求性的疑问，而不是指令（左思民）。例如：

（2）你听不听【呢】？

例（2）形式上是一个疑问句，但是说话者愈想得到的答案只是"是"，他用"呢"来请求听者注意听他说什么。"呢"说明说话人在双方共享预设的基础上点明某一点，提醒听话人注意（徐晶凝）。也即是说，这里的"呢"并不表示疑问，而是表达说话人对听话人的提醒，起着缓和语气的添加功能和追究功能。

"呢"也可通过微妙夸张而指明事实（吕叔湘）。说话人表达两方面的内容：1）他事先知道或预设听话人会有某种行为或想法；2）他将要讲的话是与听话人的观点或见识不同，因此，点明这一点并提醒听话人注意（左思民；徐晶凝）。有时可用于停顿，例如：

（3）告诉你【呢】，没话可说！她跑啦！跑啦！

例（3）是一个陈述句，"呢"带有"你不知道吧，让我告诉你的"的意思。一方面告诉听话人他即将讲述的事情与听话人已经知道的某些事情是有关系的，也唤起听话人的注意，使他们对即将讲述的话题感兴趣（徐晶凝）。

语气词"吧"的认知语义功能

"吧"用在疑问句句尾表示推测，包含明显的揣测语气，带有半信半疑的意思。将"吧"用在疑问句，说话人将判断权交给听话人。例如：

（1）你心里一定嫌麻烦对【吧】。

例（1）是一个陈述句，说话者提出其设想，想让听者来确认说话者的推断。

"吧"的另外一个重要的作用为表示请求、劝告。刘月华指出，将"吧"用在表示请求、命令的句子中，句尾语调较低，命令语气带有缓和、劝告的意味。虽然祈使是说话人发出的，但是执行与否却由听话人决定，因此，用"吧"的祈使句能够给听话人足够的面子，带有"委婉口气"（徐晶凝）。例如：

（2）让我请你【吧】，你想上哪里，我就请你上哪里，我请求你答允。

（3）危险少些，动手【吧】。

例（2）是一个祈使句，"吧"表示一个请求，说话者希望得到听者的确认。同样，例（3）也是一个祈使句，这里"吧"表达的意思是指出命令，不过，"吧"带有"委婉口气"，所以，虽然是说话者发出命令，但是，最后是否执行是要听者所决定。

与上述几个语气词一样，"吧"也能用在句中，但是它表示强化延宕的口气，也就是说说话人对要讲的话有怀疑的态度，例如：

（4）如今的青年人我对您说【吧】，太爱出风头了。

例（4）是一个陈述句，"吧"带有"左右为难"的感觉，表示说话人对后面要说的内容有怀疑的态度，而且，给说话人机会再次考虑后面要讲的话。

语气词"啦"的认知语义功能

语气词"啦"是语气词"了"和语气词"啊"的复合形式，有时表示"界变"，其基本语气功能是"语气积极化"，适用于轻松随意的交际场合及关系较近的交际对象（易娟，2004）。一般带有"高昂口气"，表示情况已经有变化或将要出现新的情况，例如：

（1）快点儿！客人快要来【啦】！

例（1）是一个感叹句，"啦"表示情况马上就要改了，此外，说话人也想催促听话人，这就是"啦"里面的"啊"祈使口气影响，"啦"表示"弱传信式告知求应"（易娟，2004）。

运用"啦"表达肯定，说话人表示他对命题确信无疑，又表示听话人应倾听接受所说的信息。因此，它一般用在关系亲密的人之间，其作用为帮助交际参与者保持或建立亲密的关系（徐晶凝，2008）。例如：

（2）说实话，我觉得80戈比一个，就是最好的价钱【啦】！

例（2）是一个陈述句，它表达，说话人对所说的内容有自我肯定，也想使听者相信他所言的正确性。

语气词"哈"的认知语义功能

语气词"哈"出现于北京话，作为典型的方言语气词。"哈"的流行在网络和新闻媒体中随处可见，无论是作为方言词还是作为普通话中原本的一个不常用的语气词，句末语气词"哈"已经进入普通话，其语气意义正在不断地变化（吴宝安，韩小红，2013）。

语气词"哈"表示说话人对所说的内容有确认，有"事情是这样的意思"，经常用来询问听话人是否与说话人有相同的感受、看法或评判，是否赞同说话人的意见。在对话中"哈"也常常用来要求听话人对说话人虽有所认定，但又不能完全肯定的说话内容加以确认（贺阳，1994）。例如：

（1）对不对【哈】？

（2）晚上还会开车【哈】？

例（1）是一个疑问句，说话人用询问形式来表示，他对所言的内容无疑而问，而且，想使听者也确定该信息，给肯定的答案。同样，例（2）也是一个疑问句，而且，"哈"带有怀疑语气，因为说话者不知道，听者的答复是否肯定，所以他用缓和语气的"哈"来询问，情况是否如此。

"哈"在句尾表达一种善意的提醒或是对命令的事情的缓和语气，但是没有"吗"、"吧"那么强的祈使口气。例如：

（3）来，外婆来给你治好，乖乖别再哭了【哈】。

虽然例（3）是一个祈使句，而且，说话人适用"哈"明显带有缓和语气，虽然这是个请求，但整个句子委婉；因此，使听者更容易接受此请求。

总体而言，上述语气词的功能比较多，而且每个都有自己的特色，一般都用于句尾，而且所表达的含义并不一样，修饰命题作用也有差异。

四、五种语气词使用情况调查分析

为了更好地了解语气词的使用情况，我们通过问卷和访谈方法，调查语气词的使用情况。调查方法主要为定量分析，由问卷调查法和访谈法四个部分组成。

进行调查的区域为重庆某高校，被访者共有 72 人（其中男性 35 人，女性 37 人，见下图）。被访者平均年龄 24—25 岁，35 岁以上仅有 5 人。被访者中，68 人家乡为中国（重庆 18 人，四川 13 人，河南 13 人，湖北 5 人，山东 4 人，安徽、贵州、江苏、江西、山西各 2 人，辽宁、湖南、甘肃、陕西、西藏各 1 人），4 人为有一定汉语基础的外国人。

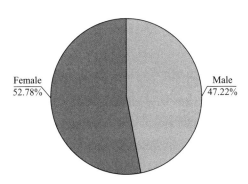

调查题目为最常用／最少用的语气词及原因。被访者需要将"啦"、"吗"、"吧"、"呢"、"哈"五个语气词依常用度进行排序，并说明为什么最常用／最少用该语气词。

按照上述定量分析的结果，最常用的语气词是"吗"，最少用的语气词是"啦"。下面说明出现此结果的原因。

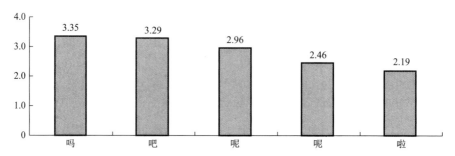

根据调查结果显示，说话人在疑问、反问时选用"吗"语气词，也许是因为中国人不习惯直接问或确认某件事。在 26 名常用"吗"的被访者中，女性有 8 人，男性有 18 人。其中，有男性被访者指出，他们是问问题的比较多，他们在询问或委婉请求时常用这个语气词，而且等待听者的确定答案，因为"用这个语气词会得到他人的正面回答"。此外，有被访者也指出，用"吗"时感觉给听者一种被责备感，这使有人不愿意在交际中多用这个词。

对于"吧"语气词而言，被访者强调，用这个语气词会表达不确定（不绝对），给听者被尊重的感觉，并让语气更加委婉、缓和，因此，很符合中国人的文化和性格，而且是中国人思维的特色。"吧"表示征询意见及尊重对方，甚至在要求、命令时带有礼貌的含义，所以有人提出，用此语气词感觉好像在等待听者的同意。

第三个最常用的语气词是"哈"。人们使用这个语气词大概和它本来的意思有关系，所以很多被访者提出，交际时用"哈"显得比较亲切，并能给人一种愉快、亲密感。调查再次证明，"哈"语气词的用法与区域有很大关系，因为根据相关研究（吴宝安，韩小红，2013），它在四川话中最具代表性，多用于祈使句，表达提醒、强调、请求、劝告等语气，表示用商量的语气征求听话人的意见。在我们进行调查问卷答案中，也有被访者提出用"哈"的原因，其中大多数人称有方言习惯的原因，比如说，"哈"在四川话中很常用。此外，也有被访者强调，他们不常用这个语气词是因为觉得它很奇怪、不自然，受到的影响比较小，用的情况不多。大概是因为这个语气词比较"年轻"，是最近 40 年才开始流行。

我们通过比较发现，人们不太常用"呢"是因为感觉这个语气词太扭捏，或是没有用这个语气词的习惯。其中，还有一种原因涉及地方特色，与进行调查的区域有关系，因为"发'呢'音时，有个鼻音'n'，感觉不方便"，不符合语音习惯。

调查显示，最不常用的语气词是"啦"，原因如下：有人觉得这个语气词"有点可爱"，"太娘"（男性被访者提出），"不符合自己的性别"（男性被访者提出）；有人强调这个语气词给听者不礼貌的感觉，常在不耐烦或着急的状况下使用（这大概和"啦"的语义功能有关系，因为它由"了"与"啊"组成，而"啊"语气词有下命令、催促的意思）。

五、结论

根据以上研究和调查可以看出，使用现代汉语中的语气词来进行人际功能表达，是交际中不可避免的重要成分。作为语气标记，现代汉语语气词认知语义功能有两种：一是表达说话人对语句内容的态度；二是表明说话人对听话人交际身份的主观定位，还有说话人和听话人的关系和对交际过程的把握。这再次证明语气词是交际和认知最重要的手段，而且值得进一步研究。

Analysis of Cognitive Semantic Functions of Modal Particles in Modern Chinese

Liubymova Yuliia Serhiivna / Ukraine

Vice Director of Confucius Institute at Kiev National Linguistic University, Vice Professor, Director of Chinese-teaching Office in the Department of Oriental Language

1. Introduction

To choose the statement to complete the communicative act, the speaker must first make the correct analysis of the communicative context, consider the relative relationship between himself and the listener in terms of power and familiarity, and then decide which language means to use to convey the content of the sentence and his attitude. Modal particles are one of the important means of conveying one's ideas or feelings in modern Chinese.

As a composite multi-layer structure, human consciousness manifests itself as perception of the world, intention and social relations. The mood (modality) reflects the speaker's emotions, tone and perception of the context. We usually speak with a certain tone, and if a sentence has no tone, it cannot be called a sentence. There are different ways to achieve tone. In Chinese, the same sentence with different modal particles can express a variety of subtle and rich tones. The use of modal particles to express tone is a major feature of Chinese grammar; therefore, modal particles play an important role in Chinese grammar and are the main content to be discussed in the genre category.

From the perspective of interactive subjectivity, the modal particles are used to express the speaker's attitude towards the hearer and express certain cognitive semantic functions. All in all, as a grammatical category, modal particles are still unstudied from the perspective of cognitive-functional semantics, and little is done by means of actual corpus investigation.

2. Research Status of Modal Particles in Modern Chinese

The modal particle has come from ancient times. The ancient Chinese " 乎、也、矣、哉 ", modern Chinese " 啊、吧、呢、吗、哈 ", etc. constitute the Chinese modal particle system. In ancient Chinese, modal particles were often used as empty words (function words). Many scholars have studied ancient Chinese modal particles. For example, Wang Li (2003), in his research of the development of modal particles, introduced semantic functions of the most important modal particles in ancient Chinese. According to his statement (1985: 160), being an empty word in Chinese, the modal particle makes the expression of various emotions more obvious by means of intonation. Although modal words are not the central means of expression in the category of modality, its role of explicit expressing of the mood and emotions cannot be ignored.

Modern Chinese language researchers are also concerned about this issue, as they mainly study this issue from the perspective of functional and cognitive linguistics. In the process of studying modal particles in modern Chinese, Fang Yuqing (1992) introduced the classification of modal particles and their relations with the type of mood. The following nine types of mood are emphasized: determining tone, exaggeration tone, pause tone, doubt tone, rhetorical tone, hypothetical tone, measure tone, imperative tone and exclamatory tone. Liu Yuehua (2006: 411) pays more attention to the functions of modal words (such as making sentences longer, slowing the rhythm, and soothing the tone) when examining the most commonly used modal particles in modern Chinese. Zuo Simin (2009) mainly focuses on the grammatical role of the basic modal particles in modern Chinese, stating that modal words are not expressing the manner of speaking, but the intention of the speaker. In other words, with the help of modal particles the recipient can accept the speech content spoken by the speaker to a greater extent. Xu Jingning (2008: 4) pointed out from the perspective of cognitive semantics that in terms of language characteristics, sentence content, modality and meaning belong to objectivity, subjectivity and intersubjectivity respectively. For this reason, not only the speaker's attitude towards the content should be noted, but also the emotional interaction between the two parties of the communicative act.

In summary, modal particles are a very abstract and complex phenomenon, and they are one of the means of the tone expressing. They play an important role in the category of modality. That is to say, the modal particle is a part of the modal category, and its meaning depends on the speaker's perception of the relevant communication situation, therefore, when conveying different meanings, the use of modal words is also different. The modal category of modal particles is closely related to the subjectivity of interaction. Therefore, this research object not only includes the speaker's intention and attitude towards the relevant communication situation, but is also focused on the research of his understanding and attitude towards the listener.

3. Cognitive Semantic Functions of the Main Modal Particles in Modern Chinese

3.1 The Category of Modality in Modern Chinese

Scholars have different understandings of the category of modality, which has a lot to do with the interpretation of this problem. For example, when Halliday (1985) studied cognitive modality and non-cognitive modality, he referred to the ambiguity, fusion and median situation between epistemic modality and non-epistemic modality. Lyons (1977: 809-823) distinguishes subjectiveandobjectivemodality. According to Lyons' analysis of modality, all propositional elements that express the subjective attitude of the speaker and the propositional components related to the possibility and inevitability express modal meaning, so modality meaning can be expressed in many forms.According to his theory, modal verbs, modal adverbs, modal adjectives, modal particles, etc. can be used as expressions of the category of modality (朱冠明 , 2005:17-18). Perkins (1983) discusses the expression of modality more comprehensively: in addition to what Lyons mentioned, there are quasi-modal auxiliary verbs, modal nouns, modal verbs, interrogative sentences and rhetorical questions.

The above scholars all advocate that the study of modality should be based on grammaticalization. For example, Palmer (1986) believes that although the modal expression of human language is very rich, because the research of modality itself is a grammatical study, he uses grammaticalization of modal expression as an important criterion, mainly studying auxiliary verbs, mood, particles and clitics, excluding adjectives, adverbs, nouns, verbs, intonation and other prosodic features are excluded from the scope of research of modality (徐晶凝 , 2008: 17) .

Although there are many ways to express modal meaning in modern Chinese, if modality is considered as a grammatical category, the members of this category are required to be a closed system consisting of a set of linguistic components with common form features. The study of modality as a grammatical category in the Chinese linguistic community is rare, but the study of the auxiliary words that mainly express modal meanings has already begun. Later, Lv Shuxiang (1944) and Zhao Yuanren (1979) also paid close attention to this topic. In the study of modern Chinese modal categories, the most important thing is to analyze the modal expression system and the attitude, which can be expressed by the speaker / listener to the content of the sentence, taking into the account the peculiarities of the Chinese language.

3.2 The Status of Modern Chinese Modal Particles in the Category of Modality

As we have discussed above, the means of expressing modality are rich and varied, while the modal particles in Chinese are the means of expression with the highest level of grammaticalization. The modal particle as an empty word in the end of the sentence modifies the whole proposition. As the marker, modal particles are also highly likely to be associated with temporal markers, which act as modal markers and utterance markers. Xu Jingning (2008: 133) proposed that modern Chinese modal particles have three important characteristics:(1) grammatically,it is not a necessary component of grammatical structure, and does not affect the grammatical structure of the sentence; (2) with or without a particle, it cannot influence the proposition; (3) in terms of modality, it is an essential component, so its purpose is to express the relevance of the sentence to the context and to meet the needs of the listener, to better ensure the success of communication. It can be seen that although the modal particle does not affect the sentence structure and cannot completely change the meaning of the sentence, it will prompt the meaning of the proposition and let the speaker and the listener understand the subtle details of the dialogue. In short, the modal particle reflects the speaker's psychological attitude towards the proposition and the subjective positioning of the speaker's communicative identity. One of the most important functions of language is communication; therefore, being able to use and understand modal particles properly can promote communication more smoothly.

3.3 Analysis of Cognitive Semantic Functions of the Five Main Modal Particles

The modern Chinese modal particle system is quite large. In view of the length of this article, this article discusses only the most commonly used modal particles in modern Chinese. According to the relevant literature, the main modal particles in Chinese are "啊" *a* (the variants are "啦" *la*, "哇" *wa*, "呀" *ya*, "哪" *na*), "吗" *ma*, "吧" *ba*, "呢" *ne* and so on. The modal particles we want to discuss are "啦" *la*, "吗" *ma*, "吧" *ba*, "呢" *ne* and recently become popular particle "哈" *ha*. We will analyze the cognitive and semantic functions of the above modal particles separately.

3.3.1 Cognitive semantic function of the modal particle" 吗 " (*ma*)

The history of "吗" ma is unclear in the academic world, but it is undeniable that it is a recognized most typical modal particle, which means a simple interrogative tone and can convey the inquiry information alone. It is a "question mark". E.g:

（1）他来了【吗】？

Example (1) is a question, and "吗" ***ma*** is a question mark. The sentence indicates that the speaker's judgment ratio is equal, and the answer may be "yes" or "no". Liu Yuehua (刘月华) (2006: 415-419) proposed that "吗" ma, in addition to constituting a yes-no question sentence (the speaker usually has an expected answer), sometimes indicates the affirmation of the speaker (negative sentence), which can also indicate questioning, blaming and differentiating meaning (rhetorical question), for example:

（2）他不会游泳【吗】？

（3）看你，这还是领导【吗】？

Example(2) is formally a yes-no question, but actually expresses the self-affirmation of the speaker's content that is, the speaker thinks, "He can swim." Similarly, example

(3) is also a form of yes-no question, but it does not need to make a yes/no judgment, it expresses the speaker's attitude and tone of questioning and reproach.

In general, the usage of " 吗 " ***ma*** can indicate the speaker's right and wrong judgment, and it also indicates that the speaker wants to express his tone and attitude towards the content in question. When " 吗 " ***ma*** is paused in the sentence, it can also arouse the listener's attention or helps the speaker to consider what to say next (with low and slow intonation), for example:

（4）你说的这件事【吗】，我完全不同意。

The example (4) is a declarative sentence in the form, and " 吗 " ma used by the speaker is followed by a pause in the voice, which indicates that he wants the listener to listen more clearly and understand what he wants to express.

3.3.2 Cognitive semantic functions of the modal particle"呢"(*ne*)

"呢" *ne* appears at the end of the interrogative sentence as an interrogative modal particle, for example:

（1）这是谁【呢】？

Example (1) has the form of a question. The speaker uses "呢" *ne*, as he wants to get information about "who", and "呢" *ne* here has the meaning of exploration. Sometimes, the "呢" *ne* at the end of the question also has the meaning of the request, although the meaning of this sentence is passed without depending on the intonation, the sentence itself usually has a questioning tone, and its role is to make the sentence sound more like a request, but not an order. E.g:

（2）你听不听【呢】？ Example (2) has a question form, but the speaker just wants to get the answer "yes",

he uses "呢" *ne* to ask the listener to pay attention to what he said. "呢" ne indicates that the speaker points out a certain point on the basis of sharing the presupposition between the two parties, reminding the listener to pay attention. That is to say, "呢" *ne* here does not express doubts, but expresses the speaker's reminder to the listener, and plays the function of adding and easing the tone.

"呢" *ne* can also indicate facts through subtle exaggeration. The speaker expresses two aspects: 1) he knows or presupposes that the listener will have some kind of behaviour or thought; 2) he will speak differently from the listener`s point of view or insight, so he points this out and reminds the listener to pay attention to what has been said. Sometimes it is used for pauses, for example:

（3）告诉你【呢】，没话可说！她跑啦！跑啦！

Example (3) is a declarative sentence; "呢" ne expresses the meaning "you don't know, let me tell you". On the one hand, it means that what the speaker is about to tell is related to something that the listener already knows, and also evokes the attention of the listener, making him interested in the topic to betold (徐晶凝 , 2008:169).

3.3.3 Cognitive semantic functions of the modal particle "吧" (ba)

"吧" *ba* is used at the end of the question to indicate conjecture, including obvious guess tone, with a half belief meaning. The use of " 吧 " *ba* in the interrogative sentence means that the speaker will give the judgment to the listener. E.g:

（1）你心里一定嫌麻烦对【吧】。

Example (1) is a declarative sentence in which the speaker proposes his or her idea and wants the listener to confirm the speaker's inference.

Another important role of "吧" *ba* is to express requests and advice. Liu Yuehua (2006: 424-427) pointed out that the use of "吧" *ba* in the sentences that express requests and orders has a low tone at the end of the sentence, and the tone of the command has the meaning of easing and advising. Although the speaker issues the imperative, it is the listener who determines the execution. Therefore, the imperative sentence with "吧" *ba* shows the speaker's respect to the listener and has a "tactful meaning" (徐晶凝 , 2008: 191).E.g:

（2）让我请你【吧】，你想上哪里，我就请你上哪里，我请求你答允。

（3）危险少些，动手【吧】。

Example (2) is an imperative sentence, "吧" *ba* means a request, and the speaker wants to be confirmed by the listener. Similarly, example (3) is also an imperative sentence. Here, "吧" *ba* is used to indicate the order. However, "吧" *ba* here has a "tactful tone". Therefore, although the speaker gives an order, the listener decides the final execution.

Like the above mentioned modal particles, "吧" *ba* can also be used in the middle of the sentence, but it is used to strengthen the tone of delay, that is to say, the speaker has a doubtful attitude towards what to say next, for example:

（4）如今的青年人我对您说【吧】，太爱出风头了。

Example (4) is a declarative sentence. "吧" ba here gives the feeling of "dilemma", indicating that the speaker has a doubtful attitude towards what is to be said later, and gives the speaker the opportunity to consider the words to be mentioned later.

3.3.4 Cognitive semantic functions of the modal particle "啦" (la)

The modal particle "啦" la is a composite form of the modal particle "了" le and the modal particle "啊" a, sometimes it means "boundary change", and its basic tone function is the "tone activation", which is suitable for easy and casual communication occasions and close relationship with the communicative object (易娟 , 2004). Generally it has an "exalted tone", indicating that the situation has changed or new situations will occur, for example:

（1）快点儿! 客人快要来【啦】!

Example (1) is an exclamatory sentence. "啦" la means that the situation will soon be changed. In addition, the speaker also wants to urge the listener. It is the particle "啊" a in "啦" la that gives a the influence of the imperative tone, "啦" la means "the weak form of expressing the request" (易娟 , 2004).

Using "啦" la to express affirmation, the speaker shows that he is convinced of the proposition, and that the listener should listen to accept the information. Therefore, it is generally used between people with close relationships, and its role is to help communicative participants maintain or establish intimate relationships (徐晶凝 , 2008: 150). E.g:

（2）说实话，我觉得八十戈比一个，就是最好的价钱【啦】!

Example (2) is a statement that expresses that the speaker has self-affirmation of what he said and wants to convince the listener that he is correct.

3.3.5 Cognitive Semantic Function of the Modal Particle "哈" (*ha*)

The modal particle "哈" *ha* appears in the Beijing dialect as a typical dialect modal particle. The popularity of "哈" *ha* can be seen everywhere in the Internet and in the news media. Whether it is used as a dialect or as an unusual temperament in Mandarin, the modal particle "哈" *ha* has entered Mandarin, and its tone of meaning is constantly changing(吴宝安，韩小红 ,2013:73).

The modal particle "哈" *ha* means that the speaker has confirmed the content ("things are like this"), often used to ask whether the listener has the same feelings, opinions or judgments as the speaker, and whether he agrees with the speaker's opinion. In the dialogue, "哈" *ha* is often used to express that although the listener confirms the speaker's assertion in a certain way, but still is not completely sure (贺阳 , 1994:60-61).

（1）对不对【哈】?

（2）晚上还会开车【哈】?

Example (1) is a question. The speaker uses in the form of inquiry to express doubt to the content of the proposition, and wants to make the listener also determine the information and give a positive answer. Similarly, case (2) is also a question, and "哈" *ha* has a doubtful tone, because the speaker does not know, whether the listener's reply is affirmative, so he uses the particle "哈" *ha* to ease up the tone to ask whether the situation is so or not.

"哈" *ha* at the end of the sentence expresses a kind reminder or adds a mitigating tone to the order sentence, but it does not have such a strong imperative tone as "吧" ba or "吗" *ma*. E.g:

（3）来，外婆来给你治好，乖乖别再哭了【哈】。

Although sentence (3) is imperative, but the speaker applies "哈" *ha* obviously with a mitigating tone, although this is a request, the whole sentence has a tactful tone, thus making it easier for the listener to accept the request.

In general, the above modal particles have a lot of functions, and each has its own characteristics, they are all generally used at the end of the sentence, but the meanings expressed are not the same, and the role of the modifying the proposition is also different.

4. The Research and the Analysis of the Use of Five Main Modal Particles

In order to better understand the use of modal particles, we researched the use of modal particles through questionnaires and interviews. The survey method is mainly quantitative analysis, which consists of four parts including questionnaires method and interview method.

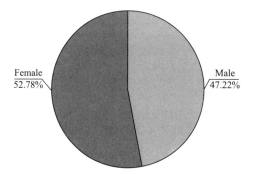

The investigation area was one of Chongqing universities with 72 participants (including 35 males and 37 females, see left). The average age of the respondents was 2425 years old, and there were only 5 people over the age of 35. Among the respondents, 68 were from China (18 in Chongqing, 13 in Sichuan, 13 in Henan, 5 in Hubei, 4 in Shandong, 2 in Anhui, Guizhou, Jiangsu, Jiangxi, Shanxi, Liaoning, Hunan, Gansu respectively, 1 in Shaanxi and Tibet respectively, and 4 people are foreigners with a certain level of Chinese.

The survey title is "the most frequently / rarely used modal particle" and the reason for its use. Respondents had to sort the five modal particles " 啦 " *la*, " 吗 "

ma, " 吧 " *ba*, " 呢 " *ne*, " 哈 " *ha according to the frequency degree, and explain
why they most frequently /*rarely use this or that particle.

According to the results of the above quantitative analysis, the most frequently
used modal particle is "吗" *ma*, and the most rarely used one is the modal particle
"啦" *la*. The reason for this result is explained below.

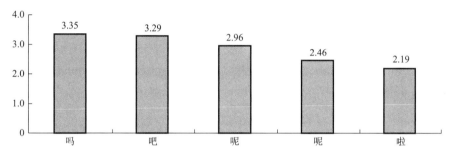

According to the survey results, the speaker uses modal particle "吗" ma in
interrogative or rhetorical questions, perhaps because the Chinese are not
used to asking or confirming something directly. Among the 26 respondents
frequently using "吗" ma, there are 8 women and 18 men. Among them, male
respondents pointed out that they are usually asking more questions. They use
this tone of speech when asking or tactfully requesting, and waiting for the
listener's answer, because "using this modal particle I can get positive answers
from others". In addition, there were some respondents who also pointed out
that using "吗" ma gives a sense of blame to the listener, which makes people
reluctant to use this word in communication.

As for the modal particle "吧" ba, the respondents stressed that with this modal
word they can express uncertainty (not absolute), giving the listener the feeling
of being respected, and also makes tone more tactful and ease, so it is in line with
the Chinese people culture and character, and is also the peculiarity of the Chinese
people way of thinking. "吧" ba expresses asking for opinions and respecting each
other, even when requesting or ordering it adds certain politeness, so some
respondents mention that using this modal particle gives the feeling like waiting for
the listener to agree to what has been said or asked.

The third most commonly used modal particle is "哈" ha. The reason people use this modal particle has to do with its original meaning, so many respondents suggested that using "哈" *ha* in communication is more intimate and can give people a happy and intimate feeling. The survey once again proves that the usage of the modal particle "哈" *ha* has a lot to do with the region, because according to related research (吴宝安，韩小红, 2013: 73), it is mostly represented in Sichuan dialect, mostly used in imperative sentences, expresses reminders, emphasis, requests, advice, etc., indicating that the tone of the proposition is used to seek the opinions of the listener. In the answers to our questionnaires, some respondents also suggested the reasons for using "哈" *ha*. Most of them said that it has to deal with the dialect habits, as "哈" ha is very common in Sichuan dialect. In addition, some respondents stressed that they do not use this modal particle because they feel that it is very strange and unnatural, and the impact is relatively small, and there are not many situations where they can use this particle, probably because this modal particle is quite "young" and it has only become popular in the last forty years.

Through the comparison we have found out that people rarely use particle "呢" *ne*, because they feel that the tone of speech is too tweaked or that they are not in the habit of using this modal word. Among them, there is another reason related to local characteristics, which has to do with the area where the research was conducted, because "呢" *ne* has a nasal sound 'n'when it is pronounced, so "it is inconvenient" and does not conform to the voice habit.

The survey shows that the most rarely used modal particle is "啦" *la* for the following reasons: some people think that this modal particle is "a bit cute", "very feminine" (mentioned by male respondents), "does not meet their own gender" (mentioned by male respondents); it was stressed that this modal particle gives the feeling of impoliteness to the listener, and is often used in the impatient or anxious situation (and this probably has to deal with the semantic functions of "啦" *la*, as it consists of "了，呢" le and "啊" "呢" a, as "啊，呢" a is modal particle with the meaning of order, urging).

5. Conclusion

According to the above research and investigation, it can be seen that the use of modal particles in modern Chinese to express interpersonal functions is an inevitable important component in the process of communication. There are two kinds of cognitive semantic functions of modern Chinese modal particles surveying as the mood markers: one is to express the speaker's attitude towards the content of the sentence; the other is to indicate the subjective orientation of the speaker's communicative identity, pointing out the relationship between the speaker and the listener and the grasp of the process of communication. This again demonstrates that modal particles are one of the most important tools in the process of communication and cognition, and are also worthy of further study.

"一带一路"倡议背景下的阿中文化交流

雅斯敏·萨曼【埃及】
开罗大学文学院中文系讲师

几千年来，中国和阿拉伯世界有着相当频繁的文化往来。作为连接东西方桥梁的阿拉伯人，将中国的丝织品、瓷器、茶叶等闻名遐迩的货物传入西方，推动了全世界经济贸易发展的进程。而著名的丝绸之路和海上丝绸之路很早就把中国和阿拉伯世界联系在一起，使得双方经济关系日益密切，为中国和阿拉伯世界的共同繁荣做出了重要贡献。

一、古代丝绸之路和海上丝绸之路

中国文明和地中海沿岸文明开始时互不了解，到了公元前 7 世纪左右，古希腊人开始知道有一个东方的古国，但对这个古国文明的情况并不了解。虽然在丝绸之路没有开通之前，埃及尼罗河流域的草原上已经有人踩出了一条时断时续的草原贸易小道，但是中国和欧亚大陆各国真正的交往只有丝绸之路开通以后才有的。丝绸之路不仅是一条古代通商的道路，它更是连接古代中华文明、埃及文明、印度文明、希腊文明和美索不达米亚文明的道路，是东西方文化和科学技术交流的桥梁。

古代中国和阿拉伯的商贸和交通路线主要有丝绸之路和海上丝绸之路，两条商贸道路是公元前 2 世纪开始出现的，由于两条道路开始时以丝绸贸易为主，所以人们便称它们为"丝绸之路"。

陆上丝绸之路的开辟者是西汉时期的一位宫廷侍郎，名叫张骞。当时，中国西边有一个经常骚扰汉朝边境的部落，名叫匈奴。为了解西域和匈奴的情况，公元前138年，张骞率领100多人从长安出发，出使西域。但刚进入河西走廊，张骞就被匈奴俘获。10多年后，张骞逃离西域回到长安并带回了有关西域的情况，为汉朝的人们打开了一扇通往新世界的大门。

张骞第一次出使西域的旅程，又被称为"凿空"之旅——意思是本来不通的两地，硬是被开辟出一条道路。从此，通向西方的道路开启了，其路线由长安（今西安）出发，经河西走廊至敦煌，出玉门阳关，西越葱岭（帕米尔高原），穿过中亚，取道波斯，到达伊拉克和叙利亚。汉朝的商人接踵西行，商人也纷纷东来。大量的中国蚕丝、丝织品和其他货物，通过这条陆路，运往阿拉伯各地。

如果说陆上丝绸之路与阿拉伯国家的关系不够密切，那么海上丝绸之路则对阿拉伯国家有着直接的影响。其实，在陆上丝绸之路形成之前，人们已经开始从海上探索连接外部世界的道路。在埃及史书《地理志》中，最早记载了中国，书中称中国为秦尼国。据考证，中国与古罗马之间的海上航线早在公元1世纪初就已相接，当时的相接点在斯里兰卡，中间经过亚历山大等地。

随着航海业的发展，中阿双方很早就开始了双向的航行。海上丝绸之路从广州、泉州、明州（今宁波）等地南航，穿过印度至阿拉伯湾和红海。大批的陶瓷、丝、绢、棉等货物，通过这条海路，运到阿拉伯各地和其他地方。当时，"丝绸之路"上的骆驼商队络绎不绝，"海上丝绸之路"上的商船来往频繁，这两条交通大动脉将中国和阿拉伯联系在一起，给双方的经济往来提供了很大的便利。

就这样，通向中国以西的道路经过张骞两次出使西域而开启了，西行道路上许多经商的人来来往往，不同文明之间的往来真正地建立了起来，包括中阿文明的交往也相当繁盛。通过丝路，印度、东南亚、中东、非洲和欧洲之间的贸易交流也迅速活跃起来，无数新奇的商品以及新颖的技术在大陆中交换，从而推进了各自文明的发展。

二、古代中国与阿拉伯世界的经济交往

随着阿拉伯国家的建立和对外联络的开展，中阿经济关系日益密切。在唐代，阿拉伯第三任哈里发奥斯曼正式遣使到中国长安。当时，中国人将到中国经商的阿拉伯商人称为"大食"，也就是阿拉伯语"商人"（条枝）的对音。可见，在中

国唐宋时期，一大批阿拉伯大食陆续到中国经商，他们运去香料、珠宝、药物、玻璃制品等数百种商品；运回中国的陶瓷、丝绸、茶叶等闻名遐迩的特产。中国商船则远航到阿拉伯世界的阿曼、巴林、巴士拉和巴格达等地，与当地商人进行贸易。

阿拉伯阿巴斯王朝第二哈里发曼苏尔决定在巴格达建立新首都时曾说："此处是一个优良的营地。此外，这里有底格里斯河，可以把我们和遥远的中国联系起来。"由此可见，曼苏尔对阿拉伯和中国的经济关系给予极大的重视。后来，巴格达建立不久就开辟了专卖丝绸、瓷器等中国商品的"中国市场"；而唐代中国最大的对外交往口岸广州，被当时阿拉伯旅行家形容为"阿拉伯商货荟萃之地"。此外，在长安、扬州等地，也有专门销售阿拉伯商品的市场。

随着中阿经济关系的繁荣和日益频繁，古代中阿贸易相当活跃，运到阿拉伯的中国货物有许多种。其中，丝绸和瓷器最受阿拉伯人的喜爱。阿拉伯人称中国杭州生产的丝织品为"汉沙维叶"，意思是"杭州的"，同时还把中国瓷器叫做"绥尼"，意思是"中国的"。当时，阿拉伯人不仅购买并使用中国瓷器，他们还在当地仿制中国瓷器，这也是阿拉伯人对中国瓷器深切喜爱的表现。

在阿拉伯帝国建立以前，阿拉伯与中国的交往主要以间接的贸易往来为主。但是在阿拉伯帝国建立以后，两国之间的经济贸易关系随着双方政府开始遣使互访而更加频繁。在此期间，中阿两国长期和睦相处，互通有无，而阿拉伯文化则主要是通过贸易途径传到中国的。

自从唐代开始，阿拉伯和中国的贸易关系从过去以间接交往为主逐渐转变成以直接交往为主。因此，越来越多的阿拉伯商人来到中国经商。此时，来中国的阿拉伯商人多聚居在中国的重要国际港口——广州和首都长安。此外，在港市扬州和泉州，也住有不少阿拉伯商人。宋代时，来中国的阿拉伯商人多数住在广州和泉州。到了元代，大多数阿拉伯商人住在中国泉州、广州、杭州、温州等许多城市，他们运到中国的各类货物，丰富了中国的商贸宝库和经济贸易形态。

三、向西方开放

这条丝绸之路，对中国人的精神生活产生了极大的影响。丝绸之路促进了中国自汉代至唐代文化开放政策的形成。中国人的文化和技术通过这条道路传入西线诸国，如纸张、印刷术的传播，直接影响全世界文明的发展。而中国人通过这条文化大动脉，输入了不同国家文明的艺术、哲学和宗教思想。

丝绸之路开通之前，中国人虽然跟西方世界交往不多，但人们知道那边有人存在，有富庶的城邦，有富有魅力的物品和艺术品，更有长相不同的人，这引起了华夏民族的浓厚兴趣。

对中国文化和思想产生极大影响的佛教，就是公元前87年由丝绸之路这条文化大动脉传入中国的。佛教在中国的影响远远超过宗教范围，中国人后来的思想发展，打上了佛教的烙印。这条丝绸之路也给中国人带来了中亚、西亚和欧洲的文明，伊斯兰教是1000多年前通过相当和平的方式进入中国的，即随着阿拉伯商人与中国交往的增进，把自己的宗教也带到中国了，促成这一伟大历史事件的是中国闻名世界的"丝绸之路"，有了这条丝绸之路，才有了伊斯兰教的传入。

四、"一带一路"经济带

中阿的经济贸易关系不仅有悠久的历史，而且随着双方当代文化往来日益频繁而不断地得到提升，从而继续发挥加强中阿人民传统友谊的作用。在2014年，中国提出了建设"一带一路"经济带的倡议，即将"丝绸之路经济带"和"海上丝绸之路"简称为"一带一路"的经济倡议。这一跨越时空的宏伟项目，即将承接古今、连接中外，赋予古老的丝绸之路一种崭新的内涵，被誉为是一个高瞻远瞩的伟大项目和一条和平发展的共赢之路。

众所周知，丝路经济带最重要的意义就是"连接"。古代丝绸之路承载了中阿经济贸易交往的历史，而现代的丝绸之路，也就是"一带一路"经济带将实现更多的中阿经济贸易连接与互换。过去的阿拉伯世界就为丝绸之路沿线各国提供了连接的桥梁。而今天，阿拉伯国家也要通过丝路来吸引企业入驻以及更多的经贸往来，因此"一带一路"经济带的建设要推动中国和沿线国家的经济发展以及为中国和阿拉伯世界经济带来不可小觑的影响。

目前，"一带一路"经济带的建设项目已经获得60多个国家的支持，包括自古以来与中国保持良好经济贸易伙伴关系的阿拉伯国家。作为"一带一路"建设的重要合作伙伴，不少阿拉伯国家的发展战略都和中国提出来的"一带一路"经济带项目不谋而合。

2014年，在中国北京举办的中阿合作论坛第六届部长级会议开幕式上，习近平主席提出中阿双方根据"共商、共建、共享"的原则携手建设"一带一路"经济带的主张，并提出了"1+2+3"的中阿合作想法，意思就是以能源合作、基础设施建设和贸易及投资、核能、航天卫星和新能源为突破口，努力提升中阿经济贸易关系的合作层次。

　　在历史上，阿拉伯世界曾是古代丝绸之路重要的组成部分。而今天，中国的新丝绸之路——"一带一路"经济带的建设在阿拉伯世界的参与和共同努力下，才能继续发挥其连接世界东西方的作用，重新形成一条连接亚、非、欧洲的经济文化大动脉，使不同国家的经济关系不断地提升，经过"一带一路"经济带的相互交流和相互支持而放出光彩。

参考文献

伊本·白图泰：《伊本·白图泰游记》，科技书出版社 2010 年版。
穆罕迈德·阿卜杜哈米德：《丝绸之路的沿线文明》，埃及文化部出版社 2007 年版。
贝哲民：《新丝绸之路：阿拉伯世界如何重新发现中国》，东方出版社 2014 年版。
安惠侯、黄舍骄、陈大维、杨健：《丝路新韵：新中国和阿拉伯国家 50 年外交历程》，
　　世界知识出版社 2006 年版。

Cultural Exchanges between the Arab Countries and China under the Background of the Belt and Road

Yasmine Mohammad Elsmman Ahmed / Egypt

Chinese Department, Cairo University, Lecturer

For thousands of years, China and the Arab countries have had quite frequent cultural exchanges. The Arabs, as the bridge between the East and the West, brought Chinese famous goods such as silk, porcelain and tea to the West, which promoted the economic and trade development around the world. The famous Silk Road and the Maritime Silk Road have long linked China and the Arab countries, making the economic relations between the two sides increasingly closer and making important contribution to the common prosperity of China and the Arab countries.

1. The Ancient Silk Road and the Maritime Silk Road

The Chinese civilization and the civilization along the Mediterranean coast did not understand each other at the beginning. Around the 7th century BC, the ancient Greeks began to know that there was an ancient country in the East, but they did not understand anything of this ancient civilization. Although there has already been an intermittent steppe trade path on the grasslands of the Nile basin in Egypt before the Silk Road was opened, the real exchanges between China and the countries of

Eurasia were only available after the opening of the Silk Road. The Silk Road is not only a road for trade in the ancient times, but also connects the ancient Chinese civilization, the Egyptian civilization, the Indian civilization, the Greek civilization and the Mesopotamian civilization. It is a bridge between the East and the West for exchanges in culture, science and technology.

In the ancient times, the Chinese and the Arab world mainly depended on the Silk Road and the Maritime Silk Road for trade and commerce. The two trade routes began to appear in the 2nd century BC. Since the trade mainly involved silk, the two routes were called the "Silk Road".

The land Silk Road was opened by Zhang Qian, a court servant of the Western Han Dynasty. At that time, there was a tribe, called Xiongnu, in the west of China. It frequently harassed the border of the Han Dynasty. In order to understand the situation of the Western Regions and the Xiongnu tribe, in 138 BC, Zhang Qian led a team of more than 100 people and left Chang'an for the Western Regions. Zhang Qian was captured by the Xiongnu just after they entered the Hexi Corridor. More than a decade later, Zhang Qian fled the Western Regions and returned to Chang'an and brought back the situation concerning the Western Regions, thus opening a door to the new world for the Han Dynasty.

Zhang Qian's first journey to the Western Regions was also known as the "opening an overland route" – meaning that a path is opened up between two places that are not accessible. Since then, the road to the West has been opened. Its route starts from Chang'an (now Xi'an), through the Hexi Corridor to Dunhuang, out of Yumen Pass and Yangguan Pass, over the Pamirs, cross Central Asia, and reaches Iraq and Syria via Persia. Merchants from the Han Dynasty went to the West, and businessmen from the West came to China. A large amount of Chinese silk, silk products and other goods were transported to all parts of the Arab world through this road on the land.

If the Silk Road on the land is not closely related with the Arab countries, then, the Maritime Silk Road has a direct impact on the Arab countries. In fact, before the land Silk Road was opened, people began to explore the road connecting the outside world from the sea. The earliest record of China was found in the Egyptian history book *Records of Geography*. According to research, the sea route between China and ancient Rome was connected as early as the beginning of the first century. At that time, the contact point was in Sri Lanka, and passed through Alexandria and other places along the way.

With the development of maritime industry, China and Arab countries started two-way navigation very early. The Maritime Silk Road started from Guangzhou, Quanzhou, Mingzhou (now Ningbo), through India, to the Arabian Gulf and the Red Sea. A large number of goods such as ceramics, silk, enamel and cotton were transported to all parts of the Arabian and other places through this sea route. At that time, camel caravans on the "Silk Road" came and went in a continuous stream. Merchant ships on the "Maritime Silk Road" came and went in great number. The two major communicating arteries closely linked China and the Arab countries, providing great convenience for economic exchanges between the two sides.

In this way, the two journeys by Zhang Qian to the Western Regions opened the road to the west to China. Many business people on the westbound road came and went, and the exchanges between different civilizations were really established, including the frequent exchanges between the Chinese and Arab civilizations. Through the Silk Road, trade between India, Southeast Asia, the Middle East, Africa and Europe also became more active. Numerous novelty products and novel technologies were exchanged between the continents, thus promoting the development of their respective civilizations.

2. Economic Exchanges between Ancient China and the Arab Countries

With the establishment of Arab countries and the development of foreign liaison, China-Arab economic relations have become increasingly closer. In the Tang Dynasty, the third Arab Caliph Osman officially sent envoys to Chang'an, China. At that time, the Chinese called the Arab merchants who did business in China "Dashi", that is, the symphonic of "merchants" in Arabic (Tiaozhi). It can be seen that during the Tang and Song Dynasties in China, a large number of Arab merchants went to China for business. They carried hundreds of types of commodities such as scented goods, jewellery, medicines and glass products to China and returned with China's ceramics, silk, tea and other specialties. Chinese merchant ships sailed to Oman, Bahrain, Basra and Baghdad in the Arab countries to trade with local businessmen.

Mansur, the second Caliph of the Arab Abbsid Dynasty said when he decided to establish a new capital in Baghdad: "This is an excellent camp. In addition, there is the Tigris River, which can connect us with distant China." It can be seen that Mansur attached great importance to the economic relations between Arab and China. Later, soon after Baghdad was established, it opened up the "Chinese market" specializing in Chinese goods such as silk and porcelain. In the Tang Dynasty, Guangzhou, China's largest foreign exchange port, was described by Arab travelers as "the place where Arab merchants and goods gather". In addition, in Chang'an, Yangzhou and other places, there were also markets that sold Arabic goods.

With the prosperity and increasing frequency of the China-Arab economic exchanges, the trade between China and the Arab countries in the ancient time was quite active, and there were many kinds of Chinese goods shipped to the Arab countries. Among them, silk and porcelain were most popular among the Arabs. The Arabs called the silk fabric produced in Hangzhou, China, was "Hansha Weiye", meaning "Hangzhou", and Chinese porcelain was called "Sini", meaning "Chinese". At that time, the Arabs not only bought and used Chinese porcelain, but copied Chinese porcelain in the local area as well. This has also shown the deep love of the Arabs for Chinese porcelain.

Before the establishment of the Arab Empire, the contacts between the Arab countries and China were mainly indirect trade. However, after the establishment of the Arab Empire, the governments of both sides sent envoys and made mutual visits, making increasingly frequent exchanges in economy and trade between both sides. During this period, China and the Arab Empire lived in harmony and made exchanges for a long time, and the Arab culture was mainly transmitted to China through trade channels.

Since the Tang Dynasty, the trade relations between Arab and China gradually changed from indirect exchanges to direct ones. As a result, more and more Arab businessmen came to do business in China. At this time, Arab businessmen coming to China lived in Guangzhou, China's important international port and the capital Chang'an. In the Song Dynasty, most of the Arab businessmen who came to China lived in Guangzhou and Quanzhou. In the Yuan Dynasty, most of the Arab merchants lived in many cities of China such as Quanzhou, Guangzhou, Hangzhou and Wenzhou. They carried various goods to China, enriching China's trade treasury and economic and trade forms.

3. Open to the Western World

This Silk Road has had a tremendous impact on the spiritual life of the Chinese people. The Silk Road promoted the formation of a cultural open policy in China from the Han Dynasty to the Tang Dynasty. Through this road, Chinese culture and technology spread to the Western countries. Among them, the spread of paper-making and typography directly affects the development of civilization throughout the world. This cultural artery has helped the Chinese people introduce the artistic, philosophical and religious ideas of different civilizations.

Before the opening of the Silk Road, although the Chinese did not have many contacts with the Western world, they knew that there were people living there. There were rich cities and states, fascinating objects and works of art, and even people with different looks, which aroused great interest of the Chinese nation.

Buddhism, which has had a great influence on Chinese culture and thought, was introduced into China by this cultural artery of the Silk Road in 87 BC. The influence of Buddhism in China far exceeds the scope of religion. The later development of Chinese thoughts has been marked by Buddhism. This Silk Road has also brought the civilization of the Central Asia, West Asia and Europe to the Chinese people. Islam entered China through a fairly peaceful approach more than a thousand years ago, that is, with the increase in exchanges of Arab merchants with China, their own religion was also brought to China. It is China's world-famous "Silk Road" that has contributed to this great historical event. With this Silk Road, Islam was able to be introduced to China.

4. The Belt and Road Economic Belt

The economic and trade relations between China and the Arab countries not only have a long history, but also continue to be promoted as the cultural exchanges between the two sides in the contemporary time become more frequent, thus continuing to play a role in strengthening the traditional friendship between the Chinese and Arab peoples. In 2014, China proposed the construction of the Belt and Road economic belt, and referred to the "Silk Road Economic Belt" and "Maritime Silk Road" as the Belt and Road Initiative. This magnificent project spanning time and space will undertake the ancient and modern, connect China and foreign countries, and endow the ancient Silk Road with a brand-new connotation. It is hailed as a great project with great vision and a win-win road for peaceful development.

As we all know, the most important significance of the Silk Road Economic Belt is "connectivity". The ancient Silk Road carried the history of economic and trade exchanges between China and the Arab countries while the modern Silk Road, e.i. the Belt and Road Economic Belt, will achieve more economic and trade links and exchanges between China and the Arab countries. The Arab countries of the past provided a bridge to linking countries along the Silk Road. Today, the Arab countries also need to use the Silk Road to attract enterprises and more economic and trade exchanges. Therefore, the construction of the Belt and Road economic belt should promote the economic development of China and the countries along the Silk Road and bring great benefits to China and the Arab world economy.

At present, the construction project of the Belt and Road economic belt has been supported by more than 60 countries, including the Arab countries that have maintained good economic and trade partnerships with China since ancient times. As an important partner of the Belt and Road Initiative, the development strategy of many Arab countries coincide with the Belt and Road economic belt project proposed by China.

In 2014, the Sixth Ministerial Conference of China-Arab States Cooperation Forum was held in Beijing, China. President Xi Jinping proposed that China and Arab countries should work together to build the Belt and Road economic belt based on the principle of achieving shared growth through discussion and collaboration. He also put forward the "1+2+3" idea for cooperation between China and Arab countries. It means that with energy cooperation, infrastructure construction and trade and investment, nuclear energy, space satellite and new energy as a breakthrough, we should work hard to improve the level of cooperation between China and Arab countries.

In history, the Arab countries were an important part of the ancient Silk Road. Today, China's new Silk Road – the Belt and Road economic belt will continue to play its role in connecting the East and West of the world with the participation of Arab countries and our joint efforts and re-establish a link between Asia, Africa and Europe so as to promote the economic relations of different countries and become brilliant through mutual exchanges and mutual support of the Belt and Road economic belt.

"一带一路"倡议对阿根廷的机遇和挑战

达芙妮【阿根廷】
阿根廷中央财政部、国际金融关系部副部长

引　言

　　直到 19 世纪初，中国一直是世界上的经济强国，其产品和生产力对世界经济都产生了广泛的影响。在 1850 年以前的几个世纪里，中国在经济和社会进步发展水平方面是世界第一大国（Ríos, 2015）。其中最大的影响因素之一是连接亚欧大陆长达 1500 多年的丝绸之路。此外，全毅、林裳（2015）将 1535 至 1815 年间中国与拉丁美洲发展的贸易称之为"海上丝绸之路"。丝绸之路发展成为跨越不同国家的大市场，形成了地区间多样化的交流。

　　从 16 世纪后期起，中国与拉丁美洲之间的贸易往来逐渐频繁，此贸易又被称为"银丝贸易"（刘文龙，1994）。自 1565 年至 1815 年间，大量中国的丝绸、瓷器、茶叶等产品被运往美洲。中国与美洲之间的海上丝绸之路，对中国与世界都曾产生了巨大的影响。中国的贸易通过太平洋海上丝绸之路，建立了与拉美人民的友好往来，连接了三个大陆：亚洲、美洲、欧洲（全毅、林裳，2015）。中国和拉丁美洲已经建立了数百年的联系。丝绸之路的受阻或中断既可看作是巧合，也是历史的必然，因为它间接促进了中拉关系。然而，在 1815 年至 1972 年间，中国与拉丁美洲的贸易大幅度下降。随着拉美地区的国家大规模与中国建立外交关系以及中国的改革开放，商业交流再次起步。然而直到 20 世纪 90 年代，中拉贸易往来才飞速发展，成为互相不可或缺的伙伴。

一、什么是"一带一路"倡议？

2013 年 9 月，习近平主席在哈萨克斯坦发表演讲时提出与中亚建立"新丝绸之路经济带"。同年 10 月，在亚太经济合作组织领导人非正式会议期间，他提出与东盟国家携手共建"21 世纪海上丝绸之路"的构想（邹磊，2015）。"一带一路"虽是古代丝绸之路的继承和延伸，但由于时代的发展变化，它被赋予了新的含义，这项提议不仅着眼于经济，更多地体现为政治、经济、文化各方面的沟通与交流。因此，它必须顺应并引领当今世界潮流，追求和平、发展、合作和双赢（李广宇，2015）。在这一大背景下，这一倡议推动沿线国家和地区更广泛的合作，开发其中蕴藏的潜力，促进沿线地区经济快速发展和国际地位的提升。

在短短几年内，中国与"一带一路"沿线国家签订了一系列合作协议，同时为保障这些国家的基础设施建设、资源开发、产业合作等提供融资支持。

"一带一路"包括建设相互连通的货运运输道路，海关便利化，连接该地区所有公路的多式联运，改善港口基础设施和运输设施，民用航空设施，跨界能源网络的连接和光纤网络的密集化（信息丝绸之路），正如连接拉丁美洲的从中国到智利的跨太平洋光纤互联网电缆。

2014 年，中国设立丝路基金；2015 年，国家发改委、商务部和外交部联合发布了《推动共建丝绸之路经济带和 21 世纪海上丝绸之路的愿景与行动》文件；2016 年，成立亚洲基础设施投资银行（亚投行），目前已经有 87 个国家和地区加入，包括拉丁美洲的巴西、玻利维亚、智利、秘鲁和委内瑞拉；2017 年 5 月，"一带一路高峰论坛"在北京举行。从那时起，"一带一路"已经成为世界上最长的经济走廊，覆盖 67 个国家近 50 亿人口，主要围绕基础设施、产业提速和民生福祉三项重点主题。该倡议将起到加强政策沟通，确保贸易畅通，加强货币流通，促进人文交流互动等作用。

总之，中国希望通过经济交流与丝绸之路沿线的每个国家加强文化和政治联系，从而建立一种相互尊重和相互信任的新模式。"一带一路"倡议不仅建设一条经济贸易路线，而且还打造一个具有共同利益、命运和责任的社区。

中国支持"一带一路"倡议，提出通过基础设施开发将中国与亚洲、欧洲和非洲的市场联系起来。在 2017 年 5 月的一带一路论坛开幕式上，习近平表示 "一带一路" 倡议建设 "开放、包容、平衡和普惠的经济全球化"。为了满足发展中国家和发达国家的需求，中国还邀请世界银行和其他国际机构加入 "一带一路" 倡议。

1. 拉丁美洲和 "一带一路" 倡议

为了深化拉丁美洲融合和（据某些分析人士指出）降低美国人影响，2011 年在委内瑞拉成立了拉美和加勒比国家共同体（CELAC），作为一个不包括美国或加拿大的区域组织。2018 年 1 月 22 日，中国 - 拉美和加勒比国家共同体论坛第二届部长级会议在智利圣地亚哥举行。

中国外交部长王毅与来自 31 个拉美和加勒比国家共同体成员国的外交部长以及包括联合国拉丁美洲和加勒比经济委员会（CEPAL）在内的四个区域组织和多边机构的负责人共同出席 1 月的会议。会议特别发表中国提出的 "一带一路" 倡议声明，并呼吁该倡议将 "为中拉全面合作伙伴关系注入新的活力，开辟新的前景"，根据新华社消息报道[1]。

2. "一带一路" 倡议和阿根廷

2014 年，中国和阿根廷决定建立全面战略伙伴关系。能源基础设施和交通运输是构成伙伴关系的关键要素之一。中国企业具有技术能力，渴望与阿根廷企业建立联系并在此过程中转让知识，而且还拥有本国大型银行的资金支持。

中国国家主席习近平于 2017 年 5 月在北京欢迎阿根廷总统毛里西奥·马克里，强调 "拉美是 21 世纪海上丝绸之路的自然延伸"，同时称赞阿根廷对 "一带一路" 建设的支持和参与。中阿会议强调，"一带一路" 倡议正在迅速扩大到拉丁美洲，并为中国及其合作伙伴带来了回报。

签署的《共同行动计划》是一个路线图，指导双方为实现全面战略伙伴关系目标而努力。两国之间达成的最新《2019-2023 年共同行动计划》特别关注促进 "一带一路" 框架下的商业流动性，约定在 "一带一路" 框架下促进发展计划协调，在签订《中国—阿根廷共建 "一带一路" 谅解备忘录》基础上确定优先领域和项目合作计划。

在能源领域，中国国家开发银行提供的 47.14 亿美元的贷款在圣克鲁斯省（巴塔哥尼亚）修建两座水电站 "孔多克里夫" 和 "拉巴朗科萨"。据估计，工程建

1　新华网，"聚焦：拉丁美洲如何适应中国的 '一带一路' 倡议"，2018 年 1 月 23 日 [http://www.xinhuanet.com/english/2018-01/23/c_136918709.htm]

设将在 6 年内完成，装机容量为 1300 MV，占阿根廷整个国家电力供应的 5%。2014 年 7 月，习近平访问阿根廷时见证了贷款协议的签署。

在铁路公路基础设施领域，中国国家开发银行将提供 20.99 亿美元贷款，用于全长 1400 公里的"贝尔格拉诺货运"窄轨铁路现代化项目的铁路设备购买、工程建设和服务。

在阿根廷北部地区，"高查瑞光伏电站"项目通过中国进出口银行提供的 3.315 亿美元优惠买方信贷支持，目标是建设三个利用可再生能源的太阳能发电站，装机容量 300 兆瓦。

到目前为止，已经注意到，最重要的资金提供方是中国的两家政策性银行：中国国家开发银行和中国进出口银行。当然，对于中国国有建筑公司来说，大量资金投入让梦想成真。

阿根廷胡胡伊省的另一个项目是 Cauchari-Alaróz 锂盐湖项目。Exar 矿业公司是智利 SQM 和加拿大美洲锂业成立的合资企业。2017 年 1 月，赣锋锂业已与美洲锂业建立战略合作关系，承诺为该项目提供资金以换取购买产品的权利。赣锋锂业将收购 SQM 的 37.5% 股权，剩余 62.5% 股权由美洲锂业持有。宣布的交易金额为 8750 万美元。

中国驻阿根廷大使馆发布声明，中国银行对在阿根廷开展业务表现出兴趣。该声明在中国银行董事长访问阿根廷期间宣布。中国银行目前在 55 个国家和地区设有分支机构，包括拉丁美洲的 5 个国家：在智利新设立的办事处以及在巴西、秘鲁、开曼群岛和巴拿马的办事处。中国银行是"一带一路"倡议的出资方之一。根据最新的资产负债表，中国银行是中国在新丝绸之路沿线国家和地区设立办事处最多的银行。如果中国银行最终在阿根廷经营业务，它将跟随中国工商银行的脚步，成为第二大中资银行，中国工商银行在 2011 年收购阿根廷标准银行 80% 的本地业务。

中国的核电站建设技术是《共同行动计划》议程的一部分。阿根廷政府和中国政府签订协议，由中核集团中国中原对外工程有限公司负责，中国提供资金（90 亿美元）在 2022 年前修建一座核电站。该项目将取代今年初取消的项目，之前的项目是中国提供资金，但采用加拿大技术。[1]

1　在中国和阿根廷签订的《2019-2023 年共同行动计划》中，双方强调"支持深化两国企业在核电领域的合作，对两国企业之间达成的合作协议感到满意。两国的相关部门和企业承诺继续和加快就实施核能项目进行核安全监督、选址和财务安排方面的磋商。"

二、机会

中国政府坚决支持在和平共处原则下建立国际关系的愿景。中国和参与国以政策沟通、设施联通、贸易畅通、资金融通、民心相通为主要内容，满足不同方面和阶段的合作预期。

"一带一路"倡议符合中国的所有期望，但拉丁美洲仍有待观察。即使是现在，该倡议也以不同的方式为中拉关系的未来做出了贡献。

拉丁美洲缺乏基础设施和互联互通。此外，教育制度不完善，区域经济参与度低。这些因素引发了社会不平等、边缘化、贫困和失业等问题。明白中国可以为拉丁美洲做些什么是了解"一带一路"倡议可以提供何种类型投资的第一步。

首先，中国正在邀请更多南美国家加入亚投行，将基础设施建设作为扩大朋友圈的外交工具。此外，中国正在将"一带一路"倡议扩展到拉丁美洲，并通过光纤传输等项目帮助增强该地区与世界其他地区的连通性。

1. 亚洲基础设施银行的基础设施建设资金

总部在北京的亚洲基础设施银行于 2016 年 1 月正式启动，是中国发起并得到许多国家和地区支持的多边开发银行。亚洲基础设施银行允许向阿根廷和拉丁美洲提供大量资金，以改善当前和预期经济增长质量，同时允许该地区的政府为社会投资项目留出预算。目前已批准七个拉丁美洲国家（阿根廷、巴西、智利、厄瓜多尔、秘鲁、委内瑞拉和玻利维亚）加入亚投行，这些国家现在只需要完成其国内流程，然后分配一定数量的资金购买亚投行股份。

亚投行传播与发展部主管劳瑞尔·奥斯特菲尔德表示，"除非成为正式成员，否则亚投行无法开始为这些国家的基础设施项目提供资金，虽然已经在考虑他们的需求和如何帮助他们。"

此外，在 AEI 协定框架内，为了财政上的合作，阿根廷中央银行已经与中国中央银行之间达成货币互换协议，该协议不仅为我国提供了流动性，还支持北京取代美元作为垄断性贸易货币的努力。最近，两国续签了高达 1300 亿人民币的货币互换。

2. 开发区和电子商务

北京还相继启动了与"一带一路"倡议及其政策有关的新开发区和城市群，

例如西安国际港务区是继上海、福建、深圳和重庆之后的第五批自由贸易区。该园区的最大优势是通过陆路与通往亚欧大陆和中亚的走廊相连。此外，还为外国和中国企业提供了一个国际服务平台。预计到 2020 年，中国将聚集全球电子商务的 60%。阿根廷可以受益于这些电子商务和服务形式，学到很多东西。电子商务公司对拉丁美洲政府和代理商提供培训研讨计划。因此，人员交流方便中国企业家走出去，拉美人也可以学习之前在拉丁美洲不为人知的新型贸易形式。

3. 人员外交

民心相通是"一带一路"倡议的任务之一。人员外交是处于中间层的组织和个人建立信任、相互理解并汇集不同的文化的一种方式。在商务部、文化和旅游部以及外交部的帮助下，中国企业家可以走出去开展业务。在中国中央政府的帮助下，阿根廷企业家可以访问并了解中国，获知阿根廷产品将销往何处。2018 年青年汉学家研修计划期间，西安国际港务区管委会副主任杨祎在西安抛出这一观点。杨祎还认为，"汉学家对西安国际港务区进行为期 4 天的访问也是人员交流的一部分，这必将为未来的关系创造更多的机会"。在研修期间，汉学家还观看了中国文化展览，例如西安歌剧和中国书法表演。

三、挑战

一些作者还提醒中国应提防对其海外投资和建设项目的暴力行为，而且参与"一带一路"的弱小国家很难维持其经济独立性。例如，汤姆·米勒对巴基斯坦和斯里兰卡的案例进行了分析。不过，对于几十年来一直饱受美国困扰的拉丁美洲国家来说，这一论点似乎很难延伸。以阿根廷为例，自 1976 年以来，外债呈指数级增长，在 20 世纪 90 年代，阿根廷完全服从华盛顿共识，即在以开放和宏观经济自律为特征的市场逻辑下进行经济政策改革。这些年，经济政策不再是简单的提议，而是对有志于加入并获得高度发达经济体和国际组织认可的国家进行政治和经济控制的工具。互惠互利是中国自 20 世纪 50 年代中期以来一直倡导的和平共处五项原则之一，该原则表明，如果不以双赢的方式进行谈判，中国对拉丁美洲产生影响的可能性比较低。"一带一路"倡议在拉丁美洲和特别是阿根廷的项目和提议所面临的特殊挑战更多地与文化和法律制度有关。

1. 项目规模和复杂性

在阿根廷正在建设的项目中，拉巴朗科萨和孔多克里夫水电站都是复杂的工程。葛洲坝集团与项目业主（阿根廷能源部）于 2013 年 10 月签订商业合同，并于 2014 年 1 月签订补充协议。为此项目，中国葛洲坝集团公司与阿根廷电力工程公司成立了一家临时合资企业。最近，阿根廷电力工程公司副董事长因腐败丑闻而入狱，该丑闻涉及在 2008 年至 2015 年期间与上届克里斯蒂娜·基希纳尔政府有关的阿根廷商人和政客。虽然阿根廷官员指出，"合作没有停止，合资企业重新安排领导，"但中国企业迅速向杨大使（最近刚刚担任中国驻巴西大使职位）提出分析报告，并开始谈判以达成谈判解决方案，力求不影响去年 11 月开始的工程，即使开工时间已经比预期晚三年。鉴于必须进行新的环境影响研究，2016 年 12 月，阿根廷最高法院的一项预防措施要求暂停工程，直到符合《国家水利工程法》规定，即召开环境影响研究公开听证会。听证会于 2017 年 7 月召开。由于内部立法的无知和环境团体的压力，工程还将耽误更长的时间，在民主国家必须考虑到这一点。

高查瑞光伏电站的情况有所不同，该发电站的运行没有出现重大延误。参与该项目的本地和中国消息人士认为，因为这是一个很小的项目，仅占巴塔哥尼亚大坝的 10%，并且在执行和融资过程中仅涉及企业和中资银行，这也有助于增进理解和提高效率。

2. 语言

语言是谈判中常见的障碍之一，尤其是基础设施项目。翻译人员通常来自法律或语言专业，而不是工程专业。巴塔哥尼亚大坝的一位谈判人员解释说："一次我和一名中国翻译在一起，我看到英语缩略词 EPC，却不知道这是设计、采购和施工的缩写。"因此，通常只有中方提供的一名口译员会讲中文和西班牙语。这位谈判人员指出，"在语言上，他们准备得更好，可以使用西班牙语或英语。他们学得更快，而且拥有更多的资源。这里几乎没有人会讲中文。在一份文件中，我们就协议、合同和约定展开协商，然后翻译成中文是很复杂的。我们往往不够清晰、简洁和精确。"

3. 战略愿景

"我们的主要障碍是短视，还是采取长远的眼光看待，"一位会谈参与人员指出，"时间非常紧迫，但中国对此并不关心。"另一位官员强调，中国企业更习惯于中央政府参与谈判，阿根廷人缺乏这一意识。

4. 谈判风格

据观察，中国方面负责谈判的具体人员必须请示后才能对合作内容修改（还有另一个客观困难，即时差）。阿根廷官员的自主权更大，但每一次变更要求都意味着拖延。一位曾经参与列车采购的阿根廷消息人士指出："他们已经准备好协议，这标志着谈判节奏，我们在这方面表现较差。然后，当我们开始分析时（或者当中央政府发生变化时，又出现了另一种不对称性），我们开始做加法。铁路协议有4到5份，因为我们希望在列车上使用德国制造的制动装置。这样让事情变得复杂，给中国人增加了意想不到的成本，但他们在合作中表现得灵活而务实。此外，中国供应商以及汽车或能源之间也相互竞争。"

5. 阿根廷的工会

显然，中国人对阿根廷工会的权力感到困惑。一位中国商人曾经在接受记者的采访时承认，"对工会或环境问题的抗议为什么不在工作开始之前谈判？现在浪费时间和影响形象。简直让人筋疲力尽。"

结　论

"一带一路"倡议计划通过基础设施开发将中国与亚洲、欧洲、非洲以及后来加入的拉丁美洲市场联系起来。

事实上，中国经济的转型已经并将对第三国产生影响。中国日益增加的中等收入阶层将对外国商品和服务产生更大的需求。"一带一路"倡议是中国针对其邻国及包括拉丁美洲在内的外交战略，旨在通过大量基础设施项目促进贸易和经济一体化。

拉美本地人的期望很重要，因为这必然会改善经济要素的流动和资源分配。鉴于两个地区之间遥远的地理距离，在该战略框架下肯定会有更多的间接参与，而不是各方直接参与。作为中国资本在当地的合作伙伴，这些企业可以在政府作为股东加入后（例如亚洲基础设施银行）成为参与方。尤其是，阿根廷表示愿意通过财政支持、信贷增加、技术协助以及相关部门项目的其他服务（能源、运输、基础设施、医疗卫生、水系统、大坝等）加入该倡议。该倡议似乎增加了对基础设施的投资。还要考虑电子商务工具等服务的影响。物流和市场营销是必需的；挑战在于提供产能，以使中拉关系超越中国向国外供应和输出本地产品的范畴。该倡议将带来光明，双赢的关系将让彼此的关系和人员之间的联系更加紧密。

自奥巴马和特朗普执政以来的 15 年间，美国与拉美地区的关系在恶化，而中国一直积极拥抱拉丁美洲和加勒比国家。如果没有美国的反对，中国的"一带一路"倡议将自然而轻松地扩展到拉丁美洲。然而，与中国的竞争中，美国对拉丁美洲的影响力一旦失去，就很难恢复。

B&R Initiative in Latin America: Challenges and Opportunities for Argentina

Esteso Gil Alejandra Dafne / Argentina

Department of International Financial Relations, Central Finance Ministry of Argentina, Deputy Director

1. Introduction

Until the beginning of the 19th century, China had been an economic power due to the impact of its products and its productive capacity in the world economy. In 1850 and for several centuries, China, both for its economy and for the level of advancement and development of its society, was the first world power (Ríos, 2015). One of the greatest influence points was the Silk Road, which was developed for more than 1500 years connecting it with part of Asia and Europe. Also, Quan Yi, Lin Shang, (2015) call the "Route of the maritime Silk", which developed the trade between China and Latin America between 1535 and 1815. This route was constituted as a large market that crossed different countries and that generated exchange between very diverse regions.

Since the late sixteenth century, trade between China and Latin America has become very frequent—this trade is also known as "Silver and Silk Trade" (Liu

Wenlong, 1994). For this reason, from 1565 to 1815, a large number of products such as silk, porcelain and tea from China were transported to America. The Maritime Silk Road between China and America has had an impact on both China and the world. Through the Maritime Silk Road of the Pacific, China's trade established mutual knowledge with Latin America and its trajectory connected three continents: Asia, America and Europe (QUAN Yi, LIN Shang, 2015). China and Latin America have been connected for centuries. The blockade or interruption of the Silk Road can be seen as both a coincidence and a historical necessity, because it indirectly promoted this relationship. However, between 1815 and 1972 there was a significant reduction in trade between China and Latin America. With the passage of the massive establishment of diplomatic relations with many countries of the region and the reform and opening of China, commercial exchange began again. However, it was not until the 1990s, when the Sino-Latin American trade experienced a rapid development, both regions becoming indispensable partners with each other.

1.1 Latin America and Belt and Road Initiative

Aiming to deepen Latin American integration and, according to some analysts, reduce the American influence, Community of Latin American and Caribbean States (CELAC) has been formed in Venezuela in 2011 as a regional bloc that does not include the United States or Canada. On January 22nd 2018, the Second Ministerial Meeting of the Forum of China and CELAC was held in Santiago, Chile.

China's Foreign Minister Wang Yi, together with his counterparts from 31 Latin American and Caribbean countries as well as heads of four regional organizations and multilateral institutions, including the United Nations Economic Commission for Latin America and the Caribbean (CEPAL), attended the January's meeting. The meeting made a special announcement on the China-proposed B&R initiative, appealing that the initiative will "inject new energy into the China-CELAC comprehensive cooperative partnership and open up new prospects." according to Xinhua agency[1].

---

1 Xinhua Net, "Spotlight: How Latin America fits into China's B&R Initiative", 2018-01-23 [http://www.xinhuanet.com/english/2018-01/23/c_136918709.htm]

1.2 Belt and Road Initiative and Argentina

In 2014 China and Argentina celebrated the Integral Strategic Association. Energy infrastructure and transport are one of the key elements which constitute the association. There are Chinese companies with the technical capacity, the desire to associate with Argentine firms -and transfer knowledge during the process-, and the financial backing of large banks in their country.

Chinese President Xi Jinping welcomed Argentina's President Mauricio Macri in Beijing in May 2017 by proclaiming that "Latin America is the natural extension of the 21st century Maritime Silk Road" while applauding Argentina's support and participation in the B&R initiative. The Sino-Argentine meeting emphasized the fact that the B&R initiative is rapidly being expanded to Latin America and paying dividends for China and its partners.

The celebration of the Joint Action Plans is a roadmap that guides the efforts aimed at achieving the objectives of the integral strategic partnership. The last Joint Action Plan 2019-2023 held between the two countries gives special attention to the promotion of the commercial flow in the BRI framework.There, it was agreed to promote the alignment of the development plans within the framework of BRI, and the elaboration of the cooperation plans to define the priority areas and projects, based on the execution of the China-Argentina Memorandum on the Joint Construction of the B&R Initiative.

In the energy sector, they are being built two hydroelectric power plants in the Province of Santa Cruz (Patagonia) "Condor Cliff" and "La Barrancosa", through a loan of USD 4.714MM by China Development Bank (CDB). It is estimated that the works will be concluded in 6 years' time and will have an installed capacity of 1300 MV, 5% of the maximum consumption in Argentina. Xi Jinping witnessed the conclusion of loan agreement during his visit to Argentina in July 2014.

In the railway infrastructure and roads area, the project "Belgrano Cargas Railwail Rehabilitation", aims to acquire railway equipment, works and services for a narrow gauge railway, with a total length of 1,400 km, through a loan for USD 2,099 MM from CDB.

In the north region of Argentina the project of "Photovoltaic energy station Cauchari" has as objective the construction of three electricity generating parks from solar power source of renewable energy, contemplating an installed capacity of 300 MW, through an Export - Import Bank of China (EXIM) Concessional loan of USD 3,315 MM.

By far, it is noticed, that most significant financers are China's two policy Banks: CDB and EXIM. And, of course, the avalanche of funding is a dream come true for Chinese state-owned construction firms.

Another example in the Province of Jujuy is Cauchari-Alaróz project. The mining company Exar had been constituted as a joint venture between the Chilean SQM and the Canadian Lithium Americas for its development. In January 2017, Ganfeng Lithium had started a strategic relationship with Lithium Americas, committing to finance that project in exchange for the right to purchase the production. Since SQM Ganfeng Lithium output, they will then hold 37.5% and 62.5% Lithium Americas. The announced amount of the transaction is US D 87.5MM.

Chinese Embassy reported that Bank of China (BOC) showed interest in starting operations in Argentina. The announcement was made during the visit of the president of that entity to Argentina. BOC currently has a presence in 55 countries and regions, including 5 countries in Latin America: the newly opened office in Chile and offices in Brazil, Perú, the Cayman Islands and Panamá. BOC became one of the promoters of the B&R initiative. According to its latest balance sheet, it is the Chinese bank with the greatest presence in the countries that belongs the new silk route. If BOC finally operates in Argentina, it would become the second biggest Chinese bank after the Industrial and Commercial Bank of China (ICBC) , which had acquired 80% of Standard Bank's local businesses in 2011.

Chinese technology for the construction of a nuclear power plant is part of the agenda in the Plan of Action. Argentine and Chinese government through China Zhongyuan Engineering Corporation (CZEC), subsidiary of China National Nuclear Corporation (CNNC) have agreed the construction of a nuclear power plant in Argentina in 2022 with Chinese financing (US D 9,000MM). This project would replace the one canceled at the beginning of the year, which was to be made with Chinese funds, but with Canadian technology.[1]

2. Opportunities

Beijing defends its own vision of international relations that is instrumented around the principles of peaceful coexistence. Their expectations are met in different faces and stages of cooperation between China and the countries interested in participating, based on policy coordination, facilities and infrastructure connectivity, unimpeded trade and investment, financial integration and openness, and people to people bonds.

BRI meets all of Beijing's expectations, however these in Latin America remains to be seen. But even now, it contributes to the future of Sino-Latin American relations in different ways.

Latin America lacks infrastructure and interconnectivity. In addition, their education systems are deficient and their regional economies have low participation. This results in problems of social inequality, marginality, poverty and unemployment. Knowing what China can contribute to Latin America is the first step in understanding what kind of investment can be offered from Belt and Road Initiative.

1　In the Action Plan 2019-2023 signed by China and Argentina, both parties maintain that they "support the deepening of cooperation among their companies in the area of nuclear electricity, and note with satisfaction the cooperation agreements agreed between their companies. The relevant departments and companies of the Parties undertake to continue and expedite the consultations on nuclear safety supervision, site selection, and financial arrangements for the implementation of the nuclear energy project".

Firstly, China is building infrastructure as a diplomatic tool and expanding its circle of friends by inviting more South American countries to join the AIIB. Also, China is extending the BRI to Latin America and helping enhance the region's connectivity to the rest of the world through projects, for instance, optical fiber transmission.

2.1 Financial funds for infrastructure BAII

BAII, based in Beijing and officially launched in January 2016, is a multilateral development bank initiated by China and supported by a wide variety of countries and regions. BAII will allow Argentina and Latin America to finance significant amounts to improve the quality of economic growth (current and projected), while allowing regional governments to free up budget for social investment programs. The entity has given approval for the moment to seven Latin American countries (Argentina, Brazil, Chile, Ecuador, Peru, Venezuela and Bolivia) to become members of the BAII, and these now need to complete their internal processes to then allocate a volume of capital to the purchase of BAII shares.

Laurel Ostfield, responsible for communication and development of the BAII, said that "Until they become full members, something that the BAII cannot begin to finance infrastructure projects in those countries, although it is already investigating what their needs are and how can they help them?"

In addition, within the framework of the AEI agreements, the purpose of cooperating in financial matters, has already resulted in the swap currencies agreement between BCRA and Central Bank of China, which has not only provided our country with access to liquidity, but has also favored Beijing's interest in displacing the dollar as a monopolistic trade currency. Recently, both countries renewed up to 130,000 million RMB swap currency.

2.2 Development zones and e-commerce

Beijing has also launched in succession related to B&R initiative and its policies new development zones, and urban agglomerations as Xi'an International Trade and

Logistics Park, the fifth batch of free trade zones after Shanghai, Fujian, Shenzhen, and Chongqing. The great advantage of this park is its connection by land with the corridor to Eurasia and Central Asia. In addition, it works an international services platform there for foreign and Chinese companies. It is projected that by 2020 China will concentrate 60% of global electronic commerce. Argentina can benefit and learn a lot from these forms of electronic commerce and forms of services. There are training seminar programs for ecommerce companies for state and commercial agents to be implemented in Latin America. Here, people to people connection allows Chinese entrepreneurs to go global in their businesses and Latin Americans to learn about these novel forms of trade that are not yet fully known in Latin America.

2.3 People to people diplomacy

The creation of a method to develop people to people relationships is one of the Belt and Road Initiative tasks. People-to-people diplomacy is a way for organizations and individuals in the intermediate layers to relate to build trust, mutual understanding and bring together very different cultures. With the help of the Ministry of Commerce, Culture and Tourism and foreign affairs, Chinese entrepreneurs can go out in their businesses. With the help of the Chinese central government, Argentine entrepreneurs can visit and know China, know where Argentine products will be sold. This was expressed in Xi'an International Trade & Logistics Park (ITL) during the Visiting Program for Young Sinologists 2018 by Yi Yang, Deputy Director of Administration Committee of ITL zone. Yi Yang also believes that "the 4-day visit that Sinologists did to ITL zone is also part of people to people exchange that will surely create more opportunities for future relationships". In the program the sinologists also witnessed Chinese cultural exhibitions such as the opera of Xi'an and Chinese calligraphy performances.

3. Challenges

Some authors also cautioned that China should beware of violent reactions against its investments and construction projects abroad, and that smaller and weaker countries participating in the BRI would have difficulty maintaining their economic independence. Tom Miller, for example, analyzes this for the cases of Pakistan and Sri Lanka. However, it seems difficult to stretch this argument for the case of Latin American countries that have suffered American harassment for decades. In the case of Argentina, since 1976 the external debt increased exponentially and in the 1990s, Argentina was deeply aligned with the Washington consensus which economic policy reforms were based on a market logic characterized by openness and macroeconomic discipline. During these years, economic policies stopped being simple proposals and became an instrument of political and economic control for countries interested in inserting themselves and obtaining the stamp of approval from highly developed economies and international organizations. The goal of seeking mutual benefits, which is one of the five Principles of peaceful coexistence that China promotes since the mid-1950s, makes it clear that there are lower risks that China imposes its charm in Latin America, if not negotiating under the win- win scheme. The particular challenges regarding Belt and Road Initiative projects and initiatives in Latin America and specially Argentina are more related to cultural and law systems.

3.1 Scale and complexity of the projects

Within the works which are under construction in Argentina, La Barrancosa and Condor Cliff Hydropower Station hydroelectric are the complex ones. Gezhouba and the project owner (Ministry of Energy of Argentina) concluded the commercial contract in October 2013 and a supplementary agreement in January 2014. For this project, a transitory joint venture was formed between China Gezhouba Group Company and argentine Electroingeniería. Recently, the vice president of Electroingeniería was imprisoned for a corruption scandal that shakes Argentine businessmen and politicians linked to Cristina Kirchner's last administration between 2008 and 2015. Although Argentine officials said "it never stopped, what is there is a rearrangement of the joint venturein terms of leadership", the Chinese company accelerated the analysis proposed to Ambassador Yang (who has just assumed the position of ambassador recently in Brazil) and began talks to arrive to a negotiated solution, that does not harm the work and just started last November, three years later than expected. Due to new environmental impact study had to be carried out, and in December 2016, a precautionary measure by argentine Supreme Court of Justice suspended the works until the fulfillment of the provisions of the National Hydraulic Works Law, which requires the presentation of public hearing environmental impact study. This took place in July 2017. There was a long way to delay the work due to ignorance of the internal legislation and the pressure of the environmental groups that - in the case of a democratic regime - it must have been taken care of.

Different is the case of the Cauchari solar plant, which has been running without major delays. Local and Chinese sources participating in the project maintain that this is due to the fact that in a small project, 10% of what the dams in Patagonia imply, and because in execution and financing there are only companies and Chinese banks (EXIM) involved. This facilitates understanding and effectiveness.

3.2 Language

Language is one barrier that emerges on negotiating, especially in infrastructure projects. Translators usually come from law or language studies, not engineering. A negotiator from the dams of Patagonia explained "Once—with a Chinese translator—I saw the acronym EPC and did not know what Engineering, Procurement, Construction was." That is why, in general, Chinese and Spanish are spoken with only one interpreter from the Chinese side. This negotiator sustained "In language, they are better prepared, in Spanish or English. They learn faster, plus they are more and have more resources. Here almost nobody speaks Chinese. In a paper, we interchange agreement, contract, agreement, and then translate to Chinese is complicated. We tend not to be clear, concise, and precise".

3.3 Strategic vision

"Our main obstacle is short-term versus long-term vision of them," said a participant in talks, "Everything is urgent here, but China does not care about that." Another official stressed that Chinese businessmen are more accustomed to the presence of the Chinese central state in negotiations, an element of great absence in Argentina.

3.4 Bargain styles

It is observed in Chinese side are state instructions which a junior official cannot modify without asking before (and there is another objective difficulty that is the time difference). Argentine officials are more autonomous but every change it is asked for means a delay. An argentine source that has participated in trains buying process appointed: "they come with the armed agreement, they mark the rhythm of the negotiation, here we are weaker". Then when we started to analyze (or when central government administration changes here, another asymmetry), we started to add addends. There were 4 or 5 in railways agreements because we wanted to change to German brakes in the trains. This complicates the Chinese because it adds an unexpected cost, but they are flexible and pragmatic. In addition, they compete with each other, between Chinese companies of suppliers, as well as cars or energy.

3.5 Unions' presence in Argentina

Definitely, the Chinese are perplexed about Argentine union power. One of the interviewers remember what a Chinese business man confessed to him"If there is a union or environmental protest, ok, but why was it not negotiated before starting the work? That creates a waste of time and image. That wears."

4. Conclusions

The "Belt and Road" Initiative proposes to connect China with markets in Asia, Europe, Africa, and later Latin America, through infrastructure development.

Indeed, the transformation of the Chinese economy has and will have effects on third countries. An increasing number of middle-income Chinese will generate greater demand for foreign goods and services. Belt and road initiative is a diplomatic strategy of China towards its neighbors and beyond, including Latin America, to promote trade and economic integration, through a large number of infrastructure projects.

The local Latin American expectation is important because it will surely improve the flow of economic factors and the resources allocation. Due to the geographical distance between both regions, there will surely be a greater indirect participation than direct participation of the various actors within the framework of this strategy. Those companies, as local partners of the Chinese capitals, can be participants to the extent that their governments, as shareholders, are part of, for example, AIIB.In particular, Argentina has expressed its will to join the initiative through financial support, credit enhancement, technical assistance, among other services for projects for interest sectors (energy, transport, infrastructure, sanitation, water systems, dams, etc.). The initiative seems to deepen investments in infrastructure. It would be interesting to consider also the impact on services including ecommerce tools. Logistical and marketing aspects will invariably take place; the challenge will be to give capacity so that the China-Latin America relationship can go beyond the Chinese supply and the output of local products abroad. The outcome of the initiative will be floodlit so the win-win connection results into a greater density of the mutual relationship and the people and people bonds.

China has been actively embracing Latin American and Caribbean countries, as relations between the United States and the region appears to be deteriorating for the last 15 years, since Obama and then Trump's administration. With so little opposition from the United States, China's Belt and Road Initiative will naturally and easily extend to Latin America. But American influence in Latin America, once lost to China, will be extremely difficult to recover.

References

刘文龙：《马尼拉帆船贸易——太平洋丝绸之路》,《复旦学报（社会科学版）》, 1994 年。

全毅、林裳：《漳州月港与大帆船贸易时代的中国海上丝绸之路》,《福建行政学院学报》, 2015 年。

Esteso, D. &Restivo, N. (2017) "La piedra en el contrato" in *DangDai Magazine,* N.20, Buenos Aires, Argentina: Casa de la cultura, pp.58-60, Spring 2017.

Esteso, D. &Villagran, I. "Dimensiones de la Cooperación Académica y Cultural con la República Popular China" en *China, Rusia e India en América Latina, un enfoque multidimensional*. Buenos Aires, Argentina: UNDEF, pp.57-76, 2018.

Ríos, X. (2015). El XIII Plan: antecedentes, contexto, contenidos y expectativas. Simposio Electrónico Internacional sobre Política China.

XinhuaNet, "Spotlight: HowLatinAmericafitsintoChina's B&R Initiative", 2018-01-23 [http://www.xinhuanet.com/english/2018-01/23/c_136918709.htm]

Zhang, Y. (2005). Story of the Silk Road.China: China Intercontinental Press.

Zottele, A., Li,Y., & Santiago, M. A. (2017). *Las Pymes mexicanas y chinas ante el crecimiento acelerado de las relaciones económicas entre ambas naciones*. Xalapa, México: Universidad Veracruzana.

Zottele, E. & Wei Qian (2017) *One belt, One Road: Opportunity for Latin America and Search for Sustainable Development*. Changzhou University.

从文化"走出去"看海外书院的传承和流变

——以新加坡的书院为例

吴小红【马来西亚】

北京大学外国语学院博士

综　述

何明栋在《佛教对我国古代书院的影响》一文中，阐述了佛教对于古代书院的兴盛、建筑格局、组织形式、学规的制定、教学活动等。该文也是启发我研究书院的最初动机。鲁东大学的李成峰在其硕士论文《从传统书院到新式学堂：清末民初的教育转型》里，阐述了清末时期的书院转型状况，在清末"废书院、兴学堂"和科举废除的历史交替中书院走向学堂，展现了一场教育革命的发展历程。作者也提出了教会世界的书院概况。这一叙述弥补了书院历史中甚少被关注的部分。陈仙在其博士论文《英语世界的书院研究》里[1]，谈论了英语世界的书院（Academy），极具启发性。国外是如何接受古代书院的制度的这一主题非常鲜明。由最早的利玛窦书信中的"研究人生哲学的场所"开始，再将书院引入西方的视野。而中国国内书院研究最早起步于 20 世纪 20 年代。这种"反向研究"有助于我们更好地了解国内外的学术交流，尤其是当代的教育、宗教、制度上的传承，更是开拓了书院研究的视野。作者通过对海外不同汉学家的英语世界的书院研究

1　陈仙：《英语世界的书院研究》，湖南大学 2016 年博士论文。

为例，例如美国汉学家万安玲、麦哲维，德国汉学家卜恩礼等。其中美国麦哲维把研究视角集中在广州书院的地方研究。在他看来，"地方认同"研究已经成为西方学者的重要议题。此外，湖南大学岳麓书院的邓洪波教授，已被业界称为邓书院。他关于书院历史和文化的各类书籍，更是进入和了解书院研究必备的工具书。各学者的论文研究已经是一种跨界的硕果，教育、历史、人文、儒学都一一概括。这些研究，正是开启海外书院研究的管道。

相较之下，本地史料对书院的研究显得麟角凤毛。1995 年，早期儒家学者梁元生在《宣尼浮海到南洲》一书中，对 19 世纪以儒学思想传播的媒介书塾、义学和书院做了逐一的介绍。作者收录了新加坡最早的崇文阁和萃英书院碑记，实为研究本地书院最珍贵的资料。另外，2007 年庄钦永在《新甲华人史史料考释》在教育篇里，也记录了 1819—1944 年间新加坡华文学堂的情况。书中汇集了教会创立书院的一手资料，可说是非常珍贵的史料。令人惊喜的是，我们通过庄教授的视角，也颠覆了许多前人的研究。后来，分别从新加坡文史工作者林志强和柯木林在《新加坡早期的双语教育》和《重探崇文阁》文中，分别从新加坡早期视角说起，逐一讲述当代书塾学堂，进而探索新加坡早期双语教育，让我们看到了早期华人教育的概况。[1] 中国的学者 [2] 李勇在文章中，则从敬惜字纸的信仰习俗传承的角度来看崇文阁。

一、书院简介

从古至今，教学的方式以不同形式存在，如义学（为乡学）、私塾、书院等。书院是以聚徒讲授、研究学问为主，是高级形态的私学。而一般私塾、社学、义学等多数是启蒙教育的性质。书院具有聚众授徒讲学、研究学问、兼有藏书、出版、祭祀等功能。中国古代教育发生了一个很大的变化，即出现了官学、私学和书院相互平行发展的格局，三者成鼎立之势。直到清朝末年，它们之间既有纷争，但也存在更多的互相渗透与融合。皆促进了中国古代文化教育的发展和繁荣。

二、新加坡书院的几个概念

走出国门的书院，是书院精神的延续，也是文化的一种延伸。在新马一带的

---

1 林志强：《新加坡早期的双语教育》；柯木林：《重探崇文阁》。
2 李勇：《敬惜字纸信仰习俗在海外的传承与变迁：以新加坡崇文阁为例》，《世界宗教研究》，2013 年第 2 期。

书院概念，可说是延续光绪之际，属于"新型"的书院。"新"的概念主要是指其前所未有的西学成分。在当时，中国国内已经有中外合办的书院，或者是外国人办的书院，例如教会的书院已有百余所。在海外的新马书院，粗略可分为3种不同的类型，即中国走出去的书院，另一种是英国教会的新型书院，还有一类是以英语为媒介语的书院。本文将着重在从中国"走出去"，并以儒家、道教为基础的两所书院为例。

在新马出现一个有趣的现象是：1800 年间，伦敦会传教士沿用中国清朝所使用的"学堂"一词称呼学校。在称呼书院和学校分别为 College 和 School。传教士和教员因其学术程度高低而有分别。因为翻译不统一，所以字面上是分不清书院的性质和创办者。后来英殖民时代，书院还被翻译成 Institution 还有 Free School（参照附录）。早期的海外书院在名字方面，已经出现了"混乱"的现象。因此，唯有详读其建校历史等资料，方能得知一二。

庄钦永教授在 2007 年考证的资料里，引用了于英国伦敦大学亚非研究院图书馆内的伦敦会（London Missionary Society）美国哈佛大学豪斯登图书馆（Hougston Library）美部会（American Board of Commissioners for Foreign Missions）的观点[1]。这为一直被视为传统的书院研究输入了新血，庄钦永质疑了前人的研究。这对本地书院的研究可说是一个新里程碑。

新加坡的书院资料，往往附属于南洋早期教育、私塾等，因此显得零散。教会的记录基于宣教的基础，详细记录了当代教会在南洋的所见所闻，为后人带来宝贵的资料。由此，我们得知新加坡教会的资料较完整和齐全。

相较于本地华侨、华社或政府，伦敦会（Methodist Missionaries）早已在新加坡设立所谓的方言学堂。另有闽人创办的私塾，这些都是设立后来书院的良好基础。

三、新加坡第一所书院：崇文阁属性辨析

本地史学家陈育崧在 1972 年 1 月 11 日《南洋商报》副刊《商余》发表《新加坡第一间华文学校的发现》中认为，1849 年建，1852 年落成的崇文阁是新加坡第一间华校，第一间书院。29 年后，庄钦永于 2001 年在《南大学人》论文集上发表《新加坡崇文阁非学校考辨》，从学术角度论析崇文阁并非一所书院。

1　庄钦永：《新甲华人史史料考释》，《1819—1844 年新加坡的华文学堂》，第 182-184 页。

1. 建筑外观和空间

庄钦永教授认为，崇文阁空间狭小的塔楼，第二、三层面积是非常小，而且从楼下到二、三楼的铁梯异常得陡，很显然其设计并非专为学童所用。[1] 由《兴建崇文阁碑记》和《重修崇文阁碑记》碑文里，他提出了一些值得深思的论证：可见碑文撰稿人知道"阁"和"书院"的分别。在他看来，作为一所学堂的崇文阁，竟舍弃"书院"一词不用，而以道教建筑"阁"字取代。仅从字面上来看，以当时撰稿人对文字的敏感度，这一点确实值得注意。

崇仁阁的外观整体建筑，看起来的确不像一般书院，呈八角形，三层宝塔式的古典建筑物，古人俗称的"八卦楼"。另，崇文阁内两方碑记立置时间（同治六年 [1867]），比后来萃英书院（咸丰十二年 [1861]）迟了 6 年，创办年份只是 5 年之隔。两所都是由同一班闽商创办的，以其功能来看，两座建筑不可能属同等性质。

2. 选址准则及外部环境特征

中国古代的建筑布局素来讲究风水。书院这样一种介乎礼制与使用之间的建筑形式，更是一种物化的精神空间。崇文阁在选址布局方面，也延续了书院选址的精神。正如碑文："……地于岛屿之西偏。……斯阁也背冈峦而面江渚，左连凤寺右接龙门山川即已毓秀，文运逐卜咸亨。……"[2] 此书院选在背向起伏的山，面朝向江上一块陆地。左连接凤寺，右接龙门。山川毓秀，文运逐渐顺利。古人看来，建筑选址若背靠山水，将来一切都会顺利。

崇文阁坐落在直落亚逸街，Telok Ayer 在马来语是水湾之意，根据《新加坡风土志》作者吴彦鸿的考证，1822 年由英国工程师富兰克林（James Franklin）所绘制的地图，在新加坡河的南岸注明有"华人镇"（Chinese Town）及"马来人镇"（Malay Town），后者更接近直落亚逸。相信那是以捕鱼为生的马来人聚落。[3] 当年这就是一道海岸线，非常符合碑文的原意。在《重修崇文阁碑记》云："……前襟沧海，后枕云山，闾阎鳞比，庙宇蝉联，形势纵非廓大之观，山川颇负钟灵之胜。……"[4] 这条街原址在新加坡河的南边，海岸线也只离街道 1 公里之远。后来

1　庄钦永：《新甲华人史史料考释》，教育篇《1819—1944 年间新加坡的华文教育情况》，第 221 页。
2　陈荆和、陈育崧合编：《新加坡华文碑铭集录》，《兴建崇文阁碑记》，第 283 页。
3　Telok Ayer Street, NLB.
　　http://eresources.nlb.gov.sg/infopedia/articles/SIP_656_2004-12-31.html.
4　陈荆和、陈育崧合编：《新加坡华文碑铭集录》，《重修崇文阁碑记》，第 291 页。

的发展把原址隔着海岸线往四条街移开。因此，现在来到这里没有机会看到海岸线了。另，安祥山 [1]（Ann Siang Hill）正距离崇文阁不远，由此，我们可以看出前人在选址方面遵守了古人的各种准则。

3. 祭祀梓潼帝君

在碑记里记载了："……其巍然在上者所以崇祀梓潼帝君也……" [2]。重修崇文阁碑云："……崇祀梓潼帝君于阁中……" [3] 祭祀道教中的梓潼帝君，是宋代以后参加科举士子，顶礼膜拜的主要神明。也称文昌帝君。

我们可以理解崇文阁是以祭祀潼帝君为主。它以宏正道、宪章文武、达到入圣域为主旨。在《重修崇文阁碑记》里，也强调了"文"的重要性，道出于天，实体在于圣，流传于世则依靠文，文在的地方既是道所在之地，即是圣和。

4. 敬字惜纸文化仪式

1890 年，新加坡《星报》上的惜字报道：惜字之戒，华地为严。而我华人之族于者，见有剩纸遗书即一点一书亦无不肃然敬之，惜之，恐其或坠地也。故闽籍乐善诸君曾于道光己酉年间捐资倡建崇文阁于直落亚逸街。[4] 由此，我们可得知早期先贤，希望能借助实践敬惜字纸，让后人能对剩纸遗书表示敬崇，故建立了崇文阁。

《兴建崇文阁碑记》（同治六年 [1867]）上有一段重要文字，说明其功能。碑文称："……其巍然在上者所以崇祀梓潼帝君也，其翼然在下者所以为师生讲受也。侧为小亭，以备焚化字纸。每岁仲春，济济多士，齐明盛服以承祭祀，祭毕并送文灰而赴于江，因颜之曰崇文阁……"依据碑文，楼上是祭拜梓潼的地方，楼下为老师讲授之用，侧边的小亭子，用来焚化字纸。每年农历二月初三，贤士百官盛装参与祭祀活动。在文昌君诞辰这一天，把有名望之士聚集一块儿，在南洋的新加坡进行了敬惜字纸仪式，别具意义。大家基于敬惜字纸的传统，对于文字文化的崇敬，在建筑侧边建立小亭子，可谓类似于敬字亭，或类似字库塔、焚字炉等。活动结束后，将焚化字纸灰烬送往大海。

在《重修崇文阁碑记》里也记载了："……广收遗字以化炭，恭送率由于

1　Pioneers Trail in Ann Siang Hill Park and Telok Ayer Green, NEA.
　　https://www.nparks.gov.sg/-/media/nparks-real-content/gardens-parks-and-nature/diy-walk/diy-walk-pdf-files/pioneers-trail-ann-siang-hill-park-and-telok-ayer-green.pdf.
2　陈荆和、陈育崧合编：《新加坡华文碑铭集录》，《兴建崇文阁碑记》，第 283 页。
3　陈荆和、陈育崧合编：《新加坡华文碑铭集录》，《重修崇文阁碑记》，第 291 页。
4　《星报》，1890 年 7 月 7 日。

旧。……"这广收被丢弃了的纸张，将之化为灰烬。在中国清代，曾出现了专门的惜字会雇人在街头巷尾拾捡废纸，称拾遗人。一般的仪式收回的纸会经水洗、晒干后入炉焚烧。接着再用木勺将灰送入陶瓮中，以船送入江水或海中待水慢慢淹没，瓮自沉入水中，也称"送圣迹"。1889 年 6 月 19 日《叻报》：本坡有崇文设，系专为敬惜字纸一事而设，雇有工人多名，每日四出捡拾字纸……1892 年 3 月 3 日《星报》：闽籍绅商所设惜字会，每日捡得字纸，洗洁焚之。这些也证明了崇文阁惜字会组织的形态和功能，传承了中国的文化。

《星报》曾报道："凡诸色人等所有检拾字纸以及断简残编，均许携之阁内炉中聚而焚之，至其灰烬释于每年二月初三日传集各塾师徒及铺户之有名望者。以鼓乐、彩旗抬送海外，投于江中，使悉归清流，免郁泪浊。数十年来潜移默化，南洋各地虽属巫妇亦知崇惜，不谓有因。"[1] 在进行敬惜字纸的文化仪式上，参与者不是一般的学生，皆是有名望之士，并以鼓乐声送到海外，投进江中，使其回归清流中，免去污浊。在这几十年都进行了潜移默化的作用，南洋的各地虽属马来属地，却知道崇敬珍惜，不去置疑其因。李勇教授根据这些报道，更加确定了崇文阁的功用和当年的惜字习俗。[2] 碑记里出现的"成人小子"极有可能是聆听敬惜字纸教导的听众，而非一般学生。这些报章报道也解决了"成人小子"和送字灰的时间。这些讯息显示非为学校功能，而是当年敬惜字纸信仰习俗的痕迹。庄钦永教授推测最后 1881 年，该地为什么约莫 30 年后，新加坡宣讲圣谕善书的乐善社，以此为活动重心[3]。崇文阁门口悬有"乐善社宣讲圣谕局公寓"的招牌，说明该组织就设于崇文阁。在公启里也提到在崇文阁旁的天福宫恭设龙牌香案，宣讲圣训。一般宣讲的地方，即是清代特殊的"公民道德教育"场所。这主要是指对老百姓的进行教化工作。除去建筑色彩，崇文阁在功能上则略带学宫的色彩。学宫在设计上具有明显的庙和学校结合色彩，并进行宣讲。新加坡华社显要聚集进行活动，正符合了古代学宫的一些功能。

在崇文阁改成乐善社后，在《乐善社戊戌己亥 1898、1899 两年收支报告》《乐善社辛丑 1901 收支报告》[4] 的记录里分别出现了两项纪录，第一：拾字纸、排香案二十五个月辛工银 175 元。第二：拾字纸、排香案全年薪水 84 元。由此，我们可

---

1 《星报》，1890 年 7 月 7 日。
2 李勇《敬惜字纸信仰习俗在海外的传承与变迁——以新加坡崇文阁为例》。
3 庄钦永《新甲华人史史料考释》教育篇《1819-1944 年间新加坡的华文教育情况》，第 228 页。
4 梁元生《宣尼浮海到南洲：儒家思想与早期新加坡华人社會史料彙編》，第 68 页，70 页。

以清楚总结：敬惜字纸这一传统的传承，在当代新加坡华社曾维持了一段时间。

敬惜字纸的文化起源于仓颉造字的传说，对文字的敬惜，进而转化成为民间信仰和社会习俗。宋朝时期，为了迎合科考和社会心理，将惜字思想与文昌帝君结合成为一种习俗。东南亚国家的移民延续了中国内的传统，此信仰逐渐成为一种民间习俗甚至成为一种迷信[1]，与祸福相系。早期的学者梁元生从儒家角度出发，说明了敬惜字纸承载传播儒家思想观念的重任。而李勇通过民俗角度看这民间习俗，并带祸福关系。由此，我们可以看到民间习俗和儒学之间的交叉或者重叠。传统习俗在时间演变过程中，也正好说明了物极必反的道理。这一点是值得被关注的。

5. 文风：化固陋为文章，变鄙俗为风雅

在碑记里云：……今圣天子崇儒重道，稽古右文，六字承风，威遵圣教。虽山陬海，各自别其疆土，而户诵家弦，亦兴起于学问焉。……[2] 当代天子崇尚儒家和伦理道德，考察古事，注重文事，接受教化。无论是在角落还是海堤，在不同的疆土领域，家家户户朗诵，这也形成了学问。由此，我们看见一种文风的传承，正是文化"走出去"和传承的一种形式。

在碑记里云：……从兹成人小子，读孔孟之书，究洛闽之奥。优柔德性培养天真，化固陋为文章，变鄙俗为风雅，则斯阁之建，其有裨于世道人心者岂鲜浅哉！……[3] 此举说明了移民崇文重教，大力发展教育，起了社会净化和教化的作用，也说明了南来的祖先们，除了为讨生计外，也开始重视具有教育功能的祭祀场所。这也表达了大家对文化教育的重视和关注。

在碑记里，有一段无法被好好释读的是：……从兹成人小子，读孔孟之书，究洛闽之奥。…… 碑记中记录：研读孔子孟子，研读朱理学，即北宋程颢和南宋朱熹的理学思想。这显然是宋明理学，即新的儒学学派。诸位作者和学者对这段碑文，没有太多的着墨和争议。由此，我们可以看到新旧儒学之间交叉的证据。这种文化的融合正是海外华人的一大特色。

林纬毅《新加坡儒学在体制内的流传》把崇文阁作为第一个有迹可循的第一教育机构，[4] 他笔下的崇文阁并没有过多强调儒家和道家的学派。碑文里则以书院

1　孙荣来《敬惜字纸的习俗及其文化意义》，《民俗研究》，2006 年第 2 期。
2　陈荆和、陈育崧合编：《新加坡华文碑铭集录》，《兴建崇文阁碑记》，第 283 页。
3　陈荆和、陈育崧合编：《新加坡华文碑铭集录》，《兴建崇文阁碑记》，第 283 页。
4　林纬毅《新加坡儒学在体制内的流传》，《东方论坛》，2005 年第 6 期。

的各个格局出发，严格意义上的书院，应该具备藏书、讲学和祭祀三大基本功能，这显然是学塾等办不到的。暂不说书院性质的纷争，崇文阁在文化上确实继承了书院部分的传统。

古代书院走向国际化的这些教育形式：私塾、书院、学宫等既相互关联又相对独立。我们看到了崇文阁对后来的华文教育产生了巨大影响。其他各式华社创办的书院学堂，亦相继出现，掀开了本地华社教育史波澜壮阔的新时代，正如《重修崇文阁碑记》：信乎斯文崇而人才辈出矣。[1]

崇文阁原址在直落亚逸街（Telok Ayer Street）天福宫的左殿。崇文阁建筑费用高达 9100 元，等于规模宏大的天福宫建筑费用的三分之一，说明捐建者对它的重视。当时有许多商号与船主的捐助，说明当年倡议兴建崇文阁，获得方言帮群与社会各界的广泛支持。[2]这说明了两点，文昌信仰、惜字习俗和读书人追求学问和功名，三者之间在这里的"共生"和"共存"的构建关系，崇文阁不全然属于书院性质，却是早期华社开始重视文教的起步。当年南移的先贤移民族群文化意识觉醒的开始起点，对新加坡早期的华文教育具有重大的时代意义。而这三者的共存，正是早期海外华人最直白的写实反映。

四、萃英书院的成立

1854 年，萃英书院成立。其坐落在厦门街（远东广场的一间饮食广场），可惜它只维持了 100 年就停办了。萃英书院碑现存于新加坡宗乡联合会位于大巴窑二巷会址内露天园地上。

萃英书院为古色古香的中国庭院式建筑物。进入正门为一大庭院，接着便是一个大厅，两旁有两个房间作为课室，接着是内厅、卧房、厨房、天井、后门。每年聘请老师，在中堂左右置帐讲授，把桃李置放在门和墙边。

萃英书院碑文 (1861 年立) 云："……新嘉坡自开创以来，土俗民风虽英酋之管辖，而懋迁有无实唐人之寄旅，迄于今越四十有年矣。山川钟灵，文物华美，我闽省之人，生于斯聚于斯，亦实繁有徒矣，苟不教以学，则圣域贤关之正途，何由知所向往乎。于是，陈君巨川存兴贤劝学之盛心，捐金买地愿充为党序之基，欲以造就诸俊秀，无论贫富家子弟咸使之入学，故复举十二同人共襄董建，且又

1　陈荆和、陈育崧合编：《新加坡华文碑铭集录》，《兴建崇文阁碑记》，第 283 页。
2　柯木林：《重探崇文阁》。

继派诸君，以乐成其美，择日兴工，就地卜筑，中建一祠为书院，崇祀文昌帝君，紫阳夫子神位，东西前屋连为院中公业，经于咸丰甲寅年工成告竣，因颜其院曰萃英，盖萃者聚也，英者英才也，谓乐得英才而教育之……[1] 当时的新加坡虽属于英国殖民地，闽南省人在此地居住，必须得学习。而当时的陈君巨川先生捐地建校，教育英才。据当年报道，称："叻中华人极多……而书塾之设，则惟闽人有之，……闽之义塾，名曰萃英"。[2] 这则报道清楚说明在萃英书院之前，无论闽人或其他华人方言群，都没有像它一样性质的场地。

值得注意的是，萃英书院碑文里第一次出现了"学宫"字眼。……今者陈君巨川能首行义举，倡建学宫，不惜重金买地为址。……[3] 此"学宫"之意，估计没有像中国的学宫具有政治色彩，应只是学校之意。为何当时撰稿不直呼书院，这有待进一步的考证。

1. 祭祀文风：人人知周孔之道，使荒陬遐域，化为礼仪之邦

萃英书院碑里值得关注的是：除了祭祀文昌君外，萃英书院也祭祀紫阳夫子神位，即朱熹。这是推崇学统、学派代表人物的行为。中国书院祭祀朱熹像是非常普遍的。人们是为了纪念他和尊崇理学，这也显示了海外书院的一种精神文化传承。文昌君即是道教中的梓潼帝君。

另，碑文云：……人人知周孔之道，使荒陬遐域，化为礼仪之邦。[4] "周孔"，周公与孔子被合称为"周孔"。在唐代以后成为儒学教育的别称。在萃英书院延续了祭祀本学派先师的文化。书院祭祀对象个性化的特性尽显。此外，书院也同时祭祀了魁。在道教信仰里，魁星被认为是主宰文运之神，凡参加考试者，无不尊重。曾经有记录清代是中国书院史上供祀人物最多的时期。显然的，海外书院也继承了这一做法。

可这一习俗却在 40 年后发生了变化。

每年七月初七，院中师生焚香供祭祀文昌魁星，至光绪改在八月二十七日，恭祝至圣诞。唯有一节革旧更新，极洽众意。向例院中每逢七月初七日，院中生徒酿香供祀文昌魁星，相沿成习，不知其非。今则议定明年始，改期于八月二十七日恭祝大成至圣孔子圣诞，而七月之例概已删除。众皆称善，著为定例。

1　陈荆和、陈育崧合编：《新加坡华文碑铭集录》，《萃英书院碑文》，291-292 页。

2　《叻报》，1891 年 2 月 25 日。

3　陈荆和、陈育崧合编：《新加坡华文碑铭集录》，《萃英书院碑文》，291-292 页。

4　陈荆和、陈育崧合编：《新加坡华文碑铭集录》，《萃英书院碑文》，291-292 页。

窃思翠英书院创建至今，将垂四十年之久，今一旦改变旧制，足见诸绅董之深明大义，择善而从也。[1]

文昌帝君保佑民间主读书人的功名禄位，对于读书人如欲猎取科第，自然不可怠慢，必须祭祀。魁星是主宰文章兴衰的神，在功名的驱使下，对于这些祭祀尤其看重。这不外是谄媚的心理，必须进行祭祀。1889 年，在《日新报》记录，本坡总领事罗叔羹方伯亦命驾而至，洽询众人的意见改革废除祭祀文昌魁星的习俗，改祭祀孔诞。这一举动见证了两件重要的事情，第一：清代官员在民间的影响力和带动力。虽然在海外，新加坡也继承了书院改革改制的精神。第二："习俗"虽在 40 年的累积下，亦可以被改变。这一记载，肯定了当时的社会风气改革，在教育熏陶下改变了民风。这一点的南洋人间文化改变，不得不让人侧目。这一转变确实体现了碑文所记：人人知周孔之道，使荒陬遐域，化为礼仪之邦。

2. 人才培养

萃英书院碑上云："……于是，陈君巨川存兴贤劝学之盛心，捐金买地愿充为党序之基，欲以造就诸俊秀，无论贫富家子弟咸使之入学……"[2] 无论贫富家之子弟，各族不分身份地位都可以入学，这也体现了书院的学习精神。这正是受佛教禅林讲学的影响，体现了书院最核心的精神。海外书院不但续承，而且发挥了不分族群的大爱精神。这确实让人欣喜万分。

很有意思的是，萃英书院的英译名为：Chui Eng Free School。该书院原为义学，学生多为贫寒子弟，不收学杂费，故其所在地厦门街又称"义学口"。直到第二次世界大战后，人们生活水平提高，书院才向学生收每月 3 元的学杂费以维持开销。

1854－1912 年，书院主要讲授《三字经》《千字文》《幼学琼林》、四书五经、书法、珠算、尺牍等。在 1889 年新闻里，记录了：考试的学童大约七十人，以诗歌对联、书信、追问文章句子的形式考试。[3] 得知考试的儿童相较去年有很大的进步。从这里可以看出培养人才起效。另，每年年末将会集合各位学童备考，以辛勤程度，逐一分批。诸位董事、院长等将会命令小童列坐好，表演各自的本领。黄遵宪（1848~1905）总领事观察后逐一给予成绩，成绩分作三等。书信通顺，能自完其说的共有 8 人，列为一等奖。对联工整，能了解书中道理者，一共有 17

---

1 《书院更章》,《日新报》1899 年 10 月 13 日。
2 陈荆和、陈育崧合编：《新加坡华文碑铭集录》,《萃英书院碑文》第 291-292 页。
3 《萃英集试》,《叻报》第 2151 号，1889 年 1 月 17 日。

人，列为二等奖。大略了解书中道理者，一共 15 人，列为三等。[1] 由此，我们可得知书院课程审核有一定的规划。

值得关注的是，当代的新加坡社会华裔养而不教，当书院设立时，只有闽南人，粤人不知道，因此其儿童行为不好，竟然组织私会党，号称为山顶公司者。这些都是其父母兄长没教好所导致的。[2] 当时有三位老师勤力授课，因此栽培了很多的学生。当时的新加坡社会，由于家教所致，孩童的行为出现了偏差。这所海外书院，在当时确实起了积极净化社会的作用。社会风气也逐渐变得更好。书院为海外社会民风所带来的转变，是应该被高度赞许的。

3. 牌匾的故事

萃英书院牌匾是萃集人才、广罗精英之意，故命名为"萃英"。随着书院的停办和拆除，而原址，现在已改为主题餐厅。其牌匾也经历了一段故事。如今，牌匾辗转到了福建厦门的"华侨博物馆"。

2005 年，新加坡收藏家陈华来和这牌匾有一段故事。当时有一块 1854 年"萃英书院"的牌匾，为了买它也费了一番周折。他得悉原主人要拿到英国拍卖，他上门求购，对方不肯，陈来华反复说明自己不是为了赚钱，而是为了办展览保存历史文化，终于打动了店主，他太太拿出 3000 新元的储蓄买下它。最后"萃英书院"匾牌几经辗转之后，捐赠给了厦门华侨博物院，那次捐给厦门的藏品也是一集装箱。[3] 似乎命运注定，牌匾辗转"回到"了书院的发源地——中国。

五、书院发展的后期概况

在左秉隆莅新之前，新加坡只有一所传统学塾——萃英书院。后来在清政府鼓励下，许多的兴学运动被展开，许多书室被建立起来。[4] 在 1889 年他停止了祭拜魁星，并开始祭孔。这对净化社会，减少功利主义、贪媚心理等起了非常重要

---

1 《萃英书院课童录》，《星报》第 588 号，1892 年 1 月 16 日。
2 《开塾日期》，《叻报》第 2310 号，1891 年 2 月 2 日。
3 新加坡华人收藏家陈来华：为了侨史遗存永生不灭，2007 年 6 月 12 日。
　http://www.chinaqw.com/zgqj/qxsz/200706/12/75934.shtml?fbclid=IwAR2fin5MdULuFPKfWg0xo
　D3bubygwLE5gW9tXRwEDj9xWxhN5RBWzTpdh_I.
4 左秉隆（1850 — 1924）为清朝新加坡领事，大力兴学，在新加坡领事创立的一个文社，目的是培养文风和联络人士。1881-1891 年出任清朝领事职，广州人，授四品衔。15 岁入广州同文馆学习英语及各种西学课程，18 岁进京在总理各国事务衙门当翻译官。左氏对传统文化有着非常强烈的感情与负担。在这十年，他颇受当地华侨的爱戴。《叻报》有云："左子与太守理事新洲，政绩循声，莫能枚举"。

的作用。他大力提倡传统文化，振兴学术风气之后，士人才逐渐得以抬头。

萃英书院于 1954 年宣告停办，并入新加坡福建会馆。但由于各种法律程序，直到 1960 年萃英书院才把校产正式移交给福建会馆。

而 1913 年扩建后的崇文阁，底层有两间教室，一间为低年级与幼稚园的唱游室，另一间为普通教室，二楼有三间教室。1915 年福建会馆主办的崇福女校即在崇文阁上课，有女生 30 多名，用闽南方言教学。崇文阁与天福宫毗邻，每逢测试或考试之前，女生们都到天福宫去向天后娘娘跪拜，希望她保佑自己考试过关。后来崇福改为男女合校。20 世纪 70 年代崇福撤离崇文阁后，该建筑物闲置多年。

1989 年 4 月，新加坡福建会馆宣布修复崇文阁，辟为中国茶馆及艺术画廊，并在崇文阁塔楼底层竖立一尊孔子塑像，以保存其书院气息，吸引游客观光。现崇文阁成为一间传统餐馆，与传统文化传承延续的精神。新加坡后来建立的书院有：养正书院（1905）；另外，莱佛士书院 Raffles Institute（现新加坡书院 Singapore Institute）则是英国总督斯坦佛来佛士 1823 年建立。

六、总结

海外书院能有一定的发展和传承，主要是基于侨民对原乡的缅怀情结，善举的响应。无独有偶，以上两所建筑皆由陈金声（字巨川）所建立。他为福建永春人，也可谓是乡谊所致。祭祀朱子（朱熹）也为福建闽南的代表。中国南来商人（如：陈金声等人）及本地培养的文人外，也有一些是从商人转化为士人，或是既商亦士的人物。像"丰裕"号东主及"振裕"号股东之一的李清辉。在 19 世纪 60 年代是个非常活跃的商人，但自参与萃英书院的工作之后，就热心地推动传统教育，除了屡次捐助经费给书院外，还曾多次亲任考试考官，到院考核生徒，试以诗联、书札或诘以章句，评定等差。

另，综合这两所建筑物都符合了古人的选址特色。靠主山，面水。注重外部自然风景环境，同时也讲究风水感应。而南来南洋的移民对于海，也具有特殊情怀。建立书院也尽显侨民对原乡缅怀的一种举动。

梁元生将新加坡儒学思想教育分成三种模式，其中以萃英书院为代表的 19 世纪续承模式："是一种习惯性，而不是自觉的选择"。学者邓洪波曾这么写着，华侨书院的首要任务是传播其母体文化，发扬中华数千年文明于海外，使侨民获得一种心灵深处的抚慰。[1]

国学大师季羡林在 1988 年《论书院》中曾经提到，书院可以宣扬中国文化于海外，书院可以保存历史。[2] 对此，海外书院如这两所书院为例，已确确实实做到以上两点。这种文化传承的精神，已经从方方面面看出。

书院的流变基于其务实性、平民化而展开，后因政治经济等因素而改革或消亡。虽在不同的国度，书院的流变具有相似之处。书院的生命力在于它的民间性。流变过程的传承中具有很深的宗教信仰渊源。不论是受民间信仰，还是道教、儒教、佛教的影响，均形成了它的独特性和区域性。书院形态的多样性产生不同文化。曾经有记录，西方教会传教士（马典）在书院以马来语授课，每天 4 个钟头[3]，这是 19 世纪上半叶海外中文教育的独特之处。由于当时社会结构使然，懂地方语言——马来语很是一种方便。海外书院在传承中国的文化之外，已经融合了地域的需求，显示了教育广纳百川的特点，因而更显地域色彩。

然而，严格意义上书院的大小传统、风格和建筑格局、宗教家祠、公共管理、教学活动、开讲仪式、藏书状况等值得再关注。回到书院最初的本意，应是皇家藏书的地方，对书院海外的典籍这一块，可以在今后继续深入研究和探讨。

---

1 邓洪波：《中国书院史》，武汉大学出版社 2012 年版，第 595 页。
2 季羡林：《论书院》，1988 年 8 月 11 日。
3 Medhurst to Rev.Orn,Secretary of LMS.Dated Batavia 22July 1828[LMS].

Inheritance of and Changes in Overseas Academies from the Perspective of Cultural Output— Taking Academies in Singapore as an Example

Ng Siaw Hung/Malaysia

Peking University Foreign Department PhD Student

Introduction

In the article "The Influence of Buddhism on Ancient Academies in China", He Mingdong explored the prosperity, architectural pattern, organizational form, academic rules and teaching activities of ancient colleges. This article also inspired the initial motivation of the author to study the phenomenon of "academy". In his master's thesis "From the Traditional Academy to the New School: Educational Transformation in the Late Qing Dynasty and the Early Period of the Republic of China", Li Chengfeng of Ludong University explained the transformation of academies in the late Qing Dynasty. At that time, the revolution in education took place through "abandoning traditional academies and running new schools" and the abolition of the imperial examination system. The thesis also presented an overview of academies run by churches and made up for the part of history of the academy that has attracted little attention. In his doctoral thesis "The Studies of Academies in the English World"[1], Chen Xian investigated academies in the English world and his study was very inspirational. This topic made it very clear how foreign countries accepted the ancient academy system. Through "the place to study the philosophy of life" in the letter of Matteo Ricci, the traditional *Shuyuan* academy of China was introduced into the Western perspective. The earliest research on traditional academies began in China in the 1920s. This "reverse research" could help us better understand academic exchanges at home and abroad, especially the contemporary educational, religious and institutional inheritance. It also opened up the perspective of academy research. The author took the studies on academies in the English world by different sinologists abroad as examples, such as the American sinologists Linda Walton and Steven Miles, the German sinologist Heinrich Busch, etc. Steven Miles focused on the study of local academies of classical learning in Guangzhou. In his opinion, the study of the "local identity" had already become an important issue for Western scholars. Moreover, Professor Deng Hongbo from Yuelu Academy of Hunan University was called the "Deng Academy" in the academic circle. His books on the history and culture of traditional academies became the reference books needed in order to enter into and understand the traditional *Shuyuan* academy of China. Related studies of various scholars were already cross disciplinary and covered education, history, humanities and Confucianism. These studies might be important channels for the study of overseas academies.

In contrast, there were very few local historical materials on the study of the academy. In 1995, in Liang Yuansheng's book *Voyage of Confucius to the Southern Island*, early Confucian scholars introduced private schools, free schools and academies that taught Confucianism. The author recorded the earliest inscriptions of the Chong Wen Ge and Chui Eng Free School in Singapore, which were the most precious materials for studying local academies. Moreover, Chng Khin Yong also recorded Chinese schools in Singapore from 1819 to 1944 in the education part of his *Notes on Historical Materials for the Chinese in Singapore and Malacca* in

---

1   Chen Xian, *The Studies of Academies in the English World*, Doctoral Thesis of Hunan University, 2016.

2007. The book contained first-hand information on the establishment of church academies, which can be said to be very precious historical data. To our surprise, from the perspective of Professor Chng, many previous studies were disrupted. Later, Singaporean literature and history researchers Lin Zhiqiang and Ke Mulin, in the articles "Early Bilingual Education in Singapore" and "The Revisiting of Chong Wen Ge", explained contemporary *Shushu* schools from the early perspective of Singapore, further explored early bilingual education in Singapore and provided us with an overview of early Chinese education.[1] The Chinese scholar[2] Li Yong, in his article, looked at Chong Wen Ge from the custom of "respecting the written paper and treating it with care".

1. About the *Shuyuan* Academy

Since ancient times, teaching has existed in different forms, such as free schools (for rural residents), private schools and academies. The academy was an advanced form of the private school in teaching a group of students and doing academic research. Most of the private schools, community schools and free schools only provided enlightenment education, but academies had the functions of gathering students for lectures, academic research, the collection and publishing of books and rituals of worship. A big change in ancient Chinese education was the developmental pattern of official schools, private schools and academies in parallel, and all of them were equally important. Until the end of the Qing Dynasty, there were disputes among them, but more mutual penetration and integration. They facilitated the development and prosperity of ancient Chinese culture and education.

2. Several Concepts for Academies in Singapore

The academy going abroad was a continuation of the academy spirit and an extension of culture. The concept of "academy" in Singapore and Malaysia was

---

1 Lin Zhiqiang, "Early Bilingual Education in Singapore" ; Ke Mulin, "Revisiting of Chong Wen Ge"
2 Li Yong, "Overseas Inheritance and Changes in the Custom of 'Respecting the Written Paper and Treating It with Care' : Taking Chong Wen Ge in Singapore as an Example" , *Studies in World Religions*, 2013(2).

an inheritance from the period of Emperor Guangxu and belonged to a "new type" of academy. The concept of "new" mainly referred to Western studies that had never been taught before. At that time, there were already academies jointly run by Chinese and foreigners, or those run solely by foreigners, such as more than a hundred academies run by churches. Overseas academies in Singapore and Malaysia could be roughly divided into three different types: those going abroad from China, the new type of academies run by the English Church, and those teaching in English. This article will take the two academies "going out" from China and based on Confucianism and Taoism as examples.

An interesting phenomenon in Singapore and Malaysia was that in the 1800s, missionaries of the London Missionary Society borrowed the term *Xuetang* used in the Qing Dynasty of China as the name of schools. *Shuyuan* and *Xuexiao* were called "College" and "School", respectively. Missionaries and teachers differed in their academic proficiency. Due to different translations, it was impossible to literally distinguish between the nature and founders of academies. Later in the British colonial era, *Shuyuan* was also translated as "Institution" and "Free School". (Refer to the appendix.) Early overseas academies showed "confusion" in their names. They could be understood only by reading the history of their establishment.

In 2007, Professor Chng Khin Yong's research cited the materials of the London Missionary Society in the Library of the School of Oriental and African Studies at the University of London, and those of the American Board of Commissioners for Foreign Missions in the Houghton Library of Harvard University.[1] This increased number of new forces for the traditional academy and Chng Khin Yong questioned previous studies. This was a new milestone in the study of local academies.

Singaporean academy materials were often attached to early education and to private schools in Nanyang, so it seemed fragmented. Churches, based on the missionary work, made detailed records of the observations and hearings

---

1   Chng Khin Yong, "Chinese Schools in Singapore from 1819 to 1944" , *Notes on Historical Materials for the Chinese in Singapore and Malacca*, pp.182-184.

of contemporary churches in Nanyang and thus left precious material to later generations. The material about Singapore preserved by churches was complete and comprehensive.

Compared to local Chinese, Chinese communities or the government, the Methodist Missionaries had long established a so-called dialect school in Singapore. There were also private schools founded by those from Fujian Province. They laid a good foundation for the establishment of academies later.

3. The First Academy in Singapore: An Analysis of the Attributes of Chong Wen Ge

Tan Yeok Seong, a local historian, published an article "The Discovery of the First Chinese School in Singapore" in the supplement "Siang Yu" of the newspaper *Nanyang Siang Pau* on January 11, 1972. In his opinion, Chong Wen Ge, which was begun in 1849 and completed in 1852, was the first Chinese school and academy in Singapore. Twenty-nine years later, Chng Khin Yong published "Study on Chong Wen Ge in Singapore Not Being a School" in 2001 in the paper collection *NTU Researchers* and analyzed the fact that Chong Wen Ge was not an academy from an academic perspective.

3.1 Architectural Appearance and Space

According to Professor Chng Khin Yong, Chong Wen Ge was a small tower with very small spaces in the second and third floors, and the iron stairs from the downstairs to the second and third floors were extremely steep. Obviously, it was not designed for school children.[1] Based on the inscriptions in the "Stone Tablet in Memory of the Founding of the Chong Wen Ge" and the "Stone Tablet in Memory of the Rebuilding of the Chong Wen Ge", he put forward some thought-provoking arguments that: the inscription writer knew the difference between "*Ge*" (pavilion) and "*Shuyuan*" (academy). In his opinion, Chong Wen Ge, as a school, did not use

---

1   Chng Khin Yong, "Chinese Schools in Singapore from 1819 to 1944" , *Notes on Historical Materials for the Chinese in Singapore and Malacca*, p.221.

Inheritance of and Changes in Overseas Academies
from the Perspective of Cultural Output— Taking Academies in Singapore as an Example

/// 191

the word "*Shuyuan*" but the Taoist building "*Ge*". Literally, the sensitivity of the inscription writer to the text at that time was indeed noteworthy.

The overall architectural appearance of Chong Wen Ge does not look like an academy. It is an octagonal, classical, three-floor pagoda-like building commonly known as the "Eight Diagrams Tower" in ancient times. Also, the two stone tablets in Chong Wen Ge were put up in the Sixth Year of Tongzhi (1867), which was six years later than that of the Chui Eng Free School in the Twelfth Year of Xianfeng (1861), but its founding was only five years later. Founded by the same group of Fujian businessmen, from the perspective of their functions, the two buildings could not be of the same nature.

3.2 The Criteria for the Selection of the Site and External Environmental Features

Fengshui was always an important consideration for the design of the architectural layout of China's ancient buildings. The academy, an architectural form between rituals and use, was a materialized spiritual space. In terms of site selection and layout, Chong Wen Ge also inherited the spirit of the selection of the site for a school. As described on the inscription: "... the site is west of the island ... it backs up to hills and faces rivers, connects a temple on the left and links the mountain on the right, and its academic fortune will be very successful ..."[1] According to ancient people, if the building site was backed by mountains and rivers, everything would go smoothly in the future.

Chong Wen Ge is located on Telok Ayer Street. Telok Ayer means "water bay" in the Malayan language. According to Goh Ngan Hong, the author of *An Anecdotal History of Singapore*, a map drawn by the British engineer James Franklin in 1822 marked "Chinese Town" and "Malay Town" on the south bank of Singapore River, and the latter was closer to Telok Ayer. That might be a settlement of the Malays

---

1 Chen Ching-ho and Tan Yeok Seong (eds.), "Stone Tablet in Memory of the Founding of the Chong Wen Ge", *A Collection of Chinese Inscriptions in Singapore*, p.283.

2018"青年汉学家研修计划" 论文精选集 192 ///

who survived by fishing.[1] It was a coastline in those years and that was consistent with the original inscription. In the "Stone Tablet in Memory of the Rebuilding of the Chong Wen Ge", "... it faces the sea in the front, has the mountain at its back, it is beside many residential houses and is connected with a temple. The terrain is grand, and the mountains and rivers are very beautiful ..."[2] The street was originally situated on the south side of Singapore River and the coastline was only one km away from the street. Later, it moved to four streets from the coastline. Today, there is no chance of directly seeing the coastline here. Also, Ann Siang Hill[3] is not far from Chong Wen Ge. Hence, it can be found that the ancient rules were adhered to for the selection of the site.

3.3 Pray to the Deity *Zi Tong Di Jun*

The inscription recorded: "... the upper floor is consecrated to the deity Zi Tong Di Jun ..."[4] In the "Stone Tablet in Memory of the Rebuilding of the Chong Wen Ge", "... the deity Zi Tong Di Jun was worshipped in the pavilion ..."[5] Zi Tong Di Jun was the deity worshipped by people who participated in the imperial examination after the Song Dynasty, also known as Wen Chang Di Jun, the God of Culture and Literature.

According to our understanding, Chong Wen Ge was consecrated to the deity Zi Tong Di Jun with the tenets of advocating justice, learning and exercising martial arts, and finally becoming sacred. The "Stone Tablet in Memory of the Rebuilding

---

1 Telok Ayer Street, NLB. http://eresources.nlb.gov.sg/infopedia/articles/SIP_656_2004-12-31.html.

2 Chen Ching-ho and Tan Yeok Seong (eds.), "Stone Tablet in Memory of the Rebuilding of the Chong Wen Ge", *A Collection of Chinese Inscriptions in Singapore*, p.291.

3 Pioneers Trail in Ann Siang Hill Park and Telok Ayer Green, NEA.
https://www.nparks.gov.sg/-/media/nparks-real-content/gardens-parks-and-nature/diy-walk/diy-walk-pdf-files/pioneers-trail-ann-siang-hill-park-and-telok-ayer-green.pdf.
https://www.nparks.gov.sg/-/media/nparks-real-content/gardens-parks-and-nature/diy-walk/diywalk-pdf-fles/pioneers-trail-ann-siang-hill-park-and-telok-ayer-green.pdf

4 Chen Ching-ho and Tan Yeok Seong (eds.), "Stone Tablet in Memory of the Founding of the Chong Wen Ge", *A Collection of Chinese Inscriptions in Singapore*, p.283.

5 Chen Ching-ho and Tan Yeok Seong (eds.), "Stone Tablet in Memory of the Rebuilding of the Chong Wen Ge", *A Collection of Chinese Inscriptions in Singapore*, p.291.

of the Chong Wen Ge" emphasized the importance of "learning". Tao originated from the heavens, the entity lay in sacredness, and where there was learning, there was Tao and harmony.

3.4 Ritual of Respecting the Written Paper and Treating It with Care

In 1890, the newspaper *The Star* reported that: "The land of China respects written papers. The Chinese regard all written papers with Chinese characters as sacred and those papers ought to be carefully gathered and disposed of in a proper manner. Therefore, the gentlemen of Fujian origin donated money in 1849 to build Chong Wen Ge on Telok Ayer Street."[1] According to this report, Chong Wen Ge was constructed by our forefathers to advocate respect for the written paper.

There was an important paragraph in the "Stone Tablet in Memory of the Founding of the Chong Wen Ge" in the Sixth Year of Tongzhi (1867) to explain its function. The inscription says: "… the upper floor is consecrated to the deity Zi Tong Di Jun, and the ground floor is used for teaching or lecturing. There is a small pagoda beside the pavilion used for the burning of papers containing Chinese characters. In the spring, literati will wear their festival clothes and the ashes of the burnt papers will be disposed of in the sea. Hence, the pavilion has the name 'Chong Wen Ge' …" According to the inscription, the upper floor was consecrated to the deity Zi Tong Di Jun, and the ground floor was used for teaching. The small pagoda on the side was used for the burning of papers containing Chinese characters. On the 3rd day of the 2nd Lunar month every year, literati and officials participated in the consecration ceremony. On the birthday of Wen Chang Di Jun, celebrities gathered to perform the ritual to show respect for written papers with special significance. Based on the tradition of respecting written papers and love of Chinese characters and culture, a small pagoda was built beside the pavilion, similar to the pavilion and used for respecting written papers or as a tower of writings, for the burning of paper in a furnace. After the ritual, the ashes of the burnt papers would be disposed of in the sea.

---

1 *The Star*, July 7, 1890.

The "Stone Tablet in Memory of the Rebuilding of the Chong Wen Ge" also recorded: "... the ashes of the burnt papers are collected and disposed of with respect …" Discarded papers were collected and burnt until they became ashes. In the Qing Dynasty of China, social organizations hired people to pick up the waste paper on streets and lanes, and called them "paper pickup men". Papers collected for the ritual were washed by water, dried and put in the furnace for burning. The ashes were shoveled with a wooden spade from pottery urns, which were then put into the river or sea for submerging slowly. This was also known as "sending traces of saints". The newspaper *Lat Pau* on June 19, 1889 even reported that: "There is an organization in Singapore specially established to respect written papers. It hires several workers to pick up written papers every day …" In the newspaper *The Star* on March 3, 1892: "The gentlemen from Fujian set up an organization for respecting paper to pick up written papers, wash them and burn them." These reports also proved the form and function of the Paper Respecting Society of Chong Wen Ge and its inheritance of Chinese culture.

The Star also reported: "People from all walks of life pick up written papers and broken pieces of documents and burn them in the furnace of the pavilion. The ashes of burnt papers will be disposed of in the sea on the 3rd day of the 2nd Lunar month every year after having been gathered by teachers and students of private schools and shop owners of fame. Drums and music play and colorful flags fly during the ritual. After decades' of influence, everyone in Nanyang, even witches, knows to cherish written papers but they do not know the reason for doing this."[1] Those participating in the cultural ceremony of respecting papers were not ordinary students, but celebritics, who sent the ashes of burned papers into the sea and rivers with the sound of drums and music. In a few decades, this produced an imperceptible influence and all parts of Nanyang belonging to the Malay territory knew that written papers had to be cherished, but even they did not know the reason. According to these news reports, Professor Li Yong further confirmed the functions

---

1 *The Star*, July 7, 1890.

of Chong Wen Ge and the custom of respecting written papers in those years.[1] The "young and old" appearing in the inscription were most likely to be those listening to the teaching regarding the respect for written papers, instead of students. The newspaper reports also made the "young and old" and the time of disposing of ashes clear. This was not a school function, but a trace of the custom of respecting written papers. Professor Chng Khin Yong presumed this as the reason why in 1881, about thirty years later, it became the site for an office of the Dissemination of Imperial Decrees under the Le Shan Society.[2] The signboard of "Dissemination of Imperial Decrees under the Le Shan Society" hanging at the entrance of Chong Wen Ge indicated that the organization was established in Chong Wen Ge. It was also mentioned there that the Thian Hock Keng Temple next to Chong Wen Ge was used for preaching. Generally, the preaching site provided special "civic and moral education" during the Qing Dynasty. It mainly referred to the education of ordinary people. If the architectural style was not considered, Chong Wen Ge was like a *Xuegong* (academic palace), which was designed as an obvious combination of temple and school with the function of preaching. Chinese celebrities in Singapore gathered there for ceremonies and this coincided with some functions of ancient *Xuegong*.

After Chong Wen Ge was converted into the Le Shan Society, there were two records in the *Financial Report of the Le Shan Society in 1898 and 1899* and the *Financial Report of the Le Shan Society in 1901*[3]: First, 175 yuan were paid as the salaries of workers collecting and burning papers in 25 months; second, 84 yuan were paid as the salaries of workers collecting and burning papers in one year. Based on these records, it was clear that the tradition of respecting written papers had been maintained for a long period in the Chinese community in Singapore.

---

1   Li Yong, "Overseas Inheritance and Changes in the Custom of 'Respecting Written Paper and Treating It with Care' : Taking Chong Wen Ge in Singapore as an Example" .

2   Chng Khin Yong, "Chinese Schools in Singapore from 1819 to 1944" , *Notes on Historical Materials for the Chinese in Singapore and Malacca*, p.228.

3   Liang Yuansheng, *Voyage of Confucius to the Southern Island: Confucianism and Historical Materials of Chinese Community in Singapore*, pp.68, 70.

The culture of respecting written papers originated from the legend of "Cangjie making the characters", and the respect for the characters was transformed into folk beliefs and social customs. During the Song Dynasty, in order to cater to the imperial examination and social psychology, it became a custom to combine the idea of respecting written papers with the worship of Wen Chang Di Jun. Immigrants to Southeast Asian countries inherited this Chinese tradition and it gradually became a folk custom or even a superstition[1] that was connected with good or bad fortune. From the perspective of Confucianism, Liang Yuansheng explained that respecting written papers aimed to disseminate Confucianism. Li Yong looked at the custom from a folkloric perspective with the meaning of misfortune or good fortune. This revealed the intersection and overlapping of folk customs and Confucianism. In the evolution of traditional customs, when things reached an extreme, they could only move in the opposite direction. This point is worthy of attention.

3.5 Cultural Style: Turning Bad Habits into Learning and the Vulgar into the Elegant

In the inscription: "... The emperor advocates Confucianism and ethics, investigates ancient events, attaches importance to culture and accepts enlightenment. Even across mountains and seas, in different territories, every family reads books and learns knowledge ..."[2] This meant that the cultural system was inherited and this was a form of cultural "going out" and inheritance.

In the inscription: "... The young and old read the books of Confucius and Mencius and probe into the Study of Principle. They cultivate good virtues and turn bad habits into learning and the vulgar into the elegant. The building of the pavilion is a great benefit to the people of the world! ..."[3] This demonstrated that

---

1   Sun Ronglai, "The Custom of Respecting Written Paper and Treating It with Care and Its Cultural Significance" , *Folklore Studies*, 2006(2).
2   Chen Ching-ho and Tan Yeok Seong (eds.), "Stone Tablet in Memory of the Founding of the Chong Wen Ge" , *A Collection of Chinese Inscriptions in Singapore*, p.283.
3   Chen Ching-ho and Tan Yeok Seong (eds.), "Stone Tablet in Memory of the Founding of the Chong Wen Ge" , *A Collection of Chinese Inscriptions in Singapore*, p.283.

immigrants valued culture and vigorously developed education, and it played the role of social purification and enlightenment. It also showed that in addition to livelihood, ancestors who had immigrated to the south also began to attach importance to places of worship with educational functions. Culture and education were important for them.

In the inscription, one sentence was difficult to be interpreted well: "... The young and old read the books of Confucius and Mencius and probe into the Study of Principle ..." Here, to read the books of Confucius and Mencius and probe into the Study of Principle, that is to say, the ideas of Cheng Hao of the North Song Dynasty and Zhu Xi of the South Song Dynasty. This is obviously from Song-Ming Neo-Confucianism. Authors and scholars had little focus or dispute over this sentence. It was the evidence of intersection between old and new Confucianism. The cultural integration was a major feature of overseas Chinese.

In "The Spread of Confucianism within Institutionalization in Singapore", Lin Weiyi saw Chong Wen Ge as the first traceable educational institution.[1] In his article, Chong Wen Ge did not place much emphasis on Confucian and Taoist schools. In the inscription, from the layout of the academy, a *Shuyuan* academy in the strict sense should have three basic functions of collecting books, giving lectures and praying. This was obviously impossible for private schools *Xueshu*. If ignoring the dispute over the nature of the academy, Chong Wen Ge indeed inherited the tradition of ancient *Shuyuan* academies in culture.

Ancient academies were going international and the forms of education mentioned above: private schools, academies and academic palaces, were interrelated and relatively independent. Chong Wen Ge had an enormous influence on the subsequent Chinese education. Other academies and colleges founded by various other Chinese organizations emerged one after another and opened up a new era in the magnificent history of local Chinese education. As pointed out by the

---

1   Lin Weiyi, "The Spread of Confucianism within Institutionalization in Singapore" , *Oriental Forum*, 2005(6).

"Stone Tablet in Memory of the Rebuilding of the Chong Wen Ge", "It is no doubt that culture becomes prosperous and talents emerge generation after generation."[1]

The original site of Chong Wen Ge was the left hall of the Thian Hock Keng Temple on Telok Ayer Street. The construction cost of Chong Wen Ge was as high as 9,100 yuan, which was equal to one third of that of the magnificent Thian Hock Keng Temple, indicating that donors attached great importance to it. At that time, there were donations from many firms and ship owners, and this showed the extensive support from the population speaking dialect and from people from all walks of life.[2] This proved the truth in two points. First, the worship of Wen Chang, the custom of respecting written papers and scholars' pursuit of learning and fame were in a relationship of "symbiosis" and "coexistence" here. Second, Chong Wen Ge was not entirely academy-like, but it marked the emphasis that the Chinese community put on culture and education. It was a starting point of the awakening of the cultural consciousness of our forefather immigrants to the south that had a great significance for early Chinese education in Singapore. Their coexistence was the most straightforward and realistic reflection of early overseas Chinese.

4. The Establishment of the Chui Eng Free School

In 1854, the Chui Eng Free School was established. It was located on Amoy Street (a food center in the Far East Square), but unfortunately it only lasted for 100 years and then closed. The stone tablet of the Chui Eng Free School is now preserved in the open-air garden at the site of the Toa Payoh Lorong 2 of the Singapore Federation of Chinese Clan Association.

The Chui Eng Free School was the antique Chinese-style courtyard building. A large courtyard was behind the main entrance, followed by a big hall, with two rooms on both sides used as classrooms, and next the inner hall, bedrooms, the kitchen, patio and back door. Teachers were hired every year to give lectures to the

---

1 Chen Ching-ho and Tan Yeok Seong (eds.), "Stone Tablet in Memory of the Founding of the Chong Wen Ge", *A Collection of Chinese Inscriptions in Singapore*, p.283.
2 Ke Mulin, "The Revisiting of Chong Wen Ge"

left and right of the middle hall and peaches and plums were placed near the door and beside the wall.

The inscription on the stone tablet of the Chui Eng Free School (built in 1861) recorded that: "... Since the opening of Singapore, although it is under the administration of the British, for more than 40 years, no Chinese people did business here. The mountains are beautiful and the products are abundant. People from Fujian Province are born, grow up and populate the area here. If there is no education, we will become ignorant and will have a lack of knowledge. Therefore, Mr. Tan Kim Seng donated money to buy a piece of land and found a school to provide education to children from both rich and poor families. Twelve gentlemen agreed to jointly found the school, with the support of other gentlemen. After selecting a proper day and practicing divination, in an academy, a hall was constructed in the middle to worship the deity Wen Chang Di Jun and Zi Yang Master, and the rooms on the east and west were used for teaching. The academy was completed in 1854 and named Chui Eng, which means 'to attract and educate talents' ..."[1] Although Singapore was a British colony at that time, people from Fujian Province living there had to acquire knowledge. Mr. Tan Kim Seng donated land to build a school and educate talents. According to a news report in that year, "There are a lot of Chinese ... but only Fujian people found schools ... The free school of the Fujian people is called Chui Eng."[2] This report clearly showed that before the Chui Eng Free School, for either Fujian or other Chinese dialect groups, there was no such kind of school.

It was noteworthy that an "academic palace" appeared in the inscription on the Chui Eng Free School for the first time. "... Today, Mr. Tan Kim Seng was kind-hearted to advocate the building of an academic palace and bought a piece of land for this purpose ..."[3] The meaning of "academic palace" was probably not as

---

1   Chen Ching-ho and Tan Yeok Seong (eds.), "Stone Tablet of Chui Eng Free School" , *A Collection of Chinese Inscriptions in Singapore*, pp.291-292.

2   *Lat Pau*, February 25, 1891.

3   Chen Ching-ho and Tan Yeok Seong (eds.), "Stone Tablet of Chui Eng Free School" , *A Collection of Chinese Inscriptions in Singapore*, pp.291-292.

political as in China. It should be only a school. But why didn't the author call it an academy directly? This needed further research.

4.1 The Culture of Worshipping: Everyone Knows Zhou-Kong and Turns the Remote Land into a State of Courtesy

In the inscription of the Chui Eng Free School, it is noteworthy that: In addition to the deity Wen Chang Di Jun, the Chui Eng Free School also worshipped Zi Yang Master, namely Zhu Xi. This was an act of advocating the traditional and representative figure of an academic school. It was very common to worship Zhu Xi in Chinese academies to commemorate him and revere his thoughts. This was also reflected in the spiritual and cultural heritage of overseas academies. Wen Chang Jun was the deity Zi Tong Di Jun in Taoism.

Further, the inscription reads: "… Everyone knows Zhou-Kong and turns the remote land into a state of courtesy."[1] "Zhou-Kong" was the combination of Zhou Gong and Confucius and became another name for Confucian education after the Tang Dynasty. At the Chui Eng Free School, the culture of worshipping ancient teachers was continued. The worshipping of the academy had obviously individualized characteristics. The school also worshipped Kui Xing. In Taoist beliefs, Kui Xing was considered to be the god of culture and literature and anyone who took an examination had to worship him. According to records, the Qing Dynasty was the period when the largest number of deities was worshipped in the history of Chinese academies. Obviously, this practice was also inherited by overseas academies.

However, this custom changed 40 years later.

On the Seventh Day of the 7th Lunar month every year, teachers and students in the academy burned incense to worship Wen Chang and Kui Xing. During the reign of Emperor Guangxu, this day was changed to the Twenty-Seventh Day of

---

1 Chen Ching-ho and Tan Yeok Seong (eds.), "Stone Tablet of Chui Eng Free School" , *A Collection of Chinese Inscriptions in Singapore*, pp.291-292.

the 8th Lunar month to celebrate the birthday of Confucius. "One innovation is welcomed. In the past, on the Seventh Day of the 7th Lunar month, students in the academy worshipped Wen Chang and Kui Xing without knowing that this was wrong. From the next year on, it was to be changed to the Twenty-Seventh Day of the 8th Lunar month to celebrate the birthday of Confucius. This year's worship has been canceled. Everyone welcomes this and sets it as a rule. Forty years have passed since the establishment of the Chui Eng Free School. Today, the old rule has changed; it shows the wisdom of our gentlemen."[1]

Wen Chang Di Jun was the god of culture and literature who could determine the official ranking and fame of literati. Those who desired to become an official would not neglect worshipping him. Kui Xing was the god who determined the quality of articles. Driven by the desire to become official and pursue fame, such worshipping was particularly important. This was nothing more than psychology of praise. In 1889, a news release of *Jit Shin Pau* reported that "The Consul Luo Shugeng also came to consult with everyone for reforming and abolishing the custom of worshipping Wen Chang and Kui Xing and change to celebrating the birthday of Confucius." This behavior witnessed two important things. First, the influence of officials of the Qing Dynasty among the people. Despite being overseas, Singapore also carried forward the spirit of academy reform. Second, the "custom" lasting 40 years could be changed. This report confirmed the reform of society and changed the folk custom under the influence of education. This change in the culture of the Nanyang people was rarely great. They reflected what was recorded in the inscription: "Everyone knows Zhou-Kong and turns the remote land into a state of courtesy."

4.2 Talent Development

The inscription of the Chui Eng Free School reads, "... Therefore, Mr. Tan Kim Seng donated to buy a piece of land and found a school to provide education

---

1 *Jit Shin Pau*, news "A Change of Academy", October 13, 1899.

to children from both rich and poor families."[1] Children from both rich and poor families, regardless of ethnic groups, status and ranking, could learn in the school. This reflected the educational spirit of the academy under the influence of the Zen school of Buddhism and embodied the core spirit of the academy. Overseas academies not only inherited but also showed the spirit of great love regardless of ethnic groups. This was a really exciting phenomenon.

Interestingly, the English name of the academy was: Chui Eng Free School. It was originally a free school and most of its students were poor children. No tuition and fees were charged. So, Amoy Street where it was located was also known as "Free School Street". It was not until the living standards improved after the Second World War that the academy charged students 3 yuan for tuition fees per month for daily expenses.

From 1854 to 1912, the academy mainly taught the "Three-character Classic", "Thousand-character Classic", "The Children's Knowledge Treasury", the Four Books and Five Classics, calligraphy, abacus and writing. In a news report of 1889, "there are about seventy school children taking the examination in the form of poems, couplets, writing and questions".[2] Children made great progress during the year. This revealed the effectiveness of talent development. At the end of each year, students would be assembled to prepare for the exams and they would be divided into different groups according to the degree of diligence. The directors and deans would order the children to sit down and perform their respective skills. The Consul General Huang Zunxian (1848-1905) observed and gave them scores. The results had three levels. Eight students who could write well were given the first level. Seventeen students that could understand what was taught in the books were at the second level. Fifteen students who could approximately understand what was taught in the books were at the third level.[3] Hence, course assessment of the academy was

---

1   Chen Ching-ho and Tan Yeok Seong (eds.), "Stone Tablet of the Chui Eng Free School" , *A Collection of Chinese Inscriptions in Singapore*, pp.291-292.
2   *Lat Pau*, news "Chui Eng Examination" , No.2151, January 17, 1889.
3   *The Star*, News: "Records of Students at the Chui Eng Free School" , No. 588, January 16, 1892.

Inheritance of and Changes in Overseas Academies
from the Perspective of Cultural Output— Taking Academies in Singapore as an Example

/// 203

well planned.

It was noteworthy that Singaporean Chinese raised but did not teach their children. When the academy was established, only Fujian and Cantonese attended, so the children were ill-behaved and organized a private party called the Peak Company. The reason was that their parents and brothers did not teach them well.[1] At that time, three teachers taught diligently and made many good students cultured. In Singapore then, children's behavior deviated due to lack of family education. This overseas academy did play an active role in purifying society. The social ethos was gradually getting better. The changes that academies brought to the customs of overseas communities should be highly commended.

4.3 A Tale of Plaque

The plaque of the Chui Eng Free School meant a collection of talents and elites, so it was named "Chui Eng". With the closure and demolition of the academy, the original site has now been changed to a theme restaurant. There is also a story on its plaque. Today, the plaque has been transferred to the "Overseas Chinese Museum" in Xiamen, Fujian.

In 2005, Singapore collector Tan Lai Hua had a story about this plaque. He encountered difficulty in buying the plaque of the "Chui Eng Free School" in 1854. Learning that the owner prepared to auction it in the UK, he went to buy it. However, the owner refused. Tan Lai Hua repeatedly emphasized that he was not trying to make money, but to hold an exhibition and preserve history and culture. Finally, the owner was touched. His wife took out 3,000 Singaporean dollars to buy it. In the end, the plaque of the "Chui Eng Free School" was donated to the Xiamen Overseas Chinese Museum with a container of other collections.[2] It seemed to be destined that the plaque would get "back" to the birthplace of the academy - China.

---

1 *Lat Pau*, News: "School Opening Day", No. 2310, February 2, 1891.
2 Singaporean Chinese Collector TAN Lai Huat: For the Memory of the History of Overseas Chinese

5. Later Development of Academies

Prior to the official appointment of Tso Ping Lung to Singapore, there was only one traditional school, the Chui Eng Free School. Later, with the encouragement of the Qing government, other schools were founded.[1] In 1889 he stopped worshipping Kui Xing and turned to Confucius. This played a very important role in purifying society and reducing utilitarianism and the psychology of praise. After he vigorously advocated the traditional culture and revitalized the academic atmosphere, scholars were gradually cultivated.

The Chui Eng Free School was closed in 1954 and merged into the Singapore Hokkien Huay Kuan. However, due to various legal formalities, the Chui Eng Free School did not officially transfer the school property to the Singapore Hokkien Huay Kuan until 1960.

Chong Wen Ge after expansion in 1913 had two classrooms on the ground floor, one used as the music and play room for junior and kindergarten students, and another as an ordinary classroom, and three classrooms on the second floor. In 1915, the Chong Hock Girls' School run by Hokkien Huay Kuan took classes at Chong Wen Ge. There were more than 30 girls to teach in the Southern Fujian dialect. Chong Wen Ge was adjacent to the Thian Hock Keng Temple. Before tests or examinations, girls went to the temple kowtowing to the goddess with the hope that she would bless them and they would pass their examinations. Later, Chong Hock was changed to a school open for both boys and girls. After Chong Hock moved out of Chong Wen Ge in the 1970s, the building was left idle for many years.

---

1   Tso Ping Lung (1850-1924), the first Consul to Singapore appointed by the Qing imperial court, ran schools and established a literature society in Singapore to cultivate the literary style and communication with literati. From 1881 to 1891 he served as the Consul of the Qing Dynasty at the fourth official rank. He was born in Guangzhou and went to the School of Combined Learning in Guangzhou at the age of 15 to study English and various other Western courses. At the age of 18, he served as a translator in the Ministry of Foreign Affairs in Beijing. Zuo has a very strong feeling and burden for the traditional culture. In this decade, he has been loved by the local Chinese. According to the newspaper *Lat Pau*: "Zuo and the mayor governed Singapore with many great political achievements."

In April 1989, Singapore Hokkien Huay Kuan announced that it would renovate Chong Wen Ge as a Chinese teahouse and art gallery, and a statue of Confucius was put on the ground floor of Chong Wen Ge to preserve its aura of academy and attract tourists. Now Chong Wen Ge is a traditional restaurant with the spirit of inheriting traditional culture. Later the Yeung Ching School was founded in 1905. Moreover, the Raffles Institute (now Singapore Institute) was established in 1823 by the British Governor Stamford Raffles.

Conclusion

The development and inheritance of overseas academies to a certain extent were mainly based on the homesickness of overseas Chinese and their response to charity. Coincidentally, both buildings above were constructed with the donation of Tan Kim Seng. He was born in Yongchun, Fujian Province and the donation was due to his fellowship to his countrymen. The worship of Zhu Xi was also a typical custom in southern Fujian. In addition to businessmen from China, such as Tan Kim Seng, and local literati, there were also some who changed from businessmen to scholars or to become both businessmen and scholars. For example, Li Ging-Hui, the owner of "Fengyu" and one of the shareholders of "Zhenyu". He was a very active businessman in the 1860s, but since participating in the work of the Chui Eng Free School, he enthusiastically promoted traditional education. In addition to donating funds to the academy on many occasions, he also served as an examiner to assess students by poems, couplets or books.

Further, the two buildings also reflected the criteria for the selection of the site of ancient people being backed by mountains and facing waters. They attached importance to the external natural landscape and environment, and cared about *Fengshui*. Immigrants to Nanyang also had special feelings for the sea. The founding of academies also embodied the homesickness of overseas Chinese.

Liang Yuansheng divided Singapore's Confucian education into three models, represented by the 19th-century inheritance model of the Chui Eng Free School. He described it as "a habit, not a conscious choice." Scholar Deng Hongbo once wrote that the primary task of academies of overseas Chinese was to spread its motherland culture and promote the Chinese civilization of thousands of years overseas so that overseas Chinese could feel comfortable deep down in their hearts.[1]

Ji Xianlin, the master of Chinese culture, mentioned in his article "On *Shuyuan*" published in 1988 that the *Shuyuan* academy could promote Chinese culture overseas and preserve history.[2] In this regard, taking the two academies in this study as examples, the two points above were achieved. This spirit of cultural heritage could be observed in all aspects.

The academy education developed due to its pragmatism and popularization and later reformed or died out due to political and economic factors. Although located in different countries, academies shared similarities. The vitality of the academy lay in its folk nature. The process of evolution was deeply rooted in religious beliefs. The influence of folk beliefs, Taoism, Confucianism and Buddhism resulted in the formation of its uniqueness and regionality. The diversity of academies shaped different cultures. It was recorded that Western missionaries sometimes taught in the academy in Malay for four hours per day.[3] This was unique to overseas Chinese education in the first half of the 19th century. Due to the social structure at that time, mastery of the local language, Malay, was very convenient. In addition to inheriting Chinese culture, overseas academies had already integrated the local needs and showed that education was inclusive and native.

However, the size and tradition, style and architectural pattern, religion, public administration, teaching activities, lectures and collection of books of academies in the strict sense deserve further attention. Going back to the original intention of the academy, it should be the place for a royal collection of books. The overseas classics of the academy can be investigated and explored in the future.

1　Deng Hongbo, *The History of China's Shuyuan*, Wuhan University Press, 2012, p.595.
2　Ji Xianlin, *On Shuyuan*, August 11, 1998.
3　Medhurst to Rev.Orn, Secretary of LMS. Dated Batavia 22 July 1828[LMS].

"一带一路"沿线国家汉语教学现状及对策研究
——以乌克兰高校为例

曾子儒【乌克兰】

同济大学国际文化交流学院硕士研究生

一、引言

2013 年中国国家主席习近平提出共建"一带一路"重要倡议,获得了世界各国广泛而积极的回应。其中,"民心相通"建设是各国文化的包容和相互尊重,也是沿线国家合作的重要基础。而语言毋庸置疑是"民心相通"建设的一个重要元素之一。语言作为文化的载体是不同文明交流的重要基础,一旦语言层面的沟通出现了问题,人文交流就会受到干扰。因此,汉语传播应当作为"一带一路"倡议的重要组成部分,支撑国与国之间的人文交流,实现"一带一路"沿线国家"民心相通"建设的目标。

而为了有效开展汉语传播工作,首先需要对沿线国家汉语教学的现状有基本的认识,发现当今汉语教学存在的问题,并采取有针对性的措施弥补各国汉语教学的缺陷。

结合上述实践现状与需求,我们决定开展这一项研究,研究"一带一路"沿线国家汉语教学现状,发现目前发展阶段中存在的问题与不足,并提出相关的对策与建议。我们将"一带一路"东欧地区的重要沿线国家乌克兰作为本研究的对象,对乌克兰汉语教学现状,特别是高校汉语教学进行分析,并针对存在的问题提出对策与建议。

二、乌克兰高校汉语教学现状

目前，乌克兰汉语教学机构主要包括高等学校、孔子学院、外语培训班等。其中，高等学校及孔子学院占的比例最高，学员人数最多。

当今，乌克兰有 10 所设有汉语专业的高校，4 所在基辅市、1 所在哈尔科夫市、2 所在敖德萨市、1 所在利沃夫市、1 所在第聂伯市、1 所在卢甘斯克市（从 2014 年移到斯塔罗比里西柯市）。其中，10 所国立大学以及 1 所私立大学。相关的培养方向主要包括汉语翻译及汉语言文学两种（见表一）。

表一：乌克兰汉语教学机构

高校名称	培养方向	学位	课程
欧莱西·洪洽尔第聂伯国立大学（第聂伯市）	汉语言文学	本科学位	主要包括以下三大板块： 汉语 汉语历史 中国文学
		硕士学位	
伊万·弗兰克沃夫国立大学（利沃夫市）	英语与第二外语（汉语）语文学	本科学位	综合汉语 中国文化 东方文字（汉语） 中国文学历史 翻译理论与实践
米亥罗·德拉郭马诺夫国立师范大学（基辅市）	英语、汉语及外国文学（教育方向）	本科学位	汉语作为第二外语
		硕士学位	
	英语、汉语及外国文学（教育方向）	本科学位	
		硕士学位	
塔拉斯·舍甫琴柯基辅国立大学（基辅市）	东方语言、文学及翻译：汉语与英语	本科学位	综合汉语 汉语理论语音学
		硕士学位	汉语理论语法学 汉语实践语音学 汉语实践语法学 中国语言地理学 基础商务汉语 汉语翻译实践 汉语历史 汉语词汇学 汉语翻译理论与实践

高校名称	培养方向	学位	课程
塔拉斯·舍甫琴柯卢甘斯克国立大学（从2014以来移到斯塔罗比里西柯市）	语言文学（汉语、英语）	本科学位	无信息
		硕士学位	
	语言文学（汉语、英语，中等教育方向）	硕士学位	
基辅国立语言大学（基辅市）	汉语言文学及翻译	本科学位	综合汉语 汉语词汇学 汉语历史 汉语语文学导论 汉语理论语音学 汉语理论语法学 汉语实践语音学 汉语实践语法学 汉语修辞学 双语口译 汉语实践翻译 中国文学历史 中国语言地理学 汉语翻译理论与实践 东方学课程（含东方宗教、乌克兰与东方国家的交流等） 中国国情
		硕士学位	汉语翻译理论与实践 汉语与乌克兰语比较 汉语口语与书面语交际文化 汉语与乌克兰语词汇对比 双语口译技能 汉语经济法律文章翻译
瓦西里·卡拉津哈尔科夫国立大学（哈尔科夫市）	东方语言文学（包括翻译）	本科学位	综合汉语 商务汉语 汉语翻译理论与实践 中国文学 汉语词汇学 汉语与乌克兰语辞修对比 汉语与乌克兰语语法对比 汉语历史
		硕士学位	中国语言地理学

续表

高校名称	培养方向	学位	课程
乌克兰南方师范大学（敖德萨市）	语言文学（汉语、英语、世界文学，中等教育方向）	本科学位	综合汉语 汉语实践语音学 汉语实践语法学 汉语口语与写作实践 中国国情 汉语理论语音学 汉语理论语法学 汉语教学法
	中英乌文翻译	本科学位	综合汉语 汉语翻译理论 汉语翻译实践
波利斯·格林琴克基辅大学（基辅市）	汉语言文学及翻译	本科学位	语言学理论 东方语言教学信息技术 综合汉语 实用汉语课程（语音、语法、汉字、翻译） 汉语理论课程（词汇、语法、修辞法） 东方学（东方国家通史 中国国情 乌克兰与东方国家） 文学（古代东方文学、世界文学史、东方国家文学史） 教学与翻译实习
		硕士学位	实用汉语（交际礼仪与商务交际、文学及科学语体） 东方学（东方文明比较、东方经典文学作品、乌克兰与东方国家文化及语言文学交流、东方语言与文学研究方法论） 汉语交际策略（口语与书面交际文化、汉语口译与笔译技能） 文学理论（20-21世纪世界文学、当代东方文学） 汉语理论（汉语语法、汉语功能修辞学） 实习（翻译、助教、研究等类型）

续表

高校名称	培养方向	学位	课程
国际人文大学（敖德萨市）	汉语言文学	本科学位	无信息

三、存在的问题和不足

通过分析以上的数据，我们发现乌克兰汉语教学存在以下问题：

首先，目前设有汉语专业的乌克兰高校分布不均匀，主要集中在基辅、哈尔科夫、敖德萨、利沃夫及第聂伯五大城市。因此，其他地区的汉语学习者只能通过民营培训班等非高等教育机构学习，无法满足其对系统性汉语教育的需求。

其次，绝大多数高校的培养方向仅包括翻译和语言文学两种，限制了汉语专业毕业生的就业机会。随着科学技术的发展以及全球经济转型，各国劳务市场不断发生变化，对职员技能的要求也越来越高。目前多数招聘单位要求学习者同时具备两个以上领域的专业知识和技能（如：外语及经济学等）。因此，具备单一领域专业技能的汉语毕业生在就业过程中遇到不少困难，难以合乎招聘单位的要求。

另外，有些高校仅开设本科学位的培养项目，暂未开设硕士学位培养项目。因此，其汉语教学体系不完善，本科毕业生只能到其他学校攻读硕士学位或选择其他专业硕士学位项目。

最后，绝大多数高校的汉语课程明显侧重汉语本体教学，中国国情及中国文化相关的课程在其中的比重较小。其中，交际文化方面的课程最为少见，只有两所高校设有汉语交际礼仪、汉语交际文化等与交际文化相关的课程。此外，虽然多数高校的汉语课程包含大量的实用汉语以及汉语翻译技巧等相关的内容，但仍然很少包括行业用语的相关课程（如商务汉语）。根据研究数据，目前仅有一所高校开设商务汉语课程。

四、对策与建议

针对上述的乌克兰汉语教学存在的问题和不足，我们提出以下的对策与参考性建议：

首先，针对现有汉语专业乌克兰高校的分布不均匀的问题，我们建议各所高校利用互联网技术，建立网络汉语课程体系，包括知识点介绍、练习、作业、测试等等。课程内容载体可以包括文字材料、音频、视频，有助于学习者选择适合自己的教学方式。在资源短缺的情况下，可以采取几所高校合作共同开发汉语教学的独立网络教学平台或将网络课程上传到已有的公开在线教学平台进行教学。

其次，针对培养方向单一，专业技能无法满足招聘单位的要求，我们建议在保留独立的汉语专业同时，将汉语课程纳入其他应用型专业（如：国际关系、国际贸易等等）的培养方案，作为辅修课程。以此，给学习者提供更多的选择，让每个人根据自己的个人能力以及职业规划，选择合适的汉语学习策略。

另外，针对某些高校汉语教学体系不完善，暂时无法开设硕士学位项目，我们建议建立与中国高校的合作机制，开设共同培养汉语人才的教育项目。比如，成绩优秀的学生在乌克兰高校获得本科学位后可以被保送到中国高校攻读硕士学位，相关的费用可以由中乌双方共同承担。

最后，针对某些高校汉语课程侧重汉语本体教学，忽略中国文化教学，我们建议在保持语言本体教学高水平的前提下，加强中国文化以及汉语交际方面的教学。其中，可以突出交际文化教学的相关内容，开设汉语社交礼仪、汉语交际策略等相关课程。另外，针对课程体系中缺少行业用语相关内容，我们建议开设商务汉语、法律汉语、医学汉语等课程，提高汉语课程的实际应用价值。

五、结论

综上所述，目前乌克兰高校汉语教学的综合体系比较完善，可以为乌克兰汉语学习者提供系统性的汉语教学方案，培养高水平的汉语专业人才。与此同时，乌克兰高校汉语教学的某些方面仍然有待改善。其中，设有汉语专业高校的分布不均匀；培养方向比较有限；汉语专业毕业生的专业技能无法满足招聘单位的要求；部分高校仅设有本科学位培养项目；汉语课程缺少中国文化，特别是交际文化的内容等问题最为明显。而为了解决这些问题，乌克兰高校需要不断改进汉语教学方法；使得汉语课程具有更高的实际应用价值；与中国高校建立汉语人才的共同培养机制，帮助学习者在汉语学习中达到高级水平；在汉语教学过程中讲解中国文化以及汉语社交礼仪的相关内容，帮助学习者避免在汉语交际中可能出现的歧义和文化冲突。一旦上述的问题得以解决，乌克兰高校汉语教学水平将得到改善，而乌克兰高校培养的汉语人才综合竞争力将进一步提高，为中乌两国友好合作贡献新的力量，让"一带一路"沿线国家"民心相通"的建设达到更高的境界。

The Current State of the Chinese Language Teaching and Methods of its Improvement in Countries along the "Belt and Road"— Taking Ukrainian Universities as an Example

Pavlo Zvenyhorodskyi/Ukraine

The International School of Tongji University Master

1. Introduction

The "Belt and Road" Initiative proposed by Chinese President Xi Jinping in 2013 was extensively and positively responded to by countries all over the world. Among its priorities, a people-to-people bond, which refers to the inclusiveness and mutual respect of different cultures, lays a solid foundation for the cooperation of countries along the "Belt and Road". Language is undoubtedly one of the important elements in creating a people-to-people bond. Language as a carrier of culture is an important basis for exchanges among different civilizations. If there is a language barrier, people-to-people and cultural communication will be disrupted. Therefore, the dissemination of the Chinese language should be an important part of the Belt and Road Initiative that supports cultural exchanges among countries and achieves the goal of a people-to-people bond in the countries along the "Belt and Road".

In order to disseminate the Chinese language effectively, we must first have a basic understanding of the current situation of the teaching of Chinese in the countries along the route, then identify the problems existing in teaching Chinese today, and finally take targeted measures to make up for the deficiencies in their teaching the Chinese language.

Given the above-mentioned practice and needs, we decided to study the situation of the teaching of Chinese in countries along the "Belt and Road", find the problems and deficiencies in the current stage of development, propose a relevant strategy and make suggestions. We take Ukraine, an important country along the "Belt and Road" in Eastern Europe, as an example for this study, analyze the situation of the teaching of Chinese in Ukraine, especially in universities, and put forward a strategy and make suggestions to solve the existing problems.

2. The Situation of the Teaching of Chinese in Ukrainian Universities

Currently, Ukrainian institutions where Chinese is taught mainly include universities, Confucius Institutes and foreign language teaching classes, among which universities and Confucius Institutes account for the highest percentage,with the largest number of students.

Today, Ukraine has ten national universities and one private university that offer Chinese language programs, 4 in Kyiv, 1 in Kharkiv, 2 in Odessa, 1 in Lviv, 1 in Dnipro, and 1 in Lugansk (moved to Staro Biliškoin 2014). Relevant educational directions include Chinese translation as well as Chinese language and literature (see Table 1).

Table 1: Ukrainian Universities Teaching the Chinese Language

Name of University	Educational Program	Degree	Courses
Oles Honchar Dnipro National University (Dnipro)	Chinese Language and Literature	Bachelor's	Three major course modules:
			Chinese Language
		Master's	The History of the Chinese Language
			Chinese Literature
Ivan Franko National University of Lviv (Lviv)	English and Second Foreign Language (Chinese) Literature	Bachelor's	Comprehensive Chinese
			Chinese Culture
			Oriental Hieroglyphics (Chinese)
			The History of Chinese Literature
			Translation Theory and Practice

National Pedagogical Dragomanov University (Kyiv)	English, Chinese and Foreign Literature (Education)	Bachelor	Chinese as a Second Language
		Master's	
	English, Chinese and Foreign Literature (Education)	Bachelor's	
		Master's	
Taras Shevchenko National University of Kyiv (Kyiv)	Oriental Language, Literature and Translation: Chinese and English	Bachelor's	Comprehensive Chinese Theoretical Chinese Phonetics Theoretical Chinese Grammar Practical Chinese Phonetics Practical Chinese Grammar Geography of the Chinese Language
		Master's	Basic Business Chinese Chinese Translation Practice The History of the Chinese Language Chinese Lexicology Chinese Translation Theory and Practice
Taras ShevchenkoNational University of Lugansk (moved to Staro Biliškoin 2014)	Language and Literature (Chinese, English)	Bachelor's	No information available
		Master's	
	Language and Literature (Chinese, English, Secondary Education)	Master's	
Kyiv National Linguistic University (Kyiv)	Chinese Language, Literature and Translation	Bachelor's	Comprehensive Chinese Chinese Lexicology The History of the Chinese Language An Introduction to Chinese Philology Theoretical Chinese Phonetics Theoretical Chinese Grammar Practical Chinese Phonetics Practical Chinese Grammar Chinese Rhetoric Bilingual Interpreting Practical Chinese Translation The History of Chinese Literature Geography of the Chinese Language Chinese Translation Theory and Practice Oriental Studies (Oriental Religions, Ukraine-Oriental Relations, etc.) Country Studies

Kyiv National Linguistic University (Kyiv)	Chinese Language, Literature and Translation	Master's	Chinese Translation Theory and Practice Comparison of Chinese and Ukrainian Communication Culture of Spoken and Written Chinese Comparison of Chinese and Ukrainian Vocabulary Bilingual Interpretation Skills Translation of Chinese Economic and LegalDocuments
V. N. Karazin Kharkiv National University (Kharkiv)	Oriental Language and Literature(Translation Included)	Bachelor's	Comprehensive Chinese Business Chinese Chinese Translation Theory and Practice Chinese Literature Chinese Lexicology Comparison of Chinese and Ukrainian Rhetoric Comparison of Chinese and Ukrainian Grammar The History of the Chinese Language Geography of the Chinese Language
		Master's	
South Ukrainian National Pedagogical University (Odessa)	Language and Literature (Chinese, English, World Literature, Secondary Education)	Bachelor's	Comprehensive Chinese Practical Chinese Phonetics Practical Chinese Grammar Spoken Chinese and Writing Practice Country Studies Theoretical Chinese Phonetics Theoretical Chinese Grammar Chinese Pedagogy
	Chinese-English-UkrainianTranslation	Bachelor's	Comprehensive Chinese Chinese Translation Theory Chinese Translation Practice

Borys Grinchenko Kyiv University (Kyiv)	Chinese Language, Literature and Translation	Bachelor's	Linguistic Theories Information Technology in Oriental Languages Comprehensive Chinese Practical Coursesof Chinese (Phonetics, Grammar,Hieroglyphics, Translation) Theoretical Courses of Chinese (Lexicology, Grammar, Rhetoric) Oriental Studies (History of the East) Country Studies Ukraine-Oriental Relations Literature Studies (Ancient Oriental Literature, The History of World Literature, The History of Oriental Country Literature) Teaching and Translation Practice
		Master's	Practical Chinese (Communication Etiquette and Business Communication, Literature and Scientific Style) Oriental Studies (Comparison of Oriental Civilizations, Classical Oriental Literature, Ukraine-Oriental Cultural and Linguistic Communication, Methodology of the Studies of Oriental Languages and Literature) Chinese Communication Strategies (Spoken and Written Communication Culture, Chinese Interpretation and Translation Skills) Literature Theory (20th-21st-Century World Literature,Contemporary Oriental Literature) Chinese Theory (Chinese Grammar, Chinese Functional Rhetoric) Internship (Translation, Teaching Assistance, Research, etc.)
International Humanitarian University (Odessa)	Chinese Language and Literature	Bachelor's	No information available

3. Existing Problems and Deficiencies

By analyzing the above data, we find that the following problems exist in the teaching of Chinese in Ukraine:

First of all, Ukrainian universities with programs for the teaching of Chinese are unevenly distributed, mainly in five major cities, which are Kyiv, Kharkiv, Odessa, Lviv and Dnipro. In this case, learners of Chinese in other regions can only learn Chinese through non-higher educational institutions such as private training classes, which cannot meet their needs for systematic Chinese education.

Second, most universities only set up two directions: translation, language and literature, which restrict the employment opportunities for the graduates with a major in Chinese. With the development of science and technology and the transformation of the global economy, the labor markets of all countries are subject to constant changes and impose increasingly higher requirements regarding the skills of their employees. At present, most employers require learners to have professional knowledge and skills in more than two fields (such as foreign languages and economics, etc.). Consequently, graduates with a major in Chinese with professional skills in only a single field encounter a lot of difficulties in finding employment and cannot meet the requirements of the employers.

Moreover, some universities only offer the educational program for a Bachelor's degree without offering a Master's degree. Hence, their Chinese language teaching system is not complete, and graduates can only study for a Master's degree in other universities or turn to other majors.

Finally, courses in most universities only focus on the teaching of the Chinese language, and there is a small proportion of relevant courses, such as country studies and Chinese culture. In particular, there are few courses in communication culture, and only two universities have such courses on Chinese communication etiquette and Chinese communication culture. In addition, although most universities teach a large amount of content related to practical Chinese and Chinese translation skills, they rarely include industry-related courses (such as Business Chinese). According to our data, currently only one university offers a Business Chinese course.

4. Measures and Suggestions

Considering the above problems and deficiencies of the teaching of Chinese in Ukraine, we put forward the following measures and suggestions:

First of all, aiming at the problem of the uneven distribution of the teaching of Chinese in Ukrainian universities, we propose that universities might use Internet technology to establish online Chinese curriculum systems, including the introduction of knowledge points, exercises, assignments, tests, and so on. Course content that can be downloaded includes text materials, audio and video to help learners choose the teaching method that suits them best. In the case of the shortage of resources, multiple universities can cooperate to jointly develop an independent online Chinese teaching platform or upload courses to existing public online teaching platforms.

Second, to solve the problems of there being only one educational direction and professional skills not being able to meet the requirements of employers, we suggest that while retaining the independent Chinese major, Chinese courses might be incorporated as minor courses into the educational programs of other applied majors (such as international relations, international trade, etc.). In this way, learners are provided with more choices so that everyone can choose the appropriate Chinese learning strategy according to their personal abilities and career plans.

Furthermore, given that some universities do not have a perfect system for the teaching of Chinese and it is unable for them to open a Master's program, in our opinion, they could cooperate with Chinese universities for joint educational programs for developing young people who are talented in the Chinese language.

For example, students with excellent academic results can be sent to Chinese universities to study for a Master's degree after receiving their Bachelor's degree at Ukrainian universities. The related costs could be borne by both China and Ukraine.

Finally, because some universities focus only on the teaching of the Chinese language itself and ignore Chinese culture, we propose strengthening the teaching of Chinese culture and Chinese communication while maintaining a high level of language teaching. Communication culture could be highlighted, and related courses such as Chinese social etiquette and Chinese communication strategies can be offered. In addition, in view of the lack of industry-related content in the curriculum system, we recommend that Business Chinese, Legal Chinese, Medical Chinese and other courses be offered to improve the practical value of Chinese courses.

5. Conclusion

In summary, the current comprehensive system of the teaching of Chinese in Ukrainian universities is relatively complete so that it can provide learners with systematic Chinese teaching plans and developprofessionals with high-level abilities in Chinese. Meanwhile, some aspects of the teaching of Chinese in Ukrainian universities still need improvements. Universities teaching Chinese are distributed unevenly; there are relatively limited educational directions; the professional skills of graduates with a major in Chinese cannot meet the requirements of employers; some universities only have a Bachelor's program; and there is a lack of courses such as Chinese Culture, especially communication culture. In order to solve these problems, Ukrainian universities must continuously improve their methods of teaching Chinese; they need to give their courses in Chinese a higher value for practical applications, establish joint educational mechanisms with Chinese universities to help learners reach advanced levels in their learning of Chinese, and teach Chinese culture and social etiquette to help learners avoid ambiguities and cultural conflicts that may arise in Chinese communication. Once the above problems are solved, the level of the teaching of Chinese in Ukrainian universities will be improved, and young people who have been educated at Ukrainian universities and are talented in the Chinese language will further enhance their comprehensive competitiveness and contribute new strength to the friendly cooperation between China and Ukraine, thus allowing the people-to-people bond that has been created in countries along the "Belt and Road"to reach a higher level.

"一带一路"倡议在越南的实施情况与几点思考

黄慧英【越南】

越南社会科学翰林院中国研究所研究员

"丝绸之路经济带"和"21 世纪海上丝绸之路"（以下简称"一带一路"）从倡议到行动、从理念到实践已经走过了 4 年多的时间，成果较为显著。北京"一带一路"国际合作高峰论坛的举行，引起国际社会高度关注。"一带一路"倡议从 2013 年的一张蓝图开始，到现在已经更加务实，机制也在不断深化。越南作为"一带一路"倡议的沿线国家之一，又是中国的邻居，也是中国通往东南亚各国的重要渠道，在"一带一路"互联互通上扮演着重要的角色。笔者试图通过分析越南人对"一带一路"倡议的认识、目前越中两国在互联互通上的合作状况，分析越中进行"一带一路"和"两廊一圈"倡议对接的机遇与挑战，由此提出一些个人对越中在"一带一路"倡议背景下进行战略对接和项目建设的几点思考，希望能提供从一个沿线国家去认识"一带一路"倡议的新视角。

一、越南人如何认识"一带一路"倡议

"一带一路"倡议在中国如火如荼地进行着，"一带一路"几乎成为中国老百姓无人不知的热词。那么越南人怎么认识"一带一路"倡议？

1. 越南学术界——从模糊不清到高度关注

越南学者对"一带一路"的认识，从倡议提出到目前为止可分为两个阶段。2015 年之前，由于"一带一路"还只是一个蓝图，更多的是一个总体框架设计，

加上其涵盖的地理范围和包含的内容非常庞大，中国学术界本身对于倡议的内涵、范围、措施等问题的说法不够清晰，甚至有些混乱，没有形成统一、系统的理论体系，使得越中学者在此问题上进行学术性交流造成障碍。从 2013 年到 2015 年，研究中国问题的越南学术界对"一带一路"倡议的关注度不高，一些专家在个别文章有提到，不过只停留在介绍性和总结性的程度。胡志明市国家大学张明辉武博士在他的一项研究报告中对"一带一路"倡议进行初步梳理。他的报告分为五大部分：第一、中国为"一带一路"倡议做了些什么？第二、"一带一路"倡议为何具有重要的地位；第三、中国和各国学者如何看待"一带一路"倡议？第四、"一带一路"倡议对地区和世界的影响；第五、为越南提出一些政策建议。在一些研讨会上有个别学者提到中国的"一带一路"倡议，不过对于不专门研究中国的学者来说，这个概念是相当陌生的。

2015 年随着《愿景与行动》的出台，中国关于"一带一路"倡议的研究著作如雨后春笋般地大量出版，由中国政府部门和研究机构组织有关"一带一路"倡议的国内、国际会议连续不断，为越南学者全面了解"一带一路"提供更多的渠道和机会。研究中国问题的越南专家开始不断提及"一带一路"，研究内容从之前主要注重于弄清其概念与涵义转向更深层次的问题去探讨，如：中国发动"一带一路"倡议思考、"一带一路"的可行性、倡议的落实对地区和世界的影响等，有学者以中美关系的研究视角或以"一带一路"与"两廊一圈"的对接问题为接入点，也有的研究试图为越南政府提供一些政策建议。在《谈 21 世纪海上丝绸之路》[1] 的文章中，德紧、芳阮博士较详细阐述"一带一路"的"五通"合作原则，同时分析中国和其他国家在进行"一带一路"建设时所遇到的机遇及挑战，其中作者比较强调中国与东南亚国家的"战略互信"下降因素对各国合作造成的负面影响。由阮德成、范士成主编的《增长的新基础建设》[2] 著作有一章《中国'一带一路'倡议及对越南的多方面影响》，相当全面地概述了"一带一路"倡议的经济、外交、安全等目标。在外交方面，本书认为"一带一路"高度体现中国的第二次改革开放浪潮，通过实行"一带一路"来建立有利于中国发挥更大作用的国际秩序。在安全方面，作者提出中国能源安全危机以及中国"孤独强国"状态是中国发动"一带一路"倡议的重要意图。书中列出了中国从中央、各政府部门到省级

1　[越]《中国研究杂志》，2015 年 5 月。
2　河内国家大学出版社 2016 年版。

的有关文件和政策，中国与其他国家和国际组织的双边及多边的运行机制、金融、贷款运作等等。结论部分作者侧重于基础设施建设论述并为越南提出一些具体的政策建议。目前，越南学者关于"一带一路"倡议最为完整的专题性著作有范士成主编的《"一带一路"——中国的战略与越南政策建议》[1]。该书一共有五章：第一章对"一带一路"倡议做了总体性梳理；第二章对"一带一路"运作机制进行论述；第三章总结四年来有关项目的开展情况以及各国的反应；第四章就"一带一路"对其他国家产生的影响进行预测；第五章为越南政府提出一些政策建议。范士成博士认为："一带一路"经过了从倡议到策略的转变过程，2013年为倡议提出的一年、2014年普及到中国国家各个部门、2015年划出行动计划、2016年为实现的一年。其战略带有很强的灵活性，有一系列多边倡议支持，体现中国的"实体外交"政策。书中把世界各国对"一带一路"的反应分为三组：西方国家最引人瞩目的反应是同中国建立了欧盟—中国的ECCP论坛。在亚洲国家之中，他认为南亚国家比东南亚国家的态度更加积极，东南亚国家分为积极参与、有选择性参与和慎重观察等三种表态。非洲国家来得最晚，并相对更加支持。关于"一带一路"所面临的挑战问题，该书提出的七大挑战包括：长期的海洋思维定位、"一带一路"的完整战略、中国企业"走出去"的失败案例、社会环保的挑战、"软实力"和政治信任的挑战、AIIB的有效性和恐怖活动范围增加趋势的压力。

总体来说，越南学者关于"一带一路"的研究可分为三大主要接入点：第一是对"一带一路"进行介绍性描述。这一类占最大比例，虽然其学术含量不高但是对于越南广大读者在目前阶段来说是非常必要的，有助于大家对"一带一路"形成正确的认识和理解。公布形式主要是不出版的各个单位的研究项目。这些研究尽量弄清"一带一路"的概念，其涵盖的范围，介绍有关的银行和基金组织，说明一些运行原则如"五通原则"等，阐述一些重要文件如共建"一带一路"愿景与行动文件等，回顾重要的会议如"一带一路"高峰论坛，同时对"一带一路"开展情况进行总结。第二个接入点是划分目前各国对"一带一路"的态度，由此从越南角度去评价和借鉴。越南学者基本上把各国对"一带一路"的反应分为支持、慎重、不参与三种态度，并对此加以说明。其实，从这角度演绎"一带一路"的成果不多，也相当零散。但是其对于认识"一带一路"提供更广阔的视角，也为越南建言献策有借鉴作用。支持"一带一路"者认为，这战略对于建立多极世

---

1 [越] 世界出版社2017年版。

界、维持权力均势有积极作用。反对"一带一路"者又觉得这个倡议会增加大国竞争程度，引发资金、能源和贸易战争的危机，加大各国对中国的依赖性等。第三个接入点是从为越南提出政策建议入手。对越南来说这可能是最务实的研究部分。越南学者比较一致地认为，为了达到更好地运作效果，"一带一路"应该与"两廊一圈"进行对接，同时最好从实施、敏感成分低而且越南正在缺乏的基础设施领域开始。冯氏惠教授认为："民心相通"在越中"一带一路"对接建设中起到关键性作用。而中国和包括越南在内东南亚国家学者之间的交流是比较有效的渠道。东盟和中国智库交流为了达到三个目的：一是，交换学术研究成果。权威学者进行交谈"一带一路"有关的研究结果，从而加深相互了解、彼此借鉴，对每个国家参与"一带一路"建设提供有益信息。二是，评价"一带一路"实际开展情况。这是十分重要的环节，因为"一带一路"在各个国家开展状况就是中国—东盟合作的真实体现。学者之间交流通常十分坦白、清晰、客观，容易判断开展困境的根本原因，为"一带一路"建设充分发挥积极作用。三是，共同建议政策与措施。在研究结果交流和实际状况评价基础上，智库之间会对中国与东盟"一带一路"建设政策及措施共同提出建议。

2. 越南老百姓——从一无所知到有所认识

虽然这几年来"一带一路"成为中国最热门的话题之一，不仅受到中国高层人士的普遍关注，也得到了人民群众的热烈追捧。然而越南民众对"一带一路"相当陌生。本文分为"一带一路"高峰论坛前后两个阶段来谈越南老百姓对"一带一路"的认识。

从2013年"一带一路"倡议提出之后到2017年5月"一带一路"高峰论坛举行之前，越南普通人民对其倡议基本上一无所闻也根本不关注。原因何在？首先在这阶段里越南媒体关于"一带一路"的报道甚少。这说明中国对外宣传的力度不够。中国就此问题针对越南的宣传基本限于高层人士而没有形成大众化趋势。"一带一路"的"五通"包括政策沟通、设施联通、贸易畅通、资金融通和民心相通，其内容也不超过越中两国之前的合作范围。因此如果不加以说明，一般很难分清。其次战略互疑是目前两国展开交流合作的一大障碍因素。这种互疑心态有历史根源、也有现实原因。领土纠纷的历史遗留问题根深蒂固，潮起潮落，这两年来双方人民由于海上争端问题热化而互疑心态也呈现上升的趋势。出于现实情况，越南民众对中国项目普遍存在谨慎的心理。中国企业家进入越南市场比较晚，之前其他相当成熟的投标商如日本、韩国和一些西方国家的企业家进入越南市场很成功，中国企业家因此面临较大的竞争压力。中国商品经过小道进入越南，质量没通过检验，有的伪劣假冒商品在越南市场大规模进行销售，这样就给中国商品贴上"质量问题"标签。在越南也存在一些由中国投资的基础设施项目进度被推迟（如河内的吉玲—河东线城铁项目），或是造成环境污染，给越南老百姓生活带来一些影响。再加上中国企业"走出去"，也存在"阶段性"和"区域性"问题。越南是中国的邻居，国土接壤，走进越南的第一批中国公司大部分是南方的中小型企业，在资金规模、职业规范、国际化程度方面都存在一定的局限性。以上原因使得中国提出的"一带一路"倡议没有受到越南老百姓的积极响应。"一带一路"在将来如能有效开展，希望越南会迎来一大批中国高水准的国际性企业，"中国品牌"口碑的"历史遗留"问题将会得到解决。

2018 年 5 月份北京举办"一带一路"高峰论坛之后，此话题才相续出现在越南各媒体网站上。越南普通人民开始接触到"一带一路"的概念。论坛举行之间和之后，越南各主要网站连续登载有关会议的信息。多家报纸同时引用习近平主席在高峰论坛上的开幕式致辞，也为读者提供一系列有关信息如：29 位国家元首和政府首脑、来自 100 多个国家的 1500 位官员和各界人士、70 多个国际组织的负责人和代表出席论坛；习近平主席在"一带一路"国际合作高峰论坛上宣布向丝路基金新增资金 1000 亿元人民币，本论坛一共形成成果清单 270 多项，签署 32 个双边、多边合作文件及企业合作项目，涉及 18 个国家和 8 个国际组织；未来三年向参与"一带一路"建设的发展中国家和国际组织提供 600 亿元人民币援助，向沿线发展中国家提供 20 亿元人民币紧急粮食援助，向南南合作基金赠资 10 亿美元，在沿线国家实施 100 个"幸福家园"、100 个"爱心助困"、100 个"康复助医"，未来 5 年内安排 2500 人（次）青年科学家来华从事短期科研工作、培育 5000 人（次）科学技术和管理人员、投入运行 50 家联合实验室。提供这些数字，越南人才能对"一带一路"有了概念。《新报》2017 年 5 月 16 日评论：美国回归"保护"而中国着急"开放"[1]。《青年报》2017 年 5 月 20 日认为，"一带一路"倡议需要巨大的资金来支持，而目前的情况下只有中国才有能力满足，其战略可以缩小亚太和中亚与欧洲国家的基础设施差距。[2] 越南最受欢迎的新闻网站 vnexpress.net

---

1　http://www.baomoi.com/my-quay-ve-voi-bao-ho-trung-quoc-sot-sang-mo-cua/c/22283002.epi.

2　http://cuoituan.tuoitre.vn/tin/van-de-su-kien/quoc-te/20170520/vanh-dai-con-duong-va-trung-quoc-mong/1316505.html.

2017 年 5 月 15 日登载一篇文章，肯定通过此次高峰论坛中国逐渐把"一带一路"梦想化为现实。[1] 越南各家报纸在谈到"一带一路"的积极作用之外，对该倡议的可行性、其面临的挑战以及对地区和世界的地缘政治、地缘经济的影响都表现出一定的担忧。

二、"一带一路"在越南的可行性——与"两廊一圈"进行对接

亚投行是中国展开"一带一路"的重要基金来源和运行机制，越南很早就表示支持并成为亚投行的创立成员国之一。2017 年 1 月越共阮富仲总书记访问中国时，双方在联合公报上宣布"正式成立基础设施合作工作组和金融与货币合作工作组，同意加强上述两个组织同海上共同合作发展磋商工作组配合协调，共同推进各领域全面发展"，体现越南对"一带一路"倡议适合内容愿意与中国推进合作的诚意。2017 年 5 月 11 至 15 日，越南国家主席陈大光对中国进行国事访问并出席"一带一路"国际合作高峰论坛。在圆桌峰会上，陈大光主席认为：世界正在进入关键性阶段的大环境，每个国家、地区都不断创新，尽可能发挥自己的潜力、优势，有效地利用科学技术的成果，保证和平、安全、稳定的环境和可持续发展。在这些原则的基础上，越南欢迎包括"一带一路"倡议在内的各项经济性、区域性互联互通倡议，愿意与其他国家共同研究、建设以及开展能为各国带来福祉、有利于可持续发展的项目。陈大光主席强调各国在"一带一路"框架下进行合作时的需要：跟联合国《2030 可持续发展议程》及现有的地区性、全球性合作框架连在一起；符合高效、可持续的标准；优先务实、符合于各国、各地区发展需求的项目；在共识、平等、自愿、透明、开放、互相尊重、互利、遵守联合国宪章和国际法的原则基础上进行合作。谈到互联互通合作的问题，越南国家主席分享越南在促进与邻国经济和交通畅通问题上的努力，帮助陆地国家和没有中转条件的国家更深地融入全球贸易系统。他强调应该优先国家间有效的经济联系，注重发展各大陆之间的交通互联互通，形成连接亚洲各国之间以及亚洲和欧洲、非洲、美洲大陆之间的交通系统，提升人文交流和贸易、投资的便利化。[2] 这一切体现越南对"一带一路"倡议的积极响应。然而在短期内如想取得成效的话，还应该把"一带一路"和"两廊一圈"很好地对接起来。

1　http://vnexpress.net/tin-tuc/the-gioi/phan-tich/vanh-dai-va-con-duong-tham-vong-dan-thanh-hien-thuc-cua-trung-quoc-3584243.html.

2　http://vov.vn/chinh-tri/viet-nam-hoan-nghenh-cac-sang-kien-lien-ket-kinh-te-624661.vov.

1. "两廊一圈"为建设"一带一路"打好基础

2004 年，越南国家总理潘文凯在对中国进行国事访问时，向温家宝总理提出共建"两廊一圈"的构想。自 2005 年起，"两廊一圈"一直被纳入越中联合声明的内容当中。中国国家主席习近平于 2015 年 11 月访问越南期间，两国已达成共识并写进联合声明：要加强两国间发展对接、推动"一带一路"倡议和"两廊一圈"构想的对接，加紧成立工作组，积极商签跨境经济合作区建设共同总体方案。 越南国家主席陈大光在 2017 年 5 月访问中国期间，双方发表的联合公报也明确指出："在符合各自利益、能力和条件的基础上，加快商签对接"一带一路"倡议和"两廊一圈"框架合作备忘录。发挥陆上基础合作工作组在提升两国互联互通的作用。按计划积极推进越中陆上基础设施合作领域和能源领域五年规划研究和编制工作，推动河内城铁 2 号线（吉灵—河东线）项目如期完工"[1]。"两廊一圈"的内容涉及越中关系方方面面，包括经济、贸易关系、投资、技术合作、环境保护、旅游问题等等。"两廊"是指昆明—老街—河内—海防—广宁和南宁—凉山—河内—海防—广宁的经济走廊。"一圈"指的是环北部湾经济圈，中国境内包括广西（北海、钦州、防城），海南，广东（湛江）三省，越南境内包括广宁、海防、太平、南定、宁平、清化、艺安、何静、广平、广治等省市。目前双方在落实"两廊一圈"时的主要成就集中在经贸关系和互联互通基础设施建设上。

首先，经贸合作是"两廊一圈"的主要合作内容，也是越中关系的亮点。中国从 2004 年至今一直是越南的第一大贸易伙伴而越南目前也成为中国在东盟国家最大贸易伙伴，双方贸易规模不断扩大。虽然越中经贸合作上存在的最大问题是贸易不平衡问题，越南对中国的贸易一直处在严重的逆差状态，不过最近也看到有些缓解意向。中国驻越南大使洪小勇指出："去年（2016 年），越南对华出口增长了 20% 多，相反，中国对越南的出口呈下降趋势。今年（2017 年）上半年第一季度，这一趋势还继续保持发展势头。据统计，第一季度越南对华出口增长了 40%，总体上双边贸易结构正趋于平衡"[2]。越中贸易结构也在不断优化，技术型、资本密集型产业已逐渐代替农副产品、初级工业制成品、矿产原料，成为双边贸易的主力产品，双方合作的广度和深度不断拓展。随着"两廊一圈"与"一带一路"倡议对接成为两国领导人的共识，合作项目正在稳步向前推进。据越南计划

---

1 http://zh.vietnamplus.vn.

2 http://www.haoyidian.com/5526105/20170509A06WDV00.html.

投资部外国投资局统计,2016 年前三季度,中国对越投资协议金额达 10.1 亿美元,同比增长 304%。其中新项目 208 个,协议金额 6.7 亿美元。目前,中国在越直接投资项目数量 1492 个,协议投资 110 亿美元,中国成为越南第九大外资来源地。

第二是"两廊一圈"框架之内的互联互通基础设施建设情况。2014 年越南河内—老街高速公路全线通车,这是越南首条连接越中边境的高速公路,耗资 14.6 亿美元,这是中国昆明—越南海防经济走廊的重要项目。2015 年河内—海防高速公路全线通车。这条公路的总长度将近 106 公里,投资额为 20 多亿美元。作为连接越南首都河内与越南北方最重要港口海防的一条血脉高速路,无疑对越南经济发展和人民流动具有重要的作用。河内—谅山高速公路全长 146 公里,预计总投资额约 13 亿美元,分成三段完成:河内—北江段于 2014 年动工,2016 年初完成通车;北江—谅山段于 2015 年动工,预计 2018 年通车;友谊—支陵段 2016 年动工,预计 2019 年完成。

2. "一带一路"是"两廊一圈"的延伸与提升

中国发起建设"一带一路"秉承共商、共建、共享原则,以"政策沟通""设施联通""贸易畅通""资金融通""民心相通"的"五通",为中国和沿线国家的合作内容。中国国务院公布的《愿景与行动》也指出,设施联通是"一带一路"建设的优先合作领域[1]。而这恰恰与越中两国的"两廊一圈"构想有很多契合之处。习近平主席在"一带一路"高峰论坛开幕式上的演讲中宣布,中国将把"一带一路"建成一条"和平之路""繁荣之路""开放之路""创新之路"和"文明之路"。他强调:"中国愿在和平共处五项原则基础上,发展同所有'一带一路'建设参与国的友好合作。中国愿同世界各国分享发展经验,但不会干涉他国内政,不会输出社会制度和发展模式,更不会强加于人。我们推进'一带一路'建设不会重复地缘博弈的老套路,而将开创合作共赢的新模式,不会形成破坏稳定的小集团,而将建设和谐共存的大家庭"[2]。在倡导"一带一路"建设的过程中,中国也很强调"共同安全"原则,由此形成"人类命运共同体"。按照中国的说法,"共同安全"是指自己国家的安全建立在保证其他国家安全的基础上,在捍卫本国安全的同时也使得他国得到安全。这跟传统地缘政治的"安全观"不同。如果中国能遵循以上承诺开展"一带一路"合作的话,就会为地区乃至整个世界的和平、安全与繁

---

1 《推动共建丝绸之路经济带和21世纪海上丝绸之路的愿景与行动》,人民出版社 2015 年版,第 8 页。

2 http://news.sohu.com/20170514/n492975720.shtml.

荣做出贡献，也体现出大国姿态和大国担当。

经过四年的总结和提炼，中国对"一带一路"倡议已经形成更加完整的理论体系。"两廊一圈"是之前针对越南和中国之间所提出的合作战略，在合作理念和内容上与"一带一路"有很多契合之处，但是没有形成一套理论系统。如果能够把"一带一路"和"两廊一圈"对接起来就能延伸和深化"两廊一圈"的构想，使其更加理论化和机制化，同时也使"一带一路"倡议在越南短期内能够有效地拓展。在实现以上两个倡议战略对接的过程中，《越中跨境经济合作区》建设会起到积极作用。《越中跨境经济合作区》很早就成为两国政府的共识，如能建成不仅有利于越南和中国的互联互通，而且还有利于东南亚与中国的连通。不过当前双方还没形成共同建设方案，主要原因在于双边没有把符合两国利益的共同运行机制确定下来。由此，2017 年 5 月越中在联合公报上肯定："按照平等互利、尊重个自主权独立和领土完整的原则，在符合双方法律规定和国际惯例的基础上，加快商签越中跨境经济合作区建设共同总体方案"[1]。接下来，越中两国一方面要在适合、小范围（如云南—老街或广西—芒街）建设《跨境经济合作区》试验区，一方面要尽快沟通商讨，找出符合两国利益的共同合作机制。

三、几点建议

不用质疑，互联互通对推动越中全面战略合作伙伴关系的长期健康、稳定发展非常关键。促进与中国进行全面、有效的合作，是越南政府和人民始终不变的愿望。问题在于，如何使互联互通发挥最大作用，是两国学者要深思熟虑共同解决的问题。笔者对此提出以下几点建议。

第一，"民心相通"至关重要。

越中两国有着悠久的传统情谊。目前双方在政治、经济、文化、科技等领域的合作成果令人瞩目。然而，战略互疑长期以来被两国学者广泛认为是阻碍两国关系健康发展的重要因素。原因在于双方之间存在领土纠纷的历史性问题以及担心对方国对外战略的国际游戏性问题。近几年来，互疑的心态在两国又呈现大众化趋势，引起担忧。在互联网空前发展的今天，民众具有更多的渠道去表达自己的声音。一方面他们接受的信息更加多元化，一方面他们也有越来越多的平台来参与到国家治理。这已经成为全球性的趋势，越中两国人民也不例外。国之交在

---

1 http://www.nhandan.com.vn/chinhtri/item/32881402-thong-cao-chung-viet-nam-trung-quoc.html.

于民相亲。"一带一路"五通之中有"设施连通",基础设施建设是中国的强项,也正是越南的缺乏。但是目前来说,在实现越中两国互联互通合作当中,必须更加注重"民心相通"原则。"民心相通"是剩下"四通"的基础和保障,并且"五通"当中除了"政策沟通"以外其他"四通"都由两国人民来实现。在化解双方老百姓互相猜疑的工作当中,"舆论对接"这项"软联通"非常关键。双方媒体之间需要建立沟通对话机制,学者之间建立一个话语体系的工程,同时深化其他如旅游、教育、科技、民间组织等领域的交流活动。

第二,用行动来说话。

在实现国家工业化及现代化过程中,越南对基础设施建设需求非常大,由此实施较多开放性的外国引资政策,也期待吸收越来越多的中国投资者,其中基础设施建设是优先领域。然而,十多年来,在越南,中国承包商的基础设施工程的确存在质量不高、期限延迟、价格增多等问题。河内城铁 2 号线于 2011 年 10 月动工,预期 2015 年 12 月开通,但延期到 2018 年底估计才能完工,投资金额比预算增加 3 亿美元 [1],并且施工的过程中也发生一些安全事故,使得中国企业在越南投资的信用及形象受到损失,对中国提倡的"一带一路"形成负面影响。当然,不能把责任完全推卸到中国企业身上,越南的投标、管理经验薄弱,劳工专业水平有限、遵守纪律的态度不够严格,腐败现象等因素也影响到整个工程的质量。由此,越中企业家应该实事求是地看待此问题,用真实的行动、高质量的工程来证明自己的实力,重塑企业现代化和国家化形象。

第三,坚定不移维护越中友好情谊。

越南和中国曾经同船而行度过种种难关。越中两国一直珍惜胡志明主席和毛泽东主席等老前辈已经培育的"同志加兄弟"友好深情,并且努力推动两国全面战略合作伙伴关系。双方都认为,越中友谊是两党和两国人民的共同宝贵财富,应该得以传承和发扬光大。在"一带一路"建设背景下,两国更要坚定维护由两党针对双方友好关系所提出的"十六字"方针和"四好"精神。这绝不是一个无实质性的空白口号,而体现了越中之间的特殊性关系。越中应在维护两国友谊精神的基础上,去沟通和磋商关于"一带一路"的战略合作。越中关系因海上问题而有时发生波浪起伏状况。因此,在越南国家主席陈大光 2017 年 5 月访问中国期

1　http://vnexpress.net/infographics/giao-thong/nhung-lan-tang-von-lui-tien-do-cua-duong-sat-cat-linh-ha-dong-3591133.html.

间，双方发表的越中联合公报也一致同意继续恪守两党两国领导人达成《关于指
导解决越中海上问题基本原则协议》的重要共识[1]。越中必须要通过和平谈判，遵
守国际法律原则来妥善管控和处理、化解分歧问题，千万不能把纠纷问题复杂化，
这样才能为"一带一路"框架之下促进双方交流合作创造有利环境。

　　国际力量正在发生变化。国际秩序也在重构。基辛格在他的新作《世界秩序》
中认为：由于时代和时局的急剧变化，现在需要缔造1648年建立的威斯特伐利亚
体系和1815年建立的维也纳体系之后的第三个世界秩序[2]。在世界格局孕育着新景
象的过程当中，国际社会的治理对象会更加多元化，"一带一路"倡议给正在崛
起的中国一个从国际治理参与者飞跃到国际治理引领者身份的机会，也是中国重
估自身价值和能力的好机会。"一带一路"是一个各国"共建"的大工程，了解
沿线国家的特殊情况、有效地与沿线国家进行沟通对接，才能把"一带一路"倡
议推行下去和可持续发展。

1　http://zh.vietnamplus.vn.
2　[美]亨利·基辛格:《世界秩序》，中信出版社2015年版。

Implementation of the Belt and Road Initiative in Vietnam, and Several Thoughts

Hoang Hue Anh / Vietnam

Vietnam Academy of Social Sciences, Researcher

The "Silk Road Economic Belt" and the "21st Century Maritime Silk Road" (hereinafter referred to as the "Belt and Road") have gone through more than four years from initiative to action, from concept to practice, with remarkable results. The holding of the Belt and Road Forum for International Cooperation in Beijing attracted attention from the international community. The Belt and Road Initiative, started with a blueprint in 2013, has now become more pragmatic, and the mechanism is being continuously expanded. Vietnam is not only one of the countries along the route, but it is also a neighbor of China and an important channel for China in reaching Southeast Asian countries. It plays an important role in the "Belt and Road" connectivity. The author attempts to analyze the Vietnamese people's understanding of the "Belt and Road" and the current situation of cooperation between Vietnam and China on connectivity. Through analyzing opportunities and challenges for the integration of Vietnam and China in the "Belt and Road" and "Two Corridors and One Circle", the author puts forward several thoughts on the strategic integration of Vietnam and China and the construction of the project in the context of the "Belt and Road", with the aim of providing a new perspective on understanding the "Belt and Road" from the point of view of a country along the route.

1. The "Belt and Road" in the Eyes of the Vietnamese People

The "Belt and Road", which is in full swing in China, has become a household name that is known to almost all Chinese. Then, what is the "Belt and Road" in the eyes of the Vietnamese people?

1.1 Academia in Vietnam — From Little Knowledge to Special Attention

The understanding of the "Belt and Road" on the part of Vietnamese scholars can be divided into two stages since the Initiative was proposed. Before 2015, when the "Belt and Road" was only a blueprint, it was more like an overall framework design. Moreover, its geographical scope and content were very large. The Chinese academic statements on the connotation, scope, measures, etc. of the Initiative were not clear enough, and were even a bit confusing, and there was not a unified and systematic theoretical system yet, so it was difficult for Vietnamese and Chinese scholars to conduct academic exchanges on this issue. From 2013 to 2015, Vietnamese scholars studying Chinese issues paid little attention to the "Belt and Road". Some experts mentioned it in their articles, but only as an introduction and summary. Dr. Minh Huy Sang of the Vietnam National University, Ho Chi Minh City conducted a preliminary review of the "Belt and Road" in his research report. His report had five parts: First, what is China doing regarding the "Belt and Road"?; Second, why is the "Belt and Road" important?; Third, how do Chinese and foreign scholars view the "Belt and Road"?; Fourth, the impact of the "Belt and Road" on the region and the world; Fifth, some policy suggestions for Vietnam. Scholars also mentioned China's Belt and Road Initiative at some seminars, but this concept was quite new to scholars who are not specialized in China studies.

With the release of "Vision and Actions" in 2015, China's research publications on the "Belt and Road" sprang up like mushrooms, and domestic and international conferences on the "Belt and Road" organized by the Chinese government and research institutions emerged one after another. They provided more channels and opportunities for Vietnamese scholars to have a full understanding of the "Belt and Road". Vietnamese experts who studied China started to continuously mention the "Belt and Road". Their research turned from previous focus on clarifying the concept and meaning of the strategy to deeper issues, such as China's strategic thoughts in launching the "Belt and Road", the feasibility of the "Belt and Road" and the influence of the implementation of this initiative on the region and on the world. Some scholars took the research perspective of Sino-US relations or the connection between the "Belt and Road" and "Two Corridors and One Circle" as the entry points. Some studies attempted to provide some policy suggestions to the Vietnamese government. In the article "On the 21st Century Maritime Silk Road"[1], Dr. Duc Phuong Nguyen gave a detailed explanation of the five-connectivity cooperation principle of the "Belt and Road" and analyzed the opportunities and challenges encountered by China and other countries in the implementation of the "Belt and Road". The authors emphasized the negative impact of the decline in the "strategic mutual trust" between China and Southeast Asian countries on cooperation. A chapter entitled "China's Belt and Road Initiative and its Multi-facet Influence on Vietnam" in the book *The Construction of New Infrastructure for Growth*[2] edited by Nguyen Duc Thanh and Pham Sy Thanh provided a comprehensive overview of the economic, diplomatic and security goals of the "Belt and Road". In terms of diplomacy, the book considered the "Belt and Road" as China's second wave of reform and opening-up and as being able to establish an international order that would be conducive to China's playing a greater role through the implementation of the "Belt and Road". In terms of security, the authors pointed out that China's energy security crisis and status of "a lonely power" were important motivations for China to launch the "Belt and Road" strategy. The book enumerated China's relevant documents and policies from the central government and various departments to the provincial level, bilateral and multilateral operating mechanisms,

---

1 (Vietnam) *Journal of China Studies*, May 2015.
2 (Vietnam) Vietnam National University Hanoi Press, 2016.

finance and loan operations of China and other countries and international organizations. In the conclusive part, the authors highlighted the construction of infrastructures and put forward some specific policy suggestions for Vietnam. So far, the most comprehensive monograph on the "Belt and Road" by Vietnamese scholars is *The "Belt and Road" — China's Perspective and Vietnam's Policy Suggestions*[1] edited by Pham Sy Thanh. There are five chapters in this book: The first chapter makes a summary of the "Belt and Road" Initiative; the second chapter discusses the operating mechanism of the "Belt and Road"; the third chapter summarizes the development of relevant projects in the past four years and the responses of various countries; the fourth chapter predicts the influence of the "Belt and Road" on other countries; and the fifth chapter presents some policy suggestions for the Vietnamese government. According to Dr. Pham Sy Thanh, the "Belt and Road" has undergone a process of transformation from an initiative to a Plan. The Initiative, proposed in 2013 and popularized to various national departments in China in 2014, released an action plan in 2015 and began to realize that plan in 2016. Its strategy is highly flexible and supported by a series of multilateral initiatives, reflecting China's policy of "substantive diplomacy". The book divides the responses of countries in the world to the "Belt and Road" into three groups: the most striking response from Western countries is the establishment of the EU-China ECCP Forum. Among Asian countries, in his opinion, South Asian countries are more positive than Southeast Asian countries. Southeast Asian countries are divided into three types: active participation, selective participation and careful observation. African countries came late but have been relatively more supportive. Regarding challenges faced by the "Belt and Road", this book points out seven big challenges, including: a long-term pattern of a marine line of thought, a complete "Belt and Road" Initiative, cases of failure of the Exports of Chinese enterprises, social and environmental challenges, soft power and political trust, the effectiveness of the AIIB, and increasing terrorist activities.

Generally speaking, Vietnamese scholars' studies on the "Belt and Road" have

---

1 (Vietnam) World Publishing House, 2017.

three major points of entry: The first point is the introductory descriptions of the "Belt and Road". This category accounts for the largest proportion. Although their academic value is not high, they are essential for the majority of Vietnamese readers at this stage, because they can help everyone to form a correct idea and understanding of the "Belt and Road". The form of publication is mainly the research projects of various units that have not been published. These studies attempt to clarify the concept and scope of the "Belt and Road", introduce relevant banks and funding organizations, explain some operating principles such as the "five-connectivity principle", etc., elaborate some important documents such as the vision and actions on jointly building the "Belt and Road", review important meetings such as the "Belt and Road" forum, and summarize the development of the "Belt and Road". The second point aims at the attitudes of countries towards the "Belt and Road", and evaluates and learns from the perspective of Vietnam. Vietnamese scholars basically divide the responses of countries to the "Belt and Road" into three kinds of attitudes: support, caution and non-participation, and then they explain these responses. In fact, the interpretations of the "Belt and Road" from this perspective are not fruitful and quite fragmented, but they can provide a broader perspective on understanding the "Belt and Road" and be used as a reference for Vietnam. Proponents of the "Belt and Road" believe that this strategy will play a positive role in establishing a multipolar world, maintaining a balance of power and preventing the escalation of disputes over territorial sovereignty between China and other countries. Opponents of the "Belt and Road" argue that this initiative will intensify competition among big powers, trigger crises of capital, energy and trade wars and increase other countries' dependence on China. The third point is to make policy suggestions for Vietnam. This is probably the most pragmatic part of the studies for Vietnam. Vietnamese scholars agree that in order to achieve better results, the "Belt and Road" should be connected with "Two Corridors and One Circle" and start with the construction of infrastructures that are the easiest to implement with low sensitivity and that are needed by Vietnam. Professor Phung Thi Hue indicates that the "people-to-people bond" plays a key role in the construction of the "Belt and Road" between Vietnam and China. The exchanges between Chinese scholars and those from Southeast Asian countries including Vietnam is an effective channel. The exchanges between ASEAN and Chinese think tanks serve three purposes. First, to exchange academic research results. Authoritative scholars talk about the results of research related to the "Belt and Road", so as to deepen their mutual understanding and learn from each other and provide useful information for each country to participate in the construction of the "Belt and Road". Second, to evaluate the actual development of the "Belt and Road". This is a very important link, because the situations of the "Belt and Road" in different countries might represent the true manifestation of China-ASEAN cooperation. The exchanges among scholars are usually very frank, clear and objective, and make it easy to judge the root cause of difficulties, and they play a positive role in the "Belt and Road" construction. Third, to jointly make suggestions for policies and measures. Based on the exchange of research results and the evaluation of actual conditions, think tanks will jointly make suggestions on China's and the ASEAN countries' policies and measures regarding the construction of the "Belt and Road".

1.2 Common People in Vietnam — From Complete Ignorance to Basic Knowledge

The Belt and Road Initiative has already become one of the most popular topics in China in recent years that not only attracts attention from the top level, but also is warmly welcomed by the people. However, the Vietnamese people are quite unfamiliar with the "Belt and Road". This article explores the understanding of the "Belt and Road" by the Vietnamese people in two stages, before and after the Forum for the Belt and Road.

From the launch of the Belt and Road Initiative in 2013 to the "Belt and Road" forum held in May 2017, common Vietnamese people were for the most part oblivious of it and therefore paid no attention to it. What are the reasons? First of all, at this stage, there were very few media reports about the "Belt and Road" in Vietnam. This means that China's international communication was not enough.

China's communication with Vietnam on this issue was basically limited to the top level without touching the common people. The "five connectivity" policy of the "Belt and Road" includes policy coordination, facilities connectivity, unimpeded trade, financial integration and people-to-people bonds, so its content does not go beyond the previous cooperation between Vietnam and China. It is difficult to distinguish without explanation. Second, strategic mutual suspicion is a serious barrier to the exchange and cooperation between the two countries. This mentality of mutual suspicion has historical roots as well as practical reasons. The historical issue of territorial dispute is deeply rooted and occurs frequently. In the past two years, the people of both sides have shown an upward trend of their mutual suspicion due to the heated maritime dispute. Due to the reality, Vietnamese people are generally cautious about Chinese projects. Chinese entrepreneurs entered the Vietnamese market relatively late. Entrepreneurs from other fairly mature bidders such as those from Japan, South Korea and some Western countries have successfully penetrated the Vietnamese market. As a result, Chinese entrepreneurs face greater pressure of competition. Chinese products enter Vietnam through bypaths without any quality inspection and some fake and shoddy goods are sold on a large scale on the Vietnamese market. This gives Chinese products a label of "problems of quality". In Vietnam, there are also some projects regarding infrastructures that have been invested in by Chinese investors and whose schedules are delayed (such as the Cat Linh – Ha Dong Metro Line Project in Hanoi) or which cause environmental pollution and this has negative impacts on the life of the Vietnamese people. Chinese enterprises' "going out" is also faced with "phased" and "regional" issues. Vietnam is China's neighbor with a border on land. Most of the first Chinese enterprises that have entered Vietnam are small and medium-sized enterprises from southern China. They have certain limitations in the scale of capital, professional code of conduct and internationalization. These are reasons why China's Belt and Road Initiative fails to receive a positive response from the Vietnamese people. If the "Belt and Road" can be effectively implemented in the future, Vietnam will usher in a large number of high-level Chinese international enterprises, and the "legacy of history" problem in the reputation of the "Chinese brand" will be resolved.

After the "Belt and Road" forum was held in Beijing in May this year, this topic began to appear on various Vietnamese media websites. Common people in Vietnam thus came into contact with the concept of the "Belt and Road". During and after the forum, information about the conference was continuously posted on big websites in Vietnam. Many newspapers cited President Xi Jinping's opening speech at the forum and provided readers with a series of relevant information, for example: 29 heads of state and government, 1,500 officials from more than 100 countries and people from all walks of life, more than 70 responsible persons and representatives of international organizations attended the forum; President Xi Jinping announced at the Belt and Road Forum for International Cooperation that 100 billion yuan would be added to the Silk Road Fund. This forum produced more than 270 results and 32 bilateral and multilateral cooperation documents and corporate cooperation projects were signed involving 18 countries and 8 international organizations; in the next three years, 60 billion yuan would be provided as aid to developing countries and international organizations participating in the construction of the "Belt and Road", 2 billion yuan to developing countries along the route for emergency food aid, and 1 billion US dollars to the South-South Cooperation Fund, and it would also implement 100 "happy homes", 100 "loves to help the poor", 100 incidents of "rehabilitation aid" in countries along the route, arrange for 2,500 young scientists to go to China in the next 5 years to engage in short-term scientific research, cultivate 5,000 science and technology and management personnel and put 50 joint laboratories into operation. Only by providing these numbers could the Vietnamese have a concept of the "Belt and Road". The *Baomoi* commented on May 16, 2017 that: The United States returned to "protection" and China was eager to "open up"[1]. The *Tuoitre* pointed out in May 20, 2017 that the "Belt and Road" strategy required huge supporting funds, only China could meet this need under the current

---

1 http://www.baomoi.com/my-quay-ve-voi-bao-ho-trung-quoc-sot-sang-mo-cua/c/22283002.epi.

situation, and its strategy could narrow the gap in the construction of infrastructures among Asia Pacific and Central Asian and European countries.[1] The most popular news website in Vietnam, vnexpress.net published an article on May 15, 2017, which confirmed that this forum would enable China to gradually bring the "Belt and Road" dream into reality.[2] In addition to the positive effects of the Belt and Road Initiative, Vietnamese newspapers also expressed some concerns about the feasibility of the strategy, the challenges it faces, and the impact on the regional and global geopolitics and geo-economics.

2. Feasibility of the "Belt and Road" in Vietnam — Connected with "Two Corridors and One Circle"

The Asian Infrastructure Investment Bank (AIIB) is an important source of funds and operating mechanism for China in launching the Belt and Road Initiative. Vietnam has long supported and become one of the founding members of the AIIB. When General Secretary Nguyễn Phú Trọng of the Communist Party of Vietnam visited China in January 2017, the two sides announced, in a joint communiqué, that "the cooperation on a working group for infrastructure and one for financial and monetary cooperation will be formally established, and we agree to strengthen the cooperation and coordination between the two organizations and the maritime joint cooperative development consultation working group for the joint promotion of all-round development in various fields". This could reflect Vietnam's sincerity in advancing cooperation with China on the appropriate content of the "Belt and Road". From May 11th to 15th, 2017, Vietnamese President Tran Dai Quang paid a state visit to China and attended the "Belt and Road" international cooperation forum. Presented at the Roundtable Summit, Chairman Tran Dai Quang opined that the world was entering a critical stage in the big environment, and every country and region was continuing to innovate, maximize their potential and advantages,

---

1 http://cuoituan.tuoitre.vn/tin/van-de-su-kien/quoc-te/20170520/vanh-dai-con-duong-va-trung-quocmong/1316505.html.

2 http://vnexpress.net/tin-tuc/the-gioi/phan-tich/vanh-dai-va-con-duong-tham-vong-dan-thanh-hien thuc-cua-trung-quoc-3584243.html.

make effective use of the achievements of science and technology, and ensure a peaceful, secure and stable environment and sustainable development. On the basis of these principles, Vietnam welcomed various economic and regional connectivity initiatives, including the Belt and Road Initiative and was willing to work with other countries to explore, construct and implement projects that could bring benefits to all countries and contribute to sustainable development. President Tran Dai Quang emphasized the need for cooperation among countries under the "Belt and Road" framework to: link with the *United Nations 2030 Agenda for Sustainable Development* and existing regional and global cooperation frameworks; meet efficient and sustainable standards; give priority to projects that are pragmatic and meet the developmental needs of countries and regions; cooperate on the basis of consensus, equality, willingness, transparency, openness, mutual respect, mutual benefit and compliance with the principles of the UN Charter and international laws. Talking about the issue of connectivity and cooperation, the Vietnamese President shared Vietnam's efforts in promoting unimpeded economic trading and traffic with neighboring countries, helping landlocked countries and those without transit conditions to integrate more deeply into the global trading system. He emphasized that priority should be given to effective economic ties among countries, the development of transportation connectivity among continents, the formation of a transportation system that connects Asian countries and between Asia and Europe, Africa and the American continent, and the ease of cultural exchanges and trade and investment.[1] These statements reflected Vietnam's positive response to the Belt and Road Initiative. However, in the short term, to be effective, we should also make a good link between the "Belt and Road" and "Two Corridors and One Circle".

2.1 "Two Corridors and One Circle" Laying a Solid Foundation for the Construction of the "Belt and Road"

In 2004, during a state visit to China, Vietnamese Prime Minister Phan Van Khai proposed to Premier Wen Jiabao the idea of building the "Two Corridors

---

1 http://vov.vn/chinh-tri/viet-nam-hoan-nghenh-cac-sang-kien-lien-ket-kinh-te-624661.vov.

and One Circle" together. Since 2005, the "Two Corridors and One Circle" was included in the content of the China-Vietnam Joint Statement. During Chinese President Xi Jinping's visit to Vietnam in November 2015, the two countries reached a consensus and wrote these points into the joint statement: to enhance the connectivity of developmental strategies between the two countries; promote the connectivity between the framework of "Two Corridors and One Circle" and the Belt and Road Initiative, and quickly establish working groups while working closely towards signing a master plan to build a cross-border economic co-operation zone. During a visit to China by Vietnamese President Tran Dai Quang in May 2017, the joint communiqué issued by the two sides also clearly stated that: "On the basis of meeting our respective interests, capabilities and conditions, we must accelerate the signing of the memorandum of understanding on the cooperation of the Belt and Road Initiative and the framework of 'Two Corridors and One Circle'. We must give full play to the role of the working group for cooperation on land infrastructures in enhancing connectivity between the two countries. Moreover, it is necessary to actively advance the five-year planning research and preparation in the fields of Vietnam-China land infrastructure cooperation and energy as planned, and advance the Hanoi Metro Line 2 (Cat Linh – Ha Dong) project to be completed as scheduled."[1] The content of "Two Corridors and One Circle" involves all the aspects of Vietnam-China relations, covering economics, trade relations, investments, technical cooperation, environmental protection, tourism, and so on. "Two corridors" refers to the economic corridors of Kunming - Lào Cai - Hanoi - Haiphong - Quảng Ninh and Nanning - Lang Son - Hanoi - Haiphong - Quảng Ninh. "One circle" refers to the Gulf of Tonkin Economic Circle, which includes Guangxi (Beihai, Qinzhou, Fangcheng), Hainan, and Guangdong (Zhanjiang) in China, and Quảng Ninh, Haiphong, Thai Binh, Nam Dinh, Ninh Binh, Thanh Hoa, Nghe An, Ha Ninh, Quang Binh, Quang Tri and other provinces and cities. Currently, the main achievements of the two sides in implementing the "Two Corridors and One Circle" focus on economic and trade relations and the construction of connectivity infrastructures.

1　http://zh.vietnamplus.vn.

First of all, economic and trade cooperation is not only the main content of the "Two Corridors and One Circle", but it is also the highlight of Vietnam-China relations. China has been Vietnam's largest trading partner since 2004 and Vietnam has now become China's largest trading partner among the ASEAN countries. The scale of trade between two countries is continuously expanding. The biggest problem in Vietnam-China economic and trade cooperation is the trade imbalance because Vietnam has serious trade deficits with China, but the deficit has shown a trend towards a decline recently. According to Hong Xiaoyong, Chinese Ambassador to Vietnam, "Last year (2016), Vietnam's exports to China increased by more than 20%. On the contrary, China's exports to Vietnam showed a downward trend. In the first quarter of this year (2017), this trend continued. According to statistics, Vietnam's exports to China increased by 40% in the first quarter, and the overall bilateral trade structure is becoming more balanced."[1] The trade structure between Vietnam and China is also constantly being optimized. Technology- and capital-intensive industries gradually replace agricultural and sideline products, primary industrial products and mineral raw materials and they have become the main products of bilateral trade. The breadth and depth of cooperation between the two sides are continuously expanding. As the integration of the "Two Corridors and One Circle" and the "Belt and Road" strategy becomes a consensus of the leaders of the two countries, cooperation projects will be moving forward steadily. According to statistics from the Foreign Investment Agency of the Ministry of Planning and Investment of Vietnam, the amount of Chinese investment agreements with Vietnam reached 1.01 billion US dollars in the first three quarters of 2016, with a year-on-year increase of 304%. Among them, there are 208 new projects with an agreement amount of 670 million US dollars. At present, the number of projects with Chinese direct investment in Vietnam is 1,492, and the agreed investment is 11 billion US dollars. China has become the ninth largest source of foreign investment in Vietnam.

---

1   http://www.haoyidian.com/5526105/20170509A06WDV00.html.

Second, the construction of infrastructure within the framework of the "Two Corridors and One Circle". The Hanoi-Lao Cai Expressway opened to traffic in 2014. This is the first expressway in Vietnam to connect the Vietnam-China border. It cost 1.46 billion US dollars. This is an important project of the Kunming-Vietnam Coastal Economic Corridor. The Hanoi-Haiphong Expressway opened to traffic in 2015. The total length of this expressway is nearly 106 kilometers and the investment was more than 2 billion US dollars. As a lifeline expressway connecting Hanoi, the capital of Vietnam, and Haiphong, the most important port in northern Vietnam, this will undoubtedly play an important role in Vietnam's economic development and in the mobility of the people. The Hanoi-Lang Son Expressway is 146 kilometers in length, with an estimated total investment of about 1.3 billion US dollars. It was divided into three sections: construction of the Hanoi-Bac Giang section commenced in 2014 and was completed in early 2016; construction of the Bac Giang-Lang Son section commenced in 2015 and is estimated to open to traffic in 2018; construction of the Huu Nghi-Chi Lang section commenced in 2016 and is expected to be completed in 2019.

2.2 The "Belt and Road", the Extension and Elevation of the "Two Corridors and One Circle"

China initiated the construction of the "Belt and Road" adhering to the principle of jointly building through consultation to meet the interests of all and taking "policy coordination", "facilities connectivity", "unimpeded trade", "financial integration" and "people-to-people bond" as the content of cooperation with countries along the route. The "Vision and Actions" released by the State Council of China also pointed out that facility connectivity is a priority area for cooperation in the construction of the "Belt and Road"[1]. And this is very coincidental with the "Two Corridors and One Circle" concept of Vietnam and China. In his speech at the opening ceremony of the "Belt and Road" forum, President Xi Jinping announced that China would

---

1   *Vision and Actions on Jointly Building the Silk Road Economic Belt and the 21st Century Maritime Silk Road*, People's Publishing House, 2015, p.8.

build the "Belt and Road" into a "road for peace", "a road of prosperity", "a road of opening-up", "a road of innovation" and "a road connecting different civilizations". He emphasized that: "China will enhance friendship and cooperation with all of the countries involved in the Belt and Road Initiative on the basis of the Five Principles of Peaceful Co-existence. We are ready to share practices of development with other countries, but we have no intention to interfere with other countries' internal affairs, nor to export our own social system and model of development, nor to impose our own will on others. In pursuing the Belt and Road Initiative, we will not resort to outdated geopolitical maneuvering. What we hope to achieve is a new model of win-win cooperation. We have no intention to form a small group detrimental to stability, what we hope to create is a big family of harmonious co-existence."[1] In the process of advocating the construction of the "Belt and Road", China also emphasizes the principle of "common security", thus forming a "community with a shared future for mankind". According to China, "common security" means that the security of one's own country is based on guaranteeing the security of other countries, safeguarding the security of one's own country while also ensuring the security of other countries. This is different from the traditional concept of geopolitical "security". If China can implement the "Belt and Road" cooperation in accordance with the above commitments, it will contribute to the peace, security and prosperity of the region and of the world as a whole, and this can also reflect the attitude and responsibility of a big power.

After four years of summary and refinement, China has formed a more complete theoretical system for the Belt and Road Initiative. "Two Corridors and One Circle" is a cooperation strategy previously proposed for Vietnam and China. It shares many similarities with the "Belt and Road" in terms of concept and content of cooperation, but it has not formed a theoretical system. If the "Belt and Road" and "Two Corridors and One Circle" can be integrated, the concept of "Two Corridors and One Circle" can be extended and deepened, making it more theoretical and

---

1   http://news.sohu.com/20170514/n492975720.shtml.

institutionalized and enabling the "Belt and Road" to be effectively expanded in Vietnam in the short term. The construction of the Vietnam-China Cross-border Economic Cooperation Zone can also play a positive role in the integration of the two strategic initiatives. The Vietnam-China Cross-border Economic Cooperation Zone has long been the consensus of the governments of the two countries. If it is established, it will not only be conducive to the connectivity between Vietnam and China, but also to the connectivity between Southeast Asia and China. However, the two sides have not yet formed a joint plan of construction mainly because we have not determined a common operating mechanism that is in the interests of both countries. Therefore, in May 2017, Vietnam and China confirmed in a joint communiqué that: "According to the principles of equality and mutual benefit, respect for independence and territorial integrity, and in accordance with the legal provisions of the two sides and international practices, we will accelerate the signing of the overall program for the construction of the Vietnam-China Cross-border Economic Cooperation Zone."[1] Furthermore, on the one hand, Vietnam and China should build a pilot zone of the Cross-Border Economic Cooperation Zone in a suitable and small region (such as Yunnan-Lao Cai or Guangxi-Mong Cai); on the other hand, the two sides should communicate with each other and discuss in order to find a suitable mechanism of cooperation in the interests of both countries.

3. Several Suggestions

It is beyond doubt that connectivity is crucial to promoting the long-term healthy and stable development of the comprehensive strategic partnership between Vietnam and China. It is the aspiration of the Vietnamese government and people to promote comprehensive and effective cooperation with China. The problem is how to make the most of the connectivity, which is an issue that scholars of the two countries must consider together. The author makes the following suggestions.

---

1 http://www.nhandan.com.vn/chinhtri/item/32881402-thong-cao-chung-viet-nam-trung-quoc.html.

First, a "people-to-people bond" is important.

Vietnam and China have a long tradition of friendship. Currently, the achievements of cooperation between the two sides in the fields of politics, economy, culture, science and technology are remarkable. However, strategic mutual suspicion has long been widely regarded by scholars as an important factor hindering the healthy development of relations between the two countries. In recent years, the mentality of mutual suspicion has shown a popular trend in both countries, and causes concern. With the unprecedented development of the Internet today, the public has more channels to express their voice. On the one hand, the information they receive is more diversified; on the other hand, they also have more and more platforms for participating in national governance. This has become a global trend, and the people of Vietnam and China are no exception. The friendship among nations lies in the closeness of the people. There is "facility connectivity" in the "five connectivity" of the "Belt and Road". The construction of infrastructure is what China is good at and Vietnam lacks. However, at present, for the realization of connectivity and cooperation between Vietnam and China, we must pay more attention to the principle of a "people-to-people bond" because it is the foundation and guarantee for the other "four connectivities" and, except for the "policy coordination", the other "four connectivities" must be realized by the people of the two countries. In resolving the mutual suspicion of the people on both sides, the "soft connectivity" of "public opinion" is very crucial. A mechanism for communication and dialogue needs to be established among the media on both sides, as well as a project for a system of discourse among scholars. Meanwhile, other exchange activities should be expanded in the fields of tourism, education, science and technology, and non-governmental organizations.

Second, action speaks.

In the process of realizing the country's industrialization and modernization, Vietnam has a very large demand for the construction of infrastructures. As a result, it implements an open policy on foreign investment and looks forward to attracting more and more Chinese investors, with the construction of infrastructures as a priority area. However, for more than a decade, in Vietnam, the projects regarding infrastructures contracted by Chinese contractors do have problems, such as low quality, delayed schedule and increased prices. Construction of the Hanoi Metro Line 2, started in October 2011, was expected to open in December 2015, but it is currently estimated to be completed by the end of 2018. The amount of investment is 300 million US dollars higher than the budget[1], and some safety accidents have also occurred during the process of construction. This results in staining the credit and image of Chinese enterprises investing in Vietnam and has a negative impact on the Belt and Road Initiative advocated by China. Of course, it is not solely the responsibility of Chinese enterprises. Vietnam's tendering and management experience is weak. The professional level of labor is limited and their attitude of observing discipline is not strict enough. Corruption and other factors also affect the quality of the entire project. Therefore, Vietnamese and Chinese entrepreneurs should look at this issue realistically, take real actions and construct high-quality projects to prove their strength and reshape the image of modernization and nationalization of enterprises.

Third, unswervingly maintain friendship between Vietnam and China.

Vietnam and China have gone through various difficulties being in the same boat. We always cherish the "comrades and brothers" friendship inherited from our predecessors, such as President Ho Chi Minh and Chairman Mao Zedong, and we work hard to promote the comprehensive strategic partnership between the two countries. Both sides believe that Vietnam-China friendship is a common treasure for the two sides, the two countries and the two peoples, and should be passed on and carried forward. In the context of the construction of the "Belt and Road", the two countries must firmly uphold the "16-character" policy and the "four good" spirit proposed for the friendly relations between the two sides. They are by no

---

1 http://vnexpress.net/infographics/giao-thong/nhung-lan-tang-von-lui-tien-do-cua-duong-sat-cat linh-ha-dong-3591133.html.

means empty slogans without substance, but they reflect the special relationship between Vietnam and China. Vietnam and China should communicate and negotiate strategic cooperation on the "Belt and Road" on the basis of maintaining the spirit of friendship between the two countries. Due to the maritime conflict, Vietnam-China relations sometimes are subject to a rise and fall. Therefore, during the visit of Vietnamese President Tran Dai Quang to China in May 2017, the Vietnam-China Joint Communiqué issued also agreed to continue to abide by the important consensus reached by the leaders of the two parties and the two countries in the *Basic Principle Agreement on Guiding the Solution of Vietnam-China Maritime Problems*[1]. Vietnam and China should properly manage, handle and resolve differences through peaceful negotiations and abide by the principles of international law. Disputes should not be complicated, so as to create a favorable environment for promoting exchanges and cooperation between the two sides under the "Belt and Road" framework.

International powers are changing. The international order is being rebuilt. Kissinger argues in his new book *World Order* that: Due to drastic changes in the times and situations, it is now necessary to build a third world order after the Westphalian system established in 1648 and the Vienna system established in 1815[2]. In the process of designing a new landscape in the world, the objects of governance in the international community will become more diversified. The "Belt and Road" will give the emerging China an opportunity to elevate itself from a participant to a leader of international governance. It is also a good opportunity for China to reevaluate its own value and ability. The "Belt and Road" is a big project that should be jointly built by all countries. The "Belt and Road" can be promoted and sustainable development can become possible only with an understanding of the specific conditions of countries along the route and effective communication among them.

1　http://zh.vietnamplus.vn.
2　[USA] Henry Kissinger, *World Order*, China CITIC Press, 2015.

从传统的概念谈中国现代化的道路选择

木固烈【罗马尼亚】
布加勒斯特大学讲师

现代化中国在自己的传统和西方思想的冲突或博弈中，从反对古老的传统文化走到传统和现代思想融合在一起。从 20 世纪初的"五四运动"到今天才 100 年，但在这 100 年中，发生了前所未有的巨大变化。即使有人认为，中国现代化仍然在进行当中，我们能肯定地说，目前的社会已经不是 20 世纪初的传统社会，但这并不意味着传统消失了。

为中国带来现代化的许多事件都发生在过去，已经属于历史了，我们今天只能感觉到其影响，却不能有与当时参与运动的人同样的经验。德国历史哲学家科塞雷克指出，要了解过去或过去的经验，我们只能通过语言，通过文字才能做得到。[1]

我们在讨论社会变化的时候，一定要注意政治或知识分子话语中最重要的概念，因为概念不仅表达具体发生了什么，也可以告诉我们事情是怎么发生的。拿"modern"这个概念为例，20 世纪初，汉语中本来没有这一概念，当时的知识分子要么使用直接从英文音译的"摩登"（有"现代"和"时髦"的意思），要么从日语借用的"现代"（*gendai*）描述他们想象未发生的变化，也就是说，这一概念形容了他们还没有的一种经验。在当时的中国，这些知识分子不是从具体实物了

---

1 Koselleck, R. (2004). *Futures Past. On the Semantics of Historical Time*.New York: Columbia University Press.

解现代化，而是从语言上开始意识到这种现象的存在。可以说，现代这个概念先于历史，它的出现带来了具体的变化，或者使用语用学的术语，语言先起了行事的作用。而事情发生以后，用同样的概念陈述刚发生的；从以言行事变成为以言述事。概念有双重功能，可以引起变化，同时是变化的结果；实物的变化使概念的意义变得丰富，出现滚雪球的效应。

为了解中国近100年来的现代化，单独看"现代"这个概念不够，因为从一开始"现代"就离不开"传统"。五四运动期间，"现代"和"传统"本身出现得较少，经常由"新"和"旧"替代，即，来自西方的被视为"新"，中国本土的以"旧"来形容。在五四时期的知识分子眼里，新的是合适的、好的，旧的等于过期的、应放弃的。陈独秀在《敬告青年》中写道："吾宁忍过去国粹之消亡，而不忍现在及将来之民族，不适世界之生存而归削灭也。"[1] 五四运动把现代化和传统对立起来了，激进者想要彻底打倒孔家店，保守者拒绝所有来自西方的思想，不可能把这两个融合起来，旧的先要去，新的才能来："新旧两种法子，好像水火冰炭，断然不能相容；要想两样并行，必至弄得非牛非马，一样不成。"[2] 周作人不否认古人有自己的精华，但是这种精华在模仿者手中成为糟粕："创作的古人自有他的神髓，但模仿者的所得却只有皮毛，便是所谓糟粕。"[3]

对五四运动人物来讲，放弃宗教，相信科学是现代社会的一种标志，陈独秀警告他的同胞说"国人而欲脱蒙昧时代，羞为浅化之民也，则急起直追，当以科学与人权并重。"他们不仅反对孔子和儒家思想，反对一切传统文化，因为在过去2000多年，没有任何学说没受到儒学的传染。胡适也认为"我确信中国哲学的将来，有赖于从儒学的道德伦理和理性的枷锁中得到解放。这种解放，不能只用大批西方哲学的输入来实现，而只能让儒学回到它本来的地位，也就是恢复它在其历史背景中的地位。儒学曾经只是盛行于古代中国的许多敌对的学派中的一派，因此，只要不把它看作精神的、道德的、哲学的权威的唯一源泉，而只是在灿烂的哲学群星中的一颗明星，那么，儒学的被废黜便不成问题了。"[4]

不是所有知识分子都全心全意地主张"全盘西化"。在五四运动人物中也有

1 陈独秀：《敬告青年》，《独秀文存》（第一册），上海亚东图书馆1933年版，第1—10页。
2 陈独秀：《今日中国之政治问题》，《独秀文存》（第一册），上海亚东图书馆1933年，第221—226页。
3 周作人：《国粹与欧化》，钟叔河（编）《周作人文类编》，湖南文艺出版社1998年版，221—227页。
4 庞朴：《继承五四、超越五四》，《历史研究》1989年第2期，第78—86页。

一些承认西方新知识的重要性，但不同意模仿西方文化。周作人在《国粹与欧华》中指出，"模仿杜少陵或泰戈尔，模仿苏东坡或胡适之，都不是我们所赞成的，但是受他们的影响是可以的，也是有益的，这便是我对于欧化问题的态度"。李大钊保留更加合理的态度说，青年与老人"急进与保守是也"。亦曰："有一义焉当牢记于心者，即此基于执性之二种世界观，不可相竞以图征服或灭尽其他。盖二者均属必要，同为永存，其竞立对抗乃为并驾齐驱以保世界之进步也。"[1]

　　同其他青年人一样，毛泽东也参与了中国现代化辩论。1919 年，在《健学会之成立及进行》中，介绍了自己对引进西方经验的想法，认为自强运动所主张的"西学"或"新法"并不是真正的革新，那时候的思想，是一种"中学为体，西学为用"的思想，"中国是一个声名文物之邦，中国的礼教甲于万国，西洋只有格致炮厉害，学来这一点便得。"设若议论稍不如此，便被人看作"心醉欧风者流"，要受一世人的唾骂了。那时候的思想是以孔子为中心的思想……却于孔老爹，仍不敢说出半个"非"字。甚至盛倡其"学问要新，道德要旧"的谬说，"道德要旧"就是'道德要从孔子'的变语。虽然作者的语气没有五四运动倡导者强，但是他对吸引国外知识的渴望很明显。健学会会则的第五条和第九条是关于如何"输入新思潮之方法"和讨论的自由。人类最可宝贵最堪自乐的一点却在于此（自由讨论），学术的研究最忌演绎式的独断态度。中国什么"师严而后道尊"，师说"道统"，"宗派"都是害了独断态度的大病。都是思想界的强权，不可不竭力打破。像我们反对孔子，有很多别的理由，单就这独霸中国，使我们思想界不能自由，郁郁做 2000 年偶像的奴隶，也是不能不反对的。"当然，成为革命领导之后，毛泽东的立场有所改变。作为一名共产党员，他不能反对吸引来自国外的新知识，同时也不可能支持全盘西化。为了能够在中国这块土地生根，马克思主义需要适应中国的现实，否则"离开中国特点来谈马克思主义，只是抽象的空洞的马克思主义"。[2]

　　尽管"五四运动"反对传统，在 20 世纪 20、30 年代，儒家思想仍然对中国老百姓的生活影响很大。想要使马克思主义"在中国具体化"，起码在政治话语中，不能保持五四运动类似的态度。毛泽东指出，"我们这个民族有数千年的历史，有它的特点，有它的许多珍贵品。对于这些，我们还是小学生。今天的中国

1　李大钊：《青年与老人》，http://cpc.people.com.cn/GB/69112/71148/71151/4848661.html.
2　毛泽东：《中国共产党在民族战争中的地位》，https://www.marxists.org/chinese/maozedong/marxist.org-chinese-mao-19381014.htm.

是历史的中国的一个发展；我们是马克思主义的历史主义者，我们不应当割断历史。从孔夫子到孙中山，我们应当给以总结，承继这一份珍贵的遗产。"

随着中国共产党地位的巩固以及马克思主义的传播，毛泽东坚持中国需要吸收西方的新知识的立场，但是对吸收的东西应该跟对食物一样，"必须经过自己的口腔咀嚼和胃肠运动，送进唾液胃液肠液，把它分解为精华和糟粕两部分，然后排泄其糟粕，吸收其精华，才能对我们的身体有益，决不能生吞活剥地毫无批判地吸收。"[1] 五四运动主张的"全盘西化"是错的，它仅是一种形式主义，根本不可能直接把外国的经验用于中国。马克思主义也不例外，"中国共产主义者对于马克思主义在中国的应用也是这样，必须将马克思主义的普遍真理和中国革命的具体实践完全地恰当地统一起来，就是说，和民族的特点相结合，经过一定的民族形式，才有用处，决不能主观地公式地应用它。"理性地把理论和实践结合起来的态度才算是正确的科学态度。

虽然最后毛泽东以批判的精神对待"五四运动"，但是他没有否认运动的重要性，不断强调共产党是"五四运动"精神的继承者，并使用了"五四运动"话语中的概念。不过社会的变化引起了这些概念意义的变化。谈到西方新知识的时候，毛泽东主张取其精华、去其糟粕，并且什么是精华，什么是糟粕，要用历史唯物主义来判断。毛泽东对传统的态度不仅没有新的意识形态和传统对立起来，正相反，他强调新意识形态唯一成功的方法是吸纳中国古老传统的精华。

2013 年，国家主席习近平指出，"在 5000 多年文明发展进程中，中华民族创造了博大精深的灿烂文化，要使中华民族最基本的文化基因与当代文化相适应、与现代社会相协调，以人们喜闻乐见、具有广泛参与性的方式推广开来，把跨越时空、超越国度、富有永恒魅力、具有当代价值的文化精神弘扬起来，把继承传统优秀文化又弘扬时代精神、立足本国又面向世界的当代中国文化创新成果传播出去。要系统梳理传统文化资源，让收藏在禁宫里的文物、陈列在广阔大地上的遗产、书写在古籍里的文字都活起来。"[2]

习近平提出的中国梦和社会主义核心价值观都涉及传统文化。2014 年，习近平在巴黎联合国教科文组织总部发言时，强调"实现中国梦，是物质文明和精神文明均衡发展、相互促进的结果。没有文明的继承和发展，没有文化的弘扬和繁

1　毛泽东：《新民主主义论》，https://www.marxists.org/chinese/maozedong/marxist.org-chinese-mao-194001.htm.
2　《习近平谈治国理政》，外文出版社 2014 年版，第 160—162 页。

荣，就没有中国梦的实现。"[1] 同年，与北京大学师生见面的时候，明确指出"中华优秀传统文化已经成为中华民族的基因，植根在中国人内心，潜移默化影响着中国人的思想方式和行为方式。今天，我们提倡和弘扬社会主义核心价值观，必须从中汲取丰富营养，否则就不会有生命力和影响力。"[2]

在不断强调中国文化的重要性的情况下，全盘西化绝不可能。传统文化不仅有助于马克思主义的中国化，近十几年来有不少马克思主义学者承认传统文化对中国马克思主义的影响，更重要的是，在目前的政治话语中，中国文化被视为"民族的灵魂"[3]，涉及中国人的民族认同。21 世纪的中国不能再关闭国家大门，但也不能像五四运动激进者那样否认一切中国的东西，要学习他国优秀的成果，不要简单地模仿。"外国有益、好的东西，我们要虚心学习。但是，不能全盘照搬外国，更不能接受外国不好的东西；不能妄自菲薄，不能数典忘祖。"[4] 马克思主义也一样，"对国外马克思主义研究新成果，我们要密切关注和研究，有分析、有鉴别，既不能采取一概排斥的态度，也不能搞全盘照搬。"[5]

在新的世纪，尤其是自从传统文化在政治话语中占有较重要的位置以来，有些知识分子把马克思主义和传统的儒家思想对立起来了，讨论了各种意识形态对现代社会的作用。习近平在孔子诞辰 2565 周年国际学术研讨会上发言："春秋战国时期，儒家和法家、道家、墨家、农家、兵家等各个思想流派相互切磋、相互激荡，形成了百家争鸣的文化大观，丰富了当时中国人的精神世界。虽然后来儒家思想在中国思想文化领域长期取得了主导地位，但中国思想文化依然是多向多元发展的。"[6]

在目前的政治话语中，传统文化这一概念很少单独出现，一般来说跟"优秀"搭配在一起。使用优秀传统文化意味着也有非优秀的传统文化，而且总书记谈传

1　《习近平在联合国教科文组织总部的演讲（全文）》，http://www.xinhuanet.com/world/2014-03/28/c_119982831.htm.

2　2014 年 5 月 5 日，《青年要自觉践行社会主义核心价值观》，《习近平谈治国理政》，外文出版社 2014 年版，第 166-179 页。

3　《习近平十九大报告全文（实录）》，http://finance.sina.com.cn/china/gncj/2017-10-18/doc-ifymvuyt4098830.shtml

4　《努力开创中国特色社会主义事业更加广阔的前景》，《习近平谈治国理政（第二卷）》，外文出版社 2017 年版，第 12-13 页。

5　《继续推进马克思主义中国化时代化大众化》，《习近平谈治国理政（第二卷）》，外文出版社 2017 年版，第 67 页。

6　习近平：《在纪念孔子诞辰 2565 周年国际学术研讨会暨国际儒学联合会第五届会员大会开幕会上的讲话》，http://www.xinhuanet.com//politics/2014-09/24/c_1112612018_2.htm.

统文化时，就像他以前的领导人，数次提出过"取其精华，去其糟粕"。传统文化的这种理解并不是新的，是整个 20 世纪的一个大问题，而且在新的世纪里仍然没有收到答案。今天的领导和知识分子面临着跟"五四运动"创导者同样的问题，把传统二分化需要决定放弃什么、保留什么、怎么放弃、要走多远。

如今回头看，谁都不能否认，"五四运动"知识分子的斗争为中国现代化打好了基础，虽然他们很多行为的极端性相当强，但这跟当时的历史条件有密切关系。20 世纪初的知识分子明白了他们国家需要彻底的变化。对他们来讲，现代化等于西化很正常，因为现代化的起源本来就是欧洲西方国家。更重要的是，长时间以来受到中国文化影响的日本，就是因为引进了西方国家的改革经验超越了中国。"五四运动"人士了解到现代化不能限于物质变化，新的武器和旧的思想不能保卫国家，一定要从人们的思维方式开始，因此把传统和现代化对立起来了。

以西方文化替代传统文化根本没有解决中国社会的问题，也没有带来"五四运动"倡导者所希望的现代化。许多 20 世纪初的问题归于新的领导人来解决。我们认为，中国真正的现代化是在国家领导人和其他知识分子，意识到要放弃把传统和现代对立对待的那个时刻开始的，因为现代化不可能是从外边强加的。只有把来自国外的新知识跟传统并列起来，才能得到现代化。现代化是从传统的现代化说起，而传统只有遇到新因素的时候才能开始转换，就像李大钊所说的，两者缺一不可。

On the Selection of China's Path Towards Modernization from Traditional Concepts

Zlotea Mugurel Dan / Romania

Bucharest University, Lecturer

In the conflict or game between its own tradition and Western thoughts, modernized China has gone from opposing the ancient traditional culture to the integration of traditional and modern thoughts. It has only been one hundred years since the May Fourth Movement in the early 20th century, but in one hundred years, unprecedented changes have taken place. Even if some people think that China's modernization is still in progress, we can say with certainty that the current society is no longer the traditional society of the early 20th century, but this does not mean that tradition has already disappeared.

Numerous events that brought modernization to China happened in the past and became parts of history. Today we can only feel their influence, but cannot have the same experience as those who participated in the movement at that time. German historian and philosopher Reinhart Koselleck pointed out that to understand the past or past experience, we can only achieve it through language and words.[1]

---

1 Koselleck, R. (2004). *Futures Past. On the Semantics of Historical Time*. New York: Columbia University Press.

When discussing social changes, we must pay attention to the most important concepts in the discourse of politics or intellectuals because concepts not only express what happened specifically, but also tell us how things happened. Take the concept of "modern" as an example. At the beginning of the 20th century, there was no such concept in Chinese. At that time, intellectuals either used "modeng" (means "modern" and "fashionable") directly transliterated from English or "xiandai" (*gendai*) borrowed from Japanese to describe changes they imagined, that is, the concept described an experience they had not yet had. In the China of that time, these intellectuals did not understand modernization from concrete objects, but began to realize the existence of this phenomenon from the language. It could be said that the concept of modernity preceded history, its emergence brought concrete changes or used pragmatic terms, and language played a leading role. After it happened, the same concept was used to state what had just happened; it changed from "act with words" to "be described with words". The concept had a dual function, which could cause changes and at the same time be the result of changes; the changes of objects could enrich the meaning of the concept and the snowball effect appeared.

In order to understand China's modernization in the past 100 years, it is not enough to look at the concept of "modern" alone because "modern" cannot be separated from "tradition" from the very beginning. During the May Fourth Movement, "modern" and "traditional" appeared less often by themselves but were often replaced by "new" and "old", that is, those from the west were regarded as "new" and Chinese natives were "old". In the eyes of intellectuals during the May Fourth period, the new was appropriate and good and the old was outdated and should be abandoned. Chen Duxiu wrote in "A Letter to Youth" that: "I would rather endure the demise of the past, but not the nation of the present and the future being destroyed for not fitting the world."[1] The May Fourth Movement antagonized modernization and tradition, radicals wanted to completely destroy Confucius, but conservatives rejected all ideas from the West. It was impossible to fuse them, the

---

1 Chen Duxiu, "A Letter to Youth", *Collected Writings of Duxiu (Volume 1)*, Shanghai: The Oriental Book Company, 1933, pp.1-10.

old must be removed first, and then the new could come: "New and old methods, like water and fire, cannot be compatible; if you want to go both ways, the result will be neither ox nor horse, and nothing can be achieved."[1] Zhou Zuoren did not deny that ancients had their own essence, but this essence became the dross in the hands of imitators: "The ancient people who created them have their own essence, but the imitators could only obtain superficial knowledge, the so-called dross."[2]

For those who participated in the May Fourth Movement, abandoning religion and believing in science was a sign of modern society. Chen Duxiu warned his compatriots that "If our Chinese people want to get rid of the uncivilized age, people who are ashamed to become uncultured must rush to catch up. Science and human rights are equally important." They opposed not only Confucius and Confucianism, but also all parts of the traditional culture, because in the past two thousand years, no theory had not been infected by Confucianism. According to Hu Shi, "I am convinced that the future of Chinese philosophy depends on liberation from the shackles of the ethics and rationality of Confucianism. This liberation cannot be achieved only by introducing plenty of Western philosophy, but by sending Confucianism back to its original state; that is, its position in the historical background. Confucianism was once only one of the many opposing schools that used to prevail in ancient China. Therefore, as long as it is not regarded as the only source of spiritual, moral and philosophical authority, but just a star among the brilliant philosophical stars, then the dethronement of Confucianism will not be a problem."[3]

Not all intellectuals wholeheartedly advocated "wholesale westernization". Some intellectuals in the May Fourth Movement acknowledged the importance of new Western knowledge, but did not agree to imitate Western culture. Zhou

---

1 Chen Duxiu, "Political Issues in China Today" , *Collected Writings of Duxiu (Volume 1)*, Shanghai: The Oriental Book Company, 1933, pp.221-226.

2 Zhou Zuoren, "National Essence and Europeanization" , Zhong Shuhe (ed.), *The Edited Writings of Zhou Zuoren 1 · Chinese Taste · Ideology, Society, Current Affairs*, Changsha: Hunan Literature and Art Publishing House, 1998, pp.221-227.

3 Hu Shi, "Introduction to the Development of the Logical Method in Ancient China" , Pang Pu, "Inheritance and Transcendence of May Fourth" , *Historical Research*, 1989(2), pp.78-86.

Zuoren pointed out in his "National Essence and Europeanization" that "imitating Du Shaoling or Tagore, imitating Su Dongpo or Hu Shi is not what we approve of, but it is possible and beneficial to be influenced by them. This is my attitude on the issue of Europeanization." Li Dazhao took a more rational attitude, saying that young people and the elders "are also radical and conservative. I also say that: 'We must keep this in mind, that is, the two world views cannot compete to conquer or destroy the other. Both are necessary, and both are permanent. They compete to go hand in hand and keep the world progressing."[1]

Like other young people, Mao Zedong also participated in the debate on China's modernization. In 1919, he briefed his thoughts on the introduction of Western experience in the "Establishment and Progress of the Education Society" and opined that the "Western studies" or "new methods" advocated by the Self-Strengthening Movement were not true innovations. "The idea then was 'Chinese learning as the fundamental structure, Western learning for practical use'. China is a state of prestigious culture and relics, China's rites and religions are best among the nations, and only Western science is powerful. This is what we need to learn. If your idea is a little bit different, you will be regarded as "being infatuated with European style" and reviled by the people. At that time, the thoughts were centered on Confucius ... and no one dared to say 'no' to Confucius. They even advocated the fallacy of 'new knowledge, old morality'. 'Old morality' was a variant of obedience to Confucius." Although the author's tone was not as strong as that of the advocates of the May Fourth Movement, his desire to learn foreign knowledge was obvious. Articles 5 and 9 of the Association of the Education Society involve how to "input new ideas" and freedom of discussion. "One of the most precious and enjoyable aspects of mankind is the [free discussion]. Academic research is most afraid of deductive assertiveness. In China, 'the teacher is strict and the Tao is respected.' 'Unity under Tao' or 'sects' said by teachers are serious illnesses that have the attitude of assertiveness. In the ideological world, they are hegemony that must be removed. For example, there are

---

1   Li Dazhao, "Youth and Elders". http://cpc.people.com.cn/GB/69112/71148/71151/4848661.html.

many other reasons for us to oppose Confucius. Dominating China alone shackles our ideological world and we must oppose being a slave to idols in the two thousand years." Of course, after becoming a revolutionary leader, Mao's ideas changed. As a communist, he could neither oppose absorbing new knowledge from abroad, nor support wholesale Westernization. In order to take root in China, Marxism had to be localized and adapt to the reality of China. Otherwise, "any talk about Marxism in isolation from China's characteristics is merely Marxism in the abstract, Marxism in a vacuum."[1]

Although the "May Fourth Movement" opposed tradition, in the 1920s and 1930s, Confucianism still had a great influence on the lives of Chinese people. In order to make Marxism "materialize in China", at least in political discourse, a similar attitude to the May Fourth Movement could not be maintained. Mao Zedong pointed out that "Our nation, with a history of thousands of years, has its characteristics and many valuables. In this regard, we are still elementary school students. China today is a development of historical China; we are Marxist historians, so we should not cut off history. From Confucius to Sun Yat-sen, we should sum up and inherit this precious legacy."

With the consolidation of the status of the Communist Party and the spread of Marxism, Mao Zedong kept a certain distance from the May Fourth Movement. He insisted that China should absorb new knowledge from the west, but must treat it as we did our food — "first chew it, then submit it to the working of the stomach and intestines with their juices and secretions, and separate it into nutriments to be absorbed and waste matter to be discarded — before it can nourish us."[2] The "wholesale Westernization" advocated by the May Fourth Movement was wrong. It was only a formalism because foreign experience could not be directly applied to China. Marxism was no exception. "Similarly, in applying Marxism to China, Chinese communists must fully and properly integrate the universal truth of

---

1   Mao Zedong, "The Role of the Chinese Communist Party in the National War" . https://www. marxists.org/chinese/maozedong/marxist.org-chinese-mao-19381014.htm.

2   Mao Zedong, *On New Democracy.* https://www.marxists.org/chinese/maozedong/marxist.org-chinesemao-194001.htm.

Marxism with the concrete practice of the Chinese revolution, or in other words, the universal truth of Marxism must be combined with specific national characteristics and acquire a definite national form if it is to be useful, and in no circumstances can it be applied subjectively as a mere formula." An attitude rationally combining theory with practice was regarded as the correct scientific attitude.

Although in the end Mao Zedong treated the May Fourth Movement with a critical spirit, he did not deny the importance of the movement, constantly emphasizing that the Communist Party was the heir to the spirit of the May Fourth Movement, and he used the concepts in the discourse of the May Fourth Movement. However, changes in society caused changes in the meaning of these concepts. When talking about new Western knowledge, Mao Zedong advocated taking its essence and removing its dross, and what was the essence and what was the dross should be judged by historical materialism. An important difference from the May Fourth Movement was Mao's attitude towards tradition. Not just did he not antagonize new ideology with tradition, on the contrary, he emphasized that the only successful approach to new ideology was to absorb the essence of ancient Chinese tradition. It was difficult to determine what the essence of tradition was.

Traditional culture is currently at the center of political discourse. National leaders rarely give important speeches without mentioning China's long-standing traditional culture. Traditional culture is the main part of China's rejuvenation policy, and it can also be used to solve some public moral issues in contemporary society. China's soft power is also inseparable from traditional culture. In 2013, President Xi Jinping pointed out that "During its 5,000-year history, the Chinese nation has created a brilliant and profound culture. We should disseminate the most fundamental Chinese culture in a popular way to attract more people to participate in it, matching modern culture and society. We should popularize our cultural spirit across countries as well as across time and space, with contemporary values and the eternal charm of Chinese culture. We should tell the rest of the world about the new achievements of modern Chinese culture, which feature both excellent tradition and modern spirit, both national and international. To this end, efforts should be made to sort out traditional cultural resources and bring back to life relics that have been sleeping in closed palaces, legacies of the vast land of China and records in ancient books."[1]

Both the Chinese dream and the core socialist values proposed by Xi Jinping involve traditional culture. In 2014, when delivering a speech at UNESCO headquarters in Paris, Xi Jinping emphasized that "The Chinese dream requires balanced development and mutual reinforcement of material and cultural progress. Without the continuation and development of civilization or the promotion and prosperity of culture, the Chinese dream will not come true."[2] In the same year, when meeting with teachers and students of Peking University, he clearly pointed out that "The brilliant traditional Chinese culture is the essence of the nation and has deep roots in the Chinese people's mentality, unconsciously influencing their way of thinking and behavior. Today, we advocate and carry forward the core socialist values by absorbing the rich nourishment of Chinese culture, so as to invigorate its vitality and broaden its influence."[3]

With the ever-increasing importance of Chinese culture, total Westernization is absolutely impossible in any aspect. Traditional culture can contribute to the Sinicization of Marxism. In recent decades, many Marxist scholars have recognized the influence of traditional culture on Chinese Marxism. More importantly, in the current political discourse, Chinese culture is regarded as the "nation's soul"[4], which involves the national identity of the Chinese. China in the 21st century should by no means close its door, but denying everything in China like the May Fourth Movement activists is also not acceptable. It is necessary to learn the outstanding

---

1 *Xi Jinping: The Governance of China*, Foreign Languages Press, 2014, pp.160-162.
2 Xi Jinping, March 28, 2014, "Speech by Chinese President Xi Jinping at UNESCO Headquarters (full text)" . http://www. xinhuanet.com/world/2014-03/28/c_119982831.htm.
3 Xi Jinping, May 5, 2014, "Young People Should Practice the Core Socialist Values" , *Xi Jinping: The Governance of China*, Beijing: Foreign Languages Press, 2014, pp.166-179.
4 Xi Jinping, October 18, 2017, "Report of Xi Jinping Delivered at the 19th National Congress of the Communist Party of China" . http://fifinance.sina.com.cn/ china/gncj/2017-10-18/doc-ifymvuyt4098830.shtml

achievements of other countries instead of simply imitating them. "We should learn everything beneficial and good in other countries with an open mind. However, we can neither copy other countries, nor accept anything bad from them; we should not improperly belittle ourselves and forget our roots."[1] Marxism is no exception. "We must pay close attention to and study new achievements of Marxist research in other countries, and analyze and discriminate between the good and the bad. We must neither totally exclude nor follow suit."[2]

In the new century, especially since traditional culture occupies a relatively important position in political discourse, some intellectuals oppose Marxism and traditional Confucianism and explore the role of various ideologies on modern society. The idea of Xi Jinping at the International Conference in Commemoration of the 2,565th Anniversary of Confucius' Birth reflected Hu Shi's point in the early 20th century: "In the Spring and Autumn and Warring States periods, Confucian, Taoist, Mohist, Agriculturist, and Warist schools of thought contended and compared notes with each other, presenting the magnificent cultural landscape of the contention of a hundred schools of thoughts, enriching the spiritual world of the Chinese of the time. Although Confucianism has long assumed a dominant position in the field of Chinese ideology and culture, the development of Chinese ideology and culture has been plural and multi-dimensional."[3]

In the current political discourse, the concept of traditional culture rarely appears alone, but is generally paired with "excellent". The expression of excellent traditional culture means that there is also non-excellent traditional culture. When our General Secretary talks about traditional culture, like previous leaders, he

---

1 Xi Jinping, "Strive to Open up Broader Prospects for Socialism with Chinese Characteristics" , *Xi Jinping: The Governance of China (Volume Two)*, Beijing: Foreign Languages Press, pp.12-13.

2 Xi Jinping, September 29, 2017, "Continue to Advance the Sinicization, Modernization and Popularization of Marxism" , *Xi Jinping: The Governance of China (Volume Two)*, Beijing: Foreign Languages Press, p.67.

3 Xi Jinping, September 24, 2014, Speech at the Opening Ceremony of the International Conference in Commemoration of the 2,565th Anniversary of Confucius' Birth and the Fifth Congress of the International Confucian Association. http://www.xinhuanet.com//politics/2014-09/24/c_1112612018_2.htm.

proposes "taking the essence and removing the dross" on several occasions. This understanding of traditional culture is not new, but it was a big problem throughout the 20th century, and still does not have an answer in the new century. Today's leaders and intellectuals are facing the same problem as the advocates of the May Fourth Movement. The dichotomy of tradition requires deciding what to give up, what to keep, how to give it up and how far to go.

Looking back today, no one can deny that the struggle of intellectuals in the May Fourth Movement laid a good foundation for the modernization of China. Although many of their behaviors were extreme, they were closely linked with the historical conditions of that time. Intellectuals in the early 20th century understood that their country needed radical change. To them, modernization being equal to Westernization was normal because modernization originated from European countries in the West. More importantly, Japan, which had been influenced by Chinese culture for a long period of time, surpassed China because of the introduction of the experience of the reform of Western countries. People in the May Fourth Movement learned that modernization could not be limited to material changes and that new weapons and old minds could not defend the country. They had to start with people's way of thinking, so they contrasted tradition with modernization.

Substituting Western culture for traditional culture did not solve the problems of Chinese society at all, nor did it bring about the modernization that the advocates of the May Fourth Movement hoped for. Many problems in the early 20th century were left to new leaders. In our opinion, the modernization of China can truly begin at the moment when national leaders and other intellectuals decide to abandon the tradition-modern opposition because modernization cannot be imposed from the outside. Only by juxtaposing new knowledge from abroad with tradition can modernization be achieved. Modernization begins with the modernization of tradition, and tradition can only begin to change when it encounters new elements. As Li Dazhao said, both are indispensable.

二十世纪中越文艺理论的现代转型研究

吴越环【越南】

越南社会科学院文学研究所研究员

引 言

研究中越文学、文论关系时，越南学者常强调在中国文学如此深刻影响的背景下，越南文学如何超越现有体系，以现代转型及建设具有民族特色的新文学体系。回顾越南文学的运动与发展历程可以看出，近千年的越南古典文学几乎都是以汉字与喃字为主要创作文字，而在创作思路、审美观点、创作题材以及文学作品中所使用的典故典籍等方面，中国文化元素的体现均为明显。甚至1945 年之后当国语字成了越南全国范围的官方文字后，现代国语字中来源于汉语的词语比例仍然非常高。不过作为"儒家文化圈"的成员国之一，中越文化、文学具有紧密相连的关系是可以理解的。毕竟，在韩国、日本等其他"儒家文化圈"成员国的文学之中，儒家思想和中国古典文化的影响和越南一样都较为深刻。本文通过针对中越两国文学、文论在 20 世纪的文论体系现代转型及马克思主义文论作为中越两国文学发展的核心价值观的形成和发展等两大问题，进行全面及深入的讨论。从此指出中越文论在综上问题的历史演变及主要发展特征，以及中越两国文论在不断更新与发展的过程中所存在的相同与差异之处，为研究东方文论史，特别是中越文学比较研究提供具有理论依据和实际考察的相关参考。

一、从传统东方文学体系迈向现代转型轨道

中国文化、文学对越南的影响，最为全面也是最为深刻的时间段，正是越南封建自主建国时期，其主要表现在于汉字、中国古典文学体裁及各类典故、典籍在越南文学之中的普遍性。首先要强调的是，汉字文学是越南文学史中非常重要的组成部分之一，它是越南历代贤哲和文豪用来表达自己的世界观、人生观或文学思想、彰显才华的重要方式。而喃字文学是越南古人在繁体字的基础上将其与越南人的发音特征相结合而成的，虽然在文字使用方面上其不是一种很理想的文字体系，但从民族意识方面讲，其却反映了历代越南人对外来因素的改造及创新精神。从 15、16 世纪开始直到 19 世纪末，喃字文学日渐成为越南文学史中非常重要的组成部分。阮廌的《国音诗集》、阮攸的喃字诗歌、胡春香的诗歌等都属于喃字文学，同时也是越南文学的发展象征及民族精神的标杆。从某种意义上来讲，喃字文学就是越南文学对中国文学的接受、改变、本土化及不断创新的重要成就。

在创作领域上，越南陈庭史教授致力于研究中国古典文学体裁对越南的接受及影响，他认为："越南与中国，虽然在疆域、风俗习惯已有一些区别，但在文学领域，人们仍然感到有某种谈不清楚的继承。每当提到中国古典名作，大部分越南儒家知识分子都把其当作自己历代祖宗所创作的作品似的，并把自己称之为继承者（黎贵惇、潘辉注等人的文学评论文章之中，这一点非常明显）。因此，越南古典作家使用来自于中国文学的体裁、故事、典籍等元素，都不以为是在借用外来的元素。"[1]

众所周知，古典文学的创作规律，一方面是允许使用主题、手法、故事等原有因素，另一方面也允许文学作家在原有文学因素的基础上，重新创作或变作以能够符合时代的转变及更好地表现出作者的情怀、思想和文采风格。因而，对于古典文学来讲，改变或重新创作是非常重要的特征。因此，越南著名文学家邓陈昆用汉文创作的《征妇吟曲》，竟然有了八个国语字的阐释版本；借用青心才人章回小说《金云翘传》的故事，阮攸创作出《断肠新声》六八诗律喃字叙事诗；后来阮攸的亲友范贵释又在《金云翘传》的基础上创作出汉文小说《金云翘新传》。

在任何时代，不同国家文学之间的影响都通过接受、选择和创作实现，而不

---

[1] Trần Đình Sử, *Lý luận và phê bình văn học*, Nxb Giáo dục, 2013./ 陈庭史，《文学理论与批评》，越南教育出版社 2013 年版，第 230 页。

是简单重复或抄写。越南文学作为一个独立和具有特色的民族文学，其对外来文学的影响持有什么样的态度是非常重要的。基本上可以划分为如下几点：一是，越南文学一般会选择国家情怀、民族情感等相关题材为主要创作内容。二是，虽然也受佛教、儒家、道教等东方古典哲学思想的影响，但越南作家和越南学者均有不同的认识和理解。因此，不难理解为何中国文学作品中的人道、故乡、家族情怀、朋友之间的信任和情义等内容，能受到越南读者的欢迎和喜爱。

由于前期阶段，越南知识分子可以直接阅读和欣赏汉字文学作品，因此，从某种意义上讲中国文学、文论在越南自20世纪初才开始存在翻译的问题。也就在20世纪初，随着与西方文化、文论的相遇，越南文学实现了第一次现代转型，而这一过程同时也发生在中国。从某种程度上讲，中国文论作为一种外来文论，它的现代化进程对于越南文论的现代转型或多或少都产生一定的影响。只不过，中国文学、文论对于越南文学、文论的影响是双重的：作为外国文学的身份，中国现代文学及文论对于现代越南文论来讲，其影响力与其他国家文学是相同的；但越南同中国具有"儒家文学圈"中心和边缘的关系，中国文化对越南文化来讲具有长久而深刻的影响，因此中国文学、文论对于越南文学、文论的影响还具有内在性和潜在性问题。虽然自从20世纪起，汉字、儒学科举等汉文化元素在越南的接受与传播已大不如前，但作为越南文化本身的重要构成因素，其影响是无法消灭的，只不过影响的范围、程度和表现有所不同而已。那么在20世纪的新背景之中，越南文论和中国文论的发展特征有何不同、两国文论的现代转型是否相似？

20世纪前，中国和越南都是典型的东方文化国家。作为"儒家文化圈"的中心，中国早已建设出属于自己的文论体系，而这一体系对于日本、韩国、越南等"儒家文化圈"非中心国家都有着非常深刻的影响。具有几千年的儒学科举制度和知识体系的中国和越南，让世人误认为这两个国家会执着地守护包括文学、文论体系在内的传统文化。但20世纪的历史巨变，不仅改变了这两个国家的政治和社会的面貌，在文艺领域，各种革新和新颖的观念也陆续萌生，经过激烈的斗争最后成了主流思想。在中国，鲁迅提倡："世界的时代思潮已六面袭来，而自己还拘禁在三千年陈旧的桎梏里。于是觉醒、挣扎、反叛、要出而参与世界的事业……"[1] 在越南，潘佩珠、潘周桢、黄促抗等爱国知识分子也提倡了"西学东渐"文化运动。只不过，中国学者想通过这一次现代转型来实现摆脱几千年的桎

---

1 《而已集·当陶元庆君的绘画展览时》，《鲁迅全集》（第三卷），人民文学出版社1956年版。

桔、吸收现代西方知识体系精髓并参与世界文艺事业的目的，而越南学者的文艺现代化运动目的则在于摆脱几千年封建制度的统治，并通过文艺运动寻找救国之路。侵略者的入侵无意中打破了中国几千年和越南近千年的东方传统社会制度的格局，给两国人民带来了翻身和革新运动的机会。从公元 1900 年开始的西方列强侵略到 1937~1945 年的抗日战争再到 1927~1949 年的国共内战，中国人民的生活一直挣扎在民族解放、国家统一的艰苦长征之中。而从 1858 年开始，法国对越南的殖民地统治也开始了越南人民近百年的抗法战争、20 余年抗美战争的艰苦历史，其中 60 年代末至 1975 年的抗美战争从某种程度上来讲就是南越和北越两派的内战。越南文论与中国文论就在这样的历史环境下，进行了其发展过程中的第一次现代转型。

　　20 世纪初的越南，在潘佩珠、潘周桢所提倡的"东游"运动，由梁文玕、陶元普、潘俊丰等人所倡导的"东京义塾"运动，以阮太学为领袖的越南国民党，以胡志明为领袖的越南共产党的救国革命倡导之下，越南文论正式踏入现代化进程。而在中国，从 1840 年鸦片战争起，经过八国联军侵华战争到 1919 年的五四运动，随着维护国家和解放民族伟大事业的发展，中国人民的文化革新进程也拉开了帷幕。就在 20 世纪初至 20 年代，中国文学观念已从"诗言志"的传统观念转换为以梁启超为代表的"重政治实用"、以鲁迅为代表的"重主观表现"和以王国维为代表的"重文学本体"等三种不同的文论观点。五四运动后，"在以现实主义为主、现实主义、浪漫主义、现代主义三种文学思潮交错推动和影响之下，重现实政治、时代人生、重自我表现、主体创造以及重文学实体的构成和显现等批评观念、类型和模式，又显然是近代三个基本格局的重复和发展。"[1] 19 世纪末至 1949 年这一阶段，可以看作为中国文论的多元化发展阶段。20 世纪初的中国知识分子通过吸收和学习法国、日本、苏俄、英国、美国、德国等世界现代文论体系，进行文论观念更新和现代转型。梁启超受日本现代文论的影响提倡"救国小说"，王国维受德国美学的影响主张从审美观点和视角来研究《红楼梦》，胡适接受美国实证哲学主张运用实证方法来研究《红楼梦》，受启蒙文学、现实主义影响的鲁迅主张创作现实主义文学，受资产阶级思想影响的周作人主张"个人主义——人道主义"，受无产阶级思想影响的太阳社、创造社则倡导"革命文学"，冯雪峰等受苏俄文学的影响支持和鼓励无产阶级文学，受现实主义文学影响的茅

1　黄曼君：《中国 20 世纪文学理论批评教程》，华中师范大学出版社 2010 年版，第 4 页。

盾则主张"为人生而艺术"和自然主义，郭沫若被浪漫主义影响，主张浪漫主义文学，等等。可见，20世纪初的中国，在文艺观念上可以说已形成了"百家争鸣"的文论格局。

而20世纪初，半封建半殖民地社会历史背景下的越南文论，虽然新文学观念还较为模糊，没形成像中国上述如此明显的格局，但现代化的种子已开始发芽。全国日渐形成了不同研究流派、不同发展倾向和追求目的的民主、革新运动。"勤王运动"的爆发与失败成为越南社会、文化现代化转型的起点。以现代民族精神为动力，越南学者积极地把阮攸的《金云翘传》、胡春香的喃字诗歌、阮廌的《平吴大诰》《国音诗集》等越南古典汉字、喃字文学音译成现代国语字，同时组织编撰和注释了多部越南古典文学史。这一切都反映了越南知识分子对本民族国学经典的传承与呵护，同时也确定了越南知识分子对国家、民族的独立和发展事业的责任担当。与此同时，法国对越南的殖民政策及其在越南全国范围创建的各类现代模式高等教育的快速发展，使越南知识分子第一次能够全面、系统化地接受和把握西方文化、文论的知识体系。除此之外，从国外留学回来的知识分子以及他们对越南文论的革新及现代化的渴望，也是越南文论现代化转型的重要元素之一。海潮、邓泰梅、张酒、梁德铁、范琼、梁维次、阮文永、张永记等20世纪一批优秀知识分子正是越南构建文论现代体系的重要和主要力量。

译介和传播西方现代文论，编撰、注释越南古典汉字、喃字文学，研究阮攸《金云翘传》，支持国语字文学的发展等，均是越南传统文论的现代转型的重要内容。范琼、范维存等人倡导实用主义文学观念，而这一文学革新思路却与少山所倡导的以文学作品本身的审美价值为主要研究对象的文艺观念有所冲突。范琼与吴德继关于阮攸《金云翘传》的文艺争议，从某种意义上来讲反映了当时越南文论的传统与现代化交叉、挣扎的复杂状态。散陀等新诗运动的诗人们则主张打碎一切破旧的创作规矩、解放个性、解放诗歌。

进入1932—1945阶段，越南文论的现代转型已有了进一步的发展：文学创作活动与文艺批评理论协同发展。怀清和少山的作家自主意识文艺观念可以看作为这一阶段越南文论现代转型的重要起点。这一观点同时也被春妙、制兰园、韩默子等新诗运动诗人们接受并出色地表现在他们的诗品之中。"为人生而艺术"和"为艺术而艺术"的文艺争议也因此而发生。这场文艺争议同时还被看作为资产阶级、唯心文学观念和无产阶级、唯物文学观念之间思想斗争的一种表现。

在中国，第一次现代转型如综上所述，"是从突破'诗文评'传统文论形态、接受和转化外国文论的过程中实现的，其间主要经历了接受日本及欧美文论和转化苏联文论两个阶段，经历了从多元探索到多元归一、形成统一的理论系统的漫长过程。"[1]可见，中越文论的现代转型与发展不在于其传统文艺观念自身所发生的变革，而是受西方文论思想影响后发生的。不过由于这一过程在中越两国是经过不同渠道、不同方式，接受不同内容而产生差异。《世纪文学理论批评教程》中指出，中国文论的初次现代转型具有四大特征。一是："冲决封建道统、文学观念的罗网，摒弃了为封建伦理道德服务的文学批评目的论，并在进化论思想指引下，主逆、求变、尚用，开始建立起新的文学理论批评价值观。"二是："古代注重和谐美的文艺美学观念和强调批评主体作用的表现论批评观念已不再是唯一的、主要的文学观念和批评观念。"三是："文学理论批评开始走向科学化、逻辑化、打破了印象批评、评点式批评等批评方法的旧格局，出现了从大处着眼进行科学分析的文学理论批评方法和运思方式。"四是："文体观念发生了重大变化，小说被提到文学正宗地位。文体属文学形式的范畴、文学观念和批评观念的变革也体现在文学形式上。"[2]本文认为，从发展流程和文论知识体系的主要特征等方面来讲，越南文论初次现代转型在表面上似乎与中国十分相似，但从具体性问题来讲，中越文论的现代转型则存在很大的区别。

同中国一样，现代转型也是越南文学超越和摆脱数千年传统文论体系格局并建立起新文艺体系模式的过程。中国是东方文化的中心之一，其对日本、韩国、越南等周边国家都有着较为深刻的影响。随着"儒家文化圈"的不断扩大，中国古典文艺观念和审美价值也慢慢成为这些国家传统文化的重要组成元素。这也是人类发展史中的自然发展规律。日本、韩国、越南等受中国文化影响的国家在发展的过程中，一方面学习和吸收了中国哲学、美学等古典知识体系的精髓，另一方面，在本土文化的基础上也不断努力创新和建设具有本国特色的知识体系。越南喃字及喃字文学正是越南民族在这一方面的努力。因此，对于越南文化来讲，儒学文化、东方传统文论既是其内在价值，需要维护、继承和发扬，又是需要脱离的外来文化与文论。鲁迅之所以提倡"要出而参与世界的事业"[3]是因为中国知

1　赖大仁：《20世纪中国文论的现代转型与发展》，《当代文艺理论与思潮新探索》，2001年第5期，第99页。

2　黄曼君：《中国20世纪文学理论批评教程》，华中师范大学出版社2010年版，第17—19页。

3　《而已集·当陶元庆君的绘画展览时》，《鲁迅全集》（第三卷），人民文学出版社1956年版。

识分子 2000 年来所继承的中国古典文论是该国民族的魂魄和精髓，且其有资格与西方文化与文论知识体系并立。但越南文论却没有那个姿态和动力，也无法凭借属于别人的东西去参与世界的事业。因此，接受西方现代文论既是越南文论自我革新和现代化进程必走之路，同时也是其超越传统、创建具有民族特色的文论体系的良好机遇。20 世纪初，越南文论生活中所发生的国学文艺争论、传统诗歌与新诗文艺争议等均是文化、文艺话语体系不断变换与更新的重要表现。几乎仅需要仅仅 30 余年时间，越南文论已从东方文论的典型模式成功转换为现代、多元化的文论模式。当然，在这整个过程中，法国殖民者以及其对越的侵略政策，无意中也发挥了很大的作用。

中国文论的初次现代化转型，大部分都通过日本来学习西方，因此日本维新革命对当时中国知识分子均产生较为深刻的影响。越南从 19 世纪中下叶开始就成为法国的殖民地，因而越南学者对于西方现代文论的接受，主要是通过法文和法国文论这一重要渠道。从这一点来讲，越南对西方文化、文论的接受更为直接、也较为全面。受中国"新书"和资产革命运动影响，越南多名学者如潘佩珠、潘周征等人也倡导了"东游"运动，但最后都因失败而告终，因此，日本的维新革命精神对于当时的越南政治、社会几乎没有较为直接影响。而在法国全面着力建设现代型教育系统和现代文明的背景下，越南文论却有着较为自由和健康的发展空间。新诗、浪漫主义小说、现实主义小说、现代戏剧等现代文学体裁以及新文艺理论批评的萌生与其在 1932—1945 阶段的快速发展和所取得的丰硕成果，正是越南文论的现代化转型所取得的成就。

而对同一个发展阶段的中国文论来讲，"从文学观念和文学理论批评的发展上看，虽然还在很大程度上具有过渡性特征，但它本身仍然是一个取得重大成就的历史阶段。在中外文化、文学思潮的冲撞、交汇中，文学理论批评的现代品格正在形成，现代化过程亦已展开，许多重大问题都预示着今后发展的方向。"[1] 但同时，宋剑华也指出："20 世纪中国文学对现代主义文学具有强烈的排斥性，五四时代，是以传统文化心理抗拒现代主义，30 年代以后，则使用政治意识形态观念批判和否定现代主义……"[2] 这种情况与越南有所区别，19 世纪末至 1945 年的整整 50 余年时间，越南文学、文论对西方文学、文论的接受是较为主动的。而且

1　黄曼君：《中国 20 世纪文学理论批评教程》，华中师范大学出版社 2010 年版，第 19 页。
2　宋剑华：《现代性与中国文学》，山东教育出版社 1999 年版，第 101 页。

也不仅限于西学知识分子，成名于儒家科举的老一代知识分子如散陀、梁维次等人，也开始通过不同的渠道学习法文并把其作为学习西方知识的重要工具。1945年，越南民主共和国正式成立，也就是从那时候开始，越南将马克思主义文艺理论当作唯一的文艺理论体系并几乎拒绝和批判所有非马克思主义文论。这种情况同样也发生在中国，当然其历史形态和发展特征因两国社会、文化、历史背景的不同而产生差异，这一点是可以理解的。

二、引进马克思主义文论并将其当作文艺理论发展的核心价值观

马克思主义文艺理论在中国乃至越南都具有非常重要的历史地位。作为中越两国社会主义发展倾向的核心价值观，马克思主义理论体系不仅成为中越两国的建国指导思想，在文艺领域上也发挥很大的作用，甚至完全改变了中越两国在前期所建造的文论体系。从 20 世纪初多元化的文论体系，中越文论开始走进单一化文论体系。马克思主义文艺理论几乎全面、彻底地影响了两国的文艺生活及文论体系建设。

在中国，从 19 世纪末梁启超所著的《自由书》之中的《中国之社会主义》的出现，可以看作为社会主义思想正式传入中国的标杆。1903 年由日本社会主义先驱者幸德秋水所编撰的《社会主义神髓》以及大杉荣的《劳动运动的精神》《社会的理想轮》、河上肇的《马克思之经济论》、山川均的《从科学的社会主义到行动的社会主义》、平林处之辅的《民众艺术底理论与实践》等日本社会主义先驱者的作品都被翻译成中文，并"成为许多中国留日学生和早期革命民主主义者受社会主义思想启蒙教育的重要著作"[1]。而在这一探索时期，翻译无产阶级有关文艺理论（其实是日本学者对于俄国文学的研究）最为积极的是冯雪峰，他在北新书局上连续发表的《新俄文艺的曙光》《新俄的演剧运动与跳舞》《新俄的无产阶级文学》等文章都引起了当时中国文坛的关注。在《日本马克思主义文艺理论在中国的译介》一文中，王志松认为："中国无产阶级文学运动在 1928 年杂志《文化批判》和《太阳月刊》同时创刊拉开帷幕，之后历经 1930 年'左翼联盟'成立，至 1936 年'左翼联盟'解散落下帷幕。"[2] 1926 年，郭沫若在《创造月刊》发表

1　王志松：《日本马克思主义文艺理论在中国的译介》，《东北亚外语研究》，2015 年第 2 期，第 10—16 页。

2　王志松：《日本马克思主义文艺理论在中国的译介》，《东北亚外语研究》，2015 年第 2 期，第 10—16 页。

了《革命与文学》一文，文章就革命和文学的关系进行了系统化论述。这篇文章后来被李初梨看作中国第一篇倡导革命文学的文章。其外，在1926—1930阶段，中国学者也集中将无产阶级文学运动的基本特征与创作的文章翻译成中文，如藏原惟人的《到新现实主义》、青野季吉的《日本无产阶级文学理论的开展》、田口宪一的《日本艺术运动底指导理论的发展》、片上坤的《现代新兴文学的诸问题》等文章，这些文章在中国文坛上都具有广泛的影响。

除了来源于日本文坛的"第三种人""超越阶级文学"等范畴之外，据胡永钦、耿睿勤、袁延恒等人在《马克思恩格斯在中国的传播》中的统计，仅从1920年至1927年，在鲁迅、冯雪峰、周扬、瞿秋白等人的努力之下，就有20余种马克思、恩格斯的经典作品被翻译成中文并在全国范围推广和传播。从这一点可以说明，马克思主义文艺理论在中国的译介与传播首先是受日本革命文学的影响，后来是在中国社会政治的实际要求的环境下，其才得以系统化地翻译和推广。至于马克思主义文艺理论如何在中国得以萌生，黄曼君也作了总结："一则译介活动中与马克思主义文艺思想掺杂在一起的也有苏联的'无产阶级文化派''拉普派'，乃至日本福本和夫'左'倾路线影响下的庸俗社会学和机械论的文艺观点；二则马克思主义文艺思想从其诞生的文化场横向移到我国文化场，是一个跨越不同文化时空的接受和重构过程，外来的马克思主义文艺思想既可能因此而在中国得到新的丰富和发展，又可能因误导或曲解而导致不同程度的'变形'和'失真'。"[1]本文认为，黄曼君的这一总结已概括出中国马克思主义文艺理论思想初期发展的主要特征。但不管马克思主义在中国是怎么"变形"和"失真"，其首先是中国文艺理论本身发展的需求，而不是因为某些社会政治原因。这种情况与马克思主义文论在越南的初期发展有所不同。

中国马克思主义文艺理论的滥觞期，主要通过译介日本学者发表关于"革命文学""无产阶级"、苏俄文学等有关问题的文章，以及马克思恩格斯的原著翻译等渠道，而得以传播并很快取得统治地位。而越南马克思主义文艺理论却在1935~1939阶段"为艺术而艺术还是为人生而艺术"的文艺争论之中萌生的。在这场文学争议中，海潮在多家媒体报刊上发表了多篇介绍马克思主义文艺理论的文章。不过"为艺术而艺术还是为人生而艺术"的文学争论，并未直接提出和谈论马克思主义文艺理论有关范畴，而是主要围绕及开展文学与社会的关系、文学

---

1 黄曼君：《中国20世纪文学理论批评教程》，华中师范大学出版社2010年版，第28页。

艺术的职能、自由创作等相关问题的讨论。但在这场争议之中，海潮以及裴功惩、山茶、石洞、胡青等人，已为越南马克思主义文艺理论和批判现实主义打好了基础。在《文学之两种观念》一文中，少山把文学划分为两种，包括以伦理道德和以创作美为主要创作目的。1935年，海潮在《新生活》上发表了《为艺术而艺术还是为人生而艺术》一文，文章中，其反对少山的文学观念，认为任何艺术创作的目的，都在于反映和描画生活，反映劳动人民的思想、情感和抱负，同时其还发挥着改造社会的重要作用，也就是说任何艺术都是"为人生而艺术"；而少山提倡所谓"文艺奉献美"的观念仅代表社会中的衰朽力量的艺术而已。1937年，海潮在《香江》杂志上发表了《文学与唯物主义》一文，文章中海潮提出并深入论述了文学与社会生活的关系、文学与阶级斗争、革命文学、反革命文学等马克思主义文艺理论有关问题。其外，海潮、怀清、裴功惩、仲明、文明、如风、蓝开等人也在《星期六小说》和《骚坛》上发表了多篇论述马克思主义文艺理论问题的文章，如海潮的《迈向文学中之写实主义：小说体裁之几个发展倾向》、怀清的《文学中之诚实与自由》、《文学之意义与作用》、裴功惩的《赞成创建越南新文化》等。

在中国，日本"革命文学"以及俄国十月革命的成功都有着非常深刻的影响，但在越南，俄国十月革命几乎没有引起任何影响。随着中国的"新书"运动，20世纪初的越南知识分子也开始向往、学习日本，因此，潘佩珠、潘周征提倡"东游"运动，这场社会革命运动虽然也引起了爱国青年分子的关注但最终也没能发挥太大作用。因此，马克思主义文艺理论在越南的译介与传播不像中国从文艺理论自身的需要出发，而是越南共产党人对马克思—列宁主义的强烈推崇和当时越南文艺理论家对文学的理解相结合而产生的结果。1925~1927阶段，随着由阮爱国[1]所创办的共产主义思想立场培训班的出现，以及越南国内的越南国民党、越南青年革命同志会、新越革命党、越南工会、越南农会等革命组织的成立，马克思主义在越南才正式被引进和传播。1938年，陈庭龙在《信息》上发表了《在苏俄的这三年时间》一文，文章中系统化地介绍了苏俄文学以及马克思主义文艺理论，并提出越南文学马克思主义发展倾向的规划。因此，马克思主义文艺理论在越南的译介与传播和中国相比而言稍微晚了一些，且也没有系统化地将马克思主义的经典原著翻译成越南语或广泛的传播。马克思主义文艺理论在中国的译介、传播与

1　胡志明的别称。

快速发展，主要是通过鲁迅、瞿秋白、周扬或梁启超等进步文学家、思想家的努力，而在越南最早接受马克思主义的却不是文学家或思想家，而是越南第一位共产党人的胡志明，之后通过他自己以及陈富、李洪峰等越南共产党先锋队的努力，马克思主义才被全面和快速地传播。这一点就是中国和越南马克思主义文艺理论早期发展最大的差异。

不过在这一阶段，中越文艺理论生活不管是从文学观念、研究类型和方法等方面，都具有多样化的发展姿态。"巴金、老舍、曹禺等人的创作经验谈，林语堂、戴望舒等人的文论，朱光潜、刘西渭（李健吾）、梁宗岱、钱谷融、巴人等人的理论译著和文艺论评，'九叶'诗人的诗论，等等。"[1]这些成果丰富和多样化了中国文艺理论生活的发展局面。而在越南，怀清、世旅、少山等人倡导的浪漫主义文学的文学观念革新，海潮、裴功惩、范琼等人推崇的现实主义文学观念革新以及六场文艺争论的连续出现，使越南文论生活的现代化转型进程取得了快速发展和丰硕成就。换句话说，不管是在越南还是在中国，马克思主义文论在其初期发展之中，相对而言与其他文艺思想流派都具有较为平等的关系。

至于马克思主义文艺理论作为一个完全陌生的思想流派，为何却能够在如此短暂的时间内被译介与传播并成为中国和越南文坛上独尊的指导思想，本文认为，张宝贵的以下总结是非常正确的："译文的数量、经典程度及翻译、传入时间的先后，意味着逻辑上的主从关系，这说明如果不是呼应马克思主义所针对的社会实际问题，这种主义的文艺理论就失去了传入的理由。"[2]换句话说，马克思主义文艺理论之所以能够在中国和越南生根发芽不仅是因为当时中越两国文艺理论本身的需求，而还在于马克思主义本身的社会针对性以及中共、越共对解放民族、统一国家的革命路线的选择。

1899 年，列宁在谈论俄国社会主义建设有关问题时曾指出："对于俄国社会主义者来说，尤其需要独立地探讨马克思的理论，因为他所提供的只是一般的指导原理，而这些原理的应用，具体地说，在英国不同于法国，在法国不同于德国，在德国不同于俄国。"[3]列宁的这一观点概括了马克思主义的实践性本质，也让苏联后的社会主义国家能够更灵活地运用马克思主义来实现无产阶级革命、解放民

1　黄曼君：《中国 20 世纪文学理论批评教程》，华中师范大学出版社，2010 年，第 28 页。
2　张宝贵：《马克思主义文艺理论中国化的早期历程》，《中国社会科学》2008 年第 2 期，第 140—151 页。
3　《列宁选集》（第一卷），人民出版社 1995 年版，第 274 页。

族和建立新国家的伟大事业。

对于中国的实际情况，李春华在《中国特色社会主义：马克思主义民族化的成功典范》一文中曾作出如下总结："20 世纪 40 年代至 70 年代末，马克思主义民族化的理论标志，是以毛泽东思想为代表性的一系列马克思主义民族化理论形成……以毛泽东为代表的中国共产党人，堪称是马克思主义民族化的杰出代表。毛泽东以超凡的勇气冲破教条主义的束缚，以马克思主义立场、观点和方法为指导，将马克思主义普遍真理和中国具体实际相结合，找到了具有中国特色的新民主主义革命道路……"[1] 在这篇文章中，李春华也提到了朝鲜、古巴等社会主义国家的马克思主义本土化建设。对于越南的发展情况，他肯定："越南共产党坚持马列主义和胡志明思想，领导人民克服困难，在社会主义建设中取得了许多重大成就。"[2] 李春华所提到的"胡志明思想"，正是马克思主义越南化最典范的例子。越共全国人大第九次大会对"胡志明思想"作出如下定义："胡志明思想是胡志明关于越南革命基础问题的全面和深入的观点系统，是胡志明主席在我国的实践情况的基础上对马列主义运用和发展的结果，同时也是继承和发挥民族传统美德和解放阶层、解放民族的观点系统"。[3] 按照越共第九次大会的观点，胡志明思想系统民族和解放民族革命，社会主义以及社会主义的过渡期，越南共产党，民族大团结，军事，建设属于民族、因民族、为民族之国家，民族力量和时代力量相结合，道德思想，人文思想，文化思想等内容。并且胡志明也曾经肯定："开始的时候，就是爱国主义而不是共产主义让我信从列宁、信从第三国际。"[4] 可见，马克思主义不管是在中国还是越南，都通过不同方式在不同的时期有了新发展，而那种发展就是以马克思主义为思想指导的原理与各国实际情况相结合并通过各国杰出共产党人的阐释、运用和发展所获得的成就。所以马克思主义"中国化""越南化"，既属于马克思主义在中国和越南的具体发展历史所取得的成就，又具有马克思主

1 李春华：《中国特色社会主义：马克思主义民族化的成功典范》，《马克思主义研究》，2011 年第 6 期。

2 李春华：《中国特色社会主义：马克思主义民族化的成功典范》，《马克思主义研究》，2011 年第 6 期。

3 Trung tâm lý luận chính trị, Đại học Quốc gia Thành phố Hồ Chí Minh, *Sức sống của chủ nghĩa Mác - Lênin trong thời đại ngày nay*, Nxb Chính trị Quốc gia, 2014./ 胡志明市国家大学政治理论中心：《现代时期中之马列主义的活力》，河内国家政治出版社 2014 年。

4 参 Hellmut Kapfenberger, *Hồ Chí Minh: Một biên niên sử*, Đinh Hương, Thiên Hà dịch, Nxb Thế kỷ mới, 2010./【德】Hellmut Kapfenberger：《胡志明：一本编年记》，丁香、天河译，胡志明：新世界出版社，2010 年。

义本身的国际性发展特征。

总的来讲，马克思主义文艺理论在中国和越南经过接受和传播的初期发展之后，根据两国不同的实际情况以及两国领导的文艺思想转变而得以改造并取得了不同程度的发展。

三、结语

中越两国山水相连，文化相通，在文学交流方面因此也有着密切和悠久的关系。处于东方文明之中心地位，中国文化特别是其儒家思想对周围国家有着非常深刻的影响。中国古典文学的题材、体裁、表达方式等曾被越南先贤积极接受、学习并在其基础上创新属于自我的文学体系。因此在 20 世纪之前，中越文学、文论关系均属于越南文学主动接受中国文学的精髓并在本国文化和人文情怀的基础上进行创新和创作的基本状态。而从 20 世纪初开始，在两国社会政治巨变的背景下，中越两国文论从纯粹的传统东方文论体系已日渐转换为现代文论体系。如果单纯从发展阶段及形态来看，两国文论的现代转型进程，特别是马克思主义在中越两国的译介与传播的历史演变都较为相同，但把两者放在一起并就具体问题进行客观、合理地比较研究时，就能看出其确实存在非常大的差异，而这些差异正是反映了中国以及越南文论体系的民族意识和独特之处。

A Study of the Modern Transformation of Sino-Vietnamese Literary Theories in the 20th Century

Ngo Viet Hoan / Vietnam

Institute of Literature, Vietnamese Academy of Social Sciences, Researcher

Introduction

When studying the relations of Chinese and Vietnamese literature and literary theories, Vietnamese scholars often emphasize how Vietnamese literature can transcend the existing system in order to realize the contemporary transformation and build a new system of literature with national characteristics under such profound influence from Chinese literature. Looking back on the movements and developments of Vietnamese literature, it is obvious that almost all Vietnamese classical literature in the past thousand years mainly used Chinese characters and Chu-Nom as the languages for literary creation, and Chinese cultural elements are manifested in creative ideas, aesthetic viewpoints, creative themes and allusions in literary works. After 1945, even when Chữ Quốc Ngữ, the modern writing system in Vietnam, became the official national language of Vietnam, there have been many Chinese-derived words. However, as a member of the "Confucian Cultural Circle", it is understandable that the Chinese and Vietnamese culture and literature are closely connected. After all, in the literature of other countries in the "Confucian Cultural Circle", such as South Korea and Japan, the influence of Confucianism and Chinese classical culture is as profound as it is in Vietnam. This article conducts a comprehensive and in-depth discussion on the two major issues of Chinese and Vietnamese literature and literary theories, namely the modern transformation of literary theory in the twentieth century, and the formation and development of the Marxist literary theory as the core values for Chinese and Vietnamese literature. Hence, this article reveals the historical evolution and main developmental characteristics of Chinese and Vietnamese literary theories and the similarities and differences between the Chinese and Vietnamese literary theories in the process of continuous updating and development. It can provide reference with a theoretical basis and a practical survey for studying the history of oriental literary theories, especially the comparison of Chinese and Vietnamese literature.

1. From the Traditional System of Oriental Literature to the Modern Transformational Track

The period when Chinese culture and literature has the most comprehensive and profound influence on Vietnam was in the feudal society after Vietnam became an independent country. Its main manifestation was the universality of Chinese characters, Chinese classical literature genres and various allusions and books in Vietnamese literature. First of all, the literature in Chinese characters was a very important part in the history of Vietnamese literature. It was an important way for Vietnamese sages and literati to express their world view, life philosophy or literary ideas and to show their talents. The Chu-Nom literature was created by ancient Vietnamese integrating traditional characters with pronunciations of Vietnamese. Although not an ideal writing system for language use, from the perspective of national consciousness, it reflected the spirit of transformation and innovation of Vietnamese to exotic elements. From the fifteenth and sixteenth centuries to the late nineteenth century, Chu-Nom literature gradually grew to be a very important part of the history of Vietnamese literature. Nguyen Trai's *Poems of National*

Pronunciation, Nguyen Du's Chu-Nom poems, Ho Xuan Huong's poems, etc. belonged to Chu-Nom literature and served as a symbol of the development of Vietnamese literature and a benchmark of the national spirit. In a sense, Chu-Nom literature is an important achievement of Vietnamese literature's acceptance of, change in, localization of and continuous innovation to Chinese literature.

In terms of literary creation, Professor Tran Dinh Su of Vietnam specializes in the study of the acceptance and influence of Chinese classical literary genres in Vietnam. According to him, "Vietnam and China, although there are some differences in territory and customs, in the field of literature, there is something difficult to say about the inheritance. When mentioning Chinese classical masterpieces, most Vietnamese Confucian intellectuals regard them as works created by our ancestors, and they call themselves the heirs (this point is very clear in the articles of literary review by Le Quy Don, Phan Huy Chu and others). Therefore, Vietnamese classical writers do not think that their use of genres, stories, classics and other classics from the Chinese literature are exotic elements."[1]

As we all know, the rules of creation of classical literature, on the one hand, allow the use of original factors such as themes, techniques, stories, etc., and on the other hand, they allow writers to re-create or transform based on the original literary factors to adapt to changes of the times and better express their feelings, thoughts and literary style. For classical literature, adaptation or re-creation is a very important feature. *The Song of a Soldiers Wife (Chinh Phu Ngam Khuc)* written by the well-known Vietnamese writer Dang Tran Con in Chinese has eight interpreted versions by the national pronunciation; based on the novel *The Stories of Jin Yun Qiao* created by Qingxincairen, Nguyen Du wrote a Chu-Nom narrative poem *Đoạn Trường Tân Thanh* (A New Cry from a Broken Heart) in six-eight rhythm; later, Phạm Quy Thich, a friend of Nguyen Du, wrote a Chinese novel *The New Tale of Kiều*.

---

1 Tran Dinh Su, *Theory and Criticism of Literature*, Hanoi: Education Publishing House, 2013, p.230.

In whatever era, the influence of national literature is achieved through acceptance, selection and creation, rather than simply repetition or transcription. It is important for Vietnamese literature, as an independent and distinctive national literature, to take an attitude towards the influence of foreign literature. Basically, it can be divided into the following points. First, the Vietnamese literature generally chooses related topics such as national feelings and emotions as its main creative content. Second, despite the influence of Buddhism, Confucianism, Taoism and other oriental classical philosophies, Vietnamese writers and scholars have a different cognition and different understandings. Therefore, it is not difficult to understand why humanity, homesickness, family feelings, trust and affection of friends in Chinese literary works are welcomed and loved by Vietnamese readers.

At the early stage, Vietnamese intellectuals could directly read and appreciate literary works written in Chinese characters. In a sense, the translation of Chinese literature and literary theory became a problem in Vietnam since the beginning of the 20th century. In this period, encountering Western culture and literary theory, the Vietnamese literature achieved its first modern transformation, and this process also occurred simultaneously in China. To some extent, as a foreign literary theory, the process of modernization of Chinese literary theory had more or less influenced the modern transformation of Vietnamese literary theory. However, the influence of Chinese literature and literary theory on its Vietnamese counterpart was twofold: as a foreign literature, modern Chinese literature and literary theory had a similar influence on modern Vietnamese literary theory as it had on those of other countries; but Vietnam and China had a central and peripheral relationship in the "Confucian Literary Circle", and Chinese culture had a long-lasting and profound influence on Vietnamese culture, so there are also inherent and potential issues. Since the twentieth century, although the reception and dissemination of Chinese cultural elements such as Chinese characters and Confucian imperial examinations became worse than before; as an important part of the Vietnamese culture, the influence of Chinese culture could not be eliminated, but with a different scope, degree and manifestation. Then, in the new context of the twentieth century, what differences are there in the developmental characteristics and the modern transformation of Vietnamese and Chinese literary theories.

Before the twentieth century, China and Vietnam were both typical countries of oriental culture. At the center of the "Confucian Cultural Circle", China had long established its own system of literary theory, and this system had a profound influence on non-central countries such as Japan, South Korea and Vietnam. The world mistakenly considers China and Vietnam, both with thousands of years of Confucian imperial examinations and system of knowledge, as two countries that would persistently guard their traditional culture including literature and literary theory. However, radical changes in the history of the twentieth century not only changed the political and social outlook of these two countries, but also in the field of literature and art, various innovations and novel ideas sprang up and finally became the mainstream thoughts after a fierce struggle. In China, Lu Xun advocated: "The ideological trend of the world has struck from six sides, but we are still detained in the 3,000-year-old obsolete trance. So, we must awaken, struggle, rebel and desire to participate in the cause of the world ..."[1] In Vietnam, patriotic intellectuals such as Phan Boi Chau, Phan Chu Trinh, Huynh Thuc Khan also advocated the cultural movement of "Western Learning Spreading to the East". However, Chinese scholars wanted to take the opportunity of this modern transformation to achieve the purposes of getting rid of the shackles of thousands of years, absorbing the essence of the modern Western knowledge system and participating in the world's literature and art cause, while the Vietnamese scholars' literature and modernization movement aimed to get rid of thousands of years of rule of the feudal system and find a way to save the country through a literary movement. The invasions inadvertently broke the pattern of the traditional oriental social system in China for thousands of years and in Vietnam for nearly a thousand years so that the people of the two countries had the opportunity to rise and carry

---

1   Lu Xun, "Er Yi · On Fine Arts Exhibition of Mr. Tao Yuanqing" , *The Complete Works of Lu Xun*, Vol.3, Beijing: People' s Literature Publishing House, 1956.

out reforms. From the invasion by Western powers in 1900 to the War of Resistance against Japan in 1937-1945 to the civil war between the Communist Party of China and the Kuomintang in 1927-1949, the Chinese people were struggling in the arduous long march to liberate the nation and unify the country. Since 1858, the French colonial rule over Vietnam also triggered a difficult period in the history of the Vietnamese people's war of resistance against France for nearly a century and the war of resistance against the United States of America for more than two decades. To a certain degree, the war of resistance against the United States of America from the late 1960s to 1975 was the civil war between the two factions in South and North Vietnam. Under such historical circumstances, Vietnamese and Chinese literary theories underwent the first modern transformation in their development.

In the Vietnam of the early twentieth century, guided by the national salvation revolution of the "Đông Du" (journey to the east) movement advocated by Phan Boi Chau and Phan Chu Trinh, the "Tonkin Free School" movement advocated by Luong Van Can, Dao Nguyen Phu and Phan Tuac Phuong, etc., the Vietnamese Nationalist Party led by Nguyen Thai Hoc and the Communist Party of Vietnam led by Ho Chi Minh, the Vietnamese literary theory officially proceeded to the process of modernization. In China, from the Opium War of 1840, the Eight-Power Allied Forces invading China, to the May Fourth Movement of 1919, with the development of the great cause of safeguarding the country and liberating the nation, the process of cultural renovation of the Chinese people also started. From the beginning of the 20th century to the 1920s, the philosophy of Chinese literature had already transformed from the traditional "poetry expressing aspirations" to three different literary theories, that is, "political and practical" represented by Liang Qichao, "valuing subjective expression" by Lu Xun and "literature ontology" by Wang Guowei. After the May Fourth Movement, "dominated by realism, under the interweaving promotion and influence of the three literary trends of realism, romanticism and modernism, the ideas, types and models of the criticism of valuing realistic politics, contemporary life, self-expression, subjective creation and literary entities were obviously clearly the repetitions and developments of the three basic patterns in modern times."[1] The period from the late 19th century to 1949 could be regarded as the stage of diversified development of Chinese literary theory. At the beginning of the 20th century, Chinese intellectuals renewed their literary theories and achieved modern transformation by assimilating and studying the world's systems of modern literary theory such as those in France, Japan, Soviet Russia, Britain, the USA and Germany. Liang Qichao advocated "salvation novels" under the influence of the modern Japanese literary theory. Wang Guowei was influenced by German aesthetics and advocated the study of *A Dream of Red Mansions* from the aesthetic point of view and perspective. Hu Shi accepted American empirical philosophy and advocated using the empirical approach to study *A Dream of Red Mansions*. Lu Xun, influenced by the literature of the enlightenment and realism, advocated the creation of realistic literature. Zhou Zuoren, who was influenced by bourgeois thought, advocated "individualism-humanitarianism". The Sun Society and the Creation Society, influenced by the proletarian thought, advocated "revolutionary literature". Feng Xuefeng and others, under the influence of Soviet Russian literature, supported and encouraged proletarian literature. Mao Dun, who was influenced by realist literature, advocated "art for life" and naturalism. Guo Moruo was influenced by romanticism and advocated romantic literature. In short, the Chinese literary theories in the early twentieth century, in terms of philosophies of literature, could be said to have formed the pattern of "a hundred schools of thoughts".

In the early twentieth century, against the social and historical background of the semi-feudal and semi-colonial society, although the concept of the new literature was still relatively vague and did not form such an obvious pattern as China's was, the seeds of modernization had begun to sprout. Movements of democracy and innovation by different academic schools with different developmental tendencies

---

1 Huang Manjun, *A Textbook of a Review of Chinese Literature Theory in the 20th Century*, Central China Normal University Press, 2010, p.4.

and pursuits gradually took shape in the country. The outbreak and failure of the "Phong trào Cần Vương" became the starting point of Vietnam's modern social and cultural transformation. Taking the modern national spirit as the driving force, Vietnamese scholars actively transliterated Nguyen Du's *The Tale of Kieu*, Ho Xuan Huong's Chu-Nom poems, Nguyen Trai's *Bình Ngô đại cáo* (literally: Great proclamation upon the pacification of the Wu), *Poems of National Pronunciation* and other classic Vietnamese characters and literature into modern national letters, and edited and annotated a number of history books of Vietnamese classical literature. All of them reflected the inheritance and care of national classics by Vietnamese intellectuals, as well as their responsibility for the independence and development of the country and nation. Also, the French colonial policy towards Vietnam and the rapid development of higher educational institutions of various types established across Vietnam allowed Vietnamese intellectuals to comprehensively and systematically accept and master the knowledge system of Western culture and literary theory for the first time. Moreover, intellectuals who had returned from studying abroad and this plus their desire for innovation and modernization of Vietnamese literary theory were also important motives for the transformation to modernized Vietnamese literary theory. A series of excellent intellectuals in the 20th century, such as Hai Trieu, Dang Thai Mai, Truong Thanh, Luong Duc Thiet, Pham Quynh, Luong Duy Thu, Nguyen Van Vinh, Truong Vinh Ky, etc., formally became the important and main force of Vietnam in building a modern system of literary theory.

Translating and disseminating modern Western literary theories, compiling and annotating Vietnam's classical Chinese characters and Chu-Nom literature, studying Nguyen Du's *The Tale of Kieu* and supporting the development of national pronunciation literature were the important content in the modern transformation of the traditional Vietnamese literary theory. Pham Quynh, Pham Duy Ton and others advocated the concept of pragmatic literature, but this idea of literary innovation conflicted with that advocated by Thieu Son with the aesthetic value of literary works as the principal object of research. In a sense, the literary dispute between Pham Quynh and Ngo Duc Ke on Nguyen Du's *The Tale of Kieu* reflected an interweaving and struggling complex state of the Vietnamese literary theory at that time. Poets in the New Poetry Movement such as Tan Da advocated eliminating all obsolete rules, liberating personality and liberating poetry.

Entering the stage from 1932 to 1945, the modern transformation of the Vietnamese literary theory further evolved: creative literary activities and the theory of literary criticism developed in concert. Hoai Thanh and Thieu Son's self-consciousness as writers could be regarded as an important starting point for the modern transformation of the Vietnamese literary theory at this stage. This point was also accepted by Xuan Dieu, Che Lan Vien, Han Mac Tu and other poets in the New Poetry Movement and outstandingly represented in their poems. Accordingly, the literary debate between "art for life" and "art for art" occurred. This literary debate was also seen as a manifestation of the ideological struggle between the bourgeoisie and the idealistic philosophy of literature and the proletarian and materialistic philosophy of literature.

In China, the first modern transformation, as mentioned above, "is achieved by breaking through the traditional literary theory of 'poetry and literary review' and accepting and transforming foreign literary theory, which experiences the two stages of accepting Japanese, European and American literary theories as well as accepting and transforming Soviet literary theory; and this has gone through a long process from diversified explorations to integration and formation of a unified theoretical system."[1] Hence, the modern transformation and development of Chinese and Vietnamese literary theories lay not in renovating their traditional literary ideas, but occurred after being influenced by Western literary theories. However, there were differences between China and Vietnam because the two countries completed this process through different channels, by different methods and by accepting

---

1   Lai Daren, "Modern Transformation and Development of Chinese Literary Theory in the 20th Century" , *Study & Exploration*, 2001(5), p.99.

different contents. According to the research results in *A Textbook of a Review of Chinese Literary Theory in the 20th Century*, the first modern transformation of Chinese literary theory showed four characteristics. First, "it broke the feudal ruling and shackles of literary ideas, abandoned the teleology that literary criticism served feudal ethics and morality, advocated rebellion, sought changes and valued practicality under the guidance of the theory of evolution, and began to establish new values of the theory of literary criticism." Second, "the ancient literary and artistic aesthetics that emphasized harmonious beauty and the expressionist criticism that emphasized the role of the subject of criticism were no longer the only and dominant ideas of literature and criticism." Third, "the criticism of literary theory begins to evolve towards science and logic, breaking the old patterns of criticism by impression and viewpoints, and bring forth methods of criticism of literary theory and a way of thinking through scientific analysis from a macroscopic perspective." Fourth, "the concept of stylistics has undergone big changes and the novels have been elevated to be a mainstream literary genre. The changes in the domain of literary form and ideas on literature and criticism are also reflected in literary form."[1] This article reveals that, in terms of the developmental process and main characteristics of the knowledge system of literary theories, the first modern transformation of literary theories in Vietnam seemed to be very similar to that in China on the surface, but in terms of specific issues, there were big differences.

Like China, the modern transformation was also the process of the Vietnamese literature transcending and getting rid of thousands of years of the traditional system of literary theory and establishing a new model of a literary system. China was one center of the oriental culture that had a profound influence on neighboring countries such as Japan, South Korea and Vietnam. With the continuous expansion of the "Confucian Cultural Circle", Chinese classical literary and artistic ideas and aesthetic values gradually became important elements in the traditional culture of these countries. This was also a law of natural development in the

---

1 Huang Manjun, *A Textbook of a Review of Chinese Literary Theory in the 20th Century*, Hubei: Central China Normal University Press, 2010, pp.17-19.

history of human development. Under the influence of Chinese culture, in their process of development, Japan, South Korea and Vietnam, on the one hand, learned and absorbed the essence of the classical system of knowledge such as Chinese philosophy and aesthetics; on the other hand, they continuously strived for innovation and for the establishment of a knowledge system with national characteristics based on the local culture. The Chu-Nom letters and literature in Vietnam were the efforts of Vietnamese people in this regard. In the case of Vietnam, the Confucian culture and the oriental traditional literary theories were not only our intrinsic values that needed to be preserved, inherited and carried forward, but also the exotic culture and literary theories that needed to be separated. The reason why Lu Xun advocated "going out to participate in the cause of the world"[1] was that the Chinese classical literary theory inherited by Chinese intellectuals for two thousand years was the soul and essence of the country's nationality and it was qualified to be juxtaposed with Western culture and knowledge system of literary theories. However, Vietnamese literary theory did not have that attitude and motivation, nor could it participate in the cause of the world by relying on what belonged to others. Thus, accepting modern Western literary theories was not just the only way for the Vietnamese literary theory to self-renovate and modernize, but also a good opportunity to transcend tradition and create a system of literary theory with national characteristics. At the beginning of the 20th century, the literary dispute and the artistic debate between traditional and new poetries that occurred within the Vietnamese literary theory were important manifestations of the continuous transformation and renovations of the system of cultural and literary discourse. It took only over thirty years for Vietnamese literary theory to successfully transform from the typical model of oriental literary theories to a modern pluralistic model of literary theories. Of course, in this process, the French colonists and their policy of aggression against Vietnam also played a significant role.

Most of the first modern transformation of Chinese literary theory was learned

---

1   Lu Xun, "Er Yi · On the Fine Arts Exhibition of Mr. Tao Yuanqing" , *The Complete Works of Lu Xun*, Vol.3, Beijing: People' s Literature Publishing House, 1956.

from the West through Japan. Consequently, the Japanese Restoration had a profound influence on Chinese intellectuals at that time. Vietnam became a French colony during the mid-nineteenth century. Accordingly, Vietnamese scholars' acceptance of modern Western literary theories was mainly through the French language and French literary theory. From this point of view, Vietnam's acceptance of Western culture and literary theories was more direct and comprehensive. Influenced by China's "New Book" and Bourgeois Revolution movements, a number of Vietnamese scholars such as Phan Boi Chau and Phan Chu Trinh, also advocated the "Đông Du" movement, but it all ended in failure. Hence, the spirit of the Japanese Restoration had almost no direct influence on Vietnam's politics and society at that time. However, against the background of France's comprehensive efforts to build a modern system of education and a modern civilization, the Vietnamese literary theory had a relatively free and healthy space for development. New poetry, romantic novels, realistic novels, modern dramas and other modern literary genres, as well as the emergence of the criticism of the new literary theory and its rapid development and fruitful results in the period of 1932-1945 were exactly the achievements of the modern transformation of Vietnamese literary theory.

Regarding the Chinese literary theory at the same stage of development, "although from the perspective of the development of literary ideas and criticism of literary theory, to a large extent, it still shows transitional characteristics, and it is still at a historical stage in which significant achievements have been made. In the collision and confluence of Chinese and foreign cultural and literary trends, the modern character of the criticism of literary theory is taking shape and a process of modernization has also begun. Many big issues indicate the direction of future development.[1] Moreover, Song Jianhua also pointed out that: "Chinese literature in the 20th century was strongly exclusive of modernist literature. During the May Fourth period, modernism was resisted by a traditional cultural psychology, but

---

1 Huang Manjun, *A Textbook of a Review of Chinese Literary Theory in the 20th Century*, Hubei: Central China Normal University Press, 2010, p.19.

after the 1930s, political ideology was used to criticize and deny modernism ..."[1]
The situation was different from that of Vietnam. For more than 50 years from the
late 19th century to 1945, Vietnam actively accepted Western literature and literary
theory. And this was not confined to scholars of Western studies. Intellectuals of
the older generation such as Tan Da and Luong Duy Thu who became famous in
the period of Confucian imperial examinations also began to learn French through
different channels as an important instrumentality for acquiring Western knowledge.
In 1945, the Democratic Republic of Vietnam was formally founded. From then on,
Vietnam regarded Marxist literary theory as the only system and rejected almost
all criticism of non-Marxist literary theory. This also occurred in China. Of course,
their historical forms and developmental characteristics differed due to the different
social, cultural and historical backgrounds of the two countries. This was quite
understandable.

2. Introduction of the Marxist Literary Theory as the Core Values for the Development of Literary Theories

The Marxist literary theory was historically important in China and Vietnam.
As the core values of socialist China and Vietnam, the Marxist theoretical system
had not only become the guiding ideology for the founding of China and Vietnam,
but it had also played a critical role in the field of literature and art, and even
completely changed the systems of literary theory built up by China and Vietnam
in the earlier period. From the diversified systems of literary theory in the early
part of the twentieth century, China and Vietnam began to adopt a single system of
literary theory. The Marxist literary theory almost comprehensively and thoroughly
influenced the literary and artistic life and the construction of the system of literary
theory in the two countries.

In China, "Socialism in China" in the *Book on Liberty* written by Liang
Qichao in the late 19th century could be regarded as a benchmark for the formal

---

1   Song Jianhua, *Modernity and Chinese Literature*, Shandong: Shandong Education Press, 1999,
    p.101.

introduction of socialism into China. In 1903, the literary works of socialist pioneers from Japan were translated into Chinese, such as *The Essence of Socialism* compiled by Kotoku Shusui, *The Spirit of Labor Movements* and *The Ideal Wheel of Society* by Osugi Sakae, *Marx's Theory on Economics* by Hajime Kawakami, *From Scientific Socialism to Socialism in Action* written by Hitoshi Yamakawa and *The Theory and Practice of Popular Art* by Hirabayashi Hatsunosuke, and they "became important works for many Chinese students studying in Japan and early revolutionary democrats in accepting socialist enlightenment education."[1] And in this period of exploration, the most active translator of proletarian literary theories (actually the study of Russian literature by Japanese scholars) was Feng Xuefeng. His articles, such as "The Dawn of New Russian Literature", "The New Russian Drama Movement and Dance" and "New Russian Proletarian Literature", captured the attention of the Chinese literary circle at that time. In the article "Translation and Introduction of the Japanese Marxist Literary Theory in China", Wang Zhisong indicated that: "The Chinese proletarian literary movement was launched when the magazines *Cultural Criticism* and *Sun Monthly* were published in 1928. Later, it experienced the establishment of the "Left Alliance" in 1930 and ended when the "Left Alliance" was dissolved in 1936."[2] In 1926, Guo Moruo published an article entitled "Revolution and Literature" in the magazine *Creation Monthly*, which systematically discussed the relationship between revolution and literature. This article was later regarded by Li Chuli as China's first article advocating revolutionary literature. Furthermore, during the period of 1926-1930, scholars also translated articles written with the basic characteristics of the proletarian literary movement into Chinese, such as "To New Realism" by Kurahara Korehito, "The Development of the Japanese Theory of Proletarian Literature" by Aono Suekichi, "Development of the Guiding Theory of the Japanese Art Movement" by Taguchi Kenichi and "Problems of Modern Emerging Literature" by Kyoiku. These articles

---

1 Wang Zhisong, "Translation and Introduction of Japan's Marxist Literary Theory in China", *Foreign Language Research in Northeast Asia*, 2015(2), pp.10-16.

2 Wang Zhisong, "Translation and Introduction of Japan's Marxist Literary Theory in China", *Foreign Language Research in Northeast Asia*, 2015(2), pp.10-16.

had a widespread influence within the Chinese literary circle.

In addition to the categories of "the third type of person" and "transcending class literature" derived from the Japanese literary circle, according to the statistics collected by Hu Yongqin, Geng Ruiqin and Yuan Yanheng *et al.* in "The Spread of Marx and Engels in China", from 1920 to 1927, by the efforts of Lu Xun, Feng Xuefeng, Zhou Yang and Qu Qiubai, etc., more than 20 kinds of classic works by Marx and Engels were translated into Chinese and promoted and disseminated nationwide. Regarding this, it could be affirmed that the translation and dissemination of the Marxist literary theory in China was first influenced by Japanese revolutionary literature, and then the translation and promotion became systematic according to the practical needs of Chinese society and politics. As regards how the Marxist literary theory could develop in China, Huang Manjun also summarized that: "First, with the activities of translation and introduction, Marxist literary ideas were mixed with the Soviet's 'proletarian cultural school' and the 'RAPP', or even with the literature and artistic ideas of the vulgar sociology and the mechanism under the influence of Japan's left-leaning line of Fukumoto Kazuo; second, Marxist literary and artistic thoughts moved horizontally from the cultural field in which they were born to our country's cultural field. This was the process of acceptance and reconstruction across different cultural times and spaces. The exotic Marxist literary theory could not only be newly enriched and developed in China, but it could also result in differing degrees of 'deformation' and 'distortion' due to being misled or misinterpreted."[1] Such statements of Huang Manjun could summarize the main characteristics during the early stage of development of the Marxist literary theory in China. No matter how "deformed" and "distorted" Marxism was in China, it was first of all out of the need for the development of a Chinese literary theory instead of social and political reasons. This situation was different from the early development of the Marxist literary theory in Vietnam.

1　Huang Manjun, *A Textbook of a Review of Chinese Literary Theory in the 20th Century*, Hubei: Central China Normal University Press, 2010, p.28.

The origin of the Marxist literary theory in China was mainly the translation of Japanese scholars' articles on "revolutionary literature", the "proletariat", Soviet literature and other related issues, as well as the translation of the works of Marx and Engels. This literary theory spread rapidly and soon became dominant. However, the Marxist literary theory in Vietnam emerged during the period 1935-1939 in the debate on "art for art" or "art for life". In this literary debate, Hai Trieu published several articles on the Marxist literary theory in newspapers. Unfortunately, the literary debate of "art for art" or "art for life" did not directly put forward and talk about the domains of the Marxist literary theory, but focused on and discussed the relationship between literature and society, the function of literature and art, and free creation. In this debate, Hai Trieu, Bui Cong Thua, Son Tra, Thach Dong and Ho Thanh laid a good foundation for the Marxist literary theory and critical realism in Vietnam. In the article "Two Concepts of Literature", Thieu Son divided literature into two types for the purposes of ethics and morality or creative beauty. In 1935, Hai Trieu published the article "Art for Art or Art for Life" in the *New Life* magazine. In this article, he opposed Thieu Son's literary idea and argued that the purpose of any artistic creation had to be describing and depicting life, reflecting the mentality, emotions and ambitions of the working people and playing an important role in transforming society, that is to say, art must be "art for life"; and the so-called "beauty in literature and art" advocated by Thieu Son only represented the decaying power in society. In 1937, Hai Trieu published "Literature and Materialism" in the *Huong River* magazine. According to the article, Hai Trieu proposed and explored in depth the related issues of the Marxist literary theory, such as the relationship between literature and social life, literature and class struggle, revolutionary literature and counter-revolutionary literature. Moreover, Hai Trieu, Hoai Thanh, Bui Cong Thua, Trong Minh, Van Minh, Nhu Gio and Mau Khai also published a series of articles on the Marxist literary theory in the magazines *Saturday Fiction* and *Literary Circle*. For example, "Toward Realism in Literature: Several Trends in the Novel Genre" by Hai Trieu, "Honesty and Freedom in Literature" and "The Significance and Role of Literature" by Hoai Thanh, and "The

Approval of the Establishment of a New Vietnamese Culture" by Bui Cong Thua, and so on.

In China, Japan's "revolutionary literature" and the success of the October Revolution in Russia had a very profound influence, but in Vietnam, the October Revolution in Russia had hardly any influence at all. With the "New Book" movement in China, Vietnamese intellectuals in the early twentieth century also began to yearn for and learn from Japan. That's why Phan Boi Chau and Phan Chu Trinh advocated the "Đông Du" movement. Although this revolutionary social movement attracted the attention of patriotic young people, it did not play any crucial role in the end. The translation and dissemination of the Marxist literary theory in Vietnam, unlike in China that started from its own theoretical needs, was the result of the combination of the Vietnamese Communists' promotion of Marxism-Leninism with the understanding of the Vietnamese literary theorists of literature at that time. At the stage of the years 1925-1927, with the emergence of communist training courses opened by Nguyen Ai Quoc[1] and the founding of revolutionary organizations such as the Vietnam Nationalist Party, the Vietnamese Revolutionary Youth League, the New Vietnamese Revolutionary Party, the Vietnamese Trade Union and the Vietnamese Farmers' Union, Marxism was officially introduced and spread throughout Vietnam. In 1938, Tran Dinh Long published an article, "Three Years in Soviet Russia", in the *Information* magazine, which systematically introduced Soviet Russian literature and the Marxist literary theory and put forward the plan for the development of Marxist Vietnamese literature. The translation and introduction of the Marxist literary theory in Vietnam arrived slightly later than in China, and the Marxist classics were not systematically translated into the Vietnamese language nor widely disseminated. The translation, dissemination and rapid development of the Marxist literary theory in China came about mainly through the efforts of progressive writers and thinkers such as Lu Xun, Qu Qiubai, Zhou Yang or Liang Qichao. However, it was not writers or

---

1   Another name for Ho Chi Minh.

thinkers who first accepted Marxism in Vietnam, but Ho Chi Minh, Vietnam's first Communist. Later, through the his own efforts and the vanguard of the Communist Party of Vietnam such as Tran Phu and Ly Hoang Phuong, Marxism was spread in a comprehensive and rapid manner. This was the biggest difference between China and Vietnam during the early stage of development of the Marxist literary theory.

However, at this stage, both China's and Vietnam's literary theories showed diversified trends of development in literary ideas, and in the types and methods of research. "The creative experience of Ba Jin, Lao She, Cao Yu, etc., the literary theory of Lin Yutang, Dai Wangshu, etc., the theoretical translations and literary criticism of Zhu Guangqian, Liu Xiwei (Li Jianwu), Liang Zongdai, Qian Gurong, Ba Ren, etc., and the theory of poetry of 'Nine-Leaf' poets, and so on."[1] These achievements enriched and diversified the development of the Chinese literary theory. In Vietnam, romantic literature innovations by Hoai Thanh, The Lu and Thieu Son, the realistic literature advocated by Hai Trieu, Bui Cong Thua and Pham Quynh, and six continuous literary debates enabled the rapid development and fruitful achievements of the Vietnamese literary theory in the process of modernization and transformation. In other words, no matter whether in Vietnam or in China, the Marxist literary theory had a relatively equal relationship with other literary schools in its early development.

As for why the Marxist literary theory, as a completely alien ideological school, could be translated and disseminated in such a short period of time and become the sole guiding ideology in the Chinese and Vietnamese literary circles, this article supports the following summary of Zhang Baogui: "The number of translations, the degree of classicism and the time sequence of translation and introduction indicate the logical master-slave relations. Without the actual social problems targeted by Marxism, there would be no reason to introduce such a literary theory."[2] In other

---

1 Huang Manjun, *A Textbook of Chinese Literary Theory Review in the 20th Century*, Hubei: Central China Normal University Press, 2010, p.28.
2 Zhang Baogui, "The Early Stage of the Sinicization of the Marxist Literary Theory", Social Sciences in China, 2008(2), pp.140-151.

words, the reasons why the Marxist literary theory could take root in China and Vietnam were not only the needs of the two countries for literary theories at that time, but also the social targets of Marxism and the choice of the Communist Party of China and the Communist Party of Vietnam to revolutionize the nation and unify the country.

In 1899, Lenin pointed out when discussing issues related to the construction of socialism in Russia: "For Russian socialists, it is especially necessary to explore Marx's theory independently, because what he provides is only general guiding principles, and the application of these principles, to be specific, differs from France to Britain, from France to Germany, and from Russia to Germany."[1] Lenin's view summarized the practical nature of Marxism and also allowed socialist countries following the Soviet Union to more flexibly apply Marxism to realize the great cause of the proletarian revolution, the liberation of the nation and the establishment of a new country.

With respect to the actual situation in China, Li Chunhua summarized in his article "Socialism with Chinese Characteristics: A Successful Example of the Nationalization of Marxism" as follows: "From the 1940s to the late 1970s, the theoretical sign of the nationalization of Marxism was the formation of a series of nationalized Marxist theories represented by Mao Zedong Thought ... The Chinese Communist Party represented by Mao Zedong could be called an excellent representative of the nationalization of Marxism. Mao Zedong broke through the restraint of dogmatism with extraordinary courage, was guided by Marxist stances, viewpoints and methods, combined the universal truth of Marxism with the specific reality of China and found a new revolutionary democratic path with Chinese characteristics ..."[2] In this article, Li Chunhua also mentioned the Marxist localization in North Korea, Cuba and other socialist countries. With regard to the development of Vietnam, he praised that: "The Communist Party of Vietnam

---

1   *The Collected Works of Lenin*, Volume 1, Beijing: People's Publishing House, 1995, p.274.
2   Li Chunhua, "Socialism with Chinese Characteristics: A Successful Example of the Nationalization of Marxism", *Studies on Marxism*, 2011(6).

adheres to Marxism-Leninism and Ho Chi Minh's Thought, leads the people to overcome difficulties, and makes numerous major achievements in the building up of socialism."[1] "Ho Chi Minh's Thought" mentioned by Li Chunhua was the best example of the Vietnamization of Marxism. The Ninth National People's Congress of the Communist Party of Vietnam gave the following definition of "Ho Chi Minh's Thought": "Ho Chi Minh's Thought is a system of Ho Chi Minh's comprehensive and in-depth viewpoints on the fundamental issues of the Vietnamese revolution, the result of the application and development of Marxism-Leninism based on the practice of Chairman Ho Chi Minh in China, and also a system of viewpoints of inheriting and giving play to the traditional virtues of the nation and liberating classes and the nation."[2] According to the Ninth National People's Congress of the Communist Party of Vietnam, Ho Chi Minh's Thought includes the content of national revolution, socialism and the period of transition of socialism, the Communist Party of Vietnam, the great unity of the nation, military affairs, the construction of a country of, to and for the nation, the combination of national power and the power of the times, moral thoughts, humanistic thoughts and cultural thoughts. Ho Chi Minh once confirmed that: "In the beginning, it was patriotism, not communism, that convinced me to follow Lenin and the Third International."[3] Thus, Marxism had new developments in different ways during different periods either in China or in Vietnam. Such developments were the achievements made through combining Marxism as the ideological guide with the realistic conditions of each country and through the interpretation, application and development by excellent Communists in different countries. Therefore, the "Sinification" and "Vietnamization" of Marxism belonged to the achievements made by Marxism in the specific developmental history of China and Vietnam, as well as in the characteristics of the international development of Marxism itself.

---

1 Li Chunhua, "Socialism with Chinese Characteristics: A Successful Example of the Nationalization of Marxism", *Studies on Marxism*, 2011(6).

2 The Political Theory Center of Vietnam National University, Ho Chi Minh City, *The Vitality of Marxism-Leninism in the Modern Era*, Hanoi: National Political Press, 2014.

3 [German] Hellmut Kapfenberger, *Ho Chi Minh: Eine Chronik*, Dinh Huong and Thien Ha (trans.), Ho Chi Minh: New World Press, 2010.

In general, after the initial development through acceptance and dissemination in China and Vietnam, the Marxist literary theory was transformed according to the different situations of the two countries and changes in the prevailing literary and artistic ideas, and achieved different degrees of development.

3. Conclusion

China and Vietnam, linked by mountains and rivers, share a similar culture, so they also have a close and long-standing relationship in literary exchanges. Being at the center of the oriental civilization, the Chinese culture, especially its Confucianism, has a profound influence on surrounding countries. The subject, genre and way of expression of Chinese classical literature were actively accepted, acquired and innovated by Vietnamese sages to create their own system of literature. Before the 20th century, the relationship between Chinese and Vietnamese literature and literary theories was in a basic condition that Vietnamese literature actively accepted the essence of Chinese literature and innovated and created its based on their own national culture and humanistic feelings. Since the beginning of the 20th century, against the background of radical social and political changes occurring in the two countries, Chinese and Vietnamese literary theories gradually changed from a purely traditional oriental system to a modern system. From the perspectives of stages and patterns of development, the modern process of transformation of literary theories in the two countries, especially the historical evolution of the translation and dissemination of Marxism in China and Vietnam, were about the same, but if the two countries were put together for objective and reasonable comparison of specific issues, there were indeed very large differences. These differences formally reflected the national consciousness and uniqueness of Chinese and Vietnamese systems of literary theories.

荀子对孔子礼学思想的继承与发展

赵荷【土耳其】

安卡拉大学助教

荀子在孔子礼学思想的基础上，创建了独特的、并且长期影响中国文化和文明发展的礼学思想体系。荀子对孔子礼学思想的继承与发展，这个主题包括很多方面：正名、义利、仁、礼治、人性，等等。本文将集中论述两个方面：一是探讨"礼的起源"。从文献看，孔子没有去探讨"礼"的起源，而荀子则积极地作了这项工作，深入地探讨了礼的起源。二是比较孔子的"以仁释礼"和荀子的"以法入礼"。孔子用"仁"对"礼"作了创造性的阐释。荀子对于道德教化的局限性有更深刻的认识，他隆礼至法，认为"礼"是"法之大分，类之纲纪"，是"法"的总则与旨归。荀子以法入礼，主张礼法兼治，对社会治理发生了更大的作用。

一、荀子礼学的时代背景

西周初年，周人取代商人统治天下，为了更好地巩固政权和社会稳定，周代统治者(主要是周公)制定新的礼乐，用来规范和统一人们的行为。在西周400多年中，周礼逐步固定化、模式化，日益成为统治者治理天下的重要工具。

春秋时代，社会中开始出现许多不稳定的因素，造成了"礼崩乐坏"的局面，社会也从稳定期转入混乱期，周礼逐步失去了控制力，于是政治家们开始对"礼"

进行反思。诸子百家便应运而生。生在春秋末期的孔子积极改造了周礼，希望周礼重新规范约束人们的行为，使社会重新从混乱恢复到稳定有序的状态。

战国时期天下大乱。诸侯国的大混战从春秋时代延续到这个时期，已经从量变走向质变。战国末期的中国社会，焦点在于怎样使社会从混乱走向统一有序。朱俊在他的论文中说："荀子生活的战国末年，政治统一的趋势日益明显。战国时代，各诸侯国为争夺土地和人口，发动了割据战争，战争的规模持续扩大。……到荀子晚年，秦王政即位亲政，距秦灭六国最后统一中国仅十几年。这个时期，统一已成民心所向。……大一统业已成为历史发展的必然趋势，荀子经常使用'调一天下''齐一天下''县天下一四海'等语来表明统一的趋势。"[1] 处于奴隶制社会向封建制社会转型的大变革中[2]，荀子继承儒家思想，认为改造后的"礼"，仍然是唯一合适的治理模式。

二、荀子探讨"礼"的起源

礼是儒学中所提到的概念之一。它的英文翻译是"Rites""Rituals"或者"Etiquette"。关于礼的来源有不同的观点。黄辉解释这些观点说："一是礼起源于祭祀[3]，以王国维、刘师培、郭沫若为代表，这种观点最为普遍；二是礼起源于风俗习惯，以杨宽、杨向奎、蔡尚思等为代表；三是礼起源于饮食分配上的差别，以杨英杰等为代表。"[4] 虽然有不同的观点，我们所提到的礼是管理政府与社会的一些准则、社会规范、国之纲纪。根据社会和政治发展，礼已经超越了宗教仪式，转变为规范人民之间交流乃至政府政策的传统规则。

孔子说："非礼无以节事天地之神也，非礼无以辨君臣上下长幼之位也，非礼无以别男女父子兄弟之亲、婚姻疏数之交也。"（《礼记·哀公问》）意思是：没有礼，就没有仪式来祭祀天地之神；没有礼，就没有办法辨君臣、上下、长幼的地位；没有礼，就没有办法区分男和女、父亲和儿子、兄弟之亲的适当地位、在婚姻中进行契约家庭间的交往。这些说明，孔子充分肯定礼的重要性，认为礼是维持社会地位、人们生活、交往的基础。

孔子对周礼的最大发展就在"以仁释礼"，最根本的特征是使礼内在化、自

1　朱俊：《荀子的礼学思想》，西北大学 2006 年硕士学位论文第，4—5 页。
2　关于奴隶制社会与封建制社会，请参见：郭沫若《奴隶制时代》，人民出版社 2005 年版。
3　*Combridge History of China*, Cambrigde University Press, 1999, p.252.
4　黄辉：《略伦先秦礼学的三次发展》，上海师范大学 2005 年硕士学位论文，第 1 页。

觉化。孔子的礼学思想为后世提供了德治的范本。

从文献看，孔子没有去探讨"礼"的起源。研究者认为孔子的礼要以仁为核心、以仁释礼。孔子的仁是德的泛称，包括社会的众多道德，是"众德之一"。对这方面有不同的说法，黄辉说大部分是"仁"字的不同阐发："一部分人认为仁是礼的本质，以李会钦、杨庆中、史华楠为代表；一部分人从哲学、人类学等角度提出孔礼揭示了人的本质、礼的心理基础是仁，以杨庆中、何锡蓉、李晓虹为代表。从礼规范自身的特点来看，孔礼是礼仪（形式）和礼义（内涵）的合一，以李晓虹为代表。"[1]从这些观点里我们可以看：孔子的"礼"是建立在他所认为的"人性本善"的基础上的，他认为"仁"是内在的、人文的，而"礼"是"仁"在制度方面的具体显现，他认为理想的社会应该是制度与人文二者的融合。总的说来，孔子的礼治思想以"仁"为标准和核心。

荀子探讨了"礼"的起源。他说："礼起于何也？曰：人生而有欲，欲而不得，则不能无求。求而无度量分界，则不能不争；争则乱，乱则穷。先王恶其乱也，故制礼义以分之，以养人之欲，给人之求。使欲必不穷于物，物必不屈于欲。两者相持而长，是礼之所起也。"（《荀子·礼论》）意思是：礼的起源是什么？说：人生来就有欲望，欲望得不到满足，他就要去求索。求索没有分界，他就要争夺；争夺造成混乱，混乱造成穷困。先王憎恨混乱，所以建立礼义来区分，来满足人的欲望，供给人的需求。使得欲望的满足不会因为物质的匮乏而终止，物质的给予不会过分地顺从于欲望。欲望和物质两者相辅相成，这是礼出现的原因。可见荀子探讨"礼"的起源，是建立在"人性本恶"的基础上面。他认为礼不能根源于人的内在本性，礼的本源只能存在于主体之外。

关于荀子论述礼的起源有不同的观点[2]：荀子的礼起源于"养欲给求"，起源于"天地"，起源于"制欲止乱"，礼是圣人的创造物，等等。朱俊说："俞荣根认为，荀子的礼法起源论基于其性恶论。因为人性恶，社会上就生出争夺祸乱。本于天地说，惠吉星持这种观点。他认为荀子的性恶论表明，礼不可能根源于人的内在本性，礼的本源只能存在于主体之外。虽然礼不能脱离社会、人类、天地万物产生和存在，但'真正具有本原地位的只有天地'。"[3]虽然有不同的观点，他们多明确说明荀子的礼注重外在规范。

1 黄辉：《略伦先秦礼学的三次发展》，上海师范大学 2005 年硕士学位论文，第 2 页。
2 黄辉：《略伦先秦礼学的三次发展》，上海师范大学 2005 年硕士学位论文，第 3 页。
3 朱俊：《荀子的礼学思想》，西北大学 2006 年硕士学位论文，第 1—2 页。

孔子的"礼"更重视"仁"。而荀子则更重礼"礼"的制度性,他认为制度性与人文并举来治国更重要,这个制度性便体现为"法"。

三、荀子"以法入礼"

"法"的意思是"method""way",当"method"描述了在某些情况下的人类行为,由国家宣布对未遵守规定的处罚,这显然是一项"law"。

孔子并不小看"法"的作用,但他觉得成文法不必要。他认为"礼"是最基本的政治原则和行为规范,而"法"并不是治理国家与社会的最好方式。孔子反对主政者高调处罚。陈荣庆说:"对提高社会成员品德和处置不守规则行为的方式是重在为政者的德行影响上,要求君主做好全体成员的表率。孔子反对主政者高调处罚不守规则者,而是力图唤起违规者的自我意识,让其自己去改正。这是一种被动的态度,相信和信赖于人的自我觉醒和自我拯救。"[1]

荀子把礼与法结合在一起,提出了"以法入礼""隆礼至法"思想。关于他的礼法思想,朱俊说:"礼法结合是这个时期的一个学术特点。在礼法关系上,这些学者大多具有以礼辅法的倾向。荀子总结了他们的理论,使礼法结合得更加紧密,所不同的是,荀子是站在儒家立场上吸收法家,援法入礼,以礼为主法为辅,形成自己的礼法关系论。"[2]对于社会治理,陈荣庆说:"孔子是'道之以德,齐之以礼',而荀子则是'道之以德,齐之以礼,再齐之以法'。"[3]荀子并不主张制定残酷的法律规定,他只是认为"礼"没有惩罚性,不可以惩恶,所以要用"法"补充"礼"的缺陷。陈荣庆还说,荀子认为治理社会、维护制度光有为政者(君主)的德行做表率还很不够,有"礼"进行规范也还不够,社会上存在着不少德行不能教化、礼义不能规范的人(如丹朱、商均、象之类),需要对他们不守规则的做法进行处罚,用"法"来强迫他们变得无害于社会。[4]可见,荀子援法入礼,实际上是把法家的法治纳入儒家的礼治系统,他的核心仍然以礼为主,他的以礼制律的思想,大大丰富和发展了孔子的礼学内容。

1　陈荣庆:《从荀子对孔子"礼"的继承与发展看荀子德礼法兼治的天下治理理念》,《宜春学院学报》,2010年第32卷。

2　朱俊:《荀子的礼学思想》,西北大学2006年硕士学位论文,第6页。

3　陈荣庆:《从荀子对孔子"礼"的继承与发展看荀子德礼法兼治的天下治理理念》,《宜春学院学报》,2010年第32卷,第90页。

4　陈荣庆:《从荀子对孔子"礼"的继承与发展看荀子德礼法兼治的天下治理理念》,《宜春学院学报》,2010年第32卷,第91页。

四、结论

孔子与荀子都认为，礼是治国理政的基体方式。孔子"以仁释礼"，将"德"内化到人的内心，礼中融入了自觉的意识，主张"仁政""德治"。孔子礼学思想的缺点，是他所要求的内在德性与当时的社会现实、人性特点不相符合，所以他的礼学思想也很难为社会所用。

荀子从"性恶"的基础上探讨"礼"的起源，认为光强调"礼"的自觉性是不够的，还要"以法入礼"，强调"礼"的强制性。荀子的"隆礼重法"提出后，礼的规范性、强制性和有效性等特点就更明显了。礼与法的合力，对社会治理发生了更大的作用。这是荀子对孔子思想的继承与发展。

Xunzi: the Inheritance and Development of Confucius' Theory of Rites

Burçin Bedel / Turkey

Ankara University, Research Assistant

Xunzi, based on Confucius' theory of rites, created a unique system of theory of rites that had a long-standing influence on the development of Chinese culture and civilization. Regarding Xunzi's inheritance and development of Confucius' theory of rites, this topic covers many aspects: rectification of the name, justice and benefit, benevolence, rule of rites, human nature, etc. This article will focus on two aspects. First, it will explore the "origin of rites". According to the literature, Confucius did not explore the origin of "rites", while Xunzi actively did this work and explored it in depth. Second, it will compare Confucius' idea of "explaining rites with benevolence" with Xunzi's idea of "turning laws into rites". Confucius used "benevolence" to creatively interpret "rites". Xunzi had a deeper understanding of the limitations of moral education. He valued rites and emphasized law and considered "rites" as the "the great basis of law and the foundation of precedents", and the general principle and purpose of "law". Xunzi turned laws into rites and advocated the combination of rites and law, thus having great effects on social governance.

1. Background of the Times: Xunzi's Theory of Rites

At the beginning of the Western Zhou Dynasty, Zhou defeated Shang and ruled the country. In order to better consolidate their political power and social stability, the rulers of the Zhou Dynasty (mainly the Duke of Zhou) formulated new rites to regulate and unify people's behavior. For more than 400 years in the Western Zhou Dynasty, the rites of Zhou gradually became stereotyped and modeled, and thus were an important instrument for rulers in governing the country.

In the Spring and Autumn Period, many unstable factors began to appear in the society, which caused the situation in which "rites collapse, music spoils". The society also shifted from a period of stability to one of chaos. The rites of Zhou gradually lost their controlling effect, so politicians began to rethink the concept of "rites", and hundreds of schools of thoughts emerged. Born in the late Spring and Autumn Period, Confucius actively transformed the rites of Zhou with the hope of re-regulating and restraining the people's behavior and restoring society from a state of chaos to a stable and orderly state.

The country was in a chaotic state during the Warring States Period. The large-scale dogfight of vassal states continued from the Spring and Autumn Period to this period and evolved from quantitative to qualitative changes. In the late Warring States Period, the focus of Chinese society was how to change from a state of chaos to one of unity and order. In his article, Zhu Jun said: "In the late Warring States Period, where Xunzi lived, the trend of political unification became increasingly apparent. In the Warring States Period, vassal states launched wars to scramble for land and population. Wars became full-scale ... In the old age of Xunzi, King Zheng of Qin ascended the throne and there were only a little more than ten years left before the final unification of the six states by Qin. In this period, reunification was the will of the people ... Unification had already become an inevitable trend in historical development. Xunzi often used "reunification of the country", "conquering the country and unifying the four seas" to indicate the trend of unification."[1] It

---

1　Zhu Jun, *Xunzi's Theory of Rites*, Master's Thesis of Northwest University, 2006, pp.4-5.

was the great transformation from slavery to the feudal system[1]. Xunzi inherited Confucianism and considered the "rites" after the transformation as the only appropriate model of governance.

2. Xunzi's Exploration of the Origin of "Rites"

"*Li*" is one of the concepts mentioned in Confucianism. Its English translation is "Rites", "Rituals" or "Etiquette". There are different opinions about the origin of rites. Huang Hui gave an explanation: "First, rites originated from sacrifice[2], represented by Wang Guowei, Liu Shipei and Guo Moruo, which is the most popular opinion; second, rites originated from customs, represented by Yang Kuan, Yang Xiangkui, Cai Shangsi, etc.; third, rites originated from the differences in food allocation, represented by Yang Yingjie and others."[3] Although there are different opinions, the rites we mention are some rules, social norms and national disciplines governing the government and society. According to the social and political developments, rites have transcended religious rituals and have become traditional rules that regulate communication among people and even among government policies.

Confucius says: "Without them they would have no means of regulating the services paid to the spirits of heaven and earth; without them they would have no means of distinguishing the positions proper to the monarch and the minister, to high and low, to old and young; without them they would have no means of maintaining the separate character of the intimate relations between male and female, father and son, elder brother and younger, and of conducting the intercourse between the contracting families in a marriage, and the frequency or infrequency (of the reciprocities between friends)." (*Book of Rites · Questions of Duke Ai*) This means that Confucius fully confirms the importance of rites and believes that rites are the basis for maintaining social status, people's lives, and contacts.

---

1   Regarding a slave society and a feudal society, please refer to: Guo Moruo, *Slavery Era*, People's Publishing House, 2005.

2   *Cambridge History of China*, Cambridge University Press, 1999, P252.

3   Huang Hui, *Brief Comment on Three Developments of the Theory of Rites in the Pre-Qin Period*, Master's Thesis of College of Philosophy, Law & Political Science, Shanghai Normal University, 2005, p.1.

The biggest development of Confucius to the rites of Zhou was to "explain rites with benevolence". The most fundamental feature is the internalization and self-awareness of rites. Confucius' theory of rites provided a model for a rule of virtue for later generations.

According to the literature, Confucius did not explore the origin of "rites". Researchers revealed that the core of Confucius's rites was benevolence, to explain rites with benevolence. Benevolence for Confucius was just a general reference to morality, including the many morals of society and to being "one of the virtues". There are different opinions regarding this; Huang Hui said that most of them are different interpretations of the word "ren" (benevolence): "Some researchers indicated that benevolence was the essence of rites, represented by Li Huiqin, Yang Qingzhong and Shi Huanan; other scholars proposed, from the perspectives of philosophy and anthropology, that Confucius's rites revealed the nature of human beings, and the psychological basis of rites was benevolence, represented by Yang Qingzhong, He Xirong and Li Xiaohong. From the characteristics of ritual norms themselves, Confucius' rites were the unity of ritual (form) and etiquette (connotation), represented by Li Xiaohong."[1] As stated above, we can find that: Confucius' rites were constructed on what he believed, that is "human nature is good". In his opinion, "benevolence" was inherent and humanistic, but "rites" were the concrete manifestation of "benevolence" in terms of institution. He believed that an ideal society should be the fusion of institution and humanities. Generally speaking, Confucius' theory of rites regarded "benevolence" as the standard and core.

Xunzi explored the origin of "rites". He said: "What is the origin of rites? I reply: 'Man is born with desires. If his desires are not satisfied, he is bound to pursue them. If in what he pursues there is no measure nor limits, he is bound to contend with other men. Contention leads to disorder. Disorder leads to poverty. The ancient kings depised such disorder, and so established ritual righteousness to curb it, to

---

1 Huang Hui, *Brief Comment on Three Developments of the Theory of Rites in the Pre-Qin Period*, Master's Thesis of College of Philosophy, Law & Political Science, Shanghai Normal University, 2005, p.2.

nourish men's desires, and to provide them with what they pursue. They made sure that desires would not fall short of their objects, and that the objects would not be beyond what is desired. In this way, desires and their objects sustained each other over a long period of time. This is the origin of rites.'" (*Xunzi· Discourse on Ritual Principles*) It can be found that the origin of "rites" from the perspective of Xunzi is constructed on the idea that "human nature is evil". His point is that "rites" cannot be rooted in the inherent nature of man, but the origin of "rites" can only exist outside of the subject.

There are different views on Xunzi's discussion of the origin of rites[1]. Xunzi's rites originated from "nourishing men's desires", "heaven and earth", or "satisfying desires and curbing disoder", and the rites were the creation of saints, and so on. Zhu Jun said: "According to Yu Ronggen, Xunzi's origin of rites was based on his theory that human nature is evil. Because human nature is evil, there is contention in society. Hui Jixing supported the belief that in the origin from heaven and earth. In his opinion, Xunzi's idea on human nature being evil indicated that rites could not be rooted in the inherent nature of human beings, but outside of the subject. Although rites could not be separated from society, human beings, and everything in the world, and 'the only origin was heaven and earth'."[2] Despite the different views, they mostly made it clear that Xunzi's rites focused on external norms.

Confucius' "rites" paid more attention to "benevolence", but Xunzi emphasized the institutional nature of "ritual". According to him, institutional nature and humanism were important for governance of the country, and this institutional nature was reflected as a "law".

3. Xunzi "Turn Laws into Rites"

"Law" means "method" and "way". When "method" describes human behavior under certain circumstances, the State declares a penalty for non-compliance, which

---

1 Huang Hui, *Brief Comment on Three Developments of the Theory of Rites in the Pre-Qin Period*, Master's Thesis of College of Philosophy, Law & Political Science, Shanghai Normal University, 2005, p.3.

2 Zhu Jun, *Xunzi's Theory of Rites*, Master's Thesis of Northwest University, 2006, pp.1-2.

is obviously a "law".

Confucius did not underestimate the role of a "law", but he did not believe that the law had to be written down. According to him, "rites" were the most basic political principle and code of conduct, and with "laws" was not the best way to govern the country and society. Confucius opposed high-profile punishment by those in power. Chen Rongqing said: "The way to improve the morality of members in the society and deal with non-disciplinary behavior was that the moral influence of politicians and the monarch must set a good example for all members of the society. Confucius opposed high-profile punishment of offenders, and attempted to arouse their self-awareness and allow them to correct themselves. This is a passive attitude, believing and trusting in people's self-awakening and self-salvation."[1]

Xunzi combined rites with law and proposed "turning laws into rites" and "value rites and observing the law". Regarding his theory on rites and law, Zhu Jun said: "The combination of rites and law was an academic feature of this period. In terms of the relationship between rites and the law, most scholars tended to use rites to support laws. Xunzi summarized the theories to make rites and law more closely integrated. The difference lay in that Xunzi was a Confucianist who absorbed the legalist theories and turned laws into rites. Rites were dominant, but the law was supplementary to forming his own theory on the relationship between rites and the law."[2] With a view of social governance, Chen Rongqing said: "Confucius was 'the way of morality and the governance of rites', but Xunzi was 'the way of morality, the governance of rites and the governance of law'.[3] Xunzi did not advocate brutal legal provisions, but considered "rites" as without a punitive nature and the ability to punish evil, so a "law" was to be used to remedy the defects of "rites". Chen Rongqing also said: "According to Xunzi,

---

1 Chen Rongqing, "Viewing on Xunzi's Ruling Thoughts that Morality, Rites and Laws Work Together for His Inheritance and Development of Confucius' Thoughts on 'Rites'", *Journal of Yichun College*, 2010, Vol. 32.

2 Zhu Jun, *Xunzi's Theory of Rites*, Master's Thesis of Northwest University, 2006, p.6.

3 Chen Rongqing, "Viewing on Xunzi's Ruling Thoughts that Morality, Rites and Laws Work Together for His Inheritance and Development of Confucius' Thoughts on 'Rites'", *Journal of Yichun College*, 2010, Vol. 32, p.90.

it was far from enough to govern the society and maintain the system only by the ruler (monarch) setting a good example, or the regulation of "rites". There were many people that could not be educated by morality and rites (such as Danzhu, Shangjun, Xiang, etc.), so the law should be used to punish their non-disciplinary behavior and force them to become harmless to the society."[1] Hence, Xunzi turned laws into rites to incorporate the rule of law in the Confucian system of the rule of rites. His core was still rites. His theory of rites with laws greatly enriched and developed the content of Confucius' rites.

4. Conclusion

Both Confucius and Xunzi considered rites to be the basic way of governing the country. Confucius preferred to "explain rites with benevolence", internalize "morality" into people's minds, integrate the self- consciousness into rites, and he advocated "benevolent politics" and "rule by virtue". The shortcoming of Confucius' theory of rites was that the inherent virtue he required was not consistent with the social reality and human nature at that time, so his theory of rites was hardly practiced at all by the society.

Xunzi explored the origin of "rites" based on the belief that "human nature is evil". In his opinion, to emphasize the self-awareness of "rites" was not enough, and to "turn laws into rites" was required to emphasize the compulsory nature of "rites". After he proposed "valuing rites and observing the law", the rites became more obviously normative, mandatory and effectively legal. The combination of rites and law played a greater role in social governance. This was Xunzi's inheritance and development of Confucius' theory.

---

1   Chen Rongqing, "Viewing on Xunzi's Ruling Thoughts that Morality, Rites and Laws Work Together for His Inheritance and Development of Confucius' Thoughts on 'Rites'", *Journal of Yichun College*, 2010, Vol. 32, p.91.

"腾笼换鸟"定义的商讨与拟定

苏尔【波兰】

比得哥熙卡基米日维尔基大学教师

根据浙江省的报告,浙江将会按照"八八战略"的指引继续实施"腾笼换鸟、凤凰涅槃"的政策[1],其中"腾笼换鸟"是浙江省委书记习近平提出并强调的概念(洪晓)。据中国学者的阐释,该政策所指是中国"部分发达地区将低端产业转移至其他地区,以实现发达地区经济转型和产业升级的战略目标"(李曼)。

然而,遗憾的是,笔者翻阅了许多词典依然找不到关于"腾笼换鸟"的准确解释,如此一来,既无法判断它到底是成语、俗语或其他词语,也无法获得关于此概念的全面知识。因此,找出"腾笼换鸟"这类词语适于外国人理解的定义可以说是一大挑战——第一,书本和在线词典的缺项。我们能够找到海词网站提供的英文翻译为"emptying-cage-changing-birds"这是作为汉语学习者完全无法理解的说明[2],此外只有汉语辞典之类提供的复杂义项[3];第二,网上、学术期刊、政府报告中的说明是很难理解的,使用的词汇过于专业,而外文的翻译只提供字面的意思,无法全面地表现出中国的国情。

对学习中文的外国人来讲,由于文化差异和国与国之间空间距离的关系,使用或借助词典和教科书,成为了解一个国家文化和语言图景的重要工具。反应中

---

1 https://baijiahao.baidu.com/s?id=1590530674839803811&wfr=spider&for=pc.

2 http://dict.cn/%E8%85%BE%E7%AC%BC%E6%8D%A2%E9%B8%9F.

3 http://twdict.lookup.tw/%E9%A8%B0%E7%B1%A0%E6%8F%9B%E9%B3%A5.html#.XA2MA2j0nIU.

国国情的词语对外国人本就是极难理解的。从事汉语国际教育的研究员和教师，应该寻找适合汉语学习者理解的定义，以便对中国语言、文化、政治感兴趣的外国人更好地了解它深层次的含义。本文便是基于这一考量，对"腾笼换鸟"的含义进行一系列研究，并最终拟定定义。

为较好地达到研究目的，笔者对 11 名浙江工商大学的教师进行了录音访谈，请受访者解释"腾笼换鸟"的意思。在采访的过程当中，本人使用意义协商的方法来解决沟通障碍，使受访者用更简单的语言。接下来，笔者将内容转成文字，对此进行以语义为主、定性与定量结合的研究方法的分析，提取关键词并拟定了适合外国人理解的"腾笼换鸟"的定义。

笔者研究发现，在笔者收集的与"腾笼换鸟"相关的访谈记录中，有 27 个重复出现的关键词，其中有 16 个是名词（个体或物质名词：笼子、浙江、企业或产业、污染，抽象概念名词：字面、比喻、经济、高科技、发展、原来、技术、劳动、成语、手段或措施、过程、里面），4 个是动词（升级、腾出、换成、移）、6 个是形容词（旧、落后、新、密集、创新、漂亮或好看），还有 1 个是副词（重新），出现频率请见下表（计数单位：人）：

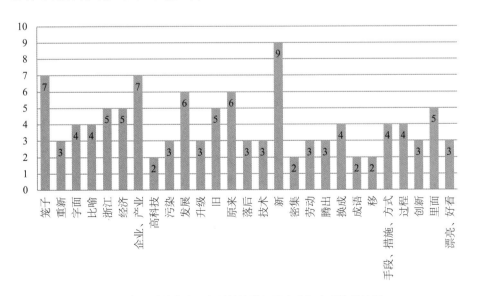

图1：与"腾笼换鸟"相关的访谈记录中重复出现的关键词

由表 1 可知，采访时最常出现的词语为"新"，11 位教师中有 9 位使用"新"来解释"腾笼换鸟"的概念。而"旧"作为"新"的反义词却并未对应地频繁出现（只有 5 位受访者用到这个词）。考虑到索绪尔的语言价值理论和部分波兰语言学家的研究成果，原因可能在于口语中消极价值的词语是相对较少使用的（参见：Laskowska 1993：129）。除"旧"以外，在该语言语境下，受访者还曾使用"落后"作为"旧"的相近词（3/11）。

值得注意的是，"过程""手段""劳动""密集""技术""升级""发展""高科技""企业"等与经济发展相关的词语"结伴"出现，强调了"腾笼换鸟"概念与该方面的紧密联系。当然，这也有可能与受试者皆为"工商学校"的教师有关；但也有研究指出"腾笼换鸟"主要是一种经济发展方式的转变。有一些研究者提到，"腾笼换鸟"也会涉及教育、出版、文化等产业的优化转型升级过程，但这样的联想意义仍属少数。

受访者也强调地方发展的因素，比如在我们研究中出现的高频词语"浙江"。这与采访的地点相关，但也与习近平曾担任浙江省省委书记，以及浙江省在全国率先采用这一经济发展策略相关。浙江省作为中国东部经济增长最快的省份之一，其采取的以"腾笼换鸟"为基础的发展策略注重于以下三个方面，即：1. 优农业；2. 强工业；3. 兴三业。

近年来，浙江省政府与大中小企业坚持全力推行这一政策，目前收益显著：浙江省产业协调发展，民营经济发展有效本土化，"绿色浙江"建设与两山理论成果喜人。从更具体的角度来说，安吉的美丽乡村、义乌的小商品市场、宁波市的循环经济、温州市的"一号工程"和绍兴市的"高大优"等，无不在展现"腾笼换鸟"政策的高屋建瓴，细小之处见大观。

除此之外，教师们也点明了"腾笼换鸟"的双层意义：字面义和比喻义。第二层含义一般与经济战略有关，受访者举出与劳动力密集产业、解雇员工、杭州市下沙开发区、环境污染等现象有关的例子。

"比如说我们工作单位在一个部门当中，上司（……）对员工说：【你们经常不好好干，我就"腾笼换鸟"，解雇你们，让新的员工进来】"

至于字面义，教师们大部分都试图分别说明每个字和四个字相连时的意义，如：

"腾笼换鸟就是……中国是以前的这个鸟放在笼子里面吧，就是，把这个……把一个鸟拿开重新换一个鸟进去，这是字面的意思。"

或者：

"就是就字面意义来说，它就是把这个笼子，本来鸟在笼子里面吧，要把这个笼子腾出来，把鸟换了。"

以下的例子解说更为详细：

"它字面的意思是指过去我们在养鸟的时候，会有一个笼子，把鸟放在一个笼子里面，然后是，因为要换一只鸟进去，把那个笼子先腾空，把那只鸟放出来，再换新的鸟进去，那么现在的，可能原来的那个鸟生病了，或者说不好看，但是它占了一个位置，那么我现在要换进去的那只鸟会是更珍贵的更漂亮的鸟，比如说那个笼子很好看，但是里面有一只不好看的鸟，我现在要换出来，换一只更漂亮的进去，所以最初的意思，大概是这个意思。"

值得一提的是，每一位受访者解释"腾笼换鸟"概念的时候都用到了"把字句"。"把字句"涉及汉语语法层面，但它在语义上也有一些强烈的表现。"把字句"强调的是主语的主动性，同时也强调变化。就此而论，"主动性"和"变化"是腾笼换鸟政策的关键，因此我们可以大胆推断，使用"把字句"来讲解"腾笼换鸟"的意义是一种得当的措施，能够抓住此概念的本质。"腾笼换鸟"的"变化"特性还表现在动词的选择："移""腾出""换成"等。

总结起来，在向外国人解释"腾笼换鸟"的意义时，我们应当注意以下几点，即：1. 字面义和比喻义；2. 文化因素（中国国情、政治、经济方面）；3. 语言形式的选择，包括简洁、准确的用词，强调"腾笼换鸟"意义的语法手段。

考虑到外国汉语学习者的语言水平和理解能力，"腾笼换鸟"这一类的词语与说法适合在中文系中级阶段中国文化、中国经济或中国常识这类课程中讲解。在学习过程中，除了介绍大致的中国政治与经济发展的趋势和概念以外，教师应当按照克拉申的"i+1"语言输入假说来引入"腾笼换鸟"的学习。据观察，汉语中级学习阶段的学生对"腾笼换鸟"中的"换"和"鸟"已经较为熟悉。"腾"和"笼"这两个字需用两个不同的方法进行解释："腾"用直接释义法解释——最简单的方式为使用《现代汉语词典》的第三个义项："使空"。在解释"笼"时，最好是利用图画辅助手段。

这样一来，确定学生对"腾笼换鸟"的每一字都有一定的理解，再给学生介绍它简化的定义。根据研究中所参考的理论知识与自己的研究分析结果，我们最终拟定适于外国汉语学习者理解的"腾笼换鸟"的简单化定义：

腾笼换鸟有两个意义（字面意义和比喻意义），它是一种类似成语的说法，也是一种理念。字面意义是：把笼子腾出来，把老鸟换成新鸟。比喻意义主要用在经济发展和企业发展方面上，也就是做事方式的变化，把不太好的换成更好的，把旧的换成新的，把落后的换成先进的。

向学生介绍了这样的定义后，可以再补充几个简单的例子，例如：

1. 企业使用的技术比较落后，对环境不太好，所以它应该"腾笼换鸟"，应该发展高技术、环保、创新的服务。

2. 你在工作上表现得不好，所以你的老板会"腾笼换鸟"，意思就是解雇你，找一个更好的员工。

老师也可以结合具体教学场景，教授几个比较难的关键词（如：劳动力、密集、升级），以便让学生更好地理解"腾笼换鸟"等文化词的语境。

当然，"腾笼换鸟"这一类词语体现了中国经济发展、国情、现代文化方面的重要部分，但尚属沧海一粟。像"腾笼换鸟"这样外国人不易理解的词汇数量还有很多，因为空间与时间关系，笔者无法对中国 21 世纪其他与文化相关的关键词语一一进行分析。然而，本人的研究旨在启发从事汉语国际教育的教师、中外、外中翻译家以及其他接触外国人的中国人等人群，寻找突破汉语和中国文化带来的理解困境的途径，即用简单的语言来解释复杂的概念，把表面知识转换成深层次的理解，将汉语和本色本真的中国文化变为一种为更多人所知悉的潮流。

参考文献

Laskowska Elżbieta. 1993. Wartościowanie w języku potocznym. Bydgoszcz : Wydawnictwo Uczelniane Wyższej Szkoły Pedagogicznej w Bydgoszczy, 1993.

张浩然：《"腾笼换鸟"能提升承接城市的经济效率吗？》，《经济问题探索》2015 年第 6 期，第 126-129 页。

李曼：《比较优势理论视角下"腾笼换鸟"战略的再思考》，《学术园地》2010 年第 5 期，第 14—15 页。

李汉学：《"腾笼换鸟"：城区中小学布局调整的一种模式探索》，《教育理论与实践》2016 年卷 36, 7，第 35—38 页。

沈水荣：《中国出版业数字化转型：腾笼换鸟？》，《科技与出版》2014 年第 2 期，第 32—36 页。

《读懂八八战略》，浙江人民出版社 2018 年版。

赵渊:《"腾笼换鸟":文化产业转型升级新路径》,《经济论坛》2012 年第 9 期,第 125—127 页。

陈建忠:《突出"三个统筹"深入推进"腾笼换鸟"》,《浙江经济》2014 年第 16 期,第 10—11 页。

Discussion and Definition of the Expression "Emptying the Cage, Changing the Birds"

Anna Sroka-Gradziel / Poland

Kazimierz Wielki University, Chinese Teacher

The report of Zhejiang Province pointed out that Zhejiang would continue to implement the policy of "empty the cage, change birds and rising from the ashes like a reborn phoenix"[1] under the guidance of the "Double-Eight Strategy". Here, "empty the cage, change birds" was a concept coined by the then Secretary of the Zhejiang Provincial Party Committee Xi Jinping. According to the interpretation of Chinese scholars, this policy refers to China's "strategic goal of transferring low-end industries from developed regions to other regions to realize their economic transformation and industrial upgrading".

However, it is a pity that the author has looked up in many dictionaries without finding an accurate explanation of the phrase "empty the cage, change birds". In this case, we can neither judge whether it is an idiom, slang or another kind of word, nor can we have a comprehensive understanding of this concept. Hence,

---

1 Zhejiang News. Opening Ceremony of the First Session of the 13th People's Congress of Zhejiang Province (Report) [Online] [Citation Date: December 9, 2018.]
https://baijiahao.baidu.com/s?id=1590530674839803811&wfr=spider&for=pc.

finding a definition that foreigners can understand of phrases like "empty the cage, change birds" is a big challenge. First, the author is unable to look up this phrase in books and online dictionaries. Only an English translation as "empty-cage-change-birds" can be found on dict.cn, but this explanation makes no sense to foreigners who are learning Chinese[1]. In addition, there is a complicated meaning given on twdict.lookup.tw[2]. Second, the clarifications online or in academic journals and government reports are quite difficult to understand because they use words that are too specialized, but the translation into foreign languages only provides literal meanings, which cannot reflect the situation in China.

For foreign learners, dictionaries and textbooks can be used as important instruments to understand the culture and language of China due to cultural differences and spatial distance among countries. Words that reflect the situation in China are extremely difficult for foreigners to understand. Researchers and teachers engaged in international education of the Chinese language should look for a circular definition without language and that is easily comprehensible for foreign learners so that foreigners who feel interested in the Chinese language, culture and politics can better understand its deeper meaning. For this purpose, this article conducts a series of studies on the meaning of "empty the cage, change birds" and finally determines a definition.

In order to better achieve the purpose of this study, the author recorded the interviews of 11 teachers from Zhejiang Gongshang University and requested the interviewees to explain the meaning of "empty the cage, change birds". During the interviews, the author adopted the method of negotiation of meaning to resolve communication barriers and the interviewees gave explanations in simple language. Next, the author converted the recorded audio content into text, made an analysis using the research method that mainly focused on semantics and combined qualitative and quantitative approaches, extracted keywords and determined a definition of "empty

---

1 dict.cn. dict.cn—Learning Words by dict.cn. [Online] [Citation Date: December 9, 2018.] http://dict. cn/%E8%85%BE%E7%AC%BC%E6%8D%A2%E9%B8%9F.

2 See: Chinese Dictionary. 腾笼换鸟 (Empty Cage, Change Bird). [Online] [Citation Date: December 9, 2018.] http://twdict.lookup.tw/%E9%A8%B0%E7%B1%A0%E6%8F%9B%E9%B3%A5.html#.XA2MA2j0nIU.

the cage, change birds" that is easy for foreigners to understand.

According to the study, in the collected interview records, the author finds 27 repeated keywords, of which, 16 are nouns (individual or material nouns: cage, Zhejiang, enterprise or industry, pollution; abstract conceptual nouns: literalness, figurativeness, economy, high-tech, development, originality, technology, labor, idiom, means or measures, process, inside), 4 are verbs (upgrade, empty, replace with, transfer), 6 are adjectives (old, backward, new, intensive, innovative, beautiful or good-looking) and 1 is an adverb (anew). Please refer to the figure below for the frequency of occurrence (in unit of: persons):

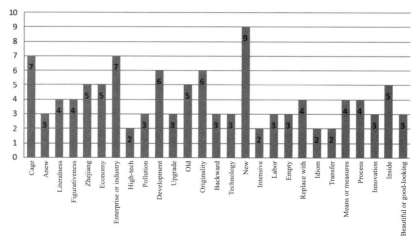

Figure 1 Keywords used by interviewees to explain the concept of "empty the cage, change birds"
Source: Interview results of the author

As can be seen from Figure 1, the most common word used in interviews is "new". Nine out of eleven teachers used "new" to explain the concept of "empty the cage, change birds". The word "old" as an antonym of "new" did not appear frequently (only 5 interviewees used this word). Considering Saussure's theory of linguistic value and some research results by Polish linguists, the reason may be that negative words are relatively rare in spoken language (see: Laskowska 1993:129). In addition to "old", in this language context, interviewees also used "backward" as a synonymous word for "old" (3/11).

It is important to note that "process", "means", "labor", "intensive", "technology", "upgrade", "development", "high-tech", "enterprise" and other words related to economic development go "together" to highlight the close links between the concept of "empty the cage, change birds" and this aspect. Of course, the reason may also be that the interviewees are teachers of "business schools"; however, some studies point out that "empty the cage, change birds" is mainly a change in the way of economic development. Some researchers have mentioned that "empty the cage, change birds" also involves optimization, transformation and upgrading of educational, publishing, and cultural industries, but such associations are few.

Interviewees also laid stress on local development, such as the frequent word "Zhejiang" appearing in our study. The reasons may include the location of interviews, Xi Jinping's previous position as the Secretary of the Zhejiang Provincial Party Committee, and Zhejiang as the first province which implemented this economic developmental strategy. As one of the fastest-growing provinces in eastern China, Zhejiang adopted the developmental strategy based on "empty the cage, change birds" that focuses on the following three aspects, namely:

1. Optimizing agriculture;
2. Invigorating industry;
3. Prospering the tertiary industry.

In recent years, the People's Government of Zhejiang Province and large enterprises and SMEs insist on implementing this policy with significant achievements in: coordinated development of industries, effective localization of the private economy, and satisfactory results of the "Green Zhejiang" construction and the theory of "lucid waters and lush mountains are invaluable assets". To be specific, the beautiful country in Anji, the small commodities market in Yiwu, the circular economy in Ningbo, the "No. 1 Project" in Wenzhou and the "high-end, large and fine quality" project in Shaoxing reflect the connotation of "empty the cage, change birds".

Moreover, teachers also clarified the double meanings of "empty the cage, change birds": the literal meaning and the figurative meaning. The second meaning is generally related to economic strategy. Interviewees cited the examples of labor-intensive industries, layoffs, Hangzhou Xiasha Development Zone and environmental pollution.

"For example, if the boss of the department (...) tells the employee that: [the cage will be emptied for new birds, and you will be replaced by new employees if you fail to work hard]"

As for the literal meaning, most teachers try to explain the meaning of the phrase when the four words are combined together, for instance:

"Empty the cage, change birds ... in the past, Chinese often kept birds in cages, literally, it means ... remove the bird and put another bird in the cage."

Or:

"Literally, a bird is kept in the cage, but the cage will be emptied and the bird will be replaces with another bird."

The following example explains it in more detail:

"It literally means that in the past when we raised a bird, there would be a cage, and we put the bird in the cage. Then, if we needed to replace it with another bird, the cage had to be emptied first to remove that bird and replace it with a new bird. It was probably that if the old bird was sick or looked bad, but it occupied the cage, I would replace it with a more precious and more beautiful bird. If the cage was very elegant, but the bird was not good-looking, I wanted to replace it with a more beautiful one. This was probably the original meaning."

It is noteworthy that every interviewee used the "ba" predicate verb sentence pattern to explain the concept of "empty the cage, change birds". The "ba" predicate verb sentence pattern, while involving Chinese grammar, also has strong manifestations in semantics. It emphasizes both the positiveness of the subject and the changes. Thus, "positiveness" and "changes" are the key to the policy. We can boldly infer that the use of the "ba" predicate verb sentence pattern to explain the meaning of "empty the cage, change birds" is a proper measure that can capture the essence of this concept. The "changes" of "empty the cage, change birds" are also reflected in the choice of verbs: "transfer", "empty", "replace with" and so on.

To sum up, when explaining the meaning of "empty the cage, change birds" to foreigners, we should pay attention to the following points, namely:

1. Literal meaning and figurative meaning;

2. Cultural factors (situation in China, politics and economics);

3. Choice of linguistic form, including succinct and accurate wording, and grammatical means of "empty the cage, change birds".

Considering the language proficiency and understandability of foreign learners, it is appropriate to explain the phrase "empty the cage, change birds" in the intermediate courses such as Chinese culture, Chinese economy or Chinese knowledge in the Department of Chinese Language. In the learning process, in addition to introducing general trends and concepts of Chinese political and economic development, teachers should guide learners to the learning of "empty the cage, change birds" according to Krashen's language input hypothesis "i+1". It has been observed that students at the intermediate level of the learning of Chinese are already familiar with "change" and "bird" in the phrase "empty the cage, change birds". The two words "empty" and "cage" need to be clarified in two different ways: "empty" should be explained by direct interpretation — the simplest way is to use the third meaning in the *Modern Chinese Dictionary*: "make empty". When explaining "cage", it is best to use a picture.

In this way, students will have a certain understanding of each word of the phrase. Then, its simplified definition should be explained to students. Based on the theoretical knowledge referenced in this study and the results of our own research and analysis, we finally determine a simplified definition of "empty the cage, change birds" that is suitable for foreign learners to understand:

"Empty the cage, change birds" has two meanings (a literal meaning and a figurative meaning). It is a phrase similar to four-word idioms and also a concept. The literal meaning is: vacate the cage and replace the old bird with a new bird. The figurative meaning is mainly used in economic development and enterprise development, that is, changes in the way of doing things, replacing the less good with the better, the old with the new, and the backward with the advanced.

After introducing the definition to students, a few simple examples can be added, such as:

1. If an enterprise uses a relatively backward technology that is not friendly to the environment, it should "empty the cage, and change birds" and develop high-tech, environmentally friendly and innovative services.

2. When you don't perform well at work, your boss will "empty the cage, and change birds", which means he will fire you and find a better replacement.

Teachers can also teach several difficult keywords (such as labor, intensive and upgrade) in combination with specific teaching scenarios, so that students can better understand the context of cultural words such as "empty the cage, change birds".

Of course, phrases like "empty the cage, change birds" can reflect the important facets of China's economic development, situation and modern culture, but it is only a drop in the ocean. There are still a lot of phrases that are difficult for foreign learners to understand. Due to the space and time limit, the author cannot analyze other keywords related to Chinese culture in the 21st century. However, this study aims at inspiring teachers of international education, Chinese and foreign translators and other Chinese people who keep in touch with foreigners to find ways to break through the dilemma of the understanding of Chinese and Chinese culture, that is, the use of simple language to explain complex concepts, the transformation of superficial knowledge into deeper understanding, and turning Chinese and authentic Chinese culture into a trend that is more widely known.

中国的网络安全法

胡瑞雪【美国】
宾夕法尼亚大学博士生

一、引言

  信息革命和跨境动态数据交换给世界带来政治威胁和新的安全问题。随着数据日益成为经济社会交流的重要组成部分，权力正在从资本密集型转向数据密集型，信息系统在国家基础设施建设中占据更重要的地位。[1] 虽然人工智能通过革命性地改变战争形态和商业技术带来政治收益，但在很大程度上还是依赖大数据和强大的计算力开发机器学习功能。高级别的数字商务和沟通交流可以创造出大量的数据输入计算机系统进行处理，由此产生优势。在信息时代，数据已成为与石油同等重要的战略资源，对国家进步和未来技术发展至关重要。然而，数据与石油有着重要的区别，因为数字信息在有限的国家管制和法规限制下可以随时跨越边界，迅速发展的全球交流对各国监管和保护数字资源带来了挑战。

  大数据让人类社会受益匪浅，但不受监管的特点也为国家带来风险，并产生了一个独特的审查领域，即审查规则制定和法律边界制定过程。中国面临着技术发展带来的更大脆弱性，也为审查网络空间治理和法律制度演进提供了理想的案例。网络安全风险与整体国家安全的相关度越来越高，因为"没有网络安全，就没有国家

---

1 Nye, *Power in the Global Information Age*, P.75.

安全"。[1] 在这种模式下，法治被视为是制订国内数据使用政策和标准的策略方法。

中国《网络安全法》的法律策略可以用来分析和评估网络空间的治理机制。本文旨在研究网络空间治理和私有的数字化趋势。通过查阅中文文献，对政治、法律以及与数据相关学科领域的中国学者访谈，我们将探讨中国面临独有的威胁。在结论部分，我们分析中国的《网络安全法》和网络空间治理的法律创新，以期得出关于制订网络空间数据保护和规则制度的结论。

二、网络空间的治理缺失

全球社会面临着严重的网络空间治理缺失，特别是在全球数据交换规则的国际协议方面。随着时间的推移，多个利益相关方将监管标准确立为规则制度，通过"积少成多，逐渐取得新的理解"，采取与普通法类似的运作方式，努力在网络空间中实现多边条约范式的国际法律体系。网络技术的迅猛发展超越传统的立法方式，规范被作为去中心化过程中的主要监管工具，创建多个规则矩阵，而不是全体一致的全球网络安全制度。在关于如何将现行国际法适用于信息通信技术的谈判中，各方充满了分歧，甚至在 2017 年联合国信息安全政府专家组（GGE）会议都陷入僵局，无法就如何适用《联合国宪章》达成共识。谈判的失败造成松散治理结构的真空地带，没有任何数字环境的软性或非约束性法律来塑造网络空间的行为。

鉴于国家不再是解决问题的自然单元，全球社会正在提供许多类似政府的职能。[2] 国家政府缺乏数字能力，逐渐将责任委托给跨国公司，因此非国家行为者具有更大的权力，可以影响和决定互联网的国际标准并赢得立法和司法机构的支持。[3] 非国家行为者拥有跨越国界并发展全球治理能力的平台。在欧盟内部，欧洲法院裁定谷歌有权决定如何平衡欧洲人的隐私自由（"被遗忘权"）和言论自由。该案件表明，相对于国家机关制订规则的传统模式，非国家行为者对网络空间内可接受行为边界的决定权正在加强。谷歌发起一项内部流程，设立高级员工组成的审查小组对什么内容删除进行表决，通过非正式监管结构形成广泛的隐私定义，

---

1 《中央网络安全和信息化领导小组第一次会议召开 习近平发表重要讲话》，www.cac.gov.cn/2014-02/27.

2 Slaughter, *A New World Order*; Mathews, *Power Shift*.

3 Büthe, *The New Global Rulers*. 对于非国家行为者的影响参见 Keck and Sikkink, *Activists beyond Borders*.

以确定"被遗忘权"的大致范围，而该案件代表决定技术企业决定网络空间标准的不对称权力。

市场行为者监管数据并承担传统上由国家承担的许多职能，并在数字环境中挑战国家主权。二十多年前，杰西卡·马修斯预测，由于技术的发展，国家行为者拥有决策权的传统威斯特伐利亚权力体系即将转变为非国家行为者的权力形式，以绕开国家控制的提高效率和实现自动化。网络空间权力涉及所有权问题，因为私营公司能生成和控制大量数据并且对相关制度的设计拥有巨大的影响力。跨国活动和在全球范围内数字信息转移的能力使企业拥有超越传统的主权观念和国家权力的权力，在网络空间它们可以随时进出"领土"和管理国界内和跨越国界的信息。Facebook 和 Cambridge Analytica 案件最明显地揭示了控制全球网络空间活动的竞争，由于美国和英国未经用户同意而共享私人信息，国家监管机构正努力在数据传输方面发挥更大的作用并起诉全球数字信息窃用行为。

三、中国数字信息风险的类型

互联网的商业化及其应用在世界范围内迅速扩张，由此造成互联空间进入人们生活的方方面面。数据传播有利于国内技术、资本和人才的发展，但是这种现象也使人们更容易受到全球交流的冲击，并且挑战政府维持秩序和提供国内治理的能力。[1] 中国共产党的合法性依赖于受互联网影响的经济和社会发展要素。由于经济、安全和社会治理方面的主权被削弱，网络空间治理的私有化放大了中共面临的风险。

1. 经济发展

中国维持经济发展速度的能力取决于由私营企业控制的数字化生产要素。习近平总书记将数字知识和信息定义为重要生产要素和社会财富，因为"信息掌握的多寡成为国家软实力和竞争力的重要标志"。"互联网＋"战略等国内政策指出，互联网已作为发展的驱动力渗透进入国家基础设施的每个组成部分，从软件开发的技术数字经济到将信息服务集成到传统行业中。信息服务发展迅速并给国家带来挑战，因为"不进步的人将落后，行动迟缓的人也将落后"，国家需要加强管理，以确保跨行业的技术发展节奏。需要全面协调才能够继续实现增长和满足市场需求，但企业在不受国家直接控制的全球范围内开展业务，因此要控制这些服务具

1　Xi, "Build China into a Cyberpower," p.453.

有挑战性。

数据存储的地理位置和先进技术的来源对经济发展构成威胁。大数据时代的国家竞争力是科技企业自行努力的结果，并且很大程度上在国有企业之外。绝大多数核心技术由中国境外的公司开发和提供，它们反映电子商务和跨境活动在技术供应链中的重要环节。发展的最大危险在于跨国公司对技术的控制以及中国对外国开发者的依赖，因为突然撤离或无法从国外购买必要的供应品可能会严重破坏国民经济和国内产业。中国的战略是力求从国外引进核心技术转变为本土创新，利用本地人才构建经济基础。数据存储的位置也被认为是中国的风险来源，因为数据离开了国境，被转移到国家控制范围以外的地区，从而限制国内企业访问有价值数据的可靠性和安全性。

2. 国家安全

关键信息基础设施的非国有权是中国国家安全的重大漏洞。可能存在的病毒制作和传播以及未经授权的网络中断被认为是最严重的威胁。中国共产党认识到数据传输和聚合会影响国家层面的安全利益，此前国家保留大量公民和国家产业的珍贵信息，但近年来相关数据主要掌握在私人企业手中。公民信息以及金融、通信和能源领域的策略和漏洞受到私人网络安全提供商的控制，因此国家无法阻止信息意外泄露和黑客攻击。跨国公司并不完全独立于外国政府的监督，数据存储在国外也带来了巨大的风险。斯诺登透露，总部位于美国的科技公司是"棱镜"计划下美国政府进行数据监控的一部分，这引发对中国境外设施存储国内信息的担忧。

私人公司对数字信息的控制会带来很大的不确定性和风险，因为外国公司可能会采取危害中国公民的做法。私人公司在各平台上提供防御措施，区域决策对国家安全影响深远。2014 年，微软公司停止对中国区 Windows XP 系统漏洞修复服务，使数以亿计的中国用户受到病毒的潜在威胁，这就凸显依赖外国网络运营商的风险。

3. 社会稳定

互联网服务提供商管理网络活动并控制大量数据，从而削弱了国家维护社会稳定的能力。市场行为者以某种方式操纵社交媒体和技术平台，使公民暴露在风险中并限制政府为公众提供可靠和有效信息服务的能力。由于社交媒体可用于操纵舆论和散布破坏国家秩序稳定的虚假信息，政府抵御外国政府的破坏活动的能力被削弱。假新闻的传播给政府制造麻烦，政府也已经在进行内容监控和删除。如果内容仍然保留在互联网上，公众很容易以为是真实的，政府没有删除消息，将会引发更大范围的混乱，削弱国家制止谣言和有害信息在网络环境中传播的能力。由于缺乏对内容传播的控制，导致中央政府无法在网络空间中发出最强大的声音。

非政府行为者对网络空间事务具有很大的影响力，这也限制了政府维持积极数字生态系统的能力。技术是一把"双刃剑"，它既带来了新的联系，但也以更快的速度渗透到文化中，并制约国家的掌控能力。截至 2016 年底，中国有 7.3 亿互联网用户，他们每天都受到数字内容波动及数字媒体公司发表观点的影响。暴力视频和淫秽内容与社会主义核心价值观相矛盾，对维护国内意识形态构成威胁。政府意识到去中心化内容管理的危险，发布"清洁和清除"和"保护年轻人"等命令，这表明有必要控制淫秽内容对年轻人和普通人群构成的风险，并制订全面的内容管理规则和制度。

虽然互联网的危险是显而易见的，但在减轻全球政府间私有化风险的策略和法律方面进行的探索很少。下一部分将分析中国解决网络空间治理缺陷的总体战略，然后分析中国解决该问题的具体法律创新。

四、中国的内容管理策略：法治

根据"网络主权"原则，中国提倡在国家边界内控制信息流动的权力，而不仅仅是根据界定网络国家领土的法律保护通信避免未经授权的访问。[1] 中国制订的策略采取法律措施维护国家内部秩序和稳定，赋予国家允许或禁止数字内容在国家领土内流通的最终权限，并在以前无边界的开放式互联网中划定国家领土。[2] 中国和俄罗斯在 2011 年向联合国大会提出的《确保国际信息安全的行为准则》（草案）包含以下原则：互联网相关问题的政策授权是国家的权利，支持依据国家法律监管内容。该原则提倡基于领土边界的法律领域概念，并尊重每个国家制订的内部互联网管理政策并拥有对国内信息基础设施的管辖权。

中国解决互联网中国家主权受损的策略是将权力集中于国家，以更好地监管非国家行为者的活动。核心目标是通过改革网络空间的内部治理结构和构建全面

1　惠志斌：《新安全观下中国网络信息安全战略的理论构建》，《国际观察》2012 年 第 2 期。

2　Cai, "Cybersecurity in the Chinese Context", p.477.

的网络治理能力，实现更大程度的"自主可控"并降低波动造成的影响。

党的十八大以来，习近平总书记着力推动网络安全管理改革，将互联网管理领导系统的构建作为十八届中央委员会制定的 60 项改革任务之一。因此，成立中央网络安全和信息化领导小组，以计划和协调跨区域的重要网络安全问题，并加强中央政府对数字活动的控制。该小组是一个常设的委员会，可以调动大量资源，被赋予国家（而非私有）级别数据保护权限。策略关键在于详细界定内部治理结构中的职责，因此党可以在保护关键信息基础架构方面发挥着最重要的作用并有权规范和控制网络空间。

随着互联网日益复杂和快速发展，监管框架被视为安全的必要组成部分，法律作为推进国家对互联网实施控制和标准化管理的新范式。法治是中国法律体系的核心，也是随着技术的不断现代化而确保治理和秩序的基本策略。由于中国的政治制度，通过法治管理网络空间的策略特别有效。一党制使北京可以颁布与技术的快速发展保持同步的法律，而议会制的立法通常因各党派之间旷日持久的辩论和协商而无法迅速通过法律。中国的策略是首先发布草案，并通过一系列磋商征求受到这些规定影响的国内外团体的反馈。在与社会成员和商业团体商谈之后，进行必要的修订并将法律草案发布为正式法律。中国的法律法规是一个综合的系统，最高级别的法律作为适应不断变化的技术发展的广泛框架发布。这允许跟随技术快速进步的步伐制订法律，提供解决新治理问题的有效手段。

五、网络空间的法律创新

中国的《网络安全法》（CSL）于 2017 年 6 月 1 日生效，是网络安全领域中监管出站数据流动和保护数字信息的根本法律。颁布该法律是为了保护网络数据的完整性、保密性和可用性，防止信息泄露或被窃取，支持在数字时代保护国家安全和主权的更广泛战略。

1. 加强国家的自主可控能力，降低安全威胁

《网络安全法》首先影响数据交换，为数据存储制订新规则，并被视为中国新兴数字基础设施的根本法律。该法律规定，在中国大陆收集的重要数据必须存储在中国境内，强制要求本地存储。《网络安全法》第三十七条规定，运营者在中华人民共和国境内运营中收集和产生的个人信息和重要数据应当在境内存储。在《网络安全法》制订过程中，全国人民代表大会的立法者从"重要业务数据"

一词中删除"业务"一词，以扩大治理业务和社会内容要求的适用范围。该法律的制订表明，法律超越了简单的分类方法，允许内容存储在境外之前需要评估特定数据对国家和公共利益的影响。

新法律要求改变业务运营方式，加强中国境内的数据安全，将数据限制在国界之内。数据本地存储要求出台之前，跨国公司拥有更大的回旋余地，可以将在中国境内收集的数据存储在地理位置最适合业务运营的服务器上，并根据业务需求迁移数据。《网络安全法》规定跨国公司必须在中国境内的基础设施上存储数据，而不是将信息发送到国外进行数据处理，因此需要在本地市场进行额外的投资和建设。该要求源自于2011年制订的前期本地化规定，"禁止银行在中国境外存储、处理或分析在中国境内收集的任何个人金融信息（PFI），不得向境外提供在中国境内收集的个人金融信息"，但法律扩大了要求的适用范围，不仅限于金融业，还将公司的义务从阻止特定数据传输到境外的被动要求转变为对重要数据进行本地存储的主动责任。

《网络安全法》通过创建本地化数据库保证境内运营的可用性并确保数字资源的可操作性，更好地防止波动造成的影响。在《个人信息和重要数据出境安全评估办法》（以下简称《办法》）中，重要数据被定义为"与国家安全、经济发展，以及社会公共利益密切相关的数据"，法律旨在降低网络空间治理私有化和境外存储带来的风险。中国共产党以前在境外调查网络犯罪和保护公民的个人信息方面受制于通过司法协助条约（MLAT）联系外国政府等耗时的方法。新的法律措施减少安全保护对境外的依赖性并培养竞争优势。实施该法律后，中国的数字经济建立在国内资源的基础上，可以促进稳定的发展，同时降低在国外设施中保留或篡改数据的风险。

2. 通过安全审查实现以国家为中心的方法

《网络安全法》要求政府对网络安全运营和网络硬件进行审查，赋予国家更大的权限。安全审查制度旨在构建网络综合治理能力，以减轻全球科技公司对网络空间不受约束和广泛的影响。根据第二十三条规定，网络关键设备和网络安全专用产品必须在安全检测符合要求后方可在中国境内运营，随后的通知规定负责信息技术产品和服务检测以及颁发网络业务许可证的机构。

国家数据出境安全控制办法对于重要信息向中国境外的转移做出规定。虽然数据本地存储是总体要求，但新法律规定允许必要的数据传输的某些情况，并赋予国家有关部门明确的职责，要求强制分析信息和在国家层面保护数据。根据《网络安全法》第五十一条和五十二条规定，关键信息基础架构的运营商必须提交产品和服务以进行数据出境安全评估。《数据出境安全评估指南》（以下简称"指南"）将数据出境定义为将在中华人民共和国境内收集和产生的电子形式的个人信息和重要数据，提供给境外机构、组织、个人的一次性活动或连续性活动。如果数据存储在境外或者在境外访问，均依法确定为出境，要求在传输之前由政府机构进行安全评估。办法规定，该法律不仅适用于"关键信息基础设施运营商"，还适用于包括网络所有者和网络服务提供商在内的更广泛的"网络运营商"。

六、结论

中国的《网络安全法》通过本地存储要求和法律创新对开放和无限制的互联网划定边界。这些规定旨在减轻网络空间治理私有化带来的威胁，并通过法治保障稳定性。中国的法律可以降低非国家行为者构成的威胁，要求将个人信息和重要数据保留在中国境内，从而将本地存储与安全联系起来。本地存储规定保护数据和战略信息，以实现技术"安全可控"，从而限制数字信息的自由流通，以免干扰国家产业的成长。

安全审查规定有助于在国家和非国家行为者之间重新分配权力，并将权力的核心转移到中央政府手中。政府的数据审查旨在缓解信息自由传输到中国境外造成的安全威胁。因此，中央政府的关注重点从对治理问题的响应转移到预防性管理，允许国家作为网络空间运营的集中管理者。之前互联网公司为去中心化的单个网络空间平台设置规则，《网络安全法》力求通过国家控制数据传输重构互联网治理的性质。未来的研究应继续探讨网络空间的法律创新及其对互联网治理的意义。

China's Cybersecurity Law

Rachel Ann Hulvey / United States of America

University of Pennsylvania, Ph.D. Student

1. Introduction

The information revolution and the dynamic exchange of data across borders creates political threats and novel security issues. As data increasingly becomes a critical component of economic and social interactions, power is shifting from capital-intensive to data-intensive sources with information systems commanding greater importance in the national infrastructure.[1]Artificial intelligence creates political gains by revolutionizing the battlefield and commercial technologies but relies heavily on big data and tremendous computing power to develop machine learning functionality. Advantages develop from higher levels of digital commerce and communication exchanges that create large pools of data feeding into computer systems for processing. In the information age, data has become a strategic resource equal in importance to oil for national progress and is critical for future advancements in technology. Data, however, has an important distinction from oil

---

1   Nye, *Power in the Global Information Age*, P.75.

since digital information instantly crosses borders with limited state control and regulation and the rapid global exchange creates challenges for states to regulate and protect digital resources.

Although the big data era brings benefits to global society, the unregulated nature also generates risks for the state and creates a unique area to examine the process of developing rules systems and legal boundaries. China faces heightened vulnerability from technological development and presents an ideal case for examining cyberspace governance and legal evolution. Cybersecurity risks are increasingly relevant for overall security as "without cybersecurity, there is no national security" （没有网络安全就没有国家安全）. Under this model, rule of law is used as the strategic method to develop policies and standards of appropriate data usage domestically.

The legal strategy of *China's Cybersecurity* Law will be reviewed to analyze and assess governance mechanisms for cyberspace. The article proceeds by examining cyberspace governance and the *digital trend of privatization*. The unique threats facing China is examined by conducting a review of the Chinese language sources and interviews with Chinese scholars from political, legal, and data science disciplines. The concluding section analyzes China's Cybersecurity Law and the legal innovations for cyberspace governance to draw conclusions about the mechanisms for developing data protection and rule systems in cyberspace.

2. The Governance Deficit in Cyberspace

Global society faces a critical governance deficit in cyberspace, particularly with respect to international agreement concerning the global rules of data exchange. The paradigmatic international legal system with multilateral treaties is struggling to materialize in cyberspace as standards of regulation are created by multiple stakeholders into a body of rules over time and operate analogous to common law where through "small understandings new understandings get made". The blistering speed of technical developments online often outpaces traditional legislative approaches and norms are used as the dominant regulatory tool in a decentralized process that creates multiple matrixes of rules rather than a consistent global regime for cybersecurity. Negotiations on how to apply existing international law to the use of information communication technologies are fraught with disagreement, with consensus on how to apply the United Nations Charter reaching a deadlock during a 2017 United Nations Group of Government Experts (GGE) meeting. The failed negotiations created a vacuum for loose governance structures to instead shape behavior within cyberspace with soft or non-binding law regulating the digital environment.

Global society is providing many functions of government as the nation-state is no longer the natural problem-solving unit.[1]State authorities lack digital capabilities and increasingly delegate responsibilities to multinational corporations, creating greater authority for non-state actors to influence and decide international standards for the Internet and gain legislative and judicial agency.[2]Non-state actors own the platforms that cross national boundaries and develop global governance capabilities. Within the European Union, the European Court of Justice delegated Google with the authority to determine how European freedoms granting privacy ("the right to be forgotten") and free speech are to be balanced and the case represents the growing authority non-state actors have to define the boundaries of acceptable conduct in cyberspace in contrast to a traditional model where rules are developed by organs within the state apparatus. Google initiated an internal process to determine the contours of the "right to be forgotten" norm by creating a review panel of senior employees to vote on content deletion and more broadly shaped definitions of privacy through an informal regulatory structure and the case represents the disproportionate power of technology firms to decide the

---

1   Slaughter, *A New World Order* ; Mathews, *Power Shift.*

2   Büthe, *The New Global Rulers.* For the influence of non-state actors more generally see Keck and Sikkink, *Activists beyond Borders.*

standards for cyberspace.[1]

Market actors regulate data and assume many of the functions traditionally held by state and challenge state sovereignty within digital environments.[2]Over 20 years ago, Jessica Matthews predicted an imminent power shift from the traditional Westphalian hierarchy with state actors commanding decision-making power to new forms of authority for non-state actors due to the technological developments that allow for efficiency and automation that circumvents state control.[3]Authority over cyberspace involves an aspect of ownership as private corporations generate and control vast amounts of data and possessed outsized influence over the development of rule systems.[4] Transnational activities and the ability to transfer digital information globally imbues corporations with power that contests traditional notions of sovereignty and the authority of states to grant territorial access and regulate material within and across borders.[5] The competition for control over global cyberspace activity is most prominently revealed by the Facebook and Cambridge Analytica case, as private information shared without user consent between the United States and the United Kingdom left state regulators struggling to exert greater authority over data transfer and prosecute global digital activities.[6]

1　Lisa Fleisher and Sam Schechner, How Google's Top Minds Decide What to ForgetWSJ, https://www.wsj.com/articles/how-googles-top-minds-decide-what-to-forget-1431462018 (last visited May 18, 2018); See Case C-131/12, *Google Spain SL v. Agencia Espanola de Proteccion de Datos* (AEPD) (Eur. Ct. Justice May 13, 2014). The opinion of the Court of Justice of the European Union are available at its website, http://curia.europa.eu.

2　蔡翠红:《国家－市场－社会互助中网络空间的全球治理》;鲁传颖:《主权概念的演进及其在网络时代面临的挑战》,《国际关系研究》2014 年第 1 期。

3　Mathews, "Power Shift"; Wexler, "Life, Liberty, and Trade Secrets".

4　Nash et al., "Public Policy in the Platform Society"; Farwell, "Industry's Vital Role in National Cyber Security", *Stategic Studies Quarterly*, 6, No.4.

5　Krasner, "Power Politics, Institutions, and Transnational Relations" ; Johnson and Post, "Law and Borders".

6　In the United States currently there is no comprehensive law regulating the collection and use of personal data, for more details see: Keane Woods, "The Cambridge Analytica-Facebook Debacle".

3. A Typology of China's Digital Risks

The commercialized Internet and its applications have spread quickly around the world creating an interconnected space that is integrated into nearly every facets of life. The dissemination of data benefits domestic developments of technology, capital, and talent, however, this phenomenon also heightenssusceptibility to shocks from global exchange and challenges the government's ability to maintain order and provide domestic governance functions.[1] The legitimacy of the Chinese Communist Party (CCP) rests on economic and social development factors that are both influenced by the Internet. The privatization of cyberspace governance amplifies risks to the CPC due to diminished sovereignty over economic, security, and social aspects of governance.

3.1 Economic Development

China's ability to continue the pace of economic development rests on digital factors of production that are controlled by private companies. President Xi Jinping identifies digital knowledge and information as critical to factors of production and social wealth as "the amount of information a country possesses has become a major indicator of its soft power and competitiveness".[2] Domestic policies such as the Internet plus strategy recognize that the Internet is integrated into every component of the national infrastructure as the driving force for development,from the technical digital economy for software development to the integration of information services into traditional industries.[3] Information services are developing rapidly and present challenges to the state as, "those who do not move forward will fall behind, and those who move too slowly also fall behind" and identified the need for greater state management to ensure the pace of technological development across national

---

1   Xi, "Build China into a Cyberpower", p.453.
2   Xi, p.451.
3   司 et al., " '互联网 +' 是什么 ?"

industries.[1]Comprehensive coordination is needed to continue achieving growth and maintain pace with market demands, however, these services are challenging to control as firms operate globally outside of direct state control.

The geographic location of data storage and the source of advanced technologies presents threats to economic development. National competitiveness in the big data era is a result of the private efforts of technology firms and largely develops outside of state-owned enterprises. A large majority of core technologies are developed and supplied by companies outside of China and represent a vital link in the technological supply chain through e-commerce and cross border activities. The greatest danger to development lies in the control of technology by global firms and China's reliance on foreign developers as the sudden removal or inability to procure necessary supplies from abroad could severely disrupt the national economy and domestic industries.[2] China seeks to shift strategies from importing core technologies from foreign sources to creating indigenous innovations and building an economic foundation from local ingenuity.[3] The location of data storage is also considered a source of risk for China as data leaves national boundaries and is transferred to territories outside of national control, limiting the reliability and security of domestic firm's access to valuable data.

3.2 National Security

Non-state ownership of critical information infrastructure is a large vulnerability to China's national security. The potential for the production and dissemination of viruses and the unauthorized interruption of the network are considered the most

---

1 Xi, "在网络安全和信息化工作座谈会上的讲话"; Hui et al., "2017 年全球数字经济发展报告 [Annual Report on Development of Global Digital Economy Competiveness]," pp.5–6. Note the different types of digital economies from the "resource based digital economy" which includes data collection, data storage, data mining, and the "technical digital economy" which includes the manufacture of hardware and software development.

2 Hui and Tan, "全球治理变革背景下的中国网络空间安全发展［China's Cyberspace Security Development in the Context of Global Governance Reform]," p.9; Xi, "在网络安全和信息化工作座谈会上的讲话".

3 国务院, 新一代人工智能发展规划的通知 [New Generation Artificial Intelligence Development Plan].

severe threats.[1]The Chinese Communist Party (CCP) recognizes data transmission and aggregation influences security interests at the national level as previously the state maintained large amounts of valuable information about citizens and national industries but recent years have led to a shift of data held largely in the hands of private companies. Information about citizens plus tactics and vulnerabilities in finance, communication, and energy sectors are under control of private cybersecurity providers leaving the state less capable to prevent unintended information disclosures and hacking attempts.[2]Foreign multinational firms are not fully independent from the surveillance of foreign governments and data storage abroad creates large risks.[3] The Snowden revelations revealed technology firms based in the United States were part of data monitoring by the American government under the PRISM program generating concern over storage of domestic information in facilities located outside of China.[4]

The control of digital information by private firms creates large levels of uncertainty and risk as foreign companies can implement practices that harm Chinese citizens and in turn hinder the legitimacy of the CCP. Private companies maintain defenses on individual platforms and regional decisions have a profound impact on national security.In 2014, Microsoft stopped a vulnerability patching system service for Windows XP system products in China, exposing millions of Chinese users to viruses and highlighting risks from dependencies on foreign network operators.[5]The danger of digital viruses for national security and political stability is represented by the 2018 biotechnology scandal in China's northeastern Jilin Province. A pharmaceutical company fabricated the production and inspection data of thousands of infant vaccines leading to large levels of outcry from Chinese

1   惠，"中国互联网的法治之路"，p.32.
2   Hong, "The Cross-Border Data Flows Security Assessment: An Important Part of Protecting China's Basic Strategic Resources".
3   Cai, "Cybersecurity in the Chinese Context," p.486.
4   Cai, "云时代数据主权概念及其运用前景 [The Concept of Data Sovereignty in the Cloud Age]", P.58; Lu, "网络空间治理的力量博弈、理念演变与中国战略 [The Power Game of Cyberspace Governance and Chinese Strategy]."
5   Cai, "Cybersecurity in the Chinese Context", pp.483–84.

netizens directed at the government and state anxiety over the likelihood of public protests.[1] The national outrage diminishes the credibility of the CPC to protect public health and safety and signals that a similar episode could easily arise in the digital sphere from private negligence and the lack of central control over technology firms.[2]

3.3 Social Stability

Internet service providers manage online activities and control large swaths of data diminishing the ability of the state to protect social stability. Market actors manipulate social media and technology platforms in a manner that exposes citizens to risks and limits the ability of the government to ensure reliable and valid information services for the public.[3] The government is less able to protect against nefarious activity from foreign governments as social media can be used to manipulate public opinion and spread false information that destabilizes national order.[4] The spread of fake news is particularly troubling for the CPC as authorities already engage in content monitoring and deletion. If content remains online, the public is apt to assume it is indeed real since the government has not removed the story generating larger levels of confusion and diminishing the ability of the state to prevent the spread of rumors and harmful information in the online environment. The lack of control over the dissemination of content diminishes the ability of the CPC to maintain an internal position as the strongest voice in cyberspace.[5]

The relatively large influence of non-governmental actors on cyberspace affairs also limits the ability of the government to maintain a positive digital ecosystem. Technology is a "double-edged sword" as it brings new connections but also

---

1 Hancock and Xueqiao, "China Detains Company Chairwoman in Vaccine Scandal"; Wei, Lung, and Hong, "Chinese Parents Panic Over Infant Vaccine Safety."

2 Interview with industry experts in China.

3 Cai, "国家—市场—社会互动中网络空间的全球治理," p.93.

4 Hui, "用法律和情怀超越'后真相'时代 [Surpassing the Post Truth Era with Law]"; Hui and Tan, "全球治理变革背景下的中国网络空间安全发展 [China's Cyberspace Security Development in the Context of Global Governance Reform]," p.5.

5 Interview with industry experts in China.

permeates at a higher rate into culture and limits the state's control capability.[1] At the end of 2016, China had 730 million Internet users who are exposed to daily fluctuations in digital content and shaped by the ideas promoted by digital media companies. Violent videos and salacious content are a contradiction to core socialist values and present a threat to the maintenance of domestic ideology. The government recognizes the dangers of de-centralized content management through orders such as "Clean and Clear," and "Protecting the Young," which indicate the need to control the risks posed to the youth and general population by obscene content and develop a more comprehensive system of rules for content management.[2]

Although the dangers of the Internet are apparent, less has been explored on the strategies and legal methods for mitigating the risks of privatization among global governments. China's overarching strategy for addressing governance deficits in cyberspace will be analyzed in the next section before turning to an analysis of China's specific legal innovations for resolving the issue.

4. China's Strategy for Content Management: Rule of Law

Under the "Cyber Sovereignty" doctrine, China promotes the right to control the flow of information within national boundaries that goes beyond protecting communications from unauthorized access by using the law to define national territory online.[3] Strategies developed by China employ legal measures that protect internal order and stability by vesting the state with the ultimate authority to allow or prohibit the circulation of digital content within national territory and create a sense of national territory in the previously unbounded and open Internet.[4] The 2011 Draft International Code of Conduct for Information Security proposed by China and Russia to the United Nations General Assembly includes the principle that the

---

1   Xi, "在网络安全和信息化工作座谈会上的讲话".

2   胡 and 史 , "全国 '扫黄打非' 办公布一批网络 '扫黄打非' 大案要案".

3   Hui, "新安全观下中国网络信息安全战略的理论构建 [The Theoretical Construction of China's Network Security Strategy]".

4   Cai, "Cybersecurity in the Chinese Context", p.477.

policy authority for Internet-related issues is the right of states and supports the ability to regulate content based on national laws. The doctrine promotes the notion of legal spheres based on territorial boundaries and respect for each country's ability to define internal Internet management policies and have jurisdiction over domestic information infrastructure.[1]

China's strategy for addressing diminished sovereignty from the interconnected nature of the Internet is to centralize power with the state to better regulate the activities of non-state actors.[2] The central aim is to achieve greater self-sufficiency ("自主可控") and mitigate against fluctuations by reforming the internal governance structure of cyberspace and creating comprehensive cyber governance capabilities.[3]

Since the 18th Party Congress, General Secretary Xi Jinping has attached importance to cybersecurity governance reforms by promoting the creation of an Internet Management Leadership System as one of the 60 reform tasks created by the 18th Central Committee. As a result, the Central Cybersecurity and Informatization Leading Small Group was established to plan and coordinate important issues of cybersecurity across domains and to increase control of the central government over digital activities.[4] The new organization is a permanent and well-resourced commission that is imbued with authority to ensure data protection from a state rather than private level. The strategy delineates roles within the internal governance structure,so the Party plays the strongest role in protecting critical information infrastructure and is empowered to regulate and control cyberspace.

With the complexity and rapid development of the Internet, a regulatory framework is viewed as the necessary component for security with law as the

---

1   Yuan, "Where Are the National Borders of Cyberspace".
2   Cai, "The Concept of Data Sovereignty in the Cloud Age", p.60.
3   吴，李，and 陈，"打造自主可控的大数据资源网络［Building an Autonomous and Controllable Large Data Resource Network］".
4   中央网信办理论学习中心组 [Theoretical Studies Center Group, Cyberspace Administration of China], "深入贯彻习近平总书记网络强国战略思想扎实推进网络安全和信息化工作 [Deepening the Implementation of General Secretary Xi Jinping's Strategic Thinking on Building China into a Cyber Superpower: Steadily Advancing Cybersecurity and Informatization Work]".

new paradigm for advancing state control over the Internet and standardizing management.[1]Rule of law is the core of the Chinese legal system and the fundamental strategy for ensuring governance and order as technology continues to modernize.[2]The strategy of using rule of law to govern cyberspace is particularly advantageous due to China's political system. The one-party system allows Beijing to promulgate law that keeps pace with the fast development of technology more rapidly than parliamentary systems that are often delayed from expeditiously passing legislation by protracted debate and negotiation between parties.[3] China's strategy is to first issue a draft and solicit feedback from domestic and international groups impacted by the provisions through a series of consultations. Following the meetings with community members and business groups, necessary revisions are made and the draft law is promulgated into official law. The legal code in China is developed as a comprehensive system where the highest order law is issued asa broad framework designed to adapt to changing technical development. This allows for accompanying measures to be implemented that clarify the law as technology rapidly progresses and provides an efficient means to address new governance issues.

5. Legal Innovations for Cyberspace

China's Cybersecurity Law (CSL) went into effect on June 1, 2017 as the foundational law for the field of cybersecurity to regulate outbound data flows and safeguard digital information. The law was issued to protect the integrity, confidentiality, and availability of network data and prevent leakages or theft of information and supports a broader strategy of protecting national security and sovereignty in the digital age.[4] The article examines how China's legal innovations mitigate the threats of privatization compared with the strategies of legal systems in

---

1　Wang and Ceng, " 中 国 网 络 安 全 立 法 的 模 式 构 建 [The Model of China' s Cybersecurity Legislation]". Cyberspace Administration of China, "习近平: 自主创新推进网络强国建设 - 中共中央网络安全和信息化委员会办公室 ".
2　周 , "习近平互联网法治思想研究" ; 张 , "法治与国家治理现代化 ", p.6.
3　Interview with cybersecurity expert in China.
4　中华人民共和国网络安全法 , art. 1 and 11.

the United States and Europe.

5.1 Increases the self-sufficiency of the state and mitigates security threats

The first major component of the CSL influencing data exchange creates new rules for data storage and is viewed as foundational to China's emerging digital infrastructure. The law mandates that important data collected in the mainland be stored in China and requires data localization. Article 37 of the CSL states that personal information and important data collected and generated while operating within the borders of the People's Republic of China must be stored within China. During the development of the CSL, the legislators of the National People's Congress removed the word "business" from the phrase "important business data" to issue broad requirements governing content for both business and social purposes. The drafting decision indicates the law goes beyond a simple classification method to assess the value of specific data to the state and public interests before allowing content to be stored outside of national boundaries.[1]

The new measures require changes in business operations to tighten security within China and encumber data within national borders. Prior to data localization requirements, multinational companies possessed greater leeway to store data collected in China on servers in the geographic location that was most optimal for business operations with the movement of data corresponding to the demands of commerce. Under the CSL, multinational companies must secure infrastructure in China to store data rather than sending the information abroad for data processing, often entailing additional investment and construction in local markets. The requirements build from earlier localization rules in 2011 that "prohibits Banks from storing, processing or analyzing outside China any Personal Financial Information (PFI) which has been collected in China, or providing PFI collected in China to an offshore entity" but broaden the requirements beyond the financial industry and shift the obligations of companies from negative requirements to prevent the export of specific

---

1 Hong, "THE CROSS-BORDER DATA FLOWS SECURITY ASSESSMENT: An Important Part of Protecting China's Basic Strategic Resources."

data to positive duties explicitly necessitating localization of important data.[1]

The Cybersecurity Law develops greater protection against fluctuations by creating a localized pool of data to guarantee availability for domestic operations and ensure the operability of digital resources. In the *Measures on the Security Assessment of Cross-Border Transfer of Personal Information and Important Data* (hereinafter "Measures") important data is defined as "data closely related to national security, economic development, and the society's public interests" and the law reduces the risks from the privatization of cyberspace governance and storage in foreign locations. The CPC was previously beholden to foreign governments to investigate cybercrime and protect the personal information of citizens abroad through time-consuming methods such as mutual legal assistance treaties (MLAT).[2]The new legal measures reduce outside reliance for security protection and foster competitive advantages. Following the implementation of the law,China's digital economy builds from a foundation of domestic resources that allows for more stable development with decreased risk of data being withheld or tampered with whilestored at foreign facilities.[3]

5.2 Develop a state-centric approach through security reviews

The Cybersecurity Law establishes greater authority for the state by mandating government reviews of cybersecurity operations and network hardware. The security review regime is designed to build comprehensive governance capabilities (网络综合治理能力) that mitigate the unbridled and far-reaching power of global technology firms over cyberspace.[4]Under Article 23, critical network equipment and specialized cybersecurity products must meet the requirements of a security

---

1   Notice on Urging Banking Financial Institutions to Do a Good Job in Protecting Personal Financial Information] (promulgated by the People's Bank of China, Jan. 21, 2011), http://www.gov.cn/gongbao/content/2011/content_1918924.htm.

2   Lovelock, "Regulating for a Digital Economy". Note the U.S.-U.K. mutual legal assistance treaty as an example.

3   Big Data Security Standardization White Paper. Also, note Big data is a free resource of the industrial society, whoever controls big data gains the advantage.

4   "'4.20' Speech at a Second Cybersecurity and Informatization Work Conference".

inspection to operate within China and subsequent notices define the agencies responsible fortesting information technology products and services and providing network access licenses.[1]

National data exit control measures provide rules for transfers of important information outside of Chinese territory. Although data localization is the overarching requirement, the new law identifies certain situations where necessary data transfer is permissible and provides relevant national departments with a clear mandate to analyze information and ensure data protection at the national level. Under Articles 51 and 52 of the CSL, operators of critical information infrastructure must submit products and services for a data outbound security assessment. The *Guidelines for the Cross-Border Data Flows Security Assessment* (hereinafter "Guidelines") define data export as a one-time or continuous activity of providing personal information and important data collected within China to organizations outside the country. Data is legally categorized as exported if stored or accessed overseas and a security assessment by government agencies is required before conducting such a transfer.[2]The Measures specify that the law applies not only to "critical information infrastructure operators" but to a broader group of "network operators" that includes network owners and network service providers.[3]

6. Conclusion

China's Cybersecurity Law creates borders around an open and unbounded Internet through localization requirements and legal innovation. The provisions work to mitigate the threats from the privatization of cyberspace governance and ensure stability through rule of law. The Chinese law mitigates the threats posed by non-state actors and links localization with security by requiring personal information and important data to remain within China's borders. Localization provisions protect

---

1 "Announcement of China National Certification and Accreditation Administration Committee."

2 Information Security Technology- Guidelines for Data Cross-Border Transfer Security Assessment, art. 3.6.

3 Measures regarding Security Assessments for Cross-Border Transfers of Personal or Important Data, art. 2.

data and strategic information to achieve "secure and controllable" technology to limit the free movement of digital information from disrupting the growth of national industries.

Provisions for security reviews serve to redistribute authority between state and non-state actors and shift the locus of power to the central government. Government reviews of data focus on mitigating security threats from the free transfer of information to locations outside of China's border. This shifts the focus of the central government from responding to governance issues to preventative management and allows the state to serve as the central manager of cyberspace operations. Internet firms previously created rules for individual platforms that decentralizes cyberspace and the Cybersecurity Law provisions seek to reorganize the nature of Internet governance with the state in control of data movement. Future research should continue to review legal innovations for cyberspace and the resulting implications for Internet governance.

中国与"一带一路"倡议的价值创造

安德烈·马卡拉格维【秘鲁】
秘鲁天主教大学教授

引　言

　　管理学以经济、文化、社会学和心理学等学科为基础，分析组织现象以及如何在市场上相互作用和实现目标。许多管理学理论都提到融合对于发展价值链的重要性（Porter，1985），不仅能够带来组织的成长，价值链中所有要素也将成长。因此，我们理解，真正的价值创造通过在决策过程中融合利益、文化、良好实践和价值观的和平关系实现。

　　本文的目的是揭示改革开放以来中国如何通过融入世界创造和提供价值。为此，首先重要的是要了解什么是价值，以及如何在战略管理中创造价值。本文从学术研究的角度关注"一带一路"倡议，最后将这两个要素结合起来，指出中国如何从战略上借助于"一带一路"创造并向世界提供价值。

什么是价值？

　　可以从不同的视角理解价值一词。甚至存在一个常见的错误，将价值与价值观混淆，价值观的含义更加广泛（Hoag & Cooper，2006）。在商业管理中，价值通常是愿景和使命陈述的组成部分，或者是要求公司员工具有的价值观。在下文中我将讨论若干定义，方便理解本文中价值的含义。

基于价值的管理（也称作价值管理）是源于大量国际组织实践的一种模式，例如可口可乐公司和 AT&T，用于衡量组织如何推动创造价值的战略（Ray,2001）。在谈及价值时，有必要了解价值管理一词的含义。

在组织发展中，价值过去通常与股东财务方面的增长有关（Hoag & Cooper,2006）。价值增加是另一种观察视角。在这方面，当组织明智地使用资源并有所增益时，价值得以创造。然后，企业将创造价值的重点放在结果更好、效率更高的活动上。另一个用途是在组织的人员方面，换言之，企业可能会尝试使员工感到自身有价值（Hoag & Cooper, 2006）。

Hoag 和 Cooper 提出一个更加合适的价值驱动组织的定义："价值驱动组织，其价值本质上包含于价值交换手段之内。价值通过价值转移实现交换，价值转移是对供应商和顾客之间持续进行平等价值交换的追求和承诺"（Hoag & Cooper,2006, 第 76 页）。

在这种管理模式下，领导者不仅应该考虑为希望获取利润的股东创造价值，而且必须意识到还有许多其他利益团体向组织寻求某种类型的价值，在某些情况下，这些可能重合甚至产生矛盾。良好的价值管理可以防止这些矛盾的发生（Young & O'Byrne, 2000）。

在上面给出的定义中，交换，即提供商和客户之间的关系极其重要。当组织满足其利益相关者的期望并以某种方式为获得这种满足而提供回报时，价值得以创造并提供。价值在三个不同的维度创造：经济、社会和环境。我们必须明白，当今组织对于价值管理的目的是实现这三个维度的增长。

获取的收益或满足超出成本或投入的情况下创造价值（Malmi & Ikäheimo,2003）。因此，投资者对某个项目或企业进行的投资获取利润时将获得价值；当客户希望通过某个产品满足一项需求时，如果现实超过预期，客户将获得价值；工人的努力和工作表现获得财务奖励和情感上的认可时，工人将发现自己的价值。这只是一些范例，因为价值管理模式寻求为所有利益相关者创造价值。

考虑到这一点，Miguel Córdova 提出网络与战略之间的联系。他认为，牢固的关系有助于在利用资源方面取得更好的结果，在战略价值创造方面相互帮助（Córdova, 2017）。因此，为了发展和提供价值，管理者必须建立战略联盟。

Brandenburger 和 Stuart (1996) 得出的结论是，组织为了实现价值增加，必须确保其价值链成员的成长。并非所有组织在所有方面都是专家；某些组织在特定活动方面拥有更好的资源，因此，共同努力可以为两个组织增加价值。

我们认为，价值通过合作与融合创造。价值管理组织通过在决策过程中融合利益、文化、良好实践和价值观发展关系，创造价值。融合过程并不容易，尤其是因为价值链中每个成员的利益和组织文化之间存在差异。而这是组织领导人在谈判中必须克服的困难。

中国通过国际关系创造价值

中国已经证明在战略上实现目标并创造价值的能力（Albrow, 2016）。然而，不仅如此。中国可以看作是一家以提供和创造价值为目标的管理型公司，这就是我希望在下文的"一带一路"倡议部分进行解释的内容。

"一带一路"倡议（BRI）

自改革开放以来，尤其是第三阶段的"一带一路"，中国坚持采用融合战略。习近平主席在北京举行的"一带一路"论坛开幕式上的讲话指出，古代中国丝绸之路的本质是和平与合作、开放与包容、相互学习和互惠互利（习，2017）。经济增长是战略融合的结果；也是该倡议的基础。

中国政府正在推动对其他国家的投资和共同发展，以寻求双赢的关系。目的是推动经济走廊建立，融合每个沿线成员的市场、资源和能力，以实现其经济发展目标（Silin, Kapustina, Trevisan, & Drevalev, 2017）。已经有研究表明该倡议内的国家对经济增长的预测更高（香港贸发局经贸研究，2018）。

众所周知，工业和基础设施项目的外国投资有助于创造价值，特别是在创造就业、企业发展和国际商业方面。"一带一路"倡议针对这些类型的项目，旨在帮助其他国家建设更好的基础设施和通信系统，作为回报，中国将更容易从这些国家获得资源和产品。

一项研究得出的结论是，"一带一路"倡议将有利于尼日利亚经济增长（Ayokunle O. & A.O, 2018）。在同一项研究中，作者指出，中国被认为是尼日利亚一个非常重要的盟友，90% 的尼日利亚人民对中国感到亲切。中国和尼日利亚并不是最近才发展关系，但"如今一带一路项目计划在尼日利亚修建一条 1042 公里的沿海铁路，价值一百二十亿美元，经过十（10）个州将该国的东部与卡拉巴尔连接起来。"（Ayokunle O. & A.O, 2018, 第 20477 页）。该研究的作者强调这类项目对尼日利亚国家发展的重要性。

除尼日利亚外，欧洲也受到该倡议的影响。对港口、铁路和其他一带一路相关基础设施的投资正在使欧洲国家重塑其经济战略（Fardella & Prodi, 2018）。根据这项研究，对铁路和港口的投资将使欧洲国家与中国之间的贸易受益，从而推动双方的经济增长。

这两个案例可以证明"一带一路"倡议的意图是通过战略伙伴关系之间的合作创造价值。在西方模式下，不同的旗帜和国家被看作是分歧，而持久支持这一倡议的东方愿景则基于资源的融合和有效利用，让所有人实现共赢；那就是创造价值。这项倡议有望为该地区乃至世界带来非常重要的经济、社会、政治和生态发展（香港贸发局经贸研究，2018）。

建 议

必须指出，"一带一路"倡议并没有试图改变每个国家的主权和文化。中国政府正在亚欧大陆促进融合。需要考虑不同类型的文化、历史背景、宗教以及其他特征，才能实现该倡议的目标。中国作为领导方，需要在参与国中推动这一愿景，让人民成为建立在和平与合作基础上的新世界秩序的一部分。

"一带一路"倡议需要被视为双赢战略，对双方都有帮助的战略联盟。为了实现这一点，需要分享更多关于"一带一路"倡议的信息。如果没有战略性的管理，不同国家的文化差异和历史背景可能会成为一个问题。

其他方面也可以作为中国价值创造和提供的补充，例如教育体系和近期改革，在政治层面上制定战略决策的方式，大量的企业和国家组织，为实现可持续发展目标等而制定的规范和法规。这些主题可以用于未来的研究。

China and the Value Creation through the Belt and Road Initiative

Andres Macarachvili / Perú

Department of Management Science at

Pontifical Catholic University of Perú, Professor

Introduction

Management sciences is based in economic, cultural, sociological and psychological disciplines. It analyzes the phenomenon of organizations and how they interact in the market and achieve their goals.Many theories of management sciences mention the importance of integration to develop a value chain(Porter, 1985) that allows not only the growth of an organization, but of all those that are in that chain. This allows us to understand that true value is created through peaceful relationships that integrate interests, culture, good practices and values in decision-making.

The intention of this paper is to showhow China is creating and delivering value by integrating itself to the world since the reform and opening-up. For this purpose, first it is important to understand what value is and how is it created in strategic management. Then the paper presents the Belt and Road Initiative (BRI) based on academic research and, finally, integrate those two elements to show how China is, strategically, creating and delivering value to the world by the BRI.

What is value?

There are different perspectives to understand the world value. Even there is a common error confusing the singular -value- with the plural -values- covering even more meanings to the word(Hoag & Cooper, 2006). In business management, values are usually part of the vision and mission statements, or the values required by the employees of the company. In the next lines is discussed several definitions to understand what value in the context of this paper is.

Value Based Management (VBM) is a model that is born from the practice of many international organizations, such as Coca Cola and AT&T for example, to measure how they are promoting strategies that create value(Ray, 2001).It's necessary to understand what the VBM refers to when it talks about value.

In organization development, value was used to be related to the growth of the financial aspect to the shareholders(Hoag & Cooper, 2006). Added value is another way to see it. In this aspect, value is created when an organization use wisely the resource and adds something to it. Companies then creates value focusing on those activities that presents better results and are efficient. Another use is in the human aspect of the organization, in other words, a company may try to make their employees feel valued(Hoag & Cooper, 2006).

> Hoag and Cooper present a definition more adequate for a value-based organization: "The essence of value in a value-based organization is contained within the means of the value exchange. Value is exchanged through the value transposition, which is the pursuit of and commitment to the continuous exchange of equal worth between a supplier and a customer" (Hoag & Cooper, 2006, p. 76).

Under this management model, leaders should not only think about creating value for shareholders, who expect their profits to increase, but recognizing that there are also many other interest groups that seek some type of value from organizations and some cases these can be superimposed and even contradict. Good management based on value can prevent these contradictions from occurring(Young & O'Byrne, 2000).

In the definition presented, the exchange, the relations between providers and clients are extremely important. Value will be created and delivered when the organization satisfies their stakeholders expectations and those somehow retributes for that satisfaction. Value is created in three different dimensions: economic, social and environmental. It must be understood that, today, the purpose of organizations in the VBM must be to develop growth in these three aspects.

Value is created to the extent that the gain or satisfaction obtained is greater than the cost or investment that had to be made(Malmi & Ikäheimo, 2003). Thus, an investor will receive value when obtaining profits for the investment made in a certain project or company; a customer will receive value when the reality exceeds the expectation when he seeks to satisfy a need with a certain product; and a worker will find value when he feels well rewarded financially and emotionally recognized in exchange for his effort and work. These are only some examples, because the VBM model seeks to create value for all stakeholders.

Considering this, Miguel Córdova propose the link between networks and strategies. He argues that strong relations help to obtain better results in the use of resources, helping each other in the strategic value creation (Córdova, 2017). So, to develop and deliver value, strategic alliances must be created by managers.

From Brandenburger and Stuart (1996), it is possible to conclude that, for the value of an organization to increase, it must ensure the growth of the members of its value chain. Not all organizations are specialists in everything; some have better resources for a certain activity, so the union of efforts can increase the value for both organizations.

This allows us to understand that value is created through cooperation and integration. VBM organizations create value by developing relationships that integrate interests, culture, good practices and values in decision-making process. This integration process is never easy, especially due to the differences that may exist between the interests and the organizational culture of each member of this chain. And this difficulty is the one that the leaders of the corporations must overcome in the negotiations.

China Creates Value Through Its International Relationships

China have proven its ability to strategically achieve its objectives and, doing so, creating value(Albrow, 2016). However, it is not only that. China can be seen like a corporation managed with the purpose of delivering and creating value, and this is what I would like to explain in the following part based on the BRI

Belt and Road Initiative (BRI)

China has been able to apply this integration Innovation since the reform and opening-up and, especially in this third stage, with the BRI, since 2013. President Xi Jinping, in his speech at the opening ceremony of the Belt and Road Forum in Beijing, said that the essence of the Silk Road of ancient China was about peace and cooperation, openness and inclusiveness, mutual learning and mutual benefit (Xi, 2017). Economic growth is intended to be the result of this important and strategic integration; that is the foundation of the initiative.

The Chinese government is promoting investment and joint development with other nations in search of a win-win relationship. The intention is to facilitate the creation of a corridor to integrate markets, resources and capacities of each member of the initiative to achieve their economic development objectives(Silin, Kapustina, Trevisan, & Drevalev, 2017). There are already studies that show that countries inside the initiative have higher growth projections(HKTDC Research, 2018).

It is known that foreign investment orientated to industrial and infrastructural projects helps to create value, especially in the job generation, entrepreneurial development and international business. BRI is orientated to those kinds of projects, helping other countries to obtain better infrastructure and communication systems and, in return, China will have better ways to obtain resources and products from those countries.

A study concludes that the BRI will benefit Nigeria's economic growth(Ayokunle O. & A.O, 2018). In that same research, the authors indicate that China is considered as a very important ally to Nigeria and that the people of Nigeria is 90% pro-China. Relations between China and Nigeria is not recent, but "Now,the B&R project intends to build a 1,042km coastal railway worth Twelve (12) billion Dollars in Nigeria, which will connect Calabar to the Eastern part of the country, passing through Ten (10) states." (Ayokunle O. & A.O, 2018, p. 20477). The authors of this research emphasizes on the importance of this kind of projects for the development of the Nigerian nation.

As well as Nigeria, Europe is also being affected by the initiative. The investments in ports, railroads and other kind of infrastructure related to the road or belt, are making European countries to reshape their economic strategies (Fardella & Prodi, 2018). According to this research, the investment in railways and ports will benefit trade between European countries and China, increasing the economic growth for both nations.

Those two examples can evidence that the BRI intention is the value creation through collaboration between strategic partnership. In the Western model, flags and nations were viewed as divisions, while the Eastern vision that endures the initiative is based on the integration and efficient use of resources to win all together; that is creating value. This initiative promises a very important economic, social, political and ecological development for the region and for the world(HKTDC Research, 2018).

Recommendations

It is important to say that the Belt and Road Initiative does not attempt to change each countries' sovereignty and culture. The Chinese Government is promoting this integration through the Eurasian area. In this objective, different kind of cultures, historical background, religions, among other characteristics, need to be considered to achieve the initiative´s goal. China, as the leading party, needs to promote this vision along the countries participating, so people can be part of this new world order based in peace and collaboration.

BRI needs to be viewed as a win-win strategy, a strategic alliance that helps both parties. To achieve this, more information about the BRI needs to be shared. Cultural differences and historic background of the countries can be a problem if it´s not managed strategically.

There are other aspects that could complement the idea that China creates and deliver value, as, for example, the education system and recent reform, the way strategic decisions are made at a political level, the considerable number of companies and state organizations that holds, the norms and regulations created to meet the Sustainable Development Goals, etc. These topics could be considered for future studies.

References

Albrow, M. (2016). Philosophical Social Science as a Bridge from "Belt and Road" to Global Governance. *Collected Works at the Symposium on China Studies 2016*, pp. 12 - 22.

Ayokunle O., I., & A.O, A. (2018). Belt and Road Initiative: Analysis of Possible Effects on Nigeria's Economy. *International Journal of Contemporary Research and Review, 09*(06), 20475 - 20182. doi:https://doi.org/10.15520/ijcrr/2018/9/06/536

Brandenburger, A., & Stuart Jr, H. (1996). Value - based Business Strategy. *Journal of Economics and Mangement Strategy*, pp. 5-24.

Córdova, M. (2017). Are networks important in order to secure a firm´s strategy? *360: Revista de ciencias de la gestión*, pp. 106 - 118.

Fardella, E., & Prodi, G. (2018). Existential Alternative fot Europe? The Belt and Road Initiative and Its Impact on Europe. *Russia in Global Affairs*, 164 - 176.

doi:10.31278/1810-6374-2018-16-2-164-176

HKTDC Research. (2018, 05 03). *HKTDC*. Retrieved from The Belt and Road Initiative: http://china-trade-research.hktdc.com/business-news/article/The-Belt-and-Road-Initiative/ The-Belt-and-Road-Initiative/obor/en/1/1X3CGF6L/1X0A36B7.htm.

Hoag, B., & Cooper, C. L. (2006). *Managing value-based organizations it′s ot what you think.* Massachusetts: New Horizons in Management.

Malmi, T., & Ikäheimo, S. (2003). Value Based Management practices - some evidence from the field. *Management Accounting Research*, pp. 235 - 254.

Porter, M. E. (1985). *The Competitive Advantage: Creating and Sustaining Superior Performance.* NY: Free Press.

Ray, R. (2001). Economic value added: Theory, evidence, a missing link. *Review of Business*, pp. 66 - 70.

Silin, Y., Kapustina, L., Trevisan, I., & Drevalev, A. (2017). China's economic interests in the "One Belt, One Road" initiative. *SHS Web of Conferences*, sp. doi:https://doi.org/10.1051/ shsconf/20173901025.

Xi, Y. (2017, 05 14). Work Together to Build the Silk Road Economic Belt and The 21st Century Maritime Silk Road. *Belt and Road Forum (BRF) for International Cooperation in Beijing.* Beijing, Xinhua, China: Xinhuanet. Retrieved from http://www.xinhuanet. com//english/2017-05/14/c_136282982.htm.

Young, S., & O'Byrne, S. (2000). *EVA and Value-Based Management.* McGraw-Hill.

汉语新词对社会发展的影响

夏谙特【秘鲁】

里卡尔多·帕尔玛大学教授

一、引言

社会的日益进步对不同领域的发展都产生了巨大的影响，而这就需要对已有的技术、想法和概念进行不断的创新。语言就是其中的一个方面，因为语言是人类进步最重要的工具之一；随着新世界进入了一个联系紧密的全球化时代，需要用词汇和术语来描述当前的现象和概念，语言在积极参与了社会的发展并起到了至关重要的作用。这种前所未有的进化过程引起了许多语言学派、语言学家及语言爱好者的关注。

此外，最重要和令人惊讶的（对某些人）变化之一，是普通话的使用范围越来越广了。在过去的 10 年中，提供汉语课程的语言学校越来越多。在这种汉语教学扩大的同时也产生了很多新的词汇。它们由越来越多的普通话学习者传播到世界各地，这不仅影响了中国，也影响了世界上许多其他国家。正如中国社会语言学家认为的那样"中国的新词汇是反映社会生活及中国变化的先锋"。

二、新词的定义

"新词"最早于 1772 年在英语中率先使用，它借用了法语 néologisme(1734) 一词，根据 James Aderson "新词"，源于希腊语，其含义为 νέο - néo-，"新的"

和 λόγος lógos "言语，话语"，可以定义为一个相对较新或孤立的术语、单词或短语。它正在进入一个共同使用的过程中，但尚未被主流语言完全接受。根据 Gryniuk 的观点，一些新词通常直接用于特定的人、出版物、时期或事件。在语言形成的过程中，新词比原始语言更为成熟。

国内外许多学者和语言学家对此持不同看法。英国著名学者彼得·纽马克（Peter Newmark）在他的"翻译教科书"中定义了"新词"："新创造的词汇单位或现有的具有新意义的词汇单位"。根据牛津高级英汉词典（第 7 版），新词被描述为"一个词的新词语或表达新词义"。朗文当代英语词典将新词定义为"一个新词汇或表达，或为旧词的新意义"。王铁坤（1992）指出，"新词是指新近创造或是从其他语言中借用的新词汇，它可以是从本国语言中的方言词、古文或是行业语言中产生的，也可以指现有的新词义和新用法。"刘树新指出，一个词语不仅被创造出来，而且也得到了普遍的接受，并被人们广泛使用，其在词汇系统中占有一席之地，可被称之为新词。

郑艳霞将汉语新词定义为新创造的汉语词汇，或从其他语言中借用的词语，或是具有新意义的现有汉语词汇，它可以表达新事物、新概念、新思想、新体验或是中国社会和文化的新问题。此外，汉语新词汇应该遵循汉语形成的规律，应该被人们普遍接受和广泛使用。郑艳霞根据其性质也将新词分为三类。

1. 根据来源分类

郑艳霞说，汉语新词汇有三个主要来源。首先，创造汉语新词来描述新的思想、现象和新概念，例如："打车神器""断网恐惧症""多代住房"等；其次，一些汉语新词用现有的短语或单词发展出新的含义，而这些新的短语或单词可能与原有词意没有关系，例如："土豪""正能量""单细胞动物"等；再次，一些汉语新词借用了其他语言的词汇，例如"阿尔法男""慕课"等。

2. 按内容分类

根据郑艳霞的说法，汉语新词汇也可以根据其内容进行分类。随着中国社会的发生，中国在政治、经济、教育、娱乐等多个领域发生了翻天覆地的变化。结果，在这些领域中产生了许多汉语新词汇。根据这一点，汉语新词主要被归类为关于政治和经济的新词，例如："制度笼子""微博外交""过渡性贷款"等；关于科学技术的新词，例如："云服务""微世界"；关于社会生活的新词，例如："橡皮婚姻""半塘夫妻""低碳旅游"等。当然，除了以上提到的三个方面，汉语的新词还反映不同的领域新事物。

3．根据组合模式进行分类

根据其组合模式，汉语新词可以主要分为五种类型：词缀、复合词、转换词、缩写词和重叠词。

我们还要思考一下新词产生的原因。根据周序林"社会发展与新词汇的涌现"的研究，我们能了解社会的发展深刻地影响着新词的出现。一方面巨大的社会变革为新词的出现提供了社会与物质的基础，另一方面，西方文化的渗入与传播，也给新词的出现提供更大的发展空间。自从改革开放以来，中国社会与经济的发展可谓日新月异，在这样的历史变革中，在经济体制改革和政治体制改革的双重推动下，各种新思想、新事物应运而生，政治、经济、文化等各方面都发生着翻天覆地的变化，新事物在人们的生活中不断涌现。为了更直接地表达这些新事物、新现象，大量的新词随之被创造出来，并以惊人的速度广泛传播，迅速进入了人们日常生活的方方面面。

根据陈元解释的新词创作原理，社会或其他类型变化的元素，如社会结构、经济基础、上层建筑和民俗的变化，以及科学上的新发现、发明、技术和突破，如新概念，新观念、新观点、新观念，所有这些都不可避免地受到语言交流系统的影响和再生产，而这些变化则可以通过语言的媒介被我们很好地观察到。这就是发明新词汇的主要原因。

此外，根据周序林研究，汉语素来都有吸收外来语的传统，比如著名的上海洋泾邦汉语，随着改革开放，国门进一步地敞开，西方文化不断深入，传统文化正在接受着外来文化前所未有的挑战，在中西方文化不断碰撞、此消彼长的过程中，大量具有西方特色的、表达西方生活方式的、融入西方文化色彩的词汇进入中国，并逐渐深入到人们的日常语言中。此外，随着网络时代的到来，互联网深入家家户户，其对语言的影响也是不容小觑的，近年来网络新词大量涌现，不但在网络上被创造出来，还逐渐走入了人们的日常生活中。

三、新词呈现的新特征

1．政治词呈新义

改革开放以来，具有强烈阶级斗争色彩的政治语言已经逐渐退出了历史的舞台，从人们的生活中淡出。与此同时，体现着时代新风貌的词汇如"改革开放""一国两制""三个代表""与时俱进"开始被人们熟悉。其中还有一些曾经在特定时期，打着时代烙印的政治词汇，被以幽默的方式沿用下来，指代日常生活中的某些事物与行为，比如："影响市容"（其貌不扬）、"码长城"（打麻将）等。

另一个值得注意的汉语语言现象就是人与人之间的称呼，也是随时代而变化的，比如从新中国成立到改革开放前人们彼此、甚至夫妻间都以"战友""同志"相称，20世纪80年代，"师傅""小王""老赵"开始广泛使用，进入21世纪"先生""小姐""太太"又逐渐流行起来。

2．经济词汇大量涌现

改革开放以后，特别20世纪90年代，中国的政治经济体制改革出现长足进步，尤其是市场经济的蓬勃发展，一些前所未闻的新鲜事物走入了人们的生活，这就要求与之适应的新鲜词汇补充进来以满足人们表达新思想、新生活的需求。比如："超市""按揭""直销""传销""楼市""回扣"，等等。随着股民数量的增长与股票相关的词汇也变得耳熟能详，比如："股市""涨停板""套牢""绩优股""蓝筹"。市场经济的发展也让更多的人开始经商，逐渐富裕起来，甚至有些人还被金钱所迷惑，随之而来产生的新词也有："下海""款爷""富姐""炫富"。当然在这样的市场环境下，也有越来越多的农民来到城市谋生，他们常被叫作"民工""外来妹""钟点工""小阿姨"。

3．饮食和娱乐休闲词汇

随着物质生活水平的不断提高，人们越来越重视精神生活的丰富，各种各样的休闲娱乐方式层出不穷，从20世纪80年代的"霹雳舞""搓麻"，到90年代的"桑拿""蹦迪"，再到新世纪的"上网""电游"，直到近年来的"网游""网购"，与"玩"相关的词汇被越来越广泛地使用。与"吃"相关的词汇，如"吃醋""吃亏""吃豆腐"也有了新搭配，引申出了新含义；"宰鸡""宰鸭"到"宰人"，"宰"的含义也从"杀害生命"演变成"骗取钱财"。

4．外来词

国门打开后，思想开放的都市年轻人更多地接触到了外国的生活与行为方式，随着思想文化领域交流的不断深入，人们喝"可乐""雪碧"，吃"汉堡""热狗"，唱"卡拉OK"开"派对"。在直接引进外来词的同时，汉语还引申创造，如英语的taxi进入中国后叫"的士"，从而又衍生出了"面的""的哥""打的"等。"酒吧"源自英文的bar，自此之后，各种各样的"吧"，"餐吧""网吧""书吧""氧吧"

——出现，"泡吧"已经成为人们生活的新时尚。

5．科技词汇

21 世纪以来，随着科技的进步，特别是生物技术，网络信息技术的迅速发展与进步，人们越来越深刻地认识到，科学技术与日常生活的密不可分，因此那些高大上的科技词汇例如："克隆""纳米"也变得耳熟能详，更有一些原本的科技词汇已经完全融入了人们的日常生活，比如"多媒体""VCD、DVD"。

四、新词与社会

在过去的几十年中，学者们对新词出现的原因进行了大量的研究，社会语言学家们认为，语言与社会发展存在着密不可分的联系，这种联系是复杂又多样的。

1．新词汇映射出社会发展

社会政治、经济、文化及科技等各方面的发展与变化都会影响到新词的出现，新词就像镜子一样映射出社会的发展。首先，词汇的丰富程度反映出人们对社会的理解程度，拥有丰富词汇语言的民族，往往对世界的发展有着更广泛、透彻的理解，而这样的民族也会更加强大。近年来汉语的新词辈出，也从一方面折射出中国国力的迅速发展。其次，新词本身就是一种文化现象，展示了社会文化发展与前进的脚步，当城市中的人先富裕起来，开始有帮助他人的愿望的时候出现了"希望工程"，当人们对经济发展过程中一小撮人利用手中权力换取利益产生不满时候，就出现了"反腐倡廉"。此外随着社会的进步，人们自我意识的觉醒，从最初尊重自我权力出现的"隐私权""肖像权"，到向往自由、张扬个性的"新人类"，近年来甚至还出现了"后现代"的"二次元"生活。当然，在社会文化发展速度滞后于经济发展速度时，一些负面的、不健康的思想与观念不可避免地出现了，映射到语言上，精神空虚产生了"郁闷"，没事找事就要"玩心跳"，精神压力过大还会产生"抑郁症"。

2．21 世纪的汉语

新词的出现无疑是对汉语表达功能的极大丰富，有利于保持汉语的活力，从而促进其繁荣与发展。加速传播的外国文化带来的大量新词，在丰富汉语词汇的同时，也给语言本身带来了诸多负面影响，是否应当全盘接受？社会经济文化发展不平衡中出现的负面的、不健康的词汇，甚至污言秽语是否应当进入汉语词典？这些都要成为语言规划工作者必须考虑与面对的重要课题。

基于这些宝贵的研究，我们可以将新词与其例子分类如下：

表一：新词分类

分类	例子
根据发展进程： 使用常规单词来表达一个新词汇，一个新的概念或想法。	"走出去"是中国企业寻求发展的一项国家战略，随着"一带一路"共同倡议的实施和推进，往哪里走？如何走？走什么？怎么走得好，走得稳，走得持久，就变成政商两界必须系统思考的问题。
通过简化： 将汉语中较长的单词变成更短的版本，仍代表其原始的含义。	东盟四国行，见证中企海外重生"走出去"
根据文化背景： 使用古典诗歌或文学中的单词或短语，并将其带入现代语境中，它可以在不同情境中表达不同含义。	尽管这些对象只是4国数千家中企庞大队伍中的凤毛麟角，但不同以往的"孔雀东南飞"以及埋头精耕细作，证明"走出去"有助于企业浴火重生。

五、结论

基于这项研究，我们可以理解新词汇是社会和人类发展的一部分，它们不应被视为违反常态或破坏语言形式的工具。新词汇现象从一开始就是人类发展的一部分，并在需要时它将继续努力对语言进行修改。我们必须记住，新词汇是人类在不同领域及整个社会的一面镜子。现阶段，随着中国经济的迅速增长及其在世界上的影响力，普通话的扩张也随之而来，这不可避免地给世界和中国社会带来新的概念和思想，因此新词汇的作用仍然至关重要。我相信，在不久的将来，中国不仅会出口产品，还会"出口"词汇，这将对整个世界全球化发展起到有益的影响。

参考文献

1. Anderson, James M. (2006). Malmkjær, Kirsten, ed. The Linguistics encyclopedia (Ebook ed.). London: Routledge. p. 601. ISBN 0-203-43286-X.

2. Gryniuk, D (2015). On Institutionalization and De-Institutionalization of Late 1990s Neologisms. Cambridge Scholars Publishing. p. 150.

3. "Neologism" (draft revision). Oxford English Dictionary. December 2009.

4. Zuckermann, Ghil'ad (2003). Language contact and lexical enrichment in Israeli Hebrew (2nd ed.). New York, NY: Palgrave Macmillan. p. 3. ISBN 978-1403917232.

5. 陈建民：《中国语言和中国社会》，广东教育出版社。

6.《新潮青年爱说什么话》，《青年一代》。

7. 新华社：《网语进入生活》。

8.《什么时代说什么话：百年流行词快速浏览》，《中国青年》。

9. 周序林：《社会发展与新词汇的涌现》（人文社科版），2004 年。

The Influence of Chinese Neologisms on Social Development

Armando Zarate Alvarado / Perú

Ricardo Palma University, Professor

1. Introduction

Rapid social progress has a profound influence on the development of different sectors, so it is inevitable to continuously innovate existing technologies, ideas and concepts. Language is one facet of them since it is one of man's most important tools; as the new world enters an era of closely connected globalization, vocabulary and terminology are needed to describe the contemporary phenomena and concepts, and language actively participates and plays a vital role in social development. This unprecedented evolution has attracted the attention of many linguistic schools, linguists and language lovers.

Furthermore, one of the most important and surprising (to some people) changes is the growing use of Putonghua. The number of language schools teaching Chinese courses has been on the rise over the past decade. Along with this expansion of the teaching of the Chinese language, many new words and expressions have also been coined. They are spreading by more and more Putonghua learners all over the world, which influences not only China, but also many other countries in the world. As claimed by the Chinese sociolinguists (1999), "China's neologisms are in the vanguard reflecting social life and China's changes".

2. Definition of Neologism

The term "neologism" is first attested in English in 1772, borrowing a French word "néologisme" (1734). According to James Aderson (2006), "neologism" derived from Greek and contained two parts: "νέο- néo-", which means "new", and "λόγος logos", which means "speech". It may be defined as a relatively recent or isolated term, word, or phrase that may be in the process of entering common use, but has not yet been accepted into mainstream language. According to Gryniuk (2015), neologisms are often directly attributable to a specific person, publication, period, or event. In the process of language formation, neologisms are more mature than protologisms.

Different definitions have been given by scholars and linguists at home and abroad. Peter Newmark (2001), a famous British scholar, defined "neologism" in *A Textbook of Translation* as: "newly come lexical or existing units that acquire a new sense". According to the Oxford Advanced Learner's Dictionary (7th edition), a "neologism" is "a new word or expression or a new meaning of a word" (2009). The Longman Dictionary of Contemporary English defines a neologism as "a new word or expression, or a word with a new meaning" (2002). Wang Tiekun (1992) pointed out that "neologisms refer to new words that have been newly coined or borrowed from other languages, and they can be derived from dialect, ancient language, or industrial jargons of local languages, or they can refer to new meanings and new usages of existing words." Liu Shuxin (1990) defined that a word that is not only created, but also universally accepted and widely used, and has a place in the lexical system can be called a neologism.

Zheng Yanxia (2016) defined Chinese neologisms as newly coined Chinese words, or words borrowed from other languages, or existing Chinese words with new meanings, which can express new things, new concepts, new ideas, new experiences or new issues in Chinese society and culture. Moreover, Chinese neologisms should follow the rules of the language formation of Chinese and be widely accepted and used. Zheng Yanxia (2016) also classified neologisms into three categories based on their nature.

Classification based on sources

Zheng Yanxia explained that there are three sources of Chinese neologisms. First, some neologisms are coined to describe new ideas, phenomena, and concepts, such as "find-taxi app", "no Internet phobia", "multi-generation housing"; second, new meanings are evolved from existing phrases or words, and they possibly have no connections with the original meanings, such as: "Tuhao", "positive energy", "single-cell animals", etc.; and third, Chinese neologisms borrow from other languages, such as "alpha male", "MOOC".

Classification based on content

According to Zheng Yanxia, Chinese neologisms can also be classified based on their content. With the development of Chinese society, China has undergone tremendous changes in many fields such as politics, the economy, education, and entertainment. As a result, a large number of Chinese neologisms appear in these fields. Thus, Chinese neologisms are mainly classified as neologisms about politics and economy, such as: "institutional cage", "micro-blog diplomacy", "bridging loan"; neologisms about science and technology, such as: "cloud service", "micro world"; new words about social life, such as: "plastic marriage", "half sugar couple", "low-carbon tourism". Of course, in addition to the three aspects mentioned above, neologisms in Chinese reflect new things in different fields.

Classification based on the combination mode

According to the combination mode, Chinese neologisms can be divided into five types: affixes, compound words, converted words, abbreviations and overlapping words.

The reasons why neologisms come into being should also be considered. Based on the article of Zhou Xulin (2004) entitled *Social Development and Emergence of Neologisms*, we can find that social development has profoundly influenced the eme.........: of neologisms. On the one hand, drastic social changes can provide a social and ......rial basis; on the other hand, the infiltration and diffusion of Western culture ....ffers plenty of room for the emergence of neologisms. Since the reform and ......ng-up, China's social and economic development has been changing with each ......ing day. In the face of historical changes, under the dual promotion of econom.... and political reforms, various new ideas and new things have emerged at the hi......... moment, staggering changes have occurred in politics, economy, culture a.... .....er aspects, and new things in people's life are springing up like mushroo...... In order to express these new things and new phenomena more directly, a large .....ber of neologisms have been created and have spread widely at an amazing spee....... and have quickly entered all aspects of our daily life.

As explained by the principle of the creation of neologisms of Chen Yuan (1998), all social or other types of elements of change, such as changes in social structure, economic foundations, superstructure and folklore, as well as new scientific discoveries, inventions, technologies and breakthroughs, such as new concepts and new ideas, are inevitably influenced and reproduced by the system of language communication. These changes can be well observed by us through the medium of language. This is the main reason for creating neologisms.

Moreover, according to Zhou Xulin's research (2014), Chinese has a tradition of absorbing words from foreign languages, such as well-know» Pidgin in Shanghai. With the reform and opening-up, the country further opens ... .or wide, Western culture begins to infiltrate and the traditional culture is faci..... un.precedented challenges presented by foreign cultures. In the constant process of cu...... collision and the waning and waxing between Chinese and Western cultures, a lar.... ...mber of words with Western characteristics and reflecting Western lifestyle and c......

have gradually penetrated into people's daily language. Also, with the advent of the Internet age, the Internet has penetrated into every household, and its influence on language cannot be underestimated. In recent years, numerous netizen's neologisms have emerged. They are not only created on the Internet, but also gradually enter people's daily lives.

3. New Characteristics Reflected by Neologisms

New meanings of political words

Since the reform and opening-up, the political language with a distinctive style of class struggle gradually has left the stage of history and faded out of people's lives. In the meantime, people have become familiar with words that reflect the new style of the times, such as "reform and opening-up", "one country, two systems", "three represents", and "keep pace with the times". Some political words that had been marks of a brand of the times in a specific period are used in a humorous way to refer to certain things and behaviors in daily life, such as: "influencing the city appearance" (today means a person is not good-looking), "building the Great Wall" (today means playing mahjong).

Another noteworthy phenomenon in Chinese language is the form of address, which also changes with the times. For example, from the founding of the People's Republic of China to the period of the reform and opening-up, people and even husband and wife called each other "comrade in arms" or "comrades". In the 1980s, "master", "younger Wang" and "elder Zhao" began to be widely used. In the 21st century, "Mr.", "Miss", and "Mrs." have become popular again.

Emergence of economic neologism

Since the reform and opening-up, especially in the 1990s, China's political and economic reforms have made great progress, especially the booming development of the market economy. Some new things that people had never heard of have begun to come into people's lives. As a result, new words have been needed by people to express new ideas and new lives, such as "supermarket", "mortgage", "direct sales", "pyramid sale", "real property market", "rebate" and so on. As the number of speculators increases, terms related to stocks also become popular, such as "stock market", "limit up", "lock-in", "performance stock", "blue chips". The development of the market economy has also allowed more people to start businesses and obtain wealth. Some people are even captivated by money. The related neologisms include: "go to sea" (means starting a business), "wealthy grandpa" (means a rich man), "sister of wealth" (means a rich woman), "flaunt one's wealth". Of course, in such a market environment, more and more peasants come to cities to make a living. They are often called "migrant workers", "outsider sisters", "hourly workers", and "little aunt".

Food, entertainment and leisure words

With the continuous improvement of material life, people have begun to pursue the richness of their spiritual life, and a variety of leisure and entertainment activities have emerged. From "break dancing" and "playing mahjong" in the 1980s, "sauna" and "disco" in the 1990s, "surf on the Internet" and "electronic game" in the new century to "online game" and "online shopping" in recent years, words associated with "play" are on the increase. Words regarding "eating" also have new collocations and new meanings, such as "eat vinegar" (means being jealous), "eat loss" (means suffering a loss) or "eat tofu" (means suffer harassment); like "slaughter" in "slaughter chicken" and "slaughter duck" or in "slaughter people", the meaning of this word changes from "killing animals" to "cheating money".

Loan words

After China opened up to the outside world, young urban people with open minds have become more exposed to foreign lifestyles and behaviors. With the ideological and cultural exchanges, people drink "Cola", "Sprite", eat "hamburgers", "hot dogs", sing "Karaoke" and hold "parties". While borrowing foreign words directly, the Chinese also create new words. For example, taxi in English was originally called "taxi" in Chinese, and then new words appeared like "face taxi" (another name for taxi), "taxi brother" (means a taxi driver) or "beat a taxi" (means take a taxi). "Bar" comes from English, and then various "bars" emerged, such as "dining bar", "Internet bar", "book bar" and "oxygen bar". "Pao bar" (leisure in bars) is already a new fashion in people's lives.

Technical terms

Since entering the 21st century, with the advancement of science and technology, especially the rapid development and progress of biotechnology and network and information technology, people have become increasingly aware of the inseparability of science and technology and daily life. Technical terms, such as "clone" and "nano", have become household terms. Some technical terms have completely penetrated into people's daily lives, such as "multimedia", "VCD" and "DVD".

4. Neologisms and Society

In the past few decades, scholars have done a lot of research on the reasons why neologisms are coined. According to sociolinguists, there are inseparable connections between language and social development. These connections are complex and diverse.

Neologisms, a reflection of social development

Developments and changes in social, political, economic, cultural and technological aspects can influence vocabulary and generate neologisms, which are like mirrors reflecting the social development. First, the richness of vocabulary reflects the people's understanding of society. A nation with a language full of rich vocabulary items usually has a broader and more thorough understanding of the global development, and such a nation is more powerful than those lacking these aspects. The emergence of Chinese neologisms in recent years also reflects the rapid development of China's national strength from the point of view of one aspect. Second, the neologism itself is a cultural phenomenon showing the pace of social and cultural development and progress. When people in cities get rich first and begin to have the desire to help others, there is a "Hope Project". When people feel dissatisfied with a small group of people who use their powers in exchange for their interests, there is "anti-corruption and upholding integrity". Also, with social progress, people's self-awareness has awakened. From the "privacy right" and "portrait right" that respect our self-rights to the "new generation people" who long for freedom and show their individuality, in recent years, the term "postmodern" "two-dimensional" life has even appeared. Of course, if the social and cultural development lags behind the economic development, some negative and unhealthy thoughts and concepts will inevitably appear, which are mapped to language. There is the term "depression" used to describe spiritual emptiness, "playing thrilling" to talk about someone having nothing to do and "having a depressive disorder" if one is overly stressed.

Chinese language in the 21st century

The emergence of neologisms is undoubtedly a great enrichment of the expressive function of the Chinese language, which may be conducive to keeping Chinese alive and thus promoting its prosperity and development. A large number of neologisms brought by the accelerated spread of foreign cultures, while enriching Chinese vocabulary, also have many negative effects on the language itself. Should they be accepted in their entirety? Should negative and unhealthy words or even vulgar words emerging due to the imbalance of socioeconomic and cultural development be included in Chinese dictionaries? These are important issues that language planners must consider and face.

Based on these valuable studies, we can classify neologisms and their examples as follows:

Table 1   Classification of Neologisms

Classification	Example
By developmental process: Use ordinary words to express a new word, a new concept or idea.	"Going out" is a national strategy for Chinese companies seeking development. With the implementation and promotion of the Belt and Road Initiative, where to go? How to go? What's going on? How to go well, steadily and long-lasting? These are problems that must be systematically considered by both the political and business circles.
By simplification: Simplify long Chinese words into shorter ones, but still represent the original meaning.	Four ASEAN countries witness the rebirth of Chinese companies overseas by "going out"
By cultural background: Use words or phrases from classical poetry or literature and bring them into the modern context to express different meanings in different contexts.	Although only a few among thousands of Chinese companies in 4 countries, they are different from the previously "peacock flying southeast" and intensive cultivation and proof that "going out" can help companies be re-born.

5. Conclusion

Based on this research, we can understand that neologisms constitute part of social and human development. They should not be regarded as tools that violate norms or disrupt language forms. The phenomenon of neologisms has been part of human development since the beginning of language, and they will continue to change language when needed. We must bear in mind that neologisms are mirrors of humanity in different fields and in the entire society. At the current stage, with the rapid growth of China's economy and its influence in the world, Mandarin is becoming popular. This will inevitably bring new concepts and ideas to the world and to Chinese society, so neologisms play an important role. From my point of view, in the near future, China will not only export products, but it will also "export" words, which will have a beneficial influence on the globalization of the world.

"一带一路"背景下中国对老挝投资的文化适应性研究

拉沙米【老挝】

老挝国立大学助理教授

一、对外投资要特别重视文化适应问题

对外直接投资是投资人将资本直接注入国外的工业或商业企业，并以自己的名义和责任从事生产或经营。投资是在一定的社会文化环境中进行的。投资与社会文化环境是一对矛盾，它们相互依存、相互影响，并在一定条件下相互转化。投资对文化环境起到决定作用，同时又受文化环境的制约。因此在研究投资时，我们不能不研究社会文化环境与投资的文化适应性关系。社会文化环境对投资的影响表现在两个方面；一是促进投资，一是阻碍投资。究竟采取那种影响方式则要视投资对文化的反应方式而定。一般而言，投资若与文化相适应，那么文化就会促进投资实现效率最大化，反之则不然。具体来说，社会文化环境对投资的影响表现在：投资活动受制于一国的物质文化、投资活动受制于一国的制度文化、投资活动受制于一国的精神文化、投资活动受制于投资人的文化背景、投资活动受制于受益人的文化背景。

二、中国"一带一路"倡议与老挝投资的总体发展情况

从老挝计划与投资局发布的统计数据来看，中国已经成为老挝外来投资最大来源国，投资涉及的行业涵盖了木材加工、农业种植、城市基础建设、水电站建

设、铁路建设、银行服务业、旅游业等所有开放的行业。从 2008 年到 2018 年上半年，中国是老挝第一大投资来源国，占老挝经济特区投资的 23%，在老挝开展了一系列投资项目，覆盖从水电到农业、矿业以及服务部门的运作等各个方面。中国投资老挝 2214 个项目，投资金额达到 60.29 亿美元。其中，制造业 939 项，投资金额 25.38 亿美元；贸易业 523 项，投资金额 8.04 亿美元；服务业 752 项，投资金额 26.87 亿美元。

三、中国"一带一路"倡议与老挝投资的文化适应性评价

老挝自 1986 开始实行革新开放，逐步实现从计划经济向市场经济转变，20 世纪 90 年代加速转型，目前基本属于社会主义市场经济。基本保持 GDP 每年以超过 7% 速度的快速增长。为了促进经济发展，老挝注重吸收外资，促进对外开放和贸易。根据中华人民共和国驻老挝人民民主共和国大使馆经济商务参赞处的统计，以 2013 财年为例，老挝进出口贸易总额 47.12 亿美元，同比增长 10.53%，其中进口 28.14 亿美元，同比增长 3.45%，出口 18.98 亿美元，同比增长 18.49%，对外出口增长明显，另外吸引外资 17 亿美元。

老挝和中国多年来一直坚持在不同发展领域进行合作，中国主要在老挝进行商业援助和项目投资。首先，从老挝自身经济发展现状来看，老挝由于历史上长期遭受殖民主义剥削和封建君主专制的压迫，经济发展基础差，底子薄。按照世界银行的划分，老挝属于世界上最不发达的国家之一，2017 年 GDP 总量 168.53 亿美元，不到中国的 1/800，在东盟十国中基本属于下游水平。

四.中国"一带一路"倡议与老挝投资的文化冲突案例

老挝某大型水电站项目，是老挝国家政府使用中国政府出口信贷与某中资承包商在 2000 年签订的总承包建设合同，由中资承包商带资承建，其中老方配套资金占投资总额的 10%。该水电站装机 1200 千瓦，总投资 987 万美元，于 2001 年 3 月开工建设，2003 年 3 月全部完工。该水电站项目主要工程有：拦水大坝，石砌滚水坝以及混凝土涵洞、抽水系统、两台发电机组、两台变压设备等。中资承包商在老挝的项目开展经历了艰难的探索过程，尤其是初期，因为对当地市场不够熟悉，东道国的文化观念、风俗习惯、思维方式、生活方式等与国内差异很大，跨文化冲突频繁出现，主要表现在两个层面：一是国际工程项目内部层面。项目

初期，中方外派人员与老挝当地沟通较少，工作与生活相对闭塞。思想上，由于远离祖国和亲人，由刚到一个新的国家时的新鲜、好奇逐渐产生失落、烦恼、焦虑的情绪，并会对自身价值观念、未来发展前景等产生质疑；工作中，由于对当地人思维习惯、工作方式缺乏了解，常常事倍功半，甚至适得其反；生活上，每天不仅要面对风俗人情、生活方式不同的压力，还要面对语言沟通的障碍。为提高本土化经营运作能力，加强与东道国的联合，项目组内部聘用很多当地人员，这些人员由于各自所处的文化环境不同，在项目组内部造成文化冲突。此外，项目本身的一次性和项目组织的临时性，以及项目建设环境的特殊性，决定了项目组是一种以项目为中心，以承包任务为目标的短期性组织，其内部在组织结构与沟通渠道上，存在矛盾和冲突。国际工程项目中领导层的权利是一种临时性的授权，是按照项目任务和专业分工，以内部承包合同或聘任合同的形式所授予的权力。项目组成员之间彼此了解不多，信任程度低，人际关系松散。授权的短期性和临时性使得领导层的权威和对项目成员约束力较弱，而项目组在初期一般采取高度集中的领导方式，一定程度上压制员工的积极性与创造性，造成员工的不满和抵触情绪。二是国际工程项目外部层面。项目组来到老挝后，受到老挝外在文化环境的影响，如当地分包商、材料供应商，当地的宗教信仰、法律法规、政治团体以及政府机构等。当时的老挝官员办事效率较低，特别是在涉及项目手续审批时表现得尤为突出，使中资承包商深感头痛，有时不得不请中国驻老挝大使馆及经商处出面催促才能解决。此外，老方部分项目配套资金不能及时到位，也在一定程度上影响了工程进度。从中老边境到万象的 830 余公里道路沿线，设有 10 多处种类繁多的收费站，给过往的中资承包商带来了不必要的负担。老挝政府当时对道路运输车辆超重标准的不合理定位，也给中资承包工程企业车辆出行带来不便。该国虽不发达，但该国法律对企业员工工作、生活条件要求很高。工程初期各方面条件比较艰苦，职工四人一间，住在简易板房里。当地劳工部门来检查，要求每个房间住宿不得超过三人，否则不许施工。另外，当地法律非常注重保护当地职工权益，规定外国企业必须招聘 30% 以上的本地员工，企业不得随便辞退工人，辞退工人要多付 2—3 个月工资。所以，聘用当地工人是件棘手的事，稍有不慎便会陷入法律纠纷。项目组在项目管理过程中所面临的跨文化冲突，可能是由环境因素造成的，也可能与个体认知有关。

1. 沟通方式和语言导致的跨文化冲突

中方人员在老挝生活会遭遇语言沟通障碍。由于语言、文字的深层内涵及其表达方式上的不同，造成沟通上的误会，因而易产生文化冲突。沟通方式，无论是语言的还是非语言的，都可以将不同文化的人群分开。语言是人类相互沟通的主要手段，并体现一个社会的文化，表达出某种文化的思维模式。因此，掌握语言是了解它所体现的文化的关键。另外，由于项目组人员来自不同文化背景，人们对同一事物的描述和表达有着不同的方式。人们在通过翻译对同一事物进行交流时，往往只是语言符号的一一对应，而对包含在事物深层的各国、各民族、各地区在其长期生产实践中所形成的风俗习惯，则无法用语言准确表达，这往往成为文化冲突的导火线。

2. 固有观念导致的跨文化冲突

人们在对本国文化和东道国异文化进行评价时，常使用一些先入为主的"定型观念"。定型观念来自个体有限的经验，并借由间接获取的信息而形成。由于对老挝文化不了解，中方员工常无意识地使用自己熟悉的文化标准去衡量和评判老挝文化中人们的行为，认为自己的文化价值体系较有优越而产生种族优越感，忽视东道国文化的存在及其在工程项目进程中的影响，较易形成以自我为中心的管理，经常遭到项目组内老挝当地员工的抵制，引发各种冲突，成为项目顺利进行的绊脚石。

五．结论与启示

国际工程项目管理中的文化冲突，主要表现在项目内部冲突和外部冲突两方面，其产生的主要原因有沟通方式、语言障碍、风俗习惯和文化定型观念，根本原因是文化差异。国际工程项目应坚持文化宽容原则，利用文化差异，兼顾共性与个性，进行文化整合，取长补短，实现人力资源本土化，并积极开展跨文化培训，来解决项目管理中的文化冲突，保证工程项目顺利完成。要想把本土人才培养成具备全球思维的国际人才，除了前期的人才测评与甄选，还需多给员工一些激励和动力，多提供一些跨国学习与实践的机会。一部分中资企业认为，东道国语言和文化是海外经营区位选择中最次要的因素，这非常令人担忧。有关专业机构的研究表明，在培养最紧缺的全球领导力人才时，可借鉴以下一些举措，如短期或长期境外派驻、跨文化管理专项培训、引入教练 / 导师制、属地化语言培训、体验式/行动学习、短期境外商务旅行、国际跨部门团队合作等。

除了外派的本土人才外，当地员工、中国的海外留学人员，也是培养跨文化国际人才的重要来源。开展全球化经营的中资企业，必须抛弃一个陈旧的观念："我只是一个中国企业"。要培养具有全球化思维和跨文化能力的优秀国际人才，企业要把自己提升至"我是世界企业"的高度，树立全球公民的社会责任，而不是花大价钱去雇佣管理者。

A Study on the Cultural Adaptation of China's Investments in Laos under the Belt and Road Initiative

Vongsengchanh Latsamy / Laos

National University of Laos, Assistant Professor

1. Foreign Investments Should Pay Special Attention to Cultural Adaptation

Outbound direct investment means that investors directly put capital into foreign industrial or commercial enterprises and engage in production or management under their own names and responsibility. Investments are made in a certain social and cultural environment. Investments and the social and cultural environment are contradictory, interdependent and mutually influenced, and they can be changed under certain conditions. Investments play a decisive role in, while being constrained by the cultural environment. Therefore, when studying investments, we must also study the relationship between the social and cultural environment and the cultural adaptation of investments. The influence of the social and cultural environment on the investments is manifested in two aspects: One is to promote investments and the other is to hinder them. The way influence occurs depends on how the investments adapt to culture. Generally speaking, if investments can adapt themselves to the culture, then culture will promote investments to maximize its efficiency, and vice versa. To be specific, the influence of social and cultural environment on investments is reflected in: investment activities are subject to the material culture, institutional culture and spiritual culture of the host country, and they are also subject to the cultural background of investor and beneficiaries.

2. The Overall Development of China's Investments in Laos under the Belt and Road Initiative

According to statistics released by the Lao Ministry of Planning and Investment, China became the largest source country of foreign investments in Laos. Industries involved in the investments include wood processing, agricultural planting, the construction of urban infrastructures, hydropower stations and railways, banking services, tourism and other open industries. From 2008 to the first half of 2018, China was the largest source of investment in Laos, accounting for 23% of the investments in special economic zones, and launched a series of investment projects in Laos, covering operations from hydropower to agriculture, mining and service sectors. China invested in 2,214 projects in Laos with a total amount of investments of 6.029 billion US dollars. Among them, there were 939 manufacturing projects with a total amount of investments of 2.538 billion US dollars, 523 trade projects with a total amount of investments of 0.804 billion US dollars, and 752 service projects with a total amount of investments of 2.687 billion US dollars.

3. Evaluation of the Cultural Adaptation of China's Investments in Laos under the Belt and Road Initiative

Laos began to introduce the reform and opening-up in 1986 and gradually realized the transition from a planned economy to a market economy. The transformation accelerated in the 1990s and currently basically belongs to a socialist market economy. At present, it maintains the rapid growth of the GDP at an annual rate of more than 7%. In order to promote economic development, Laos attaches importance to attracting foreign investments and promoting the opening-up and trade. According to statistics of the Economic and Commercial Counsellor's Office of the Embassy of the People's Republic of China in the Lao People's Democratic Republic, taking the fiscal year 2013 as an example, Laos's total import and export trade was 4.712 billion US dollars, seeing a year-on-year increase of 10.53%, of which imports were 2.814 billion US dollars, with a year-on-year increase of 3.45%, and exports were 1.898 billion US dollars, with a year-on-year increase of 18.49%. Exports increased significantly. Moreover, foreign investments of a total of 1.7 billion US dollars were attracted.

Laos and China continued their cooperation in different development fields for many years. China mainly provided business assistance and project investments in Laos. First, from the perspective of Laos' economic development, the country has suffered from a long history of colonial exploitation and the oppression of a feudal monarchy. It has a weak foundation for economic development. According to the World Bank's classification, Laos is one of the least developed countries in the world, with a total GDP of 16.853 billion US dollars in 2017, less than 1/800th of China's. It is basically at a downstream level among the ten ASEAN countries.

4. A Case Study of the Cultural Conflicts in China's Investments in Laos under the Belt and Road Initiative

For a large hydropower project in Laos, a general construction contract was signed by the Lao government with a Chinese contractor in 2000 using export credits of the Chinese government. The Chinese contractor was responsible for construction with funding, and the fund provided by the Lao side only accounted for 10% of the total amount of investment. The hydropower station, with an installed capacity of 1,200 kilowatts, had a total amount of investment of 9.87 million US dollars. Construction commenced in March 2001 and was completed in March 2003. The main works of this hydropower station project included: a water dam, an overflow rockfill dam and concrete culverts, a pumping system, two generating units, two transformers, etc. Manifestations and causes of cross-cultural conflicts: the Chinese contractor's project development in Laos went through a difficult process of exploration, especially at the initial stage, because it was not familiar with the local market and the host country's culture, customs, ways of thinking and lifestyle were quite different from those in China. Cross-cultural conflicts frequently occurred, mainly on two levels: first of all, the internal level of the international project. At the beginning of the project, Chinese expatriate employees had virtually no communication with Lao locals and their work and life were relatively isolated. In mind, because of being far away from the motherland and their loved ones, they changed from a kind of freshness and curiosity when they first arrived in the new country to become gradually lost, annoyed and anxious, and then they questioned their own values and future developmental prospects. At work, due to a lack of understanding of local ways of thinking, habits and work styles, they often got half the result with twice the effort, or even became counterproductive. In daily life, they not only faced the pressure of different customs and lifestyle every day, but also barriers to communication through language. In order to enhance localized operations and strengthen cooperation with the host country, the project team employed many local workers, who caused cultural conflicts within the project team due to different cultural environments. Moreover, owing to the one-off nature of the project and the temporary nature of the project organization, as well as the particularity of the environment of the construction of the project, the project team was inevitably a short-term organization centered on the project and targeted at contracting tasks. There were contradictions and conflicts in the internal structure and channels of communication. The powers of the leadership in international projects were temporarily authorized in the form of internal contracts or employment contracts according to the project tasks and professional division of labor. The project team members did not know much about each other, with a low degree of trust and loose interpersonal relations. The short-term and temporary nature of the authorization resulted in weak authority on the part of the leaders and a binding force on project members. The project team generally adopted a highly centralized approach to leadership in the early stage, which suppressed the enthusiasm and creativity of employees to a certain extent and led to their dissatisfaction and resistance. Second, the external level of the international project. After the project team came to Laos, it was influenced by the external cultural environment of Laos, such as local subcontractors, material suppliers, local religious belief, laws and regulations, political groups and government agencies; Lao officials were less efficient at that time, particularly involving the approval of project formalities. The Chinese contractor found this painful and sometimes they could do nothing but turn to the embassy and the business office for help. Further, the progress of the project was also influenced by the fact that the fund from the Lao side could not be allocated in a timely manner. There were more than 10 toll stations of various types along the 830-kilometer road from the border between China and Laos to Vientiane that placed an unnecessary burden on the Chinese contractor. The Lao government's unreasonable standard for overweight road transportation vehicles at that time also caused inconvenience for the transportation by the Chinese contractor. Although the country was underdeveloped, its laws had demanding requirements for the working and living conditions of workers. At the beginning of the project, the working conditions were very unfavorable with four workers living in one room in a prefab house. The local labor department came to inspect, and requested that no more than three workers should live in one room, otherwise construction was not allowed. Also, local laws attached great importance to protecting the rights and interests of employees by stipulating that foreign companies were to recruit more than 30% of their employees from local workers, and that companies must not arbitrarily dismiss workers, and if so, they should pay an additional 2-3 months' wages. Therefore, hiring local workers was a tricky task and legal disputes were possible traps. The cross-cultural conflicts faced by the project team in the project management process could be caused by environmental factors or linked to individual cognition. Of the following causes of cross-cultural conflict, the first two were related to the environment, and the third was related to individuals.

4.1. Cross-cultural conflicts caused by the style and language of communication

The Chinese might encounter barriers to communication due to language when living in Laos. The differences in the deep connotations of languages and words and their expressions lead to misunderstandings in communication and cultural conflicts. Methods of communication, whether verbal or non-verbal, can separate people of different cultures. Language, one of the main ways for humans to communicate with each other, reflects the culture of a society and expresses a certain manner of cultural thinking. Therefore, knowing the language is a key to understanding the culture it embodies. Also, because project team members come from different cultural backgrounds, they have different ways to describe and express the same thing. When people communicate the same thing through translation, this is only a one-to-one correspondence of language symbols. However, customs and habits formed in the long-term practices of production of countries, peoples and local regions that are deeply rooted in things cannot be expressed accurately through language. This often becomes the triggering factor for cultural conflicts.

4.2. Cross-cultural conflicts caused by religious belief and customs

Religious belief, a truly enduring gene in culture, is something that is deeply rooted in the culture and condenses the history and culture of a nation. Different religions have different preferences and taboos, which affect the way people perceive things, their code of conduct and their values. Different ideas of people from different countries often confuse project team managers and lead to cultural conflicts in management. In Laos, the locals worship within Theravada Buddhism. Compared with Mahayana Buddhism introduced into China, they have their own unique customs and habits, which are manifested in their unique use of traditions, preferences and taboos. Failure to understand those customs can lead to a failure of management.

4.3. Cross-cultural conflicts caused by the concept of state ownership

People often have preconceived "stereotypes" when evaluating the cultures of their own country and the host country. Stereotypes, coming from the limited experience of individuals, are formed from information that has been obtained indirectly. Due to their lack of understanding of Lao culture, Chinese employees often unconsciously use their familiar cultural standards to measure and judge the behavior of people in the Lao culture. They see their culture and value system as superior and have a sense of racial superiority. While ignoring the culture of the host country and its influence in the process of the construction of the project, they are prone to forming a self-centered type of management that local Lao employees often resist within the project team, it triggers conflicts and becomes a stumbling block to the smooth progress of the projects.

5. Conclusions and Implications

Cultural conflicts in the management of international projects are reflected in internal and external conflicts. The main reasons include communication methods, language barriers, customs, habits and cultural stereotypes, and the root cause is cultural differences. International projects should adhere to the principle of cultural tolerance, make use of cultural differences, take into account commonality and individuality, realize cultural integration, learn from each other's strengths, localize human resources, and actively carry out cross-cultural training to resolve cultural conflicts in project management and ensure the smooth progress of the construction of the project. In order to develop local talents into international talents with a global insight, in addition to the preliminary talent assessment and screening, more incentives and motivation should be provided to employees, such as more opportunities for transnational learning and practice. Some Chinese enterprises think that the host country's language and culture are the least important factors in choosing an overseas business location, and this thought can be worrying. Studies of relevant professional institutions have shown that when cultivating the urgently-needed global leadership talents, the following measures can be used for reference, such as short-term or long-term overseas dispatchment, special training of cross-cultural management, introduction of the coach/mentor system, localized language training, experiential/action learning, short-term overseas business travel, international cross-departmental teamwork, etc.

In addition to expatriating local talents, local employees and Chinese students studying abroad are also important sources of cross-cultural international talents. Chinese enterprises that carry out global operations must abandon an old idea: "We are nothing but a Chinese enterprise." To cultivate excellent international talents with a global insight and cross-cultural communication abilities, enterprises must elevate themselves to the height that "we are a global enterprise" and assume their social responsibility as global citizens, rather than spending large amounts of money on hiring managers.

东南亚华人与"文化"[1]

新沼雅代【日本】
横滨国立大学副教授

一、前言

目前"多元文化主义 / 社会"、"多元语言主义 / 社会",这些词很流行。日本学者西山长夫在 1999 指出:因为文化包括语言,所以在理论上"多元文化主义 / 社会"应该包括"多元语言主义 / 社会"。但是,"文化"和"语言"之间有一些语意上的区别,"语言"的前提是被"使用"的,"文化"的对象很模糊,并没有被"使用"(西山)。学术界对英语区域(加拿大、澳大利亚、美国)、欧洲(欧盟诸国,尤其是法国)的多元文化的研究很多。加拿大是双语言多种文化,澳大利亚是单语言多种文化,法国是多语言单一文化。国家可以决定国家的语言(比如,公用语言),还可以决定国家的文化?

东南亚的很多国家,在形成民族国家的过程中,试图融合人们,并在传统文化的基础上形成民族文化(西山)。已经是多元民族和多元文化国家,是否以哪一个种族的传统文化为基础形成民族文化呢? "文化"指的究竟是什么?[2]

1　本文是在"陈六使研究所系列专题讲座"(15)Tan Lark Sye Institute Lecture Series No 15,(New Era University College,2018 年 3 月)、"御茶水女子大学中国文学会例会"(2018 年 7 月)上发表的报告,经笔者修改,此处作为论文为首次发表,内容有所增删,特此说明。

2　为了容易掌握东南亚华人的情况,在本文把东南亚国家用"东南亚"做为整体地推进论证,但是实际上,东南亚华人的情况因东南亚的各个国家(新加坡、马来西亚、印度尼西亚、越南、柬埔寨、缅甸、老挝、泰国、菲律宾、文莱、东帝汶)而异。在东亚的各个国家情况也类似。

二、文化是什么?

在日文、中文和英文中,"文化"的词汇怎样使用呢? 从下面的例子可以看出,无论哪种语言"文化",都用于代表一个国家或民族的个别风俗,也用于委婉地表示具有高品格、高教育水平或广泛的知识等。

(1) これは日本の文化だ。(这是日本的文化。)

(2) 彼は文化的な人だ。(他是很有文化素养的人。)

(3) 彼は文化人だ。(他是个文化人。)

(4) 怎样让中国的文化输出到全世界。

(5) 人们都会说他很有文化。

(6) 明星文化水平高吗?

(7) Tips for understanding American Culture.

(8) He is a cultured person.   (= well educated, sophisticated)

(9) He has no culture. (culture   ↔   barbarian)

Terry Eagleton 对"文化"做如下的定义:第一,文化是构成特定群体生活方式的价值观、习俗、宗教的复合体。第二,文化是帮助人们在特定环境下探索适当的行为模式的默认同意或实际指导方针。总之,文化不只是反映或代表社会实践,而是建立其他社会实践。Eagleton 还指出:自 20 世纪 60 年代以来,"文化"的轴心已经指向了与 Culture(指普遍的文化)相反的 culture(指特定的文化)。"文化"从超越一种特殊的个人身份,比如,根据民族、性别、种族、地区等的认同(identity),偏向于肯定这些特殊个人身份(Eagleton 2000 : 91)。他的观点可以如下图所示:

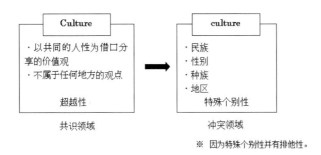

图 1   Culture 与 culture

(本图参照 Eagleton 2000,91—92)

图 1 显示以下内容。大写 C 的 Culture 具有以共同人性为借口的价值观，并且具有不属于任何地方的观点（所谓上帝的眼睛）。从这个角度来看，Culture 具有"超越性"并且是"共识"的领域。另一方面，小写 c 的 culture 具有民族性、性别性、种族性、地区性的特殊个别的概念。有时候 culture 的差异会导致族群之间的矛盾和冲突。由于 culture 具有个别性，因此它也具有排他性。从此，可以说 culture 是一个"冲突"的领域。

三、东南亚的殖民地

东南亚的许多国家曾经经历过欧洲和美国的殖民（泰国以外）。

英国：缅甸，马来西亚，新加坡，文莱；

法国：越南，柬埔寨，老挝；

荷兰：印尼；

葡萄牙：东帝汶；

西班牙，美国：菲律宾。

从 8 世纪左右开始，东南亚海上贸易很发达。中国、印度、阿拉伯的商人到南洋来往频繁。可以说，当时的东南亚已经成为多元种族、多元文化社会。多元民族和多元文化国家，是否以哪一个种族的传统文化为基础形成民族文化呢？一般来说，在中心而且占多数的种族代表国家的种族。日本学者山本信人在 1997 指出[1]：理想无论怎么样，民族国家作为一个民族国家，由中心和周边、多数和少数的等级秩序来维持下去（山本）。

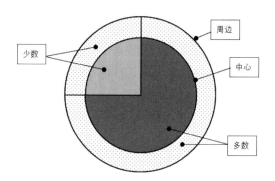

图 2　中心、周边、多数、少数

1　本文引用日本学者的研究说明的部分比较多，这些著作没有中文版。本文笔者认为，通过本文里的翻译引用，把日本的东南亚华人研究介绍给中文使用地区的学者，也具有重要的意义。

但是，殖民地的人口比率来说。殖民者虽然是中心，但不是多数。当时的东南亚，各个地区是由几个社群而构成的。殖民者采用社会地位的等级制度来控制社会。殖民地社群之间的关系可概括为如下图：

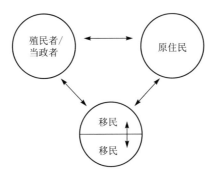

图 3　殖民地社群之间的关系

日本学者清水昭俊在 1998 指出，欧洲列强的殖民地有两种：第一是殖民型（比如，澳大利亚、亚马逊流域），入侵的白人完全排除本地原住民，不能对原住民进行榨取。第二是榨取型，入侵的白人不完全排除本地原住民，能对原住民进行榨取（除了澳大利亚、亚马逊流域外，殖民地是殖民型和榨取型的混合）（清水）。榨取型的殖民地，在当地人的社会状况下，殖民方可以用于他们的政治和经济利益的条件保存下去。这个政策让本地的各民族分裂对抗，殖民政府容易支配本地人。这可以说，间接统治本地人也可以说"温存和活用"（清水）。16 世纪以后，葡萄牙、荷兰、英国等国在南洋形成了活动据点和殖民地。尤其是英国，采用的殖民形式是上述的榨取型。结果，英国的殖民政策唤醒了居民的种族意识和文化多样性意识（西川）。

四、欧洲列强关注南洋华人

16 世纪以后，葡萄牙、荷兰、英国等国在南洋形成了活动据点和殖民地。19 世纪末开始，欧洲列强在东南亚开始殖民地化。要注意的是，开始殖民地化之前在东南亚的欧洲列强的人们也是移民。山本信人在 1997 还指出：欧洲人以提高政治权力和控制效率，需要建立自己的社会模式。在这个新的社会模式里，重现了殖民地社会的居民，并有自己的社会表现。

梅斯蒂索他人被强迫分为东洋外国人或原住民。根据山本 1997 关于东洋外国人的类别，经过如上而成。原则上，不承认存在于类别之间的"种族"。"复合社会"的本质是经济。社会按照种族被"分裂",而由于制定没有社会共同意识的逻辑,来进行"种族"是已经确定的一种事实化。

殖民统治者忽略了居民的种族、宗教等多样性,"想象"了这些种类。我们应该要注意的是"东洋外国人"。"东洋外国人"是以中国人为基础而形成的种类。以"东洋"为假设与"西洋"的欧洲人不同,以"外国人"为假设与"原住民"不同的人。此外,那时欧洲人已经注意到,拥有广泛而强大的网络,擅长买卖的特殊人们。欧洲人重新确认了东洋外国人(=当时在东南亚的华人),他们也开始认识到自己是东洋的外国人(山本)。本文笔者认为,"东洋外国人"是现今东南亚华人心态的基础。

当时的东南亚也可以说是一种很特殊的地方。山本还指出:清朝原来禁止国民出国,海外华人的存在没有被接受,并被视为叛民。1860 年代开始,中国开始关注东南亚华人社区作为中国现代化的资金和技术来源。当时,南洋并不仅仅指南中国海,而是一个人、物、钱和信息往来的空间。这种空间是开放的,灵活的,并且不受区域性限制,山本 1997 称之领域为"Frontier"。这个"南洋"是一个通常与"中国"形成鲜明对比的空间。这种"南洋"的空间感,似乎在 19 世纪末,欧洲列强和中国发现南洋华人的存在,东南亚的华人自己也开始自我调节"南洋华人"的时候形成的(山本)。

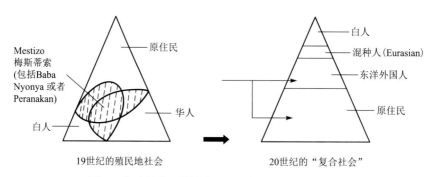

图 4 "复合社会"的模式(本图参照山本 1997,274)

五、南洋华人的空间感和民族主义对的形成

19 世纪末开始,南洋华人团结感的现象逐渐形成,表现在 1911 年辛亥革命前后和 1937 年抗日战争时期。那时候,有些南洋华人认识到殖民地的现实,拥有殖民地人民的个人身份,更倾向于当地的民族主义。在南洋华人中,占优势的

群体主要是对其所属东南亚华人社区感兴趣的人群（山本）。

举个新加坡的例子。新加坡李显龙总理在 2017 年新加坡华族文化中心的开幕式时，提到新加坡的华族国民要拥有"新加坡华人"的文化：

> 新加坡华族文化既有中华传统文化的面向，也有新加坡多元文化的特色。他因此认为华族文化中心所发展的本土华族文化，必须是从"以新加坡人为本位"的定位出发。（略）

> 新加坡华人在对自己的华族文化感到骄傲的同时，越来越清楚意识到，自己的华族文化有别于马来西亚华人，印度尼西亚华人的华族文化，也和中国及中国香港或中国台湾的华族文化有所不同。（略）

"历经建国半世纪新加坡华人拥有独特面貌文化身份"

《联合早报》，2017 年 5 月 20 日

笔者认为一个国家的总理亲自向人民呼吁建立自己的"文化"，是一个多元民族国家所特有的行为。实现经济发展之后，近年来新加坡已转向关注国内的文化和艺术方面。然而，本文笔者认为，从结果来说，让新加坡华人感到新加坡华人的传统文化和艺术大部分都来自中国，却又给大家"寻找独特文化的压力"，并敦促年轻人喜欢欧美文化的趋向。

文化问题与身份认同有很强的关系。被殖民过的国家，国民可能会向殖民的宗主国寻求身份认同。为了捕捉整个东南亚华人的心态，不限于新加坡，不仅要考虑民族根源的中国的影响，还要考虑殖民时的宗主国的影响。

从 20 世纪中叶开始，东南亚国家已经独立于殖民地。政府试图将人民团结在一个传统文化中，但在一个多元民族社会中，问题在于哪个民族文化处于中心位置。从处于边缘地位的民族群体来说，独立于殖民地却是让他们重新关注自己的文化和身份认同的一个契机。

此外，现在东南亚的许多国家还是多元民族社会，除了官方语言问题以外，母语也重要，这主要与身份认同有关。说到东南亚华人的文化，情况非常复杂，也有很多要考虑的因素。笔者认为，把南亚华人的这个复杂情况可以表达如下图。

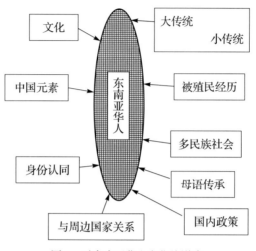

图 5　对东南亚华人文化的影响

对于有关南洋华人的个人身份的趋向性问题，山本 1997 指出：南洋华人的空间感和个人身份，有时甚至会超越华人社区、殖民地、南洋和殖民地宗主国（山本）。本文笔者认为，南洋华人的个人身份取向性，可以分为：

1. 中国取向性；

2. 本地取向性；

3. 华人社区取向性；

4. 前殖民地宗主国取向性。

身份认同（identity）只有在与其他人有关系时才建立。因此，身份认同受到对其他人的认同的变化，以及其他人自身的变化的影响。另外，个人身份是可变的和超越的。南洋华人会受到他们所居住的社会，以及那里的历史和法律地位的影响。南洋华人的存在，随着时代、社会、环境的变化而会变得明显、消失和复活。总之，在这个十分复杂的情况下，南洋华人的身份认同自然是多样的。山本 1997还指出："中国元素（Chineseness）"是被文化的"纽带"绑住的（山本）。在年轻一代的马来西亚华人中，母语已转为英语（洪丽芬），印尼华裔学生的母语已转为印尼语（李明欢・黄猷）。 在马来西亚和印度尼西亚等多元文化和多元民族社会中，许多世代的母语渐渐地变为在他们国家里广泛使用的语言。在语言方面，虽然民族之间正在推进"融合"，但当需要按族群划分时，例如"华人""印尼人"等，主要以那个人在平时生活中实行的"文化"为分类的标准。如果他们采用中国式的文化习俗过着生活，大家会判断他们拥有中国元素，并将他们称为"华人"。

六、总结

图6的内容可将南洋华人的文化形成概括如下：

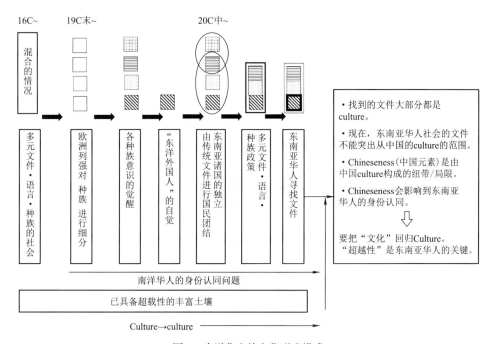

图6　南洋华人的文化形成模式

8世纪开始从各地来南洋的移民，形成了多元种族共存的社会。16世纪开始白人也进入这个社群。自19世纪末，随着欧洲列强的殖民地化，进行"种族"细分以及等级化，促使各种族意识的觉醒。居住在南洋的华人，也开始认识到他们是"东洋外国人（东南亚华人）"。20世纪中叶以后，东南亚很多国家独立了，各个政府主要从传统文化所构成的种族社群团结人民。发表者认为传统是文化的具体表现，文化和认同意识（identity）有互相影响。20世纪60年代开始，"文化"却从大写C的Culture变成小写C的culture。小写c的culture指的是特殊性的、个别性的东西。这是东南亚各个国家独立时期开始形成的。

　　南洋本来就是个多样种族的地方，南洋华人拥有超越性、可变性的认同意识，也就顺理成章了。南洋既已拥有创造超越性认同的土壤，而身份认同是可变的，因此，可变性不算南洋的特点。对东南亚华人的认同有深刻影响的是Chineseness（中国元素）。Chineseness是中国跟海外华人之间的"文化"纽带。另一方面，

Chineseness 是被中国的 culture 所局限。本文笔者认为"超越性"是未来东南亚华
人的关键词。

参考文献

西山長夫:「多文化主義・多言語主義をアジアから問う」、『言語文化研究』、立命館
　　大学国際言語文化研究所 1999 年 11 卷 3 号。

清水昭俊:『周辺民族の現在』、世界思想社 1998 年版。

山本信人:「国民国家の相対化へ向けて — 東南アジア華人の可変性と越境性」、『地
　　域史とは何か』、山川出版社 1997 年版。

テリー・イーグルトン 2006、大橋洋一訳『文化とは何か』、松柏社（Eagleton2000,
　　The Idea of Culture）。

REDFIELD, R.1956、*"Peasant Society and Culture: an anthropological approach to
　　civilization"*, University of Chicago Press.

《四大种族共建新加坡 50 年辉煌》，新加坡宗鄉会馆联合总会《源》，2016 年第 1 期。

洪丽芬:《试析马来西亚华人母语的转移现象》,《华侨华人历史研究》,2008 年 第 1 期。

李明欢、黄猷:《东南亚华人族群文化与华文教育》,《海外华文教育》,2008 年第 1 期。

"历经建国半世纪 新加坡华人拥有独特面貌文化身份",《联合早报》，2017 年 5 月 20
　　日，https://www.zaobao.com.sg/znews/singapore/story20170520-762042

Southeast Asian Chinese and "Culture"[1]

Niinuma Masayo / Japan

Yokohama National University, Associate Professor

1. Introduction

Today, "multiculturalism/society" and "multilingualism/society" are very popular words. Japanese scholar Nishikawa Nagao pointed out in 1999 that in theory "multiculturalism/society" should include "multilingualism/society" since culture includes language. However, semantic differences exist between "culture" and "language". The premise of "language" is "used", and the object of "culture" is vague and not "used" . There are a lot of studies on the multiculturalism of English-speaking regions (Canada, Australia, the USA) and Europe (EU countries, especially France). Canada is bilingual and multicultural, Australia is monolingual and multicultural, and France is multilingual and has a single culture. Can countries determine not only their languages (for example, the common language), but also their culture?

---

1 This article is a report published on Tan Lark Sye Institute Lecture Series No. 15, (New Era University College, March 2018) and the Routine Conference of Ochanomizu University on Chinese Literature (July 2018), and it was revised by the author. This is the first publication with some additions and deletions of the contents.

Many countries in Southeast Asia, in the process of forming a nation state, attempt to integrate people and shape a national culture on the basis of traditional culture (Nishikawa, 1999:12). But if it is a multi-ethnic and multi-cultural country, which ethnic culture is chosen as a base to shape the traditional culture on ? What exactly does "culture" mean?[1]

2. What is culture?

How is the word "culture" used in Japanese, Chinese and English? As indicated from the examples below, in no matter what language, "culture" is used to represent the individual custom of a country or nation, or euphemistically indicate noble character, good education or extensive knowledge.

(1) これは日本の文化だ。(This is the culture of Japan.)

(2) 彼は文化的な人だ。(He is a cultured person.)

(3) 彼は文化人だ。(He is an intellectual.)

(4) 怎样让中国的文化输出到全世界。(How can the Chinese culture be exported to the world?)

(5) 人们都会说他很有文化。(People say that he is cultured.)

(6) 明星文化水平高吗？ (Are the celebrities well cultured?)

(7) Tips for understanding American Culture.

(8) He is a cultured person. (= well educated, sophisticated)

(9) He has no culture. (culture ↔ barbarian)

Terry Eagleton (2000) gave the following definition of "culture": First, culture is the complex of values, customs, beliefs and practices which constitute the way of life of a specific group. Second, culture is the implicit knowledge of the world by which people negotiate appropriate ways of acting in specific contexts. In short,

---

1 In order to easily know the situation of Chinese in Southeast Asia, this article will bundle all of the countries of the area into the term "Southeast Asia" for demonstration. However, in fact, the situations of Chinese in different Southeast Asian countries are different (Singapore, Malaysia, Indonesia, Vietnam, Myanmar, Laos, Thailand, Philippines, Brunei, Timor-Leste). The situations in East Asian countries are also obvious.

culture does not merely reflect or represent social practices, but establishes other social practices. Eagleton (2000) also indicated that since the 1960s, the axis of "culture" has pointed to culture (specific culture) as opposed to Culture (universal culture). "Culture" goes beyond a particular personal identity (for example, the identity according to ethnicity, gender, race, region, etc.) and tends to confirm these special personal identities (Eagleton 2000:91). His points can be shown in Figure 1.

Culture	culture
· Values shared on the pretext of common humanity · Views that do not belong anywhere Transcendence	· Ethnicity · Gender · Race · Region Particular individuality
Area of consensus	Area of conflict

※ Due to particular individuality and exclusivity
Figure 1 Culture and culture
(Refer to Eagleton 2000:91-92, plotted by the author)

Figure 1 shows the following content. "Culture" with the uppercase "C" has the values on the pretext of common humanity and views that do not belong anywhere (the so-called "God's eye"). From this perspective, "Culture" is characterized by "transcendence" and an area of "consensus". On the other hand, "culture" with the lowercase "c" indicates special concepts of nationality, gender, ethnicity and regionality. Sometimes differences in "culture" can lead to contradictions and conflicts between ethnic groups. The "culture" is individual, so it is also exclusive. It can be said that "culture" is an area of "conflict".

3. Colonies in Southeast Asia

Except for Thailand, many countries in Southeast Asia have been colonized by Europe and the United States.

The United Kingdom: Myanmar, Malaysia, Singapore, Brunei
France: Vietnam, Cambodia, Laos

The Netherlands: Indonesia

Portugal: Timor-Leste

Spain and the United States: The Philippines

From around the 8th century, Southeast Asia's maritime trade was well developed. Chinese, Indian, and Arabian merchants frequently passed through the South Seas. Southeast Asia at that time was multi-ethnic and had multi-cultural communities. In multi-ethnic and multi-cultural countries, from the traditional culture of which race is the national culture shaped? Generally speaking, the race at the center that accounted for the majority of people represented the race of the country. As pointed out by Japanese scholar Yamamoto Nobuto in 1997[1]: ideally, a nation-state is maintained by the center and peripheral, a majority and minority hierarchy (Yamamoto, 1997:257).

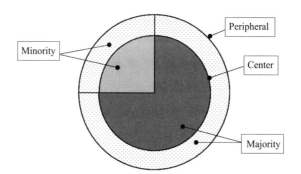

Figure 2   Center-peripheral, majority-minority
(Refer to Yamamoto 1997, plotted by the author)

However, in terms of the structure of the population in the colonies, the colonists were the center, but not the majority. At that time, in Southeast Asia, each region was made up of several communities. The colonists adopted a hierarchical system of social status to control them. The relations between different communities can be

1   This article often cited studies of Japanese scholars, but their works are not available in Chinese. The author of this article believes that it is also of great significance to introduce Japanese studies on Chinese in Southeast Asia to scholars in Chinese-speaking regions through translation and quotes in this article.

summarized as follows:

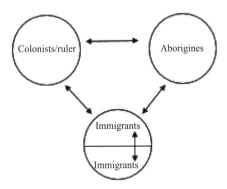

Figure 3   Relations among the different communities in colonies
(Plotted by the author)

Japanese scholar Akitoshi Shimizu revealed in 1998 that there were two types of colonies of European countries: First, the colonial type (for example, Australia and the Amazon basin), because the invading whites completely ruled out the indigenous peoples without exploiting them; second, the squeezing type, because the invading whites could not completely exclude the native aborigines but could squeeze them (the colonies were the mixture of colonial and squeezing types except Australia and the Amazon basin) (Shimizu 1998:30-32). In colonies of the squeezing type, under the social conditions of locals, colonists could preserve their political and economic interests. They implemented the policy of divide and rule over local ethnic groups so that the colonial government could easily dominate local people. That is to say, indirectly ruling locals was "gentle and flexible" (Shimizu 1998:30-32). After the 16th century, Portugal, the Netherlands, the United Kingdom and other countries formed strongholds and colonies in the *Nan Yang*. In particular, the United Kingdom practiced the squeezing type of colonies. As a result, their colonial policy awakened locals' awareness of race and cultural diversity (Nishikawa, 1999:11).

4. European countries' focus on the Chinese in the *Nan Yang*

After the 16th century, Portugal, the Netherlands, the United Kingdom and other countries formed strongholds and colonies in the *Nan Yang*. Since the late 19th century, European countries began to colonize Southeast Asia. It should be noted that Europeans immigrated to Southeast Asia before the start of colonization. Yamamoto Nobuto also pointed out in 1997 that: Europeans needed to establish their own social model in order to strengthen their political power and the efficiency of their control over the locals. In this new social model, the inhabitants of the colonial society were reproduced and gave their own social performance (Yamamoto 1997: 273, 278).

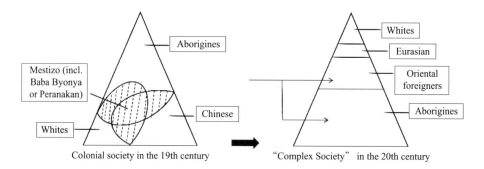

Figure 4   The "Complex Society" model
(Cited from Yamamoto 1997:274, partially revised by the author)

People other than mestizo were forcibly classified as oriental foreigners or aborigines. According to Yamamoto (1997), the category of oriental foreigners was formed in the following way. In principle, no "race" among categories was recognized. The essence of a "complex society" is the economy. Society is "split" by race, and without the logic of social common sense, "race" was an established fact.

Colonial rulers, while ignoring ethnic, religious and other diversities of the local residents, "imagined" these categories. Attention should be paid to "oriental foreigners", which was a category based on Chinese. "Oriental" meant that they were different from "Western" Europeans, and "foreigners" meant that they were not aborigines. Moreover, Europeans at that time had already noticed that there was a wide and strong network of special people who were good at buying and selling. Europeans reconfirmed the oriental foreigners (= Chinese in Southeast Asia then) and they also began to recognize that they were oriental foreigners (Yamamoto 1997:276). The author of this article held the opinion that "oriental foreigners" are the basis of the mentality of the Chinese in Southeast Asia today.

Southeast Asia was also a very special region at that time. Yamamoto (1997) also indicated that the Qing Dynasty originally banned nationals from going abroad and the presence of overseas Chinese was not accepted and were considered traitors. From the 1860s, China began to pay attention to the Southeast Asian Chinese communities as a source of funds and technology for the modernization of China. The *Nan Yang* referred to a space for the exchange of people, things, money and information. This space was open, flexible and free from regional restrictions, and Yamamoto (1997) called it the "frontier". The "*Nan Yang*" was a space usually in sharp contrast with "China". This sense of space of called the "*Nan Yang*" seemed to be formed in the late 19th century when European countries and China discovered the existence of Chinese in the *Nan Yang*, and Chinese in Southeast Asia also began to self-regulate as the "Chinese in the *Nan Yang*" (Yamamoto 1997:260-262, 282, 285).

5. A sense of space for the Chinese in the *Nan Yang* and the formation of nationalism

Since the late 19th century, the Chinese in the *Nan Yang* gradually demonstrated solidarity, which was reflected before and after the Revolution of 1911 and the Anti-Japanese War in 1937. At that time, some Chinese in the *Nan Yang* recognized the reality of the colony and the identity of being colonized people, so they were inclined to local nationalism. Among the Chinese in the *Nan Yang*, the dominant group was those interested in the Chinese community in Southeast Asia which they belonged to (Yamamoto 1997:286, 389).

Take Singapore as an example, at the opening ceremony of the Singapore Chinese

Cultural Centre, in 2017, Prime Minister Lee Hsien Loong of Singapore mentioned that Chinese nationals in Singapore should have a "Singaporean Chinese" culture:

The Chinese culture in Singapore includes both the traditional Chinese culture and Singapore's multicultural characteristics. He therefore believes that the local Chinese culture developed by the Chinese Cultural Centre must be based on a "Singapore-oriented" positioning. (Omitted)

Thus, the Chinese Singaporean is proud of his Chinese culture – but also increasingly conscious that his "Chineseness" is different from the Chineseness of Malaysian and Indonesian Chinese, or the Chineseness of people in China, Hong Kong or Taiwan. (Omitted)

"Singaporean Chinese Has a Unique Cultural Identity Half a Century after the Country Was Founded" (*Lianhe Zaobao*, May 20, 2017)

In the author's opinion, a country's prime minister appealing to the people to establish their own "culture" is a unique behavior of a multi-ethnic country. After achieving economic development, Singapore has in recent years shifted its attention to the domestic cultural and artistic aspects. However, the author of this article presumes that the result will allow Singapore Chinese to feel that most of their traditional culture and art comes from China, but it can place everyone under "the pressure to find a unique culture" and urge young people to follow the trend of European and American culture.

Culture is strongly related to identity. In colonized countries, nationals may seek identity from their suzerain states. In order to capture the mentality of the Chinese in Southeast Asia as a whole, this article is not limited to Singapore. We must consider not only the influence of China with a national origin, but also the influence of suzerain states at the time of colonization.

Since the middle of the 20th century, Southeast Asian countries have been independent of their suzerain states. The government tries to unite the people in a traditional culture, but in a multi-ethnic society, the question is which national culture is at the center. For marginalized ethnic groups, independence from colonies is an opportunity for them to refocus their culture and identity.

Furthermore, many countries in Southeast Asia are still multi-ethnic societies. In addition to the official language, the mother tongue is also important because it is related to identity. Speaking of Chinese culture in Southeast Asia, the situation is very complicated, and there are many factors to consider. The author depicts the complex situation of the Chinese in Southeast Asia as follows.

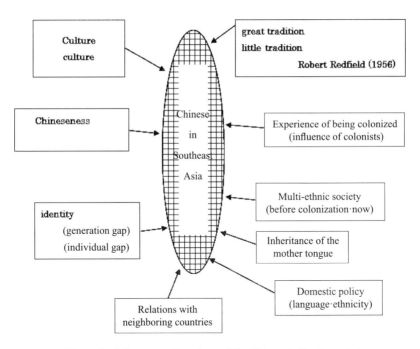

Figure 5   Influence on the culture of the Chinese in Southeast Asia
(Plotted by the author)

Regarding the trend of the personal identity of the Chinese in the *Nan Yang*, Yamamoto (1997) pointed out that the sense of space and personal identity of the Chinese in the *Nan Yang* sometimes even surpassed the Chinese communities, colonies, the *Nan Yang* and the suzerain state (Yamamoto 1997:289). The author of this article divides the personal identity of the Chinese in the *Nan Yang* into:

1. China orientation;
2. Local orientation;
3. Chinese community orientation;
4. Former suzerain state orientation.

Identity is established only when it is related with other people. Therefore, identity is influenced by changes in the identity of others, as well as changes in others. Moreover, personal identity is variable and transcendent. The Chinese in the *Nan Yang* are influenced by the society in which they live, and their historical and legal status there. The presence of Chinese in the *Nan Yang* can become obvious, disappear and resurrect as the times, society and environment change. In any case, in this very complicated situation, the identity of the Chinese in the *Nan Yang* is naturally diverse. Yamamoto (1997) indicated that "Chineseness" is bound by cultural "ties" (Yamamoto 1997:256). For the younger generation Malaysian Chinese, their mother tongue has been changed to English (Ang Lay Hoon 2008:34), and that of Indonesian Chinese students has changed to Indonesian (Li Minghuan and Huang You, 2008:59). In multicultural and multiethnic societies such as Malaysia and Indonesia, the mother tongue of many generations is gradually changing to be the language widely used in their respective countries. In terms of language, although "integration" is being promoted among ethnic groups, when it is necessary to divide by ethnic groups, such as "Chinese", "Indonesian", etc., the classification is based on the "culture" of that person in his/her daily life. If they live in an environment with Chinese culture and customs, everyone will judge that they have Chineseness, and will call them "Chinese".

6. Conclusion

Figure 6 can summarize the cultural formation of the Chinese in the *Nan Yang* as follows:

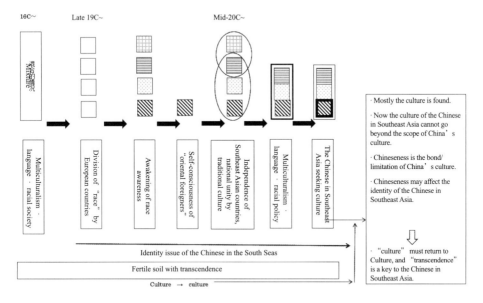

Figure 6　Model of the cultural formation of the Chinese in the *Nan Yang*

(Plotted by the author)

In the 8th century, immigrants from various other regions to the *Nan Yang* constituted a multi-ethnic community. From the 16th century, whites also entered this community. Since the late 19th century, with the colonization by European countries, the "ethnic" subdivision and hierarchization awakened the ethnic sense of all races. The Chinese living in the *Nan Yang* also began to realize that they were "Foreign Orientals (Chinese in Southeast Asia)". After the middle of the 20th century, countries in Southeast Asia became independent, and each government united the people based on the ethnic community made up of a traditional culture. The author considered tradition as a concrete manifestation of culture, and culture and identity influence each other. Since the 1960s, "culture" has changed from the uppercase "Culture" to the lowercase "culture". The lowercase "c" referred to something special and individual. This was formed during the period of the independence of Southeast Asian countries.

The *Nan Yang* is a region of diverse races. It is logical that the Chinese in the *Nan Yang* have a transcendent and variable sense of identity. The *Nan Yang* already has the soil for brewing transcendental identity. Identity is variable, so variability is not characteristic of the *Nan Yang*. Chineseness has a profound influence on the identity of the Chinese in Southeast Asia because it is the "cultural" bond between China and the overseas Chinese. On the other hand, Chineseness is limited to Chinese culture. The author of this article believes that "transcendence" is the key word for the Chinese in Southeast Asia in the future.

鲁迅故事的嬗变

——从"祥林嫂之死"谈《祝福》的影视舞台改编

安娜【意大利】

慕尼黑大学副教授

不管是埃斯库罗斯、莎士比亚，还是中国剧作家曹禺的戏剧，主人公之死都是舞台上最常见的情节、主题之一。尽管古希腊、伊丽莎白时代的英国与现代中国舞台上讲述的故事不同，但它们对死亡的表达却有一些相似的地方：首先，戏剧里的人物经常不是死于自然原因——阿伽门农被他的妻子和她的情人杀害，哈姆莱特死于一个由克洛狄斯阴谋的决斗中，周冲和四凤触电而死、周萍开枪自杀。其次，舞台上的死亡通常会被提前暗示，这就使得主人公遇到死亡的时候，观众已经有了一定的准备。[1] 再次，死去之前，舞台上的人物经常会说一些非常重要的话，比如，哈姆莱特所说的"此外仅余沉默而已。"[2] 其实，关于舞台上的死亡应该还有很多方面可以讨论，这里还有一点值得提到，那就是，由于主人公的死亡经常发生在一部戏的结尾，因此，它经常会影响到整个戏剧的含义，换句话说，对死亡的处理决定一部戏到底是一部悲剧还是一部喜剧。

《祝福》是鲁迅最重要的作品之一。从研究《祝福》的文章可以看到，不少人讨论"祥林嫂之死"，即，《祝福》的女主人公祥林嫂"为什么死了""怎么死

---

1 Susanne Marschall: Letzte Augenblicke im Kino. Gedanken über filmische (Vor-)Zeichen des Abschieds. ENDE Mediale Inszenierungen von Tod und Sterben. Augen Blick 43 (2008:29).

2 https://www.douban.com/group/topic/86741767/.

了""谁害死了祥林嫂"。本文受这些文章启发，希望对"祥林嫂之死"的研究有所新的发现。不过，笔者想从另外一个角度入手，也就是《祝福》的影视舞台改编，探讨不同改编版本对"祥林嫂之死"有一个什么样的表现和理解。随着分析不同时代、不同戏剧类型的《祝福》改编，我发现，对"祥林嫂之死"的描写与表达其实存在着非常大的差异。

笔者认为，从"祥林嫂之死"的处理，可以将《祝福》的改编作品分为三种类型：第一，悲剧式的处理；第二，正剧式的处理；第三，传奇式的处理。[1] 以下笔者将通过 1946 年和 1978 年越剧《祥林嫂》，1956 年电影《祝福》和 1953 年评剧《祥林嫂》剧本来分析这一问题。而在分析每一部戏对"祥林嫂之死"的处理时，主要会谈到以下几个问题：在整个叙事当中，"祥林嫂之死"发生在什么位置？它和之前、之后的叙事有什么关系？祥林嫂的最后几句话说什么？对死亡的处理对整个故事有什么影响？谈到改编作品之前，我首先要用同样的标准来分析鲁迅的小说《祝福》，简单地谈一下小说里对"祥林嫂之死"是一种什么样的表达。

一、鲁迅小说《祝福》对"祥林嫂之死"的描写

鲁迅的短篇小说《祝福》写于 1924 年 2 月 7 日，后来成为小说集《彷徨》的第一部作品。从叙述的角度来看，《祝福》是一部典型的框架小说：叙述人是"我"，大概是一个受到现代教育的人，为了过年回到自己的老家鲁镇，因为在那里已经没有住的地方，于是便住在一个叔叔家。这个叙述的时间持续四天，"我"第一天回到鲁镇，第二天和第三天看朋友，第四天过节。"我"的心态比较复杂，一方面并不喜欢在鲁镇的生活，一方面还是欣赏过节的气氛。然而，"我"在鲁镇过节的故事很快就和另外一个故事交接起来，那就是祥林嫂的故事。"我"第二天见到她，发现她老了很多，因为她的一个问题而吓坏了，那就是"一个人死了之后，究竟有没有灵魂的"。第三天，"我"听到祥林嫂死了，在记忆中怀念了祥林嫂的一生。第四天，从记忆醒来之后过节。新年的祝福是贯穿于整个小说的主题，既是第一个故事里的"我"在经历的情况，也是第二个故事里祥林嫂几次经历的，从另外一个角度来看，也是鲁迅在写作时的经历，1924 年的新年正好是 2 月 5 日，也就是创作《祝福》的前夕。不管在哪里，这个"祝福"都不是一个

1　在《史元：十九世纪欧洲的历史意象》中海登·怀特提到，历史叙事主要可以归纳为四个模式，传奇原型、喜剧原型、悲剧原型、反讽原型。

值得庆祝的事情，由一件很悲伤的事情展现出"祝福"是非常残酷、冷漠的，这件事就是"祥林嫂之死"。

"祥林嫂之死"是小说的叙事动机，因为祥林嫂之死，"我"才开始回忆她的一生。因此，"祥林嫂之死"在小说中处在比较靠前的叙述位置。它有一定的暗示，那就是，"我"第二天见到祥林嫂，发现她变化很大，听到她对人死了以后发生什么的问题。不过，这些叙述很突然，而且很短。

> "不早不迟，偏偏要在这时候，——这就可见是一个谬种！"我先是诧异，接着是很不安，似乎这话于我有关系。试望门外，谁也没有。好容易待到晚饭前他们的短工来冲茶，我才得了打听消息的机会。"刚才，四老爷和谁生气呢？"我问。"还不是和祥林嫂？"那短工简捷的说。"祥林嫂？怎么了？"我又赶紧的问。"老了。""死了？"我的心突然紧缩，几乎跳起来，脸上大约也变了色。但他始终没有抬头，所以全不觉。我也就镇定了自己，接着问："什么时候死的？""什么时候？——昨天夜里，或者就是今天罢。——我说不清。""怎么死的？""怎么死的？——还不是穷死的？"他淡然的回答，仍然没有抬头向我看，出去了。[1]

这些叙述很多方面是比较模糊的：首先，我们不知道祥林嫂具体什么时候死的，我们也不知道她在哪里死的，而且也不知道她为什么死——反正"穷死"不是真正的原因。我们也不知道她生活中最后几句话说的什么，有可能是对"我"说的，不过，这也不清楚。我们唯一知道的是三个人物对祥林嫂的死亡的反应：首先是四叔，他不但不可怜她，反而还骂他。这个描写主要告诉我们，四叔是一个非常残酷、自私的人。其次是短工，他好像根本没有将这件事情放到心上。第三个反应是小说中的"我"：他也不是好人，我们可以读到他听到这个消息之后"心地已经渐渐轻松"，不过从叙事来看，他应该还有一定的良心，因为他后来开始回忆祥林嫂。这个回忆也是小说中最长的一部分，也就是祥林嫂的一生。从整个小说的结构和功能来开，可以说鲁迅在《祝福》里完成了一个类似于《阿Q正传》的任务：也就是说，给祥林嫂写了一部传记，让一个历史学家不会在乎的人进入历史。不过，这并不影响到具体的现实，鲁镇到最后还要和平时一样过节，祥林嫂之死不带来任何变化。值得注意的是，在讲述祥林嫂一生的部分，第一人称的叙述者几乎消失了，因此我们感觉这是一个比较客观的叙述，"祥林嫂之死"

---

1 《祝福——从小说到电影》，中国电影出版社1979年版，第6页。

则有一个很小的空间，而且关于她的死，叙述是非常主观的："我"只是重复鲁四爷和短工的反应，再加一点自己的感受，对"祥林嫂之死"的具体情况，全是一片空白。

二、《祝福》影视舞台剧的改编

回到《祝福》影视舞台剧的改编，笔者发现目前所看过的都有一些共同的地方：第一，都将《祝福》中的"我"去掉，换成一个客观的、全能的叙述角度。第二，都将"我"的比较随意的、散乱的回忆模式去掉，将祥林嫂的一生根据线性时间顺序叙述。第三，这个叙述似乎自然到最后带来"祥林嫂之死"，因此，死亡不再是作品的动机而是作品的结局，在这个位置它对整个作品的含义有更强烈的影响。虽然有这些相似的地方，但不同的艺术表现形式还是存在很多不同。

第一，悲剧式的处理。

有一部分改编作品给"祥林嫂之死"留下了很大的空间，将她的死亡描写得很详细。同时，这些作品非常动人，完全让观众进入到人物的内心世界。我想用"悲剧式"来概括这种处理方式。以1946年和1978年的越剧版本为例。

《祝福》的越剧改编和著名演员袁雪芬是分不开的。她四次改编了《祝福》，第一次是1946年，那时她才二十几岁，还不是一位著名演员。当时的演出地是在由国民党统治的上海，根据鲁迅小说改编的作品立刻引起上海大量文学和艺术家的兴趣。[1]中华人民共和国成立之后，袁雪芬成了人民表演艺术家，她在1956年和1962年继续改编《祥林嫂》。"文化大革命"结束之后，50多岁的袁雪芬推出了第四个《祥林嫂》版本。以下着重分析1946年和1978年的剧本以及演出。[2]

越剧《祥林嫂》用很长的时间来表现"祥林嫂之死"。在越剧改编中，祥林嫂死去之前说了几句很丰富的话，回忆自己的一生。这一点在1946年的改编中已经可以看到：

> 尾声是在高升客店外。袁雪芬演的祥林嫂两眼茫然，拖着疲惫的脚步上场。她手里拿着鲁家奶奶发付的五百文工钱，铜钱一枚一枚地撒落在地上而好不知觉。她见人就问："一个人死了之后究竟有没有灵魂？"但得不到回答。在恍惚之间，她回忆起前尘，这里用类似电影的手法表

---

1 章力挥、高义龙：《袁雪芬的艺术道路》，上海文艺出版社1984年版，第114页。
2 1956年和1962年版本笔者未找到。

现她的幻觉，概括了她的一生：

　　祥林嫂：祥林！祥林！

　　祥林：你快逃走！你快逃走！

　　祥林嫂：癞大叔！癞大叔！

　　卫癞子：祥林嫂！二十千！三十千！

　　祥林嫂：阿毛爹！

　　贺老六：你要好好照顾孩子！

　　祥林嫂：大伯！

　　贺老三：弟媳妇，明天我来收房子！

　　祥林嫂：老爷！老爷！

　　鲁阿牛：祥林嫂，你已经老了，这里用不着你了，你还是别处去吧！

　　祥林嫂昏倒死在桥头的一个凉亭边。[1]

在 1978 年的版本里，祥林嫂死去之前有一首优美的长歌《抬头问苍天》，这首歌早就变成了一个单独的作品，在演出的时候需要大概十分钟的时间。由于篇幅太长，在这里只列出一部分：

　　我要告诉去……我一定要告诉去……（走了两步又站住）我到哪里告诉去？……我到哪里告诉去啊！……天呀！（唱）我只有抬头问苍天……

　　（幕后合唱）抬头问苍天，祥林嫂魂灵究竟有没有？有没有？（幕后合唱）苍天不开言。祥林嫂我低头问人间……你说，地狱到底有没有？……死了的一家人，都能见面吗？……告诉我……告诉我……

　　（幕后合唱）人间也无言……[2]

可以看到，越剧版中，祥林嫂的最后几句话非常丰富，一方面包括鲁迅小说里祥林嫂所说的话，一方面包括鲁迅小说叙述者关于祥林嫂的一生的报告，另一方面也包含着一些对人生的思考。通过这些话，祥林嫂之死变成一个很长的过程。从这里，还可以看到悲剧式处理的另一个特点：改编作品不强调《祝福》的故事时间，而是挖掘这个故事在演出时间当下的联系和意义。关于第一次改编祥林嫂的结尾，我们可以读到：

1　《袁雪芬的艺术道路》，第 116 页。

2　吴琛等：《越剧祥林嫂》，上海文艺出版社 1979 年版，第 63 页。

祥林嫂昏倒死在桥头的一个凉亭边。灯暗后复亮，又是大年初一了。一个十九岁的小姑娘阿香由母亲领着去鲁府帮佣。她们走过祥林嫂的遗体，掩鼻皱眉，觉得不吉利。这段戏没有一句话，但与序幕相呼应。它形象地告诉人们：祥林嫂地悲剧还在继续，新的祥林嫂还在产生。阿香面临着的，不也将是祥林嫂那样的命运么？[1]

1978 年，在《重演祥林嫂》一文中，袁雪芬也强调这部戏剧和当下现实的关系，从鲁迅《祝福》里的人物和事情来思考她自己在"文化大革命"时期的生活经验：

作为一个演员，却不能唱，不能演，也不能讲，我被剥夺了为人民服务的革命权力。看，"四人帮"眼中的袁雪芬，简直就跟鲁四老爷眼中的祥林嫂一样，是个"谬种"，是个"不祥之物"！在"四害"横行的地方，经受这种祥林嫂式遭遇的人又何止我一个！多少作家、艺术家，不能写，不能唱；多少科学家，不能搞科研，不准钻技术；多少老工人、老模范，不能搞生产；多少革命老干部，被他们视为眼中钉啊！"四人帮"在迫害人民这一点上，跟鲁迅先生笔下的鲁四老爷很有相似之处，他们表面上道貌岸然，满肚子却是吃人的虎狼之心。他们在精神上折磨你、摧残你，剥夺你的劳动权利，毁败你的一切希望，还要诬蔑你是不干净的"臭老九"。[2]

总之，悲剧式的处理一方面给祥林嫂之死设计了一个很大的时空，也给主人公写出很长的、很有魅力的最后几句话，另一个方面，悲剧式的处理强调祥林嫂的普遍性，也就是说，她不是一个时代和一个空间的代表，而是在不同的时代、不同的地方都可以展现出她的意义。

第二，正剧式的处理。

和悲剧式的处理不同，还有一部分作品用一个比较理性的态度来叙述"祥林嫂之死"。在叙事中，"祥林嫂之死"不再是重要的细节，叙述宁可将焦点放在一些其他方面上。以 1956 年的电影《祝福》为例。

电影《祝福》是 1956 年为纪念鲁迅逝世二十周年而创作的作品，导演是桑弧，编剧是著名的剧作家和当时任文化部副部长的夏衍，主演是著名的演员白杨。与上文的越剧作品做比较，可以发现电影《祝福》没有给"祥林嫂之死"留下足

---

1 《袁雪芬的艺术道路》，第 117 页。
2 　袁雪芬：《重演＜祥林嫂＞》，《越剧祥林嫂》，第 113 页。

够的时长，在一百分钟的电影中，"祥林嫂之死"只用了两分钟。和越剧改编作比较的话，祥林嫂的最后几句话也非常短，在这里用的是鲁迅小说里祥林嫂对"我"说的话，因为影片里没有"我"，这句话没有具体的听众，编剧说"经过权衡之后，我保留了祥林嫂的这个疑问或者希望，而把它改为绝望中的自问式的独白"。[1] 在文学剧本中，祥林嫂之死有以下的表现：

> 鲁镇（外、夜）
>
> 人们在放鞭。
>
> 祥林嫂坐在桥边，冷得缩成一团。（出画）
>
> 祥林嫂远远走来。
>
> 祥：一个人死了以后到底有没有灵魂？一个人死了以后到底有没有
>
> 灵魂？告诉我！告诉我！
>
> 祥林嫂走向村口，终于不支倒下死去。[2]

在电影里，另外一个比较明显的方法是，祥林嫂还没有倒在地上的时候，已经有旁白开始解释说，这是很久以前发生的事情。祥林嫂去世之后接着电影开头回音的旁白，"在50年代的当下"这和祥林嫂的故事明确拉开一个距离，似乎是告诉观众这是很久以前的事情，和我们这个时代没有关系：

> 旁白：祥林嫂，一个勤谨、善良的女人，经受了数不清的苦难和凌
>
> 辱之后，倒下了，死了。这是四十多年以前的事情，对，这是过去了的
>
> 时代的事情，应该庆幸的是，这样的时代了，终于过去了，终于一去不
>
> 复返了。[3]

为什么设计这样一个旁白？夏衍曾解释说："为了使生活在今天这样一个幸福时代的观众不要因为看了这部影片而感到过分的沉重，就是说，不必为古人流泪。对于后一点，直到今天，我还没有改变原来的想法。我总觉得今天的青年人应该了解过去那个悲痛的时代，但只应该为了这个时代的一去不复返而感到庆幸，而不必再为这些过了的人物的遭际而感到沉重和悲哀。"[4]

祥林嫂的最后一句话，在电影《祝福》里是祥林嫂死亡前的一天对"我"所说的那一句话。在电影里，这句话的功能和小说有一定的相似的地方，也就是说

1　《祝福——从小说到电影》，中国电影出版社1979年版，第120页。

2　同上，第114页。

3　同上，第114页。

4　同上，第123页。

都宣布死亡的到来。虽然编剧将它解释为独白，但是，我们作为电影观众会将它理解为祥林嫂向我们提出来的问题，从这个角度来看，我们就变成了她的对话对象，或者甚至是小说中的"我"。值得注意的是，从主演白杨的笔记可以读到，她直到 20 年后即 20 世纪 70 年代末，还在思考祥林嫂的最后几句话："任何时候，只要心里一想到这些不称心的镜头，真想再重拍一次。"[1] "我多么想再重演一下这个镜头啊，影片公映后我似乎'有了'她这一瞬间的神态了，可以为人物传神。但'木已成舟'，再说也是'后话'了。"[2] 从某些方面来看，正是祥林嫂这个最后一句话可以看作是电影《祝福》一个充满着悬念的地方。编剧夏衍提到："我接受这一改编工作就是把它看作是一件严肃的政治任务"[3]，虽然他在这里说的主要是改编鲁迅的作品，但从今天的角度来看，"政治任务"在 50 年代恐怕不仅和改编鲁迅的作品有关系，更多涉及拍电影本身。从这个角度来看，电影的主要任务应该是歌颂新中国，电影《祝福》对祥林嫂之死的处理和这一点是一致的。

第三，传奇式的处理。

最后还要谈到另外一种处理方式，可以称之为传奇式处理。有一部分的改编作品根本就没有让祥林嫂死去，不仅在舞台上没有"祥林嫂之死"，而且最后还增加了一位想改变她命运的人物。通过这个方法，祥林嫂的一生不再有悲剧的结局，不再是反复上演的固定的祝福，而到最后暗示这个一成不变的状态会有变化。结局不是充满着悲剧的气氛，而是表现出一种新鲜的、充满着乐观主义的情绪。祥林嫂不再是一个被杀害者，而是一个主动的、积极的反抗者形象。虽然这里只能谈到 1953 年的评剧剧本《祥林嫂》，但是笔者估计还有其他的类似的改编。在这个剧本中，我们可以看到，祥林嫂不仅没死，反而更变成了一个反抗社会、反抗命运、反抗鲁迅给她安排的结局的人物。

> 嫂:（唱）见此情不由我心中暗想，倒叫我一阵阵心中惨伤。我只说捐了门槛赔了罪，那知道罪未减反倒遭殃。看起来捐门槛我上了当，六嫂子！你不是说捐了门槛千人踩万人过，就赔了罪了吗？
>
> 柳:啊！也许是白捐了吧！
>
> 嫂:那么，神也不能治我的命了？
>
> 柳:我也糊涂了！

---

1 白杨:《电影表演探索》，中国电影出版社 1979 年版，第 81 页。
2 同上，第 82 页。
3 《祝福——从小说到电影》，第 119 页。

嫂：你说一个人死了真有鬼，在阴间能见面么？

柳：我也只是听人说，谁知道真——

嫂：你也不知道那我还怕什么？（看爷子）

柳：祥林嫂……

嫂：哈……哈……（唱）悔不该听信了你的话，捐了条门槛在庙堂，哪有神来哪有鬼，逼得我家破人又亡！我要到庙里去走一趟，倒看看我砍断那门槛有何妨，

柳：祥林嫂……你要干什么？

嫂：我？！我要砍断那条门槛！

（幕急落）

附第五场鲁太太念佛词，（天论佛，地论佛，天论八宝护身佛，阿弥陀佛。）[1]

1953 年的评剧剧本《祥林嫂》，情节的结局不是祥林嫂之死，而是祥林嫂准备去砍门槛的戏。这个戏在鲁迅的小说里本来是没有的，鲁迅的小说只提到刘妈和祥林嫂说，如果她去寺庙里捐一个门槛她可以变成"无罪"。祥林嫂用了很多钱去捐一个门槛，结果完全没有用，鲁四爷根本不管。后来有一些戏剧改编在这里填了一个戏，那就是"砍门槛"的戏：祥林嫂一知道捐门槛是没有用的，非常生气，决定到寺庙去将门槛砍掉。"砍门槛"的戏似乎在好几个版本，包括夏衍的电影都可以找到，袁雪芬在文章中也谈到这个戏：

关于戏的结尾，祥林嫂要不要砍门槛的问题，袁雪芬也作了慎重的考虑。一九四八年拍摄电影《祥林嫂》时，为了加强人物的反抗性，曾设计了祥林嫂砍门槛的细节。这种处理，解放后被故事片《祝福》（夏衍改编，白杨主演）吸收了。有的地方剧种（如评剧）的演出本，在砍门槛时还设计了大段唱。袁雪芬在一九五六年演出时，已割舍了这个情节。这次修改，她的看法更明确了：门槛应该让观众去砍，艺术作品不应随意拔高人物，而要给观众留下想象的余地。鲁迅写道祥林嫂对命运、灵魂发出了怀疑，正是恰到好处，改编本没有必要把这样一个行动强加给这个人物。[2]

1　王雁、李凤阳：《祥林嫂（新评剧）》，北京宝文堂书店 1953 年版，第 35—36 页。

2　《袁雪芬的艺术道路》，第 269—270 页。

可以看到，"砍门槛"不仅是一个情节的处理，更多地涉及怎么理解鲁迅，怎么将鲁迅和当下现实连接起来的问题。祥林嫂到底有没有反抗意识？在当时有很多文章讨论过这个问题，因为它是涉及当时政治社会的大问题，那就是革命。和其他作品不同的是，1953 年的评剧版本《祥林嫂》中，砍门槛不再是祥林嫂去世之前的一个情节，而是这个故事的结局，就是让她不死。从某些方面来看，将祥林嫂的死改成祥林嫂的反抗或甚至革命，将悲剧改成传奇。

三、结语

从以上的分析可以看到，讨论《祝福》的影视舞台改编是一个比较复杂的问题，它涉及很多方面，如不同时代的历史背景，不同戏剧艺术类型的表现方式与习惯，不同时代对鲁迅的理解等。同时，在 20 和 21 世纪的中国，这些都在不断地改变。然而，"祥林嫂之死"涉及一个非常关键的问题，那就是如何处理底层民众的苦难，而且这个问题本身和"中国革命"是分不开的。人们经常说，戏剧是社会的一面镜子，通过不同时代对《祝福》的改编，特别是对"祥林嫂之死"的处理，我们也可以更好地理解不同时代的社会、历史背景。

A Lu Xun's Story in Transformation

Anna Stecher / Italy

Ludwig Maximillians University of Munich, Assistant Professor

In dramas of either Aeschylus, Shakespeare or the Chinese playwright Cao Yu, the protagonist's death is one of the most common plots and themes on the stage. Although stories told on stages of ancient Greece, Elizabethan England and modern China are different, they share some similarities in the manifestation of death. First, characters in dramas often do not die for natural reasons — Agamemnon was murdered by his wife and her lover, Hamlet died in a duel conspired by Claudius, Zhou Chong and Sifeng were electrocuted and Zhou Ping shot himself. Second, death on the stage is usually hinted at in advance, which prepares the audience for when the protagonist encounters death.[1] Third, before death, characters on the stage often say something very important. For example, Hamlet said, "The rest is silence."[2] In fact, death on stage has many other facets that may be investigated. It is worth mentioning here that because the death of the protagonist often occurs at the end of the play, it influences the meaning of the whole work. In other words, the

---

1   Susanne Marschall: Letzte Augenblicke im Kino. Gedanken über filmische (Vor-)Zeichen des Abschieds. ENDE Mediale Inszenierungen von Tod und Sterben. AugenBlick 43 (2008:29).

2   https://www.douban.com/group/topic/86741767/.

emplotment of death determines whether the drama is a tragedy or a comedy.

The New Year's Sacrifice is one of Lu Xun's most important works. Many articles regarding research on the *The New Year's Sacrifice* discussed the "death of Hsiang Lin's wife"; in other words, "why" and "how" did the heroine of *The New Year's Sacrifice* die, or "who should be blamed for the death of Hsiang Lin's wife"? Inspired by related studies, this article aims to discover something new in the study of the "death of Hsiang Lin's wife". From another perspective, that is, the adaptations of *The New Year's Sacrifice* to films and dramas, the author explores the manifestation and understanding of the "death of Hsiang Lin's wife" by the different versions of its adaptation. With the analysis of the adaptations of *The New Year's Sacrifice* to different types of plays at different historical moments, the author reveals that there are actually large differences in narration and in the embodiment of the "death of Hsiang Lin's wife".

In the opinion of the author, according to different emplotments of the "death of Hsiang Lin's wife", the adaptations of *The New Year's Sacrifice* can be divided into three types: First, a tragic emplotment; second, a serious dramatic emplotment; third, a legendary emplotment.[1] In the following sections, the author will analyze this issue through the scripts of the Yue Opera "*Hsiang Lin's Wife*" in 1946 and 1978, the film "*The New Year's Sacrifice*" in 1956 and the Pingju Opera "*Hsiang Lin's Wife*". The following questions will be discussed during the analysis of emplotments of the "death of Hsiang Lin's wife" in each play. Where does the "death of Hsiang Lin's wife" occur in the entire narrative? What relations does it have with the narrative before and after? What are the last words of Hsiang Lin's wife? How does her death influence the whole story? Before examining the adapted works, an analysis must be made of Lu Xun's novel *The New Year's Sacrifice* with the same criteria in order to briefly explain how the "death of Hsiang Lin's wife" is expressed in the novel.

---

1 In *Metahistory: The Historical Imagination in Nineteenth-Century Europe*, Hayden White summarized the historical emplotments by the four archetypical genres of romance, comedy, tragedy and satire.

1. Narration of the Death of Hsiang Lin's Wife in Lu Xun's Novel *The New Year's Sacrifice*

Lu Xun's short story *The New Year's Sacrifice* was completed on February 7, 1924 and later became the first work in the collection of novels called *Wandering*. From a narrative point of view, *The New Year's Sacrifice* is a typical framework novel: the narrator is the first-person "I", probably a person who had received a modern education and returned to his hometown Lu Town to celebrate the New Year. Without a home there, he had to live temporarily in the home of an uncle. This narrative lasted for four days. The person "I" returned to Lu Town on the first day, visited friends on the second and third days and celebrated the festival on the fourth day. The I's mentality was very complicated. On the one hand, "I" disliked the life in Lu Town. On the other hand, "I" still appreciated the atmosphere of the festival. But the story of "I" in Lu Town was soon connected with another story, that is, the story of Hsiang Lin's wife. "I" saw her the next day, found that she looked much older and was terrified by her question, that is, "After a person dies, does she turn into a ghost or not?" On the third day, "I" heard of the death of Hsiang Lin's wife and recalled her life in his memory. On the fourth day, the festival came after waking up from the memory. The New Year's blessing was the theme throughout the novel. It was not only the situation of "I" in the first story, but also the experience of Hsiang Lin's wife in the second story. From another perspective, it was also the experience of Lu Xun while writing. The new year in 1924 happened on February 5th, the eve of the writing of *The New Year's Sacrifice*. No matter where it is, the "blessing" is not something to be celebrated, but a very sad thing. This shows that "blessing" is very cruel and indifferent. This event is the "death of Hsiang Lin's wife".

The "death of Hsiang Lin's wife" is the narrative motivation of this novel. Because of her death, "I" began to recall her life. The "death of Hsiang Lin's wife" is narrated early in the novel. There is a hint that when seeing Hsiang Lin's wife on the next day, "I" found that she had changed a lot and asked what would happen after death. However, these narratives are sudden and short.

"Not earlier nor later, but just at this time—sure sign of a bad character!" At first, I felt astonished, then very uncomfortable, thinking these words must refer to me. I looked outside the door, but no one was there. I contained myself with difficulty till their servant came in before dinner to brew a pot of tea, when at last I had a chance to make some enquiries. "Just now whom was Fourth Master mad at?", I asked. "Why, still with Hsiang Lin's Wife," he replied briefly. "Hsiang Lin's Wife? How was that?" I asked again. "She's dead." "Dead?" My heart suddenly missed a beat. I started, and probably changed color too. But since he did not raise his head, he was probably quite unaware of how I felt. Then I controlled myself, and asked: "When did she die?" "When? Last night, or else today, I'm not sure." "How did she die?" "How did she die? Why, of poverty of course." He answered placidly and, still without having raised his head to look at me, went out.[1]

These narratives are vague in many aspects. First of all, we know neither when Hsiang Lin's wife died, nor why she died — "poverty" was not the real reason anyway. We do not know what her last words were about, probably she spoke to me, but that was not clear. The only thing we know is the responses of three characters to the death of Hsiang Lin's wife. First of all, that of her uncle, not only did he not pity her, but he even blamed her. Such a description mainly tells us that the uncle was a very cruel and selfish person. Then, the servant did not seem to take this matter to heart at all. Third, "I" in the novel: He was not a good man when we read that his "heart already felt lighter" at hearing the news, but from the narrative point of view, he should still have some conscience because he began to recall the story of Hsiang Lin's wife. This memory is also the longest part in the novel, which reflects on the life of Hsiang Lin's wife. From the structure and function of the entire novel, it can be said that in *The New Year's Sacrifice*, Lu Xun completed a task similar to *The True Story of Ah Q*. In other words, he wrote a biography for Hsiang Lin's wife and recorded a person in history that no historian cared about. However, the practical

---

1 *The New Year's Sacrifice — From Novel to Film*, China Film Press, 1979, p.6.

reality was not affected. In the end, Lu Town celebrated the festival as usual and the death of Hsiang Lin's wife did not bring any change. It is noteworthy that in the part narrating the life of Hsiang Lin's wife, the first-person narrator almost disappeared, and we felt that an objective narration had developed. There is a small space for the "death of Hsiang Lin's wife". Regarding her death, the narration is very subjective: "I" just expressed the responses of the Fourth Master and the servant, plus a bit of my own feelings, and the specific situation of the "death of Hsiang Lin's wife" is completely blank.

2. Adaptations of The New Year's Sacrifice to Films and Dramas

Returning to the adaptations of *The New Year's Sacrifice* to films and dramas, the author finds some common points. First, "I" in *The New Year's Sacrifice* was deleted and replaced with an objective and all-around narrative angle. Second, they removed the casual and scattered memory mode of "I" and described the life of Hsiang Lin's wife in a linear, chronological order. Third, the narration seems to naturally lead to the "death of Hsiang Lin's wife" in the end. Therefore, death is no longer the motivation but the ending of the works. Then, it has a stronger influence on the meaning of the entire work. Despite these similarities, there are still many differences in different artistic expressions.

2.1 Tragic Emplotment

Some adaptations leave ample space for the "death of Hsiang Lin's wife" and describe her death in great detail. Furthermore, these works are very moving and bring the audience completely to the inner world of these characters. The author summarizes this approach as "tragic emplotment". Take the Yue opera versions in 1946 and 1978 as examples.

The adaptation of *The New Year's Sacrifice* to a Yue opera was inseparable from the famous actor Yuan Xuefen. She adapted *The New Year's Sacrifice* four times. The first adaptation was completed in 1946 when she was in her twenties and was not yet well known. At that time, the venue was in Shanghai ruled by the

Kuomintang and the opera adapted from Lu Xun's novel immediately attracted special attention from writers and artists in Shanghai.[1] After the founding of the People's Republic of China, Yuan Xuefen became a people's performing artist and she continued to adapt the opera *Hsiang Lin's Wife,* in 1956 and 1962. After the Cultural Revolution ended, Yuan Xuefen, who was in her fifties, launched the fourth version of *Hsiang Lin's Wife.* The following analysis will focus on the scripts and performances of 1946 and 1978.[2]

The Yue opera *Hsiang Lin's Wife* spent a long time to embody the "death of Hsiang Lin's wife". In the adapted Yue operas, Hsiang Lin's wife said a few words with enriched meanings and which recalled her life before death. This can already be found in the 1946 adaptation:

The epilogue is outside Gao Sheng Inn. Hsiang Lin's wife, played by Yuan Xuefen, with a vacant expression, was dragging her tired legs. She was holding copper coins of the value of five hundred given to her by the Madam Lu, and she did not realize that the copper coins were being scattered on the ground one by one. She asked anyone she met, "After a person dies, does she turn into a ghost or not?" But she could not get an answer. In a trance, she recalled the past, and here her hallucinations were presented in a film-like manner to summarize her life:

Hsiang Lin's Wife: Hsiang Lin! Hsiang Lin!

Hsiang Lin: Run away! Run away!

Hsiang Lin's Wife: Uncle Mange! Uncle Mange!

Mange Wei: Hsiang Lin's wife! Twenty thousand! Thirty thousand!

Hsiang Lin's Wife: Father of Ah Mao!

He Lao Liu: You have to take good care of the child!

Hsiang Lin's Wife: Elder Brother!

---

1   Zhang Lihui and Gao Yilong, *Yuan Xuefen's Art Career*, Shanghai Literature and Art Publishing House, 1984, p.114.

2   The author cannot find the versions of 1956 and 1962.

He Lao San: Sister-in-law, I will take over the house tomorrow!

Hsiang Lin's Wife: Master! Master!

Lu Ah Niu: Hsiang Lin's wife, you are old, you are not needed here, you should go elsewhere!

Hsiang Lin's wife fainted and died near a gazebo at the bridge.[1]

In the 1978 version, before the death of Hsiang Lin's wife, a beautiful long song sings "*Look up and Ask God*". This song long ago became a separate piece of art, which takes almost ten minutes when performing. Due to the length, only a part of it is given here:

I want to tell ... I must tell ... (two steps and stand still) Where do I tell? ... where do I tell! ... Oh my God! (Singing) I can only look up and ask God ...

(Chorus behind the scenes) Look up and ask God, after death, will Hsiang Lin's wife turn into a ghost or not? Does she or doesn't she? (Chorus behind the scenes) God does not speak. Hsiang Lin's wife, looks down to ask Satan ... you tell me, is there a Hell? ... will all the people of one family who have died see each other again? ... tell me ... tell me ...

(Chorus behind the scenes) Satan does not speak ...[2]

It can be seen that in the Yue opera version, the last words of Hsiang Lin's wife have very enriched meanings, which include, on the one hand, words spoken by Hsiang Lin's wife in Lu Xun's novel, the report of her life in the novel, and on the other hand, some thoughts on life. With these words, the death of Hsiang Lin's wife becomes a long process. Here, this is another feature of the tragic emplotment: The adaptation does not emphasize the time line in the story of *The New Year's Sacrifice*, but unveils the current connection and meaning of the story at the

---

1 Ibid, p.116.

2 Wu Chen et al., *Yue Opera Hsiang Lin's Wife*, Shanghai Literature and Art Publishing House, 1979, p.63.

time of the performance. In the ending of the first adaptation of *Hsiang Lin's Wife*, we can read:

Hsiang Lin's wife fainted and died near a gazebo at the bridge. The lights turned on again after darkness, it was a New Year's Day. A 19-year-old girl, Ah Xiang, was led by her mother to become a servant in the Family of Lu. They walked past the corpse of Hsiang Lin's wife, covering their noses and frowning, feeling an ill-boding. There is not a single word in this scene, but it echoes the prologue. It vividly tells people that: The tragedy of Hsiang Lin's wife is still going on, and a new Hsiang Lin's wife is still being produced. Wouldn't Ah Xiang face a fate like Hsiang Lin's wife?[1]

In 1978, in the article "Replay of Hsiang Lin's Wife", Yuan Xuefen also pointed out the relationship between the drama and the contemporary reality; her own experience in the Cultural Revolution was reflected by characters and events in Lu Xun's *The New Year's Sacrifice*:

As an actor, I couldn't sing, I couldn't perform, I couldn't speak, I was deprived of the right to serve the people. Look, Yuan Xuefen in the eyes of the Gang of Four was just like Hsiang Lin's wife in the eyes of the Fourth Master, a "sure sign of a bad character"! Where "Four Harms" were rampant, where there were many who had an experience resembling that of Hsiang Lin's wife! Many writers and artists could neither write nor sing; many scientists could neither engage in scientific research nor be allowed to develop technologies; many veteran and model workers could not make products; and many old revolutionary cadres were hurt by them! In persecution of the people, the Gang of Four was very similar to the Fourth Master in the novel of Mr. Lu Xun. On the surface, they were morally correct, but their hearts were full of cannibalism. They mentally tortured you, destroyed you, deprived you of the right to work, destroyed all your hopes, and slandered you as dirty "stinky old ninth".[2]

---

1   *Yuan Xuefen's Art Career*, p.117.
2   Yuan Xuefen, "Replay of Hsiang Lin' s Wife", *Yue Opera Hsiang Lin's Wife*, p.113.

In short, the tragic emplotment, on the one hand, designed a big time and space for the death of Hsiang Lin's wife and wrote the protagonist's long and charming last words, and on the other hand, emphasized the universality of Hsiang Lin's wife. In other words, she is not a representative of one era and one space, but significant in different times and different places.

2.2 Serious Emplotment

Unlike the tragic emplotment, there are also some works that take a relatively rational attitude in narrating the "death of Hsiang Lin's wife". In the narration, the "death of Hsiang Lin's wife" is no longer an important detail, the focus is on some other aspects. Take the film *The New Year's Sacrifice* in 1956 as an example.

The film *The New Year's Sacrifice* was shot in 1956 in commemoration of the 20th anniversary of Lu Xun's death. The director was Sang Hu, the screenwriter was Xia Yan, a famous playwright and the then Deputy Minister of Culture, and the star was the famous actress Bai Yang. In comparison with the Yue opera mentioned above, the film *The New Year's Sacrifice* did not give enough time for the "death of Hsiang Lin's wife". In the 100-minute film, the "death of Hsiang Lin's wife" took only two minutes. If compared with the adaptation of the Yue opera, the last words of Hsiang Lin's wife were also very short. Here the words spoken by Hsiang Lin's wife to "I" in Lu Xun's novel was used because "I" did not exist in the film and there was no specific listener to these words. The screenwriter said, "after serious consideration, I retained this question or hope of Hsiang Lin's wife, and changed it to a self-questioning monologue in despair."[1] In the literary script, the death of Hsiang Lin's wife was manifested as follows:

Lu Town (outdoors, night)

Firecrackers explode.

Hsiang Lin's wife sat by the bridge, shrinking with cold. (Fading out)

Hsiang Lin's wife walked near from afar.

---

1   *The New Year's Sacrifice — From Novel to Film*, China Film Press, 1979, p.120.

Hsiang Lin's Wife: After a person dies, does she turn into a ghost or not? Does she turn into a ghost or not? Tell me! Tell me!

Hsiang Lin's wife walked to the village entrance and finally fell down and died.[1]

In the film, another obvious technique was that before Hsiang Lin's wife fell to the ground, a narrator began to explain that this happened a long time ago. After Hsiang Lin's wife died, a voice-over echoed with what was at the beginning of the film, "in the 1950s", which clearly became distant from the story of Hsiang Lin's wife. It seemed to tell the audience that this was a story from a long time ago and had nothing to do with our times:

Voice-over: Hsiang Lin's wife, a diligent and kind woman, fell down and died after much suffering and abuse. This happened more than forty years ago. Yes, it was a story of the past. Fortunately, such an era finally passed away and finally went away with the wind.[2]

Why was this voice-over designed? Xia Yan once explained, "In order to make the audience live a happy life today, so as not to feel overly grave after watching the film, that is to say, there is no need to shed tears for the past. For the latter point, I have not changed my mind until today. I always feel that today's young people should understand the sad times of the past, but should only be grateful that the times are gone, and it is not necessary for them to have to feel sad and uncomfortable about the suffering of these characters from the past."[3]

The last words of Hsiang Lin's wife, in the film *The New Year's Sacrifice*, were those spoken to "I" the day before the death of Hsiang Lin's wife. In the film, the function of those words was similar to that of the novel, that is, to hint at the arrival of death. Although the screenwriter embodied it as a monologue, we as the audience could understand it as a question that Hsiang Lin's wife asked us. From

---

1 *The New Year's Sacrifice — From Novel to Film*, China Film Press, 1979, p.114.

2 Ibid., p.114.

3 Ibid., p.123.

this point of view, we become the object of her conversation, or even the "I" in the novel. According to the notes of the film star Bai Yang, she still thought over the last words of Hsiang Lin's wife until the late 1970s, which was about two decades later: "Whenever I think of these unsatisfactory shots, I really want to re-shoot it again."[1] "I truly want to re-shoot the scene. After the film was screened, I seemed to have 'the moment' of her facial expression and can vividly embody her. But 'the timber has been turned into a boat already', I can do nothing."[2] In some ways, the last words of Hsiang Lin's wife could be regarded as a place full of suspense in the film *The New Year's Sacrifice*. The screenwriter Xia Yan mentioned: "I accept this work of adaptation as a serious political mission."[3] Although he talked about adapting Lu Xun's works, from today's perspective, the "political mission" in the 1950s was probably not only related to the adaptation of Lu Xun's works, but also involved the shooting of the film itself. From this perspective, the main task of the film should be an ode to the People's Republic of China. The emplotment of the death of Hsiang Lin's wife by the film *The New Year's Sacrifice* was consistent with this point.

2.3 Legendary Emplotment

Finally, there is another approach that can be called the legendary emplotment. Some adaptations did not allow Hsiang Lin's wife to die. Not only was there no "death of Hsiang Lin's wife" on stage, but also a character who wanted to change her fate was added. By this approach, Hsiang Lin's wife no longer had a tragic ending. It was not the stereotyped blessing repeatedly performed, but in the end it hinted that this immutable state would be changed. The ending was not a tragedy again, but it was full of a positive and optimistic mood. Hsiang Lin's wife was not a victim, but an active and positive resister. Although only the script of the Pingju opera *Hsiang Lin's Wife* in 1953 was analyzed here, the author estimated that there might be other similar adaptations.

---

1   Bai Yang, *Exploration of Film Performance*, China Film Press, 1979, p.81.
2   Ibid., p.82.
3   *The New Year's Sacrifice — From Novel to Film*, China Film Press, p.119.

In this script, Hsiang Lin's wife not only did not die, but she also became a character who rebelled against society, rebelled against fate and rebelled against the ending arranged by Lu Xun.

> Wife: (singing) Seeing this, I couldn't help pondering and feeling sad. I had bought a threshold to atone for my sins in this life, but the sins were not atoned and I still suffered. It seemed that I was fooled to buy a threshold. Liu Ma, didn't you say that thousands of people walked over and trampled on the threshold to atone for sins in this life?

> Liu: Ah! Maybe it was in vain!

> Wife: So, God can't control my fate?

> Liu: I'm confused too!

> Wife: You said that we could turn into a ghost after death and meet our family in the underworld?

> Liu: A little bird told me, who knows—

> Wife: Even you don't know, what else do I fear? (looking towards God)

> Liu: Hsiang Lin's wife ...

> Wife: Ha ... Ha ... (singing) Regrets that I should not heed your words and buy a threshold to atone for my sins. Where there are gods and ghosts, which forced my family to part and die! I am going to the temple to see if I cut the threshold,

> Liu: Hsiang Lin's wife ... what are you going to do?

> Wife: Me?!! I want to cut that threshold!

> (The curtain falls rapidly)

Attached to Scene 5, Mrs. Lu preached Buddha (Heaven on Buddha, Earth on

Buddha, Heaven on Buddha of Eight Treasures, Amitabha.)[1]

In the script of the Pingju opera *Hsiang Lin's Wife* in 1953, the ending of the plot was not the death of Hsiang Lin's wife, but that she was going to cut the threshold. This plot was absent in Lu Xun's novel. Lu Xun's novel only mentioned that Liu Ma told Hsiang Lin's wife to buy a threshold to be her substitute in order to atone for her sins in this life. Hsiang Lin's wife spent a lot of money on buying a threshold, but as a result, this was useless. The Fourth Master did not care about this. Later, some adaptations added the plot of "cutting the threshold": After knowing that buying a threshold was useless, Hsiang Lin's wife was very angry and decided to go to the temple and cut the threshold. The plot of "cutting the threshold" had several versions, including Xia Yan's film, and Yuan Xuefen also mentioned this in her article.

Regarding whether Hsiang Lin's wife would cut the threshold at the end of the drama, Yuan Xuefen also made a careful consideration. When the film *Hsiang Lin's Wife* was shot in 1948, in order to strengthen the character's resistance, the detail of Hsiang Lin's wife cutting the threshold was never designed. This emplotment was absorbed by the feature film *The New Year's Sacrifice* (adapted by Xia Yan and starring Bai Yang). The scripts of local dramas (such as the Pingju) designed songs about her cutting the threshold. When Yuan Xuefen performed in 1956, she had given up the plot. In this adaptation, her opinion was even clearer: The threshold should be cut by the audience and the artwork should not arbitrarily exalt the character, but leave the audience to their imagination. In Lu Xun's novel, Hsiang Lin's wife questioned her fate and ghost, and that was proper. The adaptation does not need to impose such an action on this character.[2]

It can be found that "cutting the threshold" is not only a new plot, but also involves how to understand Lu Xun and how to connect Lu Xun with the current

---

1   Wang Yan and Li Fengyang, *Hsiang Lin's Wife (New Pingju Opera)*, Beijing Baowentang Bookstore, 1953, pp.35-36.
2   Zhang Lihui and Gao Yilong, 1984, pp.269-270.

reality. Did Hsiang Lin's wife have a sense of resistance? Many articles at that time discussed this issue because it was important in politics then, that is, at the time of the revolution. Unlike other works, in the 1953 script of the Pingju opera *Hsiang Lin's Wife*, cutting the threshold was no longer part of the plot before the death of Hsiang Lin's wife, but the ending of the story in which she did not die. In some ways, the death of Hsiang Lin's wife was changed into a kind of resistance or even a revolution, and the tragedy was adapted as a legend.

3. Conclusion

According to the above analysis, it is relatively complicated to explore the adaptations of *The New Year's Sacrifice* into films and dramas because it is related to many aspects, such as the historical background of different times, the expression and habits of different types of dramatic arts, and the understanding of Lu Xun in different times, etc. Moreover, in China in the 20th and 21st centuries, these are constantly changing. However, the "death of Hsiang Lin's wife" involves a very critical issue, that is, how to deal with the sufferings of the lower-class people, and this issue itself is inseparable from the "Chinese Revolution". It is often said that drama is a mirror of the society. Through the adaptations of *The New Year's Sacrifice* in different times, especially the emplotments of the "death of Hsiang Lin's wife", we can better understand the social and historical background of different eras.

中国对科特迪瓦的贡献

爱比【科特迪瓦】

菲利克斯·乌弗埃·博瓦尼大学研究员

引 言

中国在非洲的主要目标之一是帮助非洲国家发展。作为非洲西部的沿海国家，科特迪瓦像其他非洲国家一样，利用中国的资金建设各种类型的基础设施。因此，我们提出以下问题：科特迪瓦如何看待中国？此外，1996 年至 2016 年期间，中国与科特迪瓦合作建设了哪些大型公共工程，其影响如何？

本文的分析基于我们从诸多文献中心和地方机构（外交部、公共债务部）收集的一手和二手资料以及在科特迪瓦进行的书面和口头调查。

在本研究中，我们将"公共工程"定义为中国在文化、供水、能源、医疗卫生、道路和行政建筑等各个领域中资助的所有建设、翻新和维护工程，这些工程对社会经济的发展不可或缺，实际上可以增加科特迪瓦的建筑财产。1996 年是科特迪瓦第一座大型文化建筑的竣工年份，而 2016 年标志着科特迪瓦最伟大体育建筑的开端，所有这些工程均由中国提供资金。

本研究有两大目标，第一个目标是审查在该期间中国在科特迪瓦不同部门中已经完成的一些重要项目，第二个目标是揭示这些项目对双方的影响（中国 - 科特迪瓦）。因此，通过四个不同的轴展示一些已经完成的伟大公共工程；这些工程为科特迪瓦和中国带来的利益；以及两国面对的挑战。

一、中国在科特迪瓦完成的一些项目

自 1983 年两国正式建交以来，中国对科特迪瓦的发展提供的财政支持不仅日益增多，而且形式多样。通常是在各个领域建设公共工程，例如：文化、医疗卫生、教育、道路、供水、能源、行政等。因此，在本研究第一部分，我们选择关注中国从 1996 年到 2016 年在不同领域完成的 9 个重要项目。具体名单如下：阿比让文化宫（1996—1999）、亚穆苏克罗议员之家（2004—2009）、科特迪瓦外交部会议中心（2007—2009）、加尼奥阿综合医院（2009—2010）、外交部办公楼整体翻修工程（2011—2015）、阿比让－大巴萨姆高速公路（2012—2015）、博努阿自来水厂（2012—2015）、苏布雷水电站（2012—2017）、Ébimpé 奥林匹克体育场（2016 年 12 月至今）。

表 1：1996-2016 年中国在科特迪瓦完成的大型项目

项目名称	建设期间	施工企业	项目资金来源，单位：十亿西非法郎		项目总金额，单位：十亿西非法郎
			中国	科特迪瓦	
阿比让文化宫	1996 年 7 月—1999 年 10 月	中国成套设备进出口集团有限公司；甘肃海外工程总公司	12	9	21
亚穆苏克罗议员之家	2004 年 5 月—2006 年 5 月	武汉市建筑设计院	16	6.3	22.3
加尼奥阿综合医院	2009 年 4 月—2010 年	中国海外工程有限责任公司；武汉市建筑设计院	4.5	2.5	7
科特迪瓦外交部会议中心	2007 年—2009 年	江苏省建筑工程集团有限公司	1.53	-	1.53
外交部办公楼整体翻修工程	2011 年—2015 年	江苏省建筑工程集团有限公司	7.3836	-	7.3836
阿比让－大巴萨姆高速公路	2012 年 8 月—2015 年 9 月	中国机械设备工程股份有限公司（CMEC）	52.686466 24	9.30147026	61.9879365
博努阿自来水厂 1 期	2012 年 8 月—2015 年 3 月	中国地质工程集团有限公司	50	9.5	59.5
苏布雷水电站	2013 年 2 月—2017 年 11 月	中国水利水电建设集团（中国电建）	198	140	338

续表

项目名称	建设期间	施工企业	项目资金来源，单位：十亿西非法郎		项目总金额，单位：十亿西非法郎
			中国	科特迪瓦	
阿尼亚马奥林匹克体育场	2016 年 12 月起（正在建设）	北京建工集团有限责任公司	63.99024324	-	63.99024324

来源：作者从科特迪瓦的一些部门获取本表制作的资助，例如国家技术研究与发展局、外交部、公共债务部、Fraternité Matin

上表揭示了一些值得强调的事实。中国的确在很多领域进行了投资。因此，我们注意到，我国最重要的项目主要与公共领域有关，涉及两国在双边合作期间提出的基础设施项目。另外我们还发现，科特迪瓦的工程完全由中国企业提供资金。资金主要来源于大量的捐赠以及长期无息贷款（PSILT）与政府担保优惠利率贷款（PPBG）的组合。这两种类型的贷款都必须偿还，但与 PSILT 不同，PPBG 的利率从 1.5% 到 5% 不等。

例如，阿比让文化宫建设获得三批 PSILT 贷款的资助，协议分别于 1992 年 7 月 10 日、1995 年 11 月 16 日和 1997 年 5 月 14 日签订。亚穆苏克罗议员之家的资金也来自于无息贷款。相比之下，阿比让－大巴萨姆高速公路、博努阿自来水厂和苏布雷水电站（项目资金数量最多）获得 PPBG 贷款。科特迪瓦外交部会议中心由中国无偿援建。其他项目通过经济合作贷款提供资金。科特迪瓦一共取得大约由 7000 多亿西非法郎的资金用于完成这些项目。

中国政府不直接借款给科特迪瓦，而是指定中国企业（例如中国海外工程有限责任公司、中国成套设备进出口集团有限公司、中国机械设备工程股份有限公司、中国地质工程集团有限公司……）负责项目建设。因此，如上表所示，所有工程均由中国企业负责。我们有必要分析这些项目对两国的影响以及对科特迪瓦状况的改善。

二、科特迪瓦的利益

在科特迪瓦的发展过程中，中国的承诺和行动在多个层面上创造了财富。这一承诺在某种程度上有助于改善科特迪瓦人民的福祉，并为经济增长提供特定视角。

1. 社会福祉的改善

中国在科特迪瓦建设的项目在许多方面有助于改善科特迪瓦人民的福祉。

在医疗卫生领域，各个地区建设的医院和医疗中心使人们容易获得医疗服务。这可以降低过去因缺乏医疗带来的高死亡率。加尼奥阿综合医院建设就是一个很好的例证。供水领域的许多其他项目也为人民的福祉和休闲做出了贡献。通过建设自来水厂并且使用柴油发电机在村庄和城市钻井，中国为本地人提供可靠的饮用水。此外，道路建设有利于货物和人员运输，也为贸易等经济活动提供便利。

综上所述，中国在科特迪瓦的活动对人民的福祉起着至关重要的作用。中国企业在不同领域建设的基础设施非常重要，可能有助于消除贫困。事实上，中国为我们的国家发展和社会福祉提供帮助，也有利于我国实现可持续的经济增长。

2. 经济发展的视角

中国为科特迪瓦带来了更多的机会，可以提振我国的经济。

中国开展的项目确实能为科特迪瓦带来很多好处，可以在就业市场上发挥作用。此外，建筑工地雇用工人让一部分科特迪瓦年轻人能够临时就业。除了临时就业机会外，中国建设的项目还为一定数量的人提供了好工作。基础设施完全建成并正式移交给科特迪瓦政府后，科特迪瓦将安排新的合格人员进行管理。例如，为了保持良好的运转，议员之家聘用多个领域的工作人员。阿比让文化宫也是如此，永久雇佣60多名人员。这些项目有助于解决科特迪瓦持续的失业问题。

除了建立新的伙伴关系，加强两国之间的联系明显有助于提高某些资源（例如可可、棉花和石油）的出口数量。2010年以来，科特迪瓦向中国出售大量棉花。科特迪瓦对中国的棉花出口量约为"58300吨，占产量的80%"，2005年棉花是科特迪瓦对中国的第二大出口产品。从2005年起，其他产品（例如木材和橡胶）也销往中国。除了上述产品外，科特迪瓦也将石油出口到中国。石油是2006年销量最大的产品，占对中国出口总额的54.2%。这有助于提升科特迪瓦的经济，可以作为科特迪瓦政府让该行业更具有活力以推动产量增长和提高国内生产总值（GDP）的一种方式。

此外，两国之间的密切联系让科特迪瓦拥有新的伙伴关系，方便两国直接交流，作为科特迪瓦传统伙伴关系的补充。中国的参与对于科特迪瓦降低公共项目开发成本起到重要的作用。这可以保证科特迪瓦与适当伙伴合作的同时拥有更多的自主权和自由。例如，就基础设施项目的资金来源和实际用途而言，科特迪瓦可以决定与资金和条件更加宽松的企业合作。同样，中国也受益于与科特迪瓦的合作。

三、中国获取新建筑工程和新市场

中国在科特迪瓦的存在和行动为中国政府带来真正的好处，值得一提的是：中国企业及工人可以获取新工程，进入其他新市场，出口工业产品，例如建筑材料，而这些市场亦可提供自然资源。

1. 中国企业的新建筑工程

中国凭借两国良好的双边关系在科特迪瓦资助项目是中国企业获取建筑工程的重要手段。事实上，自 1996 年以来很多项目都是由中国企业完成。这些项目包括中国地质工程集团有限公司（CGC-CI）承建的博努阿自来水厂、中国机械设备工程股份有限公司（CMEC）承建的阿比让 - 大巴萨姆高速公路、中国电建集团承建的苏布雷水电站、江苏省建筑工程集团有限公司承建的阿比让文化宫和外交部大楼翻新改造项目、北京建筑设计研究院有限公司承建的奥林匹克体育场。所有这些都是中国企业在科特迪瓦建设的工程项目。

此外，上述工程建设还有利于中国增加就业，因为项目施工期间的很大一部分工人来自中国。关于这一点，Mema DIABATE 指出，"在签订合约时，其中一项条款是允许中国政府提供部分工人"。因此，与科特迪瓦建立和维持良好关系对中国而言是至关重要的利益，因为这可以保证获取更多的建筑项目。

在科特迪瓦获取新的建筑和公共工程项目是将科特迪瓦与中国联系在一起的真正利益。即使在科特迪瓦有强大的欧洲老牌公司，中国只需要在科特迪瓦取得建筑项目输出其建筑企业的价值，并且进行植入和推广。科特迪瓦也是中国与前欧洲公司进行合作的合适地点。中国可以证明本国企业完成大型项目的能力。除了获取新的建筑工程和良好的国际计划宣传外，这些活动还能保证中国进入科特迪瓦市场。

2. 中国进入新消费市场

中国进入科特迪瓦后可以接近科特迪瓦的消费市场。除了不同项目建设所需的材料外，中国还出口各种工业制成品。

使用中国企业生产的建筑材料，对于中国而言是实实在在的利益。事实上，中国企业自行提供基础设施建设项目所需的全部建筑材料。根据 2015 年以来对不同项目负责人的访谈和调查，我们可以得出结论，建筑材料基本上都来自中国。这一结论适用于中国建设 的所有大型工程项目。

参与亚穆苏克罗议员之家建设的工人 Rodolph SANHIN 称"项目几乎所有的材料都来自中国"。此外，Désiré Boua AKA 告诉我们："阿比让 - 大巴萨姆高速公路的建筑材料也来自中国，因为该项目由中国出资 85%，科特迪瓦出资 15%"。Mema DIABATE 指出，"在中国和科特迪瓦签订的项目建设合约中，有一项条款要求中国提供部分建筑材料。"同时，科特迪瓦政府对于建筑材料的进口完全免税。

除了基础设施建设使用的材料外，我们在本地市场上也发现标注"中国制造"的商品。从这个意义上讲，科特迪瓦正在成为中国的一个重要市场。

中国不但将工业产品出口到科特迪瓦，还从科特迪瓦进口自然资源。原材料是中国与部分非洲国家合作的重要方面。中国进入科特迪瓦市场后，可以获得科特迪瓦供应的各种原材料。中国从科特迪瓦进口的商品类型可以证明这一事实。主要进口商品包括棉花、可可、石油等原材料。2006 年，"中国从科特迪瓦进口的商品中 92% 是农产品"，这个亚洲国家受益于科特迪瓦丰富的能源资源。因此，科特迪瓦是中国资源供应保障和多样化战略中重要的一个国家。除了工程建设和市场外，中国在推动国内和国际计划的外交进程中还可以获得科特迪瓦政府的有力支持。

如上文所述，我们认为中国受益于在科特迪瓦的行动。科特迪瓦政府的信任是中国在科特迪瓦获取支持的关键所在，更重要的是，中国可以赢得新的建设项目和市场。总之，中国可以提升本国企业和劳动力，还可以出口产品并获得原材料供应。

四、项目实施过程中遭遇的挑战

与其他国家一样，中国公司在科特迪瓦的大型项目建设也面临着诸多挑战。在这方面，我们主要关注普遍存在的问题，例如本地劳动力的附属地位、投资性质和基础设施建设质量，以及不遵守环境规范。

1. 本地劳动力在建筑工程中的附属地位

中国企业在工程施工过程中对工人的管理通常是保证项目顺利实施的重要

因素。

事实上，与西方的建筑企业不同，除了本地劳动力之外，中国的企业还招聘大量的中国工人。我们在其他非洲国家也观察到类似的情况。例如，在加纳，Anthony Yaw BAAH 等指出："上海建工集团负责加纳塔克拉迪体育馆项目施工，聘用的 230 名工人中 150 名是中国人"。这表明中国工人在大型工程施工过程中非常重要。

过去在科特迪瓦建筑工地上这种现象很常见。我们在建筑工地上先后实施两次调查，亚穆苏克罗议员之家（2004—2006）和外交部大楼翻新改造项目（2011—2015），都证明这一情况的存在。亚穆苏克罗议员之家（2004—2006）工程建设监督人员指出，"在项目初期，从厨师、洗衣工到最高级别人员，还有工人，基本上都是中国人"。

相比之下，Mema DIABATE 称，"在外交部大楼翻新改造项目的 130 多位工人中，有 30 名中国工人和 100 名本地工人"。这些例子表明，过去建筑工地上的中国工人数量很多，但在中国和科特迪瓦政府的介入下，近年来趋势开始扭转。因此，面临的最大挑战仍然是本地工人在建筑工地上的工作岗位类型和待遇。

不同企业对本地工人的待遇也有所不同，但大多数企业还是具有一定的相似之处。Anthony Yaw BAAH 等对此做出如下总结："工作关系，对工会的敌视态度，不尊重工人的权利，恶劣的工作条件和各种各样的歧视"。这些问题引发反抗，还削弱中国和非洲的合作关系。

在科特迪瓦的建筑工地上这些现象并不明显。但也存在其他类似的问题，例如本地工人无法担任负责。本地工人很少被任命为负责人。我们对 Rodolphe SANHIN 的访谈确认，"亚穆苏克罗议员之家建筑工地上的所有小组负责人全部来自中国。"此外，在建筑工地上，不论本地工人在何时签订合同，他们都被视为是临时工。本地工人没有交通、住宿和医疗津贴。我们特别强调工资待遇差的问题。

最终，本地工人的工作条件非常糟糕。但不是任何中国企业、任何员工都是这种情况。因此，我们需要从工人待遇的角度认真思考中国雇主和本地员工之间的关系。除了工人管理外，科特迪瓦和中国政府还要求关注项目实施过程中的其他问题。

2. 环境影响和人口居住条件等挑战

不仅存在工人的问题，工程施工对环境和人口居住条件的影响也值得关注。

项目对科特迪瓦的环境影响不大，因为在建筑工地开工之前，本地监督人员将分析企业的安全和卫生计划。只有在计划批准后，企业才能开工。真正的问题在于建筑工地所在地原居民的管理。

企业所在的工地既是居住场所，也是经济活动发生的空间，例如本地社区赖以生存的农地。因此，在安全方面可能造成的后果是社区搬迁。例如，为了修建阿比让－大巴萨姆高速公路，很多居住点被拆除，但本地居民发现故土难离，很难适应其他居住地点。加尼奥阿综合医院大楼项目也是如此，拆除了建筑工地上原有的三座基督教福音派教堂。

项目也会对社会经济活动产生不良影响。在毫无准备的情况下全部或部分征用土地。某些地区的项目建设会涉及农地。根据国家技术和发展研究局收集的数据，1994年迪沃格格杜水稻垦区大约158户农民的农地被征用。

社区搬迁往往导致社会失衡，改变本地人口的生活轨迹。据我们所知，空间概念是非洲人民身份认同和本地化的关键元素，特别是科特迪瓦人，因此搬迁并不容易。在大多数情况下，搬迁会引发民众不满，甚至造成暴乱，妨碍建筑工地上的工程施工。阿比让－大巴萨姆高速公路、苏布雷水电站、苏布雷奥林匹克体育场等项目开工时就意识到这样的问题。此外，还面临其他现实挑战，例如沟通问题、人员培养和技术转让。

对劳动力管理、环境影响和人口居住条件的分析表明，中国企业在科特迪瓦的项目施工尚需解决某些问题。鉴于大型工程主要采用中国工人，科特迪瓦政府对此做出一些努力。建筑工地上的本地工人数量增加可以发现这一点。因此，各方之间必须继续合作，以解决可能妨碍完美协作的所有分歧。

结 论

综上所述，笔者认为，通过与科特迪瓦的双边合作，中国能够顺利完成各个活动领域的开发项目。这些行为对中国和科特迪瓦都有影响。不仅存在积极的方面，也有值得商榷的方面，在未来的合作过程中需要进一步思考。

中国在科特迪瓦的活动受益于科特迪瓦政府的信任。中国赢得一些工程项目，这对于中国企业和劳动力的发展有好处。此外，科特迪瓦的消费市场也让中国受益匪浅，可以购买项目施工材料，还可以获得自然资源供应。除了强化在基础设施领域的经历外，中国的活动可以为科特迪瓦的求职者提供工作岗位，还允许与其他合作伙伴交流。这意味着长期发展的前景。

虽然两国都能够受益，但在劳动力管理和环境方面仍面临一些挑战。双方在合作过程中有必要考虑上述事项。制订具体的战略会让合作的项目更加顺利和富有成效。

The Contribution of China for the Supplies of Côte D'Ivoire: Synthesis on Public Works, from 1996 to 2016

Ebi N'godo Filomene / The Republic of Côte D'Ivoire

University of Flix Houphouet Boigny, Researcher

Introduction

One of the main goals of the popular Republic of China in Africa, is to help African countries in their process of development. Côte d'Ivoire, as a coastal and West African country, takes advantage of some funding from China, for the creation of some infrastructures of all kind, like other African countries. This raises up the following question: On which basis is China perceived on the Ivorian land? Furthermore, what are the public huge works made by China, in terms of the cooperation with Côte d'Ivoire, from 1996 to 2016, and their impact?

This analysis is made possible thanks to primary and secondary sources collected from many documentation centers and local institution(ministry of foreign affairs, Direction of Public Debt), and some investigations, oral surveys made in Côte d'Ivoire.

In this study, we define public works as the entire works realized in the domain of building, rehabilitation, maintenance, funded by China in diverse areas such as, culture, hydraulics, energy, health, roads, and administrativebuilding, which are necessary to the socioeconomic development, indeed for the reinforcement of the architectural patrimony of Côte d'Ivoire. The year 1996, shows the achievement of the very first big cultural building in Côte d'Ivoire. As well as the year 2016, which marks the beginning of the greatest Ivorian sportive building, all of them funded by China.

This study deals with two main objectives, the first is about viewing some important projects already done by China in different sectors of the Ivorian activities during that period, the second is about revealing the impacts of these achievements on both parts (China-Côte d'Ivoire). Thus, through four distinct axes, while showing some great public works that have already been achieved; then the interests of these works for Côte d'Ivoire, and China; and some challenges that the two nations have to reach.

1. Some Projects Fulfilled by China in Côte D'Ivoire

The financial support for development that China provides to Côte d'Ivoire, since their diplomatic relations became official in 1983, is more and more visible and multiform. It is largely perceived through the realization of some public works in various sectors of activities, such as: culture, health, education, roads, hydraulics, energy, administration, Therefore, in the first part of our study, we choose to be focused on about nine important projects performed by China in these different domains of activities, from 1996 to 2016. They are as follow: The cultural palace of Abidjan (1996-1999),the house of representatives of Yamoussoukro (2004-2009), the conference center of the Ivorian Ministry of foreign Affairs (2007-2009). The general hospital of Gagnoa (2009-2010), the rehabilitation of the ministerial block (2011-2015), the highway linking Abidjan to Grand-Bassam (2012-2015), the station of water treatment in Bonoua (2012-2015), the hydraulic power of Soubré (2012-2017), the Olympic stadium of Ébimpé (since December 2016).

Table1   The tremendous projects fulfil led by china in côted'ivoire from 1996 to 2016

Different projects	Period of fulfillment	Companies in charge of the projects	Financial Contribution in billions of FCFA		Total amount of the project in billions of FCFA
			China	Côte d'Ivoire	
cultural palace of Abidjan	July 1996 -October 1999	COMPLANT; Gansu Oversea Engineering corporation	12	9	21
house of representatives of Yamoussoukro	May 2004 - May 2006	Institut d'Etudes d'Architecture de Wuhan	16	6.3	22.3
general hospital of Gagnoa	April 2009- 2010	COVEC ; Institut d'Etudes d'Architecture de Wuhan	4.5	2.5	7
conference center of the Ivorian Ministry of foreign Affairs	2007– 2009	Jiangsu Provincial Construction Group	1.53	-	1.53
rehabilitation of the ministerial block	2011 – 2015	Jiangsu Provincial Construction Group	7.3836	-	7.3836
highway liking Abidjan to Grand-Bassam	August 2012 - september 2015	China Machinery and Equipment Import Export Corporation (CMEC)	52.68646624	9.30147026	61.9879365
station of water treatment in Bonouaphase1	August 2012 - March 2015	CGC -CI	50	9.5	59.5
hydraulic power of Soubré	Febrary 2013- November 2017	Sinohydro (power china)	198	140	338
Olympic stadium of Anyama	Since Décember 2016 (being built)	BCEG	63.99024324	-	63.99024324

The observation of this chart, shows a certain number of facts which are worth to be underlining. Really, China invests in a lot of domains of activities. Therefore, we notice that the most important projects that the country fulfils are mainly related to the public domain, and they concern infrastructural projects broached during the bilateral cooperation between the two States. Another notice made from that chart is that, those works fulfilled in Côte d'Ivoire are all fully funded by Chinese companies. These achievements are the outcomes of too many donations, but also the combination of loans without interests in the long run (PSILT), and some loans with preferential rates and governmental improvement (PPBG). These two types of loans are to be reimbursed, but at the difference of PSILT, the PPBG is invoiced to a rate going from 1,5% to 5%(Direction de la DettePublique of Côte d'Ivoire, 2018, pp.4-6)

For example, the building of the cultural palace of Abidjan (see figure 1 and 2) is the outcome of three PSILT, (6 370 000 000, 3 185 000 000, and 1 911 000 000 fcfa), which successively were signed on July 10th 1992; November 16th 1995; and may 14th 1997. The house of representatives in Yamoussoukro (see figure 3 and 4) is also the outcome of a loan without any benefit amounting to 5 096 000 000 Fcfa. Contrary to, the highway linking Abidjan to Grand-Bassam (see figure 5 and 6), the project of water treatment from Bonoua, and the hydraulic power of Soubré (the highest project in terms of funds) are funded by the PPBG. Concerning the conference room of MEMAE, it is a donation from the Chinese republic. Some diverse other projects are about to be realized thanks to these same loans derived from the economic cooperation. In Total, Côte d'Ivoire was beneficiary of a sum around 703891779740 Fcfa, for the achievement of these projects.

The Chinese government does not directly lend some amount of money to Côte d'Ivoire, but appoints a Chinese company such as (COVEC, COPLANT, CMEC, CGC...) for the project to be fulfilled. Thus, as mentioned in the chart the entire works are made by some Chinese companies. The impact of these projects upon the two States and, the improving conditions of ivorians must be analysed.

2. The Interests of Côte D'Ivoire

The commitment and actions of China results in an asset in the process of development of Côte d'Ivoire, at several levels. This commitment contributes to a certain level to the welfare of the Ivorian population and offers some perspectives of economic growth.

2.1 The development of social well being

The projects undertaken by China in Côte d'Ivoire contribute to a social welfare of the Ivorian population at many levels.

In the domain of health, the construction of hospital and health centers in a variety of areas, allows the population to easily have access to health. This permit to reduce mortality often caused by lack of care. The construction of the general hospital of Gagnoa is a good illustration.Many other actions carried out in the sector of hydraulics contribute to the welfare and entertainment of the population. This is perceived through the construction of water stations, some drillings equipped with diesel engines in villages and the drillings for the urban hydraulics, China opens the access to drinking water of the population. Also, the building of roads facilitates the traffic of goods and people, but also allows the practice of economic activities such as trade.

To sum up, the intervention of China in Côte d'Ivoire plays a very crucial role in the wellbeing of the population. The infrastructures built by China in different domains, by means of its companies are very important and likely to help in the fight against poverty. Indeed, help for the development and social well-being, China can also allow a sustainable economic growth of the country.

2.2 The perspectives for economic growth

The presence of China in Côte d'Ivoire, is a means of more opportunities, likely to lift up the economy of the country.

The activities undertaken by China are really beneficial for Côte d'Ivoire, in the way that they contribute a lot in the market of employment. In addition, the fact of employing some workforce on the building sites allows first of all to temporarily occupy a part of the Ivoirian youth.Besides the temporary employment, the activities undertaken by China offer good jobs to a certain number of people. After the infrastructure are totally built and officially given to the Ivorian government, Côte d'Ivoire will appeal a new human qualified resource for its management. For example, for a good functioning, the House of Representativesemploys some workers from several domains. It is as the same for the cultural palace of Abidjan that permanently employs about 60 persons. All these help solve the matter of unemployment going on in Côte d'Ivoire.

Besides acquiring new partnerships, it is clear that reinforcement of the relationship between the two nations helps raise the rate of exportation of some resources such as cocoa, cotton and petrol. An important quantity of the Ivorian cotton production is sold to China since 2010. With a volume of about "58 300 tons, about 80%" (Anthony Caubin, 2010, p. 63) of the Ivorian exportations towards China, cotton, is the second most exported product in China in 2005. Other products such as wood, and latex are also sold in China since 2005. Apart from the products mentioned above, it is clear that Côte d'Ivoire also exports its petrol to China. It is the most sold product in 2006 with a rate reaching 54, 2% (Pierre Roche Séka, et al., 2008, p. 17) of the total value of the exportations in China. This contributes to elevate the economy of Côte d'Ivoire and may be a means for the Ivorian government to make this sector more dynamic for the growth of the production and lifting up the level of its Gross Domestic Product (GDP).

Moreover, the relationship between the two States allow Côte d'Ivoire to have a new partnership that will permit the two nations to exchange directly, added to the traditional partners of Côte d'Ivoire. This intervention from China plays a huge role in the reduction of costs of public development projects on the Ivorian territory. It guarantees to Côte d'Ivoire more sovereignty and freedom to cooperate with the suitable partner. For example, for the funding and practical application of an infrastructural project, Côte d'Ivoire can decide to cooperate with the company whose cost and conditions are more accessible. As the same, China also has some benefits from it presence in Côte d'Ivoire.

3. The Acquisition of New Building Sites and Markets by China

The presence and actions of China in Côte d'Ivoire, represent for the Chinese government a real source of benefits, let mention of: the acquisition of new building sites for these firms and its workforce, the access to new other markets on which it will be easy to export a part of its industrial production such as the construction materials, but also these markets will help supply natural resources

3.1 Some new building sites for Chinese firms

The projects funded by China in Côte d'Ivoire through the bilateral relation between the two nations, is an important means for the Chinese firms in acquiring more building sites. Indeed, the entire projects are fulfilled by the Chinese companies since 1996. Among those building sites we can mention the construction of water station located in Bonoua assigned to the Chinese geological engineering company in Côte d'Ivoire (CGC-CI) , The highway linking Abidjan to Grand-Bassam assigned to CMEC , the hydraulic power of Soubré assigned to Sinohydro, the rehabilitation of the cultural palace of Abidjan and the ministry of foreign Affairs made by CNCCU, and Jiangsu Provincial Group Co, the building of the Olympic stadium assigned by the Chinese company Beijing Institute Architectural Design. All these building sites are a means for some companies to be implemented and make visible the Chinese work in Côte d'Ivoire.

Furthermore, those building sites also allow China to facilitate its employment system, because a large part of workforce during the achievement of the projects originates from China. Concerning this, Mema DIABATE argues "In the signing of the contracts, there is a convention that permits the Chinese government to supply a part of the workforce". It is therefore, a crucial benefit for China to keep and have good relationship with Côte d'Ivoire, because this way guarantees a lot of coming building sites.

The acquisition of new building sites in the domain of construction and public works in Côte d'Ivoire, is a real stake in the relation that binds Côte d'Ivoire and China. Despite the presence of old and powerful Europeans companies in Côte d'Ivoire, China needs to find some building sites in Côte d'Ivoire to export the values of its companies of construction but to also implant and promote them. It is the appropriate spot for China to cooperate with former European companies in Côte d'Ivoire. This is a means for China to show the extent to which its companies are able to work on huge projects. Beside the acquisition of new building sites, and a good press on the international plan, these activities also guarantee China to have access to the Ivorian market.

3.2 The access of China to new consumption markets

The arrival of China in Côte d'Ivoire is a means to access the Ivorian consumption market. In addition to the materials for the implementation of the different projects, China also exports a variety range of manufactured products.

The use of some construction materials originating from Chinese firms, is a real benefit for the Popular Republic of China. In fact, for the execution of infrastructural projects, the Chinese companies come with all the needed construction materials. Then different interviews and investigations made since 2015, with supervisors of the works, draw a conventional conclusion according to which the basic construction materials always come from China. For all these huge works performed by China.

For his contribution in the achievement of the House of Representatives in Yamoussoukro, the worker Rodolph Sanhin, asserts that "for this project almost all the materials originated from China". Furthermore, Désiré Boua AKA, explains to us that "the construction materials used for the highway linking Abidjan to Grand-Bassam, also originates from China, because this project was funded at 85% by China and at 15% by Côte d'Ivoire". For Mema Diabate, "In the clause of the contracts signed by China and Côte d'Ivoire for the execution of the building sites, there is an agreement that requires China to provide a part of the construction materials". Moreover, the whole of these materials is exonerated of taxes by the Ivorian government.

Apart from the materials meant for the fulfilment of these infrastructures, we can underline the presence of articles labelled "Made in China" on the local markets. In this sense, Côte d'Ivoire is becoming an important market for China.

Besides exporting a part of its industrial production in Côte d'Ivoire, China has also a real benefit of some natural resources in Côte d'Ivoire. The raw material is an essential means in the cooperation existing between China and some African States. Thanks to its access to the Ivorian market, China now benefits of the variety of raw materials of Côte d'Ivoire, in terms of supply. The type of the importations from Côte d'Ivoire testifies that reality. Those importations are made up of raw materials such as cotton, cocoa, petrol, and so on. In 2006, "92% of the Chinese importations from Côte d'Ivoire are mainly agricultural products" (Séka Pierre Roche Séka, et al., 2008, p. 17), This Asian country also benefits of the energetic resources of Côte d'Ivoire. In this case, Côte d'Ivoire represents an essential territory for China in its strategy of reinforcement and diversification of these resources. Besides building sites and markets, China can also rely on the strong ideological support of Ivorian authorities, to reinforce its diplomatic courses on the national and international plans.

After the above, we can bear in mind that China remains beneficiary out of its actions in Côte d'Ivoire. The Chinese support in Côte d'Ivoire is a crucial element to obtain confidence from the Ivorian authorities, and most importantly it allows to get new building sites and markets. This aspect allows China to promote its own companies, its workforce, it also allows to export its products but also the reinforcement of its supply sources in raw material.

4. Some Challenges to Face in the Practical Application of the Projects

Like other nations, there is a number of challenges to face in the execution of huge projects by Chinese companies in Côte d'Ivoire. In this production, we mainly focus on the most recurrent problems, such as the subordination of local workforce, the nature of investments and the quality of fulfilled infrastructures, and the non-respect of environmental norms.

4.1 The subordination of local workforce on building sites

The management of workers on the building sites held by the Chinese companies often represents an essential element in the implementation of the projects

Indeed, contrary to Western companies of construction, Pékin and its companies recruit a large number of Chinese' workers besides the local workforce. We can observe the similar case in some African States. For example, in Ghana, Anthony Yaw Baah, et al. (2011, p. 67), reports that "The company Shanghai Construction Group, responsible of the building sites of the stadium in Takoradi, employed 150 Chinese out of 230 workers". This shows that the Chinese workers are very important in the accomplishment of huge works.

This situation that was frequent in the past on the Ivorian building sites tends to be normal. Two respectively investigations was done on the construction building site notably, The House of Representatives in Yamoussoukro (2004-2006) and the renovation of the ministerial block (2011-2015) testify this reality . The head in charge of the control of construction works of The House of Representatives in Yamoussoukro (2004-2006), argues that "at the beginning of the works, the workforce from the cook, the launderer to the most ranked workers, and also the workforces, was essentially Chinese ".

On the contrary, Mema Diabate argues that "on about 130 workers, committed in the work of the ministerial block renovation, we can mention about 30 Chinese and 100 local workers". These examples show that if the number of Chinese workers was high on building sites before, the trend changes over the years, Thanks to the different intervention of the Chinese and Ivorian government. Therefore, the greatest challenge to face remains the type of job, and the treatment reserved to these local recruits in the construction sites

Even though the treatment of local workers differs from one company to other, there are still some similarities that characterize most of them. Anthony Yaw Baah, et al. (2011, p.75) deal with those similarities through these words "The relations of work held, hostile attitude towards syndicates, non-respect of workers' rights, awful working conditions and many types of discrimination". These acts interpretation, bring about revolts and show that there are some problems which weaken the partnership between China and Africa.

These remarks are not forcibly perceived on all the building sites in Côte d'Ivoire. Therefore, there are some similar issues such as the non-accountability of local workers. Local workers are rarely appointed for charges of responsibilities. The interaction we had with Rodolphe Sanhin confirms that "The entireheads of groups on the building site of the House of representatives in Yamoussoukro were completely from China". Moreover, local workers are also considered as temporary workers no matter the time of their contracts on a building site. The local workers are not given allowance for their transportation, accommodation and Health care. We can also underline the issue of weak wages.

Ultimately, the working conditions of the local workers are unpleasant. But this situation is not always the same in all Chinese firms, and for all employees. Therefore, this situation requires a review of the relation between Chinese employers and local employees in terms of the worker treatment. Apart from the management of workforce, the Ivorian and Chinese authorities are appeal to have a look on other issues in the implementation of the projects.

4.2 Challenges at the level of environment and the living conditions of the population

Despite the question of workforce, the impact of the works upon the environment and the living conditions of the population, remains alarming.

The influence of the projects upon the environment in Côte d'Ivoire is much less demanding, because before a company starts working on a building site, its security and hygienic plan is analyzed by some local supervisors. It is only after the approval of the plan, that the company starts working. The real matter is rather perceived through the management of the population pre-established on the building sites.

Further, the sites on which companies are working serve whether as dwelling place or a space meant for the growth of economic activities, such as the plantations for these communities to survival. Therefore, concerning the question of security, these communities are displaced. For example, for the fulfilment of the highway linking Abidjan to Grand-Bassam many dwelling places have been destroyed, the residents found themselves in a situation where it was hard to leave their original places for somewhere else, where they had to adapt. It is the same for the building of the general hospital of Gagnoa, which caused the destruction of three Evangelical churches, seen in advance on the building sites.

The projects also have bad consequences upon the economic activities of these communities. They cause the systematic or partial destruction, often without warming. Thus, the activities undertaken in some areas within the country are mostly linked to these plantations. According to the data collected by Bnetd (2000, p.12) the arrangement of the rice perimeter in Guiguidou, in 1994, damages the plantations for about "158" peasants.

The relocation of communities creates a social imbalance within the population and often changes its own story. This situation is not easy when we know that the notion of space is crucial in terms of identifying and localizing peoples in Africa, mainly in Côte d'Ivoire. Most of the time this matter generates the dissatisfaction of populations and creates some uprisings likely to really prevent companies from working on the building sites. This was perceived at the beginning of the practical application of the projects for the highway linking Abidjan to Grand-Bassam, the hydraulic power of Soubré and the Olympic stadium of Soubré. Moreover, to those realities, it remains other challenges such as the problem of communication, brewing of people, and transfer of technology.

The analysis of the questions in relation with the workforce management, environment, and the living conditions of populations, shows that the completion of the projects by the Chinese companies in Côte d'Ivoire, leave some issues to deal with.Some efforts are made by the Ivorian government with Chinese workers committed for the realization of the huge works. This is perceived through the increasing of the number of local workers committed on the building sites. Therefore, these different entities must keep on working together, so as to solve all the issues of differences that can impede a perfectcollaboration.

Conclusion

To sum up, we can confirm that through its bilateral cooperation with Côte d'Ivoire, China identities itself through the completion of outstanding development projects in various domains of activities. These deeds have impacts both on China and Côte d'Ivoire. There are some positive aspects, but also aspects which are at the core of many discussions, and need to be analyzed for the future cooperation.

Thanks to its actions in Côte d'Ivoire, China benefits from the Ivorian authorities confidence. China also gets some sites for the promotion of its companies and workforce. Moreover, China, benefits from the Ivorian consumption market, on which some materials for the construction of projects are carried, and in turn supplies itself with some natural resources. Besides reinforcing its gained experience in the domain of infrastructure, the actions undertaken by China allows Côte d'Ivoire to occupy a part in these jobseekers and also to deal with other partners with whom to start. This represents a perspective of a long-term development.

Besides the profits that the two nations may have, there are some challenges to go through at the level of the management of workforce, and the environment. It is therefore crucial for the two States committed in that collaboration, to take into account the above issues mentioned. In order, to seek for some concrete strategies, that will make more useful and more productive these projects of cooperation.

Reference

1. Oral survey

Boua Aka Désiré, born on February the 15th 1953, chief of department of Infrastructural road works at Bnetd , in charge of the project for the highway liking Abidjan to Grand-Bassam, October 1st 2015 and January 2018 Abidjan.

Diabaet Mema , born on March, 20th 1970, Supervisor of infrastructural works , by BNETD, in charge of the works supervision of The house of representatives, the general hospital of Gagnoa, the rehabilitation of the ministerial block on October 1rt 2015 , august 28th2018, in Abidjan.

Kouakou Sanhin Rodolphe, born on June, 24th 1982, worker on the building site of The house of representatives, on September 21st 2015 , in Yamoussoukro, under the supervision of KOIDIO Konan Armel Didier , commercial agent, and KONAN Marcelin , commercial agent .

2. Printed sources

Bnetd," Projetd'Amenagement Hydro-Agricole de Guiguidou", August 2000, p. 32.

Caubin Anthony,*La coopérationéconomiquechinoiseen Afrique de l'Ouest: l'exemple de la Côted'Ivoire, research* memoir, sciences pro Toulouse, 2010, p. 100.

Direction of Public Debt,,"Conventions de prêt signées avec la Chine", march 01th 2018, pp.4-6.

Ministèred'ÉtatMinistère des Affaires Étagères, "Report on Chine/ Côte D'Ivoire, cooperation" MEMAE/CAB/DGCB/APO/BAB/14, Abidjan, september 20th 2014, 9.

Seka Pierre Roche, KOUAKOU Kouadio, "Relations economique entre la Chine et l'Afrique de l'Ouest :l'exemple de la Côte d'Ivoire", March 11th 2008 , p. 26.

3. journal articles

Yedagne Honorat (de), "5 milliards de FCFA pour la maison de la culture", *FraternitéMatin, n° 8327,* july12 th1992, pp.6-7.

Xu Yi Ching, "China and the United States in Africa: coming conflict or commercial coexistence?" *Australian journal of international affairs*, Vol 62, n°1, 2008, pp. 16-37

Yaw BAAH Anthony and JAUCH Herbert, "investissement Chinois en Afrique: Condition de travail et relations professionelles" *Alternative sud*, Vol. 18 n°2, 2011, pp. 63-82.

Zheng Ruolin, "De la françafrique à la chinafrique", *revue pour l'intelligence du monde,* November-december 2007, pp.64-75.

巴勃罗·德·罗卡与中国: 革命诗人的旅行、翻译和印象

何塞·米格尔·比达尔【智利】
华东师范大学拉丁美洲和跨文化研究中心博士生

引 言

受毛泽东邀请,智利诗人巴勃罗·德·罗卡(Carlos Ignacio Díaz Loyola 的笔名,1894—1968)和他的儿子于 1964 年访问中华人民共和国并居住了 5 个半月。[1] 在此之前,拉美前卫文学运动的先驱和坚定的马克思主义者巴勃罗·德·罗卡已经被中国的革命事业和毛主席的个人魅力所吸引,在他的许多作品中都提到这些。[2] 德·罗卡也坚持认为艺术可以而且必须用于革命目的,文学应将政治和社会正义作为其创作的核心。[3] 除了文学观点相似外,其他因素也使他更接近毛泽东。在这方面,德·罗卡于 1938 年被智利共产党(CHCP)边缘化,他对智利左派运动的幻想破灭,同时他还反对苏联修正主义和真诚关心农民,这是他倾向于中国

---

[1] 五个半月这个数字参见孙维学、林地等主编《新中国对外文化交流史略》,中国友谊出版公司 1999 年版,第 213 页。其他作者,比如 Eugenio Matus (1929-1997),认为 De Rokha 在中国待了六个月,参见 Eugenio Matus, "Pablo de Rokha," *Revista Trilce* 14 (1968): 3-6; 6, http://www.memoriachilena.cl/archivos2/pdfs/MC0013714.pdf.

[2] Pablo de Rokha, ed., *Antología 1916-1953*, (Santiago: Multitud, 1954), 89, 358, 360, 491, 497, 522, 524, 527; Pablo de Rokha, *Neruda y yo-Tercetos dantescos a Casiano Basualto* (Santiago: Ediciones Tácitas y Fundación de Rokha, 2016), 16,20, 98, 129.

[3] On De Rokha's revolutionary interest in his poetry, see Alejandro Lavquén, ed., *Antología de las obras completas de Pablo de Rokha* (Santiago: Pehuén, 2016), 21; 在本文的第三和第四部分中也进行了讨论。

共产主义计划的部分关键因素。[1]

　　德·罗卡在访问中国一年前创作的一首长诗表现出对中国革命道路和文学思潮的坚定支持，这首诗名为《中华人民共和国火之歌》（1963）。在这首诗中，他对中国的社会主义发展推崇备至。[2]随后他对社会主义中国的访问强化这种崇拜，他继续以与《火之歌》相同的意识形态创作关于中国的诗歌。这些诗歌从未出版过西班牙语版本，现存的只有《红色中国》打印稿（1964）。然而，1965年在中国出版二十首德·罗卡中文诗汇编，书名为《献给北京的颂歌》。

图1　巴勃罗·德·罗卡作品《红色中国》手稿封面。

　　虽然近年来巴勃罗·德·罗卡的文学作品受到广泛关注，但仍未有人研究他的中国诗歌和前往中国的旅行。[3]造成这种情况的主要原因之一是，许多研究

1　有关德·罗卡生平和政治观点的传记处理，请参见 Mario Ferrero, *Pablo de Rokha. Guerillero de la poesia* (Santiago: Sociedad de Escritores de Chile, 1967); Fernando Lamberg, *Vida y obra de Pablo de Rokha* (Santiago: Zig Zag, 1966); Naín Nómez, *Pablo de Rokha. Una escritura en movimiento* (Santiago: Documentas, 1988) and his "Introducción," in Naín Nómez, ed., *Canto del macho anciano y otros poemas*, 13-22, (Madrid: Editorial Biblioteca Nueva, 2003); also Lavquén, ed., *Antología de las obras completas de Pablo de Rokha*, pp. 15-22. 然而，这两项研究都没有充分探讨德·罗卡与毛泽东思想的密切关系。

2　Pablo de Rokha, ed., *Antología 1916-1953*, (Santiago: Multitud, 1954), 89, 358, 360, 491, 497, 522, 524, 527; Pablo de Rokha, *Neruda y yo-Tercetos dantescos a Casiano Basualto* (Santiago: Ediciones Tácitas y Fundación de Rokha, 2016), 16, 20, 98, 129.

3　On De Rokha's revolutionary interest in his poetry, see Alejandro Lavquén, ed., *Antología de las obras completas de Pablo de Rokha* (Santiago: Pehuén, 2016), 21; 在本文的第三和第四部分中也进行了讨论.

德·罗卡的学者认为那些作品未能反映德·罗卡复杂诗意假设的多方面声音。[1]
因此，在探讨诗人的贡献时，德·罗卡诗歌的文学评论家选择其他作品作为最具
代表性和最有价值的作品。另一个重要原因是，很难获取《红色中国》手稿，因
为原始文本和现存的少量影印本都由私人持有。实际上，直到最近，公众和部分
专家甚至都搞不清楚手稿是否仍然存在。[2]最后，中国和拉丁美洲文化关系在学
术领域缺乏关注的状态限制对拉美旅行者在中国的历史背景和印象的研究。[3]本
文的具体案例研究，通过探讨德·罗卡的旅行填补这一空白，这是所谓的"全球
六十年代"广泛背景下中国和智利交流的组成部分。[4]

中国旅行

巴勃罗·德·罗卡对中国的访问采取 20 世纪 50 年代以来中国对拉美文化外
交的核心形式：在精心挑选的中国地方进行安排好的旅行。中国中央政府不会直
接发出旅行邀请，而是通过为赞助中国与其他国家文化交流而成立的组织发出。
在德·罗卡的案例中，赞助组织是中国拉丁美洲友好协会。[5]旅行期间，旅行者通
常会与和自己职业相同的杰出中国人以及致力于中外友好的协会成员见面。在大
多数情况下，他们受到毛泽东、周恩来或其他中国最高领导人的接见并参加全国
性的庆祝活动。在国家代表的安排下，向他们展示新制度的物质和非物质成就以
及传统文化的亮点。在中国期间，来访者还受到中国东道主的鼓励，就不同问题

1　有关德·罗卡生平和政治观点的传记处理，请参见 Mario Ferrero, *Pablo de Rokha. Guerillero
　　de la poesía* (Santiago: Sociedad de Escritores de Chile, 1967); Fernando Lamberg, *Vida y obra
　　de Pablo de Rokha* (Santiago: Zig Zag, 1966); Naín Nómez, *Pablo de Rokha. Una escritura en
　　movimiento* (Santiago: Documentas, 1988) and his "Introducción," in Naín Nómez, ed., *Canto
　　del macho anciano y otros poemas*, pp. 13-22, (Madrid: Editorial Biblioteca Nueva, 2003); also
　　Lavquén, ed., *Antología de las obras completas de Pablo de Rokha*, pp. 15-22. 然而，这两项研究
　　都没有充分探讨德·罗卡与毛泽东思想的密切关系。
2　对于原稿下落背后的"侦探"故事，见 Pedro Pablo Guerrero, "*China Roja*: El libro perdido
　　de Pablo de Rokha," El Mercurio, Sección Artes y Letras, May 11, 2014. Accessed on 24 /12/2014
　　at: http://impresa.elmercurio.com/Pages/NewsDetail.aspx?dt=11-05-2014%200:00:00&NewsID
　　=226411&dtB=02-04-2017%200:00:00&BodyID=6&PaginaId=12; Alejandro Lavquén, "China
　　Roja de Pablo de Rokha," Punto Final 303, (April, 2014); "China Roja de Pablo de Rokha II,"
　　accessed on 13/12/2018 at http://letras.mysite.com/alav140514.html.
3　Pablo de Rokha, *Canto de Fuego a China Popular*, *Multitud* 89 (1963): pp. 1-6.
4　论冷战时期拉美研究的新视角，见 Eric Zolov, "Introduction: Latin America in the Global
　　Sixties," The Americas 70, 3 (January, 2014): pp. 349-362.
5　人民日报，1964-06-12.

（例如他们所来自国家的主要特征和革命前景）发表演讲并撰写文章并提出他们
对中国现实的看法。希望他们回国后写作关于访问期间所见、所闻和所读内容的
有利报告。[1]

　　根据中国报纸的报道、对诗人朋友和亲戚的采访、德·罗卡旅行和诗歌的照
片，诗人在中国的行程可以得到一定程度的重现。[2] 行程大致分为两个阶段。第
一阶段对应前三个月，从德·罗卡于 1964 年 6 月 10 日抵达中国到 9 月初。按照
欧金尼奥·马特斯（Eugenio Matus）与巴勃罗·德·罗卡在中国见面的报告和
中国报纸上对诗人在这三个月期间参加官方活动的报道；这段期间遵照中国为
德·罗卡访问安排的最初行程。[3] 在此期间，诗人创作出《红色中国》的大部分
诗歌。[4]

　　就诗人去过的地方而言，这三个月也是最活跃的。在《红色中国》的五十
首诗中有几首提及这些地方。根据中国报纸上的诗词和解说可以重现他的行程，
诗人在这三个月中非常活跃，去过的地方从北方的满洲里到南方的上海。在穿
越城市和乡村地区时，德·罗卡探索古代和近代的历史遗址，包括长城、中国
国家博物馆、天安门广场、颐和园和杭州西湖。他还参观重要的社会和工业
项目，例如小学、养老院、人民公社和钢铁厂。最后，灌溉系统、水坝、桥梁
和其他公共工程也是他这次旅行的重要部分。总之，德·罗卡是历史现实的见
证人。

　　在前三个月中，德·罗卡出席会议和活动，与中国著名的文化领袖见面。例
如，他见到 20 世纪中国的两位重要作家，中国文化部长兼中国作家协会主席茅盾
（1896-1981）；全国人民代表大会常务委员会副委员长和中国文学艺术界联合会主
席，诗人郭沫若（1892-1978）。根据私人秘书马里奥·费雷罗（Mario Ferrero）的

1　Ratliff, "Chinese Communist Cultural Diplomacy toward Latin America," 59-60; Hubert,
　　"Intellectual Cartographies of the Cold War," 337; Montt Strabucchi, "The PRC's Cultural
　　Diplomacy towards Latin America in the 1950s and 1960s," pp. 69-70.
2　以下是德·罗卡的中国之行和有关中国的诗歌简介：Ferrero, *Pablo de Rokha. Guerillero de
　　la poesía*, 37, 81-82; Lamberg, *Vida y obra de Pablo de Rokha*, 183; Nómez, *Pablo de Rokha. Un
　　escritura en movimiento*, pp. 207-209.
3　Matus, "Pablo de Rokha," 6. Matus 指出，这位诗人最初被邀请了两个月。然而，在这三个月
　　里进行的一系列官方活动表明，最初的邀请可能会持续三个月。
4　比如，Eugenio Matus 的报告中指出 "两个月后" 诗人发表了 "五十首伟大的诗"。Matus, "Pablo
　　de Rokha", 3. 人民日报和上海文汇报上的一些报道也表明，到那年九月，诗人已经写了 "五十
　　多首诗"，人民日报，1964-09-12；文汇报，1964-09-12。

说法，德·罗卡与后者建立密切的友谊。[1] 几个月来他参加的活动，最重要的是在哈尔滨举行的一次示威，目的是谴责美国对越南的军事介入。这次会议上，诗人的儿子在众多听众面前朗诵一首诗《谴责美帝国主义》，这首诗后来被收录到《献给北京的颂歌》。[2]

图 2　巴勃罗·德·罗卡（左四）在颐和园。经德·罗卡基金会同意发布。

1　见 José Miguel Curet Arana 和 Naín Nómez 的评论：José Miguel Curet Aranam "Pablo de Rokha: Vanguardia y Geocrítica: La poesía de *U* (1926) y *Carta Magna de América* (1949)," 博士论文，Universidad de Salamanca, Salamanca, 2015, 242; Nómez, *Pablo de Rokha. Una escritura en movimiento*, 208; 然而，Nómez 仍然认为，在一些诗歌中，如德·罗卡的 "Gran oda popular al río Yangtsé" (Great Ode to the Yangzi River) 中，"有时会表现出他那富有远见的大嗓门"。在提到同一首诗时，Eugenio Matus 也指出，这只是一个天才的作品，见 Matus, "Pablo de Rokha," 6.

2　对于原稿下落背后的"侦探"故事，见 Pedro Pablo Guerrero, "*China Roja*: El libro perdido de Pablo de Rokha," *El Mercurio*, Sección Artes y Letras, May 11, 2014. Accessed on 24 /12/2014 at: http://impresa.elmercurio.com/Pages/NewsDetail.aspx?dt=11-05-2014%200:00:00&NewsID=226411&dtB=02-04-2017%200:00:00&BodyID=6&PaginaId=12; Alejandro Lavquén, "*China Roja* de Pablo de Rokha," *Punto Final* 303, (April, 2014); "*China Roja* de Pablo de Rokha II," accessed on 13/12/2018 at http://letras.mysite.com/alav140514.html.

图3　巴勃罗·德·罗卡和他的儿子在中国的小学。经德·罗卡基金会同意发布。

第二阶段从 9 月初到 1964 年 11 月下旬或 12 月初返回智利。这个阶段对应"额外期间"，诗人决定将访问期间延长三个月。据称延长访问期间主要出于三个原因。第一，他对直接参与自身诗歌翻译的兴趣。第二，德·罗卡对中国的流连忘返。例如，访问前三个月结束时有一次与郭沫若会面，他强烈表达对中国的最深切的感情。在那个场合，除其他外，诗人告诉郭，我到过许多国家，而中国给我留下的印象是我一生中获得的最深刻最良好的印象，是任何人都无法把它磨灭掉的。[1] 第三，延长访问期的决定还与以下事实有关，即诗人到达后不久就患上重病，需要康复治疗。[2]

在后几个月中，诗人显然很少出行，大部分时候都在北京。同时，与中国官

1　人民日报，1964-09-12; 文汇报，1964-09-12.

2　然而，关于这个问题的一些研究已经证明是近年来一些特别吸引人的奖学金的丰硕源泉。比如，María Montt Strabucchi, " 'Writing about China.' Latin American Travelogues during the Cold War: Bernardo Kordon' s '600 millones y uno' (1958), and Luis Oyarzún' s 'Diario de Oriente, Unión Soviética, China e India' (1960)," *Revista Caminhos da História*, 21, 1 (2016): 93-124; "Viajeros chilenos a la RPC en los años cincuenta y sesenta," in Stefan Rinke, ed., *Entre espacios: la historia latinoamericana en el contexto global. Actas del XVII Congreso Internacional de la Asociación de Historiadores Latinoamericanistas Europeos (AHILA)*, Freie Universität, pp. 9-13 September, 2014, Colegio Internacional de Graduados "Entre Espacios" : pp. 3027-3035; Rosario Hubert, "Intellectual Cartographies of the Cold War. Latin American visitors to the People' s Republic of China, 1952-1958." In Robert T. Tally Jr., ed., *The Routledge Handbook of Literature and Space*, 337-348, (Abingdon, Oxon and New York: Routledge, 2017).

方的见面和参加活动频率低于前几个月。在此期间最重要的活动是纪念中华人民
共和国成立 15 周年举行的传统阅兵，这是德·罗卡参加的少数活动之一。在该
活动上，德·罗卡和他的儿子以及何塞·万图勒里是智利的唯一代表。[1] 他为这个
活动所创作的诗歌标题为《欢呼国庆》- 作为《红色中国》手稿的附件得以保留，
这是诗人在中国最后几个月唯——首关于中国的诗歌。剩下的时间似乎都花在校
正《红色中国》手稿以及其他诗歌翻译和写作上。[2]

图 4   巴勃罗·德·罗卡和他的儿子以及陪同翻译赵金平（1933-?）（右一）庆祝中华人民共和
国成立 15 周年。经德·罗卡基金会同意发布。

　　虽然中国方面精心安排巴勃罗·德·罗卡的访问，但值得一提的是他也享有
自由活动的时间。例如，费尔南多·兰伯格（Fernando Lamberg）在《德·罗卡

1　人民日报，1964-10-01. 两天后，德·罗卡还参加了由不同中国友好协会组织的仪式。所有参
　　加过中国革命 15 周年庆祝活动的外国代表都参加了这次聚会。人民日报，1964-10-04.

2　从 1964 年 10 月起，中国的杂志和报纸上刊登了他的八首诗的中文译本，这表明翻译工作
　　在当年的 9 月和 10 月间加强了。据我所知，在这些翻译之前，德罗哈的诗中只有另外两首
　　可以在中文出版物上找到。见人民日报，1964-07-05，1964-08-13，1964-10-10，1965-02-
　　16; Pablo de Rokha, 赵金（译）., "孟泰同志，" 鸭绿江，10 (October, 1964): pp. 61-62; "献给
　　上海的热情之歌，" 文汇报，10 (October 1964): 4; 赵金平（译）., "给美帝国主义的公开信，"
　　世界文学，12 (December, 1964): 11-18; "诗四首: 毛泽东，伟大的榜样，中国儿童，" 诗刊，
　　10, (October 1964): pp. 39-46。Mario Ferrero 还肯定，德·罗卡的诗也在其他中国报纸上发表
　　过。遗憾的是，我还没有机会查阅到那些出版物。Pablo de Rokha, Guerillero de la Poesía, 37.

传记》中写道，到达后，"主人面带微笑和友好的表情，允许他随意闲逛数周"。[1]
此外，欧金尼奥·马特斯也评论说："下午，完成工作后（写作并回答中国翻译对
诗歌的疑问），[他]来到外国专家居住的友谊宾馆和一群朋友聊天。我们在宾馆
的公园散步。如果天气不好，他会待在我们的公寓里。"[2] 马特斯提到，一天德·罗
卡和他的儿子费利克斯（中文非常好）前往王府井街买鞋，还有一次他们在前门
大街购买外套，这些服装在许多最后照片中成为他经典形象的一部分。[3]

翻　译

邀请巴勃罗·德·罗卡访问的主要目的之一是全面报告中国的现实。然而，
这个想法被诗人部分拒绝。[4] 根据费尔南多·兰伯格的说法，德·罗卡意识到，"在
了解这个国家不平凡现实"之后，他需要"至少五年时间完成这个主题"。[5] 然后，
对于德·罗卡来说，为了说明这一现实的伟大之处 - 无法全面描述 - 最合乎逻辑
的解决方案是创作一系列诗歌。他将自己的决定传达给茅盾，茅盾毫不犹豫地接
受该建议。[6]

中国人对翻译德·罗卡诗歌感兴趣主要是认为中国当年流行的文学观念和智
利诗人接近。对于德·罗卡而言，大众和无产阶级艺术理念是英雄和史诗风格写
作的一部分，这是他将悲剧定义为"美洲社会史诗"的典型代表。这种写作风格
基于意象的直觉发展，从而将诗人转变为专业的政治家。因此，对于智利诗人而
言，没有中立的形式，实现的一切形式都应具有社会性和史诗性：他们必须讲述
大陆民众的悲惨历史。德·罗卡认为，为了使诗歌具有社会期望，诗人需要依赖
传说和史诗，因为这是人们的诗意直觉，人是创造者。对于德·罗卡来说，这是
对现实的真正艺术诠释，是对客观现实的升华，并使人们的思想孤立。因此，"为
艺术而艺术"的格言是美学唯心主义的模糊神秘化。[7]

考虑到德·罗卡对艺术首先必须作为推动社会变革渠道的看法，毛泽东当政

1　Lamberg, Vida y obra de Pablo de Rokha, p. 183.

2　论冷战时期拉美研究的新视角，见 Eric Zolov, "Introduction: Latin America in the Global Sixties," *The Americas* 70, 3 (January, 2014): pp. 349-362.

3　Matus, "Pablo de Rokha," pp. 5-6.

4　Lamberg, *Vida y obra de Pablo de Rokha*, p. 183; Matus, "Pablo de Rokha," p. 3.

5　Lamberg, *Vida y obra de Pablo de Rokha*, p. 183.

6　Lamberg, *Vida y obra de Pablo de Rokha*, p. 183.

7　On this point, see Lavquén, ed. *Antología de las obras completas de Pablo de Rokha*, p. 21.

时中国文学界对德·罗卡的诗歌感兴趣，反之亦然，这一点丝毫不觉得奇怪。在中国，从 1949 年到 1966 年的小说和诗歌被描述为"革命浪漫主义与革命现实主义相结合"。这种明显自相矛盾元素的结合是社会主义的现实主义实践中固有悖论的逻辑延伸，由毛泽东在《在延安文艺座谈会上的讲话》（1942 年）中继承。他探讨艺术和文学在革命背景下的作用，并得出两个结论。首先作者需要吸收农民的日常用语并适应大众艺术的形式，因为这些是人民的真实审美形式和内容。其次文学不应原封不动地表现出残酷的现实。相反，它必须按照党的艺术标准，以一种富有想象力的方式改变表面上的现实，唤醒群众并鼓励他们团结起来，实现为改变自身所处环境而奋斗的乌托邦理想。[1]

中国的拉美文学翻译与上述文学趋势并没有任何不同。20 世纪 50、60 年代几乎完全限于当代或以前的作品，根据中国人的说法，它们反映人民的生活并使该地区被压迫群体的革命或民族民主运动理想化。[2] 译者在译后记中的德·罗卡生平简介和在《献给北京的颂歌》中包含的书签凸显译者对强调德·罗卡诗歌政治内容的兴趣。在这些作品中，德·罗卡的入选作品主要集中在最激进的作品上，包括《海沟之歌》（1933 年）、《五首红歌》（1938 年）、《红军歌》（1944 年）、《朝鲜战争烈士葬礼》（1950 年）和《中华人民共和国火之歌》[3]。考虑到德·罗卡对中国文学形式和政治运动的拥护，诗歌翻译成中文让诗人感到高兴，不仅因为正如马图斯指出的那样，"他被拥有数亿中国读者的说法所感动"[4]，或许更重要的是，因为他的文学作品被中国公开确认为毛泽东和斯大林"宏伟艺术黄金标准"诗人的范例，代表"人民的胜利"。[5]

即使对翻译质量进行完整而详尽的分析超出本文的研究范围，但对西班牙语和中文版本的诗歌及标题的比较可以为译者所享有的自由提供启发。然而，重要

1 人民日报，1964-06-12.

2 Ratliff, "Chinese Communist Cultural Diplomacy toward Latin America," 72; Teng, *Bianjing zhinan*, pp. 29-43.

3 Ratliff, "Chinese Communist Cultural Diplomacy toward Latin America," 59-60; Hubert, "Intellectual Cartographies of the Cold War," 337; Montt Strabucchi, "The PRC's Cultural Diplomacy towards Latin America in the 1950s and 1960s," pp. 69-70.

4 关于诗人访华之旅中的德·罗卡熟人访谈录，见 Diego Meza, dir., Eduado Lobos, prod., *Pablo de Rokha. El amigo piedra* (Chile: La Cresta Producciones y Deboom Studio, 2010). Accessed on 5/11/2018 at: https://www.youtube.com/watch?v=s5tu-VEJ2QE&t=52s.

5 Matus, "Pablo de Rokha," 6. Matus 指出，这位诗人最初被邀请了两个月。然而，在这三个月里进行的一系列官方活动表明，最初的邀请可能会持续三个月。

地是，不仅因为翻译者遭遇的困难，还为了吸引中国读者的兴趣，必须这样做。其中一个例子是德·罗卡诗集中包含的最后一首诗对应 *Ovación universal* 的删节版本。赵金平选择将标题译为"欢呼国庆"。他通过将"大众"替换为"国庆"明确这首诗的主旨；即中华人民共和国成立庆典，而原始名称中没有明确指出。

另一个证明译者希望吸引中国读者关注的例子是最容易翻译的诗歌之一《北京欢笑》中。这首诗的第一节是西班牙原文：

> Excited among these kind people
>
> their full laugh I would compare
>
> to peaches or oat,
>
> or to almonds, or to poetry

> (Emocionado entre esta gente buena
>
> su risa llena la compararía
>
> a los melocotones o la avena,
>
> o a las almendras, o a la poesía)[1]

而中文版为：

> 在这些善良的人们 中间，我很激动，
>
> 他们的美丽的欢笑，
>
> 好比鲜桃和红杏，
>
> 好比诗歌和芦笙．

显然，中文译本使用的名词和形容词存在一些差异。首先，在中文版本中，形容词"丰满"被"美丽"代替。其次，增加形容词"红"和"鲜"。第三，"燕麦"和"杏树"这两个名词被对中国读者具有文化含义的其他名词所取代："红杏"和"芦笙"。

第一个词语"红杏"是著名的诗词典故，出自宋代诗人（960-1279）叶绍翁

---

1   De Rokha, *China Roja*, 手写稿，中国，1964. 本文作者将这首诗的中文译本译成西班牙文，见 Lavquén, *Antología de las obras completas de Pablo de Rokha*, pp. 139-141.

的诗《游园不值》。字面意思是春天的红色杏花怒放。然而，从隐喻的角度来看，这个词语暗示带有哲学意味的典型春天景象的诗意形象。[1] 同时，第二个词语"芦笙"是一种苗族簧管乐器，主要由中国西南农村地区以及老挝和越南等周边国家的不同民族演奏。因此，赵金平决定用"芦笙"和"红杏"代替"杏仁"和"燕麦"的做法创造出两个原文不存在的现象：两种水果（红杏和桃子）和两种艺术表现形式（音乐和诗歌）。这种变化不容忽视，因为中国的艺术表达总是追求对仗。如前文所述，翻译决定可以反映出译者的努力和采取的机制，以使德·罗卡的诗歌对中国读者更具吸引力。

赵金平与德·罗卡合作翻译《红色中国》手稿现存 51 首诗中的至少 21 首。[2] 这项工作的成果在 1965 年 9 月为世人所知，二十首诗被收录在《献给北京的颂歌》。这本诗集由作家出版社出版，新华书店发行。诗集标题与《红色中国》第 17 首诗《献给北京的红色颂歌》（中文译本第 11 首诗）呼应。封底也出现西班牙语的"北京欢乐与其他诗词"标题。封面由著名插图画家张守义（1930-）设计，除了创作个人作品外，为外国文学书籍译本制作封面和插图也是其职业生涯的重要部分。[3] 就这本书而言，张守义设计的封面反映时代的流行主题，新旧交织在一起。从这个意义上讲，北京的古代皇宫与建筑用起重机、城市的现代灯具和建筑物融为一体，而燕子和挂在气球上的红色宣传布可以理解为唤起人们对中国共产党领导下实现美好未来的期望（见图 5）。

关于入选的诗歌，在自由翻译的情况下，改造的内容主要是为了吸引中国读者的注意。不完全否认时间的缺乏和翻译某些诗歌的困难可能也是选择的考虑因素。举例来说，译者抛弃标题中不直接涉及任何中国事件、社会工程、城市或人民的诗歌，这明显是为了吸引中国读者。《实验》、《历史的篡改》或《革命意志》等诗歌就是这种情况。唯一包含抽象内容的诗歌是《伟大的榜样》，把中国比作一个伟大的诚信典范。同样，译者也不考虑与文化相关的诗歌，例如《大众文化宫》、《诗意共和国》和《美食交响团》，做出决定的原因可能是这些诗歌不是以"革命"为焦点。最后，另一种特殊情况，诗歌《在中国看古巴》是对古巴的推崇，

1　出自宋祁 (980-1061) 的《玉楼春·春景》。

2　已经翻译但未在《献给北京的颂歌》中收录的唯一一首诗是《致北美帝国主义的公开信》，巧合的是，这本诗是本研究收集到的《红色中国》手稿中遗漏的一首诗。关于诗歌翻译，详见注释47。

3　张守义：《张守义外国文学插图集》，湖南美术出版社 1982 年版；张守义：《我的设计生活》中国旅游出版社 2007 年版。

将其排除在外极有可能是因为与中国没有直接关系。相比之下，译者收录献给中国城市的八首诗中的七首、两首围绕革命人物（《毛泽东》和《孟泰同志》[1]）的诗、社会项目或公共工程四首诗中的三首（《人民公社》、《灌溉水的胜利》和《蕃瓜弄》[2]）、中国不同人群的九首诗中的四首（《北京的人和街道》、《北京欢乐》、《中国儿童》和《公社社员》）。

图5：《献给北京的颂歌》封面

后三首诗包括并代表相同的编辑决策模式。因此，诗歌《谴责美帝国主义》不仅是对中国最大敌人之一的直接攻击，还提到1964年8月在哈尔滨举行的针对美国介入越南的示威。《长城》一诗可以将中国的过去转变为新中国的象征，其入选毋须进一步解释。最后一首诗《欢呼国庆》是《欢呼大众》的改编版本，是对新中国成立十五周年的歌颂，体现德·罗卡和毛泽东文学思想的意识形态导向。

最后，赵金平还将读者的注意力引向诗集附上的德·罗卡生平简介中。在最后一段，赵金平感谢德·罗卡对新中国的支持，译者总结诗人访问的最重要

1　孟泰（1898-1967），中国钢铁工人，在20世纪50、60年代是中国工人劳动模范。

2　蕃瓜弄是位于上海市闸北（如今的静安区）的棚户区，聚集着第二次世界大战期间从其他中国城市来到上海的难民。1963年，蕃瓜弄第一阶段翻新建设标志着上海市政府几十年消除贫民窟努力的开始。

方面："他热情地进行诗歌创作，支持我国人民反对帝国主义，反对修正主义的斗争，赞扬我国的社会主义建设成就，歌颂我国人民的伟大领袖毛主席。"[1] 因此在中国至今唯一的官方版本中，赵金平让智利诗人的毛主义形象在中国永不磨灭。

诗人的印象

德·罗卡的《中华人民共和国火之歌》、《红色中国》和《欢呼国庆》充分体现中国革命在诗人心目中最深刻的积极印象。在这些文字中，诗人始终如一地展示田园诗般的中国社会主义现实的美好形象，同时无条件地支持中国的事业。德·罗卡认为中国是非常独特的，是公正和道德优越社会的典型代表。为了揭示这种乌托邦式的中国形象，他经常使用副词和代词，例如 "hasta"（甚至）、"todo"（一切/每个人）、"nunca"（从未）、"siempre"（总是）、"solo"（仅）和 "nadie"（没有人），这些词有助于德·罗卡强调中国的特殊性。例如，在这一行中，诗人描述中国群众时写道："我从未见过比他们更快乐的平民面孔/伟大而朴素的人民"）。[2] 同样，灾难，例如过去的饥荒，被描述为在"可爱的胜利大众中国"完全消失，据诗人所说，"没有人挨饿"。[3]

提到人民的品格，中国人的独特和积极的特点也被凸显。对于德·罗卡来说，"所有人相似/或平等"，中国人民表现出特别之处：中国人民 "为英雄事业而生/；中国人清醒而公正，懂得并做了必须做的事情……"[4] 通过描述中国群众作为整体人群的特点进一步强化中国当前的积极整体性，尽管规模庞大，但作为整体和统一的集体发挥作用（例如 "大潮"[5]、"广大的中国父母和子女"[6]、"广大人民群众"[7] 或 "像海沙一样数不胜数的人民"[8]）。德·罗卡将团结如此庞大人口的能力视为毛泽东在中国成功的另一个重要因素。通过这种方式，他远离任何个人主义的观点，因为这种观点试图将个人置于社会和共同利益之上。因此，德·罗卡将

1　De Rokha, *Xiangei Beijing de songge*, p. 85.
2　De Rokha, *China Roja*, p. 37.
3　De Rokha, *China Roja*, p. 8.
4　De Rokha, *China Roja*, p. 84.
5　De Rokha, *China Roja*, p. 1.
6　De Rokha, *China Roja*, p. 16.
7　De Rokha, *China Roja*, p. 106.
8　De Rokha, *Canto de fuego a China Popular*, p. 3.

构成中国人口的不同群体变为"无个性特征"，这是"伟大中国人民"的正确观点，
"为人类的伟大事业服务 /，为工人阶级和全体人民服务"[1]。—"在群众内部，群众
是伟大的！"[2] — 德·罗卡强调。因此，人类不能够在社会以外实现自己的个性，
而是能够参与整个中国社会事业，参与由此产生的共产主义建设。从这个意义上
讲，新中国在德·罗卡的诗歌形象中是由举措、改革和行动方案组成的整体单元，
以整个社会横向蓬勃发展的形式运作。反过来，这表明与资本主义社会相比，社
会主义社会生活具有生产力和非常和谐。

德·罗卡对中国历史的看法也渗透着中国的经验无与伦比的想法。例如，智
利作家解释说，"不再被欺辱的国家 / 不再受伤害的国家"[3]。因此，对中国现状的
推崇不可避免地回对过去帝国时代的伟大和艰难，这种话语只是为了解释新中国
是长期遭受压迫和原本智慧的产物。根据德·罗卡的说法，社会主义中国代表着
"最新，最古老"的矛盾。[4]

德·罗卡创作的中国作品另一个关键问题是他相信中国强大经验的全球意
义。诗人评论道，这个社会主义国家具有"国际化的思维和行动"。[5] 德·罗卡认
为中国的政治模式与整个国际革命运动的全球未来有关。中苏冲突发生后，中华
人民共和国已经崛起成为真正的引领者。德·罗卡夸张地提问："六亿五 / 千万中
国人，/ 举起红旗，在这里，说："现在"？ …… / 不。史诗政党 / 的背后，有一个
世界，强大的 / 世界，自由的世界，/ 巨大的花朵在颤抖，这是整个工人阶级 /，
为数众多"。[6] 中国成为"站在世纪的开端"[7]的政治实体，写下"地球上全体人民
/ 有血有肉的伟大诗歌"[8]，"有意识和 / 不断地向所有人 / 劳动人民开放"[9]，推进"从
社会主义到共产主义的道路，为了所有人的国际幸福"[10]。此外，在这种充满希望的
毛主义中国形象中预言不久的将来实现共产主义将是不可避免的："今天伟大的

1　De Rokha, *China Roja*, p. 107.

2　De Rokha, *China Roja*, p. 107.

3　De Rokha, *China Roja*, p. 122. 我的重点.

4　人民日报，1964-08-12。这首诗的中文译本是在这一演示后的第二天在同一家报纸上发表的，
　见人民日报，1964-06-13.

5　De Rokha, *China Roja*, p. 53.

6　De Rokha, *Ovación universal*, p. 5.

7　De Rokha, *China Roja*, p. 130.

8　De Rokha, *China Roja*, p. 57.

9　De Rokha, *China Roja*, p. 130. 原文的重点.

10　De Rokha, *Canto de Fuego a China Popular*, p. 4.

社会主义中国和明天共产主义的聆听者"[1] 将成为"世界的推动者 /，在人类生活的最高峰 /，屹立……"[2]

德·罗卡的诗也暴露他的偏好，将中国的描述转化为客观和值得信赖的信息。诗人持续将见证者身份作为支持其主张真实性的修辞手段，这是他有意追求的目标。以这种方式，德·罗卡如同当代的马可·波罗，讲述人民公社的见闻："我见证伟大的发展 /，反抗的发展 /，组织的具体事实 /，尊严和成功。/（...）我没有看到旧时的苦痛。"[3] 更为重要的是，对现实的直接观察让他有机会反击中国的敌人："他们（中国的敌人）说公社失败 /，什么失败？修正主义者的诽谤失败（...）帝国主义者和垄断者的帮派失败……捏造失败的人失败 / 反马克思主义的人失败……"。[4] 德·罗卡进一步批评并提出另一个问题："那么，臭名昭著的诽谤依据什么 /，兽性的谎言散播 /，仿佛巨大的垃圾袋 / 在下水道中？"[5] 随后，将经验观察作为证明新中国光辉未来的基础，他迅速回应对中国的批评："这就是这样：事物是事物，不是事物的形象，这是经验的事实（...）只有看不到太阳的傻瓜才会否认"。[6]

除了作为见证者的经历，德·罗卡还利用更深层次的元素证明他对中国的判断。首先是他作为诗人的天才。德·罗卡是一位有远见卓识的诗人，这是他诗歌的核心特征，他诗化了世界，触及宇宙运动的价值，揭示现实的意义。诗歌是世界的中介，诗人充满创造的力量，成为上帝的模仿者。正是这句话的力量使诗人免于灭绝，这句话使他得以履行英勇的角色：征服者、革命者、超人和英雄。在革命追求的背景下，正是德·罗卡的诗意天才使他能够同情并向人们传播历史革命意识。弥赛亚格调的这一使命出现在他创作的中国作品不同部分中，帮助他克服毛主义共和国可能存在的文化差异。因此，通过反思世界各地被剥削者生活中的普遍性，中国的经验变得可理解："我听到中国人民、国家、兄弟和所有国家同志们的伟大话语"[7]。在《欢呼国庆》中也有一种相似的感觉："我把他们 [人民] 放入我的灵魂中 /；没有人对我陌生 /，也没有人想念我 /，因为我是诗写就的人 /；如果我的话是我的步枪或匕首，我的口音 /，是我受欢迎的胆魄 /；我很了解这个

1　De Rokha, *Ovación universal*, p. 13.
2　De Rokha, *China Roja*, p. 129,
3　De Rokha, *China Roja*, p. 5. 增加的重点 .
4　De Rokha, *China Roja*, p. 5.
5　Lamberg, *Vida y obra de Pablo de Rokha*, p. 183.
6　De Rokha, *China Roja*, p. 97.
7　Matus, "Pablo de Rokha," pp. 3-4.

伟大的现代国家……"。[1]

　　德·罗卡采用另一种个性化的话语强调他理解中国经验并指出文本的核心观点是他的个人背景以及与中国人的密切关系。德·罗卡在其所有诗作中都清楚地表明，正是他的智利/拉美身份使他有可能了解中国（["美洲智利人"]；[2] ["我是印第安裔西班牙人"]；[3] ["来自拉美的老诗人"]；[4] ["我，拉美人，人民的诗人"]；[5] [智利人][6]）。亲近感的一个例子出现在德·罗卡的《中华人民共和国火之歌》一诗中，他吸引人们关注这种联系："您的革命仿佛拉丁美洲的革命，仿佛智利盛夏的西瓜（......）我向您唱出"共和国火之歌"，如同国际主义智利战士，是您的内心革命"[7]。同样，《在中国看古巴》一诗中德·罗卡明确提到，不仅是革命运动的思想交流，还是拉丁美洲了解这种关系的能力。德·罗卡在这首诗中写道："一个巨大的声音，从中国传到古巴/，从古巴传到中国，拉丁美洲/了解它，这是它的命运，理解为自己的……"[8]。最后，联系这两种经验的核心要素是在帝国主义霸权下遭受的苦难和剥削："帝国主义/，英国人，美国人/！他们发现我们很富有/让我们变得饥饿！......抢到！......我理解/并钦佩，发出自己的声音，为你们的英雄国家，歌唱/他们的天才（......）我与众人战斗/，咆哮/，作一首火之歌/，我了解的人们"。[9]

　　在其他诗歌中，青年时代在智利高山和田野的经历有利于他理解农民在中国革命中的作用。从这个意义上，德·罗卡将自己描述为"山林间出生，山坡上长大"的人，接受"马克思主义和使人坚强的苦难"教育，他能够理解中国"前行"中"英勇、坦诚的老面孔，和反抗暴行"。[10] 为了进一步表达对中国农业建设的认同感，诗人在《人民公社》一诗中写道："我的出生和成长仿佛山林的/飞鸟，狂野地/，在马鞍和骑手之间（…）我睡在小木屋里/，和劳工分享面包/，我看到月亮穿越/幽

1　Matus, "Pablo de Rokha," pp. 5-6.
2　De Rokha, *China Roja*, p. 101.
3　De Rokha, *China Roja*, p. 101.
4　De Rokha, *China Roja*, p. 10.
5　De Rokha, *China Roja*, p. 82.
6　De Rokha, *Ovación universal*, p. 13
7　De Rokha, *Canto de fuego a China Popular*, p. 2.
8　De Rokha, *China Roja*, p. 67.
9　De Rokha, *China Roja*, pp. 129-131. 增加的重点.
10　Lamberg, *Vida y obra de Pablo de Rokha*, p. 183.

深的夜空。我理解人民公社 / 史诗般的工作，从成功走向成功 / 怀着坚定的信念"[1]。在讨论中国北方的大型林业项目时，他的早年生活经历再次被提起。这次与他的智利身份的关系得到明确："我是智利山林间的骑士，清楚林业人物的无限诗意"。[2]

在德·罗卡的诗歌中，中国以这种方式变得可以理解，并成为环境控制以及被剥削人民不断斗争的普遍经验的一部分。中国的革命似乎并不属于另一个"世界"，而是一种熟悉的农业和革命现实，与拉丁美洲的痛苦联系颇深。

最后的思考

巴勃罗·德·罗卡的生活以及与中国的关系受到冷战期间三个关键事件的重要影响：中国革命、古巴革命和中苏分裂。他的旅行反映中国对拉美革命前景日益浓厚的兴趣。特别是对于中国和智利而言，德·罗卡的访问有助于提升亲华派国际运动在当地和全球的重要性。德·罗卡诗歌在中国的出版、他参加活动以及与中国外交人员的密切联系[3]，表明著名的国家和 / 或国际人物在构成全球冷战的不同左派之间的国际和国家冲突所起的核心作用。

德·罗卡作品中的中国形象也说明智利诗人如何将自身的活动视为本地和全球斗争的有机组成部分。考虑到他的作品对国家的重要性，德·罗卡创作的中国诗歌不能仅仅看作是对中国宣传的复制。相反，它们是在两个不同地区跨国革命背景下根据第一手经验所构思的富有想象力的作品，为中国和拉美的讨论提供来源。德·罗卡中国作品的跨国性或许在文学上可以更好地表现，将对中国文化、历史和人民的史诗般的描绘纳入文学作品极为丰富的超现实和民族大众的想象中。

尽管德·罗卡强调按照与拉美的同一性介绍中国，但由于固定的变化而暂时中断，而且如同外国人的任何其他文明叙事，文化差异的观念并没有完全消失。德·罗卡对中国的表现造成一种他者的感觉，反映出中国现在和过去现实的刻板印象、整体化和理想化，并倾向于以独特的方式呈现和美化。这些形象在简化和异域化方面继承传统的"东方主义"观点，但不会破坏德·罗卡对中华人民共和国的积极评价。相反，它们有助于强化良好的形象。因此，德·罗卡采用"东方

1　De Rokha, *China Roja*, pp. 58-59. 我的重点 .

2　De Rokha, *China Roja*, p. 44. 我的重点 .

3　例如，我们知道德·罗卡与林平关系密切。林平于 1965 年担任中国首任驻智利办事处主任，1970 年成为中国驻智利的第一任大使。

主义"话语强调中国革命的优越性并向资本主义世界（德·罗卡诗中的低劣和最终"他者"）发起挑战。

　　有趣的是，德·罗卡对中国发展的积极评价并没有对他在国内复制中国革命产生任何帮助。事实上，德·罗卡认为中国代表一个独特的历史案例，从而限制该模式在拉丁美洲的潜在适用性。在 1963 年的一次采访中，诗人明确指出这一想法："我非常尊重中国的英雄和领导者，他们是中国人民的历史表达和反映，也是中国人民及其行为总体轮廓的历史表达。在我看来，中国的变革是本世纪的重大事件之一；但人民必须根据自身的主观和客观条件进行革命；中国是中国，古巴是古巴；即使在拉丁美洲确定革命的分层，国家的民族形态将奠定革命的基调和风格……"。[1]

　　虽然德·罗卡没有否认中国在国际共产主义运动中的重要全球领导作用，但他解释称，最终应该在国家层面上找到每个国家革命的基础。对德·罗卡来说，中国革命是一场革命运动，尽管与智利的现实有相似之处，但历史、自然和人文条件不完全相同。总之，德·罗卡对中国的看法是共同人性和文化差异同时存在，因此他一方面保持自己的国家身份，另一方面又强调不同革命运动团结的重要性，"马克思 - 列宁主义国际联合，共同反对成群结队的帝国主义恶霸。"[2]

1　On this point, see Lavquén, ed. *Antología de las obras completas de Pablo de Rokha*, p. 21.

2　Ban Wang, "Revolutionary Realism and Revolutionary Romanticism: Song of Youth," in Kirk A. Denton, ed., *The Columbia Companion to Modern Chinese Literature*, pp. 237-249 (New York, Chichester and West Sussex: Columbia University Press, 2016); also Cyril Birch, "Literature under communism," in Roderick MacFarquhar and John King Fairbank, eds., *The Cambridge History of China, vol.14, The People's Republic, part 2: Revolutions within the Chinese Revolution, 1966-1982*, 743-814, (New York and Melbourne: Cambridge University Press, 1991), pp. 743-787.

Pablo de Rokha and China: The Travel, Translations and Impressions

Jose Miguel Vidal Kunstmann / Chile

Department of History, Centre for Latin-American and Intercultural Studies of East Normal University, Postdoctoral Research Fellow

Introduction

Invited by Mao Zedong, the Chilean poet Pablo de Rokha and his son Pablo Díaz Anabalón spent five months and a half visiting the People's Republic of China (PRC) in 1964.[1] Previously, Pablo de Rokha, one of the pioneers of the Latin American avant-garde literary movement and a committed Marxist, had been already captivated by the events of the Chinese Revolution and the figure of Chairman Mao, appearing references to both of them in many of his writings.[2] As Mao, de

---

1   The figure of five months and a half is given in Sun Weixue 孙维学 , Lin Di 林地 , et al., eds., *Xin Zhongguo dui wai wenhua jiaoliu shilue* 新中国对外文化交流史略 (A Brief History of New China's Foreign Cultural Exchanges) (Beijing:Zhongguo youyi chuban gongsi, 1999), 213. Other authors, such as Eugenio Matus (1929-1997), posit that De Rokha stayed in China for six months. Eugenio Matus, "Pablo de Rokha," *Revista Trilce* 14 (1968): pp. 3-6; 6. The text can be consulted at: http://www.memoriachilena.cl/archivos2/pdfs/MC0013714.pdf.

2   Pablo de Rokha, ed., *Antología 1916-1953*, (Santiago: Multitud, 1954), 89, 358, 360, 491, 497, 522, 524, 527; Pablo de Rokha, *Neruda y yo-Tercetos dantescos a Casiano Basualto* (Santiago: Ediciones Tácitas y Fundación de Rokha, 2016), 16,20, 98, 129.

Rokha also upheld that art could and must be used for revolutionary purposes; concurring with the Chinese leader in the idea that literature should put politics and social justice at the core of its creation. [1] Apart from literary affinities, other factors brought him closer to Maoism as well. In this regard, De Rokha's marginalization of the Chilean Communist Party (CHCP) occurred in 1938 and his general disillusionment with the Chilean left movement, as well as his opposition to Soviet revisionism and sincere interest in the peasant's world, seemed to have been some of the critical elements that account for his inclination towards China's communist project. [2]

His support to Chinese revolutionary path and literary trends manifested more powerfully in a lengthy poem written one year before his visit to China, entitled *Canto de fuego a China Popular* (Song of Fire to the People's Republic of China, 1963). In this, De Rokha exalted China's socialist development and attacked the critics of it passionately. [3] Shortly after, this fascination would be encouraged during his visit to the socialist country, where he continued composing poems about China in the same ideological line of his *Canto de fuego*. These poems were never published in Spanish and only survive in a typescript manuscript titled *China Roja* (Red China, 1964). In China, however, a compilation of twenty of De Rokha's "Chinese" poems, under the title *Xiangei Beijing de songge* (Anthem dedicated to Beijing), was published in 1965.

Although in recent years Pablo de Rokha's literary production has

---

1 On De Rokha' s revolutionary interest in his poetry, see Alejandro Lavquén, ed., *Antología de las obras completas de Pablo de Rokha* (Santiago: Pehuén, 2016), 21; also the discussion in the third and fourth part of this paper below.

2 For biographical treatments of De Rokha' s life and political points of view, see Mario Ferrero, *Pablo de Rokha. Guerillero de la poesía* (Santiago: Sociedad de Escritores de Chile, 1967); Fernando Lamberg, *Vida y obra de Pablo de Rokha* (Santiago: Zig Zag, 1966); Naín Nómez, *Pablo de Rokha. Una escritura en movimiento* (Santiago: Documentas, 1988) and his "Introducción," in Naín Nómez, ed., *Canto del macho anciano y otros poemas*, pp. 13-22, (Madrid: Editorial Biblioteca Nueva, 2003); also Lavquén, ed., *Antología de las obras completas de Pablo de Rokha*, pp. 15-22. Neither of these studies, however, fully explored De Rokha' s affinities with Maoist ideas.

3 Pablo de Rokha, *Canto de Fuego a China Popular*, *Multitud* 89 (1963): pp. 1-6.

received a great deal of attention, his poems on travel to China remain largely unexamined.[1] One of the main reasons for this is that many of De Rokha's scholars contend that these works do not offer the multifaceted voice that insinuates in the complexity of De Rokha's poetic postulates.[2] Therefore, literary critics of Rokhian poetry have selected other works as the most representative and valuable writings when exploring the contributions of the poet. Another crucial reason is that access to *China Roja*'s manuscript has been challenging, as the original copy and few photocopies of it that exist are in private hands. Actually, until recently, it was even unknown to both the general public and some specialists whether the manuscript had survived or not.[3] Finally, the underdeveloped state of the scholarly field of Sino-Latin American cultural relations has limited the production of investigations focused on the historical context and impressions of Latin

---

1 Brief treatments of de Rokha's trip to China and on his poems about China appear in the following texts: Ferrero, *Pablo de Rokha. Guerillero de la poesía*, 37, 81-82; Lamberg, *Vida y obra de Pablo de Rokha*, 183; Nómez, *Pablo de Rokha. Un escritura en movimiento*, pp. 207-209.

2 See, for example, the comments of José Miguel Curet Arana and Naín Nómez: José Miguel Curet Aranam "Pablo de Rokha: Vanguardia y Geocrítica: La poesía de *U* (1926) y *Carta Magna de América* (1949)," Ph.D. dissertation, Universidad de Salamanca, Salamanca, 2015, 242; Nómez, *Pablo de Rokha. Una escritura en movimiento*, 208; Nómez still, however, considers that in some poems, such as De Rokha's "Gran oda popular al río Yangtsé" (Great Ode to the Yangzi River), "sometimes surfaces the visionary *tremendismo* of his greater tone" ("A veces aflora el tremendismo visionario de su tono mayor"). Referring to the same poem, Eugenio Matus also points out that this was, simply, a genius work. See Matus,"Pablo de Rokha," p. 6.

3 For the "detective" story behind the whereabouts of the original manuscript, see Pedro Pablo Guerrero, "*China Roja*: El libro perdido de Pablo de Rokha," *El Mercurio*, Sección Artes y Letras, May 11, 2014. Accessed on 24 /12/2014 at: http://impresa.elmercurio.com/Pages/ NewsDetail.aspx?dt=11-05-2014%200:00:00&NewsID =226411&dtB=02-04-2017%20 0:00:00&BodyID=6&PaginaId=12; Alejandro Lavquén, "*China Roja* de Pablo de Rokha," *Punto Final* 303, (April, 2014); "*China Roja* de Pablo de Rokha II," accessed on 13/12/2018 at http:// letras.mysite.com/alav140514.html.

American travelers in China.[1] The specific case study around which this paper revolves contributes to fill this gap by exploring De Rokha's trip as part of the broader context of Sino-Chilean interactions during the so-called "Global Sixties."[2]

This article is divided into four parts. The first part reconstructs the details of De Rokha's stay in China. By recreating De Rokha's circuit in China, what this part sets out to do is to examine the relationship between De Rokha's visit and the system of guided tourism implemented by the PRC for foreign guests. In the third part, it turns to examine the Chinese publication of De Rokha's poem on China. Based on a comparison between *China Roja* and *Xiangei Beijing de songge*, this section offers a brief and partial survey of the history of the publication. It scrutinizes the main features of this book paying particular attention to the difficulties and political concerns involved in the process of translation and selections of the poems. Lastly, the fourth part analyzes De Rokha's representations of China as showcased, principally, in his *Canto de fuego* and *China Roja*. Drawing on the insights provided by recent scholarship that defies the use of Edward Said's formulation of Orientalism as an appropriate heuristic device for approaching Latin American's views of the Orient, this part argues that de Rokha's images on China reveal a distinct type of Orientalism. In this, a strong feeling of identification between Latin American revolutionary movements and China's political and social aspirations

---

1   The few studies that exist on this subject, however, have proven to be a fruitful source of some particularly fascinating scholarship in recent years. See, for example, María Montt Strabucchi, "'Writing about China.' Latin American Travelogues during the Cold War: Bernardo Kordon's '600 millones y uno' (1958), and Luis Oyarzún's 'Diario de Oriente, Unión Soviética, China e India' (1960)," *Revista Caminhos da História*, 21, 1 (2016): pp. 93-124; "Viajeros chilenos a la RPC en los años cincuenta y sesenta," in Stefan Rinke, ed., *Entre espacios: la historia latinoamericana en el contexto global. Actas del XVII Congreso Internacional de la Asociación de Historiadores Latinoamericanistas Europeos (AHILA)*, Freie Universität, 9-13 September, 2014, Colegio Internacional de Graduados "Entre Espacios": 3027-3035; Rosario Hubert, "Intellectual Cartographies of the Cold War. Latin American visitors to the People's Republic of China, 1952-1958." In Robert T. Tally Jr., ed., *The Routledge Handbook of Literature and Space*, pp. 337-348, (Abingdon, Oxon and New York: Routledge, 2017).

2   On new perspectives on Latin America's studies in the Cold War, see Eric Zolov, "Introduction: Latin America in the Global Sixties," *The Americas* 70, 3 (January, 2014): pp. 349-362.

can be visualized.[1] Thus, one of the main features of De Rokha's discourse on China, as opposed to traditional Orientalist tenets, is that ideas of "otherness" and "inferiority" tended to be replaced by those of "sameness" and "superiority". China in De Rokha's poetry emerges not in a marginal position vis-à-vis Latin America but as one that shares common revolutionary experiences. Ultimately, for De Rokha, the PRC became the embodiment of the communist utopia leading the global revolution.

The Travel

Pablo de Rokha's stay in China adopted the form of what had been the core of Chinese cultural diplomacy towards Latin America since the 1950s: supervised tours through carefully selected parts of the PRC. Rokha The Sino-Latin American Friendship Association (中国拉丁美洲友好协会) helped to Coordinate those tours.[2] In these tours, the travelers usually met with prominent Chinese of their own occupation and with members of associations devoted to the relations with foreign countries. In most of the cases, they had interviews with Mao, Zhou Enlai (1898-1976), or other top Chinese leaders and participated in some national celebrations. They were guided by national delegates who showed them the material and immaterial achievements of the new system and the highlights of traditional culture. While in China the visitors were also encouraged by their Chinese hosts to make speeches and write articles on different issues, such as their country's main features and revolutionary prospects, and to provide their ideas of the PRC's reality. At their return, it was expected that they would write favorable reports of what they saw,

---

1 For example, Julia Kushigian, *Orientalism in the Hispanic Literary Tradition: In Dialogue with Borges, Paz, and Sarduy* (Albuquerque, New Mexico: University of New Mexico Press, 1991); Araceli Tinajero, *Orientalismo en el modernismo hispanoamericano* (Indiana: Indiana University Press, 2003); "Asian Representations in Spanish American Modernism," *Literature and Arts of the Americas*, 39, 1 (2006): pp. 146-150; Erik Camayd-Freixas, ed., *Orientalism and Identity in Latin America: Fashioning Self and Other from the (Post) Colonial Margin* (Tucson:University of Arizona Press, 2013).

2 人民日报 (People's Daily) 5, June 12, 1964.

heard and read during their visits.[1]

Based on the information provided by Chinese newspapers, interviews to friends and relatives of the poet, photos of the De Rokha's trip and his poems, the poet's itinerary in China can be up to some extent reconstructed.[2] The stay can be roughly divided into two parts. The first stage corresponds to the first three months of the journey, a period which goes from De Rokha's arrival on June 10, 1964 until the beginning of September. Following what Eugenio Matus states in his report concerning his meeting with Pablo de Rokha in China, and also in the information contained in Chinese newspapers concerning the official activities in which the poet participated in these three months; this period seemed to have been the original time-frame considered by the Chinese for De Rokha's visit.[3]Simultaneously, it was during this period when the poet wrote most of the poems of his *China Roja*.[4]

These three months were also the most active in terms of the places the poet visited. References to these places survived in several of the fifty poems of *China Roja*. The itinerary of his trip reconstructed through information in poems and notes in Chinese newspapers, reveals that the poet was in constant movement during these three months, traveling to different locations from Manchuria to Shanghai. In his travels through both urban and rural areas, De

---

1   Ratliff, "Chinese Communist Cultural Diplomacy toward Latin America," pp. 59-60; Hubert, "Intellectual Cartographies of the Cold War," 337; Montt Strabucchi, "The PRC's Cultural Diplomacy towards Latin America in the 1950s and 1960s," pp. 69-70.

2   For interviews to acquaintances of De Rokha on the poet's trip to China, see Diego Meza, dir., Eduado Lobos, prod., *Pablo de Rokha. El amigo piedra* (Chile: La Cresta Producciones y Deboom Studio, 2010). Accessed on 5/11/2018 at: https://www.youtube.com/watch?v=s5tu-VEJ2QE&t=52s.

3   Matus, "Pablo de Rokha," 6. Matus points out that the poet had been invited, originally, for two months. However, the series of official activities carried out during these three months suggest that the original invitation could have been for three months.

4   See, for example, Eugenio Matus's report in which he points out that "after two months" ("luego de dos meses") the poet delivered "fifty great poems" ("cincuenta grandes poemas"). Matus, "Pablo de Rokha", 3. Also some notes on the *Renmin ribao* and Shanghai 上海's *Wenhui bao* 文汇报 (Wenhui's Daily) indicates that by September of that year, the poet had already written "more than fifty poems" (五十多首诗). *Renmin ribao* 4, September 12, 1964; *Wenhui bao* 3, September 12, 1964.

Rokha explored ancient and recent historical sites. These include, among others, the Great Wall, the National Museum, Tian'anmen Square, the Summer Palace and the West Lake in Hangzhou. He also visited important social and industrial projects, such as primary schools, elderly homes, people's communes and steel factories. Finally, irrigation systems, dams, bridges and other public works were also a fundamental part of his tour. All in all, De Rokha was a guided eyewitness to a reality that was the output of China's relatively successful recovery since1962.

In these first three months, De Rokha also attended meetings and events where he encountered eminent Chinese leaders linked to the Chinese world of culture. For instance, he met two of China's key writers of the twentieth century, Mao Dun — at that time China's Minister of Culture and Director of the Chinese Writers Association (中国作家协会); and the Vice Chairman of the Standing Committee of the National People's Congress and President of the Chinese Literary and Art Circle Federation (中国文学艺术界联合会), the poet Guo Moruo. With the latter, according to Mario Ferrero, the personal secretary of the poet, De Rokha established a close friendship.[1] As for the events in which he participated in these months, the most significant was a demonstration in Harbin coordinated with the aim of condemning the United States' military involvement in Vietnam. In this meeting, the poet's son read in front of a large audience, one of the poems that would be included in *Xiangei Beijing de songge*, "Denuncia del asalto imperialista Yanqui".[2]

The second period runs from the beginning of September until his return to Chile, which took place either in late November or early December of 1964. This period corresponds to an "extra time", since the poet decided to extend

---

1 Ferrero, *Pablo de Rokha. Guerillero de la poesía*, 37. For other meetings attended by De Rokha during this period, see *Renmin ribao* 5, June 12, 1964, 3, June 16, 1964, 3, August 12, 1964, 4, September 12, 1964; *Wenhui bao* 3, June 30, 1964, 3, September 12, 1964.

2 *Renmin ribao*, 2, August 12, 1964, the poem' s translation into Chinese was published one day after this demonstration in the same newspaper. See *Renmin ribao*, 6, August 13, 1964.

his visit for three more months. It can be contended, that the extension of his stay responded to three main factors. The first one was his interest in working directly in the process of translation of his poems. The second was De Rokha's fascination with China. His deepest sympathy towards China was, for example, strongly conveyed in his reunion with Guo Morou at the end of the first three months of his stay. In that occasion, among other things, the poet told Guo that "I have been in many countries, but the impressions that China has left on me are the most profound and good impressions I have ever had in my life. No one can wipe them out ". 1Thirdly, his decision to remain for an extended period in China is also connected to the fact that shortly after arriving, the poet fell seriously ill and needed recovery time.[2]

In these months the poet apparently made few trips, spending much of his time in Beijing. Also, meetings with Chinese authorities and participation in events were less than in previous months. The most important, and one of the few events attended by De Rokha during this period, was the traditional military parade held to commemorate the 15th anniversary of the founding of the PRC. On that occasion, he alongside with his son and José Venturelli were the only representatives of Chile.[3] His poem dedicated to this event called *Ovación universal* (Universal Ovation) —which survives as a kind of appendix in the manuscript of *China Roja*—, is the only poem that the poet seems to have written about China during his last months in the PRC. The rest of the time it was seemingly invested in making several of the many corrections in his handwriting that remain on the manuscript of *China Roja*, as well as in the

---

1   *Renmin ribao*, 4, September 12, 1964; *Wenhui bao*, 3, September 12, 1964.
2   Matus, "Pablo de Rokha," p. 3.
3   *Renmin ribao* 6, October 1, 1964. De Rokha also participated two days later in a ceremony organized by different Chinese friendship associations. This reunion was attended by all foreign delegates who had participated in the celebration of the 15th anniversary of the Chinese Revolution. *Renmin ribao* 6, October 4, 1964.

translation work and writing of other poems.[1]

Fernando Lamberg in his biography of De Rokha, for example, writes that after his arrival "his hosts, with a smiling and delicate kindness, allowed him to wander a bit for a few weeks," .[2]Additionally, Eugenio Matus also comments that "in the afternoon, after finishing his work day (he wrote and took care of the Chinese translator's queries of his poems), [he] came to the Friendship Hotel (友谊宾馆), where the foreign specialists lived, to chat with the small group of friends. We used to go for a walk in the hotel's park, or if the weather was bad, he stayed in our apartment." [3]. Another day, Matus also described that De Rokha went with him and his son, Félix, who spoke perfectly Chinese, to buy shoes in Wangfujing Street, and that in another occasion, they headed to Qianmen Avenue to purchase the coat that would become part of his classic image in many of the poet's last pictures.[4]

The Translation

De Rokha realized that after "knowing the extraordinary reality of the country" he would need "a minimum of five years to address the subject".[5] Then, the

---

1 The publication in Chinese magazines and newspapers of eight translations of his poems into Chinese from October 1964 onwards, suggests that the work of translation intensified during September and October of that year. To my knowledge, before these translations, only two other of De Rokha's poems can be found in Chinese publications. See *Renmin ribao* 7, July 5, 1964; 6, August 13, 1964;6, October 10, 1964; 6, February 16, 1965; Pablo de Rokha, Zhao Jinping 赵金 , trans., "Meng Tai tongzhi 孟泰同志 (The Comrade Meng Tai)," *Yalü jiang* 赵金 (The Yalü River) 10 (October, 1964): 61-62; "Xiangei Shanghai de reqing zhi ge 献给上海的热情之歌 (Warm-heart song dedicated to Shanghai)," *Wenhui bao* 文汇报 10 (October 1964): 4; Zhao Jinping 赵金 平 , trans., "Gei Mei diguozhuyi de gongkai xin 给美帝国主义的公开信 (Open Letter to American Imperialism)," *Shijie wenxue* 世界文学 (Journal of World Literature) 12, (December, 1964): 11-18; "Shi si shou: "Mao Zedong," "Weida de bangyang," "Zhongguo ertong" " 诗 四 首 : " 毛 泽 东" , "伟大的榜样" , "中国儿童" (Four poems: "Mao Zedong", "The Great Example," "Chinese Children)," *Shigan* 诗 刊 (Newspaper of Poetry) 10, (October 1964): 39-46, Mario Ferrero also affirms that De Rokha's poems were published in other Chinese newspapers. Unfortunately, I have not yet had the opportunity to check those publications. Pablo de Rokha, *Guerillero de la Poesía*, 37.
2 Lamberg, Vida y obra de Pablo de Rokha, p. 183.
3 Lamberg, *Vida y obra de Pablo de Rokha*, p. 183.
4 Matus, "Pablo de Rokha," pp. 5-6.
5 Lamberg, Vida y obra de Pablo de Rokha, p. 183.

solution that seemed most logical for De Rokha to illustrate all the grandiosity of this reality— without having a full picture of it—, was to write a series of poems. He communicates his decision to Mao Dun who accepted the suggestion without inconvenience.[1]

The Chinese interest for translating De Rokha's poem was directly related to the proximity that was considered to exist between the literary points of view in vogue in those years in China and those of the Chilean poet. For De Rokha, the concepts of popular and proletarian art were part of a heroic and epic style of writing, which was typical of a tragedy defined by him as the "American Social Epic" ("Épica Social Americana"). This style of writing was based on the intuitive development of images that transformed the poet into a professional politician. Thus, for the Chilean poet, there were no neutral forms and all the forms achieved should be social and epic: they must speak of the tragic history of the multitudes of the continent. In order to present the poetry with a social aspiration the poets needed, according to De Rokha, to rely on the legend and the epic, since these are the poetic intuition of the people, because it is the people who create them. This was for De Rokha the true artistic interpretation of reality, one that sublimates the objective reality that alienates the people's minds. The maxim of the "Art for art's sake", therefore, was a murky mystification of aesthetic idealism.[2]

Considering De Rokha's perspective on the role of art, as a channel that must above all promote social transformation, it is hardly surprising to find that period China's literary circles in an interest for De Rokha's poetry and vice versa.

De Rokha's interest in Chinese literary forms can be seen in the stylistic decisions taken by him in the poems of *China Roja* as opposed to his *Canto de fuego*. In this respect, Mario Ferrero explains the following: "…De Rokha, making a concession alien to his principles and whose theory he has attacked multiple times, breaks his usual line of non-versified epic to return to the traditional quatrain, partial rhyme

---

1   Lamberg, *Vida y obra de Pablo de Rokha*, p. 183.
2   On this point, see Lavquén, ed. *Antología de las obras completas de Pablo de Rokha*, p. 21.

or assonate. He explains this change as a faster way to reach the great masses of the people...".[1] This perspective reveals the influence of the artistic tendencies of the Great Leap Forward inserted within the slogan, "more, faster, better, and more economically" (多 , 快 , 好 , 省), which continued serving as the guideline for all industrial, scientific and artistic production. In literature, this point of view resulted in the promotion of a faster writing process through compositions of a shorter extension. Through this it was expected that these types of works would represent a more concrete revolutionary ambition allowing a faster production and a more direct language for transmitting its ideological messages.[2]

De Rokha's stylistic concession may also have been partly motivated by the need to facilitate the complex work of translating his poems into Chinese, whose burden was handed over to De Rokha's interpreter during his trip, Zhao Jinping. An example of the difficulties encountered by Zhao — a graduate of the Institute of Foreign Languages in Beijing (北 京 外 国 语 学 院) who had already made translations of Latin American works since the late 1950s—,[3] can be observed in a brief comment reproduced by Eugenio Matus on what De Rokha commented to him in relation to this process:

> The Chinese translator, who, like all Chinese speakers in Spanish, was an expert grammarian, was disconcerted by Don Pablo's often capricious syntax.
>
> Poet — he said to him— I cannot find the subject of this sentence.
>
> Don Pablo rode in rage. He did not understand how such questions could be asked.
>
> —But it is that before translating —the translator insisted—, I have to do a syntactic analysis, I have to understand the text from the grammatical point of view.

1 Ferrero, *Pablo de Rokha. Guerillero de la poesia*, p. 81.

2 Birch, "Literature under communism," pp. 768-769.

3 Lin Hui 林 辉 , ed., *Zhongguo fanyi cidian* 中 国 翻 译 词 典 (Dictionary of Chinese Translator Biographies), (Beijing: Zhongguo duiwai fanyi chubanshe gongsi, 1988), 710; Teng, "*Bianjing zhinan*," p. 163.

—You are wasting your time —Don Pablo replied —, because I have my own grammar, which surely will not coincide almost in anything with the one you learned.

(El traductor chino, que como todos los chinos hablantes en español, era un experto gramático, se desconcertaba ante la muchas veces caprichosa sintaxis de don Pablo.

—Poeta —le decía—, no encuentro el sujeto de esta oración.Don Pablo montaba en cólera. No comprendía cómo se podían hacer preguntas semejantes.

—Pero es que antes de traducir —insistía el traductor—, yo tengo que hacer un análisis sintáctico, tengo que entender el texto desde el punto de vista gramatical.

—Está usted perdiendo el tiempo —le replicaba don Pablo—, porque yo tengo mi propia Gramática, que seguramente no coincide casi en nada con la que aprendió usted.)[1]

While exaggerated in his assessment that a grammatical and syntactic analysis would not be of any help at the time of translating, De Rokha's advice to Zhao Jinping was correct in the sense that this type of approach could not be the only used in the translation process. De Rokha's automatic writing typically involves so many linked prepositional phrases and dangling adjectives that it is hard not only to tell what the subject of a sentence is but also what is modifying what, especially since the descriptions are often quasi-surrealistic. Therefore, any translator of his works to any language has the imperious need of going beyond the mere formalities of the language to translate his poems. In addition to this difficulty, De Rokha's use of a high-poetic register with frequent prosaic twists, and vernacular terms, including many *chilenismos* (Chilean Spanish's original terms) complicated the picture even more.

Although a complete and detailed analysis of the quality of the translation work

---

1   Matus, "Pablo de Rokha," p. 6.

is beyond the scope of this article, the comparison of some sections of the poems and their titles in the Spanish and Chinese versions sheds some light on the liberties taken by the translator. It is important to be clear, however, that these were not only implemented due to the difficulties encountered by the translator but also due to his interest in capturing the attention of the Chinese audience. An example of this is the last poem included in the Chinese compilation of De Rokha's poems, which corresponds to an abridged version of *Ovación universal*. Zhao chose to translate the title as "Ovation to the National Day (欢呼国庆)." By replacing "universal" for "national day" (guoqing) Zhao was making clear which was the object of this poem; that is, the PRC's founding, something that in the original title was not clearly established.

Another example that shows the interest of the translator for attracting the attention of Chinese readers occurs in the translation of one of the easiest poems for translating, "Alegría pekinesa" (Beijing Happiness). In the original Spanish version the first verse of this poem — correctly entitled by Zhao as "Beijing huanxiao 北京欢笑 " —, reads:

Excited among these kind people

their full laugh I would compare

to peaches or oat,

or to almonds, or to poetry

(Emocionado entre esta gente buena

su risa llena la compararía

a los melocotones o la avena,

o a las almendras, o a la poesía)[1]

---

1 De Rokha, *China Roja*, typescript manuscript with handwriting amendments, People's Republic of China, 1964. A complete translation of the Chinese version of this poem into Spanish made by the author of this paper, can be consulted in Lavquén, *Antología de las obras completas de Pablo de Rokha*, pp. 139-141.

Instead the Chinese version reads:

在这些善良的人们 中间，我很激动，

他们的美丽的欢笑，

好比鲜桃和红杏，

好比诗歌和芦笙．

Excited among these kind people,

their beautiful joy is like

fresh peaches and crimson apricots,

like the poetry and the *lusheng.*

As is evident, the Chinese translation presents several differences in terms of the nouns and adjectives utilized. First, in the Chinese version the adjective "llena" (full) is replaced by "beautiful" (*meili*). Second, the adjectives "red/crimson" (*hong*) and "fresh" (*xian*) have been added. Third, the nouns "avena" (oat) and "almendras" (almonds) were replaced by two other nouns that entail cultural connotations for the Chinese reader: "(red/crimson) apricots" (*hongxing*) and *lusheng*.

The first of these terms, *hong xing*, is a well-known poetic allusion that comes from the Song dynasty (960-1279) poem by Ye Shaowen 叶绍翁 , "An Unworthy Visit to the Park" (游园不值). There, it refers, literally, to the spring's crimson spray of an apricot. Metaphorically, however, the line in which the term appears has become also a famous allusion to a typical poetic image of a spring scene with a philosophical message.[1] Meanwhile, the second, a *lusheng*, is a Hmong musical instrument with multiple bamboo pipes, used primarily in the rural regions of southwestern China and in nearby countries such as Laos and Vietnam, where it is played by different ethnic groups. Zhao Jinping's decision of including "lusheng"

---

1   The last line of the poem, Hongxing chuqiang 红杏出墙 ("Over the wall peeps out a crimson spray of apricot") has, nevertheless, another figurative reading. It can be used to refer to a wife having an illicit lover. Meaning the vitality of spring, it appears also in the Song poem, "Spring Scenery in the Jade Pavilion" (玉楼春·春景) by Song Qi 宋祁 (980-1061).

and "apricots", instead of "almonds" and "oat" creates therefore two pairs that do not exist in the original: two fruits (apricots and peaches) and two artistic expressions (music and poetry). These changes should not be overlooked since the search for symmetries is a constant in Chinese artistic expressions. Translation's decisions such as those just mentioned, explicitly expose the effort and mechanism used by the translator to make De Rokha's poetry more alluring for its Chinese readership.

Working hand in hand with De Rokha, Zhao Jinping translated in total at least 21 poems out of the 51 that survive in the manuscript of *China Roja*.[1] The result of this work saw the light in September 1965, when twenty of the poems were included in the compilation *Xiangei Beijing de songge*. This was published by the Writers Editorial (作家出版社) and distributed by the New China Bookstore (新华书店). The title of the compilation corresponds to the poem number 17 of *China Roja*, "Himno rojo dedicado a Pekín" ("Red Anthem dedicated to Beijing," poem number 11 of the Chinese version). Also in the back cover, the title of "Alegría pekinesa y otros poemas" ("Beijing Happiness and other Poems") appears in Spanish. Concerning the cover, this was designed by Zhang Shouyi 张守义 (1930-), a famous cartoonist, who in addition to his more personal works, devoted an essential part of his career to make covers and illustrations for translations of foreign literature books.[2] In the case of this book, Zhang's cover reflects the usual motifs of the time, with the old and the new intertwining. In this sense, Beijing's ancient imperial palaces converge with construction cranes, and the modern luminaries and buildings of the city, while the swallows and propaganda red canvases that appear hanging on balloons can be read as evoking the hope of a better future under the line

---

1 The single poem that seems to have been translated but was not included in *Xiangei Beijing de songge* was "Carta abierta al Imperialismo Norteamericano" (Open Letter to the North American Imperialism), which coincidently, is the only poem missed in the copy of *China Roja* that I consulted for this study. For the reference of the translation of his poem see note 47 above.

2 Zhang Shouyi 张守义 , *Zhang Shouyi waiguo wenxue chatu ji* 张守义外国文学插图集 (A Compilation of Zhang Shouyi's Illustrations of Foreign Literature), (Changsha: Hunan meishu chubanshe, 1982); *Wode sheji shenghuo: Zhang Shouyi* 我的设计生活：张守义 (My Design's Life: Zhang Shouyi), (Beijing: Zhongguo lüyou chubanshe, 2007).

of the Chinese Communist Party (see Figure 6).

Regarding the poems selected for inclusion, the main editorial line seems to have been, as in the case of the liberties taken in the translation, dominated by the interest of securing the attention of Chinese readers. This, without completely rejecting that the lack of time and the difficulties in translating some poems may also have motivated the selection. The interest in reaching Chinese audiences, for example, seems to be evident in the fact that the translator discarded those poems whose titles did not refer directly to any Chinese event, social project, city, or people. This was the case of poems such as "Experimentaciones" (Experimentations), "Así se forja la historia" (This is how History is forged) or "La voluntad revolucionaria" (The Revolutionary Will). The only poem of this type of more abstract-content's poems that was incorporated was "El gran ejemplo" (The Great Example), an allegory about China as a great model of integrity. Similarly, the translator did also not consider poems related to cultural issues such as "Palacios de Cultura Popular" (Popular Culture Palaces), "La república poética" (The poetic republic) and "La orquesta gastronómica" (The Gastronomic Orchestra), in a decision that was most likely taken due to the less "revolutionary" focus of these poems. Finally, in another particular case, the poem "Cuba desde China" (Cuba from China), an exaltation to Cuba, the decision of excluding it in all likelihood responds to the fact that this did not directly concern with China. In contrast, the translator added in seven out of eight poems dedicated to Chinese cities, the two centered on revolutionary historical characters ("Mao Tse-Tung" and "El camarada Mon Tai" [Comrade Mon Tai][1]), three of four addressing social projects or public works ("Las comunas populares" [The People's Communes], "Trova al agua de regadío" [Trova to the irrigate Water] and "El callejón de la calabaza"

---

1   The last line of the poem, Hongxing chuqiang 红杏出墙 ("Over the wall peeps out a crimson spray of apricot") has, nevertheless, another figurative reading. It can be used to refer to a wife having an illicit lover. Meaning the vitality of spring, it appears also in the Song poem, "Spring Scenery in the Jade Pavilion" (玉楼春·春景) by Song Qi 宋祁 (980-1061).

[The alley of the Pumpkin]¹), and four of nine focused on different groups of the Chinese population ("Gentes y Calles de Pekín" [Peoples and streets of Beijing], "Alegría pekinesa", "Niños chinos" [Chinese Children] and "Los comuneros" [The Communers]).

The last three poems included, also represent the same editorial decision pattern. Thus, the poem "Denuncia del asalto imperialista yanki," was not only a direct attack against one of China's greatest enemies but also a reference to the demonstration held in Harbin in August of 1964 against the US infiltration in Vietnam. The presence of the poem titled "La Gran Muralla" (The Great Wall), an icon of China's past converted into a symbol of the New China, does not require further explanations. Finally, the last poem, "Ovation to the National Day," which as noted was a condensed version of *Ovación universal*, is an eulogy to the New China in honor of its 15th anniversary that embodies the ideological guidelines of both De Rokha's and the Maoist literary project.

Ultimately, Zhao also reinforced his intention of directing the reader's attention towards China's struggles in the biographies of De Rokha attached to the publication. In them, Zhao Jinping's appreciation for De Rokha's support to the New China is manifested in the last paragraph where the translator summarizes the poet's most essential aspects of his visit: "During the time of his visit he devoted himself to the creation of poems, supported the cause of my people against imperialism, and opposed revisionist disputes. He praised China's achievements in socialist construction and exalted the great leader of our people, Chairman Mao (他 热情地进行诗歌 创作 , 支持我国人民反对帝国主义 , 反对修正主义的斗争 , 赞 扬我国的社会主义 建设成就 , 歌颂我国人民的伟大领袖毛主席)."² By doing this, Zhao immortalized in China the Maoist image of the Chilean poet in the only

---

1 The single poem that seems to have been translated but was not included in *Xiangei Beijing de songge* was "Carta abierta al Imperialismo Norteamericano" (Open Letter to the North American Imperialism), which coincidently, is the only poem missed in the copy of *China Roja* that I consulted for this study. For the reference of the translation of his poem see note 47 above.

2 De Rokha, *Xiangei Beijing de songge*, p. 85.

official edition of these poems that exists until today.

The Poet's Impressions

De Rokha's *Canto de Fuego a China Popular*, *China Roja* and *Ovación universal* are a palpable testimony of the deepest and positive impressions that China's revolutionary project had in the poet's mind. Throughout these texts, the poet displays, persistently, favorable —almost idyllic—, images of China's socialist reality and an unconditional support to her cause. De Rokha regards China as unique in its character, a representative example of a just and morally superior society. In order to unveil this utopian image of the PRC, he frequently uses adverbs and pronouns such as "hasta" (even), "todos" (everyone), "todo" (everything/all), "nunca" (never), "siempre" (always), "solo" (only) and "nadie" (no one/nobody), which helps to emphasize the exceptionality of China in De Rokha's view. In this line, for example, when describing Chinese population, the poet writes: "I *never saw* in the whole world/ such a great peasant dignity/, people freer than a tumult of oceans" ("Nunca ví a lo ancho del mundo/ tan gran dignidad campesina/, gente más libre que un tumulto de oceanías"). [1] And in a similar vein, in his "Palacios de Cultura Popular," he comments concerning Chinese happiness: "*I never saw* happier faces/ of great-modest men /, among the popular people" ("Nunca ví caras más felices/ de grandes varones modestos/, entre las gentes populares"). [2] Also, disasters, such as the famines of the past, are described as something that has totally disappeared in "the beloved-triumphant Popular China" ("amada China Popular triunfante"), where, according to the poet, "nobody is hungry" anymore ("Nadie tiene hambre"). [3]

The idealization of China's Maoist society reaches its peak when the poet addresses issues such as social justice and work, generalizing his impressions in these respects to the whole Chinese community: "*Everything* is right here/, *everything* is clear and definitive of disposition/, like a mathematical chord" ("Todo

---

1   De Rokha, *China Roja*, pp. 59-60. My emphasis.
2   De Rokha, *China Roja*, p. 37. My emphasis.
3   De Rokha, *China Roja*, p. 8.

es justo aquí, todo es claro/ y definitivo de índole/, como un acorde matemático");[1] "*Everyone* works together/ for the same cause/, which is the cause of the world" ("todos trabajan juntos/ por una misma causa/, que es la causa del mundo");[2] "… *everyone* eats, produces, lives and feels/ the as their own work the social work" ("… todo el mundo come, produce, vive y siente/ como trabajo propio el trabajo social").[3] Furthermore, based on his optimistic perception of the success of Maoist policies, De Rokha defines China with adjectives that powerfully highlight the particularity of this nation. The "Chinese World" ("Mundo Chino") is, according to the Poet, "enormous" ("egregio") and "incorruptible" ("insobornable"),[4] "invincible" ("invencible") and "formidable,"[5] as well as "invulnerable" ("inexpugnable") and "unshakeable" ("inconmovible").[6]

When it comes to the people's characters, the uniqueness and positive features of Chinese people also emerges. For De Rokha while "all peoples resemble/ or are equal" ("todos los pueblos se parecen/, o son iguales"), there are people like the Chinese which present special characteristics: People as the Chinese are "made for the heroic enterprise/; the Chinese is sober and fair, understands and does what must be done …" ("hechas para la empresa heroica/; el chino es sobrio y justo, entiende y hace lo que debe hacerse…").[7] The positive totalization of China's present reality is further strengthened by characterizing Chinese population as a uniform mass of people, which despite its gigantic dimensions works as a whole and unified collective body (e.g., "huge tide" ["marea enorme"],[8] "The broad mass of Chinese parents and children" ["la amplia masa china de padres e hijos],[9] "the broad masses"

---

1 De Rokha, *China Roja*, p. 106. My empahsis
2 De Rokha, *China Roja*, p. 119.My emphasis.
3 De Rokha, *China Roja*, p. 21. My emphasis.
4 De Rokha, *China Roja*, p. 66.
5 De Rokha, *China Roja*, p. 112.
6 De Rokha, *China Roja*, p. 120.
7 De Rokha, *China Roja*, p. 84.
8 De Rokha, *China Roja*, p. 1.
9 De Rokha, *China Roja*, p. 16.

["las amplias masas"], [1] or "your multitude innumerable as the sands of the sea" ["tu multitud 'innumerable como las arenas del mar'"][2]). De Rokha sees this capacity of union of such an immense number of people as another central factor that underlies the success of China's Maoist project. With this he takes a distance of any individualistic perspective that may attempt to put the individual over the society and the common good. Accordingly, De Rokha converts the different groups that make up the Chinese population into "flags of anonymity" ("banderas del anonimato"), the correct point of view by which the "Chinese people, new and giant" ("pueblo chino, nuevo y gigante") "serves the great human cause/, in function of the working class and all the people ("…sirve la gran causa/ humana, en función de la clase/ obrera y de todo el pueblo…")[3]. — "It is gigantic to be mass, inside the mass!" ("! Es gigante ser masa, dentro de la masa!") —,[4] stressed De Rokha. Hence, the human being fulfills his/her individuality not outside society, but as long as he/ she is capable of participating in the Chinese society as a whole, and consequently, in the Communist project that this entails. The New China, in the poetic images of De Rokha, emerges, in this sense, as a whole unit composed of measures, reforms and ways of acting that work in a transversal and flourishing form for the entire society. This shows, in turn, how productive and harmonious life could be in a socialist society in contrast to capitalist ones.

The idea that the Chinese experience is unparalleled also permeates De Rokha's perspectives on China's history. The Chilean writer explains, for example, that "a country was *never* more stolen/, a country was *never* more wounded" ("nunca un país fue más robado/, nunca un país fue más herido").[5] The exaltation of China's present is carried out, therefore, not without repeatedly evoking the greatness and hardships of the imperial past, in a discourse that does nothing but to account for the fact that the New China is the result of a long history of oppression and original

---

1   De Rokha, *China Roja,* p. 106.
2   De Rokha, *Canto de fuego a China Popular*, p. 3.
3   De Rokha, *China Roja*, p. 107.
4   De Rokha, *China Roja*, p. 107.
5   De Rokha, *China Roja*, p. 122. My emphasis.

intellectual creation. Socialist China represents the paradox, according to De Rokha, of being "the newest, in the oldest" ("lo más nuevo, en lo más viejo").[1]

Informed by a Marxist's teleological view of history, De Rokha portrays China's past as an unchangeable trajectory that has only been transformed dramatically as a result of the impact of imperialism and communism on nineteenth and twentieth century China. The poet, then, describes China's historical past as four thousand years of "frightful exploitation" ("explotación espantosa"),[2] "slaverism-feudalism" ("esclavismo-feudalismo"), "Lords-Emperors-Actors, crowned with millenary murders" ("Señores-Emperadores-Actores, coronados de asesinatos milenarios"),[3] and of "emperors against emperors/ or killing or robbing, enslaving/ from between massacres to beheadings/ they took the people…" ("emperadores contra emperadores/ o matando o robando, esclavizando/ de entre masacres a degollaciones/ al pueblo lo llevaron").[4] This is a history of abuses that is also exemplified in China's recent past by the agents of European, Japanese and North American imperialism, which "like dogs of fire from an infernal conflagration/, kicked with impunity the flower of innocence" ("como perros de fuego de un incendio infernal/, pateaban impunes la flor de la inocencia"),[5] and by the Nationalist Party and Chiang Kai-shek (Jiang Zhongzheng 蒋中正 1887-1985), the "great scorpion that looks like a man" ("un gran alacrán que parece hombre").[6] This "static" and decadent past, in turn, appears, too, as the great cause that explained why some problems still existed in China: "After four thousand years/ of frightful exploitation/ it is not a rose-colored thing/ to repair all the damage/; overcame the disappointments/, there are still some suffering/ among six hundred and fifty/ million of attentive people …" ("Después de cuatro mil años/ de explotación

1 Pablo De Rokha, *Ovación universal*, typescript manuscript with handwriting amendments, Beijing, 1964, 8.
2 De Rokha, *China Roja*, p. 8.
3 De Rokha, *Canto de fuego a China Popular*, p. 3.
4 De Rokha, *China Roja*, p. 9.
5 De Rokha, *China Roja*, p. 20.
6 De Rokha, *Canto de fuego a China Popular*, p. 1.

espantosa/ no es cosa color de rosa/ reparar todo los daños; superados desengaños/, aún queda algún sufrimiento/ entre seiscientos cincuenta/ millones de gente atenta…").[1]

Although the Chinese past is, in general, evaluated negatively, it is also in it where De Rokha localizes the roots of China's positive changes. China's Revolution, using the poet's terminology, is the corollary of centuries of accumulation of hardships that led to the emergence of the "popular heroic" ("popular heroico") consciousness. This "new world from the old world" ("mundo nuevo del viejo mundo"), De Rokha writes, "is coming from the accumulated origins on the back of the abyss, or dripped by the cosmic mud, or whipped by the hurricane of human existence" ("…viene llegando desde los orígenes acumulados a la espalda del abismo, o goteado por los barros cósmicos, o azotado por el huracán de la existencia humana…").[2] China, then, is defined by De Rokha, using his rich poetic resources, by "the heroic popular, traversing four thousand years (....) crown for millenarian murders and acts of saints and bandits, simultaneously, the rebellion of the hungry, the cyclical rebellion, humble and terrible, the rebellion of the ancestral pride, digs from your dark bases, and the heroicity engenders the fact of conscience in the world culture of the illiterates of that egregious and abominable age" ("lo heroico popular, atravesando cuatro mil años [….] coronados de asesinatos milenarios y actos de santos y bandidos, simultáneamente, la rebelión de los hambrientos, la rebelión cíclica, humilde y terrible, la rebelión del orgullo ancestral, escarba desde tus bases oscuras, y la heroicidad engendra el hecho de conciencia en la cultura mundial de los analfabetos de aquella edad egregia y abominable").[3]

At the same time, this interpretation of Chinese history leads to cities and ancient buildings such as the Great Wall and Beijing to be seen as reflections and symbols of this sustained revolutionary journey. The historical fortification and the Chinese capital became the witnesses of the Chinese past and present, of the new and the old developments, portraying not the glory of emperors but that of the subjugated

---

1   De Rokha, *China Roja*, p. 8.

2   De Rokha, *Canto de fuego a China Popular*, p. 2.

3   De Rokha, *Canto de fuego a China Popular*, p. 3

people. De Rokha narrates: The Great Wall "emerging from the remote/ as a hurricane […] daughter of the whip/, she has people's bones in the guts/ [….] She is not dead/, it is only past that shipwrecks/ with her world in the unknown/, seeing the new that advances" ("Surgiendo de lo remoto como un huracán/ […] hija del látigo, tiene huesos de pueblo en la entraña/ […] Ella no está muerta/, sólo es pasado que naufraga/ con su mundo en lo ignoto/, viendo lo nuevo que avanza…").[1] While the formation of Beijing as a city summarizes the "revolutionary processes" ("los procesos revolucionarios") that have gone "for five thousand years/ […] forging the epic of your life [Beijing's life]" ("por adentro de cinco mil años/ […] forjando la epopeya de tu vida").[2]

The origins of the Chinese revolutionary consciousness, however, are not only the result of brutal assaults to the masses, but they also derived from Chinese ancient philosophical and religious ideas. These have, according to De Rokha, supplemented Marxist thought continuing to be somehow present in Communist China. The poet, thus, appreciates, like many foreign observers before him, that old ideas such as "the "*yin*" and the "*yang*" of the Tao, already divined the antagonistic terms of the dialectical contradiction" ("…el "*yin*" y el "*yang*" del Tao, ya adivinaban los términos antagónicos de la contradicción dialéctica…")[3] that permeates Marxist formulations. And as other observers, he also assesses that the polytheistic pantheon of the Chinese represents the perfect background that facilitated the implementation of atheist Maoist policies. This idea is best revealed in the following passage of *Canto de fuego*, where De Rokha writes: "…your religion [China's religion] without a unique God, is the religion of materialism that achieved the unity of the opposites between sky and earth, without evacuating the concrete facts due to metaphysical alienation, in the ancient epochs of the cosmic mud" ("…tu religión sin "Dios único", es la religión del materialismo que lograba la unidad de los contrarios entre cielo y la

---

1　De Rokha, *China Roja*, p. 11.

2　De Rokha, *China Roja*, p. 38.

3　De Rokha, *Canto de fuego a China Popular*, p. 2. Emphasis in the original.

tierra, sin evacuar los hechos concretos por la enajenación metafísica, en las épocas antiquísimas de barros cósmicos…").[1]

Finally, the notion that the past still lived in Communist China through the complementation of ancient with modern ideas is presented in allusions to classical Chinese philosophers and poets. De Rokha's support, as expected, lies on those who were elevated as revolutionary predecessors by the intellectual line of the Chinese Communist Party: the "great poet of the people" ("el gran poeta del pueblo") Bai Juyi 白居易 (772–846) and the "materialist" philosopher ("materialista") Wang Chong 王充 (27-100), "the least barbarians and the good classics, without statue, among the peoples" ("los menos bárbaros y los buenos clásicos, sin estatua, entre las gentes").[2]Conversely, more canonical thinkers like Laozi, Confucius and Mencius, although not wholly denied of their genius, are declared by De Rokha as largely surpassed by the new ideas. However, the overcoming of the old did not always in China translate into leaving aside this previous knowledge entirely. De Rokha posits, in the case of Mencius, "who was old and knew and how he knew and how much he knew, in the academic enterprise" ("…quien era viejo y sabía cómo sabía y cuánto sabía, en la empresa académica"), that his ideas have complemented the superior understanding of the most important of all wisdoms, namely: the "popular and combatant wisdom" ("la sabiduría popular y combatiente").[3]With that in mind, the poet writes: "the archaic and the contemporary are, then, united, the contemporary and the archaic in the factories, which are factory-schools or craft workshops, Mencius and Zhou Enlai, Zhou Enlai and Mencius, with Mao Zedong in the oceans of the thought-feeling, in the vanguard, in another great red and belligerent unanimity…" ("…se unen, entonces, lo arcaico y lo contemporáneo, lo contemporáneo y lo arcaico en las fábricas, que son escuelas-usinas o en talleres artesanales, Mencio y Chou En-Lai, Chou En-Lai y Mencio, con Mao

---

1 De Rokha, *Canto de fuego a China Popular*, p. 2.

2 De Rokha, *Canto de fuego a China Popular*, p. 6.

3 De Rokha, *Canto de fuego a China Popular*, p. 6.

Tzé-Tung en las oceanías del pensamiento-sentimiento, a la vanguardia, en otra gran unanimidad roja y beligerante…").[1] De Rokha, therefore, concludes that it is not the "New China against the Old China" ("la China Nueva contra la China Vieja") but rather a "New China, that overcame the old, and another one emerges above and from the same one" ("…China Nueva, por sobrepujada la anciana, y otra distinta emerge encima y de la misma…").[2]

Another critical issue in De Rokha's works on China is his belief in the global significance of China's formidable experience. The socialist country "thinks and acts internationally" ("piensa y actúa internacionalmente"), the poet comments. [3]For De Rokha, China's political model relates to the global future of the entire international revolutionary movement, of which the People's Republic has emerged, after the Sino-Soviet dispute, as the true leader. De Rokha rhetorically asks: "Are the six hundred and fifty/ million Chinese, those who/ raise the red flag, here, and say: "present"? …/ No. At the back of the epic party/, there is the world, the strong/ world, the free world, that/ enormous flower shuddering/, which is the whole working class/, multitudinous" (¿Son los seiscientos cincuenta/ millones de chinos/, quienes enarbolan la bandera/ roja, aquí, y dicen: "presente"?.../No. A la espalda de la fiesta/ épica, está el mundo, el fuerte/ mundo, el libre mundo, aquella flor egregia estremeciéndose/, que es toda la clase obrera/, multitudinaria").[4] China becomes the political entity that stands "at the head of a century" ("…a la cabeza de un siglo…")[5] writing "the great feeding poem, which is flesh and blood/, for all the peoples of the earth," ("…el gran poema/ de la alimentación/, que es carne y sangre/, para todos los pueblos de la tierra…")[6], "conscious and/ constant, open to all/ the working people" ("…consciente/ y constante, abierta/ a todas las gentes/ obreras..").[7] promoting "the

---

1 De Rokha, *Canto de fuego a China Popular*, p. 6.
2 De Rokha, *Canto de fuego a China Popular*, p. 6.
3 De Rokha, *China Roja*, p. 53.
4 De Rokha, *Ovación universal*, p. 5.
5 De Rokha, *China Roja*, p. 130.
6 De Rokha, *China Roja*, p. 57.
7 De Rokha, *China Roja*, p. 130. Emphasis in the original.

road from socialism to communism, for *the international happiness* of all men"
("…el camino del socialismo al comunismo, por *la felicidad internacional* de todos
los hombres…").[1] Moreover, in this hopeful image of Maoist China, the attainment
of communism is predicted as an inevitable conquest in the near future: "The great
Socialist China today and Communist in tomorrow's audience" ("…la gran China
socialista/ hoy y comunista en la audiencia del mañana…")[2] will be "the lever of the
world/, at the peaks of the human life/, upright…" ("…la palanca del mundo/, en las
cimas de la vida humana/, erguida…").[3]

De Rokha's poems also expose his interest in turning his representations of China
into information that could be regarded as objective and trustworthy. This goal is
deliberately pursued by the constant use of the poet's eyewitness condition as a
rhetorical instrument to backing the veracity of his claims. In this way, De Rokha,
exhibits what he saw and heard, as a contemporary Marco Polo would, when he
describes the people's commune: "*I verified* its enormous growth/, its development
in rebellion/, the concrete facts of its organizations/, the dignity and success./ (...)
And *I did not see* a remnant of the old pain." ("*Yo constaté* su crecimiento enorme/,
su desarrollo en rebelión, los hechos/ concretos de sus organizaciones/, la dignidad y
el éxito/ […] *Y no ví* un resto del dolor antiguo…")."[4]More importantly, his condition
of direct observer of the reality gives him the opportunity to counterattack China's
enemies: "They [the enemies of China] say that the Communes failed/, what failed?,
the revisionists' slander failed (...) the imperialist and the monopolists' gang failed ...
And failed those who invented defeats/ with anti-Marxist intentions ..." ("Dicen que
las Comunas fracasaron/, ¿qué fracasó?, fracasó la calumnia/de los revisionistas[…]
fracasó la pandilla imperialista y la monopolista[…]Y fracasó quien inventó
derrotas/ con intensión antimarxista…").[5] De Rokha further continues his critique
posing another question: "Where, then, does the slander base its great infamy/,

---

1   De Rokha, *Canto de Fuego a China Popular*, p. 4.

2   De Rokha, *Ovación universal*, p. 13.

3   De Rokha, *China Roja*, p. 129,

4   De Rokha, *China Roja*, p. 5. Emphasis added.

5   De Rokha, *China Roja*, p. 5.

the bestial lie scattered/, like that huge garbage bag/ in the sewers?" ("¿En dónde, entónces [sic], basa la calumnia/ su gran infamia/, la mentira bestial desparramada/, como esa enorme bolsa de basura/ de las cloacas?").[1] And subsequently he rapidly responds to China's critiques by affirming the role of empirical observation as the basis that demonstrates the glorious future of the New China: "Here it is like this: the things are the things/ and not their image/, these are empirical facts (...) Only an imbecile seeing the sun denies it" ("Así es aquí: las cosas son las cosas/ y no su imagen/, estos son hechos experimentales [...] Sólo un imbécil viendo el sol lo niega").[2]

Beyond his eyewitness experience, De Rokha uses elements of a deeper nature to legitimize his aptitude to judge China. The first of these is his genius as a poet. In something that is a central feature in De Rokha's poetry, the poetic speaker becomes a visionary who poetizes the world and gets in touch with the cosmic values that move the universe, revealing the meaning of reality. Poetry serves as an intermediary with the world, and the poet is instilled with the power of creation becoming God's imitator. It is the power of the word what saves the poet from extinction because the words allow him to fulfill heroic roles: that of the conqueror, the revolutionary, the Superman and the hero. In the context of the revolutionary quest it is De Rokha's poetic genius what enables him to empathize with and transmit to the people the historical revolutionary consciousness. This mission of messianic tones appears in different parts of his works on China, helping him to overcome cultural differences that may exist with the Maoist republic. Thus by reflecting on the universal aspects that are part of the lives of exploited people around the world, the Chinese experience becomes intelligible: "*I heard* that great word within the Chinese people, the nation, the brother and comrade people of all nations" ("yo escucho aquella gran palabra adentro del pueblo chino, el pueblo, el pueblo hermano y camarada de todos los pueblos").[3] A similar feeling is also

---

1 De Rokha, *China Roja*, pp. 96-97.
2 De Rokha, *China Roja*, p. 97.
3 De Rokha, *China Roja*, p. 125.

powerfully conveyed in his *Ovación universal*: "*I have* them [the people] *inside my soul/; no people are alien to me/ and no people miss me/ because I am people in verse/;* if my word is my rifle or a dagger my accent/, is that my guts are popular/; *and I popularly understand/* this great modern nation…" ("lo tengo adentro del alma/; ningún pueblo me es ajeno y ningún pueblo me extraña/ porque soy pueblo en verso; si mi palabra es mi fusil o puñal mi acento/, es que es popular mi entraña/; y popularmente entiendo a esta gran nación moderna…").[1]

A second— more personal— discourse used by De Rokha to emphasize his capacity to understand China's experience and legitimize the content of his texts centers on the idea that his personal background and those of the Chinese are closely related. De Rokha throughout his poems makes it clear that it is his Chilean/ Latin American identity one of the factors that makes possible for him to understand China ("Chileno de América"["Chilean of America"];[2] "yo que soy indo-español" [I who am Indian-Spanish];[3] Viejo poeta de Latinoamérica" ["Old poet from Latin America"]; [4] "yo, latinoamericano, poeta de los pueblos" ["I, Latin American, poet of the peoples"]; [5] "hombre de Chile" [Chilean man] [6]). A case in point of this sentiment of proximity appears in De Rokha's *Canto de fuego a China Popular*, where he draws attention to this connection: "Your Revolution resembles the Latin American Revolution as a watermelon to a watermelon of the wide summers of Chile (...) I sing to you my "*Song of Fire to Popular China*" feeling like an international Chilean, soldier-style, your Revolution in the guts." ("Tu Revolución se parece a la Revolución de Latinoamérica como una sandía a una sandía de los amplios veranos de Chile (….) Yo te canto mi "*Canto de Fuego a China Popular*" sintiendo como chileno internacional, soldado-estilo, tu Revolución en

---

1   De Rokha, *Ovación universal*, 8. Emphasis added.
2   De Rokha, *China Roja*, p. 101.
3   De Rokha, *China Roja*, p. 101.
4   De Rokha, *China Roja*, p. 10.
5   De Rokha, *China Roja*, p. 82.
6   De Rokha, *Ovación universal*, p. 13

las entrañas…").[1] Similarly, De Rokha explicitly mentions in his poem "Cuba desde China" not only the idea of the communion between revolutionary movements but also the capacity of Latin America to understand this relation. In this, De Rokha writes: "There is an immense voice, which goes from China to Cuba/, which goes from Cuba to China, Latin America/ understands it, it is its destiny, it understands it as its own…" ("Hay una inmensa voz, que va de China a Cuba/, que va de Cuba a China, la América Latina/ la entiende, es su destino, la entiende como suya…").[2] Finally, one central element that connects both experiences is the suffering and exploitation suffered at the hands of imperial powers: "The imperialisms/, the English, the Yankee/ ! They found us rich/ and left us hungry! ... Bandits! ... *That's why I understand/ and admire*, and I raise my voice, for your nation of heroes, singing/ their genius (...) I fight, roaring/ with the multitudes/, a verse of fire/, and the crowds I understand" (Los imperialismos/, el inglés, el yanqui/, ¡nos hallaron ricos/ y dejaron hambre!/...!Bandidos!...Por eso comprendo/ y admiro, y levanto/ mi voz, por tu pueblo/ de héroes, cantando/ su genio […] Yo lucho, rugiendo/ con las multitudes/, un verso de fuego/, y a las muchedumbres entiendo").[3]

In other poems, it is his youth's experiences in the mountains and fields of Chile what facilitates his understanding of the role of the peasants in the Chinese Revolution. De Rokha, in this sense, describes himself as a man "born between mountains, raised between hillsides" ("nacido entre montañas, criado entre laderas") and educated "in Marxism and in the sufferings that make the man strong" ("…en el marxismo y en los padecimientos que hacen al hombre fuerte"), who is able to understand "the heroic, frank old face, and the enormity" (la antigua cara heroica, franca, y la enormidad") of China's attitude "when walking" ("al caminar ")[4]. Further supporting this sense of identification with China's agricultural project, the poet writes in his poem entitled "Los comuneros" the following verse: "I was born

---

1   De Rokha, *Canto de fuego a China Popular*, p. 2.
2   De Rokha, *China Roja*, p. 67.
3   De Rokha, *China Roja*, pp. 129-131. Emphasis added.
4   De Rokha, *China Roja*, p. 23.

and grew like the birds/ of the mountain, wildly/, between saddles and good rider's horses (...) I slept in the cabins/, and I shared the bread of the peons/, I saw how the moon crossed/ the immense night. *That's why I understand* the epic/ of the People's Commune work, success to success/, with strong faith" ("Nací y crecí como los pájaros/ de la montaña, agrestemente/, entre monturas y caballos de buen jinete [....] Dormí adentro de las cabañas/, y compartí el pan de los peones/, ví [sic] cómo la luna cruzaba/ la inmensa noche. Por eso comprendo lo épico/ del trabajo de las Comunas Populares, éxito a éxito/, con fe rotunda").[1] Meanwhile, while discussing the great forestry projects of northern China his early life's experiences are again brought up. This time, the relation to his Chilean identity is explicitly established: "And since I am Chilean of the cavalry of the mountain, *I understand* the immense poetry of your forestry character" ("Y como soy chileno de la caballería de montaña, entiendo la inmensa poesía de tu carácter forestal").[2]

In the poetry of De Rokha, in this way, China becomes understandable, and part of the same universal experience associated with the control of the environment and the constant struggles of the exploited people. China's Revolution does not appear as something belonging to another "world" but a familiar agricultural and revolutionary reality connected to the same pains of Latin America.

Final Thoughts

The decision of inviting De Rokha to China and the subsequent acceptance of the invitation in 1964, demonstrate the significance of international events to the Latin American left and to China during the 1950s and 1960s. Pablo de Rokha's life and relation with China was affected by the centrality of three key events of the Cold War: the Chinese Revolution, the Cuban Revolution and the Sino-Soviet split. His travel reflects the juncture at which China's increasing interest in Latin American revolution prospects. In other words, for both Chinese and Chilean activists, De Rokha's visit represented an event that helped to strengthen the local and global

---

1   De Rokha, *China Roja*, pp. 58-59. My emphasis.
2   De Rokha, *China Roja*, p. 44.My emphasis.

significance of the International Movement. The publication of De Rokha's poems in China, his participation in the revolutionary events, as well as his close ties with Chinese diplomas,[1] put forward the central role that famous, national and/or international figures, played in the international and national disputes between the different left factions that shaped the global Cold War.

The images of the PRC in De Rokha's works also illustrate how the Chilean poet perceived his own activism as organically a part of both local and global struggles. By continually identifying his personal experiences and Latin America's social battles with China's revolutionary project, De Rokha appropriated Maoist propaganda and literary conventions with the purpose of intervening in local debates. Taking into account the national importance attached to his work, De Rokha's poems on China cannot be viewed merely as a reproduction of Chinese propaganda. Rather, they were imaginative products envisioned in the middle of a transnational revolutionary context produced in both regions and from first-hand experience that provides input to discussions on China and Latin America. The transnational character of De Rokha's writings on China is perhaps best represented in literary terms in the incorporation of epic Maoist descriptions of Chinese culture, history, and people into the extremely rich, hyperbolic, surreal and *nacional-popular* imaginary of his literary project.

And while De Rokha stresses to present China in the light of Latin American sameness, breaking for moments with fixed alterities, ideas of cultural differences, as in any other civilization's discourse on foreigners, do not entirely disappear. De Rokha's representations of China bring a sense of otherness that is represented in the stereotypization, totalization and idealization of China's present and past reality tending to present and glorify it as a unique case. These images that inherit an "Orientalist" perspective of a traditional character in terms of its reductionism

---

1　We know, for example, that De Rokha was very close to Lin Ping　林　平, who in 1965 became the first Director of the Commercial Office of the People's Republic of China in Chile. In 1970 he would became the first Ambassador in Chile of the PRC as well. See Chou, *Chile y China: inmigración y relaciones bilaterales*, 356-357; Meza, dir., Lobos, prod., *Pablo de Rokha. El amigo piedra*.

and exoticism, do not, however, undermine De Rokha's positive evaluation of the PRC. Rather, they help to reinforce the favorable image of it. De Rokha, thus, adopts "Orientalist" discourses in order to emphasize the superiority of China's revolutionary ways and challenge the capitalist world, the inferior and ultimate "other" in De Rokha's poems.

Interestingly, De Rokha's positive evaluation of the PRC's development did not translate in his favor towards the possibility of reproducing the Chinese Revolution project at home. It was, in fact, precisely De Rokha's opinion that China represented a unique historical case what limited the potential applicability of the model in Latin America. In an interview given in 1963, the poet explicitly points out this idea: "I deeply respect the Chinese Heroes and Leaders, who are the historical expression of the Chinese people and are reflected in the Chinese people, the historical expression of the Chinese people and the general outline of their behavior, and China's evolution it seems to me one of the enormous events of this century; but each people has to make their revolution according to their objective and subjective conditions, coexistent; China is China, Cuba is Cuba; and although in Latin America the revolutionary sub-layers are identified, the national morphology of their countries will give the revolutionary tonic and the style of their revolution ..." ("Yo respeto profundamente a los Heroés [sic] y Líderes chinos, que son la expresión histórica del pueblo chino y se reflejan en el pueblo, y la expresión histórica del pueblo chino y el lineamiento general de su conducta y la evolución China me parece uno de los enormes hechos de este siglo; pero cada pueblo ha de hacer su revolución de acuerdo con sus condiciones objetivas y subjetivas, coexistentes; China es China, Cuba es Cuba; y aunque en Latinoamérica los subsuelos revolucionarios se identifican, la morfología nacional de sus países dara [sic] la tónica revolucionaria y el estilo de su revolución...").[1]

---

1   Pablo de Rokha, "Entrevista" . Typescript manuscript is held at Biblioteca Nacional, Chile, digital collection, 1963 no: 000894837. Accessed on 2/11/2017 at: http://www.bncatalogo.cl/F/CSMXJ 5BYUAJ1R3AUCIIBYYQNKQR2S3KFJMYJLSC7XS2FJMUHX5\29708?func=service&doc_ library=BNC01&doc_number=000894837&line_number=0001&func_code=WEBFULL&service_ type=MEDIA.

Although De Rokha is not denying here the importance of China's global leading role in international communism, he expounds that, ultimately, it would be in the national layers where the basis of each country's revolutions should be found. The Chinese Revolution constitutes, for De Rokha, a revolutionary movement that although shares similarities with Chile's reality, it is the result of historical, natural and human conditions that are not exactly the same. In conclusion, in De Rokha's views on China, it is the coexistence of ideas of common humanity and cultural differences which enabled him to maintain, on the one hand, his national identity, while on the other; ratify the importance of solidarity among different revolutionary movements "for the international unity of Marxism-Leninism, against the hordes of imperialist murderers" ("por la unidad internacional del marxismo-lenilismo, contra las hordas de asesinos imperialistas").[1]

References

人民日报 (People's Daily)

文汇报 (Wenhui's Daily)

Birch, Cyril. "Literature under communism." In Roderick MacFarquhar and John King Fairbank, eds., *The Cambridge History of China, vol.14, The People's Republic, part 2: Revolutions within the Chinese Revolution, 1966-1982*, 743-814. New York and Melbourne: Cambridge University Press, 1991.

Camayd-Freixas, Erik, ed. *Orientalism and Identity in Latin America: Fashioning Self and Other from the (Post) Colonial Margin*. Tucson: University of Arizona Press, 2013.

Chávez, Damián Lo. "Comunismo rupturista en Chile (1960-1970)." Bachelor's thesis, Universidad de Chile, Santiago, 2012.

Chou, Diego Lin. *Chile y China: inmigración y relaciones bilaterales (1845-1970)*. Santiago: Dibam, 2004.

Connelly, Marisela, and Romer Cornejo. *China-América Latina. Génesis y desarrollo de sus relaciones*. México, D.F: El Colegio de México, 1992.

Curet Aranam, José Miguel. "Pablo de Rokha: Vanguardia y Geocrítica: La poesía de *U* (1926) y *Carta Magna de América* (1949)." Ph.D. dissertation, Universidad de Salamanca, Salamanca, 2015.

De Rokha, Pablo, ed. *Antología 1916-1953*. Santiago: Multitud, 1954.

1　Pablo de Rokha, *Estilo de Masas*, (Santiago: Editorial Quimantú, 2017), p. 9.

"Entrevista." Typescript manuscript is held at Biblioteca Nacional, Chile, digital collection, 1963, no: 000894837. Accessed on 2/11/2017 at:http://www.bncatalogo.cl/F/CSMXJ 5BYUAJ1R3AUCIIBYYQNKQR2S3KFJMYJLSC7XS2FJMUHX5\29708?func=s ervice&doc_library=BNC01&doc_number=000894837&line_number=0001&func_ code=WEBFULL&service_type=MEDIA.

Canto de Fuego a China Popular. *Multitud* 89 (1963): pp. 1-6.

China Roja. Typescript manuscript with handwriting amendments. People's Republic of China, 1964.

Ovación universal. Typescript manuscript with handwriting amendments. Beijing, 1965.

Zhao Jinping 赵金平 , trans. "Meng Tai tongzhi 孟泰同志 (The Comrade Meng Tai)." *Yalü jiang* 鸭绿江 (The Yalü River) 10 (October, 1964): pp. 61-62.

Zhao Jinping 赵金平 , trans. "Xiangei Shanghai de reqing zhi ge 献给上海的热情之歌 (Warm-heart song dedicated to Shanghai)." *Wenhui bao* 文汇报 10 (October 1964): 4.

Zhao Jinping 赵 金 平 , trans. "Shi si shou: "Mao Zedong," "Weida de bangyang," "Zhongguo ertong" " 诗四首：“毛泽东”，“伟大的榜样”，“中国儿童” (Four poems: "Mao Zedong", "The Great Example," "Chinese Children"). *Shigan* 诗刊 (Newspaper of Poetry) 10 (October 1964): pp. 39-46.

Zhao Jinping 赵金平 , trans. "Gei Mei diguozhuyi de gongkai xin 给美帝国主义的公开 信 (Open Letter to American Imperialism)." *Shijie wenxue* 世界文学 (Journal of World Literature) 12 (December, 1964): pp. 11-18.

(Baleiluo De luoka 巴勃罗·德·洛卡). *Xiangei Beijing de songge* 献给北京的颂歌 (Anthem dedicated to Beijing). Translated from Spanish into Chinese by Zhao Jinping 赵 金平 . Beijing: Zuojia chubanshe, 1965.

Neruda y yo-Tercetos dantescos a Casiano Basualto. Santiago: Ediciones Tácitas y Fundación de Rokha, 2016.

Estilo de Masas. Santiago: Editorial Quimantú, 2017.

Ferrero, Mario. *Pablo de Rokha. Guerillero de la poesía*. Santiago: Sociedad de Escritores de Chile, 1967.

Garner, William R. "The Sino-Soviet Ideological Struggle in Latin America." *Journal of Inter-American Studies* 10, 2 (1968): pp. 244-255.

Garza Elizondo, Humberto. *China y el Tercer Mundo, Teoría y práctica de la política exterior de Pequín, 1956-1966*. México D.F: El Colegio de México, 1975.

Guerrero, Pedro Pablo. "*China Roja*: El libro perdido de Pablo de Rokha." *El Mercurio*, Sección Artes y Letras, May 11, 2014.

Halperin, Ernst. "Peking and the Latin American Communists." *The China Quarterly* 29 (1967): pp. 111-154.

Hubert, Rosario. "Intellectual Cartographies of the Cold War. Latin American visitors to the People's Republic of China, 1952-1958." In Robert T. Tally Jr., ed., *The Routledge Handbook of Literature and Space*, 337-348. Abingdon, Oxon, New York: Routledge, 2017.

Johnson, Cecil. *Communist China and Latin America, 1959-1967*. New York and London: Columbia University Press, 1970.

Kushigian, Julia. *Orientalism in the Hispanic Literary Tradition: In Dialogue with Borges, Paz, and Sarduy.* Albuquerque, New Mexico: University of New Mexico Press, 1991.

Lamberg, Fernando. *Vida y obra de Pablo de Rokha*. Santiago: Zig Zag, 1966.

Lavquén, Alejandro. "*China Roja* de Pablo de Rokha." *Punto Final* 303, (April, 2014).

"*China Roja* de Pablo de Rokha II." Accessed on 13/12/2018 at: http://letras.mysite.com/alav140514.html.

ed. *Antología de las obras completas de Pablo de Rokha*. Santiago: Pehuén, 2016.

Lin, Hui 林辉 , ed. *Zhongguo fanyi cidian* 中国翻译词典 (Dictionary of Chinese Translator Biographies). Pekín: Zhongguo duiwai fanyi chubanshe gongsi, 1988.

Matus, Eugenio. "Pablo de Rokha." *Revista Trilce* 14 (1968): pp. 3-6.

Meza, Diego, dir., Eduado Lobos, prod. *Pablo de Rokha. El amigo piedra.* Chile: La Cresta Producciones y Deboom Studio, 2010. Accessed on 5/11/2018 at: https://www.youtube.com/watch?v=s5tu-VEJ2QE&t=52s.

Montt Strabucchi, María. "The PRC's Cultural Diplomacy towards Latin America in the 1950s and 1960s." *International Journal of Current Chinese Studies*, 1 (2010): pp. 53-83.

"Viajeros chilenos a la RPC en los años cincuenta y sesenta." In Stefan Rinke, ed., *Entre espacios: la historia latinoamericana en el contexto global. Actas del XVII Congreso Internacional de la Asociación de Historiadores Latinoamericanistas Europeos (AHILA)*, Freie Universität, 9-13 September, 2014, Colegio Internacional de Graduados "Entre Espacios": 3027-3035.

"'Writing about China.' Latin American Travelogues during the Cold War: Bernardo Kordon's '600 millones y uno' (1958), and Luis Oyarzún's 'Diario de Oriente, Unión Soviética, China e India' (1960). "*Revista Caminhos da História*, 21, 1 (2016): pp. 93-124.

Mora, Frank O. "The People's Republic of China and Latin America. From Indifference to Engagement." *Asian Affairs: An American Review*, 24, 1 (1997): pp. pp. 35-58.

Nómez, Naín. *Pablo de Rokha. Una escritura en movimiento*. Santiago: Documentas, 1988.

"Introducción." In Naím Nómez, ed. *Canto del macho anciano y otros poemas*, pp. 13-22. Madrid: Editorial Biblioteca Nueva, 2003.

Ratliff, William E. "Chinese Communist Cultural Diplomacy toward Latin America, 1949-1960." *The Hispanic American Historical Review*, 49, 1 (1969): 53-79.

Rothwell, Matthew D. *Transpacific Revolutionaries. The Chinese Revolution in Latin America*. New York: Routledge, 2013.

"Secret Agent for International Maoism: José Venturelli, Chinese Informal Diplomacy and Latin American Maoism." *Radical Americas* 1, 1 (2016): pp. 44-62.

Rupar, Brenda. "El debate chino-soviético y la emergencia del maoísmo como corriente política diferenciada en el Movimiento Comunista Internacional." *Historia Contemporánea* 57 (2018): pp. 559-586.

Sha, Ding 沙丁, et al., eds. *Zhongguo he Lading meizhou guangxi jianshi* 中国和拉丁美洲关系简史 (A Brief History of Sino-Latin American Relations). Henan: Henan renmin chubanshe, 1986.

Sun, Weixue 孙维学, Lin Di 林地, et al., eds. *Xin Zhongguo dui wai wenhua jiaoliu shilue* 新中国对外文化交流史略 (A Brief History of New China's Foreign Cultural Exchanges). Beijing: Zhongguo youyi chuban gongsi, 1999.

Teng, Wei 滕威. *"Bianjing zhinan." Lading Meizhou wenxue hanyi yu Zhongguo dangdai wenxue* "边境之南". 拉丁美洲文学汉译与中国当代文学 (1949-1999) ("To the South of the Frontier": The Translation of Latin American Literature and Chinese Contemporary Literature). Beijing: Beijing daxue chubanshe, 2011.

Tinajero, Araceli. "Asian Representations in Spanish American Modernism," *Literature and Arts of the Americas*, 39, 1 (2006): pp. 146-150.

Orientalismo en el modernismo hispanoamericano. Indiana: Indiana University Press, 2003.

Wang, Ban. "Revolutionary Realism and Revolutionary Romanticism: Song of Youth." In Kirk A. Denton, ed., *The Columbia Companion to Modern Chinese Literature*, 237-249. New York, Chichester and West Sussex: Columbia University Press, 2016.

Zerán, Faride. *La guerrilla literaria. Pablo de Rokha, Vicente Huidobro y Pablo Neruda*. Madrid: Editorial de Bolsillo, 2011.

Zhang, Shouyi 张守义. *Zhang Shouyi waiguo wenxue chatu ji* 张守义外国文学插图集 (A Compilation of Zhang Shouyi's Illustrations of Foreign Literature). Changsha: Hunan meishu chubanshe, 1982.

Wode sheji shenghuo: Zhang Shouyi 我的设计生活：张守义 (My Design's Life: Zhang Shouyi). Beijing: Zhongguo lüyou chubanshe, 2007.

Zolov, Eric. "Introduction: Latin America in the Global Sixties." *The Americas* 70, 3 (January 2014): pp. 349-362.

上海市非物质文化遗产纸质资料的保存

塔塔亚恩【博茨瓦纳】

博茨瓦纳大学图书管理员

引 言

文化遗产是人类进化的重要概念"镜像",它揭示了人类进化的美学、历史、科学或精神意义上的概念转变。广义的文化遗产是指"世代相承的观念、技能、实践和实物,体现社会成员身份,使他们具有一种团结感和归属感"。文化遗产可以分为物质文化遗产和非物质文化遗产两大类。物质文化遗产包括建筑设计或环境(建筑、城镇景观等)、自然环境(乡村景观、海岸和海岸线、农业遗产等)以及图书、文献、实物、照片和影音资料(联合国教科文组织,2003年)。另一方面,非物质文化遗产的定义是"被各社区、群体,有时是个人,视为其文化遗产组成部分的各种社会实践、观念表述、表现形式、知识、技能以及相关的工具、实物、手工艺品和文化场所"。这些愿望应被理解为人类持续进步的表现,因此在现实中是动态的。本质上,非物质文化遗产的定义没有界限,但可以分为特定的类别,以指导各个国家确认非物质文化遗产。非物质文化遗产包括以下五个类别[1]:

- 口头传统和表现形式,包括作为非物质文化遗产媒介的语言;
- 表演艺术,例如音乐、诗歌;

---

1 联合国教科文组织,2003年。

- 社会实践、仪式、节庆活动；

- 有关自然界和宇宙的知识和实践；

- 传统手工艺。[1]

以上五个类别清楚地表明，非物质文化遗产与无形的信仰、精神、知识技能、经历和工艺技能有关。这些是人类进化过程中在过去创造的抽象品质或属性，因此需要保存供当代和子孙后代使用。为了让人类继续拥有这些宝贵的社会财富，我们必须保存它们。通常，保存是一项管理职能，着眼于通过保证安全、提供理想的环境条件和防范各种风险，以实现各种类型的实质性照管和保护，延长文化遗产寿命。保存是指保证文化遗产世代相传的手段。对于所有类型讲述过去故事的遗产而言，这是防止损害和破坏的直接和间接措施。虽然"保存"一词的不同定义具有相同的终极目标，为了保护遗产以供当前和未来使用，这一术语在不同行业有不同用途。在本文中，"保存"和"保护"两个术语可以交换使用，是指护理和保护文化遗产的管理职能。

全球范围内普遍采用保存策略作为保护不同国家文化遗产的手段。在这一过程中，保护者可以更好地理解非物质文化遗产的本质并开始采取新的保护措施。然而，自2003年通过《保护非物质文化遗产公约》以来，非物质文化遗产的保护仍然处于起步阶段。迄今为止，各国都在努力制定保护非物质文化遗产的策略。转变带来各种挑战，例如对非物质文化遗产的理解不足以及有限的教育、创新和技术。中国对非物质文化遗产保护的挑战认识不够。在6月7日至8日于上海举行的第六届国际（上海）非物质文化遗产保护论坛上演讲时，大樋年雄感慨道："非遗保护，不仅仅是继承、守护传统和古典原来的样子，而需要时常接触从事各个领域的人，扩展自己的见识，经常挑战新的事物，绝不能甘于维持现状"。上海乃至全世界不同社会的文化遗产工艺技能、类型和组合随着时代的变迁而发生变化，从而导致情况变得更加复杂。上海虽然举行非物质文化遗产保护论坛并成立上海市群众艺术馆（SMAC）等非物质文化遗产保护机构，但似乎没有明确的文献和纸质资料保存策略。这种情况的原因可能是缺乏技能、财政拮据、管理不善以及不重视非物质文化遗产纸质出版物。

因此，本文关注中国上海市非物质文化遗产保护纸质出版物／记录的保存。

1　联合国教科文组织，2003年。

具体而言，探讨非物质文化遗产纸质资料文献的趋势/类型，确定非物质文化遗产纸质资料保存策略，揭示非物质文化遗产保存相关的挑战并提出改进建议。本文主要对已出版和未出版的历史、人类学和其他文化研究资料、记录和档案资料进行桌面研究。收集的资料还包括个人经历、观察发现以及各种保护期望的正式和非正式讨论。

上海与非物质文化遗产概述

专家们认为中国典型的区域关系是条块关系。张学良教授在 9 月 9 日至 29 日的青年汉学家研修计划（YPYS 2018）上海九月班上指出，从 1949 年到 1978 年，中国的政策分为三个部分（"块"）：内陆地区（西部）、中部地区和沿海地区（东部）。在这三大块中，上海属于中国最发达的东部地区。2000 年以来，中国的治理政策发生了变化，开始实施城市群政策。根据城市群政策，上海被归为中国乃至全球最大的城市之一。上海市人口超过 2400 万，不仅人口稠密，而且在物质和非物质文化遗产方面也潜力无限。在过去四十年中，由于中国工业快速发展，上海经历了强劲的经济转型。与此同时，上海成长为教育科研中心，拥有博物馆、档案馆、图书馆、历史建筑遗址和非物质遗产等众多文化遗产。

联合国教科文组织通过《保护非物质文化遗产公约》后，中国于 2004 年批准公约并于 2005 年在文化部的协调下启动实施程序。在此过程中，中国举行联席会议，以制定中国非物质文化遗产保护的指导方针和政策，审查、批准和协调非物质文化遗产保护计划。2015 年，中国大约有 38 项非物质文化遗产列入联合国教科文组织的《人类非物质文化遗产代表作名录》，这一数字已显著增加。与中国的其他城市相比，上海凭借其庞大的旅游和文化资源成为中国经济增长的重要引擎之一。作者有幸参观的上海市重要历史性地标包括外滩（黄浦江畔的殖民地风格建筑）、南市（上海的老城区，有壮观的花园和茶馆）以及法租界、浦东商业区的东方明珠和上海中心大厦（世界第二高的建筑）。上海的非物质文化遗产名录包括 179 项，涵盖民间音乐、民间舞蹈和传统戏剧、曲艺、民间文学、传统手工艺等。大上海地区其他理想的文化遗产和遗址包括田园诗般的古老水乡乌镇和大运河，两者均被联合国教科文组织列为世界遗产地。

非物质文化遗产纸质资料文献类型

文献是文化遗产的核心支柱之一。文献包括我们日常生活、组织、协会和社区中每个部门使用的信息管理系统。在商业场景中，文献记录过程可能包括订购、会议记录、供需、账目和财务报表等。Setlhabi 在论文中强调，文献在确保为后代妥善保存手工艺品历史方面起着至关重要的作用，特别是文化遗产。就文化遗产而言，文献"记录实物的所有特征，可以是记录册、入库单、购置单、藏品单和主文件"。在管理非物质文化遗产时收集和记录也非常重要。事实上，非物质文化遗产表达和表现形式的确认和文献记录是确定适当保护计划首先需要考虑的方面。《保护非物质文化遗产公约》（联合国教科文组织，2003 年）规定，社区必须参与确认和确定作为文化遗产组成部分的各种非物质文化遗产。针对文献问题，本研究确定上海市非物质文化遗产出版物类型和 / 或方法的文献趋势。研究发现，这里有浩如烟海的非物质文化遗产纸质出版物。然而，出版物没有根据非物质文化遗产纸质资料保护策略特别挑选出来并予以保存。

非物质文化遗产文献类型桌面研究表明，主要有三种类型的书面形式纸质资料。在上海，我们发现非物质文化遗产文献的第一种类型是制订名录。根据《保护非物质文化遗产公约》第十七条（急需保护的非物质文化遗产名录），制订名录是重要的文献记录程序。非物质文化遗产的所有特征被记入记录册、入库单、购置单、藏品单等，反映与非物质文化遗产实践相关的方面。安东尼在"非物质文化遗产研究者论坛第一届双年度会议：教科文组织《保护非物质文化遗产公约》的实施"上指出：

"立档和宣传已被证明是非物质文化遗产保护的有效手段，可以从人类学的角度解释为在世界媒体上发起或颁布遗产的方式。它们采取对传统项目异化的语言（拍摄、影片、视听记录）对文化元素进行解释"。

安东尼的定义认为，文献是遗产要素的"镜像"。换言之，文献是作为特殊非物质文化遗产模式的特质、偏好、态度、兴趣或能力等逐项清单。例如，周庆华关于香港特别行政区政府和当地社区的非物质文化遗产保护工作报告特别强调，创建名录是非物质文化遗产保护的重要措施。报告主要关注以下事项：创建名录，将本地名录项列入中国国家级非物质文化遗产名录，将粤剧列入联合国教科文组织人类非物质文化遗产代表作名录，以及本地组织保护非物质文化遗产的各种重要行动。周庆华在报告中指出，2009 年香港特别行政区调查小组提交一份桌面研究报告和一份工作计划，该计划中包含根据本地研究机构已发表和未发表来源确定的一份 280 项非物质文化遗产暂定名录。

在创建非物质文化遗产名录时，一个重要方面是让社区、传承人和所有利益相关者参与其中。联合国教科文组织《保护非物质文化遗产公约》第十五条（社区、群体和个人的参与）规定：

"缔约国在开展保护非物质文化遗产活动时，应努力确保创造、延续和传承这种遗产的社区、群体，有时是个人的最大限度的参与，并吸收他们积极地参与有关的管理。"[1]

中国通过"参与观察法"策略实现第十五条规定的社区、群体和个人的参与。例如，为了确保完整记录活动和口述历史，香港特别行政区调查小组强调采取参与观察法进行田野研究，所有研究人员都具有丰富的质性研究经验。在上海，例如上海群众艺术馆，也被视为创建非物质文化遗产名录的一种策略。

第二种类型的非物质文化遗产纸质资料主要是各种形式或格式的记录，例如纸质、DVD、VHS、CD、缩微胶卷等。这种类型的文献更多地作为非物质文化遗产实践的全面记录保存策略，而不是汇总名录。具体来说，就纸质出版物而言，研究表明，作为一种保护方式，数量巨大的书面诗歌、事件记载等在非物质文化遗产整体记录方面起到至关重要的作用，可以保存以供未来世代使用。这是非物质文化遗产的渐进式收集策略，例如，采访遗产传承人。另一种重要的文献是在上海市非物质文化遗产机构发现的灰色文献或记录。它们是重要的原始历史文献记录，或者是非物质文化遗产领域创作者或艺术家的手稿。

观察到的第三种类型非物质文化遗产纸质资料是学院风格的记录或出版物，主要对非物质文化遗产的特定方面进行科学研究。文献包括期刊、杂志、广播电台采访、电视播放等。它们不一定提供非物质文化遗产所有方面／实践的完整记录。例如，期刊出版物中的研究论文关注感兴趣的特定方面，以发掘新观点。文献的另一个来源是各个教育部门的教材出版物／记录。格式可以是 DVD、VHS、CD、缩微胶卷、YouTube 或在线视频和音频，也可以收集印刷／纸质资料或图书。

从观察到的三种类型非物质文化遗产纸质资料范围来看，对于何种类型的纸质资料适合保存没有固定的限制或边界。所有三种文献／记录类型在上海乃至全

1　联合国教科文组织，2003 年，第 5 页。

世界范围内对于非物质文化遗产的整体保存起到非常重要的作用。因此，根据不同的非物质文化遗产实践、表现形式、观念表述、知识和技能，采取不同的保存方式。下一章节详细阐述上海市非物质文化遗产纸质出版物保存策略。

上海市非物质文化遗产纸质资料保存

中国的非物质文化遗产丰富多样，昆曲、中国书法和中国剪纸都是常见的例子。联合国教科文组织指出，"为了让非物质遗产保持活力，它必须与一种文化息息相关，在社区内以及不同世代之间经常实践和学习"。为了实现这一点，任何非物质文化遗产保护计划都必须加以重视。换言之，为了使人类继续拥有这些宝贵的社会财富，我们必须予以保存。保存是指保证过去的活动或实践和资源可用，将其与现代生活关联并传承给未来世代。在非物质文化遗产保护语境下使用的"保护"一词是指"确保非物质文化遗产生命力的各种措施，包括这种遗产各个方面的确认、立档、研究、保存、保护、宣传、弘扬、传承（特别是通过正规和非正规教育）和振兴"[1]。目前正在探索将社会实践、观念表述、表现形式、知识、技能以及相关的工具、实物、手工艺品和文化场所世代相传的方法。这是避免社会实践、观念表述、表现形式、知识和技能退化或消失以及防止所有讲述过去故事的所有实物、手工艺品和文化场所被破坏的直接和间接行动。

中国非物质文化遗产保护的骨干单位是中国文化部下属的非物质文化遗产司。在中国文化部的领导下成立设立部门或制订计划，责任之一就是保护非物质文化遗产。相关保护组织包括上海市文化广播电视局、上海市人民政府外事办公室、上海市教育委员会和上海市长宁区人民政府、上海市创意产业协会、上海艺术礼品博物馆和上海工艺美术职业学院。中国的非物质文化遗产计划主要由国家非物质文化遗产保护工作专家委员会提供指导。其他重要组织还包括上海市的私人及政府博物馆和档案馆，它们都有责任保护非物质文化遗产。例如，中国文化研究中心提供有关中国非物质文化遗产的信息。作为非物质文化遗产保护工作进展的一部分，上海艺术礼品博物馆理事长胡木清与上海工艺美术职业学院院长仓平签署《关于加强工艺美术和非遗文献资料建设的合作协议书》。

具体而言，没有专门针对非物质文化遗产纸质出版物的保存策略。通常与非物质文化遗产保护计划同时并存。因此，本节将探讨上海市非物质文化遗产纸质

1　联合国教科文组织，2003 年。

资料和其他媒介的保存策略。常见保存策略的起点是非物质文化遗产领域的确认、分类和立档。通过协调计划，特定的协会、委员会或社区团体相聚在一起，目标是共同保护非物质文化遗产。位于上海中山西路 1551 号的上海市群众艺术馆就是一个存档非物质文化遗产文献的重要文化遗产中心。其中教育计划是指作为保护策略，面向公众传播诗歌、音乐、信仰 / 宗教的不同文化工艺品及节日，例如端午节。总体而言，非物质文化遗产保护计划以联合国教科文组织《保护非物质文化遗产公约》中规定的以下原则为核心：

- 确保非物质文化遗产的生命力，包括确认、立档、研究、保存、保护；
- 宣传、弘扬、传承，特别是通过正规和非正规教育，例如上海市群众艺术馆等非物质文化遗产组织；
- 以及振兴中国非物质文化遗产的各个方面。

下一章节将简要阐述中国上海市非物质文化遗产保存面临的相关挑战。

非物质文化遗产纸质资料保存面临的挑战

虽然有大量证据表明已发布上文所述三种类型的非物质文化遗产文献，但也观察到诸多挑战，尤其是在上海。首先，有研究指出非物质文化遗产保护面临各种挑战，包括很少有纸质出版物被确认和立档。非物质文化遗产保护的常见做法是设立教育中心，例如上海社会科学院博物馆致力于非物质文化遗产保护的教学。在教育过程中以视频等形式记录技能，但纸质文献非常稀缺，特别是确认口头传统（例如诗歌）并以纸质形式记录下来。我们需要思考的主要问题是：如何将非物质文化遗产实践全部收集在纸质资料中？

作为联合国教科文组织《保护非物质文化遗产公约》的主张之一，鉴于文化是不断发展的，非物质文化遗产文献记录应该是一个持续的过程。一旦社区同意增加非物质文化遗产社会实践、观念表述、表现形式、知识和技能，文献名录也需要重新创建或更新。这对非物质文化遗产文献的持续性和更新带来挑战。因此，由于文化的变动，回归到过去将当前趋势与旧的传统文化遗产活动联系起来变得非常复杂。早在 2010 年，Borg 就指出中国的文化遗产保护正面临挑战，随后在 2013 年，Safford 也表达了相同的观点，即中国文化受到侵蚀。他们举了一些例子，例如正在消失的农历新年表现形式，社会变得更加个人主义，这表明没有社区的束缚，人们倾向于追求短暂而直接的满足感。

为了给中国寻找解决方案，在中国上海市举行的国际非物质文化遗产保护论坛上指出非物质文化遗产保护面临的一些挑战。2017 年 6 月 9 日举办的第五届国际（上海）非物质文化遗产保护论坛以"共性与差异—联合国教科文组织《保护非物质文化遗产公约》实施现状及愿景"为主题，与会人员围绕这一主题进行长时间的讨论。根据 SACM 的总结，会议重点关注以下问题：

- 联合国教科文组织颁布实施《保护非物质文化遗产公约》后的情况；
- 面对非物质文化遗产保护领域的新挑战和新机遇，探讨共性；
- 各国在非物质文化遗产保护保护方法与途径中的差异；
- 世界各国在非物质文化遗产保护领域所遇到的共同课题；

分享典型经验与做法，为携手推动非遗保护事业的发展、促进各国文化交流带来新的启迪与契机 (SACM, 2018 年)。

在 2018 年 6 月 7 日至 8 日在上海举行的第六届国际（上海）非物质文化遗产保护论坛上，上海艺术礼品博物馆表示上海参与"一带一路"建设，为世界各国的利益相关方提供文化机会。特别重视世界各国非物质文化遗产保护的实施、共性、方法或实践以及共同课题。此次论坛以"传统再造——非物质文化遗产保护的新趋势"为主题，重点关注非物质文化遗产保护的最新挑战，鼓励与会人员分享经验。例如，上海市文广局副局长尼冰发表"新时期上海特色的非物质文化遗产保护传承"主题演讲。

文献确认的其他关键挑战还包括以下问题：应该研究和记录何种形式的非物质文化遗产？如何让利益相关方参与到非物质文化遗产立档过程中，应该收集哪些类型的信息？立档如何反映本地多样化的声音和观点，如何定义文化遗产？如何确定非物质文化遗产立档的合适媒介形式？立档时应取得哪些类型的权限，尤其是版权？这些权限如何随时间流逝发生变化？ 9 月 9 日至 29 日在上海举行的青年汉学家研修计划讨论中，Segaetsho 博士提出其他问题：工业化或现代化有哪些文化遗产输入，中国如何确保现代化不侵蚀文化遗产？此外，文化遗产在多大程度上影响上海乃至整个中国的经济增长？这些问题持续构成重要的现实，文化遗产保护必须证明其合理性，以便各国可以继续保护文化遗产。谈到这些问题时，张道根教授在上海举办的青年汉学家研修计划第 2 次讲课上指出，为了解决这些问题，中国正在大力发展文化遗产的产业化路线。这些措施将确保即使在中国建设小康社会的大规模经济增长中，文化遗产仍然具有相关性，对人民的生活品质、饮食、住所以及工作和生活方式的自由选择产生影响。治理和政治也被视为文化遗产的相关挑战。例如，Safford 引用了 Lily Kong 的观点，认为在上海做出设立新纪念遗址等决策时不会产生公众抗议，因为社区在此过程中没有发言权。

尽管非物质文化遗产保护面临许多挑战，上海市的文化遗产技术和投资进展良好。代理商、投资者和创新产业公司正在进入，例如上海建为历保科技股份有限公司。上海建为是一家专业从事建筑文化遗产保护规划、设计、施工和技术服务的高新技术企业。这与中国的新产业趋势方法有关，特别是在内部和外部环境保护问题上。

结论和建议

本文旨在探讨中国上海市非物质文化遗产保护纸质出版物 / 记录的保存。研究表明，非物质文化遗产纸质资料记录存在不同的过程、类型和 / 或方法。我们进一步观察到各种非物质文化遗产保护方法或策略以及面临的诸多挑战。本文的结论是，可以举办大量活动提高非物质文化遗产保护方式。例如，在第六届国际（上海）非物质文化遗产保护论坛上，许多专家指出，"一带一路"沿线国家拥有非常丰富的非物质文化遗产资源，为彼此合作奠定良好的基础。为了实现非物质文化遗产保护的繁荣，上海应借鉴其他方的国际技术并加以利用，同时创造出可以在上海应用的相关新技术。非物质文化遗产保存 / 保护计划应与中国当前的经济发展趋势保持一致，确保人民过上更好的生活而不是只关注生产。

本研究发现，虽然已存在很多非物质文化遗产保护出版物，但没有制订系统的纸质出版物保存计划。这可以归因于以下事实，即大多数出版物都采取研究出版物的形式，而不是非物质文化遗产保护方面的文献。因此，出版物主要用作研究文献，并非可以保存的文章。作为前进的方向，上海应努力做好自身定位，进行国际合作，制订不同非物质文化遗产领域的保护计划，例如纸质出版物及其确认、分类、立档和存储。

The Preservation of Intangible Cultural Heritage Paper Materials in Shanghai

Thatayaone Segaetsho / Botswana

Librarian-Conservator, University of Botswana

Introduction

Cultural heritage is an important conceptual 'mirror image' of human evolution that reveal the transition of human evolvement on concepts considered to have aesthetic, historical, scientific or of spiritual significance. Cultural heritage is broadly understood to refer to"those ideas, skills, practices and objects that are passed on from generation to generation, allowing the members of a community to identify and create a sense of unity and belonging" (Iossifova, 2014). These could be classified into two broad categories of tangible and intangible. The tangible aspect is inclined to architectural or built environment (buildings, townscapes, etc.), natural environment (rural landscapes, coasts and shorelines, agricultural heritage, etc.) and artefacts such as books, documents, objects, photographic and audio visual materials (UNESCO, 2003). On the other hand Intangible Cultural Heritage (ICH) is defined as "practices, representations, expressions, knowledge, skills – as well as the instruments, objects, artefacts and cultural spaces associated therewith

– that communities, groups and, in some cases, individuals recognize as part of their cultural heritage"(Kurin, 2004; UNESCO, 2003).Such aspirations should be understood as part of an ongoing human evolution, hence they are dynamic in reality. In essence, there are no boundaries in defining ICH but rather certain domains could be established to guide various nations on identifying their ICH. These domains are expressed in five categories of:

- Oral traditions and expressions including language as a vehicle of the intangible cultural heritage;
- Performing arts such as music, poems
- Social practices, rituals and festive events;
- Knowledge and practice about nature and the universe and;
- Traditional craftsmanship(UNESCO, 2003).

The five domains of ICH clearly indicate that ICH is associated with believes, spirituality, knowledge and skills, experiences, and craftsmanship skills which are not necessarily tangible.These are impalpable abstract qualities or attributes in human evolution that have been created in the past and therefore need to be kept for current and future generational use. In order for humanity to keep on holding these valuable social constructs we then have to preserve them. Generally, preservation is a managerial function focusing on providing care and safeguarding of whatever type of material of interest, through providing security, providing ideal environmental conditions and taking care of various risks in order to prolong the life of our cultural heritage (Harvey & Mahard, 2014).Preservation means exploring the means of making sure that cultural heritage materials are passed on from one generation to another. It is the direct and indirect actions of guarding against deterioration and prevent damage to all types of materials that tell the stories of our past.Although the definitions of the term preservation have the same ultimate goal, to protect for current and future use, the use of the terms vary from one profession to another. Therefore in this context, the terms'preservation' and 'safeguarding' will be used interchangeably in this paper to refer to managerial functions focusing on providing care and safeguarding of cultural heritage.

Preservation strategies have been applied throughout the world as means of protecting different national cultural heritages. In such a process, preservationists or conservators have developed better understanding of the nature of tangible materials and initiated newer preservation measures. However, Intangible Cultural Heritage is still at an early stage since it's enact following the establishment of the Conversion of Safeguarding Intangible Cultural Heritage in 2003. To this date countries are now immensely working hard towards coming up with preservation strategies of ICH. These transitions come with various challenges such as the lack of promotion in understanding of ICH, limited education, innovation and technology. Such transitional challenges in ICH preservation are also less understood in China. During a speech at the 6th International (Shanghai) Intangible Cultural Heritage Protection Forum that was held from June 7th to 8th in Shanghai,Toshio Ohi, OHI CHOZAEMON XI lamented that *"To protect the ICH, people need not only to inherit and guard the traditions and classics, but also to contact and meet people working in different fields, to expand their knowledge, challenge new things, and keep moving"*(SACM, 2018). The craftsmanship skills, type and combination of cultural heritage materials used in different societies in Shanghai and the world at large have changed with time leading to various complications.Despite the initiation of a forum on ICH and the establishment of ICH centres such as the Shanghai Mass Art Center (SMAC) in Shanghai, there seem to be no clear documentation and preservation strategies for ICH paper publications in Shanghai. Such a defiance is probably caused by lack of skills, financial constraints, poor administrations and lack of prioritisation of ICH paper publications.

Therefore, this paper explores the preservation of intangible cultural heritage paper publications/recordings in Shanghai, China. Specifically the study sort to explore the trends/types of documented ICHpaper materials, establish the strategies for the preservation of ICH paper materials, determine the challenges associated with ICH preservation and make recommendations for improvement. The findings discussed in this paper are mainly the explorations from desk-top research on published and non-published historical, anthropological and other cultural studies papers, records, and archival materials. The data collected also include personal experiences, observation, and formal and informal discussions from various expects in preservation fields.

A Brief Overview of Shanghai and ICH

The regional relationship of China is discussed by experts to be a representative of two forms of stripes and blocks.As Professor Zhang Xueliang posited in his guest lecture during the Visiting Program for Young Sinologists (YPYS 2018) in Shanghai, September 9th to 29th, since 1949 up to 1978 the policy in China was such that China was divided into three parts ('blocks') of; Main Land China (Western China), Middle Part China and the Coastal or Eastern Part China.Within these three major blocks, Shanghai belongs to the Eastern part which is the most developed part of China. Since the year 2000, China's policy of governance have changed leading to a system of Clustered City Policy. Using the Clustered City Policy Shanghai is classified as one of the largest cities in China and around the world. With a population of over 24 million, Shanghai is not only heavily populated, but also heavy in both tangible and intangible cultural heritage possibilities. For the past four decades, Shanghai have been experiencing robust economic transition due to fast industrial growth in China. At the same time this has culminated in increased major hubs of education, research and a vast number of cultural heritages such as museums, archives, libraries, historic buildings, sites and intangible heritages (LMI, 2018).

Following the UNESCO's Convention for the Safeguarding of the Intangible Cultural Heritage,China ratified ICH in 2004 and in 2005 implementation process was initiated under the coordination of the Ministry of Culture. In the process China conducted Joint Conferences in order to establish guidelines and policies for Chinese intangible cultural protection, and to examine, approve, and coordinate protection programs for intangible cultural heritage.In 2015 China had about 38

elements inscribed on UNESCO's Representative List of the Intangible Cultural
Heritage of Humanity(CCSC, 2018) and this number has increased significantly.
Among other cities in China,Shanghai is one of the critical sources of economic
boost in China through its vast tourism and cultural resources. One such critical
historic landmarks in Shanghai that the Author had an opportunity to visit
include the Bund (a colonial-style waterfront area on the Huangpu River), Nanshi
(Shanghai's old town with magnificent gardens and tea houses), and the French
Concession, the Pudong business district with the Oriental Pearl Tower, and the
Shanghai Tower(second-tallest building in the world). Shanghai Intangible Cultural
Heritage list covers over 179 batch list of ICH covering folk music, folk dance, and
traditional drama, Quyi, folk literature, traditional craftsmanship and many more.
Other ideal cultural heritage sites and artefacts in the greater Shanghai include the
idyllic ancient water village of Wuzhen and the Grand Canal, both of which are
inscribed in UNESCO's World Heritage Sites.

Types of Documented ICH Paper Materials

Documentation is one of the core pillars in cultural heritage. Documentation
encompass information management systems used in every sector in our daily
lives, organisations, associations and community.In a business setup, such a
process could include issues of ordering, minutes on meetings, supply and demand,
accountability, and financial statements.As highlighted by Setlhabi (2010) in her
Thesis, documentation plays a critical role, especially in cultural heritage setup,
in ensuring that essential aspects of artefacts history are properly preserved for
future generations. In cultural heritage documentation is attributed to "registration
of all attributes of an object into a record which could be a registration book,
entry form, acquisition form, accession form, and a master file"pp02 (Setlhabi,
2010). Collection and recording of ICH materials also play a crucial role in ICH
management. In fact identification and documentation of those expressions and
manifestations classified as ICH is the first aspect that is needed in establishing
an appropriate preservation programme.As articulated in UNESCO's Convention

for the Safeguarding of the Intangible Cultural Heritage,(UNESCO, 2003), the communities themselves must take part in identifying, deciding which practices are part of their cultural heritage,and defining their intangible cultural heritage.In order to address some of the issues on documentation, this study established the trends of documentation of ICH paper publications in Shanghai focusing on types and/ or methods of ICH publication. The findings of the study observed that there are millions and millions of paper publications in ICH. However such publications have not been specifically singled out and preserved as strategic principles of ICH paper publication.

A desk-top review of literature on types of documented ICH indicated that there are mainly three key broad types of documented ICH paper materials. In Shanghai the findings revealed that the first basis of documentation in ICH is on establishment of inventories. According to Article 17 (List of Intangible Cultural Heritage in Need of Urgent Safeguarding)of the Convention for the Safeguarding of the Intangible Cultural Heritage inventories serve as critical documentation processes.These are registrations of all attributes of an ICH into a record which could be a registration book, entry form, acquisition form, accession form etc. capturing aspects associated with ICH practices. Antonio A. Arantes during 'The First ICH-Researchers Forum the Implementation of UNESCO's 2003 Convention' posited that:

> documentation and promotion, which have proved to be very useful tools for safeguarding ICH, can also be interpreted – anthropologically speaking – as ways of staging or enacting heritage in the world media. They are interpretations of cultural elements made in languages (photography, film, audio visual recordings) that are foreign to traditional repertoires (IRCI, 2012:23).

Such a definition by Antonio A. Arantes posits that documentation should be a "mirror image" of the elements of heritage.In other words, documentation should be an itemized list of aspects of traits, preferences, attitudes, interests, or abilities that are classified as unique ICH modalities. For instance, in Hong Kong, a report by CHAU Hing-wah (Hing-wah; Tik-sang, 2011)on protective works undertaken by the Hong Kong Special Administrative Region (HKSAR) Government and by the local community in safeguarding Intangible Cultural Heritage (ICH) highlighted inventory as one of the critical steps in ICH.The paper discussed the issues of creation of an inventory, the inscription of local items on the national list of ICH in China, the inclusion of Cantonese Opera on UNESCO's Representative List, and various measures undertaken by local organizations as paramount steps in ICH. As part of the discussions CHAU Hing-wah observed that in 2009, HKSAR survey team submitted a desk-top research report and a working plan with a tentative inventory of some 280 local ICH items compiled from both published and unpublished documentary sources available in local research institutions.

In conducting ICH inventories, one such important aspect is engaging the communities, heritage bearers, and all related stakeholders. Article 15 in the UNESCO conversion; titled Participation of communities, groups and individuals, states that:

> Within the framework of its safeguarding activities of the intangible cultural, heritage, each State Party shall endeavor to ensure the widest possible participation of communities, groups and, where appropriate, individuals that create maintain and transmit such heritage, and to involve them actively in its management (UNESCO, 2003:5).

The point of Article 15 on participation of communities, groups and individuals is emphasized in China through strategies of 'participation observation'. For example, to ensure full recording of the activities and oral history, the HKSAR survey team emphasized that it adopted a participant observation research approach to the field work and that the field work was undertaken by researchers with experience in qualitative research.Such a strategy is also observed as the basis of ICH inventory creation strategy in Shanghai such as at the Shanghai Mass Art Center.

The second bases of documented ICH paper materials revealed was mainly on complete recordings or records of ICH in various types or formats such as paper, DVDs, VHS, CD, Microfilms, etc. This type of documentation is more into a total capturing of the ICH practices as a preservation strategy rather than a summative inventory. Specifically on paper publications, the findings revealed that as way of safeguarding ICH a significant number of written poems, songs, event capturing etc. plays a critical role in recording the totality of ICH and these could be preserved for future generations.These are step-by-step capturing strategies of aspects of ICH collections, for example,through capturing interviews with the heritage bearers. Another significantly crucial documentation is grey literature or records observed in various centers of ICH in Shanghai. These are important original documented histories, or manuscripts by various authors or artists involved in various ICH domains.

The third basis of documented ICH paper materials observed was an academician style of records or publications that mainly provide scientific research on certain aspects of ICH. Such documentations include journals, magazines, newspapers, interviews in radio stations, televisions Etc. These recordings don't necessarily provide a totality of recordings of the complete ICH aspects/practices. For instance research papers in journal publications provide information on certain aspects of the interest of the study to discover new perspectives. Another source of documentation is the publications/recordings of teaching materials in various educational sectors. These could be in the form of DVDs, VHS, CD, Microfilms,YouTube or online videos and audios, or capturing in print/paper materials or books.

From the three observed scope of documented ICH paper materials, one cannot completely have fixed limits or borderlines on which type of documentedICH paper materials is paramount for preservation purposes. All the three domains of documentation/records concomitantly play a critical role of providing the totality of the preservation of ICH in Shanghai and the world at large. As a result there are different methods of ICH preservation practices depending on the type of media in which the ICT practices, representations, expressions, knowledge and skills. The next section provides an anecdote on the strategies of the preservation of ICH paper publications in Shanghai.

Preservation of ICH Paper Materials in Shanghai

Intangible Cultural Heritage in China vary and some of the common examples include the Kunqu Opera, Chinese Calligraphy and Chinese Paper Cut. As would UNESCO advocate for, "for intangible to be kept alive, it must remain relevant to a culture and be regularly practised and learned within communities and between generations" (UNESCO, 2003:3). In order to achieve this view of keeping alive all ICH preservation programmes becomes critical. In other words, in order for humanity to keep on holding these valuable social constructs, we then have to preserve them. Preservation is all about making sure that activities or practices and resources of the past are available so that they can be linked with current life and also passed on to the future generations.In ICH preservation is used in the context of 'safeguarding' and is defined as "measures aimed at ensuring the viability of the intangible cultural heritage, including the identification, documentation, research, preservation, protection, promotion, enhancement, transmission, particularly through formal and informal education, as well as the revitalization of the various aspects of such heritage"(UNESCO, 2003). It is exploring the means of making sure that the practices, representations, expressions, knowledge and skills, including the instruments, objects artefacts and cultural spaces associated with the mare passed on from one generation to another. It is the direct and indirect actions of guarding against deterioration or loss of practices, representations, expressions, knowledge and skills and prevent damage to all objects, artefacts and cultural spaces that tell the stories of our past.

The backbone of ICH safeguarding in China is the Intangible Cultural Heritage Division under the Ministry of Culture of China. Under this Ministry of Culture of China there is a significant number of divisions or programmes that have been established with, one way or the other, the responsibility of safeguarding ICH. Among others these include the Shanghai Municipal Administration of Culture, Radio, Film & TV, Shanghai Municipal People's Government Foreign Affairs Office, Shanghai Municipal Education Commission and Shanghai Changning District People's Government, Shanghai Creative Industry Association, Shanghai Art Collection Museum and Shanghai Art & Design Academy. The ICH programmes in China are broadly directed by National Intangible Cultural Heritage Protection Experts Committees. Other various organisational structures with significant responsibilities in ICH preservation include both private and government museums and archives centers in Shanghai which have the mandate of preservation.For example the Chinese Cultural Studies Center, (CCSS, 2018), provides information about Intangible Cultural Heritage In China. As part of the progress in ICH safeguarding,an example is the signed Cooperation Agreement of Strengthening the Arts and Crafts as well as the Construction of Intangible Cultural Heritage Documents that was done between Mr. Muqing Hu, President of Shanghai Art Collection Museum and Ms. Ping Cang, President of Shanghai Art & Design Academy (SACM, 2018).

Specifically focusing on the strategies of the safeguarding of ICH paper publications, there are no singled out specific paper publication preservation strategies for ICH only. Often these are run in parallel as complete programmes for ICH safeguarding. Therefore this section will discuss the preservation strategies of ICH paper materials concomitant with other media of ICH in Shanghai. The first starting point as a common strategy in ICH preservation is identification, classification and documentation of ICH domains. These are harmonious programmes through which specific associations, committees or community groups come together with the aim of safeguarding their intangible cultural heritage. One such critical center for cultural heritage which take into consideration the ICH documentation is the Shanghai Mass Art Center (SMAC) located in 1551 Zhongshan Xi Road, Shanghai. The programme has educational programmes in which ICH domains such as poems, music, different cultural artefacts on believes/religion and festivals such as dragon boat are taught to the public as preservation strategies. In overall the preservation programmes in ICH are centred on the following principles outlined in UNESCO's Convention for the Safeguarding of the Intangible Cultural Heritage:

- ensuring the viability of the intangible cultural heritage, including the identification, documentation, research,preservation,protection,
- promotion, enhancement, transmission, particularly through formal and informal education through various ICH centres such as Shanghai Mass Art Center,
- as well as the revitalization of the various aspects of Chinese heritage

The next section provides a brief anecdote on challenges associated with ICH in Shanghai- China.

Challenges on Preservation of ICH Paper Publications

As much as there is a significant evidence of published records on ICH either in one of the three forms discussed earlier on in this paper, a significant number of challenges is observed especially in Shanghai.Firstly, a review of literature(Borg, 2010; Safford, 2013)indicates various challenges in ICH including the fact that little is done in identifying and documenting all paper publications on ICH. The common practice of ICH preservation is through creation of educational centers such the Shanghai Academy of Social Science Museum which focuses on teaching and learning of ICH domains. Although during the processes of education such skills are recorded in the form of videos and so forth, little is done on paper documentation especially identifying oral traditions such as poems and songs and recording them in paper format. The major issue of thought is; how do we capture the totally of ICH practices in to paper materials?

As part of the prepositions in the UNESCO's Convention for the Safeguarding of the Intangible Cultural Heritage, ICH documentation should be an ongoing process given that culture is dynamic. As soon as communities agree to add certain aspects as part of practices, representations, expressions, knowledge and skills in ICH, documentation inventories need to be also re-created or updated. This pose challenges of continuity and update in ICH documentation. As a result transformation as culture changes and reverting to the past to link current trends with old traditional cultural heritage activities becomes very complex. As early as 2010, Borg (2010) had indicated that cultural heritage in China was having challenges and later on in 2013, Safford (2013) shared the same sentiments that culture in China was eroded. They gave examples such as the dying lunar New Year manifestations and that the society has become individualistic indicating that there is devoid of community bondage and people tend to seek flashier and immediate gratifications (Borg, 2010).

As part of looking for solutions in China, a number of challenges in safeguarding ICH were expressed during various international intangible cultural heritage protection forums held in Shanghai China.During the 5th International (Shanghai) Intangible Cultural Heritage Protection Forum held on the 9th June 2017, participants deliberated lengthily on issues of ICH under the theme 'Commonality and Difference- The implementation and vision of the ICH Convention'. As summarised by SACM, the conference focused on the following issues:

- The situation after the implementation of the Convention for the Safeguarding of the Intangible Cultural Heritage by the UNESCO.
- Dealing with new challenges and new opportunities in the field of ICH Protection, discusses the commonality
- Different methods and ways from all over the world in ICH protection,
- The common issues encountered by different countries in the field of ICH protection,
- Typical experience and practices and brings new inspiration and opportunity for the development of ICH protection and the cultural exchanges of different countries(SACM, 2018).

The Shanghai Art Collection Museum (2018) expressed that the participation of Shanghai in the construction of "The Belt & Road", during the 6th International (Shanghai) Intangible Cultural Heritage Protection Forum that was held from the 7th to 8th June 2018 in Shanghai, gave cultural opportunities to various stakeholders all over the world. Emphasise was made especially on issues pertaining implementation, commonalities, methods or practices, and issues of ICH across the world. Under the theme "Reconstruction of Tradition: New Trends in Intangible Cultural Heritage Protection", the conference focused on the latest challenges for ICH protection and encouraged participants to share their experience working with ICH (SACM 2018). For instance Mr. Bing Ni, Deputy Director of Shanghai Municipal Administration of Culture, Radio, Film & TV gave a speech on the Topic: "Intangible Cultural Heritage Protection Inheritance with Shanghai Characteristics in the New Era".

Other key challenges identified in literature lies along questions on;which forms of intangible cultural heritages should be researched and documented? How relevant stakeholders should be involved in the process of ICH documentation and what kinds of information about ICH should be gathered? How can documentation reflect local diversity of voices and perspectives and how should cultural heritage be defined? How can appropriate forms of media be determined for documentation of ICH? What kinds of permissions should be obtained at the time of documentation especially copy rights? How might these permissions change over time?(Safford, 2013). As part of the discussions during the Visiting Program for Young Sinologists (YPYS 2018) in Shanghai, September 9th to 29th,among others, further issues raised by Dr Segaetshowere; what was the input of cultural heritage in industrialisation or modernisation, and how does China make sure that modernisation does not erode cultural heritage? Moreover, to what extent has cultural heritage imparted on the economic growth in Shanghai and China at large? These questions continue to pose as critical realities that cultural heritage preservation has to justify with no doubt so that nations could continue to preserve their cultural heritage perspectives.

Commenting on such issues, Professor Zhang Daogen during his Lecture 2 inYPYS 2018 programme in Shanghai posited that to solve such issues, China is now vigorously striving along the lines of industrialisation of cultural heritage. Such measures will ensure that cultural heritage remains relevant even in the tremendous economic growth of China leading to moderately prosperous society imparting on the quality of people's life, food, place to live, and free choice of jobs and lifestyles. Issues of governance and politics are also observed as some of the challenges associated with cultural heritage. For example, Safford (2013) cited Lily Kong (Lily, 2007) positing that in Shanghai there can be no public protest therefore in decisions made such as the emerging of new monuments,therefore the community does not have a say in the process.

Although ICH has a significant number of challenges, technology and investment on cultural heritage is progressing well in Shanghai. For example agents, investors and innovative industrial companies are immerging such as the Shanghai Jianwei Cultural Heritage Conservation Tech. Co. Ltd. The Shanghai Jianwei is a professional, high-tech enterprise that engages in plan, design, construction and technical services for conservation of cultural heritage. These are relevant to the new trends of industrial approach in China especially on issues of internal and external environmental protection.

Conclusion and Recommendation

This paper was aimed at exploring the preservation of intangible cultural heritage paper materials/recordings in Shanghai, China. The study revealed that there are different processes, types, and/or methods of documentedIntangible Cultural Heritage (ICH) paper materials. The study further observed that there are various methods or strategies of preservation in ICH and a number of challenges associated with ICH preservation were also observed. The paper concludes that quite a number of activities can be carried out as improvement for the way forward in preservation of Intangible Cultural Heritage.For instance, during the 6th International (Shanghai) Intangible Cultural Heritage Protection Forum various experts pointed out that countries along the "Belt and Road" have extremely rich ICH resources, which lay a good foundation for mutual cooperation.In order to achieve prosperity in ICH safeguarding, Shanghai should learn from other international technologies and make good use at the same time creating new technologies that are relevant for application in Shanghai. ICH preservation/safeguarding programmes should be aligned to current economic development trends in China insuring a better life for the people rather than production.

This study observed that as much as there is a lot of publication on ICH safeguarding, there is however no systematic programmes of preserving the paper publication in ICH. This could be much more attributed to the fact that most publications are in the form of journal research publications rather than documentaries on various aspects of ICH domain. Therefore the publications mainly find application in research as literature rather than the articles being preserved themselves. As a way forward, Shanghai should strive to position itself in a way that international cooperation can be achieved to establish ICH preservation programmes for different cadres of ICH such as paper publications, their identification, classification, documentation and storage.

References

Borg, V. P. (2010). National Identity Depends on Culture, too. Retrieved from http://www. chinadaily.com.co/opinion/2010-02/09/content_9447317.htm.

CCSC, . (2018). Intangible Cultural Heritage In China. Retrieved from https://www. culturalheritagechina.org/.

CCSS, . (2018). About Intagible Cultural Heritage In China. Retrieved from https://www. culturalheritagechina.org/.

Harvey, R., & Mahard, M. R. (2014). *Preservation management handbook; 21st-century guide for libraries, archives and museums,*. Lanham, Boulder, New York, Toronto, Plymouth, UK: Rowman & Littlefield.

Hing-wah, C. *Safeguarding Intangible Cultural Heritage: The Hong Kong Experience*. [Case Study of Local Heritage Studies: Cheung Chau Jiao Festival- Teachers' References].

China.

Iossifova, D. (2014). China: toward an integrated approach to cultural heritage preservation and economic development. *City Magazine*.

IRCI, I. R. C. f. I. C. H. i. t. A.-P. R. (2012). *The First ICH-Researchers Forum The Implementation of UNESCO's 2003 Convention- FINAL REPORT*. Paris, France.

Kurin, R. (2004). Safeguarding Intangible Cultural Heritage in the 2003 UNESCO Convention: a critical appraisal. *Museum international, 56*(1 - 2), pp. 66-77.

Lily, K. (2007). Cultural Icons and Urban Development in Asia: Economic Imperative, National Identity and Global City Status,. *Political Geography, 26*, pp. 383-404.

LMI, L. M. I. G. (2018). Heritage preservation international.   Retrieved from http://www. heritage-china.com/en/For-Visitors/Shanghai/.

SACM, T. S. A. C. M. (2018). The International Intangible Cultural Heritage Protection Forum, News,.   Retrieved from http://www.sh-art.org/English/news1. aspx?class=4&Class_id=22&Class_page=780.

Safford, L. B. (2013). Cultural Heritage Preservation in Modern China: Problems, Perspectives and Potentials. *ASIA Network Exchange, 21*(1), p. 13.

Setlhabi, K. G. (2010). *Documentation of material culture; a study of the ethnology division of Botswana National Museum.* (Doctor of Philosophy), University of Botswana, Gaborone- Botswana.

Tik-sang, L. (2011). Safeguarding Intangible Cultural Heritage: The Hong Kong Experience, Learning and Teaching Resource Pack for Secondary History Curriculum. .   Retrieved from https://www.youtube.com/watch?v=GJf1bJlLTss.

UNESCO. (2003). "Convention for the Safeguarding of the Intangible Cultural Heritage," Retrieved from http://unesdoc.unesco.org/images/0013/001325/132540e.pdf.

中国的法律与经济：对改革时代的研究

安必胜【印度】

贾瓦哈拉尔·尼赫鲁大学东亚研究中心助理研究员

中国的崛起是冷战后全球政治中的热门研究主题之一。学者们尝试去解读中国经济转型的重要性。研究者试图在发展中国家模式下理解中国的成长故事，统治精英有能力制定有效的经济政策，对潜在行业进行投资并获得合理的增长，国家进行干预以推动增长和促进公私部门之间的制度协调。即使如此，在这一变化和经济转性过程中，法律一直是重要的权威力量之一。中国在改革时代的法律框架对应着建立可预见的经济框架以引领增长和发展的愿望。中共政府和政治领导层一直支持这种变化。

中国改革政策的一个重要目标是，如何实现从计划经济向市场经济体制的相对平稳过渡。在此过程中，中国的根本特征之一是法律改善经济管治方面发挥作用。针对这一变化，强有力的中国政府也扮演着同样重要的角色。中国当前的法律制度根据变化情况进行补充。新的中国领导层能够理解法律在促进经济增长和发展过程中的作用。本文旨在评估中国正式法律制度的发展以及分析在后毛泽东改革时代法律对经济所起到的作用。

一、引言

中国一直在利用法律维持秩序和稳定。回溯从帝国时代到现代中国的历程，我们可以发现法律在中国政治中起到关键作用。在帝制时代，法家和儒家思想指导下制订的各种法律规范占据统治地位。中国有着丰富的法律传统，其悠久的文明跨越两千多年的历史。根据帝国统治实践，我们可以认识到，中国通常广泛接受任何一种哲学思想流派。法（实在法）和礼（道德法）这两种法律传统在中国古代发挥着重要作用。

随后在毛泽东统治时期，法律的理解主要基于马克思主义理念，对中国政治和经济领域的适用范围和绝对作用越来越小。虽然对"实在法"进行一些实验，但仅采取改革的形式，例如《婚姻法》（1951 年）允许妇女享有更好的权利，以及《土地改革法》。文化大革命（1966 年 -1976 年）让近代中国进入社会不稳定和政治混乱的时期，破坏了中国法制的发展。后来在 1978 年对中国宪法进行修正，随后又被新宪法（1982 年）取代，这标志着中国法律制度复兴和加强的新起点。以"市场经济模式"发展中国经济的呼吁力求在法制框架下实现更大的一致性、统一性和可预测性。

在既定情况下重新审视法律在经济转型和促进中国增长方面的作用。中国的发展故事是在法律和经济结合的基础上进行一系列强有力的国内改革，并且符合中国国情。在政策层面，"发展即转型"框架在中国的直接领导和经济环境下合乎逻辑，为引入法律改革奠定了基础。（Malik，2013）

在中国的"改革开放"时代，法律改革与经济发展之间的关系是共同发展的过程。一方面，这为中国开展各种类型的私营经济活动提供更大的范围，另一方面，刺激了进一步实施法律改革以应对经济增长新挑战的需要。

就中国而言，法律也能够适应中国经济的必要变化。法律与"政策工具"共同作为实现经济发展政策目标的重要机制。

二、法律和经济发展框架

法律对经济发展和增长的作用一直是政治经济学的主要课题之一。普遍认为，法律对于支持经济繁荣和增长至关重要。其背后的基本逻辑是，法律实践是可以促进经济增长的合理法制框架前提。法律的存在为贸易和投资的增加产生合理的经济增长框架。

法律和经济发展之间的因果关系已经在许多实证研究中得到检验。可以说，自 20 世纪 90 年代初以来，拉·波塔（La Porta）、拉·德·西拉内斯（Lopez-de-Silanes）、施莱弗（Sleifer）和罗伯特·维希尼（Robert Vishny）（1998:1115）的经济学著作根据确定法律在经济增长中的一般作用，尤其是在发展中的特殊作用，进行一系列的跨国经济研究。研究得出的结论是，法律和执行质量对保护证券持有人的权利、投资者决定、金融公司准备、基于健全的法律规则运行经济的合同义务及其执行方面发挥关键作用。这种经济学原理在制度经济学的著作和研究中也获得认可，可以追溯到著名的政治经济学家和社会学家马克斯·韦伯（Max Weber，1922）。

同样，道格拉斯·诺斯（Douglas North，1990）在他的著作中也涉及这种思想流派，认为稳定和更可预测的法律秩序以及清晰的财产和合同权利是经济增长的前提。法律和发展的交互还得到顶尖的现代化理论家如罗斯托（W. W. Rostow，1960）的支持，他指出发展中国家无法实现发展是由于经济的传统性和社会的保守性。他还将这些国家的发展水平差归咎于缺乏有效的政治法律制度、文化习俗和价值观。法律与发展观点称，与改革后的中国一样，经济增长将为未来的经济改革创造必要条件。

法律与发展观点的理论基础也得到实地研究和调查报告的认可。相关研究给出充分理由证明法律的存在是经济发展的必要力量。罗伯特·巴罗（Robert Barro，1998）通过研究分析 85 个国家在 1965-1975、1975-1985 以及 1985-1990 三个期间的数据。（Barro, 1997:2）在 Knack 和 Keefer（1997:593）的一项重要研究中得出的结论是：最好通过法规强制执行对经济增长至关重要的基础设施合同。

在另一项研究中，罗斯·莱文（Ross Levine，1999:8）发现，优先考虑改善经济管理和有效执行商业合同的国家通常拥有更发达的金融体系和更高的增长率。

在中国市场经济不断发展的背景下，法律与发展之间的关系形成一个适当的链条，研究如何制订法律程序，以建立增强经济权利合法化和保护的更加正式和契约性的商业制度。

三、改革时代的领导力和法律

政治话语中认可的观点是政治指导经济。政治学之父亚里士多德（Aristotle，2000）的名言强调，"政治学是一门研究人类所有活动的'主学科'"。同样的论点也被中国接受，因为没有中国共产党的政治领导支持，法律改革就不可能实现。就中国而言，考虑到领导力及其在政治中的重要性，这并不是新的做法。

在后毛泽东时代，意识形态转变以及经济复兴的兴趣变得更加重要。最重要的是，邓小平指出中国面临的主要问题不是阶级斗争，而是经济增长与发展。中国宣告处于社会主义初级阶段。而且，在进入共产主义国家理想之前有必要经历资本主义阶段。邓小平提出的"两手抓"政策原则清楚地反映出这一点。1987年1月17日，他在中央政治局常委会议上明确表达这一想法。他指出，"搞四个现代化一定要有两只手，只有一手是不行的"。（Tuebner 和 Chunyi, 2013:2）一方面，必须发展经济以促进增长；而另一方面，必须加强法律制度。（Fengcheng, 2011）改革后的中国对法律的认可和接受度更大，彭真（时任全国人大常委会委员长）总结道：法律是"党和国家的方针和政策的定型化、法制化"。（Peng 1984:160）中国法律学者将1978年视为中国现代历史上的一个新时代，也是中国法律发展的转折点。1982年的宪法修正案还推动了中国的法律改革和遵守法律。可以说，最初几年是邓小平等政治领导的大力支持最终在中国提高经济增长的法制化程度。

邓小平1992年南巡为中国的改革进程注入新的活力，特别是在对外贸易和商业投资方面。这导致在中国的外商直接投资（FDI）急剧增加。根据国家统计局数据，外商直接投资合同金额从1991年的120亿美元急剧增加至1992年的581亿美元。1993年，外商直接投资合同金额升至1110亿美元，几乎是1992年的两倍。（CSYB, 1999:597）邓小平南巡推动经济改革进程加速，同时法律改革也受益于新的精神和动力，以寻求程序的公开性和透明性。

1993年，在江泽民领导下召开中共十四届三中全会上认为中国过渡到社会主义市场经济阶段并在朱镕基的倡导下进行法律改革。

法律改革对当代中国领导层仍然非常重要。法律改革政策从1978年在邓小平领导下开始实施，江泽民和胡锦涛担任国家主席期间持续推动。即使在习近平主席的领导下，依法治国取得更大的接受度和重视。尽管中国政府对社会稳定和政治控制保持关切，但法治程度提高的可能前景仍与经济增长目标息息相关。法律仍须作为国家行政管理的指导原则。

温家宝总理在2007年承认中国的发展模式存在结构性问题，这些问题导致"经济增长不稳定、不协调、不平衡和不可持续"。（温家宝，2007）他在"第十一个五年计划"报告中列明中国的增长模式面对的主要问题，并指出中国的发展是一个复杂的过程，涉及不同层面。他重申，中国的经济、社会、法律和政治改革应该协调推进。中国前国家主席胡锦涛于2007年12月提出的"三个代表"政治

策略中，宪法和法律至高无上的地位受到高度重视。（胡锦涛，2007）

习近平主席领导下的中国新一届领导层已认可法律改革的重要性，但更加关切政治控制和社会和谐。中共十八大提出在深化司法改革的基础上进行法制改革的重要战略计划，目标是在法治的基础上打造社会主义民主。习近平主席的"四个全面"战略包括在中国共产党成立一百年时"建成小康社会"。目标包括"依法治国"、"从严治党"和深化经济改革和增长。考虑到这些目标，法制框架必须通过适当的方式建立，以不同行动领域的一系列法律为基础。

四、结论

在改革开放的进程中，中国的法律与经济关系发生根本性的转变。多年来，全国人民代表大会通过持续立法增加关键经济法律的数量，涵盖税收、银行业、合同、企业改革、所有权和财产权、劳动权、土地管理和行政等不同领域的经济法律。中国法律与经济的共同进步在改革开放以吸引对外贸易和投资的政策下实现微妙平衡。这在实质和程序层面都对中国的法律经济关系产生重大影响。为了满足直接经济需求，在后改革年代，中国强调和加快推进法律制度的重建。中国政府试图建立公正统一的法律体系，通过制度程序和保证吸引外商投资中国。

在法制建设过程中，法院、检察院和律师等法律相关部门予以重建和加强；恢复和鼓励法律研究和教育；提出并实践法律专业精神和法治等新观念。法律是经济转型的基础，制度的确定性和稳定性范围允许经济参与者可以融入不断变化的中国经济。

Law and Economy in China: A Study of Reform Era

Abhishek Pratapsingh / India

Assistant Lecturer of the Centre for East Asian Studies and Ph.D. Candidate for Economic Studies, Jawaharlal Nehru University

The rise of China has been one of the most discussed subjects in post cold war era global politics. And quite reasonably, attempts have been made to understand the importance of China's economic transformation by scholars. There have been studies, which attempt to understand China's growth story under developmental state model ,[1] led by ruling elite capable of constructing effective economic policy, investment in potential sectors with equitable growth, interventionist state in terms of growth facilitation and institutional coordination between public-private sector. Nonetheless, the role of law has also been one of the most consistent and authoritative forces towards this change and economic transformation. The existence of legal framework in China during reform era corresponds with the desire to build a predictable economic framework to usher growth and development. Party-state

---

1 Johnson, Charles. (1999), "The Developmental State: Odyssey of A Concept", in: Woo- Cumings, M. (ed.) (1999), *The Developmental State,* Cornell University Press.
    Johnson, Charles. (1982) *MITI and the Japanese Miracle; The Growth of Industrial Policy 1925-1975*, Stanford University Press.

and political leadership in China constantly backed this change.

One of the significance of China's reform policies is that how it achieved a relatively smooth transition from planned economy to market economy based system. To this process, role of law for better economic regulation served as one of the essential feature in China. To this change, no lesser and very essential role was played by strong and capable Chinese state as well. The legal system of China now was directed towards this change and to supplement this process. The new Chinese leadership was able to understand the role of law in facilitating economic growth and development. The reading seeks to assess the development of the formal legal system in China and analyze its role in the economy in the post-Mao reform era.

Introduction

The role of law has always been a consistent source of order and stability in China. Looking back to early imperial China to the contemporary times, one can find the key role for law in the politics of China. In the history of imperial China, the role of law in form of different codes being formed under the philosophy of Legalism and Confucianism remained a dominant practice. China has a rich history of legal tradition based on longevity of its civilization and history, which spans for more than two thousand years. From the practices of imperial rule, it can be well acknowledged that China often admitted to the larger acceptance for any one schools of the philosophy. And the significant role of both the legal traditions, namely *fa* (positive law) and *li* (moral code) as an instrument for governance remained present in ancient China.

Since the establishment of People's Republic of China, law was more understood in terms of Marxist notions, and found less scope and convincing role in China's politics and economy. While some experiments with the 'positive law' took place in the form of reform under Marriage Law (1951) allowing better rights for women and Land Reform Law. Later on the amendment to the Constitution of China in 1978 and its subsequent replacement with the new Constitution (1982) marked a new beginning for revival and strengthening of legal system in China. The call to develop Chinese economy on 'market economy model' strived for greater coherence, uniformity and predictability in the regulatory framework.

In the given situation, the role of law was revisited towards economic transformation and fostering growth in China. The Chinese story is about strong set of homegrown reforms, based on confluence between law and economy, given their suitability to the Chinese conditions. At the policy level, "development as transformation" framework found logic with the immediate leadership and economic context of China, preparing basis for introduction of legal reforms.[1]

During "reform and opening up" era the relationship between legal reforms and economic development was a co-evolutionary process in China. On the one hand, this allowed broader scope for different types of private economic activities to take place in China, on the other hand it stimulating a need for further set of legal reforms to address new set of challenges emerging out of economic growth.

In the case of China, law was also able to adopt and respond with necessary changes in China's economy. In keeping with the lines of "policy instrumentalism", law served as an important mechanism to achieve policy goals for economic development.

Law and Economic Development Framework

The role of law for the economic development and growth has been one of the dominant themes of political economy. It has been widely argued that importance of law is critical to support economic prosperity and growth. The fundamental logic behind this was that the practice of law is a prerequisite for reasonable regulatory framework that can propel economic growth. The presence of law invokes reasonable framework for economic growth to spur based on increased trade and investments.

---

1   Malik, Khalid (2012) *Why has China Grown so Fast for Long*, Oxford University Press.

The causal link between law and economic development has been examined under many empirical studies and works. To say, since early 1990s noted economic works from La Porta, Lopez-de-Silanes, Shleifer, and Robert Vishny [1] made series of cross-country economic studies based on drawing the logical role of law in development in particular and economic growth in general. These studies come to the conclusion that law and quality of its enforcement has key role in terms of guaranteeing security holder's rights, investors determination, readiness of financial firms, contractual obligations to run the economy based on sound legal rules and their enforcement. This economic principle has also found acceptance in the works and studies of institutional economics that dates back to noted political economist and sociologist Max Weber (1922).[2]

Similarly, Douglas North also argued in his works about this school of thought where stable and more predictable legal order with clear set of property and contractual rights is a prerequisite for economic growth. The discourse of law and development movement also found support from leading modernization theorists like W. W. Rostow,[3] who attributed the lack of development in developing countries to their economic traditionalism and social conservatism. He also attached poor level of development in these states to their lack of effective political-legal institutions, cultural practices and values. The law development movement argued that economic growth would create a necessary condition for prospective set of economic reforms as the case was in post reform China.

The theoretical foundations of law and development movement also got approval from field studies and survey reports. There have been some studies making compelling reason for the presence of law being a necessary force for economic development. Robert Barro (1998) who analyzed data from eighty- five countries for three different periods from 1965–75, 1975–85, and 1985–90, did one

---

1 Porta, Lopez-de-Silanes, Shleifer, and Robert W. Vishny, (1998) Law and Finance, *Journal of Political Economy,* Volume 106, No 6, pp. 1113-1155.

2 Max Weber (1922) Economy and Society, revised in 2013, University of California Press.

3 Rostow, W.W. (1960) *Stages of Economic Growth,* Cambridge: Cambridge University Press.

such study.[1] In another significant work done by Knack and Keefer the findings were conclusive with better regulatory provisions on contract enforceability with infrastructure being critical for economic growth.

In another similar set of work, Ross Levine (1999:8)[2] founds that states giving priority to better economic management and effective enforcement of business contracts generally have more developed financial system and higher growth rates.

In the context of China's growing market economy, relation between law and development formed a suitable link to examine how legal processes were established to formulate more formal and contractual business regime based of increased legalization and protection of economic rights.

Leadership and Law during Reform Era

It is an accepted idea in political discourse that it is the politics that guides the economy. Reasonably, the famous quote of Aristotle, father of Political Science, underlines that, "politics is the "master science" on which all other branches of human activity depends. The same line of argument founds acceptance in case of China as well, where the process of legal reforms could not have been possible without the support of political leadership led by CPC. In case of China, this was not a new practice given the importance of leadership ad its role for politics.

The ideological shift and interest for economic revival found much importance in post Mao China. Most importantly, Deng Xiaoping argued that the major problem confronting China was not a class struggle but economic growth and development. China was declared to be in the primary stages socialism. And, before it could embark upon the ideal of communist state, it was necessary to pass through the stage of capitalism. This was clearly reflected in the principles of Deng Xiaoping's 'Two-

---

1 Barro, Robert J. (1997) Determinants of Economic Growth: A Cross-Country Empirical Study," *Journal of Comparative Economics*, Elsevier, vol. 26(4).

2 R. Levine, (1998) "The legal environment, banks, and long-run economic growth", *Journal of Money, Credit and Banking*, 30.

Hand' policy. He articulated this idea at a meeting of the Standing Committee of the Political Bureau of the Central Committee on January 17th 1987. He noted that, "to achieve the four modernizations, it is essential to have two hands, not just one".[1] On the one hand, the economy must be developed to facilitate growth; and on the other hand, legal system must be strengthened. The greater approval and acceptance of law in post reform China was best summarized by Peng Zhen, (then Chairman of Standing Committee of NPC) as law being, "the fixation of party fundamental principles and policies, that is the codification of party's fundamental principles and policies". (Peng 1984:160) Legal scholars on China see 1978 as a new epoch in Chinese modern history and a turning point towards legal development in China. The constitutional amendment of 1982 also pushed for legal reforms and adherence towards law in China. To say, in initial years it was the larger support of political leadership led by Deng Xiaoping, which caused increased legalisation towards economic growth in China.

Deng Xiao Peng's Southern Tour in 1992 was able to infuse new energy for reform process in China, especially with regard to external trade and business investment. This led to steep jump in Foreign Direct Investment (FDI) in China. According to the State Statistical Bureau, contracted FDI jumped from US $12 billion in 1991 to $58.1 billion in 1992. In 1993, contracted FDI rose to $111 billion, almost doubling the amount from 1992. (CSYB, 1999:597) The larger impact of Deng's trip was that it accelerated economic reform process, and in doing so legal reform was also benefited with new spirit and motivation for openness and transparency in processes.

The 1993 Third Plenum of Central Committee of CPC, held under Jiang Zemin, set the stage for China's transition to a socialist market economy and based on legal reforms promoted by Zhu Rongji.

---

1   Gunther Tuebner and Qi Chunyi (2013), Multiple Modernities: An Alternative to Western Economists' Recommendations for China's Private Law, *Peking University Law Journal (Zhong Wai Fa Xue)*, p.2.

The question of legal reforms has remained important with the contemporary leadership of China as well. The policy of legal reforms, which began in 1978 under the leadership of Deng Xiaoping, and remained in practice under the ruling system led by the leadership of Jiang Zemin and Hu Jintao as well. Even under leadership of President Xi Jinping the question of running the country in accordance with the law has seen larger acceptance and importance. Despite the concern of party-state towards social stability and political control in China, the likely prospects for increased legalisation in China remains largely attached with the objective of economic growth. There is also a need make law as the guiding principle for the administration of the country.

In 2007, Premier Wen Jiabao acknowledged that there are structural problems to China's development model that caused "unsteady, unbalanced, uncoordinated and unsustainable growth." [1] In his report of 11th Five Year Plan (FYP) he outlined main issues confronting the growth model in China and noted that development in China is a complicated process involving different levels. He reiterated that there is a need to coordinate and implement among economic, social, legal and political reforms in China. In the political strategy of "Three Represents' as articulated by then Chinese President Hu Jintao in December 2007, supremacy for the constitution and laws was given important priority". (Hu Jintao, 2007) [2]

Under the new leadership of China led by President Xi Jinping, the importance of legal reforms has been accepted but with a greater concern for political control and social harmony. The 18th National Party Congress (NPC) of CPC put forth an important strategic plan for the legal reforms based on deepening judicial reform, aiming to build socialist democracy based on rule of law. The four-pronged strategy of President Xi Jinping comprises of 'building a moderately prosperous society',

---

1   Jiabao, Wen (2007) Press Conference of Ministry of Foreign Affairs of the People's Republic of China (PRC), March 17. Available at URL: www.fmprc.gov.cn/eng/zxxx/t304313.htm (Online accessed on July, 1, 2018).

2   Jintao, Hu (2012) Full text: Report of Hu Jintao to the 18th CPC National Congress, (Accessed on 02 July, 20168 Available at URL: http://www.china.org.cn/china/18th_cpc_congress/2011/16/content_27137540_5.htm.

by CPC in its centenary celebration marking in 2021. The objective comprises of "upholding rule of law", "enforcing party discipline", and deepening economic reform and growth in China. Given these objectives the regulatory framework has to build in a proper manner based on series of laws in different areas of action.

Conclusion

Under the process of reform and opening up a sea change in the relationship between the law and economy did occur in China. The large number of key economic legislation passed by the National People's Congress (NPC) had increased over the years covering different set of areas in economy like taxation, banking, contract, enterprise reform, ownership and property rights, labour rights, land management and administrative law. This coevolution of law and economics in China is a delicate act of balance under the policy of reform and opening up to attracts foreign trade and investment. This made significant impact on law economy relation in China at the level of substance and procedure both. Serving immediate economic needs, the rebuilding of the legal system in China was emphasized and accelerated in post reform years. An attempt was made by the party-state to establish a fair and uniform legal system, confirming with systematic processes and assurances to attract foreign investment in China.

In this process of legalisation, various legal branches such as the court, the procuratorate, and the lawyers were re-established and strengthened; legal study and education were restored and encouraged; and new notions such as legal professionalism and rule of law were proposed and put into practice. With law forming the foundational basis of this economic transformation, the scope for certainty and stability in the system allowed economic actors to integrate with the changing Chinese economy.

中国改革开放对非中关系的影响：以尼日利亚为例

白龙【尼日利亚】

尼日利亚西北大学助理讲师

引　言

1978 年中国开始实行"改革开放"政策，改革的目的是发展"中国特色社会主义"，改革的结果是中国经济的蓬勃发展。中国从市场在促进和协调经济活动中完全不起作用的体系转变为市场发挥调控作用的体系。中国经济从几乎没有外国直接投资以及低水平的国际贸易和外汇转变为与全球经济大国（西方）相比，成为全球主要的外国投资接受国和贸易国。虽然非洲不是中国的主要贸易伙伴，但在中国的全球业务中发挥着重要作用，因为非洲是原材料主要来源和制成品销售市场。中国企业对尼日利亚非常重视，因为尼日利亚拥有丰富的人力和自然资源，如果洽当地开展合作，将对双方都有利。

一、分析框架

毫无疑问，"南南合作"对于解释中非关系非常重要。南南合作由第三世界国家领导人在 1955 年的万隆会议上提出并获得联合国贸易与发展会议（UNCTAD）的支持。1978 年，联合国在布宜诺斯艾利斯设立南南合作特设局（SU/SSC）与其机构合作促进南南贸易，增强支持。他们认为国家是理性行为者，可以根据自身的偏好做出选择，并考虑权衡取舍和次优选择。一旦存在适当的激励措施和对任何冲突或战争的限制，合作将会发生。倘若南方国家认为这是最好的选择，那么"南南合作"将会蓬勃发展并使自身利益最大化。因此，自由理念对南南合作"降低交易成本"研究具有重要意义。Keohane 进一步解释道，交易成本包括谈判过程中需要的所有资源：金钱、时间、人员、权力和声望等。他解释说，各国（应该）选择多边主义而不是双边，并且进一步认为多边主义允许各国减少双边协定、谈判和外交争端解决所涉及的交易成本。降低交易成本的观点可以用来解释中非合作论坛（FOCAC）的案例。该论坛于 2000 年在北京启动，随后每三年召开一次会议，目的是推动中国与非洲大陆 53 个国家之间的南南合作。"南南合作"为各国提供了超越双边政策传输的可能性。它们可以共同设计政策方法，借鉴所有参与国的经验，解决每个国家自身的具体问题，而不仅限于将最佳做法从一个国家传播到所有其他国家的行为。南南合作是指发展中国家之间的知识和资源共享，目的是确定消除其发展挑战的最有效措施。因此，这一观念的倡导者看到了全球"南方国家"（发展中国家）在共享技术、知识、货币、技能、资源和贸易等方面的发展潜力，而不是依靠北方国家（发达国家）的发展议程。因此，我们决定并相信该理论是指导以及为本研究提供良好方向的最佳工具。

二、1978 年改革开放以来的中非关系

继邓小平于 1978 年发起经济改革之后，中非关系进入新阶段。1982 年 12 月 20 日至 1983 年 1 月 17 日国家领导人访问非洲十一国时提出新"独立政策"，将其概括为"中国同非洲国家开展经济技术合作的四项原则"。四项原则与"八项原则"有很大不同，因为它们受到经济实用主义的鼓舞，与中国国内发展优先事项和有限的财政资源保持协调。由此可见，该政策对于改革时代仍然有用。

中非关系已成为热议话题，尤其是西方媒体、政策制定者和学者，因为自 1978 年的经济改革使中国成为在非洲投资的有力竞争者。因此，双方关系围绕新市场和投资机会、发展援助与合作以及建立战略伙伴关系而展开。近年来，中国已将非洲列为具有战略重要性的区域以及重要的社会经济合作伙伴。2000 年中非合作论坛的成立和随后的成功举办得到双方领导人的认可（中国和非洲）。习近平在 2015 年中非合作论坛约翰内斯堡峰会上重申双方的承诺。当前，中非关系正处于历史上最好时期。我们应该登高望远、阔步前行。我们应该携手努力，汇聚起中非 24 亿人民的智慧和力量，共同开启中非合作共赢、共同发展的新时代！

习近平在另一次讲话中还强调了相互信任与真诚相融。

几十年来，中非始终真诚友好、团结合作，是休戚与共的命运共同体和合作共赢的利益共同体。中国将秉持真实亲诚理念和正确义利观，同其他非洲友好国家一道，加强交流，增进互信，扩大合作。（新华社，2018年9月1日）。

因此，自2000年中非合作论坛成立以来，中非关系几乎在所有领域掀开新的外交篇章，论坛已提供1300多亿美元的无息贷款、优惠贷款和专项发展基金，与非洲国家实施众多合作和倡议。习近平也重申中国政府的承诺。

中国愿以打造新时代更加紧密的中非命运共同体为指引，在推进中非'十大合作计划'（2015年世界经济合作论坛）基础上，同非洲国家密切配合，未来3年和今后一段时间重点实施'八大行动'（2018年非洲合作论坛）。（《中国日报》，2018年9月4日）。

同时，南非总统西里尔·拉马福萨在2018年中非合作论坛北京峰会上确认近年来的中非关系。

2015年宣布的'十大合作计划'已全面落实，这表明中非合作伙伴关系正在为促进中非共同利益而努力，中国履行了诺言。

拉马福萨进一步确认中非合作论坛在非洲工业化计划中的作用，该论坛可以推动非洲大陆许多地区的工业发展，在提高农业生产力的农业现代化计划以及促进非洲连通和整合的基础设施计划等经济转型领域做出贡献。这些计划也有助于推动环境保护、可持续发展、改善公共卫生服务以及和平与安全。他还证明，中国通过中非合作论坛和其他论坛，努力确保非洲的发展在国际议程上占有重要地位。

三、1978年改革开放以来中国—尼日利亚外交关系

中国和尼日利亚两国于1971年2月10日正式建立外交关系，确认和平共处五项基本原则，即互相尊重主权和领土完整、互不侵犯、互不干涉内政、平等互利、和平共处。虽然中国改革开放最初的目的是通过与国际社会建立密切关系发展国内经济并进一步加强"南南合作"，维护南半球国家在广泛领域的合作，例如贸易、投资、技术合作、工业化、能源、粮食和农业、科技等。

为了进一步加强关系，两国领导人和高级政府官员频繁互访。双方的多次互访表明两国具有共性，从区域大国到丰富的矿产和人力资源禀赋有着诸多共同点。

中国是世界上最大的单一市场，人口超过 13 亿，而尼日利亚是非洲最大的单一市场，人口接近 1.9 亿。与尼日利亚不同，中国已经能够利用其庞大的人口、人力和物力打造强有力的国内经济，对国民产生积极的影响。

此外，尼日利亚和中国都在各自所在区域承受重大负担。就人口而言，每三个亚洲人中就有一个是中国人，而每四个非洲人就有一个是尼日利亚人。中国人口超过 13 亿，是世界上人口最多的国家，而尼日利亚人口接近 1.9 亿，是世界上黑人最多的国家。在矿产资源方面，像尼日利亚一样，中国也拥有丰富的资源。

这些因素促使尼日利亚和中国在各自地区的政治和安全中发挥重要作用。双方的共性构成两国发展密切双边关系的基础，同时两国在多边外交中针对国际关注的许多问题展开合作。中国驻尼日利亚拉各斯总领事巢小良指出，中尼两国在经济结构和发展战略上具有高度互补性，双方合作潜力巨大。近年来，中尼关系取得明显进展。中尼战略合作伙伴关系全面快速发展，两国之间的合作蓬勃发展，特别是在政治、贸易、基础设施开发、信息技术、农业和文化等领域。因此，两国应携手合作，追求互惠互利和共同发展。他进一步保证，中非合作论坛北京峰会以及习近平主席与布哈里总统之间的会晤将为全面发展中尼战略合作伙伴关系带来新机遇。回顾历史，我们很高兴看到中尼关系取得的进展。展望未来，我们相信中尼关系将拥有繁荣的未来。

四、改革开放后尼日利亚与中国的双边贸易与投资

1978 年 10 月，中国副总理耿飚访问尼日利亚。这次访问见证了两国之间的谈判并在农业、工业和贸易领域达成协议。中国同意购买棕榈仁、可可、腰果、棉花及其他商品（Owoeye，1986 年）。自 20 世纪 70 年代以来，中国和尼日利亚之间的贸易和投资一直处于低迷状态并继续以低水平增长，直到 1993 年中国从原油净出口国转变为世界第二大原油进口国，才开始快速增长。这段时间恰好西方世界（美国及其盟国）借侵犯人权的指控对萨尼·阿巴查将军发起制裁。阿巴查政权诚恳地与中国保持关系，政府颁布对国外投资者（中国投资者）有利的《1995年尼日利亚投资促进委员会第 16 号法令》，以放宽尼日利亚的投资环境。根据该法令，潜在的外国投资者可以单独投资或与尼日利亚同行合作并参与任何企业的经营，极少数由于重要原因被政府排除的清单除外（Chibundu，2000 年）。因此，中国和尼日利亚在这种情况下开始建立战略外交关系，双方之间的贸易和投资一

直在稳定增长。两国签订"双边贸易和投资协定",相互提供优惠待遇。

尼日利亚前总统奥巴桑乔于 2001 年访问北京并在贸易、技能、经济、科学、技术和投资保护等领域签订大量合作协议。为了进一步加强两国当前的双边关系,中国国家主席胡锦涛于 2006 年 4 月 28 日对尼日利亚进行的访问。双方签署石油合作谅解备忘录。该协议为中国在尼日利亚石油行业投资提供机会。

奥马鲁·亚拉杜瓦总统与中国建立友好关系并于 2008 年 2 月访问北京,期间两国同意在电力、能源以及交通基础设施领域建立战略伙伴关系。双方还达成许多金融交易。其中包括向尼日利亚指定的阿布贾医院建设项目提供 5 亿美元优惠贷款并提供 420 万美元援助建设中尼文化交流中心。

古德勒克总统与中国保持牢固的关系。中国企业在尼日利亚获得授权合同。援引尼日利亚副总统纳马迪·桑博的话,"政府已在发电、输配电等电力部门投资 100 多亿美元。同时投资 20 多亿美元用于建设尼日利亚的铁路系统"(《今日报》,2010 年 8 月 27 日)。山东电力建设第三工程有限公司获得建设奥贡州 Papalanto 燃机电厂项目授权,中国土木工程集团有限公司获得建设铁路项目授权。此外,两国之间的关系继续蓬勃发展。

自 2015 年 5 月 29 日当选以来,穆罕默杜·布哈里总统分别于 2016 年 4 月和 2018 年 9 月正式访问北京。在 2016 年的访问期间,两国签订一系列双边协议,涉及金额为 10 亿美元的阿布贾—伊巴丹—拉各斯格林菲尔德高速公路、西罗罗 300 兆瓦太阳能发电厂以及住房、铁路运输和货币互换,不仅让双方经济收益,还能加强外汇储备管理(《笨拙报》,2016 年 4 月 25 日)。在 2018 年访问期间,两国领导人在天然气管道建设、直接投资、基础设施融资以及信息和通信技术等领域签订价值 100 亿美元的若干协议和谅解备忘录。

在此基础上,中国政府采取很多措施鼓励与尼日利亚的贸易和投资关系,包括:

(1)采取积极措施推动非洲产品进入中国市场,对非洲"最不发达国家"的部分出口产品实行零关税待遇,扩大贸易规模,优化贸易结构。中国已与非洲国家和地区组织签订自由贸易协定或地区贸易协定。

(2)非洲是中国政府鼓励企业进行投资的地区之一。中国政府将制定和完善有关政策,简化投资程序,加强指导和服务,支持有实力的企业在非洲投资。中国将继续签署并执行"鼓励和保证投资双边协定","避免双重征税",维护投资者合法权益。

（3）鼓励中国金融机构在非洲设立分支机构，为中非贸易提供有效的金融服务。

（4）加强信息服务系统，为开发非洲市场创造条件。

这些举措推动尼日利亚和中国贸易额近年来快速增加。自 2004 年以来，两国之间的贸易额增长近 300%，2008 年达到 72 亿美元。2009 年，两国贸易额达到 73 亿美元，2010 年 77 亿美元和 2017 年 72 美元。目前尼日利亚仍然是中国在非洲的第二大贸易伙伴，仅次于南非。与对中国的出口额相比，尼日利亚进口中国商品数量激增，导致对中国产生贸易逆差。随着双边贸易关系的加强，预计逆差将大幅增加，直到尼日利亚工业生产商能够以具有竞争力的价格供应本国产的相同替代产品。

上述数据表明，1999 年尼日利亚向民主过渡后，尼中双边贸易和投资关系继续得到加强。

五、1978 年改革开放后中国—尼日利亚关系面临的挑战

从政治上讲，中尼双边关系面临多重挑战。中国与尼日利亚具有相同的政治经历，双方关系是可以预期的。因此，有学者认为尼日利亚和中国拥有很多共同点，相互依赖、合作和经验分享的前景可期。

这些学者观点的佐证是两国在人口和经济方面具有战略和地缘政治意义，在全世界范围展示古老文明的宝贵传承，双方都有民族特色，在政治进步和社会工作方面也有自信心。学者还认为，两国在独立之前就已经与封建主义、帝国主义和殖民主义作斗争；两国在作为第三世界国家开展南南合作方面具有很多共同点，尼日利亚奉行"一个中国政策"，中国则支持尼日利亚的"不结盟政策"。

尽管中国与尼日利亚和其他非洲国家的贸易和投资逐步增加，但许多学者遗憾地发现，贸易失衡一直持续并有利于中国。他们认为，随着中国试图在非洲贸易中实现更大的顺差以平衡从发达国家的大量进口，贸易失衡的现状将加剧。此外，非洲国家的贸易体制仍然处于后殖民时代，很少为改变这种状况付出努力。目前非洲与中国的贸易一直处于逆差状态。

毫无疑问，中国与尼日利亚的双边关系正在健康成长，但是许多尼日利亚人对贸易关系表达关切。

中国在尼日利亚做生意也有一些风险。首先，武装抢劫、绑架勒索赎金及明显的暴力和混乱倾向造成社会不安定。其次，电力和供水不足，电信和基础设施水平低下，效率低下以及安保人员缺乏专业素养（例如报警的犯罪调查没有产生任何结果和贿赂）导致运营成本高昂。

六、结论和建议

尼日利亚和许多其他非洲国家一样，与中国已经建交 40 多年。通过两国政府不同级别的持续互访、会谈和交流，双边关系可以维持并且确认相互之间的承诺和信任，两国正在所有领域努力扩大关系。双方发展关系的过程中实现大量的中国投资并达成许多双边协议。虽然两国关系存在许多积极的方面，但对中国有利的贸易失衡问题仍在继续。在这方面，尼日利亚必须发展国内经济，成为制成品的出口国，而不是中国的普通原材料生产商，只有这样才能从两国关系中受益。

中国的成功并非一日之力，而是中国领导人的长期专注，因此尼日利亚应该学习中国的经济改革经验，制定发展尼日利亚经济的政策计划。例如，在中国改革进程中，外国直接投资流入中国受到许多规则和法规的控制和指导，包括严格和广泛的中国技术能力建设计划以及严格本地内容要求。尼日利亚必须采取行动，不能依赖于出售石油或中国的贸易保证。尼日利亚也应利用不断发展的双边关系，在对本国具有重要意义的事项上受益于中国的成功并从中汲取教训，以适应其自身情况。双边关系必须涵盖科学、教育、研究和技术等人类基本发展的领域。因此，尼日利亚需要明白，中国的参与为它提供实现经济增长的绝佳机会，必须制订全面的政策以满足长期需求。作为对本国具有重要意义的事项，尼日利亚政府应避免与中国达成短期固定和超前协议，并采取超越石油领域的安排。

当前的全球化和多边主义趋势必须作为尼日利亚与中国关系的标杆，还必须借鉴其他国家与中国关系的成功之处和它们的发展战略，学习它们的经验。尼日利亚应进行全面考量，研究哪些政策对尼日利亚的长期发展有利，哪些领域必须改进。尼日利亚还必须密切关注美国与中国的贸易争端并运用成功的政策。这场贸易争端无疑将为像尼日利亚这样的国家提供丰富的外交经验和知识，可以利用目前的大量专门知识来更好地应对困难的经济关系以及如何保护国民经济的重要部门免受外部竞争。

最后，良好和无私的领导制度对国家的进步至关重要。但是如果领导人无法保持长期专注并制订符合尼日利亚人期望的整体和全面的长期发展政策和战略，中国在尼日利亚的投资将成为挑战。因此，尼日利亚必须加强民主和善治，从与中国的双边关系中受益。民主和善治的改善和发展将不可避免地建立良好的领导文化并巩固善治，不仅关乎自身地位的提高，还涉及整个国家的富强。总体而言，政府应组成一个由学者、技术专家、商人、工程师、民间社会和其他机构专家组成的领导专业委员会，提出可行的解决方案或观念，以更好地利用与中国及世界上其他强大经济体的互动。

The Impact of China's Reform and Opening-Up on Sino-African Relations: A Nigerian Experience

Bello Adamu Hotoro / Nigeria

Northwestern University in Nigeria, Assistant Lecturer

Introduction

The purpose of China's reform was said to be develop 'socialism with Chinese characteristics' (Deng Xiaoping, 1984). As a result of this reform Chinese economy has transformed vigorous. It transformed from the system where the market forces absolutely play no role in facilitating and coordinating economy activity to one in which these forces virtually organize and control. China economy has gone from where virtually no foreign direct investment and low-level of international trade and foreign exchange to a position where it is a major global recipient of foreign investment and trade in comparison with major global economic power (West). Though Africa is not China's major trade partner but play significant role in Chinese global business as it served as a major source of raw materials as well as market of its finished goods. The attention of Chinese officials and their firms are more focusing on Nigerian soil as a country with abundant human and natural resources which if properly interrelated will benefits both side.

1. Framework of Analysis

The South-South Cooperation is of no doubt very relevant in explaining the Sino-African relations to its pureness form. The South-South Cooperation is a cross-fertilization of dependency and liberal school of thought which was postulated by Third World countries leaders (Bandung Conference 1955) and stimulated by United Nations (UN) under the auspices of United Nations Conference on Trade and Development (UNCTAD), it was in 1978 UN consolidated its support by launching a Special Unit for South-South Cooperation (SU/SSC) in Buenos Aires to promote South-South trade in collaboration with its agencies (see http://www.ssc.undp.org). They conceived states as rational actors that made choices on the basis of their preferences, with consideration of trade-offs and second-best options. The cooperation could take place if there are incentives in place and constraints to any conflict or war. Hence, South-South Cooperation would flourish if states of the South considered it to be the best option among others—one that would maximize their interests. Therefore, liberal conception is relevant for the study of South-South Cooperation with the idea of "reducing transaction costs" (Keohane, cited in Udeala, O. S. 2010). He further explained that the transaction costs encompasses all resources that are require in negotiations process: Money, Time, Personnel, Power and Prestige etc. He explained that States prefer (or should prefer) multilateralism as opposed to bilateral, and further believed that multilateralism allowed States to reduce the transaction costs which are involved in bilateral agreements, negotiations and diplomatic dispute resolutions. To further prove liberal position, the idea of reducing transaction costs can be used to explain case of Forum on China-African Cooperation (FOCAC) which was launched in Beijing in the year 2000 and subsequent meeting were took place (after three years each) aimed to boost South-South Cooperation between China and fifty three countries of African continent. South-South cooperation offers countries the possibility to go beyond bilateral policy transfers. They can jointly devise policy strategies and tools that draw from the experience of all participating countries and tackle the specific problems of each of them, rather than being limited to acts of transferring best-practices from one country to all the others. (Tisdell, C. 2008). South-South Cooperation refers to the sharing of knowledge and resources between developing countries with the aim of identifying the most effective steps towards the eradication of their developmental challenges (Alex, A & et'al, cited in Rose, M. R. 2015). Therefore, the advocate of this notion saw the development potentials between among the countries of the Global South (developing countries) in sharing technology, knowledge, monetary, skills, resources, and trade etc rather than rely on the Global North for their developmental agenda. Hence, this study resolved and believed that the theory is best tool in guiding and providing a good direction for this research.

2. China-Africa Relations Since Economic Reform of 1978

Following the Deng Xiaoping's economic reforms in 1978. China–Africa relations entered new phase, with postulation of the new "independent policy" which was charted by the Chinese state leader's Africa tour to eleven countries (from 20th December 1982 to 17th January 1983), aiming at launching a new African policy shortened in the "Four Principles on Sino–African Economic and Technical Cooperation". These Four Principles varied greatly from the "Eight Principles" in the sense that they were much invigorated by economic pragmatism in harmony with China's new internal developmental priorities and its limited financial resources. On this note, these policies continued to be useful by China's new leaders in the later part of the reform era.

China-African Countries' relations have become a major subject of discussion particularly among western Medias, policy makers as well as scholars, because the economic reform policy of 1978 allowed China to emerged a competitor for the Africa's vast natural resources. Therefore, their relationship are surrounded by the need for new markets and investment opportunities, development assistance and co-operation, and forging strategic relationship. In recent years, China has pointed African continent as an area of strategic political important as well as significant socio-economic partner for development. The formation of forum on China-Africa Cooperation (FOCAC) in 2000 and subsequent success of the forum as acknowledged by both leaders (China and African). Xi reaffirmed the commitment of two sides during FOCAC meeting in Johannesburg 2015. China-Africa relations have today reached a stage of growth unmatched in history. We should scale the heights, look afar and take bold steps. Let us join hands, pool the vision and strength of the 2.4 billion Chinese and Africans and open a new era of China-Africa win-win cooperation and common development. In another occasion Xi emphasized the mutual trust and sincerity accord each other.

> For decades, China and Africa have treated each other with sincerity and friendship. We are a community with a shared future and common interests, featuring solidarity and win-win cooperation. Going forward, China will continue to deepen communication, mutual trust and cooperation with other friendly African countries, based on the principles of sincerity, real results, affinity and good faith and the approach of upholding justice and pursuing shared interests' (Xinhua 2018, September 01).

Therefore, since the formation of FOCAC in 2000, China-Africa relations opened a new diplomatic chapter in almost all sphere of human endeavor, as the Forum granted more than one hundred and thirty billions dollars for interest-free loans, concessional loans and special fund for development financing and entered numerous cooperation and initiatives with African countries. Xi reiterated the Chinese government commitments.

> To build an even closer China-Africa community with a shared future in the new era, China will, on the basis of the ten cooperation plans (focac 2015) already adopted, launch eight major initiatives (focac 2018) in close collaboration with African countries in the next three years and beyond (Chinadaily 2018, September 4).

In the same vein, South African president Cyril Ramaphosa testified China African relations in recent years during the last FOCAC meeting in Beijing 2018.

We are greatly encouraged by their assessment that the ten cooperation plans announced in 2015 have been fully implemented, for it shows a partnership that is hard at work to advance the mutual interests of Africa and China.

Ramaphosa further acknowledged the position of Africa on industrialization plan by the forum which promoted industrial development in many parts of the continent and contributed to economic transformation in areas like agricultural modernization plan which promoted greater agricultural productivity as well as the infrastructure plan which also boosted African connectivity and integration. These plans have as well contributed to environmental conservation, sustainable development, improved public health services, and peace and security. He also attested that, through FOCAC and other forums, China has worked to ensure that Africa's development is prominent on the international agenda. (South Africa's official website. http://www.dirco.gov.za/docs/speeches/2018/cram0903a.htm).

3. Sino-Nigeria Diplomatic Relations after Economic Reform of 1978

Sino-Nigeria relations antedated China's economic reform of 1978, as they established formal diplomatic ties on 10 February 1971 with an understanding to tolerate set of five principles, namely mutual respect for each other's sovereignty and territorial integrity, mutual non-aggression, non-interference in each other's internal affairs, sovereign equality, and peaceful coexistence (Alex, A & et'al, cited in Rose, M. R. 2015). Though Chinese reform and opening-up was initially aimed at developing of its internal economic through cordial relations with international community and further strengthen the objectives of the South-South Cooperation which, among other things, aimed at upholding cooperation among countries of the Southern Hemisphere in a wide range of areas such as trade, investment, technical cooperation, industrialization, energy, food and agriculture, and technology (Jules, T.D & Silva, M, cited in Tisdell, C. 2008).

To further strength their relations, the two nations witnessed exchanged visits by leaders and top governmental level officials from both sides. These multiple visitations from both sides demonstrate commonality of both Nations as they shared a lot in common from regional giant to rich endowment of mineral and human resources. China is the largest single market in the world with a population of over 1.3 billion, while Nigeria is the largest single market in Africa with a population of almost 190 million. Unlike Nigeria, China has been able to harness its vast demographic, human and material resources to build a strong and potent domestic economy which has impacted positively on its citizenry (Agbu 1994).

In addition, Nigeria and China are burdened by destiny in their respective regions. In terms of population, one of every three Asians is Chinese, so also one in every four persons in Africa is a Nigerian. With a population of over 1.3 billion, China is in fact the most populous nation in the world. Nigeria on the other hand, with a population of almost 190 million people is the largest concentration of black people in the world. In terms of mineral resources China, like Nigeria, is well endowed (Oche et al. cited in Tisdell, C. 2008).

These factors, among other things, predispose Nigeria and China to play prominent roles in the politics and security of their respective regions. They also constitute a common ground that should serve as a basis for nurturing close bilateral relations between the two countries, while fostering their collaboration in multilateral diplomacy on a wide range of issues of general international concern (Akinterinwa 1994). According to Chiao Xiaoliang the consulate general of Peoples Republic of China in Lagos Nigeria, China and Nigeria are highly complementary in economy structure and development strategy, we have enormous potential in cooperation. Recent years witnessed tangible progress in China Nigeria relations. China Nigeria strategic partnership enjoyed comprehensive and rapid development, cooperation between the two countries is flourishing, especially in the fields of politics, trade, infrastructure development, IT, agriculture and culture. Therefore, the two countries should join hands to pursue mutual benefits and common development (Vanguard 2018, September 27). He further assured that the FOCAC

Beijing Summit and the meeting between President Xi Jinping and President Buhari will bring new opportunities for the comprehensive development of China-Nigeria strategic partnership. Looking back at history, we are pleased to witness the progress we have made in China- Nigeria relations. Looking to the future, we are confident that China-Nigeria relations will enjoy a prosperous future (Vanguard 2018, September 27).

4. China-Nigeria Bilateral Trade and Investment after Economic Reform

In October 1978, the Chinese Vice- Premier, Geng Biao visited Nigerian. The visit witnessed negotiations between the two countries and agreement was reached in the fields of agriculture, industry and trade. China agreed to buy palm kernels, cocoa, cashew nuts and cotton and host others (Owoeye 1986). Since 1970s the trade and investment between China and Nigeria was loomed sided and continued to grow at low levels until the rapid growth turned China in 1993 from net exporter of crude oil to the second largest crude oil importer in the World which coincide with the sanctions imposed by the Western World (USA and its allies) on the General Sani Abacha military regime because of its human rights abuses. The Abacha's regime seriously engaged China to the extent that the government promulgated the Nigerian investment and promotion commission Decree No 16 of 1995 in order favor foreign investors (Chinese Investors) and liberalize investment environment in Nigeria. With this Decree, a potential foreign investor can now invest solely or in corporation with a Nigerian counterpart and partake in the operations of any enterprise, except for very few in the exclusive-list reserved by the government for serious reasons (Chibundu 2000). Therefore, this situation made China and Nigeria to embark on the strategy diplomatic relations accordingly, trade and investment relations between the two sides has been in steady increase. They signed a number of "bilateral trade and investment agreement" to offer each other the most conducive deals.

The then Nigerian President Obasanjo visited Beijing in the 2001 and signed a number of agreements between the two nations in areas like; trade, technical, economic, scientific, technological and investment protection (Abua, 2004). To further strength the existing bilateral relations between the two states, the Chinese President Hu Jintao paid a similar visit to Nigeria on the 28th April 2006. They signed a Memorandum of Understanding (MOU) on petroleum cooperation. This deal provided an ample opportunities for Chinese investment in the Nigerian oil industry. As part of the agreement, Nigeria granted China four drilling licences in exchange for commitments to invest US$4 billion in oil and infrastructural projects (Udeala, 2010).

The President Umaru Yar'Adua administration promote a cordial relations with China, during his visit to Beijing in February 2008, they agreed to pursue a strategic partnership in power and energy as well as in transport infrastructure (Adeniyi, 2011). Numerous financial deals were also established. These include US$500 million concessionary loan for projects to be identified by Nigeria, construction of a hospital in Abuja to be facilitated by a US$4.2 million for the construction of China-Nigeria Friendship Cultural Centre in Abuja (Adeniyi, 2011).

President Goodluck administration has also upheld strong relations with China. Chinese companies have been awarded contracts in the Nigeria. The Vice-President of Nigeria, Namadi Sambo, was quoted as saying, "The government has invested over $10 billion on the generation, transmission and distribution in the power sector. And over US$2 billion has been invested in the rejuvenation of the rail system in Nigeria" (This Day, August 27, 2010). The construction of Papalanto power gas turbine plant in Ogun State was awarded to a Chinese consortium SEPCO while the rejuvenation of the rail systems was awarded to the China Civil Engineering Construction Company (CCECC) (Ogunkola 2008). Furthermore, the relations between the countries have continued to surge more potent.

Since resuming office in 29th May 2015, President Muhammad Buhari was officially visited Beijing in April 2016 and September 2018 respectively. In the 2016 visit, the two nations sealed a number of bilateral agreements from 1 billion dollars of Abuja-Ibadan-Lagos Greenfield expressway, 300 megawatt solar plant in Shiroro to the area of Housing, Rail Transport and swap currency deal which will invariably benefits the two economy and enhance the foreign exchange reserves management (Punch 2016, April 25). While 2018 visit, the two leaders signed several agreements and memorandum of understanding (MOU) worth 10 billion dollars in areas like gas pipeline construction, direct investment, infrastructure financing and information and communication technology (Adesomoju, 2018). Several plans are on the ways to the strength the bilateral ties between the two states.

On this basis, the Chinese government has implemented numerous measures to stimulate trade and investment relations with Nigeria which included:

(1) Taking positive measures to facilitate African products to enter China market, and to give zero tariff treatment to part of exports from "least developing countries" in Africa, to enlarge the trade scale, and optimize the trading structure. China has signed free trade agreement or regional trade assignment with African countries and regional organizations.

(2) Africa is one of the regions China government encourages enterprises to make investment. Chinese government will formulate and perfect related policy, simplify investment procedures, enhance guide and service, and support powerful enterprises to invest in Africa. She will continue to sign and carry out "bilateral agreement to encourage and guarantee investment", and "avoiding double taxation" to safeguard the legal rights of investors.

(3) Encouraging China's financial institutions to setup branches in Africa, to provide effective financial service for China – Africa trade.

(4) Strengthening information service system to create conditions to exploit African market (Onuoha, 2008).

These measures were responsible for recent increase and acceleration in the trade volume between Nigeria and China. The trade volume between the two countries grew by nearly 300 percent since 2004 and reached the momentous of $7.2 billion in 2008. The trade volume between the two countries in 2009 reached $ 7.3 billion, $7.7 billion in 2010 and $7.2 in 2017 respectively (Ayoola, 2103; ThisDay 2018, September 6). Now the Nigeria remained the second biggest China trade partner in Africa, after South Africa (Utomi, 2007). A surge in Nigeria imports of Chinese goods relative to Nigeria exports to China has resulted in a trade deficit with China and this is expected to grow significantly due to increased trade relations until Nigeria can offer its industrial producers home-grown alternatives of the same quality at competitive prices (Ayoola, 2013).

The abovementioned indices showed that the Nigeria- China bilateral trade and investment relations got a major boost immediately after Nigerian transition to democracy in 1999.

5. Challenges of China-Nigeria Relations after Economic Reform Since 1978

Politically speaking, there are multiples and manifold challenges in China-Nigeria bilateral relations. This is nevertheless expected in a relationship relating two countries that have diverse orientations notwithstanding the Chinese persistent talk of having the same political experiences with Nigeria. It is as a result of that, some scholars have contended that Nigeria and China share a lot in common with prospects for interdependence, collaboration and the sharing of experiences.

Corroborating to these scholars, both states have strategic and geopolitical significance in population and economy, have earliest civilizations showed in artefacts precious all over the world, and both share the national trait which upholds self – confidence even in matters of political progress and social work. These scholars also maintain that both states battled feudalism, imperialism and colonialism anterior to independence; that both states have a lot in common as both affirm South – south cooperation as a Third World Nations, Nigeria believe in "one

– China policy" while China supports Nigerian's "Non – Alignment policy" (Ezirim, 2007; Nwachukwu, 2009).

In spite of Nigeria and other African country's progressively trade and investment with China, many scholars have observed unhappily that the balance of trade has continued and will remain to continue in favor of China. They believe, the trade imbalance will upsurge as China tries to attain a greater surplus in her African trade in order to balance the substantial imports from the developed countries. Consequently, there is evident determination by the Chinese to counterweight their trade deficit with the industrialist nations, by determined to retain trade supplies with their non –industrialized trading partners. Furthermore, African states trade regime still stays post-colonial with very slight effort being made to change the condition primarily. On this note, the Africa's trade with China has persisted to be in deficit (Ezirim, 2007; Onuoha, 2008).

China's bilateral relationship with Nigeria is undoubtedly getting healthier by the day unlike the situation during the immediate post-colonial epoch. But, many Nigerians are questioning and concerned about the trade relations. Many Chinese products particularly textiles are oversupplying the Nigerian market on a daily basis. Majority of these low-cost goods, which workmanship is often poor, would never make the grade in developed countries. This has led many Nigerians to blame the Chinese of dumping cheap Chinese goods into the local markets in so doing stifling the competitiveness of local production. Hence, the China is now pressing economic gains in the same way that it pursued ideological influence many years ago (Utomi, 2008; Momoh, 2009).

On the contrary, China also has some quetches over doing business in Nigeria. Firstly, the problem of insecurity arising from armed banditry, kidnapping for ransoms and pronounced social inclination towards violence and chaos. Secondly, the high cost of operations due to poor power and water supply, the bad level of telecommunications and infrastructure facilities, inefficient and lack of professionalism of security personnel such as when reported crime investigations do not produce any results and bribery. (Bukarambe, 2005).

6. Conclusion and Recommendations

Nigeria like many other African countries engaged China in bilateral relations for many decades. This bilateral relations was possible through constant visits, meetings and exchanges at the different governmental levels of both countries, and they affirmed their commitment and trust to each other, and the relations is broadening in all sphere of endeavor. The relations between and among these two nations have witnessed a numerous Chinese investments, sealed a number of bilateral deals. While a lot of positives are apparent in the relations between the two states, the question of excessive trade imbalance in favor of China has continued. In this respect, Nigeria must take the benefit of this bilateral relations to develop on its internal economy by being an exporter of finished products than an ordinary producer of raw materials for China.

The success of China is not a one day dream but rather a long term commitments by its leaders, therefore Nigeria should learn from the China's economy reform and create a developmental policies plan in such a way that will develop the Nigeria's economy. For example, throughout the Chinese years of reform, foreign direct investment inflows to China were controlled and guided by many rules and regulations including rigorous and extensive plans on technological capacity building of Chinese, tight local content requirements. Therefore, Nigeria must do something than sell of oil or rely on China for trade guarantees. So also Nigeria should as a matter of its national important use the ongoing bilateral relations to benefit on the Chinese triumph and adapt the lessons to accommodate its own situations. The relationship must cover areas of basic human development in science, education, research and technology. Consequently, Nigeria needs to understand that China's engagement gives it exceptional opportunity to significantly amplify its growth and come out a comprehensive policy that addresses its long-term needs. As a matter of national important Nigerian government should avoid short – term fixes and front –

overloaded agreements with the China and act beyond arrangements that focus exclusively on the oil sector.

The current trend of globalization and multilateralism must serve as a yardstick of Nigerian relations with China and must learn from the success and otherwise of other states' relations with China and their strategies toward development, so also larning from their own experiences. Nigeria should undertake a comprehensive review to examine what policies have been advantageous for Nigeria's long term development and what areas must improvement. Nigeria must also closely study the United States' trade disputes with China and apply the successful policies. This trade disputes will undoubtedly provide vast diplomatic lessons and knowledge to the countries like Nigeria and could certainly tap vast range of current expertise on how to better cope with a difficult economic relationship and how to defend the important sectors of the national economy against external competition.

Finally, the institutionalization of good and selfless leadership is very paramount for the country to progress. It is totally sad to understand that the lack of commitment in the side of leaders who failed to stand and formulate a holistic and comprehensive long term development policies and strategies capable to address the desires of Nigerians in relations to the Country's engagement with China continues to be a key challenge. Therefore, Nigeria must enhance its democracy as well as good governance for it to reap her bilateral relations with China. The improvement and development of democracy and good governance will inevitably build a good culture of leadership and consolidate good governance that will not concerned about self-aggrandizement but about enriching the country as a whole. On a whole, government should constitute a committee that comprise a leading expertise from academia, technocrats, businessmen, engineers, civil society and host of others to come out with workable solutions or ideas on how best to utilize the engagement with China and other powerful economy in the World.

References

Adesomoju, A. (2018, September 9). Nigeria signs $10bn agreements in China — Presidency. *Punch Newspaper*. Retrieved 2018 from. https://punchng.com/nigeria-signs-10bn-agreements-in-china-presidency/.

Abua, J. (2008). From China, a harvest of agreements. *ThisDay* Newspaper, 16 November.

Remarks by President Cyril Ramaphosa during the FOCAC. (2018). *Department: International relations and cooperation: Republic of South Africa*. Retrieved 2018 from. http://www.dirco.gov.za/docs/speeches/2018/cram0903a.htm

Agbu, O. (1994), "Promoting Nigeria – China Relations", *Nigerian Forum*, Vol. 14, No. 11 – 12, November – December.

Akinterinwa, B. A (1994), "Nigeria and China: Perspectives and Prospects", *Nigerian Forum*, Vol. 14, No. 5 – 6, May – June.

Anyagafu, V. (2018, September 3). China-Africa trade volume hit 116billion. *Vanguard*. Retrieved 2018 from. https://www.vanguardngr.com/2018/09/china-africa-trade-volume-hit-116-billion/.

Anyagafu, V. (2018, September 27). China enjoys brighter relations with Nigeria-Amb. Xiaoliang. *Vanguard*. Retrieved 2018 from. https://www.vanguardngr.com/2018/09/china-enjoys-brighter-relations-with-nigeria-amb-xiaoliang/.

Ayoola, J.T. (2013). Nigeria-China relations: implication on the Nigerian domestic economy. *Research journal of finance and account*. Vol.4, No 17. pp. 98-104.

Bukarambe, B. (2005), "Nigeria – China Relations: The Unacknowledged Sino – Dynamics", in Ogwu, U. J. (ed.) *New Horizons for Nigeria in World Affairs*, Lagos: The Nigerian Institute of International Affairs.

Chibundu, V. N. (2000). *Nigeria-China foreign relations*, 1960-1999. Ibadan: Spectrum Books.

Chinadaily. (2018, September 4). Full text of Chinese President Xi Jinping's speech at opening ceremony of 2018 FOCAC Beijing Summit. *Chinadaily*. Retrieved 2018 from http://www.chinadaily.com.cn/a/201809/04/WS5b8d5c25a310add14f389592.html.

Deng Xiaoping (1984) "Build Socialism with Chinese Characteristics". pp. 1-5 in The Research Department of Party Literature, Central Committee of the Communist Party of China (1991) *Major Documents of the People's Republic of China –Selected Important Documents since the Third Plenary Session of the Eleventh Central Committee of the Communist Party of China (December 1978 and November 1989)*. Beijing. Foreign Languages Press.

Ezirim, G. E. (2007), "Reflections on the China – in – Africa Debate: Mercantilism,

Partnership or Resurgence of Hegemony?" *Journal of International Politics and Development Studies,* Vol. 3, No. 1, July/December.

Momoh, Siaka (2009), "How Tidy is Nigeria-China Relations". Retrieved 2018 from http:// www. businessdayonline.com/index.php?option=com_content.

Nwachukwu, L. C. (2009), "Nigeria-China Bilateral Relations: Past, Present and Future", in Okolie, A. M. (ed.) *Contemporary Readings on Nigeria's External Relations: Issues, Perspectives and Challenges,* Abakaliki: Willyrose and Appleseed Publishing Company.

Ogunkola, O. E. (2008). *Nigeria-China trade and economic relations.* Ibadan: Nigeria African Research Consortium (AERC) Publishers.

Ogunmade, O. (2018, September 6). Nigeria-China Trade Now $7.2 Billion, Says Envoy. *ThisDay.*https://www.thisdaylive.com/index.php/2018/09/06/nigeria-china-trade-now-72.

Olaita, k. (2016, April 8). Buhari's visit and prospects for Nigeria-China relations. *TheGuardia*n. Retrieved 2018 from. https://guardian.ng/features/buharis-visit-and-prospects-for-nigeria-china-relations/.

Onuoha, J. (2008), *Beyond Diplomacy: Contemporary Issues in International Relations,* Nsukka: Great AP Express Publishers Limited.

Owoeye, J. (1986). Nigeria and China. In Olusanya G.O & Akindele R.A. (eds.) *Nigeria's external relations: The first twenty-five years.* Ibadan: University Press.

Punch Newspaper. (2016, April 25). President Buhari's trade mission to china. *Punch.* Retrieved 2018 from. https://punchng.com/president-buharis-trade-mission-to-china/.

Rose, M. R. (2015). An assessment of Nigeria-China economic relations from 1999-2014. *International Journal of Arts and Humanities.* Vol. 4(1). No. 13. pp. 18-30.

ThisDay Newspaper (2010, August 27). Federal Government Spends $12 billion on Power and Rail Problems. *This Day.*

Tisdell, C. (2008). Economic theory applications and issues: *Thirty Years of Economic Reform and Openness in China: Retrospect and Prospect.* A Conference Organized by Renmin University and the Committee of Economic Education, Ministry of Education, People's Republic of China.

Udeala, O. (2008). Foreign policy and the Nigerian image project: Constraints and challenges. *The Nigerian Forum, Vol. 29,* Nos.11-12: November-December p.72.

Udeala, O, S. (2013). Nigeria-China Economic Relations under the South-South Cooperation. *African Journal of International Affairs.* Vol. 13, No. 1 & 2.

Utomi, P. (2007). China and Nigeria. Retrieved 2018 from http://csis.org/files/media on13th November.

Utomi, P. (2008), "China and Nigeria". Retrieved 2018 from http://www.csis.org/media/csis/

pubs/080603_utomi_nigeriachina_pdf_billion-says-envoy/.

Xinhua. (2018, September 1).Xi's quotable quotes on China-Africa relations.
Retrieved. 2018from. http://www.xinhuanet.com/english/2018-09/01/c_137435500.htm.

"一带一路"倡议下的华裔菲律宾人

洪秀萍【菲律宾】
亚太进步之路基金会研究分析员

自习近平于 2013 年宣布"一带一路"倡议以来，中国领导人指示政府单位、国有企业和媒体在各个层面全面推进该倡议。中国面向世界推介一项大胆的计划，旨在通过亚洲基础设施投资银行和区域组织等双边和多边方式走进参与国。合作的优先事项包括政策沟通、设施联通、贸易畅通、资金融通以及民心相通。中国企业家获得在海外开展业务的绿灯，特别是经济带沿线地区。为了进入东南亚，中国认可华人族裔社区在加速推动"一带一路"倡议过程中的作用和贡献。海外华人社区凭借人际网络以及共同的语言和文化，不但已成为吸引外来投资的推动者，还拥有本地商业环境、法律和人民方面的专门知识。虽然认为海外华人有助于"一带一路"倡议取得成功，但过去的经验和爱国主义质疑他们与中国企业家的来往。在菲律宾，华裔菲律宾人将邻国的投资视为重要机会，渴望参与"一带一路"倡议项目。然而，他们也意识到，菲律宾政府过去的交易都以失败告终，而且菲律宾与中国存在争端。近年来的事实表明，即使存在争端和怀疑的公众舆论，经济和民众联系仍可继续发展甚至改善。本文研究菲律宾的华裔社区如何平衡他们的华裔根源和菲律宾爱国主义。他们不仅爱国，而且务实，因为大部分业务都在菲律宾，第二代或第三代也可能与中国没有亲近感。在"一带一路"倡议下，他们的机遇和挑战是什么？中国如何最大限度地发挥海外华人社区的作用和贡献？希望本文能够更深入地揭示和理解"一带一路"时代下的华裔菲律宾人。

中国的经济带

五年前提出的"一带一路"倡议（BRI）是一项经济计划，提供可供选择的合作模式，其优先事项包括政策沟通、设施联通、贸易畅通、资金融通以及民心相通。它是复兴的古代丝绸之路、当代丝绸之路和最新提议新路线的组合（例如海上和北方路线）。发起这一倡议的中国正面临着金融、科技和劳动力资源过剩，因此创造性地思考如何有效利用过剩资产。发展中国家需要援助来建设基础设施和推动自身经济发展，中国将其视为推动走出去政策的机会，同时也与世界其他地区建立合作关系。换句话说，中国的过剩产能可以满足其他国家的需要。

上海社会科学院前院长王战认为，"一带一路"倡议是中国与发展中国家交流改革开放经验的平台。[1] 它的长期目标是建立一个具有共同利益和责任的人类命运共同体，以政治互信、经济融合和文化包容为特色。暨南大学国际关系学院院长张振江教授甚至将"一带一路"倡议比喻为篮子，各方都可以将其资本、产品和服务置于其中，供其他方选择。这是中国对国际贸易和全球经济的贡献[2]——习近平主席具有里程碑意义的计划目前在中国外交和国际关系中发挥领导作用。

目标非常宏大，然而面向世界推广的这五年并不是一帆风顺。虽然65个参与国[3]对该倡议表示欢迎，但一些国家仍在考虑中。以日本为例，即使与中国建立了牢固的贸易关系，也只允许其私营部门"作为倡议的一部分与中国开展业务"，其余部门则视情况而定。日本政府目前没有制订官方政策。该倡议还因缺乏透明度或使借款国陷入"债务陷阱"而受到批评。在此期间，某些双边协议被取消；某些被修改。然而，中国学者辩护称，"一带一路"倡议还很年轻。中国自身也在从交往与合作中学习，因此学者们发现，与四五年前的积极举动相比，最近的交易更为谨慎。

从政府到企业，从媒体到社会文化交流，中国在各个层面上都大力推广"一

1　上海社会科学院前院长王战于2008年6月1日亚洲太平洋协进基金会礼节性拜访期间。

2　张振江，《国际关系视角下的"一带一路"倡议》，暨南大学国际关系学院，2018年5月14日。

3　截至本论文提交日期2018年9月1日。

带一路"倡议。中国政府认可在与其他国家（特别是在后院地区）关系中，海外华人华侨起到关键作用。另一位国际关系教授鞠海龙指出，如果中国希望"一带一路"倡议在南海地区取得成功，需要有经济基础。之所以能够这样做，是因为中国与东南亚国家有着相似的文化和发展。[1] 构成该基础的一部分是东南亚的华裔社区，与中国跟非洲和欧洲的关系相比，华裔是重要因素。他们中国大陆投资和企业的进入通道，也是连接中国企业和邻国的桥梁。除了对本国商业环境、法律和程序有更好的了解外，华裔还了解两国语言并建立本地网络。

本文研究"一带一路"倡议背景下的菲律宾华裔社区及其在菲中关系中的作用。下文各章节讨论华裔菲律宾人在"一带一路"倡议下的机遇与挑战。

菲中关系下的华裔菲律宾人

菲律宾华裔社区包括老一代华侨、年轻一代华裔菲律宾人、新移民以及中国游客和临时访问者。

老一代华侨认同华人身份，已获得菲律宾国籍；在菲律宾出生的年轻一代华裔首先认为自己是菲律宾人，但仍保留中华文化身份认同。[2] 下表中的矩阵区分前两种类型的华裔，大约构成菲律宾认可的 1-2%，但由于他们主要是企业主，占有大约 50-55% 的市场资本份额。在新一期的《福布斯》杂志中，华裔大亨吴奕辉（John Gokongwei）、施至成（Henry Sy）、陈永栽（Lucio Tan）和郑少坚（George Ty）跻身亿万富翁行列。[3]

表 1：老一代华侨移民与年轻一代华裔菲律宾人 [4]

老一代	年轻一代
•生于太平洋战争之前	•生于太平洋战争之后
•出生在中国，通常有中文名字	•出生在菲律宾，通常有教名

1 鞠海龙，《南海地区推进"一带一路"建设的经济基础与政策空间》，暨南大学国际关系学院，2018年5月16日。

2 Po, Gerley, A Comparative Analysis of the Entrepreneurial Styles of Second, Third, and Fourth Generation Overseas Chinese and Filipinos in the Philippines, DLSU Business & Economics Review, 2010, 19-2, pp. 11-23.

3 Rappler, Henry Sy still leads Filipinos on Forbes' 2018 billionaire list, March 7, 2018, https://www.rappler.com/business/197591-filipinos-forbes-world-billionaires-list-2018.

4 Ang See, Teresita, Migration Trends and their Socio-economic Implications: The Ethnic Chinese Community, presented at In Search for a China Strategy symposium on August 17-18, 2016 at the UP Asian Center Auditorium.

续表

老一代	年轻一代
• 对中国有浓厚的感情，至少童年时代在中国度过	• 与菲律宾有更多接触，没有中国生活经历
• 可以轻松地跨民族障碍，在两种文化环境中分别与中国人和菲律宾人交往	• 生活和活动限制在华人社区内，更多地与华人交往
• 加入家族和乡镇协会、地方商会	• 加入扶轮社、青年商会、国际狮子会等菲律宾团体
• 第一语言是中文	• 娴熟掌握他加禄语[菲律宾语、比沙亚语]或英语
• 只上过中文学校或大学	• 就读菲律宾的学院或大学
• 外貌和生活方式非常中国化，遵守中国的礼仪和传统，采用中国形式的社会习俗和礼节	• 西化的品味、价值和生活方式，很少遵守中国传统礼仪
• 将中国视为祖国，将菲律宾视为第二祖国	• 将菲律宾视为家乡，对中国没有特别的依恋

来源：洪玉华女士在"寻找中国战略"专题讨论会上的演讲

　　本文关注年轻一代华裔菲律宾人，因为他们不仅在经济方面，还在决策和社会文化事业中为国家建设做出积极贡献。他们在菲中关系中的作用包括：商务推动者、两国政府之间的桥梁、空白填补者、协助中小微企业（MSME）的先驱者、政策制定的利益相关者以及教育和文化交流的支持者。

　　首先，华裔菲律宾人在以下两个方面是商务推动者：知识和网络。根据"走出去"政策，中国鼓励企业向海外扩展业务。加上文化和语言上的亲和力，中国人可以在更本地化的环境中与华裔菲律宾人直接接触。这种直接接触是因为中国的城市或省份的直接签约 - 姐妹城市或姐妹省份 - 因此不可避免地需要更多的本地切入点。目前，两国有 24 个姐妹城市或省份。华裔菲律宾人的知识和网络开始变得重要。他们了解所涉及的商业环境、法律、市场、政府机构；并且可以提供潜在的合作伙伴和顾问网络。优势在于，华裔菲律宾人可以缓解两国人民之间的语言障碍。除普通话外，他们还可以说福建话，方便来自福建省的合作伙。

　　其次，他们在两国政府之间架起桥梁。有影响力的华裔菲律宾人（大部分是为菲律宾与中国一级更广泛的社会关系做出重大贡献的企业家）担任特使。举个例子，上好佳集团有限公司董事长施恭旗（Carlos Chan）先生担任菲律宾总统中国特使，为两国的贸易和交流铺平道路。值得注意的是，广州一家华侨博物馆在展览中叙述他的贡献和参与。

图一　华裔菲律宾商人、菲律宾总统中国特使施恭旗先生的事迹，在广东华侨博物馆展出。

另一个例子是，菲律宾总统罗德里戈·杜特尔特 2016 年对北京进行国事访问期间，商人构成代表团的一部分。包括菲律宾领先企业集团 SM Investments 投资公司高管在内的 300 多位商业领袖陪同。[1] 两国政府见证公私部门签署协议和意向书，带来价值 240 亿美元的投资和信贷额度保证。

第三，在两国正式关系几乎没有改善的时期，华裔菲律宾人已经开始填补空白。菲律宾政府和私营部门都在防止因政治冲突造成经济影响。在南海争端

1　Yamada, Shuhei and Endo, Jun, China, Philippines forge friendship of convenience, Nikkei Asian Review, October 21, 2016, https://asia.nikkei.com/Politics/China-Philippines-forge-friendship-of-convenience.

最严重的时期，经济关系仍保持相对良好的状态。虽然中国禁止 27 家菲律宾公司出口香蕉和菠萝并发布旅游警告，但 2010 年到 2014 年贸易额继续增加，仅 2015 年下滑。事实上，从 2010 年到 2015 年，菲律宾的进口增长 135%，但 2015 年贸易额受到菲律宾出口下降的影响，导致贸易缺口扩大。[1] 菲律宾经济学家以相反的观点解释中国采取行动的结果。埃伦·帕兰卡（Ellen Palanca）教授认为，考虑到出口属于全球价值链的一部分，菲律宾对中国的出口减少是由于西方国家对中国产品的需求降低。[2] 同时，蒂娜·克莱门特（Tina Clemente）教授指出，2013 年至 2015 年的巨额贸易逆差引发人们的担忧，这一切都是争端造成的。[3]

如果海上紧张局势对双边贸易没有产生明显的影响（香蕉出口），则 Ju 教授的解释是正确的，即政治和经济平行；它们不交叉。[4] 事实上，在缺乏政府间对话的情况下，是学术机构或称为轨道 2.0 以及商业部门让双方延续关系。

第四，菲律宾工商总会（PCCI）等著名的华裔菲律宾商业组织通过培训和业务配对帮助中小微企业进行创新，从而能够参与更大的市场。中小微企业的机会将在下一部分中讨论。

巨头拥有大量资本，通常是决策中的重要利益相关者。他们帮助政府资助和运营大型基础设施项目，即所谓的"政府和社会资本合作"（PPP）。他们的业务符合"一带一路"倡议项目，涉及航空、银行、建筑、房地产和旅游业等相关行业；因此，专业知识受到重视。他们有主动提出建议、制定议程和发起项目的能力。根据地理空间和社交网络分析，菲华商联总会（FFCCCII）和菲律宾工商总会"提供将其经济实力转化为对菲律宾产生影响的潜在途径"。[5] 此外，部分人参与政治

1　Philippine Consulate General in Shanghai, Briefer for Asia Pacific Pathways to Progress Foundation, Inc. during the think tank's official visit on May 31, 2018.

2　Palanca, Ellen, Presentation at In Search of a China Strategy: Unpacking the Bilateral and Regional Dynamics of Philippines-China Relations on August 17-18, 2016 at the UP Asian Center.

3　Clemente, Tina, "Understanding the Economic Diplomacy between the Philippines and China," International Journal of China Studies, 2016, 7(2), p. 217.

4　Ju Hailong, Economic Base and Social Policy Space of the Belt and Road Initiative in the South Sea Rim of China, presented at the School for International Studies, Jinan University on May 16, 2018.

5　Fleck, Tanner and Wissler, Jonathan, Economic preparation of the environment: A selective empirical analysis of Chinese investment in the Philippines, 2016, Naval Postgraduate School, p.83.

活动和程序或就宪章变更和税制改革等问题发表意见。

华裔菲律宾人在"一带一路"中的角色

华裔菲律宾人在双边关系中的角色可以根据"一带一路"倡议的五通进行区分。在政策沟通方面，他们可以响应 21 世纪海上丝绸之路的共同价值观 - 海上丝绸之路覆盖菲律宾 - 与地方政府的发展战略和计划保持同步。具体而言，他们可以通过活动和政治贡献实现对长期计划的互补。

华裔菲律宾人可以作为工人、投资者和协调者促进互联互通；充当"丝绸之路"沿线国家贸易畅通的贡献者和促进者，联系东南亚地区的其他华人。他们还可以与亚投行、中国银行和进出口银行等相关金融机构合作，为企业提供跨境人民币结算、贷款、支付和其他金融服务，从而为周边企业提供国际环境下的参与机会。

此外，华裔菲律宾人可以按照 21 世纪海上丝绸之路的思想和精神，作为民心相通的传播者和发起者。他们可以通过教育和文化交流加强社会文化纽带，以匹配"一带一路"倡议中的民心相通。例如，陈永栽每年派遣数百名学生到中国不同的城市参加为期两个月的寻根之旅夏令营。交流不是必须在学院内，而是企业为员工和年轻专业人员提供培训和宣传活动。例如，吴奕辉为年轻的菲律宾专业人员提供奖学金，帮助他们学习中国的语言和文化。

他们的重要作用已经显现出来，但推出"一带一路"以来，要求就更高。

"一带一路"中的商业机会

竞争既是挑战，也是机遇。虽然不乏商人对进入的中国企业与居民公司的竞争感到不安，但也有人积极迎接竞争，认为可以竞争可以推动创新，同时为消费者提供更多选择。结果取决于人们的观念、反应和克服办法。一方面，将带来竞争。例如，2017 年 7 月，福建省官员表示，投资者正在关注菲律宾的农业和采矿业。[1] 传统行业因阿里巴巴等高科技公司的到来感到威胁，这些公司

1　De Vera, Dale, China's Fujian targets more investments in PH with improved Manila-Beijing relations, InterAksyon, July 17 2017, http://www.interaksyon.com/chinas-fujian-targets-more-investments-in-ph-with-improved-manila-beijing-relations/.

拥有雄厚的资本和丰富的竞争经验。[1] 它们将与菲律宾公司形成竞争关系。另一方面，双方可以合资。在达沃，MarinaTuna 连锁餐厅经营方 Davao Marinatuna Corp. 正在与中国投资者合作开发高价值海产品。首席执行官 Domingo Ang 表示，水产养殖项目将在年底之前建造 40 个网箱养殖石斑鱼。[2] 鉴于其领先地位，华裔菲律宾人实际上可以从该倡议中受益匪浅，而"一带一路"倡议欢迎每个希望参与的人。

政策沟通和贸易畅通。华裔菲律宾人可以凭借人口规模、经济实力、政治影响力、族裔社区和媒体资源等优势为自身创造积极的条件，抓住机会并使其最大化。有准备的人可以直接获取或首先看到机会、政府计划和政策。

资金融通。"一带一路"倡议还意味着菲律宾公司可能有更好的机会在中国投资。菲律宾贸易和工业部及其附属机构一直在传播信息并为准备进入中国市场的菲律宾出口商举办信息发布会。随着世界日益一体化，这不仅是双向投资，还是参与国之间的相互投资，不同国家的多元化市场促使菲律宾公司调整产品和服务，迎合不同的喜好并在其他地区开展竞争。

如上一节所述，华裔菲律宾大型企业组织帮助赋能小型企业。为了加强对海上丝绸之路贸易的参与，中国银行正在与菲律宾贸易和工业部、菲律宾工商总会（PCCI）和菲律宾国际商会合作，将中小微企业与中国的同行联系起来。该银行还举行一系列会议，为企业提供利用国家机会的场合。300 多位中国和菲律宾企业家出席在马尼拉举行的商务对接会，中国副总理汪洋在会议上发表讲话。[3] PCCI 主席蔡聪妙表示，"中国银行正在寻找 500 家菲律宾中小微企业，提供 30 亿美元融资发展和帮助菲律宾企业取得资金、技术和市场协助"。[4] 该计划属于杜

1　Wei Lu, Filipino-Chinese Entrepreneurs under the "One Belt and One Road" Initiative: The Opportunities and Challenges, Chinese Studies Program Lecture Series, Ateneo de Manila University, 2017, No 4, pp. 105-123.

2　Francisco, Carmelito, Davao MarinaTuna partners with Chinese investors, Business World, September 25, 2017, http://bworldonline.com/davao-marinatuna-partners-chinese-investors/.

3　Xinhua, More than 300 Chinese, Philippine entrepreneurs show up in business matchmaking event in Manila, New China, March 20, 2017, http://news.xinhuanet.com/english/2017-03/20/c_136142239.htm.

4　Magkilat, Bernie, Bank of China seeks 500 Filipino MSMEs, Manila Bulletin, January 1, 2017, http://business.mb.com.ph/2017/01/01/bank-of-china-seeks-500-filipino-msmes/.

特尔特总统于 2016 年访问北京期间签署战略合作协议的一部分。[1] 华裔菲律宾人，不管是巨头，还是中小微企业主或初创企业家，都可以受益于资金融通。这个计划构成东盟对中小微企业关注的补充。[2]

此外，如果菲律宾人进行良好的谈判，可以充分利用"一带一路"倡议带来的技术和专门知识。菲律宾财政部长卡洛斯·多明格斯代表菲律宾政府与阿里巴巴的马云会晤，探讨金融科技、电子商务以及中国的经验。他在一份声明中指出："潜在的伙伴关系将有助于推动我国农村社区的经济增长，并为小企业创造公平的竞争环境"。金融科技和电子商务将使菲律宾人更多地参与市场和蓬勃发展。

互联互通和民心相通。除了竞争和新市场外，如果业务与"一带一路"倡议匹配（旅游和酒店业、房地产、建筑、制造业等），华裔菲律宾人仍然可以受益。仅旅游业一项，2017 年菲律宾的中国游客数量达到近百万，而 2016 年仅为 675,663 人次。从 2017 年 1 月至 2 月，游客到访人数与 2016 年同期相比增加 25.42%。[3] 根据菲律宾驻上海领事馆的数据，长滩岛、宿雾和公主港是最受中国游客喜爱的目的地，因为中国喜欢那里的海滩。

杜特尔特对北京进行国事访问期间，两国政府签订一项关于旅游的谅解备忘录，内容涉及：交流旅游专业人士和管理人员，交换旅游行业趋势信息，保证安全质量和推动前往对方国家旅游，联合推广活动、研讨会或培训，旅游基础设施投资。政府还计划放宽对中国人的签证。目前已有几家航空公司频繁地飞往中国。领先的菲律宾国家航空公司（PAL）已将飞往中国多个城市的航班从每周 99 次增加到 103 次[4]，开辟飞往海南的免签新航线。

1 Magkilat, Bernie, Bank of China vows to help enhance PH global trade ties, Manila Bulletin, March 10, 2017, http://business.mb.com.ph/2017/03/10/bank-of-china-vows-to-help-enhance-ph-global-trade-ties/.

2 Flores, Wilson Lee, How Philippine entrepreneurs can profit the trillion dollar Belt and Road, Philippine Star, May 15, 2017, http://www.philstar.com/business-life/2017/05/15/1699956/how-philippine-entrepreneurs-can-profit-trillion-dollar-belt-road.

3 Corrales, Nestor, 200% jump in Chinese visa application for PH visit—envoy, Inquirer.net, May 18, 2018, http://globalnation.inquirer.net/156890/200-jump-chinese-visa-applications-ph-visit-envoy#ixzz4hsRhasjA.

4 Xinhua, PAL to increase flights to China, China Plus, February 1, 2018, http://chinaplus.cri.cn/news/china/9/20180201/85960.html.

表 2: 2015 年至 2018 年 1 月 -5 月前往菲律宾人的中国游客 [1]

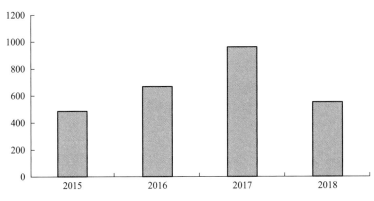

来源: 旅游部门

　　同时，在酒店行业，房地产开发商菲律宾双龙地产公司的晋江酒店是中国领先的连锁酒店，计划通过特许经营将其投资组合扩大到五家以上酒店。[2]

　　考虑到菲律宾吸引中国商务旅行人士和游客前往，蜂拥而至的人群对房地产业也产生影响。中国人的需求占到开发商向外国人销售房地产的大部分份额。自 2016 年 9 月以来，预计 100,000 名中国人涌入马尼拉。这要归功于菲律宾网络赌博行业强大的实力。自本届政府 19 个月前开始颁发执照以来，已有 50 多家离岸赌博公司获准经营。[3] 与酒店业类似，赌博行业也需要说中文的人参与市场营销、支付和回答国外客户的咨询。马尼拉大都会区的公寓销量直线上升。中国临时移民或游客的购买推高了房地产价格，对本地人而言价格昂贵。然而，如果两国间的网络赌博或移民政策突然发生变化，可能让房地产行业处于脆弱状态。[4]

　　两国政府都表示，"一带一路"倡议是菲律宾政府的"大建特建"计划的补充。根据声明，建筑业及工程和商业咨询公司都存在需求。这些公司甚至可以在项目

1　Department of Tourism, Tourists Arrivals to the Philippines 2015 – May 2018, https://drive.google.com/file/d/1oMa4U-FqqG3A1Fur-uOhCxcLbPQ-UBWJ/view.

2　Dumlao-Abadilla, Doris, DoubleDragon plans franchising Jinjiang, Inquirer.net, October 23, 2017, http://business.inquirer.net/239076/doubledragon-plans-franchising-jinjiang#ixzz4wxyoQ9Mc.

3　Bloomberg, Chinese Money Triggers a Dizzying Pally in Manila Properties, May 3, 2018, https://www.bloomberg.com/news/articles/2018-05-03/in-china-s-new-gambling-hot-spot-property-prices-are-on-a-tear.

4　Montealegre, Krista, Real estate developers cite China factor behind rising condo demand, Business World online, April 11, 2018, http://www.bworldonline.com/real-estate-developers-cite-china-factor-behind-rising-condo-demand/.

的早期阶段（例如方案提交或可行性研究）参与其中，从而允许更多的公司向政府提交创意和选择，为国家基础设施开发做出贡献。例如，在马拉维市重建过程中，"振兴马拉维财团"由 5 家中国公司和华裔菲律宾人拥有的 4 家菲律宾公司组成。然而，由于前者无法显示出重建该地区的经济能力，振兴马拉维财团目前正在考察其他前景。从长远来看，工程、城市规划等可能成为高等教育中的热门课程。

这些只是华裔菲律宾人受益于互联互通和民心相通的几个例子。此外，上述行业的投资可以为菲律宾人提供就业机会，预计将改变就业需求。

"一带一路"带来的挑战

上文讨论机会，挑战也不可避免。本节探讨菲中关系中让华裔菲律宾人处于不利地位的重要事件。

放眼来看，在授权政府同意与中国展开大规模合作的过程中，公众一直对两个关键问题持保留意见：过去菲律宾政府打交道的失败案例，例如中兴通讯菲律宾国家宽带网络项目、北方铁路项目以及领土和海上纠纷。据称中兴通讯定价过高，还涉嫌行贿某些个人和团体。丑闻起到提醒和警告的作用。出于同样的原因，前总统贝尼尼奥·阿基诺三世在与中国建立伙伴关系方面也非常谨慎。[1] 根据经验对中国资助的项目进行审查。还有关于南中国海的争端与发展、渔业事件以及其他方面的集体情感。

华裔菲律宾人是具有鲜明特点的特殊利益相关者。关于海上紧张局势，华裔菲律宾社区内部存在意见分歧。老一代华裔菲律宾人尊重菲律宾捍卫自身地位的权利，而年轻一代华裔作为菲律宾公民的观念已根深蒂固。根据中国研究教授艾琳·巴维耶拉（Aileen Baviera）的说法，不应简单认为两代人有分歧。他们都是务实的企业家，知道冲突对企业不利。[2] 他们对争端的态度因个人职业、教育或认知水平、对菲律宾和菲律宾人的看法、对中国教育的了解以及与传统中国文化

1　Mangahas, Malou, Manila, Beijing dating again: Who is the screwer, screwed? Philippine Center for Investigative Journalism, May 9, 2017, http://pcij.org/stories/manila-beijing-dating-again-who-is-the-screwer-screwed/.

2　Baviera, Aileen and Sascha Gallardo, "Filipino Media and Public Opinion on the Philippines-China Dsiputes in the South China Sea: A Preliminary Analysis" in Philippines-China Relations: Sailing beyond Disputes Waters (2013), Teresita Ang See and Chito Sta. Romana. Philippine Association for Chinese Studies, Chinese Studies Journal Volume 10. pp. 132-171.

的距离而异。[1] Baviera 和 Gallardo 表示："他们的历史和文化，也许还有商业利益，继续将部分人与中国联系起来，这一事实可以用来理解他们双重身份认同困难，但目前的社会环境、经济生活、政治经验和未来愿望与其他菲律宾人没有什么不同。"[2]

在《Tulay 双周刊》的一个专栏中，一位著名的社会活动领袖与菲律宾华裔民间协会共同创始人洪玉华女士指出："华裔菲律宾人被卷入争端。无论哪一方是对还是错，他们目前都不能表达个人偏好，避免产生不良后果或落入菲律宾鹰派将军手中。华裔菲律宾人可以做的就是利用他们的影响力作为缓和冲突的后备渠道。"[3]

华裔社区彼此之间避免讨论这些问题，特别是在公开场合。[4] 然而，在某些情况下，他们私下交谈。

虽然上届政府态度不太友好，但在阿基诺任期内也启动了菲律宾加入亚投行的谈判。[5] 分析人员丁度·曼希德（Dindo Manhit）表示，这表明马尼拉通过经济外交与北京成为朋友做出新的努力。[6] 时任财政部长 Ceasar Purisima 指出，阿基诺政府发现亚投行是西方领导机构以外的补充资金来源。

至于基础设施合作，即使政府官员参加"一带一路"倡议活动、大量投资和签署协议，外交部尚未就菲律宾参加"一带一路"倡议做出正式决定。菲律宾国家经济发展署的一位官员说，不论中国人是否将其称为"一带一路"项目，这些项目都是为菲律宾国内发展而设计的。他们补充说，"一带一路"是从中国人的角度给出的定义。[7] 官僚机构内部存在各种各样的观点，因此缺乏一致的中国政策。

例如，中菲友谊桥也因必要性和社区影响而受到批评。洪玉华女士认为"不

1　Baviera, Aileen and Sascha Gallardo, "Filipino Media and Public Opinion on the Philippines-China Dsiputes in the South China Sea: A Preliminary Analysis" in Philippines-China Relations: Sailing beyond Disputes Waters (2013), Teresita Ang See and Chito Sta. Romana. Philippine Association for Chinese Studies, Chinese Studies Journal Volume 10. pp. 132-171.

2　同上.

3　Ang See, Teresita, Tulay Fortnightly cited in Baviera and Gallardo (2013).

4　Interview with informant, a former FFCCCII official, by Baviera and Gallardo (2013).

5　Wong, Andrea Chloe, The Asian Infrastructure Investment Bank: Considerations for the Philippines, CIRSS Commentaries, Foreign Service Institute, May 2015, Vol 2, No 11.

6　Rappler, Rappler Talk: Will PH, China improve ties in 2016? January 8, 2016, https://www.rappler.com/nation/118277-rapplertalk-ph-china-ties-2016-dindo-manhit.

7　Uy, Jonathan. Interview with NEDA Public Investment Staff, March 13, 2018.

会造成交通拥堵，那不是问题"。[1] 这座桥需要道路使用者首先穿越作为文化遗产地的围墙城市狭窄街道。她指出人行桥或防洪方面的用处更大。[2]

一方面，华裔菲律宾人仍然是菲律宾人。另一方面，他们与中国有联系，一个含义接近的概念是"关系"。中国的关系概念有几种定义，但从广义上讲，它是"一种社会结构，非正式的个人联系，是指个人期待其他人提供帮助作为过去的回报或期望将来获得帮助。"[3] 人际网络中的成员密切合作，互相支持，提供最新的业务信息。[4] 然而，近些年，虽然族裔纽带得以维持，但正在改变为非正式的纽带，例如行为规范、制度和专业精神。[5]

本文并不要求华裔菲律宾人在两国之间做出选择，而是承认挑战并思考如何平衡。

在中国投资面临的挑战是对中国的新投资和市场认识不足。曾在马尼拉雅典耀大学交流的中国学者魏路（音）以福建的购物中心为例。市场有不同的客户及偏好；人们不再去逛购物中心。他在论文中详细阐述福建的购物中心并未改变业务经营方法，因此无法产生预期的结果。

展望未来

华裔菲律宾人，特别是商人，确实在推动菲中关系的进一步发展并帮助菲律宾国内发展。华裔菲律宾人的贡献非常大，特别是政府间未进行谈话时作为双方的润滑剂。这种关系得以在经济方面延续。

华裔菲律宾人是"一带一路"倡议五个优先事项的重要组成部分，在日趋一体化的世界中，一个优先事项很难与其他优先事项区分开。通过投资和跨国经营，他们与菲律宾政府共同努力改善经济状况。如果有能力，他们可以加强信息传播、宣传活动和政策讨论；越来越多的商业机构不仅为学者，还为雇员提供奖学金计划。他们与学术界、社会活动家、民间社会利益相关者（例如在能源、环境领域）

1　Robles, Raissa, 'We need it like we need a hole in our head': Chinese friendship bridge in Manila not so popular with the locals, South China Morning Post, January 18, 2018, https://www.scmp.com/news/asia/southeast-asia/article/2129448/we-need-it-we-need-hole-our-head-chinese-friendship-bridge.

2　Ibid.

3　Clemente, Tina, Guanxi in Chinese Commerce: Informal Enforcement in Spanish Philippines, Seoul Journal of Economics, 2013, Vol 26, No 2, pp. 203-237.

4　Po (2010).

5　See Clemente (2013) and Po (2010).

进一步合作,让棉兰老岛和米沙鄢群岛的组织加入对话中。

另一方面,中国应利用和通过华裔菲律宾人进行政策沟通,特别是建立互信和达成共识;在资金融通方面,他们可以走出去,搭建联系中小微企业的桥梁;关于贸易畅通,可以参与自由贸易协定、消除贸易壁垒和透明度等谈判。互联互通正在推进中。项目实施应严格遵守规定,选择具有成本效益和生态可持续性的项目,建设优质的基础设施。华裔菲律宾人商人李栋梁指出,有成本效益的项目具有动态价值,其循环效应可以改善工作和收入等其他方面。关于静态价值的项目,其价值在于人们是否情愿为此付出代价,因此项目不会产生资金。[1]菲律宾政府考虑投标人的技术专长和报价,因此中国应提供更好的议价。

在"一带一路"倡议时代,中国和菲律宾在发展上有部分相似之处,这可以作为合作的基础,共同文化的亲和力也有助于推动合作。许多合作正在进行,新机遇也伴随挑战。

1　Siy, George, Interview on March 2017.

Tsinoys in Times of the Belt and Road Initiative

Grace Guiang / Philippines

Research Analyst of Asian-Pacific Progress Foundation

Since president Xi Jinping announced the Belt and Road Initiative in 2013, the Chinese leadership has directed its government units, state-owned enterprises, and the media to promote the Initiative in full swing, at different levels. Introducing a bold plan to the world, China has approached the participating countries bilaterally, and multilaterally through the Asian Infrastructure Investment Bank and regional organizations, among others. Cooperation priorities include policy coordination, facilities connectivity, unimpeded trade, financial integration, and people-to-people bond. Chinese entrepreneurs were given the green light to conduct business overseas, especially in places along the economic belt. In effort to break into Southeast Asia, the country has also acknowledged the role and contributions of the ethnic Chinese community in accelerating the entering of the BRI. Given their personal network and shared language and culture, the overseas Chinese community have become facilitators of inward foreign investments and have the know-how in local business setting, laws and people. While they are seen as aid to the success of BRI, they are confronted with past experience and patriotism which challenge their dealing with entrepreneurs from China. In the Philippines, Chinese Filipinos embrace the pouring of investment from their neighboring country as opportunity, and are eager to participate in BRI projects. However, they are likewise aware that major dealings of the Philippine government failed in the past and that the Philippines has disputes with China. The recent years however have showed that economics and people-to-people allow relations to continue and even improved despite disputes and skeptical public opinion. This paper examines how ethnic Chinese community in the Philippines balances their Chinese roots (and guanxi) and Filipino patriotism. They are not only patriotic but also pragmatic as most of their businesses are in the Philippines, and yet their second or third generation may have little connection with China. What are their opportunities and challenges in the context of the BRI? How can China maximize the role and contributions of overseas Chinese communities? It is hoped that this paper would bring insight and understanding on the Chinese Filipinos in the era of the BRI.

China's Economic Belt

The five-year old Belt and Road Initiative (BRI) is an economic scheme that offers an alternative cooperation model whose priorities include policy coordination, facilities connectivity, unimpeded trade, policy integration, and people-to-people bond. It is a combination of revived ancient silk roads, existing ones, and recently proposed new routes (i.e., in the maritime and the Artic routes). Primarily the proponent, China, is experiencing surplus of resources in finance, technology, and labor, causing the country to think creatively of ways to use such assets productively. While developing states need assistance to build infrastructure that will boost their own economies, China sees this as an opportunity to advance its going-out policy at the same time forge cooperation with the rest of the world. In other words, China's overcapacity can fill in the demands of other countries.

According to former President of Shanghai Academy of Social Sciences (SASS) Wang Zhan, the BRI serves as a platform for China to share its experience in reform and opening-up to developing countries.[1] Its long-term vision aims to build a community of shared interests, destiny, and responsibility featuring mutual trust, economic integration, and cultural inclusiveness. International Relations professor Zhang Zhenjiang, Dean of School for International Studies in Jinan University, even described the BRI as a basket where parties could place in capital, products and services for others to choose from. It is a contribution of China to international trade and the global economy[2]—a landmark program of President Xi that is now largely taking a lead role in its diplomacy and international relations.

Grand as it seems, five years of introductory phase to the world was not smooth sailing. While 65 participating countries[3] welcomed the Initiative, some are still contemplating to get on board. Japan for instance despite a robust trade relations with China only allows its private sector to do "business with China as part of the initiative", and the rest remains on a case-to-case basis. There has been no policy for Tokyo's official line yet. The initiative has also been criticized for lack of transparency or for inducing borrowing state into a 'debt-trap'. At this period, some bilateral agreements were cancelled; some were modified. However in its defense, Chinese scholars expressed that the BRI is still young. China itself is likewise learning from all its engagements and cooperation, thus scholars observed a more careful transactions recently compared to its aggressive move four or five years ago.

The BRI is highly and widely promoted at all levels, in all fronts—from the government to enterprises, the media to socio-cultural exchanges. The Chinese government recognizes the pivotal role of the overseas Chinese to its relations with other countries specifically in its backyard region. Another professor of International Studies Ju Hailong said, if China wants BRI to succeed in the South China rim, it needs to have an economic base. It can be done because China shares similar culture

---

1 Wang Zhan, former President of Shanghai Academy of Social Science, during APPFI courtesy call on June 1, 2018.
2 Zhang Zhenjiang, The BRI from the perspective of International Relations, presented at the School for International Studies, Jinan University on May 14, 2018.
3 As of the submission of this paper, September 1, 2018.

and development with Southeast Asian countries.[1] A part of this base is the ethnic Chinese community in Southeast Asia, which is a distinguished factor as compared to China's relations in Africa and Europe. They are the gateway of Chinese inward investments and business ventures from the mainland, and the bridge that connects Chinese enterprises to its neighboring countries. Aside from having a better grasp of the business environment, laws and procedures in their home countries, they understand the languages of both nations and have acquired local network.

This paper looks into the ethnic Chinese community in the Philippines and their role in Philippines-China relations under the backdrop of BRI. The following sections also discuss the opportunities and challenges of the Chinese Filipinos under the Initiative.

Tsinoysin Philippines and China relations

The ethnic Chinese community in the Philippines is composed of the older generation Filipino-Chinese, the younger generation Chinese Filipinos or Tsinoys (TsinongPinoy), the new immigrants, and Chinese as tourists and temporary visitors.

The older generation has Chinese identity but has acquired Filipino citizenship, while Chinese Filipinos are young, native-born ethnic Chinese who identify themselves as Filipinos first but still maintain Chinese cultural identity.[2] The matrix below differentiated the first two classifications of ethnic Chinese, who make up 1-2% of the Philippine population but have a market capital share between 50-55% as they are predominantly business owners. In the recent release of *Forbes*, Tsinoy tycoons like John Gokongwei, Henry Sy, Lucio Tan, George Ty have made to its list of billionaires.[3]

1 JuHailong, Economic Base and Social Policy Space of the Belt and Road Initiative in the South Sea Rim of China, presented at the School for International Studies, Jinan University on May 16, 2018.
2 Po, Gerley, A Comparative Analysis of the Entrepreneurial Styles of Second, Third, and Fourth Generation Overseas Chinese and Filipinos in the Philippines, DLSU Business & Economics Review, 2010, 19-2, pp. 11-23.
3 Rappler, Henry Sy still leads Filipinos on Forbes' 2018 billionaire list,March 7, 2018, https://www. rappler.com/business/197591-filipinos-forbes-world-billionaires-list-2018.

Table 1　Old immigrant huaqiao vs. young generation Tsinoys[1]

Older Generation	Younger Generation
• Born before the Pacific war	• Born after the Pacific war
• Born in China, usually have Chinese name	• Born in the Philippines, usually have adopted a Christian name
• Have deep sentiments toward China and firsthand or at least childhood experiences of China	• Identify more with the Philippines and have no firsthand experience of China
• Can easily cross ethnic barriers, socialize both with Chinese and Filipinos, at ease in both environments	• Confine their lives and activities within the Chinese community, socialize more with Chinese
• Join family and hometown associations, local chambers of commerce	• Join Filipino groups like Rotary, Jaycees, Lions Club
• First language is Chinese.	• Have greater facility in using Tagalog [Filipino, Bisaya] or English
• Attend only Chinese-language schools or minimal college	• Attend Philippine colleges or universities
• Very Chinese in looks and lifestyle, observe Chinese rites and traditions, use Chinese form of social conventions and etiquette	• Westernized in taste, values, and lifestyle, observe minimum of traditional Chinese rites
• Consider China as motherland and the Philippines as second home	• Consider the Philippines as home and have no deep attachment to China

Source: Presentation of TeresitaAng See during In Search for a China Strategy symposium

This paper focuses on the young generation Tsinoys as, in present, they actively contribute to the nation-building not only through economics but also in policy-making and socio-cultural undertakings. Their roles in the Philippines-China relations are among others, business facilitator, as bridge between the two governments, as filler between gaps, frontrunner that assists micro, small and medium enterprises (MSMEs), stakeholder in policy-making, and supporter of educational and cultural exchanges.

1　Ang See, Teresita, Migration Trends and their Socio-economic Implications: The Ethnic Chinese Community, presented at In Search for a China Strategy symposium on August 17-18, 2016 at the UP Asian Center Auditorium.

First, the Chinese Filipinos wear the hat of business facilitator that involves two aspects: know-how and network. In line with its Go Global policy, China encourages its enterprises to expand business abroad. This, plus the cultural and language affinity, allows the Chinese to directly approach Tsinoys in a more local setting. A part of this direct approach can be attributed to China's signature relations by cities or provinces—known as sister-city or sister-province—hence more local entry points become unsurprising and inevitable. At present, there are 24 sister-cities or -provinces between the two neighbors. This is where the knowledge and network of Chinese Filipinos become important. They know the business environment, laws, market, government agencies involved; and can provide a network of potential partners and consultants. Advantageously, Tsinoys lessen the language barrier between both peoples. Aside from Mandarin, they can also speak Fujianese, making it easier for partners from Fujian province.

Second is their role to bridge the two governments. Influential Chinese Filipinos—mostly entrepreneurs who have significantly contributed to Philippines' relations with China and the broader societies—serve as special envoy. To take an example, Special Envoy Mr. Carlos Chan, chairman of the Oishi Group Limited Company, has paved way for trade and exchanges of the two countries. Notably, his contributions and engagements are recounted in an exhibit at an overseas Chinese museum in Guangzhou.

This banner that shows the engagements of Mr. Carlos Chan, a Chinese Filipino businessman and Philippine Special Envoy to China, was exhibited at Guangdong Overseas Chinese Museum.

Another instance, these business people were part of the delegation during Philippine president Rodrigo Duterte's state visit in Beijing in 2016. More than 300 business leaders, including an executive from leading Philippine conglomerate SM

Investments, accompanied him.[1] Both governments witnessed the signing of agreements and letters of intent between public and private officials, which brought home a $24 billion worth of investments and credit line pledges.

Third, the Chinese Filipinos act as fillers in times when official lines have very little improvement. Both the Philippine government and the private sector aimed to prevent economic consequences due to political conflicts. During the height of disputes in the South China Sea, economic relations remained relatively in good state. Despite China banning 27 Philippine companies exporting banana and

---

1   Yamada,Shuhei and Endo, Jun, China, Philippines forge friendship of convenience, Nikkei Asian Review, October 21, 2016, https://asia.nikkei.com/Politics/China-Philippines-forge-friendship-of-convenience.

pineapple and had issued a travel advisory, trade increased from 2010 to 2014 yet dropped in 2015. Philippine import in fact rose 135% from 2010 to 2015, but trade in 2015 was pulled down by Philippine export, widening the trade gap.[1] Filipino scholars of Economics interpreted this outcome of China's actions in opposing views. Prof. Ellen Palanca argues that the decrease of Philippine export to China was due to lower demands for Chinese products in the West, considering that these exports were part of global value chains.[2] Meanwhile, Prof. Tina Clemente pointed out that the big trade deficits in 2013 to 2015 raised concerns that they were caused by the disputes.[3]

If it was right that there were no recognizable effects in the bigger bilateral trade that were caused by the maritime tensions (as to the specific banana export sector), then Prof.Ju was correct in explaining that politics and economics are parallel; they do not intersect.[4] Indeed, in the absence of government-to-government talks, it is the academe or also known as the track 2.0 and the business sector that make the relations continue.

Fourth, prominent Chinese Filipino business organizations such as the Philippine Chamber of Commerce and Industry (PCCI) assist MSMEs to innovate to be able to participate in bigger markets through training and business matching. Opportunities for MSMEs will be discussed in the next section.

Due to big shares of capital, tycoons in general become important stakeholders in policy-making. They aid the government in financing and operating major infrastructure projects—the so-called Public-Private Partnership. Their businesses are in line with the BRI projects and are in relevant industries like aviation,

---

1   Philippine Consulate General in Shanghai, Briefer for Asia Pacific Pathways to Progress Foundation, Inc. during the think tank's official visit on May 31, 2018.
2   Palanca, Ellen, Presentation at In Search of a China Strategy: Unpacking the Bilateral and Regional Dynamics of Philippines-China Relations on August 17-18, 2016 at the UP Asian Center.
3   Clemente, Tina, "Understanding the Economic Diplomacy between the Philippines and China," International Journal of China Studies, 2016, 7(2), p.217.
4   JuHailong, Economic Base and Social Policy Space of the Belt and Road Initiative in the South Sea Rim of China, presented at the School for International Studies, Jinan University on May 16, 2018.

banking, construction, real estate, and tourism; and so they are consulted in matters of their expertise. They have the capability to give unsolicited advice, set agenda, and propose projects. According to a geospatial and social network analysis, the Federation of Filipino Chinese Chamber of Commerce Industry Inc. (FFCCCII) and the PCCI "provide potential pathways for translating its economic might into influence with the Philippines".[1] Further, some participate in political events and processes or speak out opinions on issues like Charter Change and tax reforms.

Tsinoys' roles under the BRI

From the bilateral relations, Tsinoys' roles cascade into the five priorities of the BRI. In policy coordination, they can echo shared values of the 21st Century Maritime Silk Road—since the Philippines would be covered by the maritime leg—and sync these with local government's development strategies and plans. Specifically, they can convey complementarity of long-term plans through campaigns and political contributions.

Tsinoys can act as workers, investors, and coordinators to promote the facilitation of connectivity; and act as contributors and promoters of unimpeded trade between or among the countries along the Silk Road, possibly linking other ethnic Chinese in the Southeast Asia region. They can also work with relevant financial institutions such as the AIIB, Bank of China, and Export-Import Bank to provide cross-border RMB settlement, loans, payments and other financial services to businesses—extendingopportunities to those from the periphery to participate in the international setting.

Moreover, they can serve as disseminators and initiators of bonds in the ideas and spirit of the 21st Century Maritime Silk Road. They can strengthen socio-culturaltiesthrough educational and cultural exchanges which fit to the people-to-people bond priority of the BRI. For instance, Lucio Tan annually sends hundreds of

---

1 Fleck, Tanner and Wissler, Jonathan, Economic preparation of the environment: A selective empirical analysis of Chinese investment in the Philippines, 2016, Naval Postgraduate School, p.83.

students to different cities in China for a two-month root-seeking camp.Exchanges do not have to remain with the academe, rather it should open for companies through trainings and awareness campaign for employees and young professionals. The Gokongwei's, for example, offers scholarships for young Filipino professionals to learn Chinese language and culture in China.

Many of these important roles have already manifested, but there is a demand for more since BRI was introduced.

Business opportunities in the BRI

Competition is both a challenge and an opportunity. While some businesspeople fret about competition between inbound Chinese enterprises and resident companies, some positively embrace competition as something that would push them to innovate and offer more, at the same time, provide options for consumers. The results depend on how people perceive it, respond to it, and approach towards overcoming it. On one hand, there will be competition. For instance in July 2017, officials from Fujian province said that investors are looking at agricultural and mining sectors in the Philippines.[1]Traditional industries feel threatened with the coming of high-tech companies like Alibaba who have strong capital and rich experience in competition.[2] This would pose competition to Filipino-owned firms. On the other hand, they can conduct joint ventures. In Davao, Davao Marinatuna Corp., operator of MarinaTuna chain of restaurants, is partnering with a Chinese investor for high-value marine products. Chief Executive Officer Domingo Ang presented that the aquaculture project would involve grouper farming through the construction of 40 fish cages before the year ends.[3] Given their lead roles, the

1   De Vera, Dale, China' s Fujian targets more investments in PH with improved Manila-Beijing relations, InterAksyon, July 17 2017, http://www.interaksyon.com/chinas-fujian-targets-more-investments-in-ph-with-improved-manila-beijing-relations/.

2   Wei Lu, Filipino-Chinese Entrepreneurs under the "Belt and Road" Initiative: The Opportunities and Challenges, Chinese Studies Program Lecture Series,Ateneo de Manila University, 2017, No 4, pp. 105-123.

3   Francisco,Carmelito, Davao MarinaTuna partners with Chinese investors, Business World, September 25, 2017, http://bworldonline.com/davao-marinatuna-partners-chinese-investors/.

Chinese Filipinos are actually one of the communities who can benefit a lot from the Initiative, but the BRI is inclusive for everyone to wants to participate.

Policy coordination and unimpeded trade. With their advantages in terms of population size, economic power, political influence, ethnic community, and media resources, Tsinoys can create positive conditions for themselves to seize and maximize the opportunities. The established ones certainly have direct access or first-glance of opportunities, government plans, and policies.

Financial integration. The BRI also means that Filipino companies may have better chance to invest in China. The Department of Trade and Industry and its attached agencies have been disseminating information and conducting info sessions for Philippine exporters to prepare before entering the China market. As the world is getting more integrated, this is not only a two-way investment, but also among participating countries whose diverse markets push Filipino companies to adjust products and services to cater different preferences as well as to compete elsewhere.

As mentioned in the previous section, Chinese Filipino big business organizations help empower small businesses. To enhance participation in the maritime silk road trade, the Bank of China is working with the DTI, PCCI, and the International Chamber of Commerce Philippines to connect MSMEs with counterparts in China. The bank also hosted a series of conferences to provide venue where they could tap international opportunities. More than 300 Chinese and Philippine entrepreneurs participated in business matchmaking in Manila, where Chinese Vice Premier Wang Yang graced the event.[1] "Bank of China is searching for 500 Filipino MSMEs that could be granted financing, technology and marketing assistance under its $3-billion program to develop and promote Philippine enterprises," PCCI Chairman Emeritus Francis Chua said.[2] This initiative falls under the inked Strategic Cooperation

---

1 Xinhua, More than 300 Chinese, Philippine entrepreneurs show up in business matchmaking event in Manila, New China, March 20, 2017, http://news.xinhuanet.com/english/2017-03/20/c_136142239.htm.

2 Magkilat, Bernie, Bank of China seeks 500 Filipino MSMEs, Manila Bulletin, January 1, 2017, http://business.mb.com.ph/2017/01/01/bank-of-china-seeks-500-filipino-msmes/.

Agreement with the parties, also signed during Duterte's visit in Beijing in 2016.[1]Here, Tsinoys—be a tycoon, a MSME owner, or a start-up entrepreneur—can also benefit from financial integration. This timely program can complement with ASEAN's focus on MSMEs as well.[2]

Moreover, the BRI brings in technology and expertise that if negotiated well the Filipinos by large could take advantage of them. Finance Chief Carlos Dominguez leads the Philippine government to explore financial technology and e-commerce and China's experience when he met with Alibaba's Jack Ma. In a statement he said that "the potential partnership would help fuel economic growth in the country's rural communities and level the playing field for small businesses". Financial technology and e-commerce will allow people to be more engaged in the market and for connectivity to thrive in the country.

Connectivity and People-to-people Bond.Aside from competition and new markets, Chinese Filipinos whose businesses are in line with the BRI—tourism and hospitality industry, real estate, construction, manufacturing, to name a few— can benefit tremendously. In tourism alone, the Chinese arrival to the Philippines reached to almost a million visitors in 2017 compared to only 675,663 arrivals recorded in 2016. From January to February 2017, a 25.42 percent increase in the number of tourist arrivals was recorded compared to the same period in 2016.[3] According to the Philippine Consulate in Shanghai, Boracay, Cebu, and Puerto Prinsesa are the most visited destinations as the Chinese are fond of enjoying the beach.

1   Magkilat, Bernie, Bank of China vows to help enhance PH global trade ties, Manila Bulletin, March 10, 2017, http://business.mb.com.ph/2017/03/10/bank-of-china-vows-to-help-enhance-ph-global-trade-ties/.

2   Flores, Wilson Lee, How Philippine entrepreneurs can profit the trillion dollar Belt and Road, Philippine Star, May 15, 2017, http://www.philstar.com/business-life/2017/05/15/1699956/how-philippine-entrepreneurs-can-profit-trillion-dollar-belt-road.

3   Corrales, Nestor, 200% jump in Chinese visa application for PH visit—envoy, Inquirer.net, May 18, 2018, http://globalnation.inquirer.net/156890/200-jump-chinese-visa-applications-ph-visit-envoy#ixzz4hsRhasjA.

Table 2: Chinese arrivals in the Philippines from 2015 – January-May 2018[1]

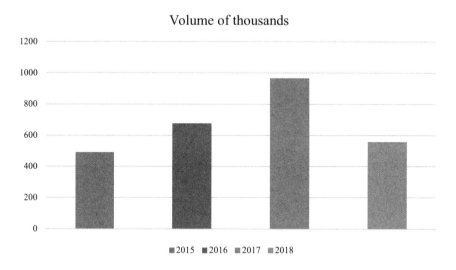

Volume of thousands

■2015 ■2016 ■2017 ■2018

Source: Department of Tourism

During Duterte's state visit in Beijing, the two governments signed a MoU on tourism which tackles: exchange of tourism professionals and administrators, trade of information on trends in tourism industry, measures to guarantee safety and quality assurance, promote the other's destinations, joint promotions and activities, workshops or trainings for the other party, and investment in tourism infrastructure. The government also plans to ease visa for the Chinese. In relation to these, several airlines are now flying more often to China. The flag carrier Philippine Airlines (PAL) has increased flights to several cities in China from 99 times to 103 times weekly[2], and has launched new route to visa-free Hainan.

Meanwhile for hospitality industry, property developer Double Dragon Properties Corps' Jinjiang Inn, a leading hotel chains in China, plans to expand its portfolio to

1 Department of Tourism, Tourists Arrivals to the Philippines 2015 – May 2018, https://drive.google. com/file/d/1oMa4U-FqqG3A1Fur-uOhCxcLbPQ-UBWJ/view.

2 Xinhua, PAL to increase flights to China, China Plus, February 1, 2018,http://chinaplus.cri.cn/news/ china/9/20180201/85960.html.

five company-owned hotels and more via franchising.[1]

As the Philippines attracts Chinese visitors primarily for business and tourism, the flock has yielded impacts on real estate. Real estate developers accounts for majority of their sales to foreigners as there is a demand from Chinese. An estimate of 100,000 Chinese have flooded into Manila since September 2016. This is due to the strength of Philippine online gaming operators industry in the country. More than 50 offshore gambling companies were permitted to operate since the current administration began awarding licenses 19 months ago.[2] Similar to the hospitality industry, the gaming industry need Chinese speakers who can attend to marketing, payment, and inquiries from customers abroad. Condominium sales in Metro Manila rose. The purchase by the Chinese temporary immigrants or visitors drive up prices, causing it be expensive for the locals. This, however, might leave the real estate industry vulnerable in the event of abrupt changes in online gaming or immigration policies from either the two countries.[3]

Both governments said the BRI complements with the Philippine government's Build Build Build program. Having claimed that, there is a demand for the construction industry as well as engineering and business consultancy firms. These firms can take part even during the early stages of a project such as proposal submission or the feasibility studies—allowing more companies to present ideas and options to the government and contribute to the infrastructure development of the country. For example in the rehabilitating Marawi City, members of the then BangonMarawi Consortium include five Chinese firms and four local firms which were owned by Chinese Filipinos. However due

1   Dumlao-Abadilla,Doris, DoubleDragon plans franchising Jinjiang, Inquirer.net, October 23, 2017, http://business.inquirer.net/239076/doubledragon-plans-franchising-jinjiang#ixzz4wxyoQ9Mc.
2   Bloomberg, Chinese Money Triggers a Dizzying Pally in Manila Properties, May 3, 2018, https://www.bloomberg.com/news/articles/2018-05-03/in-china-s-new-gambling-hot-spot-property-prices-are-on-a-tear.
3   Montealegre, Krista, Real estate developers cite China factor behind rising condo demand, Business World online, April 11, 2018, http://www.bworldonline.com/real-estate-developers-cite-china-factor-behind-rising-condo-demand/.

to the former being unable to show financial capacity to rebuild the area, the Marawi rehabilitation task force is now checking other prospects. In the long term, engineering, urban planning, and the like might become an in-demand program in tertiary education.

These are just few examples on how Chinese Filipinos can benefit from connectivity and people-to-people bond.Furthermore, investments on these industries could provide job creation and opportunity for Filipinos, but expect to have changes in employment demand.

BRI on the challenges

The opportunities discussed above are not exempted from challenges. This section brings up important events in Philippines-China relations that have put the Chinese Filipino community in an unwanted position.

To put things in perspective, two key issues have always been a source of reservation of the public in giving the government consent to have many cooperation with China: the failed past dealings with the Philippine government such as the NBN-ZTE broadband project and the North railway dealings, and the territorial and maritime disputes. The former was alleged overpricing and anomalous payment to certain individuals and groups. The scandals serve as a reminder and a warning. The same reason made former President Benigno S. Aquino III very cautious in making partnership with China.[1] From the experience, Chinese-funded projects are being scrutinized. More than that is the collective sentiments with regard to the disputes and development in the South China Sea, fishery incidents, among others.

The Tsinoys are special stakeholder with unique characteristics. There is a divided opinions within the Chinese Filipino community as regards the maritime tensions.

1　Mangahas, Malou, Manila, Beijing dating again: Who is the screwer, screwed? Philippine Center for Investigative Journalism, May 9, 2017, http://pcij.org/stories/manila-beijing-dating-again-who-is-the-screwer-screwed/.

The older Tsinoys respects the Philippines' right to defend its position, while the younger generation are already deeply rooted as Filipino citizens. According to Chinese Studies professor Aileen Baviera, one should not oversimplify them into only two divide. They are pragmatic entrepreneurs and they know that conflict are not good for business.[1] Their attitudes towards the disputes differ depending on one's occupation, level of education or awareness, perceptions of the Philippines and Filipinos, exposure to Chinese education and being far from traditional Chinese culture.[2] Baviera and Gallardo put it:

> The dilemmas of their hyphenated identity can be understood from the fact that their history and culture, and perhaps business interests, continue to connect some of them to China, but their current social context, economic life, political experiences and for the most part their aspirations for the future are the same as other Filipinos.[3]

In one column in *Tulay Fortnightly*, a prominent community leader who co-founded a Filipino-Chinese civil society group Teresita Ang See said:

> Tsinoys are the ones caught in the crossfire. No matter which side is right or wrong, they cannot play favorites at this point lest it backfire on them and they also fall into the hands of our (Filipino) hawkish generals. What Tsinoys can do is to use their influence as backdoor channels to cool the fever of conflict.[4]

The community avoided discussions on the issues whether among themselves and especially in public.[5] However, there are instances where they talked in private.

1　Baviera, Aileen and Sascha Gallardo, "Filipino Media and Public Opinion on the Philippines-China Dsiputes in the South China Sea: A Preliminary Analysis" in Philippines-China Relations: Sailing beyond Disputes Waters (2013), TeresitaAng See and Chito Sta. Romana. Philippine Association for Chinese Studies, Chinese Studies Journal Volume 10. pp. 132-171.

2　*Ibid.*

3　*Ibid.*

4　Ang See, Teresita, Tulay Fortnightly cited in Baviera and Gallardo (2013).

5　Interview with informant, a former FFCCCII official, byBaviera and Gallardo (2013).

Despite a less friendly approach of the previous administration, negotiations for the Philippines' membership to AIIB began even during Aquino's term.[1] Analyst DindoManhit said that this showed Manila's renewed effort to befriend Beijing via economic diplomacy despite the disputes.[2] The then Finance Secretary CeasarPurisima said that the Aquino government found AIIB a complementary source of funding with the Western-led institutions.

As for infrastructure cooperation, despite government officials attending BRI events, the pour of investments, and the signing of agreements, the Department of Foreign Affairs has not made official line as to the Philippines participation to the BRI. According to a NEDA official, projects are for internal development of the Philippines whether the Chinese identify or call these as BRI projects. Belt and Road is a definition from the Chinese perspective, they added.[3] There are diverse views within the bureaucracy, thus the lack of a coherent China policy.

The friendship bridge, for example, has also been criticized over necessity and community impact. Ang-See argued, "It will not decongest traffic because that's not the problem."[4] The bridge requires road users to first pass through the narrow streets of the walled city of Intramuros, a culture and heritage site. She suggested a footbridge or flood control would be more useful instead.[5]

On one hand, Tsinoys are Filipinos. On the other hand, they still have connections in China and one concept not too far off is guanxi. The Chinese concept of guanxi has several definitions, but broadly speaking it is a "social

---

1 Wong, Andrea Chloe, The Asian Infrastructure Investment Bank: Considerations for the Philippines, CIRSS Commentaries, Foreign Service Institute, May 2015, Vol 2, No 11.

2 Rappler, Rappler Talk: Will PH, China improve ties in 2016? January 8, 2016, https://www.rappler.com/nation/118277-rapplertalk-ph-china-ties-2016-dindo-manhit.

3 Uy, Jonathan. Interview with NEDA Public Investment Staff, March 13, 2018.

4 Robles, Raissa, 'We need it like we need a hole in our head': Chinese friendship bridge in Manila not so popular with the locals, South China Morning Post, January 18, 2018, https://www.scmp.com/news/asia/southeast-asia/article/2129448/we-need-it-we-need-hole-our-head-chinese-friendship-bridge.

5 *Ibid.*

construct, informal personalistic ties where one expects the other to do a favor in return for a past or in expectation of a future service."[1] Members of the network work in close cooperation, backing up each other, and providing updates of business information.[2] In recent times however, while ethnic ties lives on, they are changes into this informal ties such as standardization of practices, institutions, and professionalism.[3]

This paper, however, does not require Chinese Filipinos to choose between the two countries, rather to acknowledge that the challenge here is how to balance.

In terms of investing in China, another challenge is the insufficient understanding of the Chinese new investment and market. Wei Lu, a Chinese scholar who attended a fellowship at the Ateneo de Manila University, cited SM in Fujian as an example. Markets have different customers and their preferences; they no longer go to the mall. SM in Fujian has not changed business methods which causing it not to yield the expected results, his paper elaborated.[4]

Moving forward

The roles of Chinese Filipinos especially the businesspeople are indeed helpful in furthering Philippines-China relations and to the internal development of the Philippines. The Tsinoys have made significant contributions particularly as fillers when governments are not talking. The economic aspects made relations possible to continue.

Tsinoys are very much part of the five priorities of the BRI, in which one priority is difficult to separate from other in a world that is becoming more and more integrated. Through their investments and multinational undertakings, they work together with the Philippine government to advance economic conditions. Having

---

1   Clemente, Tina, Guanxi in Chinese Commerce: Informal Enforcement in Spanish Philippines, Seoul Journal of Economics, 2013, Vol 26, No 2, pp. 203-237.
2   Po (2010).
3   As seen in Clemente's (2013) and Po's (2010) papers.
4   Wei Lu (2017).

the means, they could intensify information dissemination, awareness campaign, and policy discussion; and more business establishments can grant scholarship programs not just for scholars but also for employees. They could further partner with the academe, social entrepreneurs, the civil society stakeholders (for example in energy, environment), and bring in the Mindanao and Visay as groups into organized dialogues.

On the other hand, China should tap and bring in Tsinoys in policy coordination especially in trust and confidence building measures and coming up with consensus; in financial integration as they have the available means to go global and the means to bridge MSEs; and in unimpeded trade negotiations such as free trade agreements, removing trade barriers, and transparency. The facilitation of connectivity is evidently on-going. The implementation of projects should carefully adhere to guidelines, choose cost-effectiveness and ecological sustainability projects, and build quality infrastructure. According to George Siy, also a Chinese Filipino businessman, cost-effective projects have dynamic value that has a cycling effect of improving other aspects such as jobs and income. As compared to static value, projects are not worth it because people are not willing to pay for it thus projects will not generate funds.[1] The Philippine government gives merit to bidders based on their technical expertise and offers, so China can focus on that to give a better bargaining deal.

In this time of the BRI, China and the Philippines share similarities partly in development that could be the basis for cooperation, and share cultural affinity that could fuel these cooperation.There are numerous cooperation ahead as there are challenges that come along with these new opportunities.

Bibliography

Ang See, Teresita (2016). Migration Trends and their Socio-economic Implications: The Ethnic Chinese Community, presented at *In Search of a China Strategy: Unpacking the Bilateral and Regional Dynamics of Philippines-China Relations* on August 17-18, 2016

---

[1] Siy, George, Interview on March 2017.

at the UP Asian Center.

Baviera, Aileen and Sascha Gallardo (2013). "Filipino Media and Public Opinion on the Philippines-China Dsiputes in the South China Sea: A Preliminary Analysis" in *Philippines-China Relations: Sailing beyond Disputes Waters*, TeresitaAng See and Chito Sta. Romana eds. Philippine Association for Chinese Studies, Chinese Studies Journal Vol 10. pp. 132-171.

Bloomberg. Chinese Money Triggers a Dizzying Pally in Manila Properties. May 3, 2018.

Clemente, Tina S. (2013) Guanxi in Chinese Commerce: Informal Enforcement in Spanish Philippines. *Seoul Journal of Economics* Vol 26, No 2, pp. 203-237.

Understanding the Economic Diplomacy between the Philippines and China.*International Journal of China Studies*. (2016)7(2).

Corrales, Nestor (2018). 200% jump in Chinese visa application for PH visit—envoy. *Inquirer.net*. May 18, 2018.

Department of Tourism, *Tourists Arrivals to the Philippines 2015 – May 2018,* released on July 27, 2018.

De Vera, Dale (2017). China's Fujian targets more investments in PH with improved Manila-Beijing relations. *InterAksyon*. July 17 2017.

Dumlao-Abadilla, Doris (2017).DoubleDragon plans franchising Jinjiang.*Inquirer.net*. October 23, 2017.

Fleck, Tanner and Wissler, Jonathan (2017). *Economic preparation of the environment: A selective empirical analysis of Chinese investment in the Philippines*. Naval Postgraduate School. Monterey, California.

Flores, Wilson Lee (2017). How Philippine entrepreneurs can profit the trillion dollar Belt and Road.*Philippine Star*. May 15, 2017.

Francisco,Carmelito (2017). Davao MarinaTuna partners with Chinese investors.*Business World*. September 25, 2017.http://bworldonline.com/davao-marinatuna-partners-chinese-investors/.

JuHailong (2018).*Economic Base and Social Policy Space of the Belt and Road Initiative in the South Sea Rim of China*.Presented at the School for International Studies, Jinan University on May 16, 2018.

Magkilat, Bernie (2017). Bank of China seeks 500 Filipino MSMEs.*Manila Bulletin*. January 1, 2017.http://business.mb.com.ph/2017/01/01/bank-of-china-seeks-500-filipino-msmes/.

Bank of China vows to help enhance PH global trade ties.*Manila Bulletin*. March (2017)10, 2017.http://business.mb.com.ph/2017/03/10/bank-of-china-vows-to-help-enhance-ph-global-trade-ties/.

Mangahas, Malou (2017). Manila, Beijing dating again: Who is the screwer, screwed? Philippine Center for Investigative Journalism. May 9, 2017.http://pcij.org/stories/manila-beijing-dating-again-who-is-the-screwer-screwed/.

Montealegre, Krista (2018). Real estate developers cite China factor behind rising condo demand.*Business World*. April 11, 2018.http://www.bworldonline.com/real-estate-developers-cite-china-factor-behind-rising-condo-demand/.

Palanca, Ellen (2016), Presentation at*In Search of a China Strategy: Unpacking the Bilateral and Regional Dynamics of Philippines-China Relations* on August 17-18, 2016 at the UP Asian Center.

Philippine Consulate General in Shanghai (2018).*Briefer for Asia Pacific Pathways to Progress Foundation, Inc*. Official visit on 31 May 2018.

Po, Gerley (2010). A Comparative Analysis of the Entrepreneurial Styles of Second, Third, and Fourth Generation Overseas Chinese and Filipinos in the Philippines. *DLSU Business & Economics Review*, 19-2, pp. 11-23.

Robles, Raissa (2018). 'We need it like we need a hole in our head': Chinese friendshipbridge in Manila not so popular with the locals.*South China Morning Post*. Jan. 18, 2018.

Rappler (2016).Rappler Talk: Will PH, China improve ties in 2016? January 8, 2016.https://www.rappler.com/nation/118277-rapplertalk-ph-china-ties-2016-dindo-manhit.

Henry Sy still leads Filipinos on Forbes' 2018 billionaire list. March 7, 2018. https://www.rappler.com/business/197591-filipinos-forbes-world-billionaires-list-2018.

Siy, George (2017). Interview on March 13, 2017.

Uy, Jonathan (2018). Interview with NEDA Public Investment Staff. March 13, 2018.

Wei Lu (2017). *Filipino-Chinese Entrepreneurs under the "One Belt and One Road" Initiative: The Opportunities and Challenges*. Chinese Studies Program Lecture Series. Ateneo de Manila University No 4, pp. 105-123.

Wang Zhan, during Pathways to Progress courtesy callto the former president of Shanghai Academy of Social Sciences, June 1, 2018.

Wong, Andrea Chloe (2015). The Asian Infrastructure Investment Bank: Considerations for the Philippines. *CIRSS Commentaries*. Foreign Service Institute. May 2015, Vol 2, No 11.

Xinhua (2017). More than 300 Chinese, Philippine entrepreneurs show up in business matchmaking event in Manila.*New China*.March 20, 2017.http://news.xinhuanet.com/english/2017-03/20/c_136142239.htm.

Xinhua (2018). PAL to increase flights to China. *China Plus*. February 1, 2018.http://chinaplus.cri.cn/news/china/9/20180201/85960.html.

Yamada,Shuhei and Endo Jun (2016). China, Philippines forge friendship of convenience.

Nikkei Asian Review. October 21, 2016.https://asia.nikkei.com/Politics/China-Philippines-forge-friendship-of-convenience.

Zhang Zhenjiang (2018).*The BRI from the perspective of International Relations*, presented at the School of International Studies, Jinan University on 14 May 2018.

京剧中的饮食文化 [1]

图娅娜【俄罗斯】
俄罗斯科学院东方学研究所研究员

中国的传统戏曲形式在全球范围内被称为京剧。俄罗斯研究人员从戏剧、音乐和舞蹈的视角对这一独特的戏剧和音乐现象进行研究。在本文中，我们主要关注京剧中似乎不太重要的元素，即饮食。细致观察这一元素可以揭示京剧中许多有趣的特点，丰富并拓展我们对这一艺术类型的理解。

在中国，传统京剧于二十世纪上半叶才开始受到大众的欢迎。众所周知，这是一个真正的艺术流派，音乐、诗歌、舞蹈和杂技艺术的结合让观众熟悉真正的民族文化和历史。京剧讲述各个社会阶层人民的生活以及神仙和奇幻生物的故事，但饮食也不容忽视。饮食是故事情节的一部分，限定舞台设计和表演的特定规则。有时候也会给观众提供食物。饮食不仅可以烘托演出的氛围，在特定情况下，还构成剧场的特殊建筑外观。

根据具体情节，食物和饮料在表演中分为两个层面：作为背景或作为情节的组成部分。前一个功能很明显：酒饮料和食物伴随情节，这在西方歌剧中也很常见。例如，莫扎特的歌剧《唐·乔瓦尼》最后一幕，骑士与主角共进晚餐；威尔第的歌剧《茶花女》宴会现场著名的"饮酒歌"；法国作曲家比才的歌剧《卡门》中的酒店场景以及意大利歌剧大师普契尼的《波西米亚人》拉丁区的酒馆等。在

1 本研究获得了 RFBR（俄罗斯基础研究基金会）的资助，项目号 15-04-00513/17 (a). 本文发表于俄文专辑 *"Taste of the East" (editor-in-chief: I. T. Prokofieva, E. Yu. Karachkova. Moscow: MGIMO-University, 2018).*

第二个层面，我们谈论食物和饮料作为情节元素，在单个场景甚至整个表演中成为焦点：例如，多尼采蒂的《爱之甘醇》和里姆斯基·柯萨科夫的《沙皇的新娘》中的毒药和神药的意象，肖斯塔科维奇歌剧《穆森斯克县的马克白夫人》中的毒蘑菇。

与西方歌剧不同，京剧的食物元素体现在原创的总体趋势框架中，每一次新的表演都与先前的表演有所不同。在传统的京剧中可以追溯许多重复的模式，这是京剧的整体特色，特别是每次表演时，也与京剧的规则有关。根据传统演绎，传统表演几乎不允许任何创新：不仅是音乐和口头剧本，还包括舞台设计、表演、服装、化妆、道具的精心保存和世代相传——这种现象在西方歌剧中很少见。所谓的"新编京剧"可能有所改变，代表传统形式和新内容的独特融合[1]。

酒是京剧中的主要饮料

京剧中经常会看到群体聚集和朋友聚会的场景，合唱从来不被用作声乐表现形式，宴会或饮食中从来不会加入群众角色或龙套角色。京剧表演时通常没有宴会，相反通常只能看到室内场景，一个或两个角色在演唱之前或之后倒掉一杯酒。很多表演都可以观察到这一点，例如《霸王别姬》。如果参与的人数比较多，饮酒很少见，京剧《连环套》中出现过这一幕。《连环套》讲述绿林好汉窦尔敦的故事，他生活在十八世纪初（角色：净）。他的复仇失败后：在一幕中，主角和四名军官两次同饮（在京剧中这可以看作是群体场景）。酒在这部京剧中也是一种武器：朱光祖（角色：武丑）将蒙汗药放入一罐酒中给窦尔敦饮用，随后酒在故事情节中起到关键作用，导致主角最终失败。

在表演时，京剧中的饮酒也很引人注目：在历史上，礼仪不允许公开展示饮酒，因此演员通常必须用左手遮住右手，然后将酒杯拿到嘴边，不仅可以使用手，宽大的白色袖子或扇子可以在更大程度上美化这一姿势。然而，某些角色在喝酒时不会掩饰自己，甚至会作秀，将一小撮胡须拉到一边。这种手势在其他场景中

1　通常，京剧表演的传统剧本、音乐和场景设计由过去数代演员和音乐家创作和发展，在大多数情况下，他们没有在历史上留下姓名。而"新编京剧"由剧本作者创作，音乐由当代剧作家和作曲家制作，舞台设计取决于导演。这就是"传统"表演没有特色的原因，但它保留京剧音乐语言清晰可辨认的传统风格，不论是唱歌、表演还是在外部特征（服装、化妆、道具）。

使用，称作"撕扎"，被认为反映该角色的独立性和叛逆性。角色通常是"净"[1]（我们以窦尔敦为代表）。

如果演员需要滑稽地刻画喝醉的人物，则不需要保持"礼仪规则"。醉酒场景通常是整个情节的关键，而在上述示例中，倒空酒杯不影响角色的正常行动。京剧《大闹天宫》中的美猴王孙悟空偷酒，把原本供奉神仙的美酒偷喝一空（角色：武生）。

京剧《豆汁记》主角的父亲金松（角色：丑）遭遇不公平的待遇后，喝得酩酊大醉，也"忘记"使用酒杯。《武松打虎》（根据施耐庵十四世纪经典小说《水浒传》其中一章改编），勇猛的武松（角色：武生）也体验到酒精的魔力。几杯酒无法让他感到满足，毫不犹豫喝掉一整桶加热后的酒。然而，即使醉酒并遭受头晕和恶心的折磨，这一点在表演中也很明显地表现出来，他仍然赤手空拳打死老虎并赢得数百年的声誉。

根据洪昇的小说《长生殿》（十七世纪）改编的京剧《贵妃醉酒》对酒精彻底改变人类行为的能力进行美学表达。中国著名的美女之一杨贵妃（角色：旦）约唐玄宗赴宴，但久候不至，经历数小时的精神折磨之后，决定借酒浇愁。首先，女主角按照礼仪要求倒掉一杯又一杯，用扇子遮挡，后来逐渐失去对自身的控制，整个饮酒过程变成纷繁的舞蹈，包括杂技的元素（详见照片3）。一直扮演女性角色的伟大演员梅兰芳（1894-1961）的表演被认为是京剧的最佳曲目之一（角色：旦）。

任何人都可以饮酒？

在京剧中，主要角色有权饮酒，或至少不是情节人物。这些人物通常属于特权阶级：皇帝、大臣、高级官员、军官及随从 - 妻子和贵妃。这很可能是由于对酒的特殊态度，认为酒是富裕生活的属性。食物也是如此 - 难怪在中国最受欢迎的见面问候方式之一仍然是"吃饭了吗？"您应该总是回答"吃了"，因为这个问题具有深刻的历史根源：每天都在为获取食物而挣扎，它是生存的象征，也是繁荣的关键。

京剧艺术具有广泛的角色体系，包括四种主要角色类型（男性角色"生"，女性角色"旦"、花脸"净"和喜剧角色"丑"）。我们注意到，最后一个角色大

1　根据作者对上海京剧院演员董炳义的采访（角色：净）（2017年7月，上海）。

多不属于上文提及的"社会"阶层，显然由于这个原因，不能够像其他群众角色和龙套角色那样饮酒。一个罕见的例子是《豆汁记》中可怜的父亲，但首先金松的角色在这部戏曲的情节中非常重要，其次他饮用的酒来自突然发达的女婿莫稽（角色：小生——青年男子）。

酒和舞台

京剧舞台上的"等级制度"通过以下事实表达，即普通人物坐在地面或地板上吃饭或喝酒，而特权人物在大椅子上庄严地坐着吃喝。研究人员确认这种模式，他们相信在某个历史时间点上，中国的高档家具属于社会精英住所的组成部分 [Baiburin, Toporkov 1990: 133]。在传统的京剧表演中，舞台家具通常限制为在舞台中央摆一张桌子和两把椅子，背景保持不变。道具也采取同样的极简主义：没有宴会场面，仅使用有一个或两个方形复古酒杯和一个酒壶的托盘，酒壶通常颈部细长。我们在京剧《武松打虎》中看到的酒桶在京剧舞台上很少见（角色：武生）。

根据罗贯中十四世纪经典小说《三国演义》改编的京剧《空城计》可以看到对经典场景的偏离。一壶酒没有出现在舞台中央的桌子上，而是摆在主角、坐在城墙旁边的聪明军师诸葛亮身边。他饮酒弹琴[1]，公开展示这座城市是空荡荡的，没有防御，误导他的精明对手司马懿，让其认为有一支部队藏在城墙下，因此未经战斗立即撤退。

这些例子充分说明京剧中饮酒广泛存在的事实，但同时也是根据场景、表演和道具规范进行安排。在京剧表演中即使发现其他饮料，也只是例外。因此，《豆汁记》主角金玉奴让丈夫喝杯热水解渴的场景事实上非常罕见。

食物：中国戏院的稀客

京剧舞台上也可以看到食物，而且食物的出现总是与吸引观众注意力的特定情节转折联系在一起。在前述京剧《大闹天宫》的场景中，美猴王孙悟空不仅喝别人的酒，还偷偷地吃掉青春永驻的仙桃，向各个方向吐出桃核，表演非常滑稽。演员通过很多次的训练模仿猴子的特殊习惯和姿势。然后孙悟空找到一个葫芦，灵活地倒出葫芦里的仙丹一粒粒吃掉，"像吃豆子一样"，如同十六世纪小说《西

1　琴——中国古代的弦乐器，现在通常称为古琴。

游记》中的描写。

仙药也出现在京剧《白蛇传》中，但以灵芝的形式存在———一种的确存在且目前仍作为中药服用的真菌。主角白素贞在救活丈夫时提到这一点。

京剧如同现实生活，仙药不是拯救垂死之人的唯一方法。在上文提及的一部戏剧中，穷人的女儿给冻得要死的穷书生莫稽一碗豆汁救活一命。豆汁是北京传统小吃，绿豆研磨制成，看起来像稀粥或浅灰色的汤，可以说是最有争议的食物之一：根据大多数中国人的说法，它以不讨人喜的酸味和味道著称，在北京以外不受欢迎。然而，莫稽对这顿饭感到非常满意，这是整个汤类饮食场景的核心思想。它首先展示中国人传统上如何吃半液体的汤类和稀饭，最后我们可以看到这位主角滑稽地舔碗、筷子和手指。

食物在京剧中可以是并非滑稽场景的核心，但是真正的马戏团风格。《时迁偷鸡》——根据《水浒传》故事改编的另一部京剧——主角是一个聪明又狡猾的小偷（角色：武丑），在烧鸡的场景中几次表演吞火。吞火是典型的川剧，而不是京剧表演。蜡烛点燃特殊的纸张包裹的烤鸡。

观众饮茶

中国传统戏剧艺术拒绝任何形式的自然主义，因此在舞台上看不到任何真正的食物，有时在西方歌剧中也是如此。但这一切都可以在……观众席发现，戏院的观众可以享用茶水和甜点。这种传统显然源于富裕人家及其客人在家中私人表演的旧例：主人在各种场合的宴请时邀请或聘请私人剧团定期表演或小圈子的安静晚宴。在中国文学中有很多证据，例如经典小说《金瓶梅》是中世纪中国人生活的真实写照。

因此，中国传统戏院建筑[1]也被设计成可以在表演时供应茶水：围绕观众席三侧提供包厢，上面还有楼上包厢，整个大厅中间区域放置桌子和椅子（如天津广东会馆戏楼）。

上图是有200-300年历史的剧院戏楼。戏楼在大城市曾经很受欢迎，但如今在北京只有其中四个和天津有一个保留下来。我们可以在北京的正乙祠戏楼和北

---

1 在古代中国，户外舞台很普遍，例如北京颐和园著名的德和园三层大戏楼和北京故宫紫禁城畅音阁大戏楼。

京湖广会馆（现在也是北京戏曲博物馆）¹观看传统戏剧表演，古老的雕梁画栋，五彩缤纷的中国灯笼，错综复杂的传统刺绣背景以及气味芬芳的中国茶和甜点有助于观众沉浸在古代的氛围中，让他们有机会欣赏戏剧。在天津广东会馆戏楼人们可以自带茶水。西式风格的剧院供应茶水，以重现过去的精神：在北京，长安大戏院和梨园都可以饮茶，观众席前排不仅摆放椅子，还有桌子。

宫廷开放式两层听鹂馆（聆听黄鹂鸟唱歌）位于颐和园，如今是一家风景如画的大型历史主题餐厅：私人庆祝活动还可以提供各种传统艺术表演。当然，在这种情况下，餐厅不是戏院，但是，另一方面，具有历史性的皇家戏台的餐厅极为罕见。

在中国，饮食与表演相结合的传统非常强大，直到今天在某些地方仍然可以看到表演结束后葵花子壳和橘子皮堆成小山，表演期间向观众提供的茶水也被积极地用作有效的营销手段，以营造特别的氛围和吸引游客。这里可以与现代西方舞台相提并论，游客亦可享用美食：例如莫斯科的"赫利肯歌剧院"不仅因其不寻常的实验和奢华的作品而闻名，表演时提供的美食也很出名，这对于俄罗斯的戏剧爱好者来说并不常见。

然而，一些中国剧院从不供应茶水，例如苏州戏曲博物馆，以示对表演者的尊重²。许多现代建筑中也不提供桌子，例如梅兰芳大剧院、北京国家大剧院，上海天蟾逸夫舞台等。

京剧与漫画

甚至在漫画中也可以发现以食物的视角看京剧。当代中国艺术家和博客作者"胖不墩儿"的京剧漫画征服众多戏迷。她通过创作有趣的漫画形象发掘自己的艺术使命，让传统戏剧艺术尽可能引起年轻人的兴趣。作为京剧的忠实粉丝，她自称是一位真正的美食家³。2012年，她发布一系列漫画，将京剧主角放在各种菜肴和饮品的背景下。例如，杨贵妃的身旁摆放着一大罐菊花酒，这是秋季重阳节的传统。

1　北京安徽会馆戏楼由于建筑结构老化，现已关闭进行翻新，平阳会馆戏楼（现为刘老根大舞台）已于几年前恢复，从那时起一直作为喜剧类型表演二人转的舞台。
2　根据作者与博物馆馆长助理浦海涅的个人访谈（2016年9月，苏州）。
3　A Bite of Beijing Opera // China radio International. CRI online Russian, 31.12.2013. [http://russian.cri.cn/841/2013/12/31/1s496290.htm].

综上所述，我们可以说京剧的饮食主题是中国戏曲传统最明显体现，提供了有趣的并置、艺术发现甚至科学见解的机会。事实证明，本质上京剧艺术受到音乐语言、歌唱、表演、严格的角色系统、化妆和服饰等规范的制约。精简和保留传统风格的努力也会影响"美食"场景，食物和饮料不仅在表演中实现独特诠释，还成为马戏和杂技艺术的重要元素，被赋予社会信息而且在特定的舞台场景中出现。根据这种以及其他通用的舞台饮食规范，我们可以发现许多因素都能证实京剧的独特性。

Beijing Opera: Food and Drinks in Plots, on Stage and in the Auditorium[1]

Tuiana B. Budaeva / Russia

Research Fellow of the Institute of Oriento Studies of the Russian Academy of Sciences

In Russian science, the traditional Chinese drama jingju (literally "capital play"), known worldwide as Beijing Opera, became the main topic of several works studying this unique theatrical and musical phenomenon from the standpoint of theater studies, musicology, choreography (Serova 1970; Xu Chengbei 2003; Budaeva 2011; Lee Chiao 2001; etc.). In this article, the reader is invited to pay attention to a seemingly less significant element in the scale of the multi-faceted art of Beijing Opera, i.e. food and drinks, for a closer look at this aspect reveals a number of interesting features that are unique to Beijing Opera, which allows to enrich and expand our understanding of this genre.

In China, the traditional jingju drama was at the height of mass popularity as late

---

1 The study was conducted by the author with the financial support of RFBR (Russian Foundation for Basic Research), Project № 15-04-00513/17 (a). The article is published in Russian in the collective monograph "Taste of the East" (editor-in-chief: I. T. Prokofieva, E. Yu. Karachkova. Moscow: MGIMO-University, 2018).

as the first half of the twentieth century, and for many people it was a real school, where music, poetry, dance and acrobatic art allowed them to get acquainted with national culture and history. Narrating about people from all social strata, as well as about gods and fantastic creatures, the theater could not ignore the food sector. Food and drinks are presented here as part of a storyline, which entails certain rules for stage design and acting. Sometimes the audience also gets offered a treat. Not only does it convey a certain mood to the performance, but in some cases it becomes the reason for the special architectural appearance of the auditorium.

Depending on the plot, the food and drinks are shown in performances at two levels: as background and as an integral part of the plot. The former function is obvious: wine drinking and food accompany the plot, which can often be seen in Western opera, as well. For example, the final scene of "Don Giovanni" by Mozart, where the Commendatore comes to dine with the protagonist; the feast scene in "La Traviata" by Verdi, featuring the famous "Brindisi"; the scene in the tavern of "Carmen" by Bizet and the one in the café in the Latin quarter in "La Boheme" by Puccini, etc. In the second case, we are talking about food and drinks as plot elements that become the focal points for individual scenes or even the entire performance: for example, the images of the potion and miracle elixir in the opera "L'elisird'amore" by Donizetti and the "Tsar's bride" by Rimsky-Korsakov, the poisoned mushrooms in "Lady Macbeth of the Mtsensk District" by Shostakovich.

Unlike Western Opera, where the food component is manifested in the framework of the general tendencies of originality, and each new performance tends to differ from the previous one, in traditional Beijing Opera many repeating patterns can be traced, being typical of the genre as a whole and for each performance in particular. They are also related to the rules of jingju, which permit almost no innovation for traditional performances in their traditional interpretation: not only the music and the verbal text, but also the stage design, acting, costumes, makeup, props are carefully conserved and transmitted from generation to generation — a phenomenon that is quite rare to find in Western Opera. Some changes are likely to appear in the so-called "re-written" Beijing Opera (xinbianjingju), which represents a unique synthesis of the traditional forms and new content[1].

Wine as the Main Beverage in Jingju

In Beijing Opera one would see scenes of mass gatherings and friendly get-togethers, the choir is never used as a vocal form, and extras and supernumeraries never get involved in feasts, eat or drink. In general, in Beijing Opera, there are no feasts, instead you can usually see only chamber scenes where one or two characters drain a cup of wine, usually before or after singing an aria. That can be found in many performances, for example, in "Bawangbieji". This infrequent, in terms of number of participants, scene is presented in the opera "Lianhuantao", a story about the leader of the rebel army DouErdun who lived in the beginning of XVIII century (typecast: "painted face" jing) and his failed revenge: in one scene the main character and the four commanders drink their cups at the same time twice (for the Beijing Opera, it can be considered a mass scene). In this opera, wine is also used as a weapon: Zhu Guangzu (typecast: military comic wuchou) puts sleeping pills in a jug of wine for Dou Erdun, which subsequently played a key role in the chain that led to the defeat of the protagonist.

Wine drinking in Beijing Opera is remarkable in terms of acting, as well: Historically, etiquette didn't allow to show the process openly, so the actor usually had to use his left hand to cover the right while taking the glass to the mouth, and not only the hand, a wide white sleeve or a fan, could also be used to aesthetize the gesture to a greater extent. However, some characters don't cover themselves while

---

1 While texts, music, and scenography for traditional performances of Beijing Opera, as a rule, were composed and developed over generations of actors and musicians of the past, and in most cases history has not preserved their names, the performances of the "re-written" Beijing Opera (xinbianjingju) are usually created by authors of the libretto and music are contemporary playwrights and composers, and stage design is up to the director. That's why it might be uncharacteristic for the "old" performances, but it retains the clearly recognizable traditional style of the musical language of Beijing Opera, both for such aspects as singing, acting and for external attributes (costumes, make-up, props).

drinking wine, they even do it for show, pulling aside a thin strand of their beards. This gesture is used in other scenic situations and received the name "sizha"and is considered to be a reflection of the independent and rebellious nature of the character who shows it. Usually those are "colored faces" (jing)[1] .

The "rules of decency" are not maintained either if the actor needs to ridiculously portray his character getting tipsy. Scenes of intoxication often are key in the plot of the entire play, whereas in the abovementioned examples, the draining of glasses usually does not matter a lot for common action. Thus, the famous Monkey King Sun Wukong from the Opera "Havoc in Heaven" ("DanaoTiangong") secretly gets drunk, drinking out of the pitcher that was intended for the feast of the gods.

Having gotten tipsy, the discouraged by the injustice Jin Song (typecast: comedian chou), the father of the protagonist of the Opera "Story of the skilly douzhi" ("Douzhiji"), also "forgets" to use a glass. The mighty warrior Wu Song(typecast: military hero wusheng) from the play "Wu Song Slaying The Tiger" ("Wu Song da hu", an opera based on an episode of a XIV century classic novel "Water Margin" by Shi Nai'an) also experienced the insidious power of the wine. When several cups seemed insufficient to him, he didn't hesitate to drain a whole barrel of the heating drink. However, even being drunk and suffering from dizziness and nausea, which is very clearly reflected in the acting, he still managed to beat the tiger who attacked him with his bare hands, gaining fame for centuries.

In the play "The Drunken Concubine" ("Guifeizuijiu" based on the novel by Hong Sheng "The Palace of Eternal Life", XVII century) the ability of alcohol to radically change human behavior also found its aesthetic expression. Yang-guifei, the concubine (typecast: dan) of the Tang Emperor Xuan-zong, one of the famous Chinese beauties of that time, got tired of waiting for her lover in vain, and after many hours of spiritual torments, decided to find solace in wine. At first, draining

---

1   From the author's interview with the actor of Shanghai Beijing Opera Theater Dong Bingyi (typecast: jing) (July 2017, Shanghai).

one glass after another, the heroine covers herself with a fan, as required by the etiquette, but then she can't control herself any longer, and the whole process of wine drinking turns into a long slow dance with elements of acrobatics. This performance, re-created by the great actor Mei Lanfang (1894-1961), who always played the female parts, is considered to be one the best plays of the Beijing Opera.

May Everyone Drink Wine?

In Beijing Opera, the right to drink wine is exclusive to the main characters or at least not episodic ones, who usually belong to the privileged class: emperors, ministers, senior officials, military leaders and their entourage — his wives and concubines. Most likely, this is due to the special attitude to wine as an attribute of prosperous life. The same applies to food — no wonder one of the most popular Chinese greetings still is "Chi fan le me?" ("Have you eaten?"). And you should always answer "yes", because this issue has deep historical roots: in terms of daily struggle for food, it was a symbol of survival and the key to prosperity.

Since the art of jingju is based on an extensive system of roles, consisting of four main types (male characters sheng, female characters dan, "painted faces" jing, and comedians chou), one can notice that the latter mostly don't belong to the abovementioned "social" layer and, apparently, for this reason don't have the honor to taste the wine as often, just like extras and supers. One of the rare examples is the already mentioned scene with the poor father from "Story of the skilly douzhi", but, firstly, the role of Jin Song is very important in the plot of this opera, and secondly, he finishes the wine of his son-in-law Mo Ji who suddenly got rich (subtypecast: xiaosheng — a young man character).

Wine and the Stage

A kind of "caste system" on the stage of Beijing Opera is manifested by the fact that common characters eat and drink, sitting on the ground or the floor, while more privileged ones do it sitting majestuously on massive chairs. This pattern is confirmed by researchers, who believe that at a certain historical point high furniture in China became an integral part of the interior of houses belonging to the social elite [Baiburin, Toporkov 1990: 133]. In traditional jingju performances, stage furniture is usually limited to one table and two chairs located in the middle of the stage against a background that never changes. The same minimalism goes for prop ware: as there are no scenes of feasts, the use of a tray with one or two square-shaped vintage glasses and a jug, often with a long narrow neck, is quite explicable. The barrel we can see in the opera "Wu Song Slaying The Tiger" is an infrequent item on the stage of Beijing Opera.

Deviation from the canonical scenery can be seen in the play "Ruse of the Empty City" ("Kong chengji") based on the classic XIV-century novel by Luo Guanzhong "Romance of the Three Kingdoms", where a jug of wine, instead of appearing on the table in the center of the stage, shows up on the side, on the city wall, where the protagonist, a shrewd strategist Zhuge Liang is sitting. Drinking wine and playing the qin^1, he openly demonstrates that the city is defenceless and free, misleading Sima Yi, his astute opponent, who decided that a troop is hiding within the city walls, and therefore retreated without fighting.

These examples speak volumes about the fact that wine drinking in the Beijing Opera is wide-spread, but at the same time is built according to a canonical palette of scenic situations, acting and the props. Other drinks, even if found in jingju performances, are rather an exception.Therefore, the scene from "Story of the skillydouzhi", where the protagonist Jin Yunu brings her husband a cup of hot water so that he could quench his thirst, can be considered highly unusual for this genre.

Food: a Rare Guest at the Chinese Theatre

Food can also be seen on the stage of Beijing Opera, and its appearance is always associated with a particular plot twist at the center of the viewers'

---

1   *Qin* — ancient Chinese stringed musical instrument of the zither type, now usually is called as guqin.

attention. In the abovementioned scene from the Opera "Havoc in Heaven" the monkey King Sun Wukong not only drinks someone else's wine, but he also secretly eats magic peaches of youth, spitting out the stones in different directions, which is comically played out by the actors, who take a lot of time training to mimic recognizable habits and gestures of monkeys. Then Sun Wukong finds a gourd, deftly takes immortality pills from within and eats them one by one, "like fried beans," as written in the XVI-century novel "Journey to the West" the play is based on.

The image of the drug is also used in the opera "Legend of the White Snake" ("Baishe zhuan"), but in the form of the lingzhi——longevity lung fungus that really exists and is still used in Chinese medicine. The protagonist Madam BaiSuzhen mentions it while reviving her husband.

In Beijing Opera, just like in real life, drugs are not the only way to save a person from death. In one of the previously mentioned plays, the daughter of a poor man offered some douzhi soup to the impoverished servant Mo Ji who was freezing, thus preventing him from starving. This dish of Beijing cuisine made from crushed green mash beans looking like very thin porridge or grayish soup can be considered one of the most controversial ones: according to most Chinese, it is notorious for its nasty sour smell and taste, but it is not that well-known outside Beijing. However, Mo Ji was incredibly happy with the meal, which is the core idea of the whole scene of soup eating, which at first shows how the Chinese traditionally eat semi-liquid soups and porridges, and in the end we can see the hero comically licking the bowl, his chopsticks, and his fingers.

In Beijing Opera, food can be the center of scene that are not just comic, but really circus-style. In the play "Shi Qian Steals the Cock" ("Shi Qiantouji"—another one of the fragments on the numerous storylines of the novel "Water Margin", the main character, a clever and cunning thief (typecast: military comic wuchou) in the scene of frying the chicken pieces several times demonstrates the trick of swallowing live fire, which is more typical for Sichuan musical drama (chuanju) than for Beijing Opera. Chicken is depicted here with sheets of special paper that instantly light up from candle flame.

Tea for the Audience

Chinese traditional theater art rejects any form of naturalism, so no real food can be seen on stage, as the case may sometimes be in Western operas. But all of this can be found in... the auditorium, where the visitors of the theater are served tea with sweets. This tradition apparently comes from the old practice of private performances in the homes for wealthy family members and their guests: private theater companies, invited or employed by the host, regularly staged shows, during feasts on all kinds of occasions, or just for quiet dinners in a narrow circle. There is a lot of evidence for that in Chinese prose, for example, in the classic novel "Jin Ping Mei, or The Plum in the Golden Vase", which is a real encyclopaedia of medieval Chinese life.

As a result, traditional Chinese theater buildings[1] were also designed so as to serve tea during performances: around the perimeter of the auditorium, boxes are located on three sides, with a balcony above them, and tables and chairs in the entire central part of the hall.

That's what the 200-300-year-old theaters built at guild halls looked like. They used to be quite popular in major cities, but only four of them in Beijing and one in Tianjin got preserved until today. In the capital, you can see traditional drama performances at Zhengyici Theater and Beijing Huguang Guild Hall (which today hosts the Beijing Opera Museum)[2], where ancient carvings, colorful Chinese lanterns, backdrops with intricate traditional embroidery and fragrant Chinese tea

---

1 In ancient China, outdoor stages were widespread, such as the famous three-tiered Imperial Theatres Deheyuan at the residence of the Yiheyuan (known as Summer Palace) and Changyinge in the Forbidden City in Beijing.

2 In Beijing, the theater of Anhui Guild Hall is now closed for renovation due to the dangerous structure of the building, the theater at Pingyang Guild Hall (Grand Stage Liu Laogen) was restored several years ago, and since then has been hosting comedy genre performanceserren-zhuan.

and sweets will surely help to immerse the viewer in the atmosphere of antiquity, giving them the opportunity to enjoy the play even more. To the Tianjin Guandong Guild Hall theater some people bring their own tea. Tea is served in some of Western style theaters, which seek to recreate the spirit of the past: in Beijing, it can be seen at the Chang'an Grand Theater (Chang'andaxiyuan) and Liyuan Theater ("Pear Garden"), where are not only chairs, but also tables are set in the first rows of the stalls.

The Imperial open two-tier Tingliguan stage("Listening to the Orioles singing"), located in the Yiheyuan Summer Palace and hosting today a large restaurant with a picturesque historic setting: private celebrations can also include different kind of traditional art performances. In this case, of course, the restaurant cannot be a theater, but on the other hand, restaurants with a historical imperial stage are extremely rare.

The tradition of combining food and performance in China is so strong that even today in some places after the performances one can see husks of sunflower seeds and tangerine peel piled up, and tea offered to the audience during the performance is actively used as an efficient marketing tool to create a special atmosphere and attract tourists. Here it is possible to draw a parallel with the modern Western stages, where visitors can also get some treats: for example, the Moscow theater "Helikon-Opera" is widely known not only for its unusual experiments and extravagant productions, but also for food accompanying some of the performances, which isn't usual for Russian theater lovers.

However, in some Chinese theaters, such as Suzhou Traditional Opera Museum, tea is never served, to demonstrate respect to the performers[1]. Tables are not provided for in many modern buildings, as well: such as Mei Lanfang Grand Theater, National Center for the Performing Arts in Beijing, TianchanYifu Stage in Shanghai, etc.

---

1 From a personal interview of the author with the assistant head of the PuHainie Museum (September 2016, Suzhou).

Beijing Opera and Comic Books

The original view of Beijing Opera through the prism of food can be found even in the comics. The contemporary Chinese artist and blogger under the alias of Sweet & Plump (Pangbu Dun'er) has conquered a large number of fans with her comic drawings on Beijing Opera. Creating funny images, she sees her own artistic mission in arousing the interest of as many young people as possible in the art of traditional theater. Being a big fan of jingju and, according to her own assurances, a real gourmet[1], and in 2012 she released a series of comics in which the heroes of the plays of the Beijing Opera are placed in the context of various dishes and drinks. For instance, the concubine Yang-guifei is depicted next to a large jug of wine of chrysanthemum flowers, which is traditional for the autumnal Double Ninth Festival, or Chongyang.

Summarizing, we can say that the theme of food and drinks in Beijing Opera, a clearest incarnation of the traditions of Chinese theater, provides an opportunity for interesting juxtapositions, art discoveries and even scientific insights. The essence of the latter is that, as it turned out, the art of Beijing Opera is regulated by the canons not only in terms of musical language, singing, acting, a strict system of roles, makeup and costumes. The effort to streamline and thus preserve the traditional image of the genre has also influenced "gastronomic" scenes, where food and drinks obtain unique interpretation not only through acting, but also through becoming elements of circus and acrobatic arts, and they get endowed with a social message and appear only in a certain scenographic context. In this and in other prevailing regulations regarding food and drinks on the stage, we can see one of the many factors confirming the uniqueness and peculiarity of the genre of Beijing Opera .

Bibliography

Baiburin, Toporkov (1990) Baiburin A., Toporkov A.At the origins of etiquette. Leningrad:

---

1   See: A Bite of Beijing Opera // China radio International. CRI online Russian, 31.12.2013. [http://russian.cri.cn/841/2013/12/31/1s496290.htm].

Science.165.

Budaeva (2011) T. B. Budaeva Music in Chinese Traditional Theater Jingju (Beijing Opera). PhD thesis.Moscow State Conservatory. p. 253.

Lee Chiao (2001) Lee Chiao.The role of dance and pantomime in musical composition of Beijing Opera. PhD thesis. Saint-Petersburg State Conservatory. p. 159.

Serova (1970) Serova S. A. Beijing musical drama (mid-XIX century-1940s). Moscow: Science. p. 195.

Xu Chengbei (2003) XuChengbei.Beijing Opera / translated from Chinese Sang Hua, He Ru. Beijing: Intercontinental Publishing House of China (Spiritual Culture of China). p. 136.

广东当代艺术

爱莲【阿根廷】
布宜诺斯艾利斯大学辅导员

当代艺术背景下的艺术与文学关系：比较文学的当前问题

玛丽亚·特雷莎·格拉穆里奥（María Teresa Gramuglio）提出三个当前具有重要意义的比较文学研究问题 / 对象：文学史、超民族文学或文化现象研究以及文学与其他艺术之间的关系。最后一个主题源自古典传统，在西方世界具有悠久的历史，从一开始就引发艺术与层次设置的对立冲突。从 19 世纪末的现代主义美学到 20 世纪初，历史前卫主义加强文学与美术，或更确切地说文学与艺术之间的关系。到 20 世纪中叶，该学科进入比较文学领域。

尽管如此，当代艺术使文学与艺术之间的联系重新焕发活力。我们可能会想到艺术展、表演、干预，简而言之，不同艺术学科实践交织而创作的作品。正如 Garramuño 所述："当代美学的某些转变倾向于让敏感变得鲜活，从而造成归属感、特异性和自治观念的危机。"从这个角度来看，当代美学将以非特异性为特征。这种趋势的背景是 20 世纪 50 和 60 年代的新艺术先锋流派提出艺术和生活的融合。在这个意义上，Garramuño 提及的非特异性不仅与不同艺术界限的交织和模糊有关，还与对艺术的质疑与实践差异化有关：

> 这种针对非特定性的想法是一种阐述普通的语言的方式，培养非归属感：不属于特定艺术的特异性，最重要的是，不属于一种特定实践的

艺术观念。

García Canclini 在谈及"后自治艺术"时也观察到这一点。后自治艺术是指近几十年来发生的过程，从基于对象向基于语境的艺术实践的转变不断加强，直到作品嵌入媒体、城市和数字空间、各种形式的社会参与，导致审美差异被稀释。如果说当代艺术的特征是其非特异性，即不仅质疑艺术之间的分离，还质疑作为差异化实践的艺术分离，那么产生的第一个问题是：如何分析艺术与文学之间的关系，如何在不失去对象特异性的情况下从比较文学的角度进行研究？关于比较文学的研究对象和方法的这些问题在其发展过程中一直存在和反复。正如 Gramuglio 指出：

> [...] 复兴总是受文学特异性的丧失和界限的模糊性所困扰，虽然在某些情况下对此感到遗憾，在其他情况下则受到赞赏；在每一个交叉路口，不确定对象的幻影和学科研究方法总是在反复。

因此有必要设计一种新的艺术研究方法，考虑当代艺术与文学关系的复杂性，同时又不丧失该研究领域的特异性。本研究的指导性问题是如何通过比较文学领域理解和分析以非特异性为特征的艺术与文学关系的新阶段。在考虑这一阶段时，我们已经确定主要困难和问题并首先提出特定趋势和过程历史化的需求。原则上，我们的目的不是回答这些问题，而是指出在比较文学领域思考艺术与文学关系时需要考虑的特定变量或组成要素。

南方中国当代艺术简史

如果说当代西方艺术中的艺术与文学关系提出很多需要分析的问题，我们必须加上中国当代艺术所呈现的特殊特征和发展情况。虽然中国当代艺术已经成功地进入全球艺术体系，但它仍然具有鲜明的特点，因为它不仅发起与西方艺术文化趋势和传统的对话，而且也是与中国艺术文化的对话。为此，许多研究者警告简化论者或肤浅的西方视角进行分析有导致偏颇的危险：

> 我们似乎已经系统性地忽略具有数千年历史的艺术传统，这种艺术无疑是非常封闭并产生对西方来说"异化"的审美对象，表扬当代的作品恰恰是相信他们采用与西方艺术相同的语言，最终趋于同质化。显然，为了研究新艺术家的作品，有必要深化其文化传统并回归其文明根源。

虽然众所周知与中国的距离导致出现简化论的观点，即对中国历史、文化和艺术传统等缺乏了解，但值得一提的是，采用与西方艺术相同语言的观点部分是因为中国当代艺术汲取西方哲学、文学和艺术思想、理念和讨论并对其进行改造。栗宪庭提到，从清朝末年（1644-1911）开始，当中国的大门被西方世界敲开，中国经历了三个主要的文化和审美转型，其标志是拒绝已建立起来的文化和审美系统并接受全新的基于现代西方的文化和审美系统。

第一阶段，即 1919 年至 1942 年之间，以对传统文学文化的幻灭和西方现实主义的引入为标志。第二个阶段（1942-1979 年）是毛泽东革命现实主义模式下的文化整合时期。对于本文而言，第三个也是最有趣的阶段是 1979 年至 1992 年，在这一时期现代艺术的主要潮流涌现。1976 年后，革命现实主义模式价值结构的丧失导致艺术家开始寻求一套新的指导方针支持其发展。正如栗宪庭说的，在引进和适应的过程中，西方体系经历不同程度的转变，因此中西方之间存在着一种相互影响和变化的文化辩证法。这些过渡现象和文化辩证法造成当代中国艺术与西方艺术的区别。在这个意义上，西方文化的元素被重新解读、诠释和表达，以符合中国艺术界的利益。

从 1979 年开始，对西方哲学和美学思想进行实验，催生新的艺术趋势和运动。西方文化受到热烈欢迎并作为拒绝前一阶段美学价值的工具。张颂仁所称的实验性或前卫艺术在 20 世纪 70 年代后期邓小平改革开放政策第一阶段出现。

经济改革进程对中国南方地区产生特别的影响。这是因为广东省深圳市被确定为"经济特区"，意味着深圳市一方面展开经济改革政策实验，另一方面作为对外开放的窗口。不仅与西方世界建立联系，还推动该地区经济迅速发展，引发艺术家的新质疑和担忧。另一个现实是靠近香港。随着中国的开放，大量流行文化产品涌入，例如电视节目和流行音乐，不仅来自中国香港，也来自中国台湾、日本和西方国家。虽然在中国大陆未出版，西方哲学、艺术和文学书籍和文章的翻译潮流也引发所谓的"阅读热"，即渴望阅读这些新的文字。艺术家陈劭雄解释说："刚好那个时候来了一盘萨特，我们就先把萨特吃了，然后他收走了。最后来了一个甜点是苏珊.朗格，又收下去。一道一道来，是翻译家给我们的"。不仅急切地阅读文字，中国南方的艺术家们还将艺术领域的阅读和实验联系起来。通常的做法是组建学习小组，后来发展成为艺术团体，甚至是艺术家团体，鼓励进行哲学和美学辩论，在艺术领域寻求技术创新。其中的一些案例包括汕头青年美术协会、一零五画室和南方艺术家沙龙。南方艺术家沙龙的艺术家们于 1986 年举办美术展，明确意图是跨越不同学科的障碍，该团体艺术家王度表示："我当时想要有一种激进的东西，就像沙龙的成员从不同领域组成的，我很希望这个《第一回实验展》是一个全新的视觉经验。"

在中国当代艺术诞生之前经验预示着某些特征。在这方面，值得一提的是，总体上在中国艺术阶段划分中，1989 年被认为是从实验艺术向当代艺术过渡的年份：

> 为什么是 1989 年？因为那是标志着中国文化领域发生重大变化的一年。此后，中国的艺术达到一个成熟的新高度，许多方面都是前十年艺术探索的成果。当年学生运动的后果是社会和经济秩序发生巨大变化。1989 年，中国开始进入 90 年代。

1988 年，杨诘苍、侯瀚如、唐颂武和陈侗在中山图书馆举行一次名为"话、对、人"的小型演出。关于此事，陈侗作如是说："虽然很少有人记得这次艺术盛会，但我们必须承认，这是当代艺术首次在广州公开展出。"然而，广东的实验艺术被"八五新潮"所忽视。广东没有积极地参与作为中国当代艺术前奏的"八五新潮"。陈侗指出，这所显示的正是一种地理上乃至文化上的极端的边缘性。[1] 然而，这种边缘性赋予广东艺术家独特而原始的特征。

如上文所述，20 世纪 80 年代的地区经济繁荣、香港流行文化产品的大量涌入和西方作品的出版让广东的艺术具有某些特征，使其与中国其他地区不同。徐坦称："在北方，他们谈现代性、现代思想时，常常是一种很学术的态度。不一定有具体的生活经验。我认为现代性肯定跟商业生活、消费生活、市场要有关系"。广东艺术家非常关注消费生活、城市化、工业化和全球化等问题。

80 年代的艺术经验在博尔赫斯书店（Libreria Borges）的创作中得到恢复和重新评价。其创办人陈侗积极参与当年的艺术和文化沸腾氛围。为了分析博尔赫斯书店案例，不能将其视为艺术家个人创作的孤立项目，而应将其视为 80 年代艺术和文化倾向的集成，并根据 90 年代的当代艺术进行更新。虽然它不间断地打上创办人的标签，但在某种程度上却是一种集体创作。

博尔赫斯书店案例

博尔赫斯书店是 1993 年创办于中国广东省广州市的一个文化艺术项目。最

1　陈侗，"保持变化与多样性：1990 年以来的广东当代艺术状况"，《广东快车》，湖南美术出版社，2003 年。

初，这里是传播外国文学作品（特别是法国作家）的场所，同时也几位广东艺术家的集会和创作场地。正如其创办人所言，1994-2001 年是试验期，在此期间主要是组织非正式的小规模活动。2002 年至 2006 年期间，来自珠江三角洲地区的当代广东艺术家参加 2002 年第四届光州双年展并参加 2003 年在第 50 届威尼斯双年展上举办的"广州快车"展览，相对于其他艺术表演表现突出。参加展览的艺术家对 20 世纪 80 年代经济改革后中国工业化、城市化，现代化和全球化等问题进行研究。书店创办人陈侗是城市艺术家，不仅在中国而且在海外都享有盛名。他拥有多个职业：不仅是广州美术学院教师，还是艺术家、策展人、艺术品收藏家、编辑和评论家。人生中的各个角色也交织投射到他拥有的书店，因为它目前是文化和艺术机构网络的组成部分。2007 年，陈侗创办博尔赫斯书店当代艺术机构，亦称作 CANTONBON，既是从书店中诞生的项目，又超越书店的概念："博尔赫斯书店艺术机构的规模比书店大得多，但书店仍然是机构的源头"。博尔赫斯书店艺术机构的主要活动是出版有关当代艺术、文学、哲学的书籍；组织阅读俱乐部和书籍相关活动；为广东艺术家提供档案作品、新小说派及其构成以及国际艺术和文化交流资料。此外，还参与录像局的项目，包括广东当代艺术家的艺术作品体系视频存档，供研究人员、学生和收藏家使用。最重要地是，在同一座城市还有设有美术馆。这些机构的资金主要来自陈侗本人出售的艺术品和书店的销售。录像局部分资金由五行会艺术机构提供。

这种机构网络可以被视为是跨越艺术与阅读的文化传播中心。正如上文所述，20 世纪 80 年代艺术与阅读开始结合。当些年的"阅读热潮"形成学习小组，后来发展成为艺术团体，甚至是艺术家团体，鼓励进行哲学和美学辩论。然而，陈侗的经历允许他不仅在艺术与阅读，还在艺术与文学方面发挥重要作用，尤其是新小说派和阿兰 - 罗伯 - 格里耶作品："罗伯 - 格里耶对我的影响是全方位的。除了理念外，他的写作技巧和生活态度也让我铭记于心。"[1] 这位作家也是一位画家，绘画和文学在他的作品《漂亮的女俘虏》中交织，配上 René Magritte 的 77 幅绘画作品。他还以电影制作而闻名。

另一方面，以博尔赫斯之名创办阅读和文学书店。改革开放后，博尔赫斯的作品进入中国。然而，"博尔赫斯"在 20 世纪 80 年代的环境中被视为"孤独"的作家。事实上，他只出版了一本书。20 世纪 90 年代他的作品开始在中国引起反

1　Liu, Tina (2014) "Chen Tong's 'Book of Sand'" in *Gallery*. Number 188, July.

响，与前卫文学有关："首先，他是格非、马原、苏童等先锋作家的导师，然后在中国文学评论界成为'后现代主义小说之父'，最后被称作是'作家中的作家'。"在这方面，20世纪90年代后期创办一间书店并冠以博尔赫斯之名意味着将其作品阅读与中国先锋文学观念关联。此外，我们将机构与广东省当代艺术家的关系视为与前瞻性思维方法相关：

> 由于发生的事件，我们可以说20世纪90年代表广州艺术的转折点。例如，成立大尾象小组，组织一系列艺术活动。1992年绘画展和1990年双年展期间，大尾象举行非正式的"分展览"，这些事件代表"当代艺术"的开端，并且因对立的偏见，广州成为当代艺术的坚定推动者。
> （Chen, 2003: 22）

众所周知，对于陈侗来说，文学占据着中心位置："[...]我不止一次提到，与绘画相比，我更重视文学"，他补充道："如果我对写作的理解像这样清楚，也许我不会继续画画。但事实并非如此。"艺术和文学的强烈交织不仅是陈侗的个人标志，也是他创办机构的标志，其核心是博尔赫斯书店，随着开创性的经验不断扩展，开始设立扮演复杂角色的机构网络。这种现象可以追溯到20世纪80年代广东艺术实验中已经存在的元素，也可以在20世纪90年代的艺术中观察到：1）创造性地运用与中国现实交互的西方思想和趋势；2）跨越分割不同艺术学科的障碍；3）扎根于广东，与外界不断对话与交流的实践。借鉴20世纪80年代经验和汲取90年代当代艺术趋势的同时，博尔赫斯书店特别强调艺术与文学的联系。在这一复杂的机构网络中既存在艺术与文学的交织，也面临艺术实践与文化产业界限的模糊。因此，博尔赫斯书店是极为相关的案例，不仅对于我们的研究，还对于非特异性或后自治阶段的艺术实践（包括文学）的理解也是如此。同时，它凸显广东艺术在全球化背景下对东西方艺术趋势与传统融合的重要性。

Contemporary Art in the Province of Guangdong: Approaches within the Field of Comparative Literature

Ayelen Goldar / Argentina

Buenos Aires University, Counselor / Ji'nan University, Postgraduate Student

The Relationship Between Art and Literature in the Context of Contemporary Art

María Teresa Gramuglio[1] poses three problems/objects of current importance in the discipline of comparative literature: the histories of literature, the study of supranational literary or cultural phenomena and the ancient topic of *ut pictura poesis*. This last topic, which originates from the classical tradition and has a long history in the Western world, raises, from its beginnings, conflicts related to the rivalry between the arts and the setting of hierarchies among them. By the end of the 19th century, aesthetic modernism, and, afterwards, by the beginning of the 20th century, the historical avant-gardes would intensify this relationship between literature and painting or, more precisely, between literature and art. By mid-20th century, the subject entered the field of comparative literature.

Nonetheless, contemporary art revitalizes the link between literature and art;

---

1 See Gramuglio, María Teresa (2006). "Tres problemas para el comparatismo" in *Orbis Tertius*. Vol. 11. No. 12.

we may think of installations, performances, interventions, in short, productions in which practices from different artistic disciplines are intertwined. As Garramuño points out: "Some transformations of contemporary aesthetics favour ways of organizing the sensitive that lead to a crisis of ideas of belonging, specificity and autonomy." (Garramuño, 2015: 13) From this perspective, contemporary aesthetics would be characterized by its nonspecificity. The background to this trend would be the experiences of the neo-avant-garde of the 1950s and 1960s, which proposed the reintegration of art and life. In this sense, the nonspecificity to which Garramuño refers not only has to do with the interweaving, the blurring of boundaries among the different arts, but also with a questioning of art as a practice differentiated from others:

> This bet for the nonspecific would be a way to elaborate a language of the ordinary that would foster various ways of not belonging: not belonging to the specificity of a particular art, but also, and above all, not belonging to an idea of art as a specific practice. (Garramuño, 2016: 19)

This is also observed by García Canclini when he speaks of "post-autonomous art"[1]. which refers to the process that has taken place in recent decades in which the shift from object-based to context-based artistic practices has increased until the works are inserted into the media, urban and digital spaces, forms of social participation where aesthetic difference seems to be diluted. If contemporary art is characterized by its nonspecificity, that is, by the questioning not only of the separation between the arts but also by the separation of art as a differentiated practice, the first question that arises is: how to analyze the relations between art and literature, how to approach its study from a discipline such as comparative literature without losing the specificity of the object? These questions about the object of study and the methods of comparative literature remain throughout their development and return constantly, as Gramuglio argues:

---

1   See García Canclini, Néstor (2010). *La sociedad sin relato. Antropología y estética de la inminencia.* Buenos Aires: Katz Editores.

[...] these renovations are always haunted by the loss of the specificity of the literary and the blurring of its limits, although in some cases it is deplored and in others, celebrated; and at each of these crossroads the ghost of the indefinite object and methods of discipline returns. (Gramuglio, 2006: 5)

It will therefore be necessary to devise new ways of approaching art, new methods that take into account the complexity of current art in its link with literature without, however, losing the specificity of this field of study. Thus, the guiding question for our research is how to understand and analyze from the field of comparative literature this new stage of the link between art and literature characterized by its nonspecificity. At this stage of the investigation, we have identified major problems and questions, and the need to historicize certain trends and processes has been raised first and foremost. In principle, our intention is not to answer these questions but rather to point out certain variables or components to be considered when thinking about this relationship between art and literature in the field of comparative literature.

Brief historization of contemporary art in Southern China

If the link between art and literature in contemporary Western art raises multiple questions for its analysis, to this we must add the particular characteristics and development that Chinese contemporary art presents. Although contemporary Chinese art has successfully entered the global art system, it still has distinctive features, as it is instituted not only in dialogue with the trends and traditions of Western art and culture, but also with those of Chinese art and culture. For this reason, many authors warn of the dangers of biased analyses from reductionist or superficial Western perspectives:

It seems as if we had gone from almost systematically ignoring a thousand-year-old artistic tradition that, undoubtedly, was very hermetic and had produced objects of a beauty that was "foreign" to the West, to praising its current productions precisely due to believing that they speak the same language of Western art, finally homogenized, when it is clear that in order to approach the work of these new artists it is essential to deepen their cultural tradition and return to the roots of their civilization. (Fernández del Campo, 2011: 154)

Although it is well known that the distance with China, i.e. the lack of knowledge of its history, cultural and artistic traditions, etc., produces reductionist perspectives, it is worth mentioning that the belief that the same language of Western art is spoken stems in part from the fact that contemporary Chinese art has taken ideas, concepts, discussions from Western philosophy, literature and art and has transformed them. As Li Xianting has emphasized[1], since the end of the Qing Dynasty (1644-1911), when the Western world burst into China, China experienced three major cultural and aesthetic transitions marked by the rejection of a cultural and aesthetic system and the adoption of a new one, which saw the modern Western system as a point of reference.

The first period, between 1919 and 1942, was marked by disillusionment with traditional literary culture and the introduction of Western realism. The second period (1942-1979) is that of cultural integration under the Maoist model. The third and most interesting for the purposes of this essay, is the period from 1979 to 1992, when the main currents of modern art emerged. In the period after 1976, the loss of structures of values from the Maoist model caused artists to begin the search for a new set of guidelines to support their development. As Li Xianting states, in the course of this process of adoption and adaptation, the Western system experienced various levels of transformation, therefore, there has been a cultural dialectic between China and the West marked by a pattern of mutual influence and change. It is the phenomenon of these transitions and the cultural dialectics that have spawned what differentiates the evolution of contemporary Chinese art from that of Western art. In this sense, we can say that the elements of Western culture are re-read,

---

1   See Li, Xianting (1993). "Major Trends in the Development of Contemporary Chinese Art" in *China's New Art, Post -1989. With a retrospective from 1979-1989.* Hong Kong: Hanart TZ Gallery.

reinterpreted and resignified to the interests of the Chinese artistic field.

From 1979 onwards, a process of experimentation with Western philosophical and aesthetic ideas came into being, giving rise to new artistic trends and movements. Thus, Western culture was welcomed with enthusiasm and as a tool to express the rejection of the aesthetic values of the previous stage. Experimental or avant-garde art[1], as Chang Tzong-zung has called it, emerged with the first stage of China's Reform Opening policy in the late 1970s.

This process of economic reform had a particular impact on Southern China. This is because the city of Shenzhen in Guangdong province was declared a "Special Economic Zone", which meant that the city would function, on the one hand, as an experimental test of economic reform policies and, on the other hand, as a window to the outside world. This generated not only a contact with the Western world but also a rapid economic development in the region that triggered new questionings and concerns among artists. Another reality is the proximity to Hong Kong. With the opening of China, a large influx of popular culture products is emerging, such as television programs, music, not only from Hong Kong, but also from Taiwan, Japan and Western countries. The advent of translations of books and articles on Western philosophy, art and literature, which had not yet been published in mainland China, led to what has been called "Reading Fever", i.e. the eagerness to read these new texts, as the artist Chen Shaoxiong explains: "If it happened to be a plate of Jean-Paul Sartre we ate Jean-Paul Sartre. And if the dessert was, for example, Susanne Langer, we ate that too. You ate whatever the translators gave you" (Asia Art Archive, Jane De Bevoise, Claire Hsu, Phoebe Wong and Anthony Yung, 2010). Not only were the texts that came in eagerly read, but the artists of Southern China also formed associations around reading and experimentation in the field of art. It was common practice to form study groups that would later become artistic

---

1   See Chang, Tzong-zung (1993). "Into the Nineties" in *China's New Art, Post -1989. With a retrospective from 1979-1989.* Hong Kong: Hanart TZ Gallery.

groups or even groups of artists in which philosophical and aesthetic debates, as well as the search for technical innovations in the field of art were encouraged. Some examples of them are *Shantao Young Artists Association, 105 Studio* and *Southern Artists Salon.* With regard to the latter group, in 1986 they held an exhibition with the clear intention of crossing the barriers that separated the different disciplines, as demonstrated by the words of Wang Du, one of the artists who formed part of that group: "At the time I wanted to do something radical, like organizing the Salon with people from all different disciplines. I wanted the First Experimental Exhibition to be a totally new visual experience" (Asia Art Archive, Jane De Bevoise, Claire Hsu, Phoebe Wong and Anthony Yung, 2010).

These experiences that are prior to the birth of contemporary Chinese art show certain characteristics that foreshadow it. In this regard, it is worth mentioning that, in general, in the periodization of Chinese art, 1989 was considered to be the year in which the transition from experimental to contemporary art took place:

> WHY 1989? Because this is the year that marks major changes in China's cultural scene. Art in China has since reached a new level of maturity which is in many ways the fruition of the previous decade of artistic exploration. Drastic changes in the social and economic order followed in the aftermath of the student movement that year. In 1989 China entered the 90s. (Chang, 1993: 1)

In 1988, a small-scale performance was held at the Sun Yatsen Library called *Language, Communication, Man* with the participation of Yang Jiechang, Hou Hanru, Tang Songwu and Chen Tong. About it, Chen Tong would say the following: "Although few people remember this art event, we must acknowledge that it represents the first time contemporary art was exhibited publicly in Canton." (Chen, 2003: 25) However, Guangdong's experimental art went unnoticed by the 1985 'New Wave Movement' which was considered the prelude to Chinese contemporary art, and in which Guangdong did not participate. This proves, as Chen Tong has expressed, the fact that Guangdong has established itself as a periphery, both geographically and culturally.[1] However, this peripheral character has provided the artists of this region with distinctive and original features.

As mentioned above, the economic boom of the region in the 1980s, the influx of both Hong Kong popular culture products and publications of Western texts has given the art of this region certain characteristics that distinguish it from other areas of China, as artist Xu Tan asserts: "In the north, people often talked about modernity and modern thought in a very academic manner. It was without any concrete life experience. I think modernity can only be discussed in the context of having experienced commerce, consumerism, and the market" (Asia Art Archive, Jane De Bevoise, Claire Hsu, Phoebe Wong and Anthony Yung, 2010). The exploration of issues such as consumerism, urbanization, industrialization and globalization have been very much present in the artists of this region.

The artistic experiences of the 80s were recovered and revalued in the creation of *Libreria Borges*. Chen Tong, its creator, has actively participated in the artistic and cultural effervescence of those years. In order to analyze the case of the *Libreria Borges* bookstore, it is necessary not to see it as an isolated project of individual creation of an artist but as a synthesis of the artistic and cultural tendencies of the 80s, which is updated in relation to the contemporary art of the 90s, and that although it does not cease to bear the hallmark of its creator, it is in a way a collective creation.

The case of *Libreria Borges*

Libreria Borges is a cultural and artistic project created in the city of Guangzhou, province of Guangdong, China, in 1993. At first, this place worked as a place for the dissemination of foreign literary texts, especially by French authors, and also as a

---

1 See Chen, Tong (2003). "Sustaining Change and Diversity: Situation of Cantonese Contemporary Art after 1990" in *Canton Express*. China: Hunan Arts Publishing House.

meeting and production place for several Guangdong artists. As its creator states,[1] 1994-2001 was a trial period during which mostly small-scale irregular programs were organized. Between 2002 and 2006, the participation of contemporary Cantonese artists from the Pearl River Delta region in the 4th Gwangju Biennale in 2002, and in "Canton Express", an exhibition presented in the 50th Venice Biennale in 2003, stood out among other artistic performances. The participating artists conducted research on issues such as the industrialization, urbanization, modernization and globalization of China after the economic reform of the 1980s. Chen Tong, the bookstore founder, is an artist of that city and is not only renowned in China but also overseas. He has several occupations: he is a teacher at the Guangzhou Fine Arts Academy, and also an artist, curator, art collector, editor and critic. This mixture of roles in his biography also reflects on the bookstore he owns since it is currently part of a network of cultural and artistic institutions. In 2007, Chen Tong created the *Libreria Borges Institute for Contemporary Art* or *CANTONBON*, a project that emerged from the bookstore but which, at the same time, goes beyond its concept: "Cantonbon is continue much more bigger than the bookstore but still the bookstore remains the father of this family"[2]. The main activities at *CANTONBON* are the publication of books on contemporary art, literature, philosophy; the organization of reading clubs and book-related events; archive works for Guangdong artists, as well as with respect to material on the Nouveau Roman movement and its own institution, and international artistic and cultural exchanges. Also, it is involved in the *Video Bureau* project, which consists in a video archive system for works of art by Guangdong contemporary artists for researchers, students and collectors. On top of that, it has an art gallery in the same city. These institutions are mainly financed with the sale of works of art produced by Chen Tong himself and the bookstore's sales. A portion of the funds for *Video Bureau* is contributed by an association called 5 Elements Art Association (五行会).

---

1   Asia Art Archive in America (April 2, 2015). *CANTONBON: A Case Study of Locality, Autonomy and Hybridity since 1993* available at: http://www.aaa-a.org/programs/cantonbon-a-case-study-of-locality-autonomy-and-hybridity-since-1993/.
2   Chen Tong, personal communication, May 23, 2018.

We can consider this network of institutions as a center of cultural diffusion that makes a cross between art and reading. As we mentioned earlier, this union between art and reading was present in the 1980s, the "Reading Fever" of those years led to the formation of study groups that later became artistic groups or even groups of artists in which philosophical and aesthetic debates were encouraged. But Chen Tong's experience has also led him to make a crossroads, not only between art and reading, but, more specifically, between art and literature, and here the Nouveau Roman and the work of Alain Robbe-Grillet play an important role: "Robbe-Grillet's influence on me is in all directions. Besides his concepts, his writing techniques and living attitudes also put something in my mind."[1] In turn, this author was also a painter and made a cross between painting and literature in his work *La Belle Captive*, in which he brings together a collection of 77 paintings by René Magritte that illustrate his writings. He has also been famous for his film production.

On the other hand, the name Borges established the bookstore in the field of reading and literature. Borges' work entered China after the reform and opening-up process. However, "Borges was seen as a 'lonesome' writer in the environment of the 1980s. In fact, he only had one book published." (Lou Yu, 2018:14) The repercussion of his work in China began in the 1990s and had to do with avant-garde literature: "First of all, he was a master for avant-garde writers such as Ge Fei, Ma Yuan, Su Tong, among others, and then he was 'the legitimizing father of postmodernism', in the opinion of several Chinese literary critics, until he became 'the writer of writers'." (Lou, 2018:15) In this regard, creating a bookstore and naming it after Borges in the 1990s meant adopting a line of reading for his work which was associated with an avant-garde Chinese literary idea. In addition to this, we may consider the relationship established between this institution and the contemporary artists of the city of Guangdong, who are also associated with a forward-thinking approach:

---

1 Liu, Tina (2014) "Chen Tong's 'Book of Sand'" in *Gallery*. Number 188, July.

Due to several happenings, one might say that 1990 represented a turning point for art in Canton. For example, the Big Tailed Elephant Group was established. This Group organized series of art events that focused on installation art. During the 1992 drawing and painting exhibition, 1990's *Biennale*, the group held unofficial "spin-off exhibitions"- those happenings represented the beginning of "contemporary art" and through opposing prejudice, Canton became a constant promoter for contemporary art. (Chen, 2003: 22)

It is well known that for Chen Tong literature occupies a central place:"[...] I have more than once mentioned that I took writing more seriously than painting", and he adds: "If I had understood writing clearly like this, perhaps I wouldn't go back to painting. But this wasn't the case." (Chen, 2014: 73) This strong interweaving of art and literature is not only Chen Tong's personal mark, but also that of the institutions he founded, whose central core is *Libreria Borges*, since this seminal experience expands to create a network of institutions as complex as the roles it plays. In this phenomenon it is possible to trace elements already present in the experiments in Cantonese art of the 1980s, which can also be observed in the art of the 1990s: 1) a creative appropriation of Western ideas and trends that interact with Chinese realities; 2) an interest in crossing the barriers that divide the different artistic disciplines; 3) a practice that is deeply rooted in Guangdong but is in constant dialogue and exchange with the outside world. While drawing on the experiences of the 1980s and feeding on the trends in contemporary art of the 1990s, *Libreria Borges* places particular emphasis on the link between art and literature. Both this intersection between art and literature and the blurring of the boundaries between artistic practices and the cultural industry are present in this complex web of institutions. For this reason, it becomes an extremely relevant case not only for our research but also for understanding artistic practices (including literature) at this stage of nonspecificity or post-autonomy. At the same time, it highlights the importance of Guangdong art as a particular synthesis between Eastern and Western artistic trends and traditions in the context of a globalizing world.

Bibliography

Asia Art Archive (Producer), Jane De Bevoise (Director), Claire Hsu (Director), Phoebe Wong (Director) and Anthony Yung (Director). (2010). From Jean-Paul Sartre to Teresa Teng [Documentary]. Siren Films.

Chang, Tzong-zung (1993). "Into The Nineties" in *China's New Art, Post -1989. With a retrospective from 1979-1989.* Hong Kong: Hanart TZ Gallery.

Chen, Tong (2003). "Sustaining Change and Diversity: Situation of Cantonese Contemporary Art after 1990" in *Canton Express*. China: Hunan Arts Publishing House.

Chen, Tong (2014). "20 years later" in *Gallery*. Number 188, July.

Fernández del Campo, Eva (2011). "El arte contemporáneo de China en el proceso de mundialización" in *Orientando. Temas de Asia Oriental,* Year II, No. 2, Universidad Veracruzana, Centro de Estudios China-Veracruz, Xalapa, México.

García Canclini, Néstor (2010). *La sociedad sin relato. Antropología y estética de la inminencia.* Buenos Aires: Katz Editores.

Garramuño, Florencia (2015). *Mundos en común. Ensayos sobre las inespecificidad en el arte.* Ciudad Autónoma de Buenos Aires: Fondo de Cultura Económica.

Garramuño, Florencia (2016). "Arte inespecífico y mundos en común" in Ayala, Matías. *Estética, medios masivos y subjetividades.* Chile: Pontificia Universidad Católica de Chile, Facultad de Filosofía, Instituto de Estética.

Gramuglio, María Teresa (2006). "Tres problemas para el comparatismo" in *Orbis Tertius.* Vol. 11. Num. 12.

Li, Xianting (1993). "Major Trends in the Development of Contemporary Chinese Art" in *China's New Art, Post -1989. With a retrospective from 1979-1989.* Hong Kong: Hanart TZ Gallery.

Liu, Tina (2014) "Chen Tong's 'Book of Sand'" in *Gallery*. Number 188, July.

Lou, Yu (2018). "Borges en China (1949-2017)" in *Variaciones Borges*. Number 45, April.

土耳其汉学研究的过去与现在

法特玛【土耳其】

内夫谢希尔·哈只·贝克塔·瓦里大学中国语言文学系助教

一、前言

土耳其共和国是一个横跨欧亚两洲的国家。土耳其三面环海，北临黑海，南临地中海，西临爱琴海。因此，土耳其是"一带一路"沿线的重要国家，也是中东地区重要大国。土总统雷杰普·塔伊普·埃尔多安赞同 2013 年由中国国家主席习近平提出建设"新丝绸之路经济带"和"21 世纪海上丝绸之路"的合作倡议。[1]他表示："我相信，'一带一路'定会成为促进和平、稳定的共赢之路。土耳其会不遗余力地参与并支持'一带一路'建设。"[2]随着"一带一路"建设的推进，土中两国关系正在不断得以加强，并且土中关系的发展引发了土耳其人学习汉语热潮。中国人经常说"团结就是力量"。我相信"一带一路"倡议让全世界人民团结起来。土耳其独特的地理位置与长久的历史对国外游客有较强的吸引力。2018 年是中国"土耳其旅游年"，这体现了中国对中土关系的高度重视。为了迎接中国"土耳其旅游年"，土耳其鼓励导游学习中文。从 2018 年开始，土耳其就在全国初级中学普遍开设汉语选修课。土中关系历史悠久，土耳其的汉学研究起源可以追溯到 16世纪。本文也分析了奥斯曼帝国的中国研究及其汉学在土耳其的起源和发展。

1　http://www.sohu.com/a/257878277_100028284?spm=smmt.mt-learning.fd-
　　d.25.1538784000023WRl5Apr, 2018-10-23.

2　http://finance.sina.com.cn/wm/2017-05-23/doc-ifyfkkme0240522.shtml,2018-10-23.

二、奥斯曼帝国的中国研究

奥斯曼时期，土耳其有关中国的知识只靠一些旅行回家的纪行。例如：1516年，奥斯曼帝国有一位叫阿里·阿克巴尔·契丹（Ali Ekber Hıtaî）的旅行家，用波斯文写成了《中国纪行》(Hıtayname)[1]。《中国纪行》记述了他对当时中国社会生活情况的见闻。16世纪末，奥斯曼帝国户部尚书塞伊菲·切莱比（Seyfi Celebi）写成了《土尔克斯坦与远东纪行》。这部纪行是16世纪关于远东的一部历史地理著作，并讲述了作者在中国的所见所闻[2]。在这两部中国纪行见闻录中，旅行家们将中国称契丹（Hitay）。1900年，奥斯曼帝国著名旅行家阿卜杜拉希德·易卜拉欣（Abdurresid Ibrahim）游历了北亚、朝鲜、日本和南亚之后写成了《伊斯兰世界》[3]。1905年，奥斯曼帝国著名旅行家苏莱曼·苏克鲁先生（Suleyman Sukru）写成了《大纪行》(Seyahatu'l Kubra)，并讲述了在上海、北京生活的穆斯林人经济生活状况。[4]

三、汉学在土耳其的起源和发展

土耳其汉学研究可以追溯到1935年，至今已有83年的历史。在土耳其国父穆斯塔法·凯末尔·阿塔图尔克（Mustafa Kemal Ataturk）建议下，安卡拉大学文史地学院于1935年成立，随后即成立了土耳其第一所汉学系，也是安卡拉大学最早成立的16个系之一。阿塔图尔克成立安卡拉大学汉学系的重要目标是为了研究土耳其的祖先突厥人的历史。相比之下，世界汉学系的目标是研究中国、中国语言、历史、文学、哲学及宗教等。不过，在土耳其成立的第一所汉学系的重要目标，是促成汉学家利用汉语作为资料源语，研究土耳其历史，并且把有关土耳其历史及文化的资料翻译成土耳其语。

1935年，阿塔图尔克邀请了世界著名的德国突厥学家葛玛丽教授（Annemarie von Gabain）在安卡拉大学汉学系授课。1937年葛玛丽教授回国之后，世界著名的德国汉学家艾伯华教授（Wolfram Eberhard）接替他的位置。从1937年至1948

1　《土耳其宗教基础伊斯兰教百科全书》，第17卷，第404、405页。

2　《土尔克斯坦与远东纪行》，2014年版。

3　欧凯：《土耳其的汉学研究及其中文教学》，《汉学研究通讯》，第十六卷，第四期，综号第64期，中国台北，1997年，第393、395页。

4　《大纪行》，安卡拉：土耳其历史协会出版社2013年版。

年，艾伯华教授到安卡拉大学汉学系任教，并担任汉学系主任。在土耳其的 11 年里，艾伯华教授为土耳其汉学做出了巨大贡献，并对土耳其的中国研究起到了重要的作用。艾伯华教授主要著作有《土耳其字母版的中文音节表》（1938）、《古汉语语法简要》（1939）、《汉学初学者重要工具书入门》（1940）、《中国北方邻族》（1942）、《汉学入门》（1946）、《中国通史》（1946）、《中国故事选》、《远东史》《土耳其民间故事选》《中国杂文》《中国民间故事选》《汉语小说在中国人生活中的地位》等出版。[1]

艾伯华教授培养的第一位土耳其汉学家是沐德累教授（Muhaddere Nabi Ozerdim）。沐德累，1916 年出生于伊兹密尔省贝尔加马小镇。1935 年进入安卡拉大学文史地学院汉学系读书。1943 年 3 月 5 日发表土耳其文博士论文《公园 4—5 世纪在中国北方建国的突厥族诗歌研究》。1948 年艾伯华教授任安卡拉大学汉学系主任一职，其间主要著作有《中国回忆录》（1987）。此外，她翻译的中国古籍包括《诗经文集》（1945）、《论语》（1963）、《老子及道德经》（1963）、《中国诗歌精华》（1961）等[2]，并翻译过《苏俄在中国》（1962）[3]。1983 年沐德累教授退休之后，艾哈迈德 . 力萨·别金（Ahmet Riza Bekin）任安卡拉大学汉学系主任一职。他著作有《丝绸之路》（1981）一书。1988 年，汉学系新任系主任欧钢教授（Pulat Otkan）接任。1975 年，发表了土耳其文博士论文《五胡乱华对中国文化、经济、社会的影响》。[4] 他重点研究中东历史及文化。2014 年他和吉莱教授合作翻译了中国古代经典《孙子兵法》。除此之外，欧钢教授遗作土耳其语版《史记·匈奴列传》，在他去世后，由吉莱教授完成并于 2018 年出版。

2005 年，欧钢教授退休之后，欧凯教授（Bulent Okay）任安卡拉大学汉学系主任一职。欧凯教授，1951 年出生于萨卡里亚省。1975 年毕业于安卡拉大学汉学专业。1977 年到政治大学读硕士。1981 年发表了硕士论文《中土原始神话比

1　阿尤布·撒勒塔史（EyupSaritas），杨晨，《1935 年以来的土耳其汉学研究》，《西亚非洲》，第二期,2014 年，第 150 、151 页；吕承璁，《长城外的记忆，万里寻古— 从安卡拉大学汉学系看土耳其汉学研究》，《国立中山大学政治学研究所硕士论文》，2015 年，第 34 页。

2　苗福光，《土耳其汉学研究与孔子学院发展现状》，《阿拉伯世界研究》，第二期，2014 年，第 116 页。

3　欧凯（Bulent Okay），《沐德累教授（Muhaddere Nabi Ozerdim）》，Dogu Dilleri Dergisi(东方语言)，第五卷，第二期，1993 年，第 85-97 页。

4　胡振华，《土耳其著名汉学家、教育家欧钢教授》，《民族教育研究》，第 15 卷，第 4 期，2004 年，第 93 页。

较研究》。他也从事中国水墨画的创作,多次举行个人中国水墨画展。[1] 1982 年,回国任教安卡拉大学汉学专业。1988 年,发表了土耳其文博士论文《隋唐汉化胡人对中国文化的贡献》,取得了博士学位。他翻译出版有《伊斯坦堡的中国宝藏》(2001)、《中国故事集》(1987)、《梅乌拉那故事集》(1986)、《沼气工程使用管理手册》(1983)、《农村沼气技术与建设》(1984),并翻译过中国古代经典《孔子·论语》(2004 年第一版,2017 年第二版)及《孙子兵法》(2016)。他主编的教材包括《使用汉语(上)》(2008)、《使用汉语(下)》(2012)、《使用汉语语法》(2011)、《汉字》(2012)、《汉土—土汉大词典》(2015)、《汉土—土汉词典》(2017)等。[2] 他在 2006 年到 2018 年的整整 12 年里,教育了 39 名年轻汉学家,其中 29 名硕士,10 名博士。[3]

阿尤布教授(Eyup Saritas),土耳其伊斯坦布尔大学中国语言文学系主任。1968 年出生于阿菲永省。1991 年本科毕业于安卡拉大学汉学专业。2005 年,发表了土耳其文博士论文《根据中国考古史料来看,伊斯兰时代之前突厥人文化生活》,取得了博士学位。自 2013 年至目前,任教于伊斯坦布尔大学中国语言文学系。主要著作包括《根据中国考古史料来看,伊斯兰时代之前突厥人文化生活》(2010)、《中国境内匈奴研究》(2010)、《裕固族通史》(2012)、《撒拉族史》(2015)、《中国乡村文学的过去与现在》(2016)等。

吉莱教授(Giray Fidan),安卡拉哈只·拜拉姆·维利大学教授、而且是中文翻译系主任。1980 年出生于安卡拉省。2010 年发表了土耳其文博士论文《根据中国史料,十六世纪奥斯曼帝国与中国的关系与奥斯曼帝国的火器向中国的传入》,取得了博士学位。主要著作包括《生存在中国》(2008)、《奥斯曼帝国的火器向中国的传入与中国的奥斯曼人》(2011)、《中国语言与中文语法》(2011)、《时间打不败的国家:中国》(2012)、《中国人眼中的奥斯曼帝国:康有为突厥游记》(2013)等。他翻译出版有《孙子兵法》(2014)、《论语》(2017)、《古船》(2017)、《凯末尔》(2018)等。

古尔罕副教授(Gurhan Kirilen),安卡拉大学汉学系新任系主任。2018 年 4 月,

---

1 欧凯(Bulent Okay),《土耳其汉学研究的现状与未来》,《土耳其汉学八十年暨首届中国学会议论文集》,五洲传播出版社 2015 年版,第 30 页。

2 法特玛(Fatma Ecem Ceylan),《中华文明:历史、文化、文学、哲学》,伊斯坦布尔 Kesit 出版社,2018 年版,第 24、25 页。

3 http://akademik.yok.gov.tr/AkademikArama/view/viewAuthorThesis.jsp,2018 年 10 月 23 日。

欧凯教授退休之后，古尔罕副教授任安卡拉大学汉学系主任一职。1977 年出生于安卡拉省。2012 年，发表了土耳其文博士论文《在中国史料中的胡人分析——浅析蛮、夷、戎、狄》，取得了博士学位。主要著作包括《古突厥人与突厥人》（2014年）、《中亚佛教——大唐西域记》（2015 年）、《古代突厥人》（2015）、《中国鸦片战争》（2014）、《中国语言》（2016）、《吐谷浑部和拓跋部》（2017）、《黄河区域出土的毗伽可汗时期的突厥雕塑》（2017）、《中国文学小说选》（2017）等。

珍珠副教授（Inci Ince Erdogdu），安卡拉大学汉学系副教授。1968 年出生于屈塔希亚省。1996 年，从安卡拉大学获得了汉学硕士学位。2002 年，发表了中文博士论文《秦汉与匈奴关系研究》，取得了博士学位。主要著作包括《中国穆斯林人口》（2015）、《汉朝时期匈奴的地名、人名和称号研究》（2017）等。主要主编的教材包括《当代中文土耳其文版》（2010）、《当代中文汉字本土耳其文版》（2010）、《当代中文练习册土耳其文版》(2010）等。

努丽娟（Nurcan Kalkir），埃尔吉耶斯大学中国语言文学助理教授。1999 年毕业于安卡拉大学汉学系。同年任教于埃尔吉耶斯大学中国语言文学系。2008 年，在安卡大学汉学系欧凯教授的门下攻读博士学位。博士毕业论文《论汉朝与匈奴的和亲政策及取得的效果》。[1] 主要著作有《汉语使用手册》（2008）一书。

依姆格（S. Imge Azerturk），埃尔吉耶斯大学中国语言文学系助理教授。1998年任教于埃尔吉耶斯大学中国语言文学系。她在安卡拉大学汉学系获得学士和硕士学位。2008~2011 年间，在厦门大学攻读博士学位。[2] 博士毕业论文《汉语后缀和土耳其语后缀的语法性质对比——以汉语后缀"者""家"和土语后缀"一c"为例》。她的研究领域是现代汉语和词汇学。

宫札（Gonca Unal Chiang），安卡拉大学汉学系助理教授。1981 年出生于内夫谢希尔省。2003 年本科毕业于安卡拉大学汉学系。2008 年硕士毕业于国立政治大学。2009~2015 年间，在安卡大学汉学系欧凯教授的门下攻读博士学位。博士毕业论文《中国思想家老子"玄德"思想的重要来源》。主要翻译著作有《土耳其出版者》（2014）、《中国现代散文选》（2016）等。

丽妃（Feyza Gorez），埃尔吉耶斯大学中国语言文学系助理教授。1987 年出生于开塞利省。2007 年本科毕业于埃尔吉耶斯大学中国语言文学系。2011 年硕士

1 努丽娟（Nurcan Kalkir），《土耳其埃尔吉耶斯大学中文系的汉学研究状况》，《土耳其汉学八十年暨首届中国学会议论文集》，五洲传播出版社，2015 年版，第 76 页。
2 同上。

毕业于安卡拉大学汉学系。2013~2017 年间，在安卡大学汉学系欧凯教授的门下攻读博士学位。博士毕业论文《中国皇权制下的宦官现象》[1]。

法特玛 (Fatma Ecem Ceylan)，是内夫谢希尔·哈只·贝克塔·瓦里 (Nevsehir Hacı Bektas Veli) 大学中国语言文学系博士。1988 年出生于代尼兹利省。2010 年本科毕业于埃尔吉耶斯大学中国语言文学系。2010~2012 年间，在东北师范大学攻读硕士学位。2013~2017 年间，在安卡拉大学汉学系欧凯教授的门下攻读博士学位。博士毕业论文《郑和下西洋在中国历史上的地位》。她土译中翻译出版包括《土耳其博物馆的变化与发展》（2014）、《尚勒乌尔法旅游》（2018）和《尚勒乌尔法旅游地图》（2018）。除此之外，2018 年法特玛、宫札助理教授和艾图龙研究员（Ertugrul Ceylan）[2] 合作编成了《中华文明：历史、文化、文学、哲学·欧凯教授纪念论文集》一书。

月光 (Nuray Pamuk Ozturk)，卡拉曼·梅赫梅特·贝 (Karaman Mehmet Bey) 大学中国语言文学系博士。1985 年出生于特拉布宗省。她在安卡拉大学汉学系获得学士、硕士和博士学位。2012~2017 年间，在安卡大学汉学系欧凯教授的门下攻读博士学位。博士毕业论文《根据中国参考文献恒罗斯之战：原因、结果及其影响》。她和燕迪研究员（Mukaddes Cihanyandi）合作翻译了《土耳其共和国，联合国教科文组织世界文化遗产预备名录》一书。除了这些汉学家之外，15 位研究员还在安卡拉大学汉学系和安卡拉哈只·拜拉姆·维利大学大学语言系攻读博士学位，并且三位研究员正在在中国攻读博士学位。

我们还可以说，安卡拉大学汉学系自 1935 年以来，与历史系一直保持着密切联系与合作。因此，著名的历史学家中，奥吉李教授（Bahaddin Ogel）、古尔琴教授（Gulcin Candarlioglu）、涂逸珊教授（Isenbike Togan）、奥纳特教授 (Ayse Onat)、蒂谢尔教授 (Ahmet Tasagil)、尔吉拉溥教授 (Konuralp Ercilasun) 对汉学研究做出了很多贡献。2005 年，奥纳特教授、塞玛助理教授和尔吉拉溥教授合作翻译了《汉书·匈奴传》。同年，涂逸珊教授翻译了《旧唐书·突厥传》。1995—2004 年间，蒂谢尔教授写成了《突厥通史（全三册）》。

---

1 努丽娟（Nurcan Kalkir），《土耳其埃尔吉耶斯大学中文系的汉学研究状况》，《土耳其汉学八十年暨首届中国学会议论文集》，五洲传播出版社，2015 年版，第 76 页。

2 艾图龙，是阿勒·易卜拉欣·车辰大学的助教。1982 年出生于托卡特省。2006 年，本科毕业于西安外国语大学。2015 年，他在安卡拉大学汉学系获得了硕士学位，并还在安卡拉大学攻读博士学位。2014 年，他和法特玛博士合作翻译了《土耳其博物馆的变化与发展》。他还编成了欧凯教授翻译的《孙子兵法》和《孔子·论语》两书。

四、结语

土中两个国家的关系可以追溯到数千年之前。近代两个国家的关系可以追溯到 1923 年。土耳其国父阿塔图尔克成立土耳其共和国之后，积极主动与中国建立和发展友好关系。由此，土耳其的汉学研究始自 1935 年。从 1935 年以来，随着汉学在土耳其的逐渐发展、土耳其新一代汉学家逐渐成长起来。虽然在这一时期，土耳其学术没有像西方那样出现很多汉学家，但是年轻一代的汉学研究者不断地增加，其研究自古而今，越来越深入。随着土耳其新一代汉学家的成长，土耳其汉学研究变得更丰富起来。我很希望土耳其新一代每个汉学家成为我们国和中国之间的一座桥梁。我觉得这样才可以使土中两个国家的关系愈加密切。

The Past and Present of Sinology in Turkey

Ceylan Fatma Ecem / Turkey

Research Assistant of Nevsehir Haci Bektas Veli University

1. Introduction

The Republic of Turkey is a country that is part of both Europe and Asia. The country is encircled by seas on three sides: the Black Sea to the north, the Mediterranean to the south and the Aegean Sea to the west. Therefore, Turkey is an important country along the "Belt and Road" and an important power in the Middle East. President Recep Tayyip Erdogan endorsed the initiative of cooperation proposed by Chinese President Xi Jinping in 2013 to build the "New Silk Road Economic Belt" and the "21st Century Maritime Silk Road".[1] He said: "I believe that the Belt and Road will be a win-win road for peace and stability. Turkey will spare no effort to participate in and support the construction of the Belt and Road."[2] With the advancement of the construction of the "Belt and Road", the relations between Turkey and China are constantly being strengthened and have triggered a wave of Chinese learning in Turks. As a Chinese saying goes, "unity is strength". I

---

1 http://www.sohu.com/a/257878277_100028284?spm=smmt.mt-learning.fd
   d.25.1538784000023WRl5Apr, 2018-10-23.
2 http://fifinance.sina.com.cn/wm/2017-05-23/doc-ifyfkkme0240522.shtml,2018-10-23.

believe that the Belt and Road Initiative can bring people around the world together. Turkey's unique geographic location and long history make it attractive to foreign tourists. The year 2018 is China's "Turkey Tourism Year", which reflects China's great importance to Sino-Turkish relations. To welcome China's "Turkey Tourism Year", Turkey encourages tour guides to learn Chinese. Since 2018, Turkey has begun to teach the elective course of Chinese in junior high schools nationwide. Turkey-China relations have a long history and the origin of sinology in Turkey can be traced back to the 16th century. This article also analyzes Chinese studies in the period of the Ottoman Empire and the origin and development of sinology in Turkey.

2. Chinese Studies in the Period of the Ottoman Empire

During the Ottoman period, Turkey's knowledge of China relied on travel notes of some travelers. For example: In 1516, a traveler named Ali Ekber Hıtaî in the Ottoman Empire wrote the *Hıtayname*[1] in Persian, which recorded his experience of the society and lifestyle in China at that time. At the end of the 16th century, Seyfifi Celebi, the Minister of Revenue of the Ottoman Empire, wrote the *Turkistan ve Uzak Dogu Seyahatnamesi*, a historic and geographic book about the Far East in the 16th century that described what the author saw and heard in China[2]. In these two works of travel notes, travelers referred to China as Hitay. In 1900, a famous Ottoman traveler called Abdurresid Ibrahim traveled to North Asia, North Korea, Japan and South Asia and wrote the *Islamic World*[3]. In 1905, another well-known Suleyman Sukru wrote the *Seyahatu'lKubra* to depict the economic life of Muslims living in Shanghai and Beijing.[4]

3. The Origin and Development of Sinology in Turkey

Sinology in Turkey, which can be traced back to 1935, has already witnessed a

---

1   Tasagil Ahmet, Hitayname, *Turkish Religious Foundation Encyclopaedia of Islam*, Vol.17, pp.404, 405.
2   Celebi Seyfi, *Turkistan ve Uzak Dogu Seyahatnamesi*. Istanbul: Selenge Press, 2014.
3   Bulent Okay, Sinology in Turkey and the Teaching of Chinese, *Newsletter for Research in Chinese Studies*, Vol.16, Issue 64(4), Taipei (China), 1997, p.393, p. 395.
4   Suleyman Sukru, *Seyahatu'lKubra*, Ankara: Turkish Historical Society Press, 2013.

history of 83 years. As proposed by Mustafa Kemal Ataturk, the Father of the Turks, Ankara University founded the Faculty of Language History and Geography in 1935 and later established the first Sinology Department in Turkey, which was also one of the sixteen earliest departments established at Ankara University. An important goal of Ataturk to found the Sinology Department of Ankara University was to study the history of Turkish ancestors. In contrast, the goal of the World Sinology Department was to study China, the Chinese language, history, literature, philosophy and religion. However, the important goal of the first Sinology department established in Turkey was to enable sinologists to use Chinese as a source language to study Turkish history and translate information about Turkish history and culture into the Turkish language.

In 1935, Ataturk invited the world-renowned German Professor Annemarie von Gabain who dealt with Turkic studies to teach in the Sinology Department of Ankara University. After Professor Annemarie returned to Germany in 1937, another famous German sinologist Professor Wolfram Eberhard took over her position. From 1937 to 1948, Professor Eberhard taught in the Sinology Department of Ankara University and served as the Chair of Sinology. In his eleven years in Turkey, Professor Eberhard made great contributions to Turkish sinology and played an important role in Turkish Chinese studies. Professor Eberhard's main works include *Chinese Syllables in the Turkish Alphabet* (1938), *A Brief Introduction to Ancient Chinese Grammar* (1939), *Introduction to Important Reference Books for Beginners of Sinology* (1940), *Northern Peoples of China* (1942), *Introduction to Sinology* (1946), *A History of China* (1946), *Chinese Stories, History of the Far East, Folktales of Turkey, Chinese Essays, Folktales of China* and *The Role of Novels in Chinese Life.*[1]

The first Turkish sinologist educated by Professor Eberhard was Professor Muhaddere Nabi Ozerdim, who was born in Bergama, Izmir Province in 1916 and

---

1   Eyup Saritas and Yang Chen, A General Look into Chinese Research in Turkey as of the Year 1935, *West Asia and Africa*, 2014(2), pp.150, 151; Cheng-Tsung Lu, *Bring Back the Memory outside the Great Wall — Turkish Sinological Research from the Perspective of the Department of Sinology, Ankara University*, Master's Thesis of the Institute of Political Science, National Sun Yat-sen University, 2015, p.34.

began her study in the Sinology Department of the Faculty of Language History and Geography at Ankara University in 1935. On March 5, 1943, she published her doctoral thesis in Turkish entitled "The Study of Turkic Poetry in Northern China during the 4th-5th Century". In 1948, Professor Eberhard served as the Chair of the Sinology Department of Ankara University, and his main works included the *Memoirs of China* (1987). Moreover, he translated ancient Chinese books including *The Book of Poetry* (1945), *The Analects of Confucius* (1963), *Laozi and Dao De Jing* (1963), and the *Essence of Chinese Poetry* (1961) etc.[1] and also *Soviet in China* (1962)[2]. After Professor Muhaddere retired in 1983, Ahmet Riza Bekin assumed the post of the Chair of the Sinology Department of Ankara University. He was the author of the book *Silk Road* (1981). In 1988, Professor Pulat Otkan became the new Chair of the Sinology Department. In 1975, he published a Turkish doctoral thesis entitled "The Infuence of the Uprising of the Five Barbarians on Chinese Culture, Economy, and Society".[3] He was interested in the history and culture of the Middle East. In 2014, he co-translated the ancient Chinese classic *Sun Tzu on Art of War* with Professor Giray Fidan. Furthermore, Professor Pulat Otkan's legacy was the Turkish version of the *Biography of Huns in Historical Records*, which was completed by Professor Giray Fidan after his death, and was published in 2018.

After Professor Pulat Otkan retired in 2005, Professor Bulent Okay served as the Chair of the Sinology Department of Ankara University. Professor Bulent Okay was born in 1951 in Sakarya Province. He graduated with a major in sinology from Ankara University in 1975. In 1977, he went on to study for a master's degree at National Chengchi University. In 1981, he published his master's thesis "Comparison of Turkish and Chinese Primitive Myths". He also painted Chinese ink paintings and

---

1   Miao Fuguang, Sinology Research and the Development of the Confucius Institute in Turkey, *Arab World Studies*, 2014(2), p.116.

2   Bulent Okay, Muhaddere Nabi Ozerdim, *Dogu Dilleri Dergisi (Oriental Language)*, Vol.5, 1993(2), pp.85-97.

3   Hu Zhenhua, Professor PULAT OTKAN — A Famous Turkish Sinologist and Educationist, *Journal of Research on Education for Ethnic Minorities*, Vol.15, 2004(4), p.93.

held many solo painting exhibitions.[1] In 1982, he returned to teach sinology at Ankara University. In 1988, he published a doctoral in Turkish entitled "The Contribution of the Hanized Hu People to Chinese Culture in the Sui and Tang Dynasties" and received a doctor's degree. He translated and published *Chinese Treasures in Istanbul* (2001), *Chinese Stories* (1987), *Mevlana Stories* (1986), *Biogas Engineering Management Handbook* (1983), *Rural Biogas Technology and Construction* (1984) and translated the Chinese classics *Confucius · The Analects* (the first edition in 2004 and the second edition in 2017) and *Sun Tzu's Art of War* (2016). His edited textbooks include *Using Chinese (Part I)* (2008), *Using Chinese (Part II)* (2012), *Using Chinese Grammar* (2011), *Chinese Characters* (2012), *Chinese-Turkish and Turkish-Chinese Great Dictionary* (2015), *Chinese-Turkish and Turkish-Chinese Dictionary* (2017), etc.[2] In the 12 years from 2006 to 2018, he educated 39 young sinologists, including 29 who got a master's degree and 10 who received a doctor's degree.[3]

Professor Eyup Saritas, Chair of the Department of Chinese Language and Literature at Istanbul University in Turkey, was born in Afyon in 1968. In 1991, he graduated from Ankara University with a bachelor's degree in sinology. In 2005, he published a doctoral thesis in Turkish entitled "The Turkish Cultural Life before the Islamic Era According to Chinese Archeological Historical Data" and received a doctor's degree. From 2013 until now, he has been teaching at the Department of Chinese Language and Literature of Istanbul University. His main works include *The Turkish Cultural Life before the Islamic Era According to Chinese Archeological Historical Data* (2010), *A Study of the Hun in China* (2010), *A History of the Yugurs* (2012), *A History of the Salars* (2015) and *The Past and Present of Chinese Rural Literature* (2016), etc.

Professor Giray Fidan, Professor of Ankara Haci Bayram Veli University and

---

1 Bulent Okay, The Present and Future of Turkish Sinology Research, *Eighty Years of Turkish Sinology and Proceedings of the First Chinese Conference*, China International Communication Center, 2015, p.30.

2 Fatma Ecem Ceylan, *Chinese Civilization: History, Culture, Literature, Philosophy*, Istanbul: Kesit Press, 2018, pp.24, 25.

3 http://akademik.yok.gov.tr/AkademikArama/view/viewAuthorThesis.jsp，2018-10 -23 .

Chair of the Department of Chinese Translation, was born in Ankara Province in 1980. In 2010, he published a doctoral thesis in Turkish on "The Relationship between the Ottoman Empire and China in the 16th Century and the Introduction of Ottoman Firearms to China" based on the Chinese historical data and received a doctor's degree. His main works include *Surviving in China* (2008), *Introduction of Firearms from the Ottoman Empire to China and the Ottoman People in China* (2011), *Chinese Language and Chinese Grammar* (2011), *An Unbeatable Country in Time: China* (2012), *The Ottoman Empire in the Eyes of the Chinese: Kang Youwei's Travels to Turks* (2013), etc. He translated and published *Sun Tzu's Art of War* (2014), *The Analects of Confucius* (2017), *Ancient Ships* (2017), *Kemal* (2018), and so on.

Associate Professor Gurhan Kirilen, the new Chair of the Sinology Department of Ankara University. In April 2018, after Professor Bulent Okay retired, Associate Professor Gurhan, who was born in Ankara Province in 1977, served as the Chair of the Sinology Department of Ankara University. In 2012, he published a doctoral thesis in Turkish on "A Hu Analysis in Chinese Historical Materials — An Analysis of Man, Yi, Rong and Di", and received a doctor's degree. His main works include *Ancient Turki and Turk* (2014), *Buddhism in Central Asia — Great Tang Records on the Western Regions* (2015), *Ancient Turki* (2015), *The Opium War of China* (2014), *The Chinese Language* (2016), *Tuyuhun and Tuoba Tribes* (2017), *Turki Sculptures of the Bilge Khan Period Unearthed in the Yellow River Region* (2017), *Selected Chinese Literary Novels* (2017), etc.

Inci Ince Erdogdu, Associate Professor in the Sinology Department of Ankara University, was born in Kutahya Province in 1968. In 1996, she obtained a master's degree in sinology from Ankara University. In 2002, she published a Chinese doctoral thesis "Research on the Relationship between Qin, Han and Huns" and obtained a doctor's degree. Her main works include *The Muslim Population in China* (2015) and *Study on Place Names, Persons' Names and Titles of Huns in the Han Dynasty* (2017). The textbooks she has edited include *Turkish Edition of Contemporary Chinese* (2010), *Turkish Edition of Contemporary Chinese Characters*

(2010), *Turkish Edition of Contemporary Chinese Workbook* (2010), etc.

Nurcan Kalkir is an assistant professor of Chinese language and Literature of Erciyes University. She graduated from the Sinology Department of Ankara University in 1999. In the same year, she taught at the Department of Chinese Language and Literature of Erciyes University. In 2008, she studied for a doctor's degree under the supervision of Professor Bulent Okay in the Sinology Department of Anka University. Her doctoral thesis was entitled "On the Marriage-for-Peace Policy of the Han Dynasty and the Huns and the Results".[1] Her main works include the *Chinese Usage Handbook* (2008).

S. Imge Azerturk is an assistant professor in the Department of Chinese Language and Literature of Erciyes University. In 1998, she began to work as a teacher there. She received bachelor's and master's degrees from the Sinology Department of Ankara University. From 2008 to 2011, she studied for a doctorate degree at Xiamen University.[2] Her doctoral thesis was "Comparison of the Grammatical Nature of Chinese and Turkish Suffixes: Taking the Chinese Suffixes 'zhe', 'jia' and the Turkish Suffix 'c' as Examples". She is interested in the research on modern Chinese and lexicology.

Gonca Unal Chiang, Assistant Professor in the Sinology Department of Ankara University, was born in 1981 in Nevsehir Province. She graduated from the Sinology Department of Ankara University in 2003. In 2008, she graduated from National Chengchi University with a master's degree. From 2009 to 2015, she studied for her doctorate degree under the supervision of Professor Bulent Okay in the Sinology Department of Anka University. Her doctoral thesis was "An Important Source of the Chinese Thinker Lao Tzu's 'Xuande' Thought". Her main translations include *Turkish Publishers* (2014), *Selected Modern Chinese Essays* (2016), etc.

---

1 Nurcan Kalkir, Sinology Research in the Chinese Department of Erciyes University in Turkey, *Eighty Years of Turkish Sinology and Proceedings of the First Chinese Conference*, China International Communication Center, 2015, p.76.

2 Ibid.

Feyza Gorez, an assistant professor in the Department of Chinese Language and Literature of Erciyes University, was born in Kayseri Province in 1987. In 2007, she graduated from the Department of Chinese Language and Literature of Erciyes University. In 2011, she graduated from the Sinology Department of Ankara University. During the period 2013-2017, she studied for a doctorate degree under Professor Bulent Okay in the Sinology Department of Anka University. Her doctoral thesis was "The Eunuch Phenomenon under Chinese Imperial Power".[1]

Fatma Ecem Ceylan, PhD in the Department of Chinese Language and Literature of Nevsehir Hacı Bektas Veli University, was born in Denizli Province in 1988. In 2010, she graduated from the Department of Chinese Language and Literature of Erciyes University. From 2010 to 2012, she studied for a master's degree at Northeast Normal University. From 2013 to 2017, she studied for a doctoral degree under the supervision of Professor Bulent Okay in the Sinology Department of Ankara University. Her doctoral thesis was "The Position of Zheng He's Voyages in Chinese History". Her translations and publications from Turkish to Chinese include *Changes and Developments of Turkish Museums* (2014), *Travel to Şanlıurfa* (2018) and *A Tourist Map of Şanlıurfa* (2018). Moreover, in 2018, she, Assistant Professor Gonca Unal Chiang and Researcher Ertugrul Ceylan[2] co-authored a book entitled the *Chinese Civilization: History, Culture, Literature, Philosophy · Papers in Memory of Professor Okay.*

Nuray Pamuk Ozturk, PhD in the Department of Chinese Language and Literature of Karaman Mehmet Bey University, was born in Trabzon Province in 1985. She received her bachelor's, master's, and doctor's degrees from the Sinology

---

1   Nurcan Kalkir, Sinology Research in the Chinese Department of Erciyes University in Turkey, *Eighty Years of Turkish Sinology and Proceedings of the First Chinese Conference*, China International Communication Center, 2015, p.76.

2   Ertugrul Ceylan, a teaching assistant at Agri Ibrahim Cecen University, was born in Tokat Province in 1982. In 2006, he graduated from Xi' an International Studies University with a bachelor' s degree. In 2015, he received a master's degree at the Sinology Department of Ankara University. He is studying for a doctor' s degree at Ankara University. In 2014, he and Dr. Fatma Ecem Ceylan co-translated the *Changes and Development of Turkish Museums*. He also edited the two books *Sun Tzu's Art of War and Confucius · The Analects* translated by Professor Bulent Okay.

Department of Ankara University. From 2012 to 2017, she studied for a doctor's degree under the supervision of Professor Bulent Okay. Her doctoral thesis was "The Battle of Talas Based on Chinese References: Causes, Results and Impacts". She co-translated the book *Republic of Turkey: UNESCO World Heritage List* with researcher Mukaddes Cihanyandi. In addition to these sinologists, 15 researchers are studying for their doctor's degrees in the Sinology Department of Ankara University and the Langauge Department of Ankara Haci Bayram Veli University, and three researchers are studying for a PhD degree in China.

It can be said that since 1935, the Sinology Department of Ankara University has kept close contact with and has cooperated with the History Department. Therefore, these famous historians, Professor Bahaddin Ogel, Professor Gulcin Candarlioglu, Professor Isenbike Togan, Professor Ayse Onat, Professor Ahmet Tasagil, and Professor Konuralp Ercilasun, have made a lot of contributions to the study of sinology. In 2005, Professor Ayse Onat, Assistant Professor Sema and Professor Konuralp Ercilasun co-translated the *History of the Han Dynasty: Biography of the Huns*. In the same year, Professor Isenbike Togan translated the *Old Tang Book — Turk Biographies*. From 1995 to 2004, Professor Ahmet Tasagil wrote *The History of Gokturks* (3 volumes).

4. Conclusions

The relations between Turkey and China can be traced back to thousands of years ago, but in modern times they started from 1923. After the founding of the Republic of Turkey, Turkish founder Atatürk actively established and developed friendly relations with China. As a result, sinology in Turkey began in 1935. Since 1935, with the steady development of sinology, a new generation of sinologists has gradually grown up in Turkey. Although during this period, there were not as many Turkish sinologists as there were in the West, the number of the younger generation of sinologists was on the increase and their studies ranged from ancient to modern times and went even deeper. With the growth of a new generation of Turkish sinologists, sinology has become enriched. I hope that every new generation of sinologists in Turkey can become a bridge between our country and China. Only in this way can the relations between Turkey and China become closer and closer.

References

1.Celebi Seyfi,《土尔克斯坦与远东纪行（Turkistan ve Uzak Dogu Seyahatnamesi）》，Istanbul: Selenge 出版社 , 2014 年版。

2. 欧凯（Okay Bulent），《土耳其的汉学研究及其中文教学》，《汉学研究通许》，第十六卷，第四期，综号第 64 期，中国台北，1997 年，第 393、395 页。

3. Sukru Suleyman, *Seyahatu'lKubra*, Ankara: Turkish Historical Society Press, 2013.

4. Tasagil Ahmet, Hitayname, *Turkish Religious Foundation Encyclopaedia of Islam*, Vol.17, pp.404, 405.

5. 努丽娟（Kalkir Nurcan），《土耳其埃尔吉耶斯大学中文系的汉学研究状况》，《土耳其汉学八十年暨首届中国学会议论文集》，五洲传播出版社，2015 年版。

6. Okay Bulent, Muhaddere Nabi Ozerdim, *Dogu Dilleri Dergisi (Oriental Language)*, Vol.5, 1993(2), pp.85-97.

7. Ceylan Fatma Ecem, *Chinese Civilization: History, Culture, Literature, Philosophy*, Istanbul: Kesit Press, 2018.

8. 胡振华，《土耳其著名汉学家、教育家欧钢教授》，《民族教育研究》，第 15 卷，第 4 期，2004 年。

9. Saritas Eyup and Yang Chen, A General Look into Chinese Research in Turkey as of the Year 1935, *West Asia and Africa*, 2014.

10. 苗福光，《土耳其汉学研究与孔子学院发展现状》，《阿拉伯世界研究》，第二期，2014 年，第 111-120 页。

11. 吕承璁，《长城外的记忆，万里寻古 - 从安卡拉大学汉学系看土耳其汉学研究》，《国立中山大学政治学研究所硕士论文》，2015 年。

12. 欧凯（Okay Bulent），《土耳其汉学研究的现状与未来》，《土耳其汉学八十年暨首届中国学会议论文集》，五洲传播出版社，2015 年版，第 29-33 页。

13. http://akademik.yok.gov.tr/AkademikArama/view/viewAuthorThesis.jsp, 2018-10-23.

14. http://fifinance.sina.com.cn/wm/2017-05-23/doc-ifyfkkme0240522.shtml, 2018-10-23.

15. http://www.sohu.com/a/257878277_100028284?spm=smmt.mt-learning.fd d.25.1538784000023WRl5Apr, 2018-10-23.

全球推进区域一体化创新实践：以欧洲和拉丁美洲为例

司芙兰【意大利】

阿根廷拉普拉塔国立大学中国研究中心主任

引　言

　　"一带一路"倡议是一个特别的国际合作项目，将亚洲、欧洲、非洲和拉丁美洲联系在一起。"一带一路"倡议开始于 5 年前，习近平主席 2013 年访问哈萨克斯坦期间提出。本文将分析"一带一路"倡议作为动态区域一体化背后的驱动因素，如何构成超越区域组织静态联系的合作平台。在与中国进行国际合作的具体实践框架下，各国必须制定共同政策以面对资源有效分配等问题。另一方面，中国被迫面对"双重"政治现实，国家和超国家。

　　值得注意的是，"一带一路"倡议在欧洲从两个方面对欧盟产生影响：一方面，质疑东欧和西欧的经济差距；另一方面，要求互联互通，覆盖欧盟和欧盟以外的国家。最终逐渐推动欧盟一体化发展。第七次"16+1"国家峰会于 2018 年 7 月在保加利亚首都索非亚举行。"16+1"是中国（作为"1"）与 16 个欧洲国家开展合作的倡议，包括 11 个欧盟成员国（保加利亚、克罗地亚、捷克共和国、爱沙尼亚、匈牙利、拉脱维亚、立陶宛、波兰、罗马尼亚、斯洛伐克和斯洛文尼亚）以及 5 个申请加入欧盟的国家（阿尔巴尼亚、波斯尼亚和黑塞哥维那、黑山、塞尔维亚和马其顿）。通过这一重要的论坛中，我们了解推动欧洲联合的驱动力。

　　至于非洲，非洲联盟已涵盖非洲大陆所有 55 个国家。尽管如此，中国过去一直在推动与非洲国家的双边合作模式，饱受非洲"去一体化"批评。然而，习近平主席于2018年9月在北京举行的中非合作论坛（FOCAC）上发表讲话时宣布，决定"和非洲联盟启动编制《中非基础设施合作规划》"，"坚定支持非洲国家和非洲联盟等地区组织以非洲方式解决非洲问题"。

在拉丁美洲有必要考虑若干一体化组织的存在，它们正在积累发展的政治动能，即使没有秩序，采用多维方法且速度不同。这些区域组织包括南方共同市场（MERCOSUR）、安第斯国家共同体（CAN）、CARICOM（加勒比共同体，英文缩写）、UNASUR（南美国家联盟）、SICA（中美洲一体化体系）、ALBA（美洲玻利瓦尔联盟）、AP（拉美太平洋联盟）和CELAC（拉美和加勒比国家共同体）。中国与拉美和加勒比经济共同体（CELAC）经常举行会议，这是唯一代表拉美所有国家并将其表示为"共同体"的区域组织。

就东南亚国家联盟（ASEAN）而言，"一带一路"倡议将通过加强东盟10个成员国之间以及东盟国家与中国之间的经济联系发挥作用，让世界上两个最具活力的区域建立联系。此外，"一带一路"倡议将允许东南亚国家缩小现有基础设施差距并促进工业发展：2015年东盟经济共同体的成立使东南亚的经济体可以联合为单一市场，而北京的战略将通过基础设施开发和稳定的贸易体制提供未来的整合。

在亚欧大陆，"一带一路"倡议对区域一体化组织也起到真正的推动作用。一开始对中国的项目有反对的声音。事实上，2014年成立欧亚经济联盟（EAEU）（俄罗斯联邦、白俄罗斯、哈萨克斯坦、亚美尼亚、吉尔吉斯斯坦），提议在中国项目框架之外进行整合。然而，中国和俄罗斯于2014年联合宣布经济合作项目同步后，2015年又产生新的大陆经济一体化，涵盖欧亚经济联盟、中国、东盟、伊朗共和国和SAARC（南亚区域合作联盟，英文缩写[1]）。

一、"一带一路"在欧盟：对抗或推动

鉴于中国的合作凸显欧洲的灰色地带，因此"一带一路"倡议在欧盟的区域一体化层面上引发多维的动态。首先，"一带一路"倡议点燃欧盟各国的激情，虽然后来该倡议因缺乏透明度和可能引发欧盟危机而受到严厉批评，因为中国的

1　成立于1985年，包括以下国家：阿富汗、孟加拉国、不丹、印度、马尔代夫、尼泊尔、巴基斯坦和斯里兰卡。

双边协议做法可能加剧成员国之间的竞争[1]。批评可能是因中国在东欧国家中的逐渐存在而开始蔓延，欧洲人担心可能逐渐失去对这些地区的影响力。

在现实中，巴尔干地区已被欧盟归为"二等欧洲公民"，不"够格"成为欧盟成员，但必须在可能加入欧盟的"诱惑"下让它们受到欧盟法律和商业影响。事实上，特别是欧洲参与"一带一路"合作方面，巴尔干地区一直被视为欧盟和中国这两个主角之间的"过渡区域"（Hackaj，2018年）。中国一直处于时刻待命状态，承认这些领土自治权，不仅是作为"中间领土"，还是具有巨大发展潜力的独立国家。

考虑到对这些领土的影响力，中国和欧盟已经走上一条对抗的道路，充分利用这些国家的优势，因此它们正处于两大势力的"争夺"中。

事实上，自2012年以来，中国已经发起一系列"16+1"峰会。中国与中东欧16个国家共同参与，包括11个欧盟成员国（保加利亚、克罗地亚、捷克共和国、爱沙尼亚、匈牙利、拉脱维亚、立陶宛、波兰、罗马尼亚、斯洛伐克和斯洛文尼亚）以及5个西巴尔干国家（阿尔巴尼亚、波斯尼亚和黑塞哥维那、黑山、塞尔维亚和马其顿），作为一种替代合作形式，代表创新的区域合作方法[2]。根据中国的说法，"16+1"是区域合作的试验模式，与中国在非洲、东亚、拉丁美洲和中东国家建立的其他多边合作平台具有共同的特点。目的是引进一种新型的"非西方南南多边合作"。值得一提的是，没有这个平台，东欧国家的重要价值不会凸显[3]。

另一方面，欧盟激烈批评这种合作模式可能导致欧洲一体化分裂[4]。实际上欧盟已经与中国制定高度完善的战略计划[5]，认为"16+1"平台是对"规则"的偏离，不会造就真正的多边合作，反而会加剧欧洲国家之间的冲突[6]。然而，正如欧洲议会文件所述[7]，欧洲的态度在2018年发生转变，特别是在欧盟成为"16+1"对话的

1　Document of the European Parliament: *China, the 16+1 cooperation format and the EU*, 2017.
2　Document of the European Parliament: *China, the 16+1 format and the EU*, 2018.
3　Document of the European Parliament: *China, the 16+1 format and the EU*, 2018.
4　Document of the European Parliament: *China, the 16+1 cooperation format and the EU*, 2017. http://www.europarl.europa.eu/sides/getDoc.do?type=TA&language=EN&reference=P8-TA-2015-0458.
5　今年也是中欧建立战略伙伴关系15周年，最近中欧关系最高水平的联合文件《中欧合作2020战略规划》明确指出这一点。2016年7月，欧盟对中国采取新策略。值得注意的是，2018年还是中欧旅游年：欧盟和中国在这一框架下力求通过青年和文化项目、节日和其他对话使双方人民相互接近。
6　Document of the European Parliament: *China, the 16+1 cooperation format and the EU*, 2017.
7　Document of the European Parliament: *China, the 16+1 format and the EU*, 2018.

观察员后，同时欧洲（尤其是德国）提出渐进发展的"柏林进程 2014-2018"[1]。

为了进一步重申对欧洲一体化的支持，在索非亚举行的"16+1"会议上通过《中欧合作 2020 战略规划》和《中国 - 中东欧国家索非亚合作纲要》，中国明确表示支持欧洲一体化并认为"16+1"合作形式是"中欧全球战略伙伴关系的补充而不是替代"[2]。中国总理李克强指出："16+1 合作绝不是地缘政治工具，有人可能会说这种合作模式让欧洲分裂，但事实并非如此。"

中国的立场取决于几个因素：中国不能忽视"一带一路"框架下对欧盟的承诺以及与欧盟的全面战略合作。另一方面，中国强调，尽管巴尔干国家尚未成为欧盟成员国，但实际上仍在欧盟法律框架内行事。"这些经济体是欧盟经济的卫星国且紧密跟随欧盟的经济周期。柏林进程为欧盟、西巴尔干国家和中国之间的以结果为导向的合作提供平台。虽然互联互通计划邀请'一带一路'倡议合作，但'16+1'合作是柏林进程下区域合作的组成部分"（Hackaj，2018 年）。

因此，在双重进程的积极推动下，欧洲正在朝着更好的区域一体化迈进：一方面，在大分裂和欧洲怀疑主义的历史时刻，各方在欧盟国家框架下寻求对"一带一路"达成共识；另一方面，"一带一路"倡议及其对"16+1"和"柏林进程"的对抗有助于巴尔干国家加入一体化和实现包容性活力[3]。虽然迄今为止欧洲仍然

1　柏林进程开始于 2014 年，是德国总理默克尔发起的一项举措，现已成为改善区域合作、支持互联互通项目以及鼓励东南欧国家进行结构改革和加入欧盟的有用平台。同时，柏林进程被证明是欧盟和潜在申请国最重要的共同倡议，着重强调欧盟在西巴尔干地区一体化的一些明确观点。虽然"柏林进程"原定于下一次伦敦峰会结束，但承诺将这一进程延续到 2018 年以后。这一承诺主要涉及人员互通，特别是作为"未来一代"的年轻人。正如欧盟委员会主席在 2017 年 9 月发表的"国情咨文"中所提到的那样，扩大欧盟的前景是可信和现实的。欧盟成员国已承诺通过区域层面的合作开始推动西巴尔干半岛转型进程。这意味着如果在柏林进程下共同努力，可以取得切实的成果。"柏林进程 2014-2018"，"柏林进程系列"报告，柏林进程 /2018 年 3 月，合作与发展研究机构，2018 年 2 月，第 6 页。

2　欧盟成员国和 16 个中东欧国家中的欧盟申请国支持欧盟和中国打造和平、增长、改革、文明伙伴关系以及《中欧合作 2020 年战略规划》，包括在中欧互联互通框架、欧洲投资计划和泛欧交通网络延长线（TEN-T）下通过试点项目积极推动实际合作平台，还支持欧盟与中国之间达成一项雄心勃勃的全面投资协议。

（9）"各方愿支持'一带一路'建设同中欧互联互通平台、泛欧交通网络西巴尔干延长线以及相关周边合作倡议相对接，这将有益于欧洲一体化进程。包括中国 - 中东欧国家合作、中欧互联互通平台、欧盟东部伙伴关系等在内的合作倡议之间在经济合作、互联互通上的协调沟通，将为有关国家深化合作提供机遇。"《中国 - 中东欧国家索菲亚合作纲要》。(http://english.gov.cn/news/international_exchanges/2018/07/16/content_281476224693086.htm)。

3　THE BERLIN PROCESS 2014-2018, Report "Berlin Process Series", Berlin Process / 3 / 2018, Cooperation and Development Institute, February 2018.

忽视这一地区，最终还是可能成为欧盟成员国（Marciacq，2017年），并有可能明确处理好与中国和中国倡议参与国的合作。

二、"一带一路"在拉丁美洲：整合或分裂？

拉丁美洲与中国的国际关系处于一个非常有利的历史时刻。中国于2008年和2016年对拉美和加勒比国家（LAC）的两份政策文件中都强调与南方国家建立"人类命运共同体"的重要性，这是联结中国和拉美人民的共同要素。

拉丁美洲于2017年加入"一带一路"倡议。当时阿根廷和智利总统参加"一带一路"倡议论坛，习近平将拉美和加勒比国家称为："一带一路"倡议的自然延伸。从那时起，许多未与中国建立外交关系的拉美国家[1]通过密集的对话，外交路线开始朝着国际承认中华人民共和国的方向迈进，特别是在"一带一路"倡议框架下。

此外，许多拉美和加勒比国家[2]2018年在智利举行的中国-拉共体论坛第二届部长级会议上[3]根据"一带一路"倡议特别声明，于"一带一路"框架下签署备忘录。还应该指出的是，一些拉美和加勒比国家已经批准与中国签订的自由贸易协定（FTA），情形和基础与我们所知的FTA不同，而且还对60年代旧经济一体化理论做出回应。这些国家包括：2005年智利，2009年秘鲁，2010年哥斯达黎加，哥伦比亚和乌拉圭正在进行自由贸易协定谈判。

然而，这些协定反映出与中国建立关系的时刻，拉丁美洲的现实情况有多个维度，区域内的国家在一体化进程中是分散的。将拉丁美洲视为一个概念单位是非常困难的，也许是不合适的。如果我们把视线投向南美洲的南锥体地区，特别是在南方共同市场，在这十年的最后几年中，现实已经发生很大的变化。南方共同市场国家经历重要的政治变革，对世界和区域经济增长的看法也不相同。通过这种方式，阿根廷和巴西之间的政治和经济分歧得到加强，乌拉圭和巴拉圭希望扩大经济开放，而安第斯共同体（南方共同市场的合作伙伴）对上述"区域协商"不感兴趣，它们的定位是走向太平洋，政策以实用主义和商业自由为基础。区域

1　Panamá, Ecuador, República Dominicana and El Salvador.

2　已经有16个拉丁美洲和加勒比国家在"一带一路"倡议框架下签署谅解备忘录：巴拿马、玻利维亚、安提瓜和巴布达、特立尼达和多巴哥、圭亚那、乌拉圭、阿根廷、哥斯达黎加、厄瓜多尔、委内瑞拉、智利等。

3　https://www.rree.go.cr/files/includes/files.php?id=1317&tipo=documentos.

联盟网络内部的各个国家都具有不同的目标，部分国家合并现有进程，而另一些国家制订新战略。因此，新的一体化进程与现有进程叠加，这意味着区域内与美国、欧盟和中国等国际权力核心有关的政治和经济战略更加分散和多样化。区域性的组织包括太平洋联盟（2011）、南美洲国家联盟（2008）以及拉丁美洲和加勒比国家共同体（2011），这些是同时并存的不同目标和模式的一体化组织。

在探讨"一带一路"在拉丁美洲的影响力时，我们有必要关注拉美和加勒比地区制定对其他国家和地区关系共同战略时遭遇的困难。通过分析南方共同市场次区域（甚至整个南方共同市场），我们将发现由于两个因素的影响，"南方共同市场未完成的外交政策"从根本上限制与中国进行集体谈判。首先，我们要提到的是，亚洲国家采取"一个中国原则"下的谈判模式，但巴拉圭在斯特罗斯纳当政期间与台湾建立外交关系，限制南方共同市场的整体谈判能力。第二，由于各个国家缺乏共同的外交政策以及奉行民族主义（和便利）政策，导致它们分别与中国进行双边谈判（巴西—中国、阿根廷—中国、智利—中国）。即使如此，最近[1]南方共同市场和中国采取新的方法，旨在恢复双方于1997年发起的中国-南方共同市场高层对话会议，根本目标是强化双边政治经济合作以及地区间的相互了解。

在对话论坛（共举行五次）上，各方同意以下优先合作事项：首先，加强商业往来，推动南方共同市场与中国的合作，扩大开放空间，商业事务在几轮总统正式访问期间已经具体化，例如：内斯托尔·基什内尔总统和卢拉·达席尔瓦总统于2004年访问中国，习近平主席于2013年和2014年两次访问本地区，第二次中国主席对南方共同市场五个成员国中的三个进行正式访问：阿根廷、巴西和委内瑞拉，中国总理温家宝2012年对南方共同市场进行正式访问。

第二，提出的目标是扩大农业合作。除了这一目标外，还建议深化科学技术领域合作，缔结技术合作协定，包括加强人力和学术资源交流。最后，文化合作也得到促进。

2004年6月在北京举行的第五次南方共同市场与中国对话会议是重要的会议。这次会议的核心内容是两点：中国坚持要求巴拉圭承认中华人民共和国，南方共同市场提议通过谈判达成《固定优惠协定》，但中国未接受，建议直接签署自由贸易协定。

1　2018年10月在蒙得维的亚举行会议，双方同意重新启动对话并承诺2019年举行另一次会议。

可以预见，随着拉美和加勒比海地区与中国和亚太地区的合作日益深入，拉丁美洲太平洋国家与大西洋国家的分裂以及南美和墨西哥之间的割裂正在逐渐消失。然而，拉美和加勒比海地区各个经济体的规模和特征以及在大陆的地缘战略地位各不相同。

如今在 2018 年，不论是特朗普风格的民族主义，还是渗透到东方国家外交政策中的"一个中国原则"逻辑，我们发现南方共同市场的商业联系在加强，试图在强化双边关系的世界生存，而不是通过集体谈判。从这个意义上讲，经济实用主义"战胜"区域一体化。

值得注意的是，南方共同市场可以作为与中国关系的主导替代方案。然而，也面临若干挑战。首先，组织发生"政治结构调整"，委内瑞拉被暂停资格（2017 年），玻利维亚将作为正式成员加入（正在等待）。巴西总统雅伊尔·博索纳罗最近当选，他指出南方共同市场对巴西政府没有任何优先权。

虽然拉美一体化进程分散且差异很大，但在寻求对中国联合行动方面，2018 年收获很大。

1 月 22 日在智利圣地亚哥举行的中国 - 拉共体论坛第二届部长级会议上：发布关于"一带一路"倡议的特别声明。拉共体成员国都认为改善全球基础设施、贸易和人民交往可以提供充分的发展机会，他们希望团结一致与中国实现共同发展。双方同意，"一带一路"建设将为中国 - 拉共体全面合作注入新的活力，开辟新的视野。双方还表示愿意在"1+3+6"框架下推动合作。

关于太平洋联盟国家（墨西哥、哥伦比亚、秘鲁和智利），4 月 18 日，第七届拉美太平洋联盟投资论坛在南京举行。太平洋联盟国家将中国视为整体增长的绝佳机会，在南京举行论坛吸引亚洲巨头公司投资，作为整体面对中国这样的大型经济体将带来实际机会和比较优势。

在南方共同市场框架下与中国的谈判开始于 1997 年，截至 2004 年一共举行"五次会议"。今年，对话机制停滞 14 年后正式恢复。第六次中国 - 南方共同市场对话会议于 10 月 18 日在乌拉圭蒙得维的亚举行[1]。南方共同市场和中国同意将这一机制固定化，恢复定期会议。

总之，在南方共同市场不断变化的背景下，拉美和加勒比国家共同体（"拉

1　http://www.mrree.gub.uy/frontend/page?1,inicio,ampliacion-actualidad,O,es,0,PAG;CONC;128;2;D;
　vi-reunion-del-dialogo-mercosur--china;3;PAG.

共体"）将承担新的角色，作为拉美与中国发展关系的替代论坛。从这个意义上讲，拉共体代表一种新机制，寻求克服次区域层面的问题，激活多层次论坛并强化多维度规划的趋势。拉美和加勒比海地区的 33 个国家首次同意组成一个区域实体考虑不同的战略目标：第一，不受限制的地域包容（克服南美洲与中美洲的分歧，加强拉美联盟的地缘政治）；第二，基于尊重政治多元性的成员资格和包容性（不考虑政治体制和政府的意识形态取向）；第三，接受经济多样性（发展模式和水平以及国际市场上不同进入方案的差异）。这在政治、经济和战略方面制造差异空间，因此对其有效性产生质疑（Llenderrozas，2013 年）。

结　论

根据本文分析我们可以发现中国提出的新国际体系（金砖国家、亚投行、一带一路项目等）不仅打开新多极化的大门，亦可发挥国家在一体化方面的积极作用，特别是新兴国家。

因此，在双重进程的积极推动下，欧洲正在朝着更好的区域一体化迈进：一方面，在大分裂和欧洲怀疑主义的历史时刻，各方在欧盟国家框架下寻求对"一带一路"达成共识；另一方面，"一带一路"倡议及其对"16+1"和"柏林进程"的对抗有助于巴尔干国家加入一体化和实现包容性活力[1]。虽然迄今为止欧洲仍然忽视这一地区，最终还是可能成为欧盟成员国（Marciacq，2017 年），并有可能明确处理好与中国和中国倡议参与国的合作。然后，我们可以发现，由于与中国扩大合作，欧洲变得更加团结，中国变得更加开放。

在拉丁美洲，可以说，随着本地区国家选择与中国合作，目前拉丁美洲太平洋国家和大西洋国家的分裂将会消失。因此，我们发现南方共同市场和太平洋联盟的商业联系在加强，试图在强化双边关系的世界生存，而不是通过集体谈判。从这个意义上讲，经济实用主义"战胜"区域一体化。然而，我们也观察到拉美国家组织正在采取新的行动，尤其是在 2018 年。同样，新的拉共体模式有利于采取集体行动，从而推动实现前所未有的拉美团结。在中国提出的"构建人类命运共同体"的挑战中，拉共体可能优先发挥作用。

1　THE BERLIN PROCESS 2014-2018, Report "Berlin Process Series", Berlin Process / 3 / 2018, Cooperation and Development Institute, February 2018.

The Belt and Road Initiative: Promoting Innovative Practices in Regional Integration at a Global Level: The Cases of Europe and Latin America

Maria Francesca Staiano / Italy

Director of the Center for China Studies at International Relations Institute, National University of La Plata (Argentina)

Introduction

The Belt and Road Initiative (BRI) is a unique project of global international cooperation, linking Asia, Europe, Africa and Latin America. Launched in 2013 by President Xi Jinping during a visit to Kazakhstan, the BRI began more than 5 years ago. This analysis will focus on the examination of the BRI as a driving force behind the dynamics of regional integration, constituting a platform for cooperation that goes beyond the static links of regional organizations. These are constantly discussed when member countries must form a common policy to face an efficient allocation of resources within the framework of a concrete practice of international cooperation with China.On the other side, China is forced to confront "dual" political realities, one national and one supranational, as well.

In particular, the BRI in Europe has generated a dynamic that is shaking the

European Union in two ways: on the one hand, it calls into question the economic gap between Eastern Europe and Western Europe; On the other hand, it requires a connectivity that includes states belonging to the EU and extra-EU countries. This is leading to a progressive promotion of the development of European integration. The VII Summit of the "16 + 1" countries took place in July 2018 in Sofia, Bulgaria. "16 + 1" is an initiative of China (the 1) aimed at generating cooperation with 16 European countries, of which 11 are members of the EU (Bulgaria, Croatia, Czech Republic, Estonia, Hungary, Latvia, Lithuania, Poland, Romania, Slovakia and Slovenia) and five are candidates to join the EU (Albania, Bosnia and Herzegovina, Montenegro, Serbia and Macedonia). From this important Forum we understand the drive towards a more united Europe.

With reference to Africa, the African Union already includes all the 55 states of the African continent. Despite this, China has in the past promoted a model of bilateral cooperation with each African country, receiving much criticism in terms of African "dis-integration". Recently, however, President Xi, during his speech to the last China-Africa Cooperation Forum (FOCAC), held in Beijing in September 2018, declared his intention to "jointly formulate a China-Africa infrastructure cooperation plan with the African Union", and to "strongly support the African countries and the African Union and other regional organizations in Africa to solve African problems in the African way".

In Latin America it is necessary to consider the presence of several integration organizations, which are going through a moment of great political momentum, albeit in a disorderly manner, with multidimensional methods and at different speeds. Among the regional organizations, we can mention MERCOSUR (Common Market of the South), CAN (Andean Community of Nations), CARICOM (Caribbean Comunity, for its acronym in English), UNASUR (Union of South American Nations), SICA (System of Central American Integration). , ALBA (Bolivarian Alliance for the Peoples of Our America), AP (Pacific Alliance) and CELAC (Community of Latin American and Caribbean States). China often faces

Latin America when it meets with CELAC, which is the only one that represents all Latin American states and presents itself as a "Community".

For the Association of Southeast Asian Nations (ASEAN), the BRI will play a key role in enabling the connection of two of the most dynamic regions in the world through the strengthening of economic ties between the 10 ASEAN members and among the ASEAN countries and China. In addition, BRI will allow the Southeast Asian countries to close the existing gap as infrastructure and promote industrial development: while the formation of the ASEAN Economic Community in 2015 has allowed the Southeast Asian economies to be united in a single market, the Beijing strategy will offer a future integration through the development of physical infrastructure and a solid trade regime.

In the Eurasian region that the BRI has played a really propulsive role for the constitution of a regional integration, as well.In a very first moment it was as an opposition to the Chinese project. In fact, in 2014 the Eurasian Economic Union, EeEU, (Russian Federation, Belarus, Kazakhstan, Armenia, Kyrgyzstan) was founded, which proposed integration outside the framework of the Chinese project. However, after China and Russia have planned a joint declaration in which they proposed to synchronize their respective economic cooperation projects in 2014, a new continental economic integration has been generated in 2015, bringing together the EaEU, the People's Republic of China, ASEAN, Republic of Iran and SAARC(Association for Regional Cooperation of South Asia, by its acronym in English[1]).

1. The BRI and its antagonistic-propulsive effects in the European Union

The BRI in Europe has provoked multidimensional dynamics at the level of regional integration, since Chinese cooperation has highlighted some gray areas of Europe. As a first result, the BRI has generated enthusiasm in the European Union

---

1 Created in 1985 and integrated by the following countries: Afghanistan, Bangladesh, Bhutan, India, Maldives, Nepal, Pakistan and Sri Lanka.

states, although subsequently the initiative has been harshly criticized for the lack of transparency and a possible EU crisis due to the Chinese practice of bilateral agreements that would have exacerbated the process of competition between the member states[1]. Probably, these criticisms have begun to spread due to the progressive presence of China in Eastern European countries, which has fueled the European fear of a possible progressive loss of influence in these areas.

In fact, the Balkan area has been relegated by the EU as a "second tier Europe", not "worthy" of being part of the Union, but which has to be subject to its legal and commercial influence, under the "temptation" of a possible membership. In fact, especially with regard to European cooperation in the BRI project, the Balkans have always been considered as a "transit zone" between the two main protagonists: the EU and China (Hackaj, 2018). This situation of stand-by has been occupied by China, which has given autonomy to these territories, not only as an "intermediate territory" but also as independent countries with a very high development potential.

Considering the possibility of gaining influence in these territories, China and the EU have embarked on an antagonistic path, which is taking full advantage of these states, which are now being "disputed" between these two great powers.

In fact, China has initiated a series of meetings called "16 + 1" since 2012. China has involved 16 countries in Central and Eastern Europe, including 11 EU Member States (Bulgaria, Croatia, Czech Republic, Estonia, Hungary , Latvia, Lithuania, Poland, Romania, Slovakia and Slovenia) and five countries of the Western Balkans (Albania, Bosnia and Herzegovina, Montenegro, Serbia and Macedonia), as part of an alternative cooperation format, representing an innovative approach to regional cooperation[2]. In fact, according to China, "16 + 1" is an experimental mode for regional cooperation that shares common characteristics with the other multilateral cooperation platforms that China has created with the countries of Africa, East Asia, Latin America and the Middle East. to introduce a new kind of "non-western

---

1   Document of the European Parliament:*China, the 16+1 cooperation format and the EU*, 2017.
2   Document of the European Parliament:*China, the 16+1 format and the EU*, 2018.

south-south multilateralism". It is important to mention that the countries of Eastern Europe would not have had such an important meaning without this platform[1].

On the other hand, the European Union has strongly criticized this format as a possible disaggregation factor for European integration[2]. The European Union has, in fact, a highly developed strategic plan with China[3] and has considered the "16 + 1" platform as a deviation from the "rule", which has not generated true multilateralism but has increased the level of conflict between countries European[4]. However, in 2018, the European attitude changed, as indicated in the Document of the European Parliament[5], especially since the EU is observer of the "16 + 1" dialogue and with the progressive development of the European (especially German) initiative of "Berlin Process 2014-2018"[6].

---

1 Document of the European Parliament:*China, the 16+1 format and the EU*, 2018.
2 Document of the European Parliament:*China, the 16+1 cooperation format and the EU*, 2017. http://www.europarl.europa.eu/sides/getDoc.do?type=TA&language=EN&reference=P8-TA-2015-0458.
3 This year also marks the 15th anniversary of the adoption of the EU-China Strategic Partnership, as expressed more recently through the EU-China 2020 Strategic Cooperation Agenda, the joint document of the highest level in EU-China relations. In July 2016, the EU adopted a new strategy on China. It should also be noted that 2018 is the year of tourism between the EU and China: in this framework the EU and China seek to bring their respective peoples closer through youth and culture projects, festivals and other dialogues.
4 Document of the European Parliament:*China, the 16+1 cooperation format and the EU*, 2017.
5 Document of the European Parliament:*China, the 16+1 format and the EU*, 2018.
6 The Berlin-Process began in 2014 as an initiative of the German Chancellor, Angela Merkel and has become a useful platform to improve regional cooperation, to support connectivity projects and to encourage the southeastern states of the EU on their way to structural reforms and accession to the EU. Meanwhile, the Berlin-Process proved to be the EU' s most important common initiative and the (potential) candidate countries to emphasize some clear perspectives of EU integration in the Western Balkans. Although the Berlin-Process is supposed to end with the next summit in London, there is a strong commitment to continue this process beyond 2018. This commitment refers mainly to the human connectivity component, especially in accordance with youth as "generation Of future" . As mentioned by the President of the European Commission in his "State of the Union" speech delivered in September 2017, the prospect of enlargement is credible and realistic. The EU member states have demonstrated their commitment to facilitate the transformation process of the Western Balkans by beginning cooperation at the regional level. This implies common efforts that could and can achieve tangible results through the Berlin-Process. THE BERLIN PROCESS 2014-2018, Report "Berlin Process Series" , Berlin Process / 3/2018, Cooperation and Development Institute, February 2018, p. 6.

To further affirm its support for European integration, in the Strategic Agenda for EU-China 2020 cooperation and in the Guidelines for cooperation between China and Eastern European countries adopted at the last "16 + 1" meeting in Sofhia, China has declared its support for European integration, and has considered the "16 + 1" cooperation format as "a complement rather than an alternative to the EU-China global strategic partnership"[1]. "16 + 1 cooperation is in no way a geopolitical platform, some may say that such cooperation can be separated from the EU, but that is not true", according to statements by Chinese Premier Li Keqiang.

This Chinese position depends on several factors: China can not set aside its commitments to the European Union within the framework of the BRI as well as in the dynamics of its comprehensive strategic cooperation with the EU. On the other hand, China has stressed that the Balkan countries, although not yet members of the EU, *de facto* act within the legal framework of the European Union. "Their economies are a satellite of the economic power of the EU and closely follow the economic cycle of the EU. The Berlin process offers a platform for results-oriented cooperation between the EU, the Western Balkans and the Chinese partners. While the Agenda for Connectivity invites cooperation with BRI, the "16 + 1" Cooperation initiative provides almost a mirror image of the Regional Cooperation component under the Berlin process" (Hackaj, 2018).

---

1   EU member states and candidate countries within the 16 CEECs support the EU-China Comprehensive Strategic Partnership of peace, growth, reform and civilization and EU-China Agenda 2020, including actively promoting practical cooperation through pilot projects in the framework of the EU-China Connectivity Platform, the Investment Plan for Europe and the extended Trans-European Network (TEN-T) and supporting the conclusion of an ambitious and comprehensive Agreement on Investment between the EU and China.
(9) "The Participants are willing to foster synergies between the Belt and Road Initiative and the Trans-European Transport Network (TEN-T) and its extension to the Western Balkans and the relevant neighborhood initiatives, which would be of benefit to European integration. Coordination on economic cooperation and connectivity between initiatives, including China-CEEC Cooperation, EU-China Connectivity Platform and EU Eastern Partnership, will provide opportunities for deepening cooperation among interested parties" .*The Sofia Guidelines for Cooperation between China and Central and Eastern European Countries.* (http://english.gov.cn/news/international_ exchanges/2018/07/16/content_281476224693086.htm).

So, what is happening in Europe is a double propulsive process towards a better regional integration: on the one hand, a common vision towards BRI is being sought within the framework of the EU countries at a historical moment of great fragmentation and Euroscepticism ; On the other hand, the BRI, together with its antagonistic demonstrations of "16 + 1" and the "Berlin Process", is supporting an integrative and inclusive dynamic of the Balkan countries[1], which until now have been left out of the European vision, eventually reaching a possible membership of the EU (Marciacq, 2017), as well as a possibility to express its potential and tangibly manage a cooperation with China and the countries parties to the Chinese initiative.

2. The BRI in Latin America:Integrative or Fragmentary Effects?

Latin America is at a very favorable historical moment in terms of international relations with China. China in the two documents of its policy towards Latin American and Caribbean Countries (LAC) in 2008 and 2016 has highlighted the importance of building with these countries of the South a "community of shared destiny" indicating the common elements that unite Chinese and the Latin American people.

The BRI has involved Latin America in 2017 when, after the participation of the Presidents of Argentina and Chile in the BRI Forum, Xi Jinping named the LAC as: "the natural extension of The Belt and Road Initiative". From that time, many Latin American countries[2] that did not have diplomatic relations with the PRC have started a diplomatic path towards the international recognition of PRC, through a very intense dialogue, especially within the framework of the implications of the BRI.

---

1   THE BERLIN PROCESS 2014-2018, Report "Berlin Process Series" , Berlin Process / 3 / 2018, Cooperation and Development Institute, February 2018.
2   Panamá, Ecuador, República Dominicana and El Salvador.

Furthermore, many LAC countries[1] have already signed a memorandum in the framework of the BRI, considering the terms of the special declaration on the BRI, signed at the II Ministerial Meeting of the China –Celac Forum, held at the beginning of 2018 in Chile[2]. It should also be noted that some LAC countries have ratified free trade agreements (FTAs) with China, which have a different dynamic and foundation than the FTAs that we know, and that respond to the old theory of economic integration of the sixties. This countries are: Chile in 2005, Peru and Costa Rica in 2009 and 2010, respectively, while they are in a negotiation phase of the FTA Colombia and Uruguay.

However, these agreements show a multidimensionality of the Latin American reality at the moment of relating to China and the countries of the region appear even more fragmented in their integration processes. Thinking of Latin America as a conceptual unit is very difficult and maybe inappropriate. If we focus on the southern cone region of South America, specifically in MERCOSUR, the reality has been quite changing in the last years of the current decade. The Mercosur countries have experienced important political changes, the vision regarding the world and economic growth of the bloc has not been homogeneous either. In such a way that political and economic differences between Argentina and Brasil enhanced, Uruguay and Paraguay increased their claims to achieve greater economic opening and some of the Andean countries (MERCOSUR partners), feeling alienated from the aforementioned "regional bids", positioned their look towards the Pacific, with policies based on pragmatism and commercial freedom. This produced a network of new alliances between the States of the region with different objectives, some of which were mixed with existing processes and others configured new strategies. In these circumstances, new integration processes emerged that were added to those in force, which meant greater regional fragmentation and diversification of

---

1   In total 16 LAC countries already signed MOU under the BRI framework: Panamá, Bolivia, Antigua y Barbuda, Trinidad y Tobago, Guyana, Uruguay, Argentina, Costa Rica, Ecuador, Venezuela, Chile, among others.

2   https://www.rree.go.cr/files/includes/files.php?id=1317&tipo=documentos.

political and economic strategies in relation to the main international axes of power: the United States, the European Union and China, to mention to the main ones. Then arose the Pacific Alliance (2011), the Unasur (2008) and the Celac (2011), as integration projects with different integration objectives and models, but which coexist with each other.

Answering to the question about the effects of BRI in Latin America, we will necessarily have to mention the difficulties LAC have had as a region to articulate common strategies regarding the relations with other countries and regions. If we analyze Mercosur sub-region in a timely manner (and even expanded Mercosur) we can detect an"unfinished Mercosur foreign policy", which has been limited the initiatives of block negotiations with China fundamentally due to two factors. First of all we can mention that the negotiation model promoted by the Asian country, under the "One-China principle", limited Mercosur's negotiation as a whole, by virtue of the establishment of diplomatic relations that Paraguay made (during the government of Stroessner) with Taiwan. Second, due to the absence of a common foreign policy and therefore to the application of nationalist (and convenience) policies by the block's States that led to bilateral negotiations with China (Brazil-China, Argentina-China, Chile- China). Notwithstanding this, recently[1] there were new approaches between MERCOSUR and China with the aim to resume the Mercosur-China High Level Dialogue Meetings that both partners initiated in 1997 and whose fundamental objective was to deepen bilateral political-economic cooperation and mutual knowledge between the regions.

In these forums of dialogue (which were held five), the parties had agreed that the cooperation priorities were the following: first, to increase business contacts to open spaces for cooperation and promotion of Mercosur in China, which became concrete in function of the business rounds that took place during the official visits of the presidents (such as: the visit of President Néstor Kirchner and Lula Da Silva

---

[1] The meeting was held in Montevideo in October 2018 and the parties agreed to re-establish the bi-regional dialogue and undertook to set another meeting for the year 2019.

to China in 2004 and the two visits that Xi Jinping made to the region in 2013 and 2014, on this last date the Chinese president formalized official visits to three of the five member countries of Mercosur: Argentina, Brazil and Venezuela or the visit of Chinese Premier Wen Jiabao in the Mercosur countries in 2012, among others).

Second, the objective they proposed was to expand agricultural cooperation. In addition to this objective, they proposed to deepen cooperation in the areas of science and technology, in order to conclude a technical cooperation agreement, which would involve enhancing exchanges of human and academic resources, among others. And finally, cultural cooperation was also promoted.

One of the main meetings was the V Mercosur-China Dialogue Meeting, held in June 2004 in Beijing. The central axis of that meeting were two: China's insistence on the need for the recognition of the People's Republic by Paraguay and Mercosur's proposal to negotiate a Fixed Preference Agreement, which was not accepted by China, who proposed to go directly to the conclusion of a Free Trade Agreement.

It is possible to foresee that with the even more deep cooperation of the LAC with China and the Asia-Pacific region, part of the existing fragmentation in Latin America between countries of the Pacific and countries of the Atlantic is falling, as well as the division between South America and Mexico. However,LAC will remain heterogeneous, due to the size and characteristics of their economies, as well as the geostrategic position in the continent.

Currently, in 2018, we are already seeing a Mercosur more linked to the commercial aspects struggling to survive in a world that tends to deepen bilateral relations over block negotiations, either from the Trump-style nationalist perspective or from the logic of the "One-China principle", which permeates the foreign policy of the eastern country. In this sense, there is a "triumph" of economic pragmatism over regional deepening.

It is remarkable that Mercosur could be a possible alternative to lead the reins of relations with China. However, it faces several challenges, firstly, the "political restructuring" of the bloc in terms of the suspension of Venezuela (2017), the future incorporation of Bolivia as a full member (a situation that is still in Stand by) and the recent triumph of the president of Brazil, Jair Bolsonaro, who said that Mercosur will not have any priority for his government.

Despite the fragmentation and heterogeneity of Latin American integration processes, 2018 was a very profitable year in the search for joint actions towards China.

The II Celac-China Forum, held on the 22th of January in Santiago del Chile: the meeting made a special announcement about the Belt and Road Initiative proposed by China. The members of CELAC unanimously said that the vision of improving infrastructure, trade and ties among people around the world has given their countries ample opportunities for development, and they hoped to unite to achieve common development with China.Both sides agreed that the joint construction of the Belt and Road Initiative will inject new energy into the China-CELAC comprehensive cooperative association and open up new perspectives.Both sides also said that they are willing to promote cooperation under the "1 + 3 + 6" framework.

On the side of the countries of the Pacific Alliance (Mexico, Colombia, Peru and Chile), on the 18th of april the VII Pacific Alliance – China Forum was held in Nanjin. The PA countries see China as the great opportunity to grow as a block and held in the city of Nanjin, a forum to attract investment from Asian giant companies, seeing a very practical opportunity and a comparative advantage of presenting itself as a block in such a big economy as China.

In the framework of MERCOSUR, the negotiations with China began in the year 1997, and "five meetings" were held until 2004, then this mechanism of dialogue returned to work this year, after 14 years of inactivity. The VI Mercosur-China

Dialogue Meeting was held on the 18th of October in Montevideo, Uruguay[1]. MERCOSUR and China agreed to systematize this mechanism and resume the dynamics of periodic meetings.

In conclusion, in the changing context of Mercosur, there is a new role for the Celac, as an alternative forum that takes the Latin American initiative in the relationship with China. In this sense, Celac represents a new mechanism, created that seeks to overcome the subregional level with the aim to activate multilevel forums and reinforce the trend towards the construction of multidimensional agendas. For the very first time, the thirty-three states of the broad Latin American and Caribbean spectrum, agree to form a regional entity, which considers different strategic goals: first, geographic inclusion without restrictions (overcoming the divisions between South America and Central America and strengthening the geopolitics of the Latin American union); second, membership and inclusion based on respect for political plurality (political regimes and ideological orientations of their governments do not matter); third, the acceptance of economic diversity (disparity in the models and levels of development and in the different insertion schemes in the international market). This has created a heterogeneous space in political, economic and strategic terms, which has generated questions about its effectiveness (Llenderrozas, 2013).

Conclusions

As emerged from the analysis of this work, it can be noted that the new international axiology that China is proposing (BRICS, AIIB Bank, BRI project, among others) has generated an opening towards a new multipolarism, also promoting a more active role of countries, especially emerging countries, specifically in terms of integration.

Therefore, in Europe we can speak of a dual pro-active process towards better regional integration: on the one hand, we are looking for a common vision towards

---

1   http://www.mrree.gub.uy/frontend/page?1,inicio,ampliacion-actualidad,O,es,0,PAG;CONC;128;2;D;
    vi-reunion-del-dialogo-mercosur--china;3;PAG.

the BRI within the framework of the EU countries in a historical moment of great fragmentation and Euroscepticism ; On the other hand, the BRI, together with its antagonistic demonstrations of "16 + 1" and "Berlin Process", is supporting an integrative and inclusive dynamic of the Balkan countries[1], which until now have been left out of the European vision, finally reaching a possible EU membership(Marciacq, 2017), as well as a possibility to express its potential and to manage tangibly a cooperation with China and the countries parties to the Chinese initiative. Then, we can see an Europe more united towards China and more open because of the extended cooperation with China.

In Latin America, it is possible to venture to affirm that with the election of the alliance of the countries of this region with China, part of the existing fragmentation in Latin America between countries of the Pacific and Atlantic countries will probably collapse. Therefore we are already seeing a Mercosur and an AP more linked to the commercial aspects struggling to survive in a world that tends to deepen bilateral relations over the block negotiations. In this sense, it could presage a "triumph" of economic pragmatism over regional deepening. However, we are witnessing new instances of acting in blocks of Latin American countries, especially in 2018. Likewise, the new CELAC model can favor a rebirth of the block action generating a propulsive dynamic towards a Latin American unity that has never been seen before. In the Chinese challenge of generating a "community of shared destiny", CELAC probably has a priority role.

Bibliography

Document of the European Parliament: *China, the 16+1 cooperation format and the EU*, 2017.

Document of the European Parliament: *China, the 16+1 format and the EU*, 2018.

HackajArdian, "China And Western Balkans", Cooperation and Development Institute,

---

1   The Berlin Process 2014-2018, Report "Berlin Process Series" , Berlin Process / 3 / 2018, Cooperation and Development Institute, February 2018.

Tirana, March 2018.

Llenderrozas Elsa, "Política exterior Latinoamericana y la Comunidad de Estados Latinoamericanos y Caribeños", in *Austral: Revista Brasileira de Estratégia e Relações Internacionais*, v.2, n.4, Jul-Dez 2013, pp.183-205.

MarciacqFlorent, "*The European Union and the Western Balkans after the Berlin Process: Reflecting on the EU Enlargement in Times of Uncertainty*" , FES Publications, Sarajevo, 2017.

PRC Government, *China's Policy Paper on Latin America and the Caribbean*, 2008,http://www.gov.cn/english/official/2008-11/05/content_1140347.htm.

PRC Government, *China's Policy Paper on Latin America and the Caribbean*, 2016, http://www.fmprc.gov.cn/mfa_eng/zxxx_662805/t1418254.shtml.

Schicheng, Xu, "China. Las relaciones con Latinoamérica en la década de los noventa". Geopolítica: Hacia una Doctrina Nacional, Buenos Aires, Editorial Pleamar, No. 67, 1999.

Staiano, M.; Bogado Bordazar, L.; y Bono, L., *Estudios sobre la República Popular China: Relaciones internacionales y Política interna,* La Plata, Ediciones IRI-UNLP, 2016.

Staiano, Maria Francesca, "¿ 法治还是人治？Una desmitificación del Estado de derecho hacia el ejemplo de la RPC", *Caminhos da História*, Brasil, 2016.

Surasky, J., "La gestión institucional de la Cooperación Internacional al Desarrollo ofrecida por la República Popular China. Buscando claridad en una voz fuerte".En: Staiano, F., El ordenamiento jurídico de la República Popular China en el marco del Derecho Internacional: planificación familiar, migraciones y cooperación. IRI-Confucio, UNLP, 2014.

The Berlin Process 2014-2018, Report "Berlin Process Series", Berlin Process / 3 / 2018, Cooperation and Development Institute, February 2018.

"一带一路"文化产业中的越中两国合作展望

陈氏水【越南】

越南社会科学院中国研究所中国文化历史研究室博士

虽然中国文化产业建立较晚，被称为新兴产业，但中国文化产业很快就成熟和发展起来，并为其国家的整体发展做出贡献。文化产业以文化和经济为本，秉承传统文化价值观，将其文化产品转化为高经济价值产品，中国政府将文化产业视为 21 世纪的经济亮点。此外，中国文化产业在向世界传递和平发展信息方面也发挥着重要的作用。中国的"一带一路"倡议（"丝绸之路经济带"和"二十一世纪海上丝绸之路"）中，文化产业的地位和作用怎样；中国已经在"一带一路"沿线国家和地区开展文化产业贸易的合作，该领域发展的初步成效和挑战如何，将是本文重点分析的问题。

一、中国文化产业在"一带一路"倡议中的作用

第一，文化产业在"一带一路"倡议中有促进经济增长的作用。作为一种经济产业，文化产业在任何战略中的第一个重要作用就是要增加价值。"丝绸之路经济带"和"21 世纪海上丝绸之路"倡议，实质上是中国的"走出去"战略。正是在"愿景与行动"中，中国强调"对外开放是中国的一项基本国策，中国将形成全面开放的格局，深度融入世界经济"。目前，中国贸易出口份额约占中国经济体总额的 20%。此外工业、农业和其他服务业对经济体具有重要的贡献，但文化产业对经济的增长也有一定的贡献。据统计，2012 年中国文化产业出口额

达到了 259 亿美元，同比增长 38.5%，贸易顺差达到了 243.45 亿美元。

文化产业对经济的贡献通常以两种方式进行。一是直接影响，即通过交易使每个国家都可以获利。其次，间接效应或者叫经济效应，除了给行业本身带来的价值外，还具有桥梁作用以及吸引其他行业发展的作用。文化产业领域通常被称为"火车头"，可以带动旅游业的发展、玩具的生产、主题公园的建设等。中国文化精髓的对外推广，正是吸引国际游客的动力之一。

当今，中国文化产业对中国经济的重要贡献之一是实现经济结构的多元化，促进了发展方式的转变。文化产业的突出优势是能耗低、无污染，符合中国产业结构调整的方向。

其次，中国的文化产品有助于加强"一带一路"沿线国家人民之间的文化交流和相互了解。中国成为世界第二大经济体后，不仅积极融入全球经济，而且逐步制定新的规则来吸引各国的参与。在这样的背景下，文化因素将有助于中国在这一倡议内建立起"和平崛起"的形象，并在各国之间建立起政治互信。在古代的陆路和海上丝绸之路到现在的新陆路和海上丝绸之路的基础上，中国希望增加其外部影响力，因此文化因素被视为除了经济和安全因素外最重要的支柱之一。到目前为止，文化产品被认为是中国增加"软实力"战略的主导模式，中国将继续推动这一卓越的作用。文化产品中的电影、出版物、服装或电子游戏等，这些文化产品将帮助中国向世界传达和平发展的信息。目前，即使不考虑中国文化产品的市场规模开发得如何，但与人民币的实力相比，中国文化产品在发展"一带一路"倡议的过程中，仍然有自己的独特地位。

总的来说，在创意经济的这个世纪，文化产业的作用和地位在任何的计划、战略或者倡议中都得到了提升。对于"一带一路"倡议而言，文化产业除了经济价值的贡献外，还有助于使沿线国家的人民更容易接受中国。

二、中国"一带一路"倡议中的文化产业发展政策

可以看出，文化产业向外部市场的出口是中国的一贯政策。中国的目标是到 2020 年能够建立起一支具有强大实力和竞争力的外向型企业队伍，意在增加出口比例，改善进出口贸易的平衡。

由于其独特的性质，文化产业出现在中国的"一带一路"倡议中，以促进经济的增长作用，同时又作为加强"一带一路"沿线国家人与人之间友好关系的一

种纽带和桥梁。2015 年 3 月，中国发布《推动共建丝绸之路经济带和 21 世纪海上丝绸之路的愿景和行动》，这份官方文件得到中国国务院授权，由国家发展和改革委员会发布。之后，中国文化部于 2016 年 12 月发布了《2016—2020 年一带一路文化发展行动计划》，这两份文件的发布体现了中国政府对"一带一路"文化产业的宏观政策。

首先，在"一带一路"倡议中，发展文化产业是加强沿途国家"民心相通"的一种方式。在中国提出的"一带一路"愿景中，文化产业将以下活动的形式具体实施：一是沿线国家间互办文化年、艺术节；二是沿线国家间互办电影节、电视周和图书展等活动；三是合作开展广播影视剧精品创作及翻译；四是联合申请世界文化遗产，共同开展世界遗产的联合保护工作；五是加强旅游合作，扩大旅游规模，互办旅游推广周、宣传月等活动，联合打造具有丝绸之路特色的国际精品旅游线路和旅游产品，提高沿线各国游客签证便利化水平，推动 21 世纪海上丝绸之路邮轮旅游合作；六是积极开展体育交流活动，支持沿线国家申办重大国际体育赛事。

在"一带一路"倡议沿线国家发展文化产业，可以提升国家的形象作用。中国方面表示："民心相通是'一带一路'建设的社会根基。传承和弘扬丝绸之路友好合作精神，广泛开展文化交流、学术往来、人才交流合作、媒体合作、青年和妇女交往、志愿者服务等，为深化双多边合作奠定坚实的民意基础"。电影周、文化年、旅游推广等活动得到中国的大力提倡和支持，将这一经济带中人们的精神价值观联系起来。

其次，文化产业的作用是在"一带一路"倡议中形成价值链。在中国"一带一路"倡议沿线国家的文化发展规划中，中国确立了加快"丝绸之路文化产业带"建设的目标。在未来一段时期，中国与沿线国家文化产业合作的一些重点领域包括：文化旅游、演艺娱乐、工艺美术、创意设计、数字文化。支持"一带一路"沿线地区根据地域特色和民族特点实施特色文化产业项目，加强与"一带一路"国家在文化资源数字化保护与开发中的合作，积极利用"一带一路"文化交流合作平台推介文化创意产品，推动动漫游戏产业面向"一带一路"国家发展。此外，促进"一带一路"文化贸易合作，围绕演艺、电影、电视、广播、音乐、动漫、游戏、数字文化、创意设计、文化科技装备、艺术品及授权产品等领域，开拓完善国际合作渠道。

到目前为止，中国正处在开辟新丝绸之路带文化产业的关键时期，中国文化产业中的文化展览内容、电影周等活动内容已初步实施。2016年，中国与"一带一路"沿线国家和地区文化产品进出口额达到了149亿美元，占文化产品进出口总额的16.8%。

1、电影和电视领域

最近，中国企业加大了对西亚地区的考察力度，寻找包括沙特阿拉伯、黎巴嫩等国家在内的西亚市场潜力。中国电影制片人表示该地区是中国电影、电视剧和电视节目的潜在市场。在合作共建21世纪经济走廊"一带一路"的构想框架内，许多专家的意见认为，"新丝绸之路"实际上也不一定要依赖陆路或者海路，特别是在通信和互联网发达的今天，中国的电影和电视剧产业可以通过网络市场走出去，建立起一条虚拟的丝绸之路。2015年9月，中国在泰国举办了电影周活动，该活动是该战略链中的重要一环。电影周活动的成功举办是中泰两国人民团结的象征，同时也为政治和经济的合作创造了一种新的动力。

2、文化展览领域

2015年5月，第十一届中国国际文化产业博览会在深圳举办。本届博览会被认为是贯彻中国正在实施的"一带一路"倡议思想的一个举措。其中一个值得注意的地方是在丝绸之路展览区，展览的主要内容是"一带一路"沿线各国的传统艺术、创意设计、非物质文化遗产、旅游和表演艺术等内容。参与展览的沿途国家有俄罗斯、印度、泰国、马来西亚等等以及西安、乌鲁木齐、广州、深圳、泉州等15个中国城市。同时，中国文化部还举办了丝绸之路文化交流论坛等。

3、旅游领域

虽然旅游业不是文化产业结构的一个领域，但是促进文化贸易交流与合作的重要基础。目前，中国和东盟国家每周约有2700趟航班，这一地区之间的人口流动性不断增加。随着世界旅游中心走向东方，中国和东盟的旅游业已经成为了不容忽视的力量。中国游客目前占越南旅游市场的三分之一。中国中产阶级的迅速崛起，外出旅游的需求，尤其是"一带一路"倡议沿线国家的需求也正在增加。旅游业的发展也将促进文化产业的发展。

但是，在"一带一路"倡议中实施的文化产业，中国也面临诸多挑战，具体体现在以下几个方面：

首先，由于不同的文化环境，增加了丝绸之路沿线文化产业的挑战。

丝绸之路的经济走廊途径许多不同文化的区域，具有鲜明的文化特色。如果说东南亚走廊拥有中国文化产品更容易接近的有利环境，那么沿着中亚和西亚沿线地区输出中国文化产品将是一个不小的挑战。

多元文化区域将在丝绸之路走廊中创造出丰富多彩的文化景观。然而，在接受另一种文化价值观时，意识形态和文化价值的差异都造成了一定的困难。因此，中国在将中国文化产品输出到"一带一路"沿线国家的过程中，必将经历重重障碍。

其次，中国"软实力"建设战略与对外发展经济关系战略的不协调性，中国"软实力"建设战略赶不上中国对外发展经济关系战略的速度。

近年来，中国特别注重扩大和提升对外开放的国家形象。中国向这些国家传递"软实力"的方式之一是文化产品输出。中国希望通过向外介绍传统文化价值观来让世界了解和接受中国的和平发展策略。然而，中国由于过分强调国家和政府在"走出去"过程中的作用，这些和平发展的指导方针并未真正发挥效果或者朝着预定的方向而发展。有分析说，中国政府的干预使文化很容易成为一种正式的意识形态。因此，许多国家不承认中国和平崛起的进程和和平的性质，而是对中国的和平崛起表示怀疑或者持一种保留的态度。例如，孔子学院、电影、出版物等并不总是受到各国的欢迎。

因此，对于中国文化产业而言，"一带一路"倡议将为寻求和拓展消费市场空间创造了机会。但是，不同的文化环境，中国文化产品"走出去"过程的局限性，将是文化产业对外发展的巨大挑战和困难。

三、越中文化产业合作前景

1、机遇

文化产业在越南和中国的发展政策中占有越来越重要的地位。尽管与其他国家或者其他行业相比，文化产业是一个发展相对较晚的行业，但凭借丰富的文化资源和巨大的市场潜力，文化产业已逐渐成为两国经济中的一个亮点。越中两国在促进文化产业的合作过程中拥有许多先天优势，例如两国地理位置相近、文化相通和政治制度相同等方面的优势。首先，地理位置上的接近和文化的相通关系在双方交换文化产业的过程中创造了一个柔和的边界。价值观念的相似性是两国文化企业降低产品宣传成本的有利条件。此外，在宏观方面一个重要的内容是，两国领导人选择文化产业作为越中文化合作中的一个重点领域。2017 年底，在中共中央总书记、国家主席习近平对越南进行国事访问期间，越南和中国两国的文化部长签署了文化产业合作谅解备忘录。该文件为两国文化产业加强合作、了解彼此市场的潜力铺平了道路。

2、挑战

越中两国文化产业合作面临的突出挑战，是两国人民之间的政治互信有待提高。岛屿之争和岛屿问题的复杂发展，影响了越中两国外交关系的稳定。根据对中国与地区国家公民"民心相通"的研究，越中共同关心的"民心相通"指数属于潜在但不平衡的群体。

具体而言，在"一带一路"倡议沿线的 63 个国家中，越南有 34 个城市跟中国的各大城市结为了友好城市，越南成为了中国"一带一路"倡议沿线国家与中国结为友好城市最多的国家。与此同时，越南和中国的旅游活动和学术合作得到了快速发展。虽然中国对越南良好评价的指数水平仅为 0.1，在东南亚国家中，越南的"民心相通"指数平均为 5.1 分，但中国人民对越南的关注程度仍相对较高。相比之下，在越南，越南国内人民对与中国相关联的因素会有着多维的反应。如 2016 年越南河静省钢铁厂事件的示威活动，导致了在河静省、平阳省的部分外国企业被打砸，以及 2018 年越南特区法有关的示威活动，等等……这些活动给中国企业在越南投资产生了犹豫的心态，其中就包括文化企业的投资。

四、越中文化产业合作的一些建议

越南作为文化产业的后来者，为了满足国内市场的需求，不断地从外部进口文化产品。中国是越南文化产品的主要供应来源之一。目前，越南 90％的网络游戏产品来自中国，中国网络文学不仅吸引了大量的越南读者，而且在一定程度上已经开始影响越南文学语言的发展。多年来，中国电视剧一直在越南从中央到地方的电视台进行热播，成为越南熟悉的文化产品。

因此，可以看出，中国促进与东南亚各国的文化合作，是越南与中国进行文化产业合作的有利前提。越南文化企业需要积极开拓中国市场，加强对越南产品需求旺盛地区的合作。越南作为中国通往东南亚的门户，中国企业非常重视与越南在文化的生产与贸易方面的合作。通过与越南的成功合作，中国可以复制这些合作模式，与东盟其他的国家合作。在出版、电视、电影、创意设计等领域，都是中国在文化产业方面的优势，越南可以加强合作，学习中国在文化产业方面的发展经验，以此来借鉴发展越南国内的文化产业。

五、结论

中国提出的"一带一路"倡议，引起了沿线地区和世界各国的关注。希望重建历史上传奇的贸易路线，中国古代丝绸之路曾经是亚欧文明和文化交流的桥梁，中国的倡议提供了两个经济弧线，一个在陆地，一个在海上，从中国各省出发，途径中亚、西亚和南亚，最后到达欧洲。这一倡议为中国经济开辟了巨大的消费市场潜力，并通过文化交流和文化推广活动，增进沿线周边国家和人民之间的相互了解。中国文化产业中的"一带一路"倡议的发展，在增加"软实力"和在国外树立中国形象的战略中发挥着重要的作用。中国越来越多的东南亚的关注和增加对东南亚的投资，为越南文化产业创造了更多的合作机会和经验。

Prospects for Vietnam-China Cooperation in the Cultural Industry under the BRI

Tran Thi Thuy / Vietnam

PhD, the Chinese Culture and History Office, the Chinese Research Institute of Vietnam Academy of Social Science

Although the cultural industry was established relatively late and is called an emerging industry, it is maturing and is developing quickly and can contribute to the overall development of China. The cultural industry is based on culture and on the economy, it holds up the banner of the traditional cultural values and transforms cultural products into products with high economic value. The Chinese government regards the cultural industry as an economic highlight in the 21st century. Furthermore, China's cultural industry plays an important role in transmitting the message of peaceful development to the world. The key issues to be analyzed in this article include what the status and role of the cultural industry is in China's Belt and Road Initiative (abbreviated as "BRI", referring to the "Silk Road Economic Belt" and the "21st Century Maritime Silk Road"); and the preliminary results and challenges of China's cooperation in developing the trade of the cultural industry in countries and regions along the Belt and Road.

1. The Role of China's Cultural Industry in the BRI

First, the cultural industry can promote economic growth under the BRI. As an economic sector, the first important role of the cultural industry in any strategy is to add value. The "Silk Road Economic Belt" and the "21st Century Maritime Silk Road" are essentially China's "going out" strategy. In the "Vision and Actions", China emphasizes that "opening up to the outside world is a basic national policy of China, and China will form a comprehensive opening-up pattern and deeply integrate into the world economy". At present, China's export trade accounts for about 20% of its economic aggregate. In addition, industry, agriculture, and other service sectors make important contributions to the economy, and the cultural industry can also contribute to the economic growth to some extent. According to statistics, in 2012,the export volume of China's cultural industry reached 25.9 billion US dollars, with an increase of 38.5% year on year, and the trade surplus was 24.345 billion US dollars.

The cultural industry makes a contribution to the economy usually in two ways. The first way is a direct impact, that is, every country can benefit from trade. The second way means indirect effects or economic effects, which, in addition to the value brought to the industry itself, also play the role of a bridge and make it possible for other industries to develop. The cultural industry is often called the "locomotive", which can promote the development of tourism, the production of toys and the construction of theme parks. The promotion of the essence of Chinese culture is one of the motivations for attracting international tourists.

Nowadays, one of the important economic contributions of China's cultural industry is to achieve the diversification of economic structure and promote the transformation of the developmental model. The outstanding advantages of the cultural industry are low energy consumption and no pollution, so it coincides with the direction of China's industrial restructuring.

Second, China's cultural products can be helpful for strengthening cultural exchanges and mutual understanding among people in countries along the Belt and Road. After China becomes the world's second largest economy, it not only actively integrates into the global economy, but it also gradually formulates new rules to attract the participation of all countries. Against this background, cultural factors are able to help China establish an image of a "peaceful rise" within this initiative and build up political trust among countries. Based on the ancient land and maritime silk roads, with the present new land and maritime silk roads, China hopes to increase its influence abroad. Therefore, cultural factors are regarded as one of the most important pillars besides economic and security factors. So far, cultural products are considered the dominant model in China's strategy of strengthening soft power, and China will continue to promote this remarkable role. Movies, publications, costumes or video games in cultural products can help China convey the message of peaceful development to the world. Currently, even if the scale of the market for Chinese cultural products is not considered, compared with the strength of the RMB, China's cultural products still have their own unique position in the development of the BRI.

Generally speaking, in this century of a creative economy, the role and status of the cultural industry is enhanced in any plan, strategy or initiative. For the BRI, in addition to the contribution of economic value, the cultural industry also helps to make it easier for people in countries along the route to recognize China.

2. The Developmental Policy for the Cultural Industry in China's BRI

The exportation of cultural products to external markets, as mentioned above, is a consistent policy of China. China's goal is to establish a strong and competitive echelon of export-oriented enterprises by 2020, with the intention of increasing the proportion of exports and improving the balance of its import and export trade.

Due to its unique nature, the cultural industry is included in China's BRI to advance the economic growth, and serve as a bond and bridge to strengthen the friendly relations of people in countries along the route. In March 2015, China released the *Vision and Actions on Jointly Building the Silk Road Economic Belt and the 21st Century Maritime Silk Road*. This official document was authorized by the State Council of China and issued by the National Development and Reform Commission. Next, the Ministry of Culture of China released the *Action Plan for Belt and Road Cultural Development (2016-2020)* in December 2016. The release of these two documents reflects the Chinese government's macro policy on cultural industry within the BRI.

First of all, in the BRI, the development of the cultural industry is a way to strengthen the "people-to-people bond" of countries along the route. In the vision of the BRI put forward by China, the cultural industry will be implemented in the form of the following activities: First, to hold culture years and arts festivals in countries along the route; second, to also hold film festivals, TV weeks and book fairs; third, to cooperate on the production and translation of fine films, radio and TV programs; fourth, to jointly apply for and protect World Cultural Heritage sites; fifth, to enhance cooperation in and expand the scale of tourism, hold tourism promotion weeks and publicity months in each other's countries, jointly create competitive international tourist routes and products with Silk Road features, make it more convenient to apply for tourist visas in countries along the Belt and Road, and push forward cooperation on the 21st Century Maritime Silk Road cruise tourism program; and sixth, to carry out sports exchanges and support countries along the Belt and Road in their bid for hosting major international sports events.

The development of the cultural industry in the countries along the BRI route can enhance the image of the country. The Chinese side stated that "A people-to-people bond provides the public support for implementing the Initiative. We should carry forward the spirit of friendly cooperation of the Silk Road by promoting extensive cultural and academic exchanges, personnel exchanges and cooperation, media cooperation, youth and women exchanges and volunteer services, so as to win public support for deepening bilateral and multilateral cooperation." Film weeks, culture years, tourism promotion and other activities are strongly advocated and supported by China to link the spiritual values of the people along the economic belt.

Second, the role of the cultural industry is to form a value chain in the BRI. In the planning for cultural development in countries along the route, China has established the goal of accelerating the construction of the "Silk Road Cultural Industry Belt". In the coming period, some key areas of cooperation within the cultural industry between China and countries along the route include: cultural tourism, performing arts and entertainment, arts and crafts, creative design and the digital culture. It will support regions along the Belt and Road in implementing special cultural industry projects based on regional and ethnic characteristics, strengthen cooperation with the BRI countries on digital protection and on the development of cultural resources, and actively use the BRI cultural exchange and cooperation platform to promote cultural creativity products and develop the animation and game industry in BRI countries. Furthermore, it will also promote cultural and trading cooperation under the BRI and develop and improve international cooperation channels around the fields of performing arts, films, television, radio, music, animation, games, the digital culture, creative design, cultural technology equipment, artwork and licensed products.

So far, China is in a critical period of opening up the cultural industry in the new Silk Road Belt. The cultural exhibition contents, film week and other activities in the Chinese cultural industry have been initially implemented. In 2016, China's imports and exports of cultural products from and to countries and regions along the Belt and Road reached 14.9 billion US dollars, accounting for 16.8% of the total imports and exports of its cultural products.

1. Films and television

Recently, Chinese enterprises have sped up their surveys in Western Asia and have looked for market potential in Western Asia, including countries such as Saudi Arabia and Lebanon. Chinese filmmakers say that the region is a potential market for Chinese films, TV series and TV shows. Within the framework of the concept of the BRI for jointly building the 21st Century Economic Corridor, many experts hold the opinion that the "New Silk Road" does not necessarily depend on land or sea routes, especially with today's well-developed telecommunications and Internet technologies. China's Film and TV industry can go out through the online market and build a virtual Silk Road. In September 2015, China held a Film Week in Thailand, which was an important part of the strategic chain. The success of the Film Week was a symbol of the solidarity of the Chinese and Thai peoples, and it also created a new impetus for political and economic cooperation.

2. Culture exhibitions

In May 2015, the 11th China International Cultural Industry Expo was held in Shenzhen. This expo is considered as a measure of the BRI that China is implementing. An important point worth noting is that in the Silk Road exhibition area, the main content of the exhibition includes traditional art, creative design, intangible cultural heritage, tourism and performing arts of countries along the route. Countries participating in the exhibition include Russia, India, Thailand, Malaysia, etc. and 15 Chinese cities such as Xi'an, Urumqi, Guangzhou, Shenzhen, and Quanzhou. At the same time, the Ministry of Culture of China also held the Silk Road Cultural Exchange Forum.

3. Tourism

Although tourism is not a sector within the cultural industry, it is an important basis for promoting cultural trade exchanges and cooperation. At present, China and ASEAN countries have about 2,700 flights per week, and the mobility of the population in this region is increasing. As the world's tourism center moves to the Orient, the tourism industry of China and the ASEAN countries will become a part that cannot be ignored. Chinese tourists currently account for one-third of Vietnam's tourism market. With the rapid rise of China's middle class, the demand for travel abroad, especially in countries along the BRI route, is also increasing.

The development of the tourism industry can also promote the development of the cultural industry.

However, China is also facing many challenges in the cultural industry implemented under the BRI, which are embodied in the following aspects:

First of all, different cultural environments increase the number of challenges that the cultural industry has to face along the Silk Road.

The Silk Road Economic Belt passes through many different cultural regions with distinctive cultural characteristics. If the Southeast Asian corridor has a favorable environment where Chinese cultural products are more accessible, then exporting Chinese cultural products in Central and Western Asia will be a big challenge.

Multicultural regions create a colorful cultural landscape in the Silk Road corridor. However, when accepting other cultural values, differences in ideology and cultural values can cause certain difficulties. Therefore, China will experience numerous obstacles in exporting its cultural products to countries along the route.

Second, China's strategy of soft power is not in concert with and cannot keep up with its foreign economic development strategy.

In recent years, China has paid special attention to expanding and enhancing the image of a country that is open to the outside world. One of the ways China shows soft power to these countries is its exportation of cultural products. China expects to introduce its traditional cultural values to the world so that they can understand and accept China's peaceful strategy of development. However, due to China's overemphasis on the role of the state and government in the process of "going out", these guidelines for peaceful development cannot really achieve their effects or develop toward the intended direction. According to analysts, the Chinese government's intervention makes it easy for culture to become a formal ideology. Therefore, many countries do not recognize the process and nature of China's peaceful rise, but express skepticism or reservation about this. For example,

Confucius Institutes, films, publications, etc. are not always welcomed by all countries.

Thus, for China's cultural industry, the BRI can create opportunities for seeking and expanding the consumer market. However, in the process of "going out", the limitation of Chinese cultural products in different cultural environments will be a big challenge and a difficulty to overcome for the external development of the cultural industry.

3. Prospects for Vietnam-China Cooperation in the Cultural Industry

1. Opportunities

The cultural industry plays an increasingly important role in the developmental policies of Vietnam and China. Although compared with other countries or other industries, the cultural industry is a relatively late-developed industry, but with rich cultural resources and huge market potential, it gradually becomes an economic highlight in the two countries. Vietnam and China have many inherent advantages in promoting cooperation in the cultural industry, such as proximity of geographical location, cultural connections and the same political system. First, their geographical proximity and cultural connections create a soft boundary in the process of exchanging the cultural industry between the two sides. The similarity of values is a favorable condition for cultural companies in both countries to reduce the cost of product promotion. In addition, an important content in the macro aspect is that the leaders of the two countries have chosen the cultural industry as a key area in cultural cooperation between Vietnam and China. At the end of 2017, during the state visit of the General Secretary of the CPC Central Committee and President Xi Jinping to Vietnam, the Ministers of Culture of Vietnam and China signed a Memorandum of Understanding on Cooperation in the Cultural Industry. The document paved the way for the two countries' cultural industries to strengthen cooperation and understand each other's market potential.

2. Challenges

A serious challenge faced by Vietnam and China's cooperation in the cultural industry is that the mutual political trust between the peoples in the two countries needs to be improved. The island dispute and the complex development of the island issue affect the stability of Vietnam-China diplomatic relations. According to a study on the people-to-people bond between the Chinese and other countries in the region, the index of the people-to-people bond between Vietnam and China belongs to a potential but unbalanced group.

To be specific, among 63 countries along the BRI route, 34 cities in Vietnam are sister cities with big cities in China, and Vietnam is becoming one of the countries with the most sister cities with China. Meanwhile, tourism and academic cooperation between Vietnam and China are growing rapidly. Although China's index of positive comments on Vietnam is only 0.1, and among Southeast Asian countries, Vietnam's index of people-to-people bonds is 5.1 on average, Chinese people are still paying special attention to Vietnam. In contrast, in Vietnam, Vietnamese people have a multidimensional response to factors associated with China. For example, the demonstration in the steel plant in Ha Tinh Province in 2016 destroyed some foreign companies in Ha Tinh Province and Binh Duong Province. As well as demonstrations related to the Vietnam Special Economic Zone Law in 2018, etc. ... these activities led to the hesitation of Chinese enterprises in investing in Vietnam, including cultural enterprises.

4. Suggestions for Vietnam-China Cooperation in the Cultural Industry

As a latecomer to the cultural industry, Vietnam has continuously imported cultural products from the outside in order to meet the needs of its domestic market. China is one of the main sources of its supply of cultural products in Vietnam. Currently, 90% of the online game products in Vietnam come from China. Chinese online literature not only attracts a large number of Vietnamese readers, but it is also beginning to influence the development of Vietnamese literary language to a certain extent. For many years, Chinese TV dramas have been hit on TV stations from central to local in Vietnam and have become familiar cultural products in Vietnam.

Therefore, it can be found that China's promotion of cultural cooperation with Southeast Asian countries is a favorable prerequisite for Vietnam's cooperation with China in the cultural industry. Vietnamese cultural enterprises need to actively explore the Chinese market and strengthen their cooperation in fields with a strong demand for Vietnamese products. Vietnam can serve as a gateway to Southeast Asia, so Chinese enterprises should attach a great deal of importance to cooperation with Vietnam on cultural production and trade. Through successful cooperation with Vietnam, China can replicate these cooperation models and cooperate with other ASEAN countries. The fields of publication, television, film, creative design, etc. are China's advantages in the cultural industry. Vietnam can strengthen its cooperation and learn from China's developmental experience in the cultural industry, so as to develop the domestic cultural industry.

5. Conclusions

China's Belt and Road Initiative has attracted the attention of regions along the route and of countries around the world. It aims to rebuild the legendary historical trade route. The ancient Silk Road used to be a bridge between Asian and European civilizations and cultural exchanges. China's initiative provides two economic arcs, one on land and one at sea, starting from provinces in China, passing through Central Asia, Western Asia and Southern Asia and finally arriving in Europe. This initiative can open up huge consumer market potentials for the Chinese economy and promote mutual understanding among countries and people along the route through cultural exchanges and cultural promotion activities. The development of China's cultural industry under the Belt and Road Initiative can play an important role in strategies to increase the "soft power" and build up a good image abroad. China's increasing attention to and investment in Southeast Asia can provide more opportunities for cooperation and experiences for the Vietnamese cultural industry.

References

Hoang Minh Loi (2013), *Countermeasures for the Rise of Soft Power in the Northeast Asian Country and Region*, Vietnam: Hanoi Science Press.

Nguyen Thi Thu Hang (2013), *Some Basic Issues of Islam in the Middle East — Culture, Society and Islamic Politics*, Vietnam: Hanoi Science Press.

Nguyen Thi Thu Phuong (2012), *The Rise of China's Soft Power and Its Implications for Vietnam*, Hanoi Encyclopedia Dictionary Press.

China's Revitalization Planning of the Cultural Industry (2009) (full text), http://guoqing. china.com.cn/2012-11/02/content_26985931.htm

Zhai Kun (2017), *The Belt and Road Initiative Report on the Five Connectivity Index*, The Economic Daily Press.

Tran Thi Thuy (2013), China's Cultural Industry in the First Decade of the 21st Century, China Research Institute of the Vietnam Academy of Social Sciences.

Tran Thi Thuy (2014), The Export Policy of China's Cultural Industry in Recent Years, China Research Institute of the Vietnam Academy of Social Sciences.

Cheng, Yung-nien, Some Major Problems of China's Silk Road, *Zaobao.sg Special Reference*, Issue 219, August 26, 2015.

Will Durant. Nguyen Hien Le (trans.), *The Story of China's Civilization*, Hanoi Information Culture Press.

新时期中医药的继承与发展

殷明花【阿根廷】

马德普拉塔国立大学助理教授

在过去几十年中，特别是最近几年中国经济、社会和文化发生深刻变化的背景下，我们有必要考虑中国文化中的传统医学体系。与中国发展有关的许多辩论和研究项目都来自汉学研究的不同领域，其中大部分来自经济学、政治和国际研究。然而，由于不可能将文化与这些以及其他领域分离，并考虑到中医（TCM）是中国数千年知识和经验的主要支柱之一，有些问题无法解决。有着千年历史的医学实践在新时代的定位和发展方式成为一个亟待探索的广阔领域。

本文的出发点在于引导我们探索这种医学体系的继承和发展，包括在当代中国与所谓的西方医学体系共存的方式、相互影响的程度以及中国人如何将两者结合。为此，我们首先追溯中医自起源以来的发展历程以及后来直到今天与西医结合的方式。研究方法包括文献研究（专著、学术文章、媒体新闻等）以及 2018 年 9 月于杭州举行青年汉学家研修计划期间的实地考察。通过参加该计划，作者有机会亲身体验西医和中医两种医学体系的动态和共存，直接参观了杭州的两家医院以及浙江中医药大学（及其浙江中医药博物馆和校史记录，其中指出自 1953 年成立以来的职业基础和进步）。同时还参观了杭州一些历史悠久的药房和诊所，特别是胡庆余堂（及其中药博物馆）和方回春堂，两家都是在杭州具有悠久和光荣传统的典型药房。

最后，鉴于"一带一路"倡议的发展，将有必要重新审视其中一些问题，不只是在中国境内，还包括一带一路沿线，随着全球人口往返中国的流动。我们还将讨论两种不同医学体系在更广阔维度上的相遇，由于中医药是中国千年智慧的主要源泉之一，有可能将"一带一路"视为"知识之路"。

中医与西医的相遇

虽然关于疾病的最早书面记录可以追溯到商代（公元前 1600-1100 年），但许多历史学家都认为中医药的确切起源年代是汉代（公元前 206 年 - 公元 220 年），在当时开始有明确的医疗技术记录。有史以来中医药界最重要的经典著作之一《黄帝内经》[1]也出现在这个年代。这本书是 2000 多年以来最具影响力的中医学典籍，目前仍在使用，并且构成了"现代临床环境中理论灵感和实践知识的宝贵来源"（Unschuld, 2003: ix）。这部多卷本典籍主要关注药物的味道和特征以及开药方的约定并提出人体机能和物质世界的相关理论。《黄帝内经》的原理目前仍是中医从业者治疗的基本思想。例如，健康即平衡的理念，疾病意味着打破人体平衡。书中还解释了一些基本的概念，例如阴阳、五行（木火土金水）和气，以及类似于当今治疗实践的方法，例如针灸或艾灸。因此人们普遍认为，该经典著作所提供的理论仍然能够为中医实践提供支持（Puerta, 2009）。

此后，经过数千年的临床经验，中医药的应用已形成特殊的理论体系并构成"历史悠久和具有实用价值的珍贵文化遗产"（Liao, 2017: 17）。事实上，在古代中国领先的四大科学领域（具有自身的知识和技术体系）中，包括天文学、算术、农学和中医，只有中医在当代中国仍在使用，未被西方科学所取代，并且在大多数中国人的生活中仍然发挥着重要作用（同上）。

虽然两种医学体系在当今社会同时存在，但必须指出的是，西医的进入导致中国已发生许多深刻的变化。因此，有必要追溯两者与最初采用方法的联系。

这是自汉代和罗马帝国时代中国和西方通过丝绸之路沟通以来，首次涉及医疗卫生方面的文化交流（Fu, 2014）。然而，西方对传教士医生的最早记载是在唐代，景教教徒从中东前往中国，于公元 635 年引进希波克拉底医学。除了这些最

1　黄帝，中国传奇性的君主和文化英雄，在中国神话中被认为是所有汉族人的祖先。他是传说中的五帝之一，公元前 2697 年至 2597 年在位。在其诸多伟大的成就中，黄帝被人们赞誉发明了中医学的原理。
　《黄帝内经》传说由黄帝在公元前 2600 年左右所著。然而，现代史学家一般认为，它是周代和汉代的学者根据古代文献汇编，比传说晚 2000 多年（约公元前 300 年）。

初的接触外，仅从鸦片战争开始，西医就开始明确被接受并给当地社会及其医疗方式带来深刻的变化。

1842 年，《天津条约》允许外国人在中国任何地方旅行，不受中国法律的约束，首次允许传教士拥有财产并在条约港口以外居住。传教士优先考虑福音传道，但医院和诊所吸引更多的人改变信仰。因此，到 19 世纪末，大多数城市都设有外国教会和教会医院，并逐步纳入西方教育和医学培训计划。随着西医影响力的不断增强，1881 年天津医学馆创建，这是中国政府最早创办的西医学校（Jackson, 2011）。

中华民国成立和中国最后一个封建王朝被废除后，一项政治运动开始试图摆脱古代中国的医学观念。事实上，中华民国首任总统孙中山先生本人是一位接受过西方医学培训的医生。作为主要人物之一，他领导政治现代化运动并提倡西医。

1910 至 1911 年的满洲鼠疫事件造成医学体系的危机，并在随后导致中医声誉下跌（Lei, 2014）。肺鼠疫夺去 60000 多满洲人的生命，"特别挑选的八十名中医医师全部感染死亡，唯一能够提供帮助的是一位在英国剑桥大学接受过医学培训的医生伍连德。他运用自己所学的科学知识指导为防止鼠疫进一步传播而必须采取的卫生和公共健康措施。这让政府当局印象深刻"（Macdonald, 2017: 2）。这场灾难造成的影响之一就是医疗卫生目标的转向，不再以个人为中心，而是以社区为中心。在这种情况下，西医被视为达成目标的唯一手段（通过注射疫苗和环境控制），从根本性削弱了中医的影响力。

根据 Lei (2000) 的说法，直到 20 世纪 20 年代，中西医从业者已经共存数十年，彼此之间没有直接的竞争。然而在国民党统治期间，两种医学体系开始长期的斗争，最终造成中医发展路线的永久改变。国民党试图实施现代化议程，在南京成立卫生部（在中国历史上首次设立一个国家行政中心负责所有与医疗卫生相关的事项）。该卫生部于 1929 年召开第一届中央卫生委员会议，在受过西方培训的医师主导下，一致通过《废止旧医以扫除医事卫生之障碍案》提案。出乎意料的是，在如此危急的情况下，中医药界接受挑战并成功捍卫了自身的地位。这一威胁并没有动摇中医，而是迫使他们参加大规模的全国医学运动，成为中医学的历史性里程碑事件。因此，在同一年，传统医学的捍卫者建立一个全国性的协会（国医学院），以应对法律和意识形态方面的挑战（Farquhar, 1994）。这种对抗"也构成认识论事件，导致许多中国医生既接受现代性话语，又在这种话语的基础上改革中医药"（Lei, 2000: 5），最终中医体系开始逐步科学化和现代化。关于废除中医的辩论引发学界反思，促使他们将文献系统化、讨论基础理论以及研究不同的思想流派。如前文所述，这项运动为进一步改进和标准化中医药奠定了基础（Liao, 2017）。

某些学者（Lei, 2000, Liao, 2017）指出，虽然西医进入中国构成一个阻碍因素，但它最终促进了中医的发展。Liao (2017) 认为，"在西医的压力下，中医医师通过建立学校、启动培训计划、出版期刊、组织社团、翻译中医书籍和开发中药等手段，采取积极措施捍卫、推动和振兴中医。所有这些变化表明，西医进入中国在某种程度上促进了中医的发展"（第15页）。更重要的是，"到20世纪末，前现代、不科学的中医不仅在中国取得与西方生物医学相当的地位，而且也逐渐传播到西方国家。在西方，中医已成为全球替代医学大家庭的一分子，并且在某种程度上也已被主流医疗卫生服务所接受。"（Lei, 2000: 3）

中华人民共和国成立后，中医药开启新的篇章。经过多年的战争，这个国家遭受数十年来的贫困、营养不良和地方病带来的沉重打击。新中国"通过大规模的社会和经济变革来应对未来的艰巨任务。（……）作为合作医疗制度的组成部分，为全体人民提供基本的卫生保健和预防服务"（Hesketh & Wei, 1997）。

毛主席根据其文化价值支持地方卫生系统，推动国家重拾对中医的兴趣，但他也相信西医取得的进步：

"我们国家的卫生工作者团队非常庞大。他们必须关心5亿多人民的健康，包括年轻人、老人和病人……目前西医医生人数很少，因此广大群众，尤其是农民，依靠中医治病。因此，我们必须努力实现中医的全面统一"（引自 Taylor, 2011）。

在此背景下，1950年召开的第一届全国卫生会议宣布了医疗卫生事业的四大基本原则：

- 医学应为工人、农民和战士服务
- 预防医学应优先于治疗医学
- 传统中医应与西医结合
- 卫生工作必须与群众运动结合

基于上述原则实现全民医疗保健可能是20世纪50、60年代中国人口死亡率和患病率降低的重要原因之一。该政策伴随着社会经济条件的改善以及对预防医学的重视，例如进行大规模的免疫运动或"除四害"运动（消灭苍蝇、蚊子、老鼠和麻雀）（Hesketh & Wei, 1997）。

根据美国人类学家冯珠娣（Judith Farquhar, 1994）所做的杰出研究，"中医药领域仅在 1949 年中华人民共和国成立后才以其现代制度形式出现。毛泽东于 1955 年宣布中国医药学是一个伟大的宝库后，当代中医机构才确定其作为完全合法实体的自身定位"（第 11 页）。

20 世纪 50 年代中后期，最初的几所中医药学院开始设立，并在公众的支持下恢复了解放前的专业协会。中医药管理局从商务部转移到卫生部。同样，"小型学术机构和家庭诊所中杂而散的中医从业者被纳入迅速发展的全国性临床和学术机构体系。中医突然获得了明确的专业身份"（同上：第 12 页）。事实上，《中医杂志》于 1955 年[1]首次出版，是中国最早、最权威和规模最大的中医期刊。十年后，中国各地开设中医药高等学府，推动统一理论教科书的编撰以及学科、药物和技术标准体系的诞生。标准的建立是该学科现代化的必要条件（Liao, 2017）。

20 世纪 60 年代，在无产阶级文化大革命（1966-1976）的背景下，许多城市医生担任乡村医生并培训当地人成为"赤脚医生"。在这一时期结束时，已经培训超过一百万名村民，他们种植中草药并以非常低的价格为社区提供医疗服务。在国际上，这一成果被视为卓越典范并成为全世界效仿的榜样。根据世界卫生组织（WHO）的报道，"赤脚医生"极大地改善了中国农村社区的医疗卫生状况，这是 1978 年在苏联加盟共和国哈萨克斯坦召开阿拉木图会议推动医疗卫生运动的主要灵感来源。世界卫生组织指出，"卫生工作者居住在他们所服务的社区，重视预防而非治疗，同时以中西医结合的方式提供培训和基本治疗"（WHO: 2008）。

随着邓小平的到来以及"改革开放"政策的制定（今年是改革开放四十周年），中医药在"四个现代化"的基础上取得新的动力：工业、农业、科学技术和国防。在这一以国家政策转变为特征的充满活力的时期，像其他学术和科学部门一样，中医机构受益匪浅（Farquhar, 1994）。

在此政治框架内，1982 年国家宪法肯定了中医药在中国卫生系统中的重要作用。1985 年强调两种医学体系地位平等并继续实施中西医结合政策，尽管重点不同。确定三种不同的临床医生类别：中医医师（TCMP）、西医医师（WMD）和

1　在改革开放政策的背景下，英语版本于 1981 年首次发布。

中西医结合医师（Griffiths 等，2010）。

在这种背景下，如今不论是国内还是国际上，中医和西医医师之间的交流开始明显增加。虽然还存在距离和不兼容的情况，但二者也彼此受益，而且许多研究者认为："交流以及对所出现问题的理解带来的好处是，可以更好地理解改善世界各地医疗卫生实践的进程"（Schnell, 1989: 44）。

目前两种医学体系的共存

尽管西医比过去更重要，但与传统中医保健知识相关的一些技术在当今中国仍然很普遍，特别是中草药、太极拳或气功等运动以及服用或饮用药用食品，主流人群是中老年人。同样，中医机构也挤满了人，他们向中医知识和技术体系寻求帮助，以应对健康问题，去看门诊医生或购买自然疗法服务。从这个意义上来说，胡庆余堂 [1] 和方回春堂，除了可以反映杭州长期以来在中国传统医学中所发挥的重要作用外，也是一个典范。两家均在清代创办（一家是 1874 年，另一家是 1649 年），都是老字号药房和诊所，包括展厅、制药车间、中药铺以及知名中医提供草药治疗和针灸（或其他技术）的各种临床治疗室。

两种医学体系共存的现象在同一家医疗机构中也可以观察到，"在大多数医疗中心和诊所中，中西医同时提供临床治疗"（Griffiths 等，2010: 387）。这种现象与西方人的观感不一致，他们认为中西医是分散的实体，彼此之间没有或很少接触。相反，在浙江中医药大学，我们发现所有医学生都接受两种体系的培训：学习西医的医学生参加一定比例的中医研讨会和实践，反之亦然。同样，专业医师（中医医师和西医医师）之间的转诊采取与专科医师（例如创伤科医生和神经病学医生）相同的方式，决定或咨询患者哪种药物更适合治疗某些特定疾病。

这种对话共存也可以在浙江省中医院观察到。该医院始建于 1931 年，是一所集医疗、教学、科研、保健、康复为一体，具有鲜明中医特色的综合性三级甲等医院，是浙江中医药大学附属第一医院和第一临床医学院。该医院以在浙江省内历史最悠久、规模最大和技术能力最强而闻名全国（被认为是浙江省设备最齐

---

1 胡庆余堂中药博物馆于 1991 年开馆，是中国唯一的国家级中药专业博物馆，也是最著名的中药博物馆之一。博物馆秉承"原址保护、原状陈列"之原则，集中药起源、陈列展示、手工作坊、营业大厅和保健诊疗五大部分于一体，展示了大量的中药传统制药器具及上万种中药植物、动物和矿物标本。

全的医院之一），并且具有中西医结合的优势。经过广泛的临床实践，该医院在中医、西医以及中西医结合领域形成三支强大的技术力量[1]。同样，医院有两种药房：西药药房和中药药房。中药药房拥有 850 多种原料药和 420 种中成药。它是浙江省最大的中药药房，每天可配制 1000 多个中药药方（约 4000 公斤）。此外，药房还设有中草药制备室和制药车间。

另一方面，如上文所述，同时 Macdonald (2017) 也指出："自 20 世纪 50 年代以来，所有医学生都必须学习现代医学和传统医学。传统医学的学生必须学习有关解剖学、生理学等方面的现代知识；现代医学的学生则必须学习各种传统医学的课程"（第 3 页）。浙江中医药大学的案例 2 提供了一个很好的例子。这家多学科的中医药专业大学始创于 1953 年，有全日制在校生 13000 多名，并且一直是中医药课程领域的先驱，提供学士、硕士、博士和博士后课程。该大学讲授的主要课程包括：中医基础理论、中医临床基础、中医内科、中医儿科、中医妇科、中医骨伤科、中西医结合基础和中西医结合临床。

关于如何在中西医提供的医疗服务之间进行选择，研修计划期间咨询消息人士以及查阅参考文献后发现，西医擅长寻找快速解决方案，而中医则疗效较慢但效果更好。因此就西医不适合治疗某些疾病这一事实达成广泛共识。相反，西医据信在治疗冠心病、肺结核、肝炎、骨折、严重消化问题等急性期疾病时更有效。相比之下，认为中医适合恢复 / 康复阶段，作为预防和促进健康的方法，也适合于治疗慢性疾病。从这个意义上来说，中医能够改善免疫系统，具有抗病毒和抗炎作用，能够保持身心平衡、缓解疼痛、降低胆固醇等（Green 等，2006）。此外，选择中医是基于这样的信念，虽然西医治疗急性疾病见效更快，但会产生副作用。有时在追求快速疗效时更需要西医治疗，但与我们的认知相反，中国人或当局不认为这会对中医造成威胁，因为在西医找不到合适的解决方案，以及发生上述其他原因时，人们通常求助于中医。

关于两种医学体系的结合，越来越多的研究致力于通过生理和生物学方式将两者同时应用于相同的治疗或疾病（Griffiths 等，2010；Dong, 2013；Li 等，2016）

1　详情见：http://www.chinatcm.org/.
2　浙江中医药大学还拥有自己的博物馆，除了介绍学校各学科的历史外，特别强调在浙江省，"就像是一幅长长的画卷，展示学校的巨大变化和伟大发展历程，饱含学校几代教职员工和行政人员的艰辛和成功，办学的优良传统（……）追随先辈的足迹，吸收他们宝贵经验和伟大思想的精髓"（根据博物馆展示的介绍文字）。

并发现一些有趣的结果，例如减少西医疗法和干预措施的副作用。两种体系的结合目前在研究和临床实践中仍然非常活跃，被认为是 21 世纪的新医学。

新时期的中医药：未来视角

从本文可以看出，中国的医疗体系发生了诸多巨大的变化，尤其是在过去的几十年中，并且继续面临着日益严峻的挑战。众所周知，中国近年来的高速发展改善了该国人民的生活水平。瑞典国家发展政策分析署指出（2013），"出于对更好和更具包容性医疗的强烈需求，中国发起了一项重大医疗改革计划，目标是建立全民医疗保障体系。新体系不仅涉及医疗卫生制度，还意识到环境、生活方式和社会经济状况对健康的影响"（第 7 页）。这项称作"健康中国 2020"的计划由卫生部部长陈竺于 2009 年公布，其中包括一项政府计划，到 2020 年为农村和城市地区的所有公民提供平等的基本医疗保健以及推行健康生活方式。习近平 2016 年在北京参加全国卫生和健康大会后发起"健康中国 2030"计划，扩大既定目标并提出新目标。在这种情况下，打造健康环境、在医疗技术创新的基础上发展强大的制药业、确保食品药品安全等也成为强制性的要求（Tan 等，2017）。

为了推行健康生活方式，该计划将中医药视为一种宝贵的资源，可以与初级卫生保健共同对预防和管理慢性病发挥重要作用。《"健康中国 2030"规划纲要》[1]指出，"到 2030 年，中医药在治未病中的主导作用、在重大疾病治疗中的协同作用、在疾病康复中的核心作用得到充分发挥"（第 25 页）。为实现这一目标，在接下来几年中有必要提高中医药的服务能力，推进中医药继承创新并依托该学科推动预防和健康保障服务项目。

该计划还提出中西医结合与支持的问题，指出："构建整合型医疗卫生服务体系，推动健康服务从规模扩张的粗放型发展转变到质量效益提升的绿色集约式发展，推动中医药和西医药相互补充、协调发展，提升健康服务水平。"（同上：第 13 页）。

总之，考虑到"一带一路"倡议的发展以及新时期中医药的继承，有必要重新审视本文涉及的一些主题，不只是在中国境内，还包括一带一路沿线，随着全球人口往返中国的流动。我们还将讨论两种不同医学体系在更广阔维度上的相遇，

---

1 引自 https://www.sahealth.sa.gov.au/wps/wcm/connect/d39abd8041032c76a711ff1afc50ebfc/1645+Ning+Zhuang.pdf?MOD=AJPERES&CACHEID=ROOTWORKSPACE-d39abd8041032c76a711ff1afc50ebfc-msgAXUQ.

由于中医药是中国千年智慧的主要源泉之一，有可能将"一带一路"视为"知识之路"。

从这个意义上讲，过去几十年来，中医药在西方国家已广泛普及，如今已成为中产阶级主要消费的一种服务，而且是生物医学的替代医学。据有关资料统计[1]，迄今为止，中医药已遍及全世界170多个国家，中国政府已与其他国家签订约180项政府间合作协议。在"一带一路"倡议的背景下，中医药被视为与发展中国家及其卫生保健系统合作的手段，也是软实力的来源。中医药代表中国传统文化的精髓（具有哲学思想和思维方式组合以及中国价值观），《中国日报》（2015年）已对此给出合理的解释[2]："随着中国经济持续高速发展，中国综合国力稳步增长，中国文化的软实力日益受到国内外的广泛关注"。

然而，在部分国家（例如阿根廷）很难接触到中药产品或合格的中医医师。在这个意义上，对于参与"一带一路"倡议的国家而言，中国政府"为政府间合作提供合作框架，这无疑将消除最大的障碍，即中医资格认证、中医教育认证、药品获取和医疗保险方面的法律障碍"[3]。目前中国的大中小型企业都可以从事国际贸易，因此这一学科的广泛拓展也会推动中医药行业的发展[4]。新时期发生的所有这些现象不仅有助于国家繁荣，还能在"知识之路"的倡议下，通过自古流传至今的知识、技术和疗法体系的国际交流开展合作，并为世界提供解决健康问题的新途径，丰富彼此之间的文化。

---

1 *One Belt and One Road* Strategy: Opportunities for International Communication of Traditional Chinese Medical Culture" (2015). China Daily. 引自 http://www.chinadaily.com.cn/interface/zaker/1143605/2015-2-1/cd_19430421.html.

2 同上。

3 "Boosted by Belt and Road Initiative, spread of TCM speeds up" (2018). China Daily. 引自 http://europe.chinadaily.com.cn/a/201806/04/WS5b14ab0fa31001b82571dfaf.html.

4 "Belt and Road Initiative Gives Traditional Chinese Medicine a Boost" (2018). Beijing Review. 引自 http://www.bjreview.com/Business/201808/t20180827_800139206.html.

Inheritance and Development of Chinese Medicine in the New Era: Reflections and Perspectives

María Florencia Incaurgarat / Argentina

Assistant Professor at National University of Mar del Plata

Within the context of profound changes that have been taking place in China for the past decades, and especially during the last years, not only in relation with economy, but also with society and culture, it is necessary to consider one of the main elements of Chinese culture in this changing context: its traditional medical system. Many debates and research projects attending to the China's development have emerged from different areas of China studies, mostly from economics, politics and international studies. However, as it is not possible to dissociate culture from these and other spheres, and considering that Traditional Chinese Medicine (TCM) constitutes one of its principal axis with thousands of years of knowledge and experience, some questions cannot remain unanswered. The ways in which this millennial practice is oriented and developed in the New Era become a wide area to be explored.

In the present article, a starting point of analysis will lead us to explore the inheritance and development of this medical system, including the ways in which it coexists in contemporary China with the so called Western medical system, the extent of mutual influence, and the ways in which Chinese people appropriate both of them. For this purpose, in the first place, the pathways of Traditional Chinese Medicine since its origins will be traced, and afterwards, the ways it intertwined with Western Medicine until nowadays. All this will be sustained by means of bibliographic research (books, academic articles, press releases, etc.) and the field study taken place during the Visiting Program for Young Sinologists, in Hangzhou, during September of 2018. By attending this program, the author had the possibility to experience at first hand the dynamics and coexistence of the two healthcare systems, Western and Chinese, visiting two hospitals in Hangzhou, as well as the Zhejiang Chinese Medical University (and its Museum of History of Chinese Medicine in Zhejiang and School History, showing the foundation and progress of the career since its beginnings in 1953). In the same way, it was possible to visit some time-honored pharmacies and clinics of Hangzhou, specifically 胡庆余堂 (and its Museum of Traditional Chinese Medicine) and 方回春堂, both representative of the long and glorious Traditional Chinese Medicine tradition of Hangzhou.

Finally, considering the development of the "One Belt One Road" initiative, it will become necessary to re-examine some of these questions, no longer within the Chinese territory, but along this corridor, with global flows that departure from and towards China. This will also lead us to discuss about the encounter of two different medical systems in a wider scale, and the possibility to think this corridor as a "knowledge road", considering Traditional Chinese Medicine as one of its main sources of millennial wisdom.

Traditional Chinese Medicine and the encounter with Western Medicine

Although the first written record of a disease dates back to Shang Dynasty (BC 1600-1100), the precise origin of Chinese Traditional Medicine is considered by many historians during the Han Dynasty (BC 206 – AD 220), when clear records of medical techniques can be found. This is the time when one of the most important classical texts in TCM ever written appeared: "The Yellow Emperor's Classic of medicine"[1](黄帝内经). This book has been the most influential treatise for more than 2,000 years and it still has validity nowadays, constituting "a valuable source of theoretical inspiration and practical knowledge in modern clinical settings" (Unschuld, 2003: *ix*). The multi-volume treatise deals with the flavor and properties of medicines as well as the convention in prescriptions, and presents views on the function of the human body and the physical world that remain the basic ideas conceived by traditional medicine practitioners, for example the conception of health as balance, and disease as rupture of that balance. Fundamental concepts are explained, like Yin and Yang, the Five Phases of nature (wood, fire, earth, metal, water) and Qi, as well as current practices like acupuncture or moxibustion are described in ways similar to those practiced nowadays.For these reasons, it is widely considered that the teachings given by this classic, still sustain the practice of Traditional Chinese Medicine (Puerta, 2009).

Since then, after thousands of years of clinical experience, the application of Chinese medicines has formed a special theoretical system, constituting a "precious cultural heritage with a long history and practical value" (Liao, 2017: 17). In fact, of the four well developed areas in Ancient China (with their own systems of knowledge and techniques), i.e. astronomy, arithmetic, agronomy and Traditional Chinese Medicine, the last one is the only one remaining in Modern China without having been replaced by Western science, and still plays an important role in most Chinese people's life (Ibid.).

---

1   Huangdi, or the Yellow Emperor, is a legendary Chinese sovereign and cultural hero who is considered in Chinese mythology to be the ancestor of all Han Chinese. He was one of the legendary Five Emperors and tradition holds that he reigned from 2697 BC to 2597 BC. Among his many accomplishments, Huangdi has been credited with the invention of the principles of Traditional Chinese medicine.
The Huangdi Neijing (also translated as "Inner Canon of Huangdi") is said to have been written by the famous Chinese emperor Huangdi around 2600 BC. However,modern historiographers generally consider it to have been compiled from ancient sources by a scholar living between the Zhou and Han dynasties, more than 2,000 years later, around 300 BC.

Although both systems coexist today, it is important to point out that the arrival of Western Medicine in China has produced many profound changes. For that reason, it is necessary to trace back their interrelation to their very first approaches.

This is how the first cultural interchanges related to healthcare can be found since the days of the Han Dynasty and the Roman Empire, when communication between China and the West was established through the silk route (Fu, 2014). Nevertheless, the first record of medical missionaries from the West is found in the Tang Dynasty, with the Nestorian Christians, who arrived from the Middle East, introducingHippocratic medicine in AD 635. Despite these first contacts,it was only at the time of the Opium Wars, that Western medicine would definitely settle and carry out profound changes in the local society and in the ways to deliver its healthcare.

In 1842, the Treaty of Tianjin allowed foreigners to travel anywhere in China and not be subject to Chinese law. For the first time missionaries were allowed to own property and reside outside the treaty ports. The missionaries' priority was the evangelization, but hospitals and clinics drew more converts than preaching. Thus, by the end of 19th century most towns had a foreign mission and a mission clinic, and progressively included western education and medical training programs. Gaining more and more influence, in 1881 the Tianjin Medical School was founded as the first to be established by the government for the teaching of Western medicine (Jackson, 2011).

Once the Republic was founded and the last Dynasty abolished, a political movement started trying to rid China of ancient medical ideas. In fact, San Yat-sen, the first president of the Republic, was himself a Western-trained medical doctor, and was one of the main figures of this movement, who led the drive for political modernization advocating Western medicine.

An unfortunate event which took place between 1910 and 1911, the Manchurian Plague, was strictly related to the crisis of the medical system, and the following loss of reputation of Traditional Chinese Medicine (Lei, 2014). During this pneumonic plague, in which60,000 people died in Manchuria, "eighty traditional physicians were specially selected to control it, but they all died of it themselves. The only person who was able to help was a young Cambridge-trained doctor, Wu Lien-te, who used his scientific knowledge to direct the sanitary and public health measures required to prevent the plague from spreading further. This made a great impression on the authorities" (Macdonald, 2017: 2). One of the repercussions caused by this catastrophe was the redirection of health care goals, which would no longer be individually focused, but rather community-centered. In that context, Western medicine was seen as a means to reach this objective (by the hand of vaccines and control of the environment) which decisively undermined the evaluation of Chinese medicine.

According to Lei (2000),until the 1920s,practitioners of the two medicines had already co-existed for decades without directly competing against each other. But it was not until the Nationalist Period when the two systems began a long struggle which would change the course of Traditional Chinese Medicine forever.As the KMT attempted to carry out a modernizing agenda, it established the Ministry of Health at Nanjing (for the first time in Chinese history, China had a national administrative center to take charge of all health care related issues). This Ministry, dominated by Western-trained physicians, during the first National Public Health Conference held in 1929, unanimously passed a proposal for *Abolishing Old Style Medicine in Order to Clear Away the Obstacles to Medicine and Public Health*. Surprisingly, under such a critical situation, the Traditional Chinese Medicine community took the challenge and defended its position, and rather than discouraging traditional Chinese doctors,this menace mobilized them into a massive National Medicine Movement, resulting in a historical milestone for the discipline.It is so, that in the same year, defenders of the traditional practice organized a national association (Institute for National Medicine), to combat these legal and ideological challenges (Farquhar, 1994). This confrontation "also constituted an *epistemological event* which led many Chinese doctors both to embrace the discourse of Modernity and to reform Chinese medicine on the basis of this discourse" (Lei, 2000: 5), leading to the progressive *scientization* and modernization of the Chinese medical system.The debate towards the dismissal of Traditional Chinese Medicine arose self-examination among the discipline community and inspired them to systematize literatures, discuss basic theories, and research into different schools of thought. This movement, as said before, laid the foundation for further improvement and standardization of TraditionalChinese Medicine (Liao, 2017).

As some authors remark (Lei, 2000, Liao, 2017), although the arrival of Western Medicine in China can be seen as a discouraging factor, it finally promoted the development of Traditional Chinese Medicine (TCM). As Liao (2017) states: "Under the pressure of Western medicine, doctors of TCM actively took measures to defend, promote and invigorate TCM by means of setting up schools, starting training programs, publishing journals, organizing societies, translating TCM books, and developing traditional Chinese drugs. All these changes show that the introduction of Western medicine into China, to some extent, has promoted the development of TCM" (p. 15). Even more, "at the end of the twentieth century, pre-modern, unscientific Chinese medicine not only stands as equal to Western biomedicine in China, but gradually has spread into western countries as well. In the West, Chinese medicine has become part of a worldwide family of alternative medicine and also has been accepted to some degree in mainstream health care services." (Lei, 2000: 3).

With the foundation of the People's Republic of China a new chapter would begin for Traditional Chinese Medicine. After years of war, the result was a country devastated by decades of poverty, malnutrition, and endemic diseases. The new Republic "responded to the daunting task ahead by introducing massive social and economic change. (…) Basic health care and preventive services were provided to everyone as part of the cooperative medical system" (Hesketh & Wei, 1997).

Chairman Mao supported the local health system relying in its cultural value, promoting the resurgence of interest by the state in traditional Chinese medicine, as he also believed in the progress carried out by Western Medicine:

"Our nation's health work teams are large. They have to concern themselves with over 500 million people [including the] young, old, and ill. ... At present, doctors of Western medicine are few, and thus the broad masses of the people, and in particular the peasants, rely on Chinese medicine to treat illness. Therefore, we must strive for the complete unification of Chinese medicine" (Quoted in Taylor, 2011).

In this context, in the First National Health Congress in 1950, four basic guidelines for the organization of health care were announced:

- Medicine should serve the workers, peasants, and soldiers
- Preventive medicine should take precedence over therapeutic medicine
- Traditional Chinese medicine should be integrated with Western scientific medicine
- Health work should be combined with mass movements

Following these guidelines, fostered the possibility to achieve almost universal access to health care, constituting one of the factors explaining the reductions in mortality and morbidity seen during the 1950s and 1960s. This policy was accompanied by the improvement in socioeconomic conditions and by the emphasis placed on prevention, for example by means of massive immunization campaigns or movements like "The Four Pests Campaign" (aimed to eliminate flies, mosquitoes, rats, and sparrows) (Hesketh & Wei, 1997).

Considering the remarkable research led by the anthropologist Judith Farquhar (1994), "the field of Traditional Chinese Medicine, came into existence in its modern institutional form only after the 1949 founding of the People's Republic of China. Contemporary TCM organizations locate their inception as fully legitimate entities with Mao Zedong's 1955 proclamation that our motherland's medicine is a great treasurehouse" (p.11).

During the mid to late 1950s, the first few colleges of Traditional Chinese Medicine were founded and the pre-Liberation professional associations were revived and enlarged with public support. The Chinese Medicine Bureau was moved from the Ministry of Commerce to the Ministry of Health. And in the same way, "the diverse and scattered practitioners of traditional medicine, with their small academies and family clinics, were organized into a rapidly growing national hierarchy of clinical and academic institutions. TCM suddenly acquired a clear-cut professional identity" (Ibíd.:12). In fact, the Journal of Traditional Chinese Medicine was first published in 1955[1] as China's earliest, most authoritative, and largest circulation TCM journal in China. In the same line, after this decade, Traditional Chinese Medicine institutions of higher learning were established throughout China, which prompted the birth of unified theory textbooks and standard system of subjects, drugs and techniques. The establishment of these criterions was a must for the modernization of the discipline (Liao, 2017).

During the '60s, in the context of the Great Proletarian Cultural Revolution (1966-1976), many urban doctors worked as village ones and trained locals to become"Barefoot doctors". By the end of this period, more than a million of villagers were trained, having grown medicinal herbs, and provided care to the community ata very low cost. Internationally speaking, this result was considered as an example of excellence and became a model for the world. According to the World Health Organization (WHO), "Barefoot doctors" have dramatically improved access to healthcare in China's rural communities and were a major inspiration to the primary healthcare movement leading up to the conference in Alma-Ata, in the former Soviet Republic of Kazakhstan in 1978. As the WHO states,"these health workers lived in the community they served, focused on prevention rather than cures while combining western and traditional medicines to educate people and provide basic treatment" (WHO: 2008).

---

1   In the context of Reform and Opening-up Policy, the English-language edition premiered in 1981.

With the upcoming of Deng Xiaoping and his "reform and opening-up" policy (this year, specifically four decades ago)Chinese Medicine received a new boost, attached to "The Four Modernizations": industry, agriculture, science and technology, and the military. This dynamic period characterized by this national policy shift, benefited the institutions of TCM as it did other academic and scientific units (Farquhar, 1994).

Within this political frame, in 1982, the formal role of Traditional Chinese Medicine in the Chinese health system was recognized at national constitutional level. Equalization of the status of the two medical systems was emphasized in 1985 and the policy of integration was continued albeit with a different emphasis. Three distinct categories of clinicians were created: Traditional Chinese Medical Practitioners (TCMP), Western Medical Doctors (WMD) and integrated TCMP-WMD (Griffiths et al, 2010).

In this context, interaction between Chinese and Western physicians started to increasesignificantly until nowadays, both in a national and an international scale.Despite having distances and incompatibilities, the two systems have also found benefits from each other, and as many authors assert: "the benefits of such interaction, and understanding some of the problems which have arisen,can lead to a better understanding of a process which can improve healthcare practices around the world" (Schnell, 1989: 44).

Current coexistence of the two medical systems

Although Western medicine has gained much more protagonism than in the past, some techniques related to traditional health care knowledge remain widely common in today's China, especially herbal medicine, exercise such as taiqi or qigong, and eating or drinking medicinal food, with predominance in adults and elder people. In the same way, Traditional Chinese Medicine establishments are crowded with people, seeking for this system of knowledge and techniques to deal with their health issues, looking for outpatient doctors or buying natural remedies.In this sense, the case of 胡庆余堂 [1] and 方回春堂 is paradigmatic, besides reflecting the vital role that Hangzhou has long played in China's bustling Traditional Chinese Medicine. Both launched during the Qing Dynasty (the first one in 1874 and the second one in 1649), constitute two time-honored pharmacies and clinics that encompass an exhibition floor, drug-making workshop, Traditional Chinese Medicine store and various clinical rooms offering herbal treatments and acupuncture (among other techniques) by renowned Chinese doctors.

The coexistence of both systems can also be seen within one same medical establishment, where "in most health centers and clinics, Traditional Chinese Medicine and Western Medicine are practiced alongside each other" (Griffiths et al., 2010: 387). This fact goes against the Western belief that in China, these systems exist like discrete entities, without or with scarce contact between each other. On the contrary, as it could be seen in the Zhejiang Chinese Medical University, all doctors are trained in both systems: those who studied Western Medicine had a percentage of Traditional Medicine seminars and practice, and vice versa. In the same way, referral between professionals (TCMD and WD) is in the same manner as between specialists (e.g. traumatologist and neurologist), deciding or consulting to the patient which kind of medicine is preferable to address some specific ailment.

This dialogical coexistence could also be seen in the Zhejiang Provincial Hospital of Traditional Chinese Medicine. Founded in 1931, this Hospital is a Grade Three Class A comprehensive hospital integrating medical treatment, medical education, scientific research, rehabilitation and health care with striking character of Traditional Chinese Medicine. It is also the First Affiliated Hospital and First Clinical College of Zhejiang Chinese Medical University. The hospital is well known nationwide for its longest history and largest scale with the best

---

1 胡庆余堂 opened in 1991 the Museum of Traditional Chinese Medicine, constituting the only state-level professional one of this kind in China, and one of the most famous TCM museums. Taking the principle of site protecting and undisturbed displaying, the Museum is divided into five parts including the history introduction of traditional Chinese Medicine, display and exhibition, manual workshops, business hall and health care and treatment. There are displayed several traditional pharmaceutical tools, plants, animals and mineral samples of Traditional Chinese Medicine.

technical capacity in Zhejiang Province (considered one of the most well-equipped hospitals in the province), and its advantages of combination of Chinese Medicine with Western medicine. After extensive clinical practice, the hospital has formed three strong technical forces in the fields of Traditional Chinese Medicine, western medicine and combination of both[1]. Likewise, the Hospital has two kinds of Pharmacies: Western and Chinese. The latter, has over 850 kinds of raw Chinese medicines and 420 patent medicines. It is the largest TCM pharmacy in Zhejiang, confecting over 1000 formulas (about 4000 kg) of Chinese medicine every day. In addition, the pharmacy has also herbal medicine preparation rooms and pharmaceutical workshops.

On the other hand, as it was mentioned above and as it is stated by Macdonald (2017): "since the 1950's all medical students have to study both modern and traditional medicine. Those students who wish to practice traditional medicine have to study the relevant modern knowledge of anatomy, physiology, and so on; while those who wish to practice modern medicine have to attend lectures on various traditional aspects" (p.3).The case of Zhejiang Chinese Medical University[2], is a good example of this training. Created in 1953, this multidisciplinary university specialized in Traditional Chinese Medicine, has more than 13,000 full-time students, and has been a pioneer in the field of Chinese medicine programs, offering Bachelor, Master, PhD and postdoctoral programs since then. The main subjects taught in this University are: TCM Basic Theory, TCM Clinical Basics, TCM Internal Medicine, TCM Pediatrics, TCM Gynecology, TCM Orthopedics & Traumatology, Basics of Integration of TCM and Western Medicine, Clinics of Integration of TCM and Western Medicine.

---

1 See more in: http://www.chinatcm.org/.
2 This University also holds its own Museum of School History, where besides showing the long history of the discipline with an specific emphasis in Zhejiang Province, "like a long picture scroll, reveals the school' s big changes and great development, signifies the hardships and success of the teaching and administrative staff through generations and the fine traditions of school running (···) tracing the footprints of the pioneering generations and absorbing the essence of their valuable experience and great thoughts" (as stated in the museum' s exhibition).

Regarding the choice in the use of Traditional and/or Western services, the informants consulted during the Program as well as the bibliography of reference, reveal that Western medicine is good at finding quick solutions, and that Chinese medicine, on the other hand, is slower but more effective. In this way, there is broad consensus on the fact that Western medicine is not suitable to treat certain diseases. On the contrary, it is believed to be more effective when treating acute stage diseases such as coronary heart disease, tuberculosis, hepatitis, cancer, fractures, severe digestive problems, among others. In contrast, it is considered that Traditional Chinese Medicine is suitable for the recovery/rehabilitation phase and as a method of prevention and health promotion, as well as for the treatment of chronic diseases. In this sense, it would produce improvements in the immune system, antiviral and anti-inflammatory effects, balance between body and mind, pain relief, cholesterol reduction, among others (Green et al, 2006).Besides this, the choice in favor of TCM, in turn, is based on the belief that, although Western Medicine is quicker to treat acute diseases, it creates several adverse effects.Sometimes, in the pursuit of rapid effectiveness among other factors, Western services are more required, but as opposed to what is believed, this is not seen by Chinese people or authorities as a menace to Chinese medical tradition, because the latter is frequently sought when the former cannot find a proper solution, as well as the other reasons mentioned above.

As regards the combination of these two systems, there is an increasing number of research studies working in the physiological and biological application of both to the same treatment or disease (Griffiths et al, 2010; Dong, 2013; Li et al, 2016), finding some interesting results, for example, related to the reduction of the side effects of Western remedies and interventions. The integration of these systems is still very active in both research and clinic practice and is considered the 21st century's new medicine.

Chinese Medicine in the New Era: Perspectives for the future

As it could be seen along this article, China's healthcare system has undergone numerous and considerable changes, especially over the past decades, and continues to face mounting challenges. As it is well known, China's great growth in recent years, has improved the country's standard of living. According to the Swedish Agency for Growth Policy Analysis (2013) this factor, "in combination with strong needs for better and more inclusive healthcare, has led China to embark on a major healthcare reform program,with the goals of establishing a universal health security system. The new system is not just a healthcare system and recognizes the impact of the environment, lifestyle and socioeconomic circumstances on health" (p.7). This program called "Healthy China in 2020", was declared in 2009 by Chen Zhu, head of the Ministry of Health, and consists in a government plan to provide basic and equal healthcare for all its citizens by 2020, in rural and urban areas, as well as promoting healthy lifestyles. In the same tune "Healthy China in 2030", launched in 2016 after the visit of Xi Jinping to the China National Health and Well-being conference in Beijing, enlarges these goals and embraces new ones. In this case, it becomes also mandatory to build healthy environments, develop a strong pharmaceutical industry based on medical technological innovation, ensure food and drug safety, among others (Tan et al, 2017).

For promoting healthy lifestyles, Traditional Chinese Medicine is considered by these plans, like a valuable resource at the same time that it can play a valuable role in the prevention and management of chronic diseases, alongside Primary Health Care. As it is stated in the Outline of the Healthy China 2030 Plan[1], by that time, Traditional Chinese Medicine "will play a key role in preventing illnesses, treating major illnesses and inrehabilitation" (p.25). For this, it will be necessary during these following years, to have improved Traditional Chinese Medicine capacity, promoted preservation and innovation, and propelled projects of preventive and health maintenance services based on this discipline.

The integration and supporting of both Traditional Chinese and Western medicine is also proposed in these plans, stating that "healthcare delivery systems should

---

1   Retrieved from: https://www.sahealth.sa.gov.au/wps/wcm/connect/d39abd8041032c76a711f
     f1afc50ebfc/1645+Ning+Zhuang.pdf?MOD=AJPERES&CACHEID=ROOTWORKSPACE-
     d39abd8041032c76a711ff1afc50ebfc-msgAXUQ.

become integrated, moving from an extensive development mode based on scale to an intensive one focusing on quality and efficiency. Efforts should be made in the complementary development of both traditional Chinese medicine (TCM) and Western medicine, as well as overall enhancement of healthcare delivery" (Ibid.: 13).

To conclude this article, and considering the development of the "One Belt One Road" initiative and the inheritance of Chinese Medicine in the *New Era*, it becomes necessary to re-examine some of the topics addressed along these pages, no longer within the Chinese territory, but along this corridor, with global flows that departure from and towards China. This will also lead us to discuss about the encounter of two different medical systems on a wider scale, and the possibility to think this corridor as a "knowledge road", considering Traditional Chinese Medicine as one of its main sources of millennial wisdom.

In this sense, Chinese Medicine since the last decades has enjoyed a widespread popularity in Western countries, being nowadays a service consumed mostly by middle-class people, and as an alternative means to Biomedical Medicine. According to relevant statistics[1], Traditional Chinese Medicine so far has spread to more than 170 countries,and the Chinese government has signed approximately 180 inter-governmentalcollaborative agreements with other countries. In the context of the One Belt One Road (OBOR) Initiative, TCM is seen as a means to collaborate with developing countries and their health care systems, as well as a source of soft power. Considering traditional Chinese medical culture as representative of the quintessence of traditional Chinese culture (with the pair of philosophical thoughts and modes of thinking as well as Chinese values), this idea is well explained in the *China Daily* newspaper (2015)[2] where it is asserted that "as the Chinese economy continuously develops at a comparatively high speed and Chinese overall national strength steadily grows, the soft power of Chinese culture is attracting stronger

---

1 "*One Belt and One Road* Strategy: Opportunities for International Communication of Traditional Chinese Medical Culture" (2015). China Daily. Retrieved from:http://www.chinadaily.com.cn/interface/zaker/1143605/2015-2-1/cd_19430421.html.

2 Ídem.

interest and wider attention at home and abroad".

Nevertheless, in some countries, like Argentina, it is highly difficult to obtain Chinese medical products or to access qualified Chinese professionals. In this sense, for countries involved in the OBOR Initiative, Chinese Government "has offered a cooperative framework for intergovernmental cooperation, which will definitely help remove the largest barrier, the legal barrier in TCM qualification, TCM education accreditation, drug access and medical insurance"[1]. This widespread expansion of the discipline is also leading to a growth of the TCM Industry since large, medium and small Chinese companies are now enabled to engage in international trade[2]. All these recent phenomenons that are taking place during this *New Era,* not only contribute to national prosperity, but also and along the whole initiative of this "knowledge road", collaborate to international exchange of this ancient set of knowledge, techniques and remedies, and provide to the World a new way to solve health problems, cultivating mutual cultural enrichment.

References

Dong, Jingcheng (2013). "The Relationship between Traditional Chinese Medicine and Modern Medicine". In: *Evidence-Based Complementary and Alternative Medicine.* Hindawi Publishing Corporation: Shanghai.

Fu, Louis (2014). "Hippocratic Medicine in China: Comparison with a 9th Century Chinese Manual on Bone Setting". In: *Journal of Orthopaedics, Trauma and Rehabilitation.* The Chinese University of Hong Kong: Hong Kong.

Green, G.; Bradby, H.; Chan, A.; Lee, M. (2006). "We are not completely Westernised: Dual medical systems and pathways to health care among Chinese migrant women in England". in: *Social Sience& Medicine.*

Griffiths, Sian; Chung, Vincent; Jin, Ling Tang (2010). "Integrating Traditional Chinese Medicine: Experiences from China". In: *Australasian Medical Journal.*

---

1 "Boosted by Belt and Road Initiative, spread of TCM speeds up" (2018). China Daily. Retrieved from: http://europe.chinadaily.com.cn/a/201806/04/WS5b14ab0fa31001b82571dfaf.html.

2 "Belt and Road Initiative Gives Traditional Chinese Medicine a Boost" (2018). Beijing Review. Retrieved from: http://www.bjreview.com/Business/201808/t20180827_800139206.html.

Hangzhou Tourist Commission (2016) *Hangzhou at a glance*. The Commercial Press.

Hesketh, Therese & Wei, Xing Zhu (1997). "Health in China. From Mao to Market Reform". In: *BMJ*.

Hesketh, Therese& Wei, Xing Zhu (1997). "Traditional Chinese medicine: one country, two systems" (1997) In: *BMJ*.

Jackson, Mark (2011). *The Oxford Handbook of the History of Medicine*. Oxford University Press

Lei, Sean Hsiang-lin (2000). "When Chinese Medicine Encountered the State, 1928-1937". Unpublished paper, retrieved from: http://www.ihp.sinica.edu.tw/~medicine/active/years/hl.PDF.

Li, Deli; Qiao, Shanshan; Shi Duozhi; Zheng Shiqi; Wang, Tengyu, Wang, Rufeng (2016) "The Combination of Traditional Chinese Medicine with Western Medicine" In: *Medicinal & Aromatic Plants*: Shanghai.

Liao, Yuqun (2017). *Traditional Chinese Medicine: Understanding its principles and practices*. China International Press: Beijing.

Macdonald, Alexander (2017). "Relationship of Modern and Traditional Schools of Chinese Medicine: Need it Remain Hostile?" In: *International Journal of Complementary & Alternative Medicine*.

Puerta, José Luis (2009). "El Canon de Medicina Internadel Emperador Amarillo". In *Revista de Humanidades:* Spain.

Schnell, James (1989). "The Merging of Traditional Chinese Medicine and Western Medicine in China: Old Ideas Cross-Culturally Communicated Through New Perspectives". In: *Explorations in Ethnic Studies*.

Swedish Agency for Growth Policy Analysis (2013). *China's Healthcare System: Overview and Quality* Improvements. Retrieved from:http://www.tillvaxtanalys.se/in-english/publications/direct-response/direct-response/2013-05-20-chinas-healthcare-system-----overview-and-quality-improvements.html.

Tan, Xiaodong; Liu Xiangxiang; Shao, Haiyan (2017). "Healthy China 2030: A Vision for Health Care". In: *Elsevier*.

Taylor, Kim (2011). *Chinese Medicine in Early Communist China, 1945-1963: A Medicine of Revolution*. Needham Research Institute Series.

Unschuld, Paul (2003). *Huang Di neijingsu wen: Nature, Knowledge, Imageryin an Ancient Chinese Medical Text*. University of California Press.

中国作为全球商品供应商在阿根廷的角色

光烈【阿根廷】
阿根廷国家参议院秘书

引　言

拉丁美洲和加勒比地区是充满潜力的地区。该地区拥有最年轻的社会。此外，一些社会是由受过良好教育的工人阶级组成，他们掌握至少两种或以上的语言。

然而，对本地区经济体的预期增长和发展所持的乐观看法，实际上仍未实现。可以肯定的是，加勒比和拉丁美洲国家需要与大国进行更深层次的合作才能发展。

我在 2018 年参加北京青年汉学家研修计划上认识的学者，来自格林纳达的戴艾美（Abbie David）指出，我们是美国的后院。尤其是加勒比海的岛国，很难打开局面，尝试与美国不认为符合自身利益的国家展开对话。然而，我在下文中将说明，2018 年中国在该地区取得了哪些重大成就。

中国的这种创新方法，成立中国—拉共体论坛就是最好的例子，能够让我的同事和我（我希望他们也会这样做）进入下一个主题：如何持续加强中国与拉丁美洲和加勒比地区的关系。当我们参加青年汉学家研修计划时，中国社会科学院拉丁美洲研究所的研究员周志伟先生在一次会议上提出了这个问题。

在本文中，我将尝试为上述问题提供答案。为此，有必要首先分析中国的合作如何在全球范围内传播，因为该国在历史上首次成为全球优秀供应商。之后，我将回顾如何建立这种合作。是中国政府独自做这件事，还是中国企业也承担一些责任？最后，我将分析拉丁美洲国家，特别是我所居住的国家阿根廷，如何利用这一机会为他们的经济带来发展。

一、中国：新的全球商品提供者

习近平在中国共产党全国代表大会上的讲话很明确：政府致力于为公民带来福祉。全面建设小康社会是今后的主要目标。

这一宏大目标意味着中国必须在世界范围内扩大合作，特别是在"南方"国家。如果中国经济发展顺利，中国人也将安居乐业，国家领导人非常清楚这一点。

为了营造有利的环境，中国必须与其他国家加强合作。许多举措都朝着这个方向努力。例如亚洲基础设施投资银行（AIIB）、"一带一路"倡议（BRI）、2016年在杭州举行的 G20 会议和峰会以及金砖国家峰会。

中国合作的第一步

自 21 世纪初以来，人们认为世界在 9·11 事件后开始发生变化。资本开始流入新兴国家，它们的经济蓬勃发展。中国当然是其中之一。与巴西、俄罗斯、印度和南非一起，这五个国家象征着不远的未来。

这些国家本应在混乱的秩序中发挥领导作用，在这种秩序下一小撮恐怖分子就可以轻易炸毁世界贸易的里程碑。除了中国之外，其他国家没有发挥作用。

在新兴国家中，只有中国成功地提供了传统布雷顿森林体系全球机构的替代方案。其他金砖国家发生了什么？一些分析人士认为，国内情况让它们失去雄心壮志（这些国家是否正在为实现这一目标而努力？）。

新兴的中国机构不仅拥有作为发展动力的资源，而且还为寻求援助的国家准备更好的答案（过去这些年世界银行在非洲做得很好）。

据说机构是对它们"创造者"利益的回应，是扩大在某个历史时刻获得影响力的来源。当然，与任何其他西方机构一样，中国机构也热衷于共同合作实现收支平衡。也许不同之处是中国诚实地承认这一点。这就是为什么西方分析家和媒体不断攻击他们的原因。

在西方国家，这被视为压制其国家伙伴主权的一种尝试。2017 年，澳大利亚走得很远，其总理马尔科姆·特恩布尔（Malcolm Turnbull）宣布"澳大利亚人民站了起来"。堪培拉的许多人认为，中国人正在寻求影响决策者。除了让大多数分析人士和学者都喜欢的话题之外，在现实生活中，行动胜于雄辩。巴基斯坦瓜德尔港是中国为合作伙伴国带来经济发展的最佳范例之一。

瓜德尔港，中国合作的最佳范例

巴基斯坦的俾路支省是瓜德尔港所在地，这是中巴经济走廊的最后一步，也是"一带一路"倡议最大的项目。修建连接新疆维吾尔自治区喀什市和印度洋沿岸港口的公路耗费多年时间。这不是一件容易的事。南南合作经常遭遇各种障碍。巴基斯坦在过去几十年中一直面对诸多困难。除了其脆弱的经济状况（国际货币基金组织财政援助记录保持者）外，它还面临着许多安全挑战。在克什米尔地区与印度的冲突永无休止，而塔利班则公然藐视伊斯兰堡建立的民主力量。

中国人带来希望，并继续前进。现在，瓜德尔港在巴基斯坦的重要性排名第三，仅次于卡拉奇和卡西姆的港口，有能力为该地区带来发展。

对于中国而言，印度洋是非常重要的地区。稍后我们将看到，通过巴基斯坦到达印度洋，可以降低马六甲海峡对中国安全利益的重要性。

瓜德尔港距霍尔木兹海峡仅 400 公里，是连接波斯湾和印度洋的关键节点。这是一个历史悠久的地点，在多个世纪以来见证了许多船只经过，实际上占据世界原油运输的三分之一。这一惊人的数字证明拥有瓜德尔港的必要性。

"一带一路"倡议，南方繁荣的框架

"一带一路"倡议是自马歇尔计划以来，迄今为止单个国家提出的最雄心勃勃的提议。幸运的是，提出这一倡议不会失去数百万人的生命，也不会摧毁成千上万个城市。中国认为该计划的触发因素是使南半球经济体蓬勃发展的机会，同时利用新能源推动中国的增长。简而言之，"一带一路"倡议是世界上最大的共赢合作。我们应该将"一带一路"倡议视为一种战略方针。这意味着它的行动不仅基于中国人的能力，而且还取决于环境的特征。当然，很难定义"一带一路"倡议的边界。最好将其视为一个想法，而不是一个刻板的计划。考虑到以前的丝绸之路。那时没有确切的路线，但每个人都知道该做什么，该去哪里。那是丝路精神，这次也是完全一样的。

习近平在中国周边发展铁路的观念反映出该国的主要利益，目前正在寻找新的方法（而且代价更低）让中国产品进入最重要的市场。有了瓜德尔港，中国商品不需要经过马六甲海峡（世界贸易的 50% 都经过）。这个地理位置确实是一个瓶颈，也是一个危险区域。这并不意味着中国将忘记对南中国海的主权主张，因为这是现任政府的优先事项。但是，在这个国家最需要的时刻，降低地缘政治在如此脆弱地点的影响将是一次巨大的胜利。请记住，主要目标是"取得决定性的胜利"。这些词的使用很有趣，因为安全范式意味着对存在威胁的广泛确认，以便做出非常规决策。可以说，"一带一路"倡议是迄今为止在这方面采取的最大举措。维持自由贸易是当今中国的主要利益，同时也是最大的威胁。

奇怪的是，澳大利亚在 2017 年发布的《外交政策白皮书》中承认保持世界贸易自由和开放是其主要优先事项之一。这是巧合吗？我不这么认为。在这一历史时刻，每条道路都通往华盛顿特区。

世界大舞台上的中国

采取习近平讲话中指出的行动后，合作正在让中国在世界秩序中发挥核心作用，特别是在"南南合作"方面。这种情况当然会引起西方大国的警觉。

在美国领导的秩序下，中国正在以非常快的速度发展，这一场景看起来与雅典和斯巴达之间的关系相似，冲突被称为"修昔底德陷阱"。中国也将陷入这个陷阱吗？习近平说，是美国想要这种情况。它可能不是陷阱，但中国的经济复兴道路上充满了许多障碍。中国不再隐藏自己的能力，也不再等待时机。去年 10 月，美国副总统迈克·彭斯在美国哈德逊研究所致辞，提到中国时，他认为中国是威胁并警告称"北京正在使用一种全政府的手段，利用政治、经济、军事工具以及宣传，在美国推进其影响和利益。"他还申明这种情况正在其他国家发生，这与澳大利亚人对中国在其国内政治中的影响的看法一致。

提到澳大利亚，前总理陆克文是最聪明、最受人尊敬的汉学家之一。几天前，他在安纳波利斯的美国海军学院发表演讲，就美国和中国之间的这一严峻形势进行了辩论。他宣称，华盛顿决定反击中国的外交政策和经济战略，这是对中国的军事和经济总实力现在已经开始挑战美国的全球主导地位这一事实的不可避免的结构性反应。

换句话说，陆克文用现实的方式描述了这种情况。随着中国能力的增强，美国应该做出反应以破坏这一上升势头。贸易战看起来像是这种思维的"合乎逻辑"结果。这位前总理目前是世界一流学者，他想知道，如果北京决定拒绝华盛顿的要求，那将会发生什么。有人思考过吗？这是一个新情况，随着事件不断揭开神秘的面纱，我们许多人将逐渐了解。然而，中国应该参与竞争吗？中国是当前世界秩序的最大受益者之一。当然，根据北京的说法，有些方面值得深思，但这并不意味着该国是修正主义者。

自 40 年前启动改革开放以来，中国经济在世界上已成为美国经济的后备军。中国通过贸易从美国获得大量美元，这对他们来说是积极的，因为总有一天这些美元将不得不回到美国。一直都是这种方式，为什么现在要改变呢？

关于美国和中国应该如何维持关系存在很多种解释。双方当前的利益是零和游戏吗？美国企业不相信这一点。例如，特斯拉几个月前宣布，该公司将在上海设立新的先进工厂生产电动汽车。

没有人能确切地说出这场贸易战是否会继续下去，但有一件事情是肯定的。中国政府将竭尽所能，为发展铺路。

分析完中国在世界秩序中的作用之后，该讨论一下拉美地区。亚太地区、欧亚大陆和非洲，一切看起来都很好。但是拉丁美洲真的很遥远。诸如"一带一路"之类的想法能否跨越大洋到达我们的海岸？

拉丁美洲和加勒比海地区的机会

我们地区不仅是美国的后院，而且距离中国还很远。在我访学期间与许多学者交谈时，我能听到他们说，除了这片大陆上有许多美丽的地方可以参观（例如阿根廷的伊瓜苏瀑布）外，到达这里要花整整一天的时间。他们是对的，没有人能改变这一点。

不论距离有多远，中国与拉丁美洲和加勒比地区之间的关系都发生了变化。北京明确申明，我们地区是"一带一路"倡议不可分割的一部分。这是完全正确的，拉丁美洲和中国非常匹配，存在着互补需求。

双方都意识到了这一点，并开始努力加强合作。例如，2018 年在智利举行了第二届中国—拉共体论坛。参加国一致认为，"一带一路"倡议是加强合作促进发展的重要机遇。

两个地区相互接近的想法已经使中国受益。多米尼加共和国、萨尔瓦多和巴拿马以意想不到的方式与中国建立了外交关系。

为我们的国家代表与中国之间制造对话机会，对于本地区而言是个好消息。拉丁美洲和加勒比地区实际上是世界范围内的第二大中国直接投资接受区域。

同时，企业有机会增加对亚洲国家的出口。2019 年 11 月，将在上海举行的 CIIE（中国国际进口博览会）将汇聚来自许多国家的商人，因为中国已成为最大的进口国之一。

哥斯达黎加对外贸易部长 Dyala Jiménez 表示，中美洲国家的出口商有机会进入中国市场。哥斯达黎加是美洲大陆与中国签署自由贸易协定的少数国家之一。

是时候把目光投向太平洋

当提及贸易,我们花了很多年才明白与亚洲国家打交道的重要性,原因之一是我们彼此之间相距甚远。几十年前,太平洋沿岸的国家确实了解进入新兴市场的重要性。因此,它们的经济保持稳定。对于阿根廷和巴西而言,情况并非如此,除了具有紧密联系外,这些国家始终偏爱欧洲(尤其是阿根廷)。在过去十年中,情况开始发生变化。中国和越南现在都是阿根廷重要的出口目的地。在巴西也发生了相同的变化,中国已成为巴西最大的贸易伙伴。

然而,今年的贸易战使事情变得更加艰难。中美对抗的后果将直接影响着我们的经济(有人会说,这是美国后院生活起伏的一部分)。

这种关系将如何发展影响阿根廷和巴西对稳定的追求。对大豆征收的关税使国际价格降至 2008 年以来的最低水平,这种情况对阿根廷经济非常有害,因为阿根廷的大部分大豆销往中国。智利、秘鲁和哥伦比亚的情况则不同,它们的经济开放得多;在新的北美自由贸易协定(现称为《美墨加三国协议》)签订之后,墨西哥也在寻找新的替代方案。

尤其对于传统的优质供应国而言,这并不是一个好消息。因此,这里的每个人都希望贸易战能够尽快结束。然而,我们应该寻求自身的解决方案,而不是让巫师去祈求停止下雨。已经有其他选择,其中之一是增加出口价值,中国企业而不是政府为这些经济体提供了机会。

二、中国大企业在共赢合作中的作用

去年十月,习近平主席鼓励企业家"把握时代大势,坚定发展信心,心无旁骛创新创造,踏踏实实办好企业,合力开创民营经济更加美好的明天,为实现中华民族伟大复兴的中国梦做出新的更大贡献"。

如果没有企业家的帮助,中国政府就无法实现其宏伟目标,即到 2050 年成为一个繁荣的中等收入经济体,消除贫困和发展高科技产业。这不仅适用于初创企业,也适用于大公司。

中国目前的大企业,著名的 BAT 三巨头,正在努力创造一个友好的经商环境。这对拉丁美洲的投资者很有用,因为在类似情况下让他们拥有合作伙伴总是比较容易。除了国家利益外,这些人都有自身的利益,中国企业也是如此。

也许对百度和腾讯知之甚少，但是阿根廷有很多人至少在阿里全球速卖通有过一次购物经历。谁能想象现在有中国消费者在类似的电子商务平台上搜寻阿根廷产品？

阿里巴巴、谅解备忘录和"光棍节"

我真的很喜欢马云在布宜诺斯艾利斯举行的会议。就个人而言，我从来没有想过有机会现场聆听最大互联网公司之一创始人的演讲。他是不断努力、创新和团队合作的典范。他在去年 9 月 10 日 50 周岁生日那天写给投资者的一封信非常完美。

然而，个人的感激无法匹配他为我们国家所做的工作。在天猫设立"国家"页面，允许阿根廷生产商将商品出售给中国人。上一次光棍节非常火爆，阿根廷商品在短短 4 个小时内就被抢购一空。这当然是正面和负面兼有的消息。只是想知道如果更多的生产者将他们的货物送到中国的库存中心会发生什么情况。

这种情况开始于几个月前，当时阿根廷政府与阿里巴巴签订谅解备忘录（MOU）。该倡议迅速升级，这在本地区并不常见。

很高兴得知中国企业开放业务。然而，在寻求解决方案时，我们地区的国家缺乏主动性。当然，有些结构性特征阻止我们的企业选择中国作为其产品的目的地。

我们地区像中国一样，曾经遭受殖民主义的影响。南美洲是一个资源丰富的大陆，因此统治帝国唯一的兴趣就是掠夺金银和其他矿产。生活在那里的人们从来不需要创新，能够满足需求的地方不会产生创造力。然而，这种情况不会永远持续下去。船开始沉没时没有人知道应该怎么办。资本主义的主要组成部分之一就是冒险。然而，阿根廷和巴西的资本家不喜欢这样做。例如阿根廷生源霸科公司在中国设立口蹄疫疫苗生产基地的例子很少见，但选择自己喜欢的任何报纸时，会读到与贿赂丑闻有关的内容。

合作意味着双方共同努力。中国可以设立游戏规则并建议拉美企业家出售他们的商品，但是由他们自己决定是否选择这样做。

我们应该怎样做？

与阿里巴巴签订备忘录预示着拉美与中国合作的未来。只有当企业经营良好时，我们地区才会变得强大，因为它们是就业的主要驱动因素。

知之非难，行之不易。正如我之前说过的那样，我们的殖民主义残留仍然存在于从未将发展观念付诸实践的地方。我们的人民在一个强大的国家的构想下成长，这个国家获得一切，付出一切，仿佛是对人类福祉的唯一责任。这种情况不能继续下去。

然而，根据美国前国务卿雷克斯·蒂勒森的说法，中国插足拉丁美洲和加勒比海地区的企图与"全球南南合作"无关，而与中国和俄罗斯在该地区新的"帝国角色"有关。因此，现任国务卿迈克·庞培严厉批评巴拿马不断增加两国之间的业务往来。作为全球南方国家的一部分，我们地区和中国有着共同的目标：发展经济。在中国—拉美和加勒比国家共同体论坛闭幕式上签署的《圣地亚哥宣言》，明确表达了为人民的发展、创新与合作而共同努力的意图。

我们正处于一个历史性的时刻，我们可以翻开新的篇章，再也不会回头。中国给了拉美地区搭乘发展快车的黄金车票，但我们将自行决定目的地是不是我们要去的地方。

三、拉美国家是否正在抓住机会？

正如我之前所说，"太平洋"国家与"大西洋"国家之间存在差异。20 世纪90 年代初以来，智利、秘鲁和哥伦比亚开始将目光投向亚太地区；阿根廷和巴西与该地区经济体的关系在几年前才开始加强。然而，拉丁美洲在这方面没有明确的战略。

这是内部国情造成的。例如，在基希内尔担任总统期间，阿根廷的肉类市场急剧下滑。目前，出口不仅与中国提供的机会（渴望消费更好产品的庞大中产阶级）有关，而且还与这样做的能力有关。目前我们有足够的牛肉可以出口。

自 2015 年毛里西奥·马克里担任阿根廷总统以来，为恢复肉类行业付出了很多努力。一旦实现该目标，下一步就是重新打开与阿根廷牛肉有关的市场。去年阿根廷和中国签订一项协议，允许各种肉类产品进入大陆。

这个案例有助于了解商人和政治家如何共同努力实现目标。我想强调这一点，因为我确实相信，我们的政治阶层有责任提出可以促进中阿两国之间贸易的政策。

同时，商人必须准备好冒险，并相信他们在世界上最大的单一市场上销售商品的能力。

政治家怎么样做才能加强合作？

我们曾多次举行政府间对话，而且中国和拉丁美洲的政党也在接触。在基希内尔担任总统期间，中国共产党和阿根廷正义党采取许多举措。如今，阿根廷执政党共和国方案党（PRO）也正在思考中国问题。去年 7 月，党的高层访问北京、西安、浙江和上海。在北京期间，中国国家副主席王岐山接待他们。助手们很惊讶，因为王岐山非常了解阿根廷的情况。他建议不要停止转型，否则发展过程也将停止。这次会议的助手包括党主席翁贝托·斯齐亚沃尼参议员。我询问他对这次旅行的印象。他坚信，阿根廷与中国保持紧密联系非常重要，因为中国是仅次于南方共同市场（巴西、巴拉圭、乌拉圭和委内瑞拉）的第二大贸易伙伴。

他还说，本党党员曾经多次来中国。同时，许多中共官员到过阿根廷，对他来说这是一个信号，表明双方之间进展顺利。

接下来，我们讨论管理问题。斯齐亚沃尼先生指出，他对中国官员为取得政府职位做好充分准备的方式感到惊讶。阿根廷的许多问题是否与政府官员缺乏经验和技能有关？他认为可能是这样。

然后他补充说，对党内官员的教育应该关注与国家利益有关的主题。例如，学习技能以找到发展更具竞争力的经济的方法。

在党内高层会见中国共产党官员的同时，还举行其他活动，例如在北京举行的青年政治学论坛。党内负责沟通的 Federico Morales 在该论坛上发表了讲话。

我询问他对中国关系的看法，他告诉我，中国正在世界范围内扩大合作，特别是在贸易方面，而同时阿根廷正在向世界开放，因此他认为我们可以把握机会。然而，政治家之间需要多次对话才能达成更好的理解。

我之前提到拉丁美洲与加勒比海地区以及中国之间的距离。这种距离是否也在文化层面发生？我询问 Morales，他是否发现两种政党管理方式有任何相似之处。他的回答令人完全惊奇。他告诉我，阿根廷总统马克里和习近平主席都热衷于将发展带入本国经济，提高生产效率和减轻贫困。然而，他确实在中国人制定长期计划上找到了不同，这在我国很少见。

"一带一路"倡议之一是文化交流。当然，每个人都对该倡议的经济方面感兴趣，不愿意花太多时间思考中国与拉丁美洲之间如何拉近距离。这些人忘记了彼此不了解的人之间无法达成协议。在中国文化中，有一个很好的概念叫作"关系"，我们拉丁美洲和加勒比地区的人们应该考虑这一点。"关系"的字面意思是关系，但是比我们想象的要深入。中国的关系意味着互惠，如果有人为我们提供帮助，我们应该在将来寻找一个机会予以回报。

了解这一点之后，我们应该首先提供帮助。当我们可以迈出第一步时，为什么还要等待呢？建立信心是任何经济流程的关键要素，"关系"是一种有效的整合策略。

结　论

对于拉丁美洲和加勒比地区而言，这是关键的几年。正如前文所述，许多国家/地区正在跃跃欲试，希望搭乘发展的快车。

中国在该地区采取的新方法带来了希望。然而，在成为美国后院的同时，很难进行深入的接触。因此，我们很怀疑中国与拉丁美洲之间的合作是否真的可持续。为了回答这个问题，分析了很多方面。最重要的发现是那些与中国成为全球优秀供应商的新地位有关的发现。中国在这些年取得了很多专业知识，方便双方签订合作协议，因为亚洲大国已成为南方许多欠发达经济体的可靠盟友。中国正在寻求共赢的协议，同时与大公司共同努力，而这些大公司已经成为通往全球最大国内市场的钥匙。拉丁美洲和加勒比地区可以而且必须抓住机会出售其商品。阿里巴巴和"国家"虚拟通道就是一个很好的例子。然而，探戈舞需要两个人一起跳。合作不仅仅是签订相互信任声明。必须遵循行动计划，拉丁美洲的私营企业和企业家必须进入舞台。私营部门拥有蓬勃发展的力量和责任，能够创造新的就业机会并为社会带来发展。

必须并且需要通过制订可以促进其活动的公共政策来帮助私营部门。如果拉美政治家不与中国同行见面交流，这一点无法实现。幸运的是，正如前文所述，交流正在发生（至少阿根廷政治家经常访问中国），而且政治家的看法也非常正面。

亚太地区已经是一个生机勃勃的地区，未来看起来更加光明，因为每年都有数千万的公民加入中产阶级，渴望尝试更好的产品和体验。拉丁美洲必须从战略上为这些人提供替代方案，否则其他地区将带走机会。

The Role of China in Argentina as a Global Good Provider

Lucas Leonardo Gualda / Argentina

Secretary of Argentina National Senate

Introduction

Latin America and the Caribbean are territories full of potential. The societies of our region are one of the youngest. In addition, some of them are composed by a well-educated working class that can speak two or more languages.

However, besides optimistic opinions, the expected growth and development of our economies are still an unfulfilled prophecy. One thing is sure, Caribbean and Latin-American countries need to engage in deeper cooperation with big players in order to develop.

How this cooperation is established. Is the Chinese government doing this alone, or are Chinese enterprises taking some responsibility too? I will analyze how Latin American countries, especially Argentina, the country where I live, are taking advantage of this opportunity to bring development to their economies.

1. China: The New Global Goods Provider

Many steps were taken in the direction of developing Cooperation Relationship with other countries. Some examples are the Asian Infrastructure Investment Bank (AIIB), the Belt and Road Initiative, the G20 2016 meetings and summit in Hangzhou, and the BRICS summit.

The first steps in Chinese cooperation

Since the beginning of this Century, things were starting to change in the world. Capital started flowing to emerging countries, and their economies flourished. China of course was among them. Along with Brazil, Russia, India, and South Africa, these five nations were the symbol of a not so distant future.

These countries were supposed to take the lead role in this messed up order, where a single group of terrorists could easily blow up the landmark of world trade. This didn't happen, except for the Chinese.

This newer Chinese institutions are not only filled with resources, which are the drivers of development, but also better prepared to come up with answers for the nations looking for aid (last years the World Bank has been doing a great job in Africa).

It is said that institutions respond to their "creators" interests, as a source to extend the influence that was obtained at some point in history. Of course, Chinese institutions, as any other Western institution, are keen on working together to make ends meet. Maybe one difference is that China honestly admits it. And that's why Western analysts and the media attack them constantly.

This is seen in the West as an attempt to overcome its nation partners' sovereignty. Australia went really far last year, its Prime Minister (now former Prime Minister) Malcolm Turnbull declared that the "Australian people have stood up". Many in Canberra believe that the Chinese are looking to influence policymakers.

Besides all that chit-chat that entertains most of analysts and scholars, in real life actions speak louder than words. Gwadar Port in Pakistan is one of the greatest examples of what China can do in order to bring development to its partner nations' economies.

Gwadar Port, the biggest example of Chinese cooperation

The pakistani province of Balochistan is where the Gwadar Port is located, the last step of the China-Pakistan Economic Corridor, the biggest project of the Belt and Road Initiative. It took many years to build the roads that connect the city of Kashgar, in the Xinjiang Uighur Autonomous Region, with the port in the Indian Ocean coast.

It wasn't an easy endeavor. The obstacles in South-South cooperation are very diverse. Pakistan is a country that has been facing many difficulties in the last decades. Apart from its fragile economic situation (it holds the record of IMF bailout grants), it also faces many security challenges. The Kashmir region is the scenery of a never-ending conflict with India, and the Taliban are constantly defying the democratic power established in Islamabad.

The Chinese maintained hope, and kept going forward. And now the Gwadar Port, the third in importance in Pakistan following the ones in Karachi and Qasim, can boast its ability to bring development to the region.

The Indian Ocean is a very important region for China. As we'll see later, reaching these waters through Pakistan reduces the importance of the Malacca Strait as one of China's main security interests.

Gwadar Port is only 400 km away from the Hormuz Strait, a chokepoint that connects the Persian Gulf with the mentioned Ocean. A historical place that has seen ships passing through it during centuries and centuries, actually witnesses one third of the world's crude oil shippings. Breathtaking figures that justify the needs of having a place like Gwadar close to it.

Belt and Road Initiative, the framework for a more prosperous South.

The Belt and Road Initiative is by far the most ambitious proposal a single country has made since the Marshall Plan. Luckily, there was no need for millions of human lives to be lost, and thousands of cities destroyed to come up with this idea. What China saw as a trigger for this plan, is the opportunity to make Southern economies thrive, and at the same time use that new energy to boost China's growth. In a few words, BRI is the biggest win-win cooperation this world has ever seen.

We should think of BRI as a strategic approach. That means that its actions are based not only in Chinese capabilities, but also in the characteristics of the context. Of course, it is hard to define which are the boundaries of the Belt and Road Initiative. It is better to think of it as an idea, instead of as a rigid plan. Take into consideration the previous Silk Road. In that time there was no precise route, but everyone there knew what to do, and where to go. That is the spirit of the proposal, and this time it is exactly the same.

Xi's idea of developing railroads through China's vicinity reflects one of the country's main interests, which is getting new ways (and cheaper ones, too) to put Chinese production in its most important markets. Via Gwadar port, Chinese goods don't need to pass through the Malacca Strait (50% of the world trade does it). This geographic point is truly a chokepoint, and that is why it is also a danger zone.

This doesn't mean that China forgets its sovereignty claim on The South China Sea, as it is a priority for its present government. But reducing the influence of geopolitics in such a delicate location would be such a triumph in a moment the country needs it the most. Remember, the main goal is to "secure a decisive victory".

It is interesting the use of those words, as the securitization paradigm implies the wide recognition of an existential threat in order to take extraordinary decisions. One could say that the Belt and Road Initiative is by far the biggest measure ever taken in that context. To keep free trade alive is todays China's main interest, and at the same time its biggest threat.

Curiously or not, Australia has acknowledged in its Foreign Policy White Paper, released in 2017 that keeping world trade free and open is one of its main priorities. Is it a coincidence? I don't think so. In this moment of history, every road leads to Washington DC.

China at the big world stage

Following the actions described by Xi in his speech, cooperation is bringing China to a central role in the world order, especially regarding the "South-South cooperation". This situation of course set up the alarms among the western big players.

A scenario where United States is leading the order, and a Chinese nation is growing at a very fast pace, looks similar to the relationship between Athens and Sparta, conflict that was labeled as the "Thucydides trap". Is China going to fall in this trap too? Xi Jinping said it was the United States that wanted that situation. It may not be a trap, but China's path to economic rejuvenation is filled with many obstacles. The country is not hiding its capabilities anymore, nor it is biding its time.

Last October, Vice-President of the United States, Mike Pence gave a speech at the Hudson Institute that set up all alarms, as he referred to China in such threatening ways, assuring that "Beijing is employing a whole-of-government approach, using political, economic, and military tools, as well as propaganda, to advance its influence and benefit its interests in the United States". He also affirmed that this situation is happening in other countries, in line with what Australians believe about the Chinese influence in their domestic politics.

Having mentioned Australia, former Prime Minister Kevin Rudd is one of the savviest and most respected sinologists. A few days ago he spoke at the US Naval Institute in Annapolis, where he debated about this challenging situation between both the United States and China. He declared that Washington's decision to push back against Chinese foreign policy and economic strategy in an inevitable structural response to the fact that China's aggregate military and economic power has now begun to challenge US global dominance.

In other words, Rudd described the situation in realistic terms. As China increases its capabilities, the United States should respond to undermine this rise. The trade war looks like a "logical" consequence of this thinking. The former Prime Minister, now a world class academic, wonders what would happen if Beijing decides to reject Washington's demands. Have any one ever thought of that? This is a new situation, and many of us will learn about it as events keep on unveiling.

However, should China enter the contest? The country has been among those who profited the most in the current order. Of course there are some features that according to Beijing deserve to be to reviewed, but that doesn't mean that the country a revisionist one.

Since the opening up and reform of the economy, 40 years ago, China found its place in the world as backup of the American economy. China's trade flow takes lots of dollars from the United States, which is positive for them, as someday those dollars will have to go back. It has been this way all this time, why should it change now?

There are many interpretations of how United States and China should maintain a relationship. Are their interests now a zero-sum game? American companies don't believe that. Tesla, for example announced months ago that the firm will start making its electric cars at a new state-of-the-art factory in Shanghai.

No one can precisely say if this trade war will eventually continue or not, but one thing is sure. The Chinese government will do everything they can to keep paving the road to development.

Having analyzed China's role in the world order, it's time to talk about our region. Everything looks really fine for the Asia-Pacific, Eurasia, and Africa. But Latin-America is really far away. Can an idea such as BRI reach the coasts of our bioceanic continent?

The chance for Latin-America and the Caribbean

Not only our region is the backyard of the United States, it is so far from China. Speaking with many scholars during my trip, I could hear them say that apart from the fact that there are many beautiful places in the continent to visit (like the Iguazú Falls in Argentina), it takes more than a complete day to get here. They are right, and no one can change that.

However far we are, there has been a transformation in the relationship between China and Latin-America and the Caribbean. Beijing clearly affirmed that our region is an inseparable part of BRI. This is completely true, our complementary needs makes both Latin-America and China a good match.

Both parts are aware of that, and started working towards increasing cooperation. This year, for example, it was celebrated in Chile the 2nd CELAC-China Forum. Participant nation agreed that BRI constitutes an important opportunity for the strengthening of cooperation for development.

This idea to bring both regions closer is already paying dividends to China. In unexpected fashion, the Dominican Republic, El Salvador, and Panama established diplomatic relationships with the Middle Kingdom.

Creating this chance for dialog between our countries representatives and the Chinese is good news for the region. Latin-America and the Caribbean is actually is the second recipient region of Chinese FDI worldwide.

At the same time, businesses have the opportunity to increase its exports to the Asian country. Next November, the CIIE (China International Importation Expo), will gather businessmen from many nations at Shanghai, as the country consolidates as one of the biggest importer countries.

Costa-Rican Foreign Trade Minister Dyala Jiménez remarked the opportunity for exporters from the Central-America country to reach further into the Chinese market. Costa Rica is among the few nations in the continent that signed a Free-

Trade Agreement with China.

It's time to look to the Pacific Ocean.

When talking about trade, it took years to understand the importance of dealing with Asian countries, and one of the reasons has been that we are so far from each other. Countries near the Pacific Ocean did understand the importance of attending those emerging markets decades ago. In consequence, its economies managed to stabilize. It hasn't been the same for Argentina and Brazil, which economies apart from being intertwined, always favored Europe (especially the Argentinian one).

In the last decade things started to change. China and Vietnam are now both the most important destinations for Argentinian exports, among other countries. The same situation occurs in Brazil, that finds in the Middle Kingdom its biggest trade partner.

This year trade war is making things a bit tougher, though. The outcome of the confrontation between the United States and China affects our economies directly (One would say, that's part of the ups and downs of living at the backyard of America).

How this relationship will evolve attempts against Argentina and Brazil search for stability. Tariffs applied on soybeans dropped the international price down to the lowest levels since 2008, a situation that is very harmful for the Argentinian economy, which sells most of its production to China. The situation is different for Chile, Perú, and Colombia, witch's economies are far more open; Mexico is also looking for new alternatives after the signing of the new-NAFTA, now called USMCA.

Especially for nations that are traditionally primary good providers, these are not good news. So everyone here hopes that the trade war ends soon. However, we ought to look for solutions that come from our own instead of asking the shaman to stop the rain. There are alternatives available, one of them is adding value to the exportations, and it's the Chinese companies, not the government, which are giving this economies the opportunity.

2. The role of Chinese Big Companies in Win-win Cooperation

Last October, President Xi Jinping encouraged entrepreneurs to "grasp the trend of the era, have firm confidence in development, innovate and create without being distracted, and work in a down-to-earth way in developing their businesses, to jointly create a better tomorrow for the private economy, and make greater contributions to realizing the Chinese Dream of national rejuvenation".

The Chinese government can't reach its big goal of being a prosperous, middle-income economy by 2050, eradicating poverty, and a hi-tech industry sector, without the helping hand of entrepreneurs. This applies not only to start-ups, but also to big companies.

Current big players in China, the famous BAT treble, are working in order to create a friendly environment for doing business. This is useful for Latin-American investors as it is always easier for them to have counterparts in a similar situation. Besides the national interest, these people have interests of their own, and so for Chinese companies.

There is little knowledge of Baidu and Tencent, but there are many people in Argentina that bought at least one time at AliExpress. Who would imagine that there are right now Chinese consumers looking for argentina products in a similar e-commerce?

Alibaba, the MOU, and the Bachelor's Day.

I really enjoyed Jack Ma conference at Buenos Aires. Personally, I've never thought of the opportunity of listening in live to the person who created one of the biggest internet companies. He's an example of constant labor, innovation, and teamwork. His last letter written to investors, released the day of its 50th birthday last September 10th, was perfect.

However, no personal appreciation compares to what he's done for our country. Opening a "national" webpage at T-Mall, allowing argentinian producers to sell their goods to the Chinese. Last Bachelor's day was a hit, in just 4 hours the argentinian goods were sold out. This is of course, positive and negative news. Just wonder what could have happened if more producers had sent their goods to the stock centers in China.

This situation began a few months before, when the argentinian government and Alibaba signed a Memorandum of Understanding (MOU). The initiative escalated very quickly, which is not usual in this part of the world.

It's nice to know that Chinese companies are open for business. However, when looking for solutions, the countries in our region have lacked initiative. Of course, there are some structural features that help to stop our businesses to choose China as a destination for its products.

Our region, as China, has suffered the effects of colonialism. South America is a land full of resources, and so the ruling empire only interest was to take away gold, silver, and other minerals. People living there never had the need to innovate, no creativity can come up in a place where your needs are fulfilled. This situation didn't last forever, though. No one knew what to do when the ship started sinking.

One of the main components of capitalism is taking risks. However, few capitalists in Argentina and Brazil like to do this. Examples like Biogenesis Bagó opening a factory in China to produce foot-and-mouth disease are not seen regularly, but choose any newspaper of your preference, and you'll read something related to bribery scandals.

Cooperation means bilateral efforts. China can open the game and propose Latin-American entrepreneurs to sell their goods, but it's up to them to decide do ir or not.

What should we do?

Signing a memorandum with Alibaba is such a good premonition of the future of Latin-America and China cooperation. Our region will grow strong only if businesses do well, as they are the main driver of employment.

This is easy to say, but not so easy to do. As I said before, our colonialist legacy is living in a place where no idea of development was ever put into action. Our people grew up with the idea of a powerful state that takes everything and gives it back in consequence, as if it were the only responsible of people's wellbeing. This situation cannot continue to.

However, according to the former United States Secretary of State Rex Tillerson, Chinese attempts to set foot in Latin-America and the Caribbean are not related with "Global South cooperation", but with a new "imperial role" China and Russia have taken in the region. Therefore, current Secretary of State Mike Pompeo heavily criticized Panama's increasing amount of business happening between both countries.

As part of the Global South, our region and China share a common goal: develop its economies. The Declaration of Santiago, signed at the end of the China-CELAC Forum expresses clearly the intention of working together for more development, innovation, and cooperation for their peoples.

We are at a moment of history where we can turn the page and never come back. China has given Latin-America a golden ticket to jump into the development train, but it's up to us to see if the destination where it takes us is where we want to go.

3. Are Latin-American countries grasping the opportunity?

As I said before, there is a difference between "Pacific" nations and "Atlantic" nations. Whereas Chile, Peru, and Colombia started looking to the Asia-Pacific since the early nineties; Argentina and Brazil ties with economies from that region began to strengthen only a few years ago. However, there is no clear strategy from this side of Latin-America.

This is a consequence of internal conditions. For example, the meat market in

Argentina fell sharply during the years of the Kirchners presidencies. Right now, the chance of exporting is related not only to the Chinese opportunity (a huge middle class eager to consume better products), but also to the capacity to do so. There is right now enough cattle to export.

Since 2015, year when Mauricio Macri took the presidency in Argentina, lot of effort was done in order to recover the meat industry. Once that goal was achieved, the next step was to re-open markets linked to argentine beef. It was last year that both Argentina and China signed an agreement allowing a wide variety of meat products to enter the continent.

This example helps to understand how businessmen and politicians can work together towards a goal. I want to highlight this, because I truly believe that it is our political class who's got the responsibility to come up with policies that could boost trade between our countries and China.

At the same time, businessmen must be ready to take risks, and trust in their capacities to sell good in the biggest single market in the world.

What can politicians do to boost cooperation?

We talked a lot about dialogue between government, but also political parties from both China and Latin-America are in contact. In Argentina during the Kirchners years, lots of initiatives were done between the CPC and the PJ (Partido Justicialista).

Nowadays, PRO, the ruling party, is also thinking of China. Last July, party authorities visited Beijing, Xi'an, Zhejiang, and Shanghai. During the stage in Beijing, they were received by Chinese Vicepresident Wang Qishan. Assistants were amazed, as Wang was pretty aware of the situation in Argentina. He suggested not to stop with the transformation, otherwise the development processes will stop too.

Among the assistants at this meeting was Senator Mr. Humberto Schiavoni,

President of PRO party. I asked him about his impressions on the trip. He is convinced that it is fundamentally important for Argentina to close ties with China, as it is the second biggest trade partner, only behind the MERCOSUR (Brazil, Paraguay, Uruguay, and Venezuela).

He also remarked that many trips to China have been made by party members. At the same time, many PCC officers came to Argentina, which is for him a signal that things are going well between both parties.

Then, we talked about management. Mr. Schiavoni mentioned he was amazed by the way officers in China are fully prepared to join government positions. Could many of Argentina's problems be related to the lack of experience and skills of government officers? He believes it could be.

He added then that education for party officers should be focused on topics related to national interests. For example, learning skills to find ways to develop a more competitive economy.

While party authorities met with Chinese Communist Party officials, there were other activities, like the Youth Political Forum that was held in Beijing. Federico Morales, who's working with the communication processes inside the party made a speech at that forum.

I asked him about his opinion about the relationship with China, and he told me that at the same time the Chinese are expanding their cooperation around the world, especially on trade, Argentina is opening to the world, therefore he sees an opportunity for us to grasp. However, much dialogue between politicians is needed in order to achieve a better understanding.

I mentioned before the distance between Latin-America and the Caribbean and China. Is this distance also happening at a cultural dimension? I asked Morales if he found any similarities between both ways of managing a political party. His answer was a complete surprise. He told me that both President Macri (Argentina) and President Xi Jinping are keen on bringing development to their countries' economies, increase the productivity of processes, and alleviating poverty. However, he did find a difference in the fact that the Chinese have long-term plans, something rarely seen in our country.

One of the dimensions of BRI is the cultural exchange. Of course everyone is interested in the economic aspects of the initiative, and don't spend so much time thinking about how can China and Latin-America get closer. This people forget that no agreement can be done between people who don't know each other.

There is a beautiful concept in Chinese culture called "guanxi" (关系), that we in Latin-America and the Caribbean should take into consideration. "Guanxi" means relationship, but in a deeper way than we think of it. The Chinese guanxi implies reciprocity, which means that if someone does us a favor, we should therefore look for an opportunity in the future to return that favor.

Knowing about this, we ought to try to do the favor first. Why wait for it when we can take the first step? Building confidence is a key element of any economical process, and "guanxi" is an efficient strategy to incorporate.

Conclusion

These are crucial years for Latin-America and the Caribbean. As it was described in the previous pages, many countries are on the blink of jumping into the development wagon.

This new Chinese approach on the region has brought about hope. However, it is hard to engage deeply while being the backyard of the United States. So it's clever to doubt if this cooperation between China and Latin America is really sustainable.

Many things were analyzed in order to answer the question. The most important findings are those related to the new status China has achieved as a global good provider. The country's acquired a lot of expertise in previous years, which makes it a lot easier for both parts to sign cooperation agreements, as the Asian nation has become a reliable ally for many undeveloped economies in the South.

China is looking for win-win agreements, and is joining efforts with big companies, which have got the key to the biggest domestic market in the world. Latin-America and the Caribbean can and must grab the opportunity to sell their goods. Alibaba and its "national" virtual aisles are a good example of this.

However, it takes two to tango. The cooperation is not only signing a joint declaration of trust. An action plan must follow, and Latin-American private companies and entrepreneurs must get into stage. It is the private sector who's got both the power and responsibility to thrive, opening new job opportunities and bringing development to their communities.

This private sector must and needs to be helped via public policies that could boost their activities. That cannot be done if Latin-American politicians don't meet their Chinese counterparts. Luckily, as you have seen in previous pages, that exchange is happening (at least, Argentinian politicians are travelling regularly to China), and the opinions of politicians are very positive.

Asia-Pacific already is a vibrant region, and the future looks much brighter, as millions of citizens enter into the middle class every year, eager to try better products and experiences. It's up to Latin-America to strategically offer these people an alternative, or let again others take the opportunity.

References

"Argentinian Institute of Statistic and Census – Dynamic Map". 2018, Retrieved from https://opex.indec.gov.ar/index.php?pagina=mapa_dinamico.

"China-CELAC Forum -Official Site." China-CELAC Forum, 2016, Retrieved from www.chinacelacforum.org/esp/.

"Gobierno firmó acuerdo para que pymes argentinas vendan por Alibaba". El Cronista Comercial. 2 May. 2017, Retrieved from https://www.cronista.com/economiapolitica/Gobierno-firmo-acuerdo-paraque-Pymes-argentinas-vendan-por-Alibaba--20170502-0070.html.

"Guanxi: The Chinese cultural concept". Commisceo Global. 19 Apr. 2016, Retrieved from https://www.commisceo-global.com/blog/guanxi-the-chinesecultural-concept.

"Full text: Action plan on the Belt and Road Initiative". Chinese Government – Official Site. 30 Mar. 2015, Retrieved from http://english.gov.cn/archive/publications/2015/03/30/content_281475080249 035.htm.

Duhalde, M., Arranz, A., Hernández, M. "China's super link to Gwadar port. A visual explainer". (no specific date). South China Morning Post, Retrieved from http://multimedia.scmp.com/news/china/article/One-Belt-OneRoad/pakistan.html.

Giusto, Patricio. "Qué Dejó El Foro Ministerial China-Celac Celebrado En Chile." Infobae, 25 Jan. 2018, Retrieved from www.infobae.com/opinion/2018/01/25/que-dejo-el-foro-ministerial-chinacelac-celebrado-en-chile/.

Hurrell, A. (2018). Beyond the BRICS: Power, Pluralism, and the Future of Global Order. *Ethics & International Affairs, 32*(1), 89-101. doi:10.1017/S0892679418000126.

Ikenberry, G. (2018). Why the Liberal World Order Will Survive. *Ethics & International Affairs, 32*(1), 17-29. doi:10.1017/S0892679418000072.

Ijaz, A. "Significance of Gwadar Port". Islamabad Policy Research Institute. 20 Aug. 2015, Retrieved from www.ipripak.org/significance-of-gwadar-port/.

Lu, H. "Xi encourages private entrepreneurs to further innovate, create, develop". Xinhua. 21 Oct. 2018, Retrieved from http://www.xinhuanet.com/english/2018-10/21/c_137548892.htm.

Pence, M. "Remarks by Vice-President Mike Pence on the Administration's Policy towards China". 4 Oct. 2018, Retrieved from https://www.whitehouse.gov/briefings-statements/remarks-vice-president-pence-administrations-policy-toward-china/.

Rodríguez Rata, A. "Si quieres dominar el mundo, empieza por estos estrechos de mar". La Vanguardia, 13 Apr. 2016, Retrieved from https://www.lavanguardia.com/internacional/20160412/401057738493/gps-dominar-mundo-estrechos-mar.html.

Rudd, K.. "How to Avoid an Avoidable War". Foreign Affairs, 23 Oct. 2018, Retrieved from https://www.foreignaffairs.com/articles/china/2018-10-22/how-avoid-avoidable-war.

Xi, Jinping. "Secure a Decisive Victory in Building a Moderately Prosperous Society in All Respects and Strive for the Great Success of Socialism with Chinese Characteristics for a New Era". Speech delivered at the 19th National Congress of the Communist Party of China. 18 Oct. 2017, Retrieved from http://www.xinhuanet.com/english/download/Xi_Jinping's_report_at_19th_C PC_National_Congress.pdf.

Waltz, R. "Why is the Strait of Hormuz so important?" The Conversation, 9 Jul. 2018, Retrieved from: https://theconversation.com/why-is-the-strait-of-hormuz-important-99496.

"一带一路"倡议下的文化和谐互通

宁羽沙【波兰】

波兰奥波莱工业大学国际经济关系学院经济与管理系讲师

在社会意识沟通的背景下,"一带一路"倡议(OBOR/BRI)涉及货物和人员的运输,即货物从一个地点运输到另外一个地点,运输方式和交通工具本身。自古以来,丝绸之路主要与商队运输有关丝绸和其他商品(包括化妆品、珠宝、玻璃、牲畜、金属、纸张、皮革、石头、烟草和木材)通常放在骆驼背上或通过海上路线"一路"运到欧洲。至于连接丝绸之路经济带和21世纪海上丝绸之路的当代倡议,媒体经常报道新的铁路路线、中国主要城市与世界其他地区之间开通的直航、现代化的港口基础设施以及不断增加的货物交易数字[1]。然而,在古代,除了货物和人员外,思想也会传播到万里之外(包括哲学和宗教思潮、艺术、科学成就等),人际沟通的同时伴随着买卖交易。

如果从人际沟通的角度分析"一带一路"倡议相关计划,以下概念将成为关键词:合作和参与。参与国的政治人物经常在发言中强调双边合作的巨大潜力和空间。"一带一路"平台面向合作项目开放,提供平等的参与机会,并通过学术和文化沟通、媒体合作、志愿服务和政治传播/公共外交(包括文化沟通计划、中文大赛、孔子学院活动等)推动人际沟通。中方还强调,倡议的精神是90多个参与国和平合作、开放包容、互学互鉴、互利共赢。本文探讨与人际合作密切

1　在过去五年中,中国与"一带一路"倡议参与国的贸易总额已超过5万亿美元,年均增长1.1%,中国已成为其中25个国家的最大贸易伙伴。

相关的有效人际沟通要素之一，即"和谐"的理念以及不同人群的感知。

与中国的学术界沟通后，人们会获得一种印象，即当代中国的"和谐"理念主要考虑两个方面：与"道"有关的古代文献以及道家（玄学意义）和儒家（伦理道德）的解释；政治方面，即中国特色的和谐社会主义社会语境下。

一方面，"道"的描述极其简单，没有名称，而且被视为一个明显的概念，因此无需解释。另一方面，它与西方的绝对（不可抗力）、万物伊始（万物）相比具有更为广泛的意义，以至于因当前知识和人类思想的局限性，无法得到充分表征。本文提到的"和谐"概念是通往"道"的唯一自然方式——一种遵循道的生活方式。对于外国人来说，将"和谐"与绝对结合往往是误解这个词的第一步。根据安娜·齐莱伊（Anna Czelej）的观察，"（...）中国人观念中的人类精神（...）与西方对此问题的感知不同，人类精神的理想状态是永远仰望，绝不低头。根据中国人的说法，只有脱离与地球和生命的联系，失去平衡后的人"，失掉和谐后才能实现这一点。"和谐"作为一个口号，也经常出现在改变和补充"阴阳"元素的符号中。最初作为太极（大同）符号，要素代替旧的符号：白虎和青龙。[1] 这种哲学理念在实践中得到运用，尤其是学习如何布置风水空间、中药和太极拳等方面，这些在中国以外也越来越受欢迎。在中国的出版市场上，人们还可以买到一些书籍，试图将"道"的思想运用于商业领域，例如《道与企业管理》、《禅道与企业管理》、《大商之道》等。

视觉化的阴阳符号在中国的城市中随处可见。中国的寺庙、招牌甚至是人行道装饰都可以看到黑白二色元素填充的圆圈（照片1）。

阴阳符号在当代世界上被视为是和谐的象征。这一点获得全球认可。作者于2017年对波兰奥波莱技术大学以及2018年对葡萄牙托马尔理工学院的学生进行调查，调查的结果可以证明这一观点[2]，三百多名调查对象一致将此符号与和谐相联系。调查对象只了解视觉维度，将其与亚洲（很少与中国）关联，既没有联想到"道"，也没有关联"变"的现象。

中国古典哲学（儒家）将"和谐"的概念与正确的行为联系在一起。细心体贴和社会认可的行为塑造人的品格和美德。在这种哲学中，按照传统方式行事，维护社会秩序，履行集体责任，可以在人际／集体层面上保证社会关系和谐。对

---

1 *Chiny*，《词汇文明》，阿卡迪，波兰华沙，2008年，第155页。
2 对以下大学经济学院学生进行调查：波兰奥波莱技术大学和葡萄牙托马尔理工学院。

于来自文化上更重视个人主义（而不是集体主义）的西方国家观察者来说，完全依赖群体和适应自上而下的规范只能间接地与和谐关联。在这种哲学中，社会受到规范的约束，构成道德框架，通常有利于社会的正常运行，但"和谐"与"自愿"结合，与自上而下的规范相抵触，个体必须寻找自身作为人类单元的路径。

如今，在"一带一路"倡议的发言中也提到孔子的言论，特别是关于多样性的建议——许多国家和谐共处与合作，达到儒家的中庸之道——平衡与和谐。

照片 1　北京语言大学附近的人行道上装饰着的阴阳符号。
来源：Katarzyna Mazur-Kajta

刚开始学习中文时，初学者对汉字特别敏感。如今，在中国旅行的外国人可能会觉得"和谐"二字有一种视觉轰炸效应。街头、广场、大楼的海报上到处都是这些汉字（照片2、3），包含该词的媒体文章数量也在不断增加。与北京年轻人（90后）进行对话时，我们可以发现，这些宣传是现任主席习近平提出的政治口号，中国特色社会主义价值观的十二个重要理念，除了"和谐"之外，还包括：富强、民主、自由、平等、公正、法治、爱国、敬业、诚信和友善。在与"一带一路"倡议有关的许多演讲中，国家领导人特别提到：推进对话、参与合作、保持开放和追求和谐。然而，他们父母一代（生于20世纪60年代和70年代）却将其与前任主席胡锦涛联系在一起。胡锦涛主席当政期间提出"三个和谐"口号：世界和平、协调一致和社会和谐。作者多次调查这个年龄段的代表人群并进行对话时，他们都惊讶于作者选择的这个主题，因为在他们看来，"和谐"口号似乎是很久以前的一个政治话题。

两个年龄段的对话者都热情分享对当代中国政策的看法，认为其目的是缓解国际舞台上的紧张局势，避免领土冲突，保障国际稳定，这是发展国际贸易的地缘战略。

照片 2   "和谐"是社会主义社会的根本理念之一，在北京的宣传栏上作为口号的背景出现两次，
其中提到造福子孙，保护自己。北京，2018 年。
来源：K. M-K.

照片 3   "和谐"是社会主义社会的根本理念之一，出现在北京语言大学一栋大楼的宣传横幅上，
北京，2018 年。
来源：K. M-K.

　　同时，关于"一带一路"倡议的正式文件和发言指出，需要关注人与自然环境关系的和谐 - 通过生态学方法预防气候变化和保护环境并考虑投资对自然环境的影响。然而，媒体上的很多言论担心大规模的倡议将对环境构成严重威胁，可能导致环境退化和自然资源枯竭。因此，虽然"和谐"一词在生活中随处可见，但似乎仍然主要指向政治领域（照片 4）。

照片4　北京语言大学校园的一块标牌上鼓励大家关注环境，共建和谐。
来源：K. M-K.

　　因此，中国人观念中的"和谐"并不是从人际沟通的角度来看待，而是与社会关系有关。中国人很难对"和谐沟通"一词给出定义，他们要求本研究的作者予以澄清，因此调查对象无法自行给出定义。

　　回到"一带一路"倡议背景下的"和谐"概念，中国文献指出"新"丝绸之路不仅继承古代丝绸之路的作用，表现为不同国家和谐共商、共建和共享，而且也指开放包容、和平相处、文化融合和共同发展。沟通主要在国家层面进行，其目的是促进不同文明之间的对话与融合。合作的范围包括：政策沟通、设施联通、贸易畅通、资金融通、民心相通。因此，"和谐"一词被多次提及，但并非在人际沟通的语境下直接提及。

　　2018年7月在北京进行的对话[1]和对现有数据的分析表明，相对较年轻的"一

1　2018年5月至7月25日中国文化部主办、省/市文化局和学术机构联合组织的"青年汉学家研修计划"期间进行本研究。

带一路"计划第一阶段在国家层面，第二阶段（目前正在进行）在企业层面，预期的第三阶段将在个人层面（人员合作）。因此，在"一带一路"倡议框架下所述的沟通目前主要是国际和全球沟通，并非跨文化沟通。"和谐"的概念在中国社会意识的思想/哲学和政策中源远流长，与人际沟通并不直接相关，而是涉及个人内部（玄学含义）和集体（关系和社会规范）。由于上述原因，很难分析这一概念在人际沟通过程中的直接作用。还值得强调的是，跨文化沟通与"和谐"是极其复杂的概念，本文知识对问题的初步研究，在未来还需要得到更广泛的认可。

对"和谐"概念的不同理解将影响沟通的有效性，特别是在地理位置和文化上遥远的市场拓展贸易时的沟通。良好的人际沟通可以使困难的决定变得容易，对话更加关注交谈的目的。有效的沟通有助于揭示计划的意图，加强沟通方的参与，共同努力对决策产生直接影响。这不仅给人留下良好的第一印象，还能促进更好的社交联系和发展商务智能。塑造人际交往能力很重要，因为沟通不清晰、不准确或粗心将造成同僚、管理者和服务接受方的不满。沟通的舒适感不仅是使用一种语言，还要求价值层次一致。为了实现这一点，必须确认感知上的相似和差异。差异决定人类的行为，包括言语和非言语沟通行为。特别是这些价值观出现在媒体信息中（文章、宣传牌等），在城市街头展示，因此在视觉上鼓励提出问题。

Harmonious Intercultural Communication on the Belt and Road - The Preliminary Research Report

Katarzyna Mazur-Kajta / Poland

Lecturer, Department of Economics and Management, Institute of International Economic Relations, Opole University of Technology

Belt and Road Initiative (BRI) in the context of communication in social consciousness is primarily associated with the transport of cargo and people, that is with moving/goods from one place to another, the movement of means of locomotion as well as the means of locomotion themselves. From the ancient times, associations with the silk route mainly concerned caravans—with silk and other goods (including cosmetics, jewels, glass, livestock, metal, paper, leather, stones, tobacco and wood) often being transported "by the way" on the backs of camels and by the sea route towards Europe. With regard to the contemporary initiative linking the Silk Road Economic Belt and the 21st Century Maritime Silk Road, the media regularly report on new rail connections, direct flights being opened between the leading Chinese cities and the rest of the world, modernized port infrastructure and numbers indicating an increasingly intense exchange of goods[1]. However, in ancient times, apart from goods and people, ideas were also transmitted for thousands of kilometers (connected, among others, with philosophical and religious currents, art, scientific achievements), and numerous purchase-sales transactions were accompanied by interpersonal communication.

By analyzing the plans related to the B&R Initiative from the point of view of interpersonal communication, the following concepts turn out to be the key words: *cooperation* and *co-participation*. Politicians of countries/regions that have joined the initiative, often emphasize in their statements the great potential and space for bilateral cooperation. The platform opened to joint projects, equal opportunities related to the possibility of participation and refer to the interpersonal relationship by promoting academic and cultural exchange, media cooperation, volunteering and political communication/public diplomacy (among others by the cultural exchange programs, Chinese language competitions, the activity of Confucius Institutes, etc.). The Chinese side also emphasizes that the spirit of the initiative should be peaceful cooperation, openness and tolerance, as well as mutual learning and mutual benefits for each of the 90 countries involved in the initiative. The aim of the article is to look at one of the elements of effective interpersonal communication, closely related to interpersonal cooperation - namely the category of *harmony* and its perception by different groups of people.

When conducting talks with the Chinese scientific community one can get the impression that the category of *harmony* in contemporary China is considered mainly in two aspects: ancient literature related to *dao* and its interpretation by the Taoists (in a more metaphysical sense) and Confucianists (in the sense of ethics and morality), and in political terms, i.e. in the context of a harmonious socialist society

---

1 China's total trade exchange with countries interested in the OBOR initiative over the past five years has exceeded USD 5 trillion, and the average annual increase was 1.1%, while China itself became the largest trading partner for 25 of them. See: *China sees trade, investment growth with B&R countries*, Belt and Road Portal, https://eng.yidaiyilu.gov.cn/qwyw/rdxw/64034.htm , access: 30.08.2018.

with a Chinese specificity.

On the one hand, the *dao* category is extremely simplified in descriptions, has no name and is perceived as a concept so obvious that it does not require explanation. On the other hand, it is compared to the western absolute (force majeure), the beginning of everything (ten thousand things), so broadly meaningful that it is not possible to be fully characterized in the present state of knowledge and limitations of the human mind. The category of *harmony* is mentioned here as the only way of nature to *dao* - a method of living in accordance with *dao*. For a foreigner, combining *harmony* with the absolute, in this meaning of the word is the first thread of misunderstanding. According to the observations of Anna Czelej "(...) the spirituality of a human being in the Chinese sense (...) differs from the Western perception of this issue, where the ideal spiritual person is someone who looks only up and never down. According to the Chinese people, only an unbalanced person who has lost contact with Earth and life"[1], who has lost harmony, can do this. *Harmony* as a slogan also appears in conjunction with the symbol of changing and complementing the elements of *yin-yang*. Which were originally a sign of *taiji* - the Great Unity, elements replacing the old symbols: white tiger and green dragon.[2] This philosophy has found its application, among others in learning to arrange *fengshui* space, Chinese natural medicine and *taijiquan* meditation gymnastics, which are also gaining popularity outside the PRC. In the Chinese publishing market, one can also buy books trying to convey the *dao* idea in the business space, indicated by the titles: "*Dao* and Business Management"《道与企业管理》, "*Zen way* and Business Management"《禅道与企业管理》, "*Dao* business"《大商之道》, etc.

Visualization of *yin-yang* symbols is visible in China even in urban space. A circle filled with white and black elements decorates Chinese temples, signs and even is a decoration of pavements (photo 1.)

---

1   Czelej A., *Magia zmian*, Studio astro psychologii, Białystok 2010, p. 84.

2   *Chiny*. Leksykon cywilizacje, Arkady, Warsaw 2008, p. 155.

The *yin-yang* symbol can be considered as a contemporary international symbol of *harmony*. This mark is practically recognized all over the world. This was confirmed in studies carried out by the author among Polish and Portuguese students in Opole in 2017 and in Tomar in 2018.[1], during which three hundred respondents unanimously associated this symbol with *harmony*. The respondents knew only its visual dimension, they connected it with Asia (less often with China), but they neither connected it with *dao* nor with the *bian* phenomenon of changing.

Chinese classical approach (Confucianism) associates the category of *harmony* with *right behavior*. Thoughtful and socially accepted deeds shape the character and virtues of man. In this approach, behaving in accordance with tradition, maintaining social order, fulfilling the duties imposed by the group harmonizes social relations on the interpersonal / group level. For a Western observer from a country with a culture more focused on individualism (rather than collectivism), full dependence on the group and adaptation to top-down norms is only indirectly connected with *harmony*. In this approach, norms discipline society, create its moral backbone and often facilitate the functioning of society, however the category of *harmony* is combined with *voluntariness* being in contradiction to top-down norms, with an individual search for one's own path by a human unit.

Nowadays, in the statements about BRI, there are also references to the formulations used by Confucius, especially those concerning diversity − harmonious coexistence and cooperation of many countries[2], achieving the Confucian golden mean − balance and harmony.

---

1   The research was conducted among students of economic faculties at the university: Opole University of Technology (Poland) and Instituto Politécnico de Tomar (Portugal).

2   See: *Chinese, foreign experts talk of shared values of Silk Road program*, https://eng.yidaiyilu.gov.cn/qwyw/rdxw/21421.htm , access: 30.08.2018.

Photo 1. *Yin-yang* symbol decorating the pavement in the area of Beijing Language and Culture University, Beijing 2018.

Source: Katarzyna Mazur-Kajta

When beginning the adventure with the Chinese language, the novice is extremely sensitive to the symbols. Today a foreigner travelling across China may get the impression that the symbols 和谐 simply bombard his sense of sight. These signs decorate posters that are hanging on the streets, green squares, buildings, etc., (photo 2, 3), and the number of articles in the media containing this word is constantly growing. When conducting conversations with the young generation of Pekingese people (generation of the 90s) one can get information that the reason for these social campaigns are the political slogans used by current chairman Xi Jinping, referring to the twelve-key principles of socialism about the Chinese specificity, to which in addition to *harmony* are also included: *prosperity, democracy, freedom, equality, justice, the rule of law, patriotism, dedication, integrity* and *friendship*. In numerous speeches related to the B&R initiative, the head of the state refers, among others, to: promote dialogue, engage in cooperation, maintain openness and seek harmony. However, their parents' generation (i.e. those born in the 1960s and 70s), mainly associates them with the chairman Hu Jintao, who during his term of office promoted the slogan of *three harmonies*: *world peace, reconciliation* and *social harmony*. The author, starting a conversation about her research (among the representatives of this age group) several times was received with surprise that she chose such a topic of research, because in their opinion the slogan of *harmony* seems to be a topic in the political realm for a long time now.

Representatives of both age groups of interlocutors eagerly share opinions on contemporary Chinese policy, aimed at alleviating tensions on the international arena, avoiding territorial conflicts and achieving international stability that is geostrategic harmony, aimed at developing international trade.

Photo 2. *Harmony* as one of the basic foundations of socialist society, it is mentioned twice on the Beijing billboard, as a background for a slogan referring to bringing benefits to future generations and securing the present, Beijing 2018.

Source: K. M-K.

Photo 3. *Harmony* as one of the basic foundations of socialist society, posted on the billboard decorating the main building of the Beijing Language and Culture University, Beijing 2018.

Source: K. M-K.

Similarly, the official documents and statements regarding the BRI indicate the need to pay attention to harmonizing the relationship between man and the natural environment – preventing climate change and protecting the environment through a pro-ecological approach and considering the impact of investments on the natural environment. However, there are opinions in the media full of fears that an initiative of such a large scale poses a serious threat to the environment and may cause its degradation and depletion of natural resources. Thus, the word *harmony* is visible in many areas of life, but it still seems to refer mainly to the political sphere (photo 4).

Photo 4. A sign set on the lawn of the Beijing Language and Culture University campus, encouraging to pay attention to the environment and jointly building harmony, Beijing 2018.

Source: K. M-K.

Harmony in Chinese therefore is not considered from the point of view of interpersonal communication but concerns social relations. The formulation *harmonious communication* [和谐 沟通] is often a difficult category to define by Chinese people, they ask for clarification what the author of the study means, which sometimes excludes the purpose of the respondents to define this concept by themselves.

Returning to the concept of *harmony* in the context of the B&R initiative, Chinese literature indicates that the "new" Silk Road not only inherits the role of the ancient Silk Road, manifested in harmonious cooperation and mutual benefits of countries co-creating it, but also refers to the slogans of *openness, tolerance, peace, cultural integration* and *development*. Communication is considered mainly at the state-state level, within which it aims to promote dialogue and integration between representatives of different civilizations. The scope of cooperation is to include: communication at the political level, infrastructure connectivity, cooperation in the field of investment and trade, monetary circulation and broadly understood agreement. Thus, the category of *harmony* is mentioned many times, but not directly in the context of interpersonal communication.

The talks held in Beijing in July 2018[1] and the analysis of existing data allow to state that the first stage of the relatively young B&R initiative is the state-state level, the second (currently being created) is the enterprise-enterprise level, and the expected third stage will be the level of individual cooperation (human-human). Because of this, communication considered in descriptions within the framework of BRI is currently mainly of international and global communication, but not intercultural yet. The category of *harmony*, which has a very rich history in China's thought/philosophy and policy in the PRC social consciousness, does not appear directly in connection with the category of interpersonal communication, but rather intrapersonal (as a metaphysical reflection) or group (relationship and social norms). Due to the above reasons, it is extremely difficult to analyze its direct role in the communication process - interpersonal communication. It is also worth emphasizing that the themes of intercultural communication and *harmony* are extremely complex

---

1   The research was carried out between 05-25.07.2018 r. under the "2018 Visiting Program for Young Sinologist" hosted by the Ministry of Culture and co-organized by Chinese Provincial/Municipal Departments of Culture and academic institutions.

issues, and this text is only an introduction to research on their problems and requires a wider recognition in the future.

Understanding the differences in the approach of the *harmony* category can affect the effectiveness of communication, especially in the case of communication accompanying trade expansion directed to geographically and culturally distant markets. Good interpersonal communication makes difficult decisions easier to solve, and conversations are more focused on the purpose of the meeting. Effective communication is conducive in showing planned intentions, strengthens the engagement of communicating parties, and combines making efforts that directly influence the decisions made. It affects not only in making a good first impression, it can promote better social contacts and develop business intelligence. It is important to shape interpersonal skills, because unclear, inaccurate or careless communication can alienate co-workers, supervisors and recipients of the services offered. Communication comfort appears not only when it is in one language, but also when there is conformity in the hierarchy of values, and to achieve this it is necessary to recognize the similarities and differences in the perception of these. These differences determine human behavior, including communication behaviors in the verbal and non-verbal aspect. Especially if the names of these values appear in the information available in the media (in articles, on billboards, etc.) and decorate the streets of cities and thus visually encourage asking questions.

References

Cabestan J-P., *Polityka zagraniczna Chin*, Dialog, Warszawa 2013.

Casaburi I., *Chinese investments trends in Europe*, 2016/2017, ESADE, 1994-2018 China Academic Journal Electronic Publishing House, www.cnki.net.

Delury J., *Harmonious in China*, 31.03.2008, https://www.hoover.org/research/harmonious-china , access on 22.10.2017.

Jaworski R., *Harmonia i konflikty*, Uniwersytet Kardynała Stefana Wyszyńskiego, Warszawa 2004.

Mazur-Kajta K., Lipińska P. *Harmonijna komunikacja w opinii młodego pokolenia Chińczyków*, [in:] ed. Mazur-Kajta K. *Przegląd Nauk Stosowanych*, 18(1)/ 2018, Politechnika Opolska, Opole 2018.

Ponomarenko L., *China's "One Belt One Road" Initiative As a method of connecting China with the Word*, International Conference on Contemporary Education, Social Sciences and Humanities (ICCESSH 2017), Advances in Social Science, Education and Humanities Research, volume 124, 1994-2018 China Academic Journal Electronic Publishing House, www.cnki.net.

Solmecke U., *Multinational Enterprises and the 'One Belt, One Road' Initiative: Sustainable Development and Innovation in a PostCrisis Global Environment*, The Copenhagen Journal of Asian Studies 34(2)/ 2016.

Su Ge, *The Belt and Road Initiative in Global Perspectives*, China International Studies 2016, 1994-2018 China Academic Journal Electronic Publishing House, www.cnki.net.

Sulej-Chhugani, K. *Komunikacja a lokalna kultura*, Poland Go Global Magazine, 1(5)/2015, The Boston Consulting Group.

Szczudlik-Tatar J., *China's New Silk Road Diplomacy*, Policy Paper, No. 34 (82)/2013, The Polish Insitute of International Affairs.

Kuzmina E.E., *The Prehistory of the Silk Road*, ed. Mair H., University of Pennsylvania Press, Philadelphia 2008.

Chiny. Leksykon cywilizacje, Arkady, Warszawa 2008.

Laozi. *Księga dao i de z komentarzami Wang Bi*. Wydawnictwo Uniwersytetu Jagiellońskiego, Kraków 2006.

China sees trade, investment growth with B&R countries, Belt and Road Portal, https://eng.yidaiyilu.gov.cn/qwyw/rdxw/64034.htm , access on 30.08.2018.

Chinese, foreign experts talk of shared values of Silk Road program, Belt and Road Portal, https://eng.yidaiyilu.gov.cn/qwyw/rdxw/21421.htm , access on 30.08.2018.

Highlights of Xi's keynote speech at the Boao Forum, China Daily, http://www.chinadaily.com.cn/a/201804/10/WS5acc15a6a3105cdcf6517259.html , access on 30.08.2018.

中国需要了解如何与西方沟通

黛安娜【哥伦比亚】

哥伦比亚国立大学副教授

"丝绸之路"是一个外来语。德国地理学家费迪南·冯·李希霍芬（Ferdinand Freiherrvon Richthofen，1833-1905）首次提出"die Seidenstrasse"（丝绸之路）的概念。他是现代地理学科的开创者之一（Osterhammel 1987, 150）。1868 年至 1872 年间，他大部分时间都在中国旅行。这些旅行的初步观察于 1872 年在上海发布英文版本（Daniel C. Waugh, 2007）。1877 到 1912 年出版五卷《中国》，但他未能在活着的时候完成全书。李希霍芬的专著构成几十年后英国地理学家哈尔福德·麦金德（Halford Mackinder）理论的原型：欧亚大陆是地缘政治的"核心地带"。介绍《中国》的意义在于揭示欧亚大陆的人类活动史。李希霍芬分析希腊和罗马文献，其中提及 *Serer*"（丝绸贸易的联系）或 *Serica*"（希腊语 *Σηρική*"）。这是古希腊和后来的罗马地理学家对遥远东方亚洲国家的印象。

一般而言，李希霍芬更喜欢使用"Verkehr"（沟通）、"Strassen"（路径或路线）、"Hauptstrassen"（主要路线）或"Handelsstrassen"（贸易路线）等词语，而不是"Seidenstrassen"（丝绸之路），尽管他强调是丝绸贸易推动亚洲内陆加强了联系（Waugh, 2007, 3）。

"丝绸之路"是源自德国历史地理学的外来语，因此中国倾向于采用其他名称，即国家主席习近平在 2013 年宣布的"丝绸之路经济带和 21 世纪海上丝绸之路"，简称"一带一路"（OBOR），而最近经常使用的说法是"一带一路"倡议

（BRI）。"一带一路"倡议是中国押注全球化的具体实施项目。中国政府将"一带一路"倡议视为所谓的"全球化 2.0"的标志，因为它象征着中国对全球化的承诺，带有"中国特色"。

"一带一路"最初只是作为一个倡议提出，但随着时间的流逝，它开始逐渐走向成熟并拥抱世界。如今，这是一项以城市为主要参与者的全球计划，从而具有可操作性，主要关注作为核心地带的欧亚大陆。"一带一路"倡议代表着城市化和发展的交叉（Chen, 2017）。"一带一路"倡议最显著的特征是，它正在成为世界最大的商业和经济区域，涉及建设基础设施工程和消除陆地、海上和水上运输通道的瓶颈。全球民用航空平台也在扩大，航空基础设施不断改善。与此同时，促进能源基础设施连通性和推动通信网络建设，例如跨越国境的光缆网络和卫星信息网络。各国之间签订科学、技术和创新方面的协定，尤其是非化石能源部门得到加强，例如水力发电、太阳能和风能。同时还鼓励使用核能。中国也在这一走廊上推广新一代信息技术和生物科技，建立工业园、经济和商业合作区以及跨境经济合作区（Scott, 2015）。

从一开始，"一带一路"倡议就被认为是与有关国家共同制订的一项提案。但由于向西方国家表述的方式不同，西方对项目的清晰性和一致性提出诸多批评，甚至产生质疑、不信任和抗拒感。美国著名智库国际战略研究中心认为："最初阶段中国对'一带一路'倡议及其实施方法的外部沟通无效。'一带一路'倡议面临着各种不同的解读和理解……（中国人）往往倾向于使用大而空的语言和理论"（Fang, 2018）。

此外，2018 年 4 月，欧盟 27 国驻华大使发布的一份报告强调对"一带一路"倡议单边性质的担忧。除匈牙利外，欧盟所有其他国家的驻华大使共同在一份声明上签字，表达欧盟对该倡议日益增加的反对声音。据《德国商报》报道，欧盟驻华大使的联合声明指出，中国的新丝绸之路"违背欧盟的贸易自由化议程，补贴中国企业将打破力量平衡"（Engdahl, 2018）。学者、政界人士和官员在西方媒体和官方声明中均认为中国隐瞒可以从"一带一路"倡议中取得的巨大利益。

短期项目建设并不重要，但它传递出关于中国在世界舞台上所扮演角色的清晰信号。下面将介绍"一带一路"倡议将对世界秩序产生影响的最显著特征。

区域发展是"一带一路"倡议的关键焦点之一。中国几乎所有的省份都自行制订计划，作为全国计划的补充。中国的目标是缩小贫困内陆地区与富裕的太平洋沿海地区的差距。中国政府从 1999 年开始实施所谓的"西部大开发战略",以发展欠发达省份(Cai, 2017, p.6)。然而,在区域发展的基础上,城市构成具体的现实:城市是"一带一路"倡议的支柱。

中国的城市转型是人类历史上规模最庞大、发展速度最快的城市革命,在改革开放的进程中发起,受到"一带一路"倡议的鼓励。城市转型的根本原因是一个国家的城市化水平与其经济增长水平息息相关。一个让人叹为观止的现实是,对于中国 35 个最大的城市,目前每个城市的 GDP 与世界上的一个国家相当。例如,上海市 GDP 规模相当于菲律宾,北京市 GDP 规模相当于阿拉伯联合酋长国,广州市经济总量相当于瑞士(世界银行,2016 年)。

中国城市的快速国际化也反映在《2018 全球城市报告》等报告中。根据该报告,国际化的中国城市从 2008 年的 7 个增加到 2018 年的 27 个。中国在过去 10 年新增加 20 个国际化城市,这表明中国城市的国际化进程在加快。数年内"一带一路"倡议将对中国人强化这一趋势,而非中国城市。

大规模铁路、机场、港口、高架桥、光纤网络和替代能源建设只不过是"一带一路"倡议的冰山一角。从这个意义上讲,该项目具有两个潜在的意义:

1."一带一路"倡议的国内影响

"一带一路"倡议首先让中国西部地区受益,这些地区位于倡议的核心地带。所谓的"共同发展"安排重要性变得突出:通过城市间的伙伴关系,中国政府力求让西部地区的发展水平追上东部地区当前的发展水平。上海、深圳和喀什之间的合作即为这一政策的雏形,距离不构成障碍。中国最国际化的城市和金融中心上海和位于东部沿海的科技资本城市深圳共同与毗邻巴基斯坦的西部边远城市喀什达成合作约定。深圳市政府已拨款 100 亿元人民币(15 亿美元)为喀什大学建设新校区,上海市的部分企业在喀什设立新工厂。这三座城市通过公共政策产生联系,建设基础设施工程和确立公私合作关系。目标是创造就业和增强喀什的经济实力。

2."一带一路"倡议的对外影响

城市化和发展之间的交叉点还包括国际层面。中国政府推行"周边外交",其中城市承担关键角色,从而将以边境城市为代表的重要区域中心与不同国家的发展中枢联系起来。目标是通过一个复杂的节点城市系统连接 93 个国家(45 个亚洲国家、39 个欧洲国家和 7 个非洲国家)和 252 座城市。为了实现这一目标,中国学者对新丝绸之路沿线城市进行精准分析。根据中国与不同国家的关系类型确定五个标准，拓展外交政策使其覆盖城市，然后研究基础设施条件、贸易流动性、财务状况和城市外交关系。构建30个指标衡量城市所在国家的双边关系类型、政治稳定性、经济自由度、货币稳定性、金融国际化水平、未来十年的城市规划人口增长率、友好城市的数量、飞往中国的航班频率以及每个国家/地区签证的便利性（Tu, 2018）。

根据上述标准确定节点城市，即"一带一路"框架下的主要增长极。评估结果对中国政府和企业以及地缘政治和地缘经济秩序都具有启示作用。这些节点城市大部分位于东南亚（22个）、南亚（21个）和东欧（16个）。莫斯科、汉堡和曼谷等城市在分析中占据最重要的位置，与中国的利益不谋而合。中国寻求加强与俄罗斯以及中亚国家的关系，在欧洲以德国作为主要合作伙伴，在东南亚将泰国作为战略核心。

在三个方面具有一定的前瞻性。首先，印度洋沿岸的城市数量最多（84个），让人联想起地缘政治学家罗伯特·卡普兰（Robert K. Kaplan）的预测。他预言印度洋将崛起为世界的战略中心。

其次，城市发展和城市国际化指标衡量沿线城市在区域和国际上的影响力高低。城市区域和城市国际化重拾昔日的荣光。

最后，根据分析，沿线城市属于中国认可的多边组织成员国，对中国政府具有重要价值。这种情况表明，自1944年签订布雷顿森林协定建立世界秩序后，一种不同的世界秩序开始浮现。中国认可的顶级多边组织包括金砖国家、上海合作组织（SCO）和亚洲基础设施投资银行（AIIB）。它们正在改变多边事务的国际基准以及国际金融体系结构。

"一带一路"倡议不仅是中国的全球化项目，而且还引发对世界秩序两个方面的重要质疑：

它打破了民族国家是现行国际体系最重要主导者的观念，即1648年《威斯特伐利亚条约》所确定的观念。城市取代国家在国际体系中起到核心作用，恢复在全球历史上的重要地位。显然，城市重拾昔日在古代丝绸之路上的繁荣昌盛。喀什、撒马尔罕、伊斯坦布尔和伊斯法罕即为这一趋势的明显写照。喀什在历史上曾经是重要的佛教、伊斯兰教和基督教城市，还是贵霜帝国或喀喇汗国的都城和主要商业中心。撒马尔罕是一个国际化大都市，特别是在600多年前它是帖木尔帝国的首都。伊斯坦布尔有着超过十五个世纪的悠久历史，是东西方之间的多元文化之都和商业枢纽。伊斯法罕在几百年中被誉为中东最美丽的城市，曾经是古波斯都城，阿契美尼德王朝、萨珊王朝和萨非王朝丝绸之路的主要中心之一。

"一带一路"倡议表明目前被归类为发展中国家的城市定位，但其未来经济增长前景广阔。中亚的阿斯塔纳和杜尚别等城市就是这种情况，它们证实发展中国家的城市经济增长稳定和逐渐加快的预测。

沿着新丝绸之路推动中国前进的伟大城市转型不仅以其巨大的规模引人注目，还允许中小城市、城市区域和城市国际化在世界变局中恢复过去的历史地位。

中国在全球化项目框架内拥抱世界，从这个意义上讲，中国在世界秩序的重构中起着决定性的作用。尽管如此，中国仍必须面对一系列挑战。特别是从拉丁美洲的角度来看，人们对拉丁美洲在"一带一路"倡议框架中的作用存在疑问。中国在与邻国或边境周边国家交往中推行"睦邻外交"或"周边外交"政策。这表明拉丁美洲未列入"一带一路"倡议。然而，有一些关键线索使我们发现拉丁美洲也不会被排除在外。2015年5月17日，中国国务院总理李克强和夫人程虹率领一百多名成员组成的代表团从北京出发开启南美之行，行程包括巴西、哥伦比亚、秘鲁和智利。此行的主要目的是通过"两洋铁路建设工程"项目再次确认"拉美新丝绸之路"（Castro, 2015）[1]。这表明，"一带一路"倡议跨越欧亚大陆边界、印度洋和南太平洋，涵盖拉丁美洲的庞大基础设施项目。

2017年5月14日，在习近平主席的领导下，为期两天的"一带一路"国际合作高峰论坛在北京举行，28个国家的元首和政府首脑以及100多个国家的1200名代表出席论坛。中国政府与68个国家签订协议，共同开发新丝绸之路贸易路线沿线的基础设施。

在此次高峰论坛上，拉丁美洲的智利和阿根廷总统出席。这两个国家坚定支持与中国开展贸易，鼓励中国对其投资。巴西也派出代表团。截至目前已有九个拉美国家签订关于"一带一路"合作的谅解备忘录。

另一方面，巴拿马运河是"一带一路"倡议从太平洋到拉丁美洲的战略要地。虽然因技术变更未对船闸进行现代化改造，导致船闸吨位和尺寸增加，但每年仍有大约3.2亿吨货物和原材料通过巴拿马运河运输（Leon-Manríquez, 2018, 114）。因此，巴拿马运河是从太平洋运输货物进入大西洋必经的战略要地。

---

1 也称作两洋铁路（trans-Amazonian railway）。

亚洲基础设施投资银行（简称"亚投行"）目前已批准七个拉丁美洲国家（阿根廷、巴西、智利、厄瓜多尔、秘鲁、委内瑞拉和玻利维亚）加入成为成员国。亚投行是一家多边开发银行并且与亚洲其他类似的金融机构合作，特别是亚洲开发银行（NDB）。最初包括 87 个成员国，其中近 40% 不是亚洲国家，欧洲国家的影响力也很强大。名单第一个加入的拉丁美洲国家是巴西。金砖国家全部作为创始成员国加入亚投行。

显然，中国将金砖国家新开发银行（NBD）作为新丝绸之路有关项目的重要补充金融机构。事实上，巴西将起到重要的领导作用，因为 2019 年将在该国设立新的 NBD 分行。

在文化和学术领域，中国还承诺每年向"一带一路"沿线国家提供 10,000 个奖学金名额。

然而，拉美各国政府尚不清楚"一带一路"倡议与该次大陆之间的联系以及如何将其纳入"人类命运共同体"的构想。由于缺乏明确性，不得不评估中国在实施"一带一路"倡议时面临的真正挑战。中国面临的真正挑战不是如何将"一带一路"建设为全球战略，更大的挑战在于跨文化沟通和理解。这是中国与其他国家和文化实现跨文化沟通和理解的机会。中国的文化范式与西方不同。从这个意义上讲，中国需要了解如何与西方沟通。文化蕴含于背景之中。它不仅仅是纯粹的"软实力"（Nye, 2004）。这不仅是现实意义上的权力问题，还涉及到权力分配（Morgenthau, 1948）。这一问题涉及对人类学意义上"他者"的真正理解：行为有形的表现通常是潜在心理现实的结果（Gertz, 1977）。

在这种背景下存在诸多误解。西方和东方对许多概念有不同的理解：和谐与社会凝聚力、军力与民主、愿望与必要性、协商民主与共同安全和自利安全、文明的对话与冲突、协商民主的团结治理与对抗民主的分而治之、军事同盟和战略伙伴。与"一带一路"倡议直接相关的另一个误解是：城市在中国被理解为行政范畴，而在西方被认为是城市事实。

这里提到的方案线索和基本目标与认识"他者"以进行有效沟通的相关性有关。中国在"一带一路"倡议中有机会向他者学习并向他者解释自身的文化。为了在特定文化背景下实现这一目标，必须提出问题：其他国家和文化如何进行沟通？在欧洲和盎格鲁 - 撒克逊文化中，沟通通常是直线型的。沟通直接进行，而且对于理解其他行动者是有必要的。指称（行动者）是思想传播的内在前提。在远东国家，沟通与特定的语境直接相关，并具有与事实相关的特定特征。言语并不是发送者和接收者之间实现沟通的唯一方式。形象、沉默、行为与言语一样重要。在拉丁美洲国家，沟通方式有所不同。诺贝尔奖获得者加夫列尔·加西亚·马尔克斯的作品《百年孤独》反映典型的拉丁美洲宇宙观，其中的沟通充斥着"魔幻现实主义"。

所有国家都可以根据其自身的需要和文化背景，选择以自己的方式自愿加入"一带一路"倡议。自 1944 年签订布雷顿森林协议以来，在一系列强制规则和机制的基础上建立现有国际体系，以美国和欧洲大国为主导，并且近距离观察世界。许多西方国家真正担心的不是中国与"一带一路"沿线国家之间的紧密联系，而是中国通过"一带一路"提出完全不同的全球化概念，这给西方国家的领导人带来巨大的挑战。中国外交的主要挑战是可以理解的。"一带一路"倡议是中国通过充满活力的外交手段实现这一目标的机会。

China Needs to Know How to Communicate with the West

Diana Andrea Gomez Diaz / Colombia[1]

Associate Professor at National University of Colombia

Silk Road is a borrowed term. The German geographer Ferdinand Freiherrvon Richthofen (1833-1905) coined the term "die Seidenstrasse" (the Silk Road). He was one of the founders of modern geography as a scholarly discipline (Osterhammel1987, 150), and between 1868 and 1872 he spent much of his time traveling in China; his initial observations from those trips already appeared in an English edition in Shanghai in1872 (Daniel C. Waugh. 2007). Then, he published five Volumes titled "China" between 1877and 1912 which he never lived to complete. In Richthofen texts there is a special emphasis in the embryo of what in Halford Mackinder, the British geographer, formulated several decades later: the geopolitical Eurasian "Heartland". His significant part of the introduction to *China* is a history of human activity across Eurasia. Richthofen analyzes Greek and Roman sources which spoke about the *Serer (*those connected with the trade in silk),or *Serica* (Σηρική in Greek) which was one of the easternmost countries of

---

1   PhD in Political Studies and International Relations, Professor at the Institute of Political Studies and International Relations (IEPRI), Universidad Nacional de Colombia (National University of Colombia). dagomezdi@unal.edu.co

Asia known to the Ancient Greek and then Roman geographers.

In general, rather than "Seidenstrassen" , Richthofen prefered the terms "Verkehr"(communication), "Strassen" (roads or routes), "Hauptstrassen"(main routes) or "Handelsstrassen"(traderoutes), even as he stressed that it was the trade in silk which fueled the development of the Inner Asian contacts (Waugh, 2007, 3).

Because it is a borrowed term of German historiography, China uses other names since it was announced by President Xi Jinping in 2013: first, Silk Road Economic Belt and 21st Century Maritime Silk Road, then abbreviated as One Belt & One Road (OBOR), and recently named as Belt and Road initiative (BRI).BRI is the concrete project of the Chinese globalizing bet. The Chinese government considers the BRI as the flag of its so-called globalization 2.0, since it symbolizes its commitment to globalization, a belt "with Chinese characteristics".

The BRI was constituted as an initiative, and with the passage of time has taken shape and begins to embrace the world. Today it is a global plan based on cities as the main actors that make the initiative operational, focusing on Eurasia as its core. BRI represents the intersection between urbanization and development (Chen, 2017). The most visible and obvious feature of BRI is that it is becoming the largest commercial and economic area in the world, involving the construction of infrastructure works and the elimination of bottlenecks in land, sea and water transport channels.Platforms for global civil aviation routes are also being expanded and the infrastructure for aviation is being improved. At the same time, the connectivity of the energy infrastructure is promoted, as well as the construction of communication networks, such as cross-border optical cable networks and satellite information networks. This lead to the signing of agreements in science, technology and innovation and, in particular, the non-fossil energy sectors are being reinforced, such as hydroelectric energy, solar energy and wind energy. Likewise, the use of nuclear energy is encouraged. Also in this corridor, China promotes new generation information technology and biotechnology. Industrial parks, zones of economic and commercial cooperation and zones of cross-border economic cooperation are built (Scott, 2015).

Since its inception, the BRI was conceived as a proposal to be built jointly with the interested countries and, given the different way of proposing it to Western countries, in the West it received many criticisms about the clearness and consistency of the project, generating suspicions, distrust and resistances. For the Center for Strategic and International Studies, recognized think-tank of the USA, "China has not been effective in the external communication on the BRI and its approach of implementation in the initial stage. There are many interpretations and understandings about the BRI ... (the Chinese) tend to speak with words and big but empty theories "(Fang, 2018).

In addition, in April 2018 twenty-seven European Union (EU) ambassadors drafted a report that increases concerns about the unilateral nature of the initiative. All EU ambassadors, with the exception of Hungary, signed the document in a statement of increasing opposition from the EU to BRI. According to the German newspaper, *Handelsblatt*, the declaration of the EU ambassadors states that China's new silk route "goes against the EU's agenda to liberalize trade and pushes the balance of power in favor of subsidized Chinese companies"(Engdahl, 2018). Scholars, politicians and officials consider in Western media and in official announcements that China must have hidden the huge interests it can gain from the BRI.

The construction of the project may not be as important in the short term as it is to convey a clear narrative about the role of China on the world stage. The following are the most preponderant features of BRI that will sooner or later impact the structure of the world order.

Regional development is one of the key aspects of the BRI initiative and almost all provinces in China have developed their own BRI plan to complement the national plan. With this, Beijing intends, among others, to close the gap between the poor inner areas and the opulent Chinese Pacific coast. Since 1999, the Chinese government has followed the so-called 'Western development strategy' to revitalize low-performing provinces (Cai, 2017, p.6). But at the base of this development by regions there are the cities as a concrete reality: cities are the pillars of the BRI.

The underlying reason of this urban transformation -the largest and fastest urban revolution in world history- initiated with the Process of Reform and Opening and encouraged by BRI, is that the level of urbanization of a country is correlated with its level of economic growth. This is a glaring reality, even today 35 Chinese cities have each one a GDP equivalent to a whole country. The GDP of Shanghai is equivalent to GDP of Philippines, Beijing's GDP to that of the Arab Emirates and Guangzhou has an economy with an equivalent size of Switzerland (World Bank, 2016).

In turn, the rapid internationalization of Chinese cities is reflected in the evident results of reports such as the Global Cities Report 2018 which registers a spectacular increase of globalized Chinese cities: from 7 in 2008 to 27 in 2018. The emergence of 20 new Chinese global cities during last 10 years demonstrates the accelerated process of cities internationalization in China. BRI will increase this trend in a few years in Chinese and not Chinese cities.

The mass production of railways, airports, ports, viaducts, optical cable networks and alternative forms of energy is only the tip of the BRI iceberg. In that sense, there are two underlying implications that outline this project:

1. Inward Impact of BRI

The BRI has as its first winner the Chinese west, located at the heart of the initiative. Arrangements such as the so-called Combined Development stand out: through the partnerships between cities, the Chinese State seeks to level the development of the west with that already existing in the east. The alliance between Shanghai, Shenzhen and Kashgar is a prototype of this policy, where distances are not an obstacle. Shanghai, the most cosmopolitan city and financial center of the country, joined to Shenzhen, the technological capital city, located on the east coast, in association with Kashgar, a remote city located on the border with Pakistan. The Shenzhen government has granted 10 billion yuan (USD $ 1.5 billion) to build a new campus for Kashgar University and some companies in Shanghai have established new factories there. Through public policies these three cities are connected in order to build infrastructure works and public and private partnerships. It seeks to generate employment as well as the economic empowerment of Kashgar.

2. Outward Impact of BRI

The intersection between urbanization and development also includes an international dimension. The Chinese government is making use of the "Periphery Diplomacy ", where the pre-eminent role is assumed by the cities, thus connecting important regional centers represented by border cities and those that are pole of development in different countries. This aims to connect 93 countries (45 Asians, 39 Europeans and 7 Africans) and 252 cities in a complex system of node-cities. For this purpose, Chinese scholars made an accurate analysis of the urban areas located along the new Silk Road.Five criteria were established based on the type of relations that China establishes with the different countries, in a kind of foreign policy extended to cities, to later examine the conditions of infrastructure, the trade flows, financial situation and the cities diplomacy relations. Even as, 30 indicators were built in order to examine the type of bilateral relations with each country to which the cities belong to, their political stability, economic freedom level, monetary stability, level of financial internationalization, growth rate of the urban population planned for the next decade, up to the number of sister cities, the frequency of flights to China and the facilities for obtaining visa in each country (Tu, 2018).

Based on these criteria, the node-cities were established, that is, the main poles within the framework of the BRI. The result of this evaluation is revealing for both the Chinese government and companies and for the geopolitical and geo-economic order. The node cities are mostly located in Southeast Asia (22), South Asia (21) and Eastern Europe (16). The cities of Moscow, Hamburg and Bangkok occupy the first places in the analysis, which is consistent with China's interest in strengthening ties with Russia -and Central Asia as a necessary step-, with Europe taking Germany as its main European partner, and with Thailand as a strategic axis of relations with Southeast Asia.

Three aspects receive in this context a great transcendence: First, the high number of cities located on the shores of the Indian Ocean (84) recalls the forecasts of the geopolitical Robert K. Kaplan who foresaw the emergence of Indian Ocean as the strategic heart of the world.

Second, the indicators of urban development and internationalization of cities measure the high level of regional and international impact of cities along the route, where city-regions and the internationalization of cities regain the importance they had in old times.

Third, in the analysis it is of great value for the Chinese government that cities along the route belong to member countries of multilateral organizations endorsed by China. This condition shows the emergence of a world order different from that proposed by the institutions created in 1944 after the Bretton Woods agreements. Those multilateral organizations considered by China as top-level are BRICS, the Shanghai Cooperation Organization (SCO) and the *Asian Infrastructure Investment Bank*(AIIB), and they are the ones that are changing the international reference in multilateral matters and the international financial system structure.

The BRI represents not only the Chinese globalization project but also engenders a crucial questioning about the world order in two dimensions:

It breaks with the idea that the Nation State is the protagonist *par excellence* of the current international system, as it had been established in the Westphalia agreements in 1648. It is no longer the State but the cities which acquire a central role in the international system, recovering their historical role in global dynamics. Particularly significant is the role recovered by cities with a prosperous and decisive past in the old Silk Road. Cities such as Kashgar, Samarkand, Istanbul and

Isfahan are an example of this trend. Kashgar was an important Buddhist, Islamic and Christian sanctuary according to the time, and one of the main commercial axes, either as capital of the Kushan kingdom or as capital of the Karakanids State. Samarkand was a cosmopolitan city especially when it was the capital of the Tamerlane Empire more than 600 years ago. Istanbul, for more than fifteen centuries, was the multicultural capital and commercial bridge between East and West. Isfahan, labeled during centuries the most beautiful city of the Middle East, was the old capital of Persia and one of the main centers of the silk route for the Aqueménide, Sasánida and Safávida commerce.

The BRI demonstrates the positioning of cities currently cataloged as belonging to countries of the developing world, but with a great horizon of economic growth in the future. This is the case of cities in Central Asia such as Astana and Dushanbe, which confirm the projections of stable and accelerated economic growth in cities of developing countries.

The great urban transformation that is driving China along the new silk route not only stands out for its monumental dimension, but also evidence that medium and small cities, city-regions and the internationalization of cities recover their historical role again in global dynamics.

Within the framework of its globalizing project, China aims to embrace the world, in this sense it is playing a decisive role in the reconfiguration of the world order. Nevertheless, a series of challenges remain that China must face. In particular, from a Latin American perspective, there is a question about the role of Latin America in the framework of the BRI. China is making use of "Neighborhood Diplomacy" or "Periphery Diplomacy" to interact with neighboring countries or those close to its borders. This denotes that Latin America does not classifies in the BRI initiative. However, there are some keys that allow us to see that Latin America is not excluded either. On May 17, 2015, Chinese Premier Li Keqiang departed from Beijing accompanied by his wife Cheng Hong and a delegation of more than one hundred people to begin a tour along South America, which took him to Brazil, Colombia, Peru and Chile. The main objective of this trip was to reaffirm the creation of the "New Silk Road to Latin America" with the bi-oceanic railway construction project (Castro, 2015)1. What this is showing is that BRI goes beyond the Eurasian borders and the Indian and South Pacific oceans, to encompass also colossal infrastructure projects that involve Latin America.

On May 14th, 2017, 28 state and government heads as well as 1200 delegates from more than 100 countries joined the two-day Belt and Road Forum for International Cooperation in Beijing lead by President Xi Jinping. Chinese government signed deals with 68 countries to jointly develop infrastructure along the new Silk Road trade routes.

In this summit Latin America sent the highest dignitaries of Chile and Argentina, two countries strongly committed with the commerce with China and the Chinese investments in their economies. Brazil also sent a delegation. Up to now, nine Latin American countries have signed some memorandums of understanding related to the "One Belt, One Road" cooperation.

On the other hand, the Panama Canal is strategic step for BRI from the Pacific Ocean to Latin America. Despite the lack of a modernization of its locks in line with the technological change that gives rise to ships of greater tonnage and size, the Panama Canal transports around 320 million tons of goods and raw materials per year (Leon-Manríquez, 2018, 114), representing a strategic step for the goods that come from the Pacific Ocean and require the passage to the Atlantic Ocean.

The AIIB has given approval for the moment to seven Latin American countries (Argentina, Brazil, Chile, Ecuador, Peru, Venezuela and Bolivia) to become members of the AIIB. This bank has been conceived as a multilateral development bank, which would cooperate with other similar institutions in Asia, in particular

---

1   It has also been called a trans-Amazonian railway or Á½ÑóÌúÂ·.

the Asian Development Bank (NDB). Its initial membership currently includes 87 countries, of which almost 40% are not Asian, and the strong presence of European countries stands out. The first Latin American country on the list is Brazil. Like this one, all the other members of the BRICS group are among the founding members of the AIIB.

Clearly Beijing envisages the New Bank Development (NBD) of the BRICS as other important financial mechanism for the projects related with the New Silk Road. In fact Brazil will has an important leadership because of in 2019 a new branch office of NBD will be inaugurated in this country.

In the cultural and academic arena, China has also committed to offering 10,000 scholarships annually to countries that are located along the Belt& Road Initiative.

But the governments of Latin America are not clear about the BRI's link with this subcontinent and how it can be included within the idea of a community of shared destiny. This lack of clarity has to compel to evaluate the real challenge that China has with BRI. The real challenge for China is not about how to build BRI as a global strategy. One bigger than this is the trans-cultural understanding. It is the opportunity for build a trans-cultural understanding with other countries and cultures. Chinese cultural codes are different from those of the West. In that sense, China needs to know how to communicate with the West. Culture is in the background. It is more than pure Soft Power (Nye, 2004). It is not only a power matter in a realistic sense, or an issue related to how to spread power (Morgenthau, 1948). It is an issue related to real knowledge of the *Other* in an anthropological sense: visible forms of behavior are the result of an underlying psychological reality (Gertz, 1977).

In the background of this situation there is a gap plenty of misunderstandings. There are many concepts with different meaning for West and for East: Harmony & Social Cohesion, Armony & Democracy, Wish& Necessity, Consultative Democracy and Common Security &Self-interest Security, Civilization Dialogue

& Civilization Clashes, United and Rule in a Consultative Democracy Vs Divided and Rule in a Confrontational Democracy, Military Allies & Strategic Partners. In a direct relation with BRI there is another misunderstanding: city is understood as an administrative category in China, and city is conceived as an urban fact in the West.

The clue and basic objective of the proposal here mentioned is related to the relevance of knowing the Others in order to communicate efficiently. China has with BRI the opportunity of learning from others and explaining to others his own culture. For reaching that objective in every specific cultural context, it is mandatory to ask: how other countries and cultures communicate? In European and Anglo-Saxon cultures, communication goes in a straight line. Communication is direct and it is indispensable to know who does the action. Pronouns (who does the action) are inherent requisite for the transmission of ideas.In far eastern countries communication use to be related directly with the specific context and has particular characteristics related to the facts. Words aren't the only way to communicate between sender and receiver. Images, silence, behavior are as relevant as words. In Latin American countries, communication use to be in a different way. The book 100 Years of Solitude, written by the Nobel prize Gabriel García Márquez reflects the typical Latin American cosmovision, where communication is plenty of "Magic Realism".

All countries can voluntarily choose their own ways and approaches to join BRI based on their own needs and cultural context. The existing international system, created since Bretton Wodds agreements in 1944, was based on a set of mandatory rules and mechanisms, dominated by United States and the European great powers, in an exclusive an close perspective of the world. What really concerns many western countries may be not the closer relations between China and countries along the BRI, but the fact that the completely different concept of globalization China introduced through BRI creates great challenges to its leadership. The leading challenge for China's Foreign Affairs is to be understood. BRI represents the opportunity for China achieve this objective by its dynamic diplomacy.

References

Cai, Peter (2017). *Understanding China's Belt and Road Initiative*. Lowy Institute. P. 6.

Castro, Patricia (2015). *La Ruta de la Seda se extiende a Sudamérica.* El Comercio (Peruvian newspaper), May 17, 2015. http://elcomercio.pe/blog/viachina/2015/05/la-ruta-de-la-seda-se-extiende-a-sudamerica (recovered: September 18, 2018).

Engdahl, F. William (2018). ¿La UE bloquear la Ruta de la Seda Económica de China? Dos modelos de desarrollo global, CEPRID. https://www.nodo50.org/ceprid/spip.php?article2339

Fang, Jin (2017). P*arallel Perspectives on the Global Economic Order. A U.S.-China Essay Collection.*"The Belt and Road Initiative: Progress, Problems and Prospects". CSIS – Center for Strategic and International Studies, Shanghai Institutes of International Studies SIIS.

Frankopan, Peter (2015). *The Silk Roads. A new history of the world*. Bloombsbury, London.

Gernet, Jacques (2006). *Le monde chinois*, Poket, France.

Gertz, Clifford (1977). *The Interpretation of Cultures*, Basic Books Classics, New York.

Kissinger, Henry. (2016). *Orden mundial*, Ed. Debate, Barcelona.

Leon-Manríquez, José Luis León (2018).*La franja y la ruta : iniciativa china de cooperación con América Latina y Caribe*. "Opciones estratégicas para LaFranja y La Ruta y conectividadmarítima entre China y América Latina y el Caribe". Ediciones UNTDF, Universidad Nacional de Tierra del Fuego, Antártida e Islas del Atlántico Sur. Argentina, pp. 113-119.

Morgenthau, Hans J. (1948). *Politics Among Nations: The Struggle for Power and Peace.* Mc Grow-Hill, USA.

Nye,Joseph S. (2004). *Soft Power: The Means To Success In World Politics*,Paperback, Cambridge.

Osterhammel, Jürgen (1987). *China. Ergebnisse eigener Reisen und darauf gegründeter Studien.*"Forschungsreiseund Kolonialprogramm.1877-1912. Ferdinand von Richthofen.. 5vols. Berlin: Reimer, 1877-1912;Vol. 1.

Richthofen, Ferdinand von (1987).Und die Erschlie ßung Chinas im 19. Jahrhundert." In:*Archiv für Kulturgeschichte* 69: pp. 150-195.

SCOTT, Emma (2015)*. China's "One Belt, One Road" strategy meets the UAE's Look East Policy*, The Jamestown Foundation, Centre for Chinese Studies, Stellenbosch University. http://www.jamestown.org/ (Recovered 20, September 2018).

Tu, Qiyu (2018). *Annual Report on World Cities*(2018), Social Sciences Academic Press, Shanghai.

Waugh, Daniel C. (2007). *The Silkroad Foundation* 5 (1), Saratoga, CA, United States. pp. 1-75.

World Bank, 2016. *Global cities initiative*. Brookings & JP Morgan. http://worldpopulationreview.com